Software and Systems Traceability

T0205344

Jane Cleland-Huang · Orlena Gotel ·
Andrea Zisman *Editors*

Software and Systems
Traceability

Foreword by Anthony Finkelstein

 Springer

Editors
Jane Cleland-Huang
DePaul University
School of Computing
243 S. Wabash Avenue
60604 Chicago
USA
jhuang@cs.depaul.edu

Orlena Gotel
New York
NY 10014
USA
olly@gotel.net

Andrea Zisman
City University
School of Informatics
London
United Kingdom
a.zisman@soi.city.ac.uk

ISBN 978-1-4471-5819-6   ISBN 978-1-4471-2239-5 (eBook)
DOI 10.1007/978-1-4471-2239-5
Springer London Dordrecht Heidelberg New York

British Library Cataloguing in Publication Data
A catalogue record for this book is available from the British Library

Printed on acid-free paper

Springer is part of Springer Science+Business Media (www.springer.com)

Requirements and Relationships: A Foreword

Software engineering is a pessimistic discipline. The glass is always half empty rather than half full. Not surprising really, we are hardened to the grind of improving quality, painstakingly testing and, never quite, eliminating bugs. Critical review is of the essence. We know there is "no silver bullet".

Traceability in software development must however, pessimism set aside, be marked as a success. We have characterised the problem. We have produced industrial strength tools that relieve a substantial part of the practical difficulties of managing traceability relations across different documents. We have arrived at a communal consensus regarding the principal notations to be used in software development, realised in UML, and characterised the relationships amongst these notations. These are all significant practical advances.

Research has gone further. One of the key challenges of traceability has been the return on investment. In essence only a few of the traceability links prove to be of value, that is are subsequently needed in support of a change. It is difficult to predict in advance however, which these might be. Given that establishing, documenting and managing traceability manually is expensive, the balance of costs and benefits is delicate one. It has been shown, convincingly in my view, that off-the-shelf information retrieval techniques will, with some judicious tuning, yield reasonable traceability links. I expect this, once industrially hardened and deployed, to drive cost reduction.

I guess with all this positivity you can sense a "but" coming ... and you are not wrong. While we have taken steps to advance the state of the art, the nature of the requirements challenge has shifted. The context has altered. Agile development has altered the way that much software is developed (just in case there is any remaining doubt, it is no longer a phenomenon of the programming fringe – it is mainstream software engineering). But agile development is really only a particular manifestation of the underlying trends in which it is becoming clear that it is cheaper to build software quickly, and change it if it fails to satisfy the emerging requirements, than to undertake the discipline of trying to get it exactly right at the outset. This is partly a technical change, the product of improved tools, environments and programming languages, but may also reflect changing business environments, that move at a pace set by a dynamic globalised economy. So we start with more change, indeed with constant change, not simply as an unwanted consequence of the inexorable laws of software evolution but embraced as the essence of software engineering.

More change means a greater need for traceability support. Of course, if you have adopted an agile approach you could argue that there is less to trace to, after all you have in large part eschewed documentation. This, I believe, is an error because it ignores the consequentially altered nature of the requirements task. I will elaborate below.

We have tended to view requirements as a discrete task in which we engage with the customer (a sort of shorthand for stakeholders) on an occasional basis. We are not, any longer, so naive as to believe that requirements elicitation is a one-shot process, but we still understand it to be something that happens from time to time, for clearly specified purposes.

Change changes things. Requirements engineering becomes instead a "relational" process in which the name of the game is continuing customer engagement. In other words, the developer tries to ensure that their application or service grows and adapts in sync with, ideally at the leading edge of, the customer's business. You could say the software is a manifestation of the relationship achieved through continuous interaction and immersion in the business. Managing this ongoing relationship and the associated knowledge of the domain is difficult and demands, I suggest, a different approach on the part of the software developer and a reimagining of requirements elicitation, specification and validation.

So, where does requirements traceability fit into this picture? It provides the information management support for these complex multi-threaded customer relationships and the technical substrate for rapid system evolution. It allows the developer to understand and account for the consequences of ongoing system change in terms of the business. It is the core of a new type of "customer relationship management" system.

I wish I had a better sense of what the new technical demands that follow from the change of view, sketched above, might be. Many of the colleagues, whose work makes up this volume, are better equipped than I am to do this.

Of course, there remains a hard core of large systems development characterised by strong safety and other constraints and bound to the co-development of complex hardware where the agility sketched above has limited impact. Defence and other mission-critical systems exemplify this. There is a continuing need to address traceability in this setting and in particular to support navigation of the complex relationships that arise. Of particular interest, and relevant in the light of the analysis above, are regulatory and compliance processes that engage a demanding framework of requirements and shifting body of stakeholders. This still remains at the edge of what can be practically accomplished and will require further research. This book sheds strong light on the challenges.

I am certain that the technical achievements marked in this volume are the basis for addressing these new frontiers for software and systems engineering and that requirements traceability will be at the forefront of engineering research. Not so pessimistic, really.

London, UK   Anthony Finkelstein

Preface

The importance of traceability is well understood in the software engineering community and adopted across numerous software development standards. Industries are often compelled to implement traceability practices by government regulations. For example, the U.S. Food and Drug Administration (FDA) states that traceability analysis must be used to verify that a software design implements all of its specified software requirements, that all aspects of the design are traceable to software requirements, and that all code is linked to established specifications and established test procedures. Other examples are found in the U.S. Federal Aviation Administration (FAA) that states that software developers need to have ways of demonstrating traceability between design and requirements, and in the Capability Maturity Model Integration (CMMI) standard that requires similar traceability practices.

Traceability supports numerous critical activities. For example, pre-requirements traceability is used to demonstrate that a product meets the stakeholders' stated requirements, or that it complies with a set of government regulations. Traceability is also used to establish and understand the relationships between requirements and downstream work products such as design documents, source code, and test cases. In this context, it supports tasks such as impact analysis which helps developers understand how a proposed change impacts the current system, and code verification which identifies superfluous and unwanted features by tracing all elements of the source code back to specific requirements. Traceability can also support reuse of parts of a software system by identifying the parts that match (new) requirements, and the evolution of software systems.

In practice, traceability links are typically created and maintained either through the use of a requirements management tool, or else in a spreadsheet or Word document directly. However, there are numerous issues that make it difficult to achieve successful traceability in practice. These issues include social ones related to communication between project stakeholders, as well as technical issues related to physically creating, maintaining, and using thousands of interrelated and relatively brittle traceability links. As a result, many organisations struggle to implement and maintain traceability links, even though it is broadly recognised as a critical element of the software development life cycle.

In order to overcome the significant challenges in creating, maintaining, and using traceability, over the last 20 years the research community has been actively addressing traceability issues through the exploration of topics related to automating the traceability process, developing strategies for cost-effective traceability, supporting the evolution and maintenance of traceability links, visualising traceability, and developing traceability practices that apply across a wide range of domains such as product lines, multi-agent systems, safety critical applications, aspect-oriented and agile software development, and various regulated industries.

Several workshops and symposia have been organised by the traceability community to bring together researchers and practitioners in order to address the challenges and discuss state-of-the-art work in the area of traceability. These events include the Traceability in Emerging Forms of Software Engineering (TEFSE) workshop series[1]; and the workshops funded by NASA (held at NASA's IV&V facility in 2006) and the NSF (held in Lexington, Kentucky in 2007 in conjunction with TEFSE 2007) that resulted in the creation of a draft Problem Statement and Grand Challenges document.

Another effort of the community was the creation of the International Center of Excellence for Software Traceability (CoEST) in 2005. The main goals of CoEST are to promote international research collaborations; advance education in the traceability area; bring together researchers, practitioners, and experts in the field; create a body of knowledge for traceability; develop a repository of benchmarks for traceability research; and develop new technologies to satisfy traceability needs. More recently, the community has also engaged in the Tracy project, funded by the NSF, with the focus of building research infrastructure, collecting and organising datasets, establishing benchmarks, and developing a tool named TraceLab to provide support for designing and executing a broad range of traceability experiments.

This book complements the current effort of the traceability community by providing a comprehensive reference for traceability theory, research, and practice and by presenting an introduction to the concepts and theoretical foundations of traceability. Several topics in this book represent areas of mature work, which have previously only appeared as research papers in conference proceedings, journals, or individual book chapters. The book therefore serves as a unifying source of information on traceability. As such, we expect the book to serve as a reference for practitioners, researchers, and students. Practitioners reading the book may be especially interested in the mature areas of traceability research, several of which have already been demonstrated to work in industry through various pilot studies, while researchers from all areas of the community may be specifically interested in the cutting edge nature of several topics and the open research challenges that need to be addressed in the future. Students new to the topic should start with a review of the fundamentals in the chapter "Traceability Fundamentals".

---

[1] TEFSE 2002: Edinburgh, UK; TEFSE 2003: Montreal, Canada; TEFSE 2005: Long Beach, CA; TEFSE 2007: also known as the Grand Challenges of Traceability, Lexington, Kentucky; TEFSE 2009, Vancouver, Canada; TEFSE 2011: Honolulu, Hawaii.

The book contains 16 chapters organised in five Parts. *Part I – Traceability Strategy* describes several traceability terms and concepts, and the activities related to traceability planning and management. *Part II – Traceability Creation* presents a variety of techniques for supporting the creation of trace links. These techniques include the use of Information Retrieval and rule-based methods, an account of the factors that impact traceability creation, methods to create traceability together with the development of software systems, and techniques for traceability creation among heterogeneous artifacts. *Part III – Traceability Maintenance* presents approaches that support traceability in evolving projects in the domains of product line systems and model-driven engineering, as well as the role of the human in the traceability process. *Part IV – Traceability Use* describes the employment of traceability in agile projects, aspect-oriented software development, non-functional requirements, and medical devices. *Part V – Traceability Challenges* presents the outstanding challenges for traceability research and practice, based on a community vision for traceability in 2035, and discusses the open traceability research topics that need to be addressed in the future.

The book also provides a copy of a glossary of traceability terms created by members of the traceability community and used in the material described in the various chapters of the book. The topics presented in these various chapters are illustrated by two case studies in the areas of electronic health care and mobile phone product line systems. The book also provides an overview of the Center of Excellence for Software Traceability and the TraceLab tool. All the above materials are presented in five different appendices in the book.

This book is the product of several years of effort. Andrea Zisman first conceived of the idea in early 2009 and the finished product was brought together in its current form as the result of numerous emails, skype calls, and face-to-face discussions between all three of the editors.

Obviously, any book of this nature demands the contributions and efforts of many different people. This book was no different, and we would like to thank members of the traceability community for their willingness to contribute their time and effort to make this book possible. The process of collecting material for the book was initiated by a call for abstracts in June 2010. At that time, we selectively invited the most promising abstracts for submission as full chapters, and also reached out to request additional chapters for a few missing topics. All submitted chapters went through a rigorous peer-review process and, as a result, we selected the chapters that are presented in this book. We thank the authors of all abstracts and chapters for their contributions to this process.

Chicago, USA   Jane Cleland-Huang
New York, USA   Orlena Gotel
London, UK   Andrea Zisman

Acknowledgments

We would like to thank the following people for their contributions.

Melissa Huang for her illustrations of Traceability Strategy, Traceability Creation, Traceability Maintenance, Traceability Use, Traceability Challenges, and the Appendices, which appear in each of the six sectional headers respectively.

Aleksandra Waliczek for managing the logistics of coordinating the final process of collecting chapters and supporting material from the authors and for integrating all of the material into the draft version of the book for delivery to Springer.

John Van Ort for compiling author information.

The US National Science Foundation (NSF) for partially funding community work on the Grand Challenges of Traceability, CoEST (Center of Excellence for Software Traceability), and TraceLab under grants CNS 0959924 and 0647443.

The US National Aeronautics and Space Administration (NASA) for providing initial seed funding for CoEST and for the first workshop on the Grand Challenges of Traceability under grant NNX06AD02G.

All of the authors who contributed abstracts and/or full chapters as a result of the initial call for chapters.

The anonymous reviewers, without whom this peer-reviewed book would not be possible.

Contents

Contributors

Nasir Ali DGIGL, École Polytechnique de Montréal, Montréal, QC, Canada, nasir.ali@polymtl.ca

Giuliano Antoniol École Polytechnique de Montréal, Montréal, QC, Canada, antoniol@ieee.org

Hazeline U. Asuncion Computing and Software Systems, University of Washington, Bothell, WA, USA, hazeline@u.washington.edu

John Burton Vitalograph Ireland Ltd., Ennis, Ireland, John.burton@vitalograph.ie

Valentine Casey Regulated Software Research Group, Lero, Dundalk Institute of Technology, Dundalk, Ireland, Val.casey@dkit.ie

Jane Cleland-Huang DePaul University, School of Computing, 60604 Chicago, USA, jhuang@cs.depaul.edu

Gerry Coleman Regulated Software Research Group, Lero, Dundalk Institute of Technology, Dundalk, Ireland, Gerry.coleman@dkit.ie

Wouter De Borger DistriNet Research Group, K.U. Leuven, B-3001 Heverlee, Belgium, wouter.deborger@cs.kuleuven.be

Alex Dekhtyar Cal Poly State University, San Luis Obispo, CA, USA, dekhtyar@calpoly.edu

Andrea De Lucia University of Salerno, Fisciano (SA), Italy, adelucia@unisa.it

Peter Donnelly Regulated Software Research Group, Lero, Dundalk Institute of Technology, Dundalk, Ireland, Peter@biobusinessni.org

Alexander Egyed Johannes Kepler University, Linz, Austria, alexander.egyed@jku.at

Anthony Finkelstein University College London, London, UK, a.Finkelstein@cs.ucl.ac.uk

Holger Giese Hasso-Plattner-Institute at the University of Potsdam, 14482 Potsdam, Germany, holger.giese@hpi.uni-potsdam.de

Orlena Gotel New York, NY 10014, USA, olly@gotel.net

Paul Grünbacher Systems Engineering and Automation, Johannes Kepler University, Linz, Austria, paul.gruenbacher@jku.at

Yann-Gäel Guéhéneuc DGIGL, École Polytechnique de Montréal, Montréal, QC, Canada, yann-gael.gueheneuc@polymtl.ca

Jane Huffman Hayes University of Kentucky, Lexington, KY, USA, hayes@cs.uky.edu

Regina Hebig Hasso-Plattner-Institute at the University of Potsdam, 14482 Potsdam, Germany, regina.hebig@hpi.uni-potsdam.de

Wolfgang Heider Christian Doppler Laboratory for Automated Software Engineering, Johannes Kepler University, Linz, Austria, heider@ase.jku.at

Claire Ingram Newcastle University, NE1 7RU, England, UK, claire.ingram@ncl.ac.uk

Waraporn Jirapanthong Faculty of Information Technology, Dhurakij Pundit University, Bangkok 10210, Thailand, waraporn.jir@dpu.ac.th

Wouter Joosen DistriNet Research Group, K.U. Leuven, B-3001 Heverlee, Belgium, wouter.joosen@cs.kuleuven.be

Bert Lagaisse DistriNet Research Group, K.U. Leuven, B-3001 Heverlee, Belgium, bert.lagaisse@cs.kuleuven.be

Martin Lehofer Siemens VAI Metals Technologies, Linz, Austria, martin.lehofer@siemens.com

Patrick Mäder Institute for Systems Engineering and Automation (SEA), Johannes Kepler University, Linz, Austria, patrick.maeder@jku.at

Jonathan Maletic Kent State University, Kent, OH, USA, jmaletic@cs.kent.edu

Andrian Marcus Wayne State University, Detroit, MI 48202, USA, amarcus@wayne.edu

Fergal Mc Caffery Regulated Software Research Group, Lero, Dundalk Institute of Technology, Dundalk, Ireland, Fergal.McCaffery@dkit.ie

Andrew Meneely Department of Software Engineering, Rochester Institute of Technology, andg@se.rit.edu

Mehdi Mirakhorli Depaul University, Chicago, IL, USA, m.mirakholi@acm.org

Rocco Oliveto University of Molise, Pesche (IS), Italy, rocco.oliveto@unimol.it

Denys Poshyvanyk The College of William and Mary, Williamsburg, VA 23185, USA, denys@cs.wm.edu

Rick Rabiser Christian Doppler Laboratory for Automated Software Engineering, Johannes Kepler University, Linz, Austria, rabiser@ase.jku.at

Steve Riddle Newcastle University, NE1 7RU, England, UK, steve.riddle@ncl.ac.uk

Andreas Seibel Hasso-Plattner-Institute, The University of Potsdam, 14482 Potsdam, Germany, andreas.seibel@hpi.uni-potsdam.de

M.S. Sivakumar Regulated Software Research Group, Lero, Dundalk Institute of Technology, Dundalk, Ireland, Smadh09@studentmail.dkit.ie

Ben Smith Department of Computer Science, North Carolina State University, Raleigh, NC 27695-8206, USA, bhsmith3@ncsu.edu

Richard N. Taylor Institute for Software Research, University of California, Irvine, CA, USA, Taylor@ics.uci.edu

Laurie Williams Department of Computer Science, North Carolina State University, Raleigh, NC 27695-8206, USA, lawilli3@ncsu.edu

Andrea Zisman School of Informatics, City University London, London, EC1V 0HB, UK, a.zisman@soi.city.ac.uk

Part I
Traceability Strategy

Traceability needs to be planned for and managed if it is to be effective and remain effective in any particular project context. Stakeholders need to be identified and requirements determined. A suitable traceability process needs to be designed and potential support from tooling explored. However, all this initial effort is mute if there is no clear understanding of the anticipated return on investment from implementing traceability within an organisation. Traceability strategy comprises all those activities associated with traceability planning and traceability management.

In this first part of the book, the chapter "Traceability Fundamentals" defines a number of traceability-related terms and concepts, as they will be used throughout the remainder of the book. A simple process for analysing the cost-benefit of traceability and selecting a strategy accordingly is described in the chapter "Cost-Benefits of Traceability". A cautionary seven-step guide for making informed decisions about tool acquisition is presented in the chapter "Acquiring Tool Support for Traceability". In combination, the chapters "Cost-Benefits of Traceability" and "Acquiring Tool Support for Traceability" highlight important considerations to help plan and manage traceability in practice.

Traceability Fundamentals

Orlena Gotel, Jane Cleland-Huang, Jane Huffman Hayes, Andrea Zisman, Alexander Egyed, Paul Grünbacher, Alex Dekhtyar, Giuliano Antoniol, Jonathan Maletic, and Patrick Mäder

1 Introduction

The role of traceability was recognised in the pioneering NATO working conference held in 1968 to discuss the problems of software engineering (Naur and Randell, 1969). One of the working papers in this conference examined the requirements for an effective methodology of computer system design and reported on the need to be able to ensure that a system being developed actually reflects its design. In a critique of three early projects focused on methodology, each was praised for the emphasis they placed on making "the system that they are designing contain explicit traces of the design process" (Randell, 1968).

Traceability was subsequently noted as a topic of interest in one of the earliest surveys on the state of the art and future trends in software engineering (Boehm, 1976), and its practice was certainly evident in those domains concerned with developing early tool support (Dorfman and Flynn, 1984; Pierce, 1978). By the 1980s, traceability could be found as a requirement in a large number of national and international standards for software and systems development, such as the high-profile DOD-STD-2167A (Dorfman and Thayer, 1990). Published research began to proliferate and diversify in the area of traceability in the late 1990s, spurred somewhat by renewed interest in the topic arising from two newly formed International Requirements Engineering professional colloquia, with two early papers focusing on the issues and problems associated with traceability (Ramesh and Edwards, 1993; Gotel and Finkelstein, 1994), the latter providing for the first systematic analysis of the traceability problem. The topic of traceability continues to receive growing research attention in the twenty-first century, with a particular focus on automated trace generation (Cleland-Huang et al., 2007; Hayes et al., 2006) and with concomitant advances in model-driven development (Aizenbud-Reshef et al., 2006; Galvao and Goknil, 2007; Winkler and von Pilgrim, 2010).

O. Gotel (✉)
New York, NY 10014, USA
e-mail: olly@gotel.net

J. Cleland-Huang et al. (eds.), *Software and Systems Traceability*,
DOI 10.1007/978-1-4471-2239-5_1, © Springer-Verlag London Limited 2012

However, despite the introduction of widely-available commercial tools claiming to support traceability in the 1980s, and substantive growth in this market through the 1990s and millennium, the actual practice of traceability remains poorly documented and, where it is examined (Mäder et al., 2009b), it appears to be little influenced by research. One confounding factor is inconsistency in the use of traceability terminology and concepts, not only between researchers and practitioners, but also within each of these communities themselves.

This chapter seeks to provide a resource on traceability fundamentals.[1] It defines the essential traceability terminology in Section 2 and is supplemented by an extensive glossary[2] that has been developed and endorsed by members of the traceability community. This glossary can be found as an appendix to this book and provides definitions for all the terms that are italicised in this chapter. The chapter also offers a model of a generic traceability process in Section 3 and describes the basic activities involved in the life cycle of a trace. This model is used as a frame of reference for articulating the grand challenge of traceability in the chapter by Gotel et al. of this book. Section 4 describes the basic types of traceability and explains some key associated concepts. Section 5 concludes the chapter.

2 Essential Traceability Terminology

At the most fundamental level, traceability is simply the potential to relate data that is stored within artifacts of some kind, along with the ability to examine this relationship. The ability to achieve traceability therefore depends upon the creation of navigable links between data held within artifacts that are otherwise disconnected. The value of traceability lies in the many software and systems engineering activities and tasks that the information provided through such interrelations can enable, such as change impact analysis, coverage analysis, dependency analysis, etc. (Gotel and Finkelstein, 1994; Lindvall and Sandahl, 1996; Ramesh and Jarke, 2001); tracing can provide visibility into required aspects of the software and systems development process and contribute to a better understanding of the software system under development.

This section defines two underlying terms, *trace artifact* and *trace link*, that are the building blocks of traceability. It subsequently uses these definitions to clarify the term *trace*. Based upon these definitions, the terms *traceability* and *tracing* are then defined.

---

[1] Section 3 of this chapter includes reproduced material from Center of Excellence for Software Traceability Technical Report #CoEST-2011-001, with permission. Please direct any feedback on this material via the CoEST website (http://www.coest.org).

[2] Version 1.0 of the traceability glossary is provided as an appendix to this book and the latest version of the glossary is maintained at http://www.coest.org. Please note that all glossary terms are defined using U.S. English.

2.1 Trace Artifact

Trace artifacts are traceable units of data. They refer to any residual data or marks of the software and systems development process that are made amenable to being traced. The term can apply to a single requirement, a cluster of requirements, or even to an entire requirements specification document. The term can apply to a Unified Modeling Language (UML) class diagram, a single class therein, or even to a particular class operation. For conceptual simplicity, the general term "artifact" is used to apply to both the object as a whole and to any internal delineation therein. What this means is that the granularity of a trace artifact is not pre-determined and may not even be consistent in any one particular project. It is this uncertainty in the granularity of trace artifacts that can lead to many problems in establishing and using traceability in practice.

> **Trace artifact** – A *traceable* unit of data (e.g., a single requirement, a cluster of requirements, a UML class, a UML class operation, a Java class or even a person). A *trace artifact* is one of the *trace elements* and is qualified as either a *source artifact* or as a *target artifact* when it participates in a *trace*. The size of the *traceable* unit of data defines the *granularity* of the related *trace*.

Three terms closely associated with trace artifact include *trace artifact type*, *source artifact* and *target artifact*. The trace artifact type serves to classify the nature and function of the artifact, and is usually a recognised and "documented" by-product of the software and systems development process. The terms source artifact and target artifact serve to characterise the role of a particular trace artifact in a specified trace.

> **Trace artifact type** – A label that characterizes those *trace artifacts* that have the same or a similar structure (syntax) and/or purpose (semantics). For example, requirements, design and test cases may be distinct *artifact types*.
>
> **Source artifact** – The *artifact* from which a *trace* originates.
>
> **Target artifact** – The *artifact* at the destination of a *trace*.

2.2 Trace Link

A *trace link* is a single association forged between two trace artifacts, one comprising the source artifact and one comprising the target artifact. This definition of trace link implies that the link has a primary direction for tracing, from the source artifact to the target artifact. Directionality between the two trace artifacts provides for the ability to traverse the trace link, or to follow it, so as to associate the two

Fig. 1 Trace link
directionality

pieces of data. It is this juxtaposition that is sought through traceability, rather than the pure retrieval of one piece of data. In practice, however, every trace link can be traversed in two directions, so the trace link also has a reverse trace link direction and is effectively bidirectional, as illustrated in Fig. 1.

> **Trace link** – A specified *association* between a pair of *artifacts*, one comprising the *source artifact* and one comprising the *target artifact*. The *trace link* is one of the *trace elements*. It may or may not be annotated to include information such as the *link type* and other semantic *attributes*. This definition of *trace link* implies that the *link* has a *primary trace link direction* for *tracing*. In practice, every *trace link* can be traversed in two directions (i.e., if A tests B then B is tested by A), so the *link* also has a *reverse trace link direction* for *tracing*. The *trace link* is effectively *bidirectional*. Where no concept of directionality is given or implied, it is referred to solely as an *association*.

The directionality of a trace link is therefore an important concept. Where a source artifact and a target artifact are defined, the semantics of the directionality is clear. Whether or not the trace link can physically be navigated in both directions, however, is usually a matter of implementation. Three terms clarify the directionality inherent in a trace link, the *primary trace link direction*, the *reverse trace link direction* and the concept of a *bidirectional trace link*.

> **Primary trace link direction** – When a *trace link* is traversed from its specified *source artifact* to its specified *target artifact*, it is being used in the primary direction as specified. Where *link semantics* are provided, they provide for a way to "read" the traversal (e.g., A implements B).
>
> **Reverse trace link direction** – When a *trace link* is traversed from its specified *target artifact* to its specified *source artifact*, it is being used in the reverse direction to its specification. The *link semantics* may no longer be valid, so a change from active to passive voice (or vice-versa) is generally required (e.g., if A replaces B then B is replaced by A).
>
> **Bidirectional trace link** – A term used to refer to the fact that a *trace link* can be used in both a *primary trace link direction* and a *reverse trace link direction*.

Two interrelated terms that are closely associated with trace link are *trace link type* and *link semantics*. The trace link type serves to classify the nature and function of the trace link. It is usually characterised according to the meaning of the relationship between the two artifacts that the link associates, so the trace link type is generally defined in terms of the link's semantic role. The trace link type is a broader term that may define a collection of links with the same link semantics.

> **Trace link type** – A label that characterizes those *trace links* that have the same or similar structure (syntax) and/or purpose (semantics). For example, "implements", "tests", "refines" and "replaces" may be distinct *trace link types*.
>
> **Link semantics** – The purpose or meaning of the *trace link*. The *link semantics* are generally specified in the *trace link type*, which is a broader term that may also capture other details regarding the nature of the *trace link*, such as how the *trace link* was created.

The term *trace relation* is frequently used interchangeably with the term trace link in many publications. In reviewing the traceability fundamentals and encouraging the more consensual use of terminology within the traceability community, the proposal is to differentiate the two terms in the future. Following from database theory, a trace relation describes all the trace links that are specified between two defined artifact types acting as source artifacts and target artifacts. It is the trace relation that is captured in the commonly used *traceability matrix*.

> **Trace relation** – All the *trace links* created between two sets of specified *trace artifact types*. The *trace relation* is the instantiation of the *trace relationship* and hence is a collection of *traces*. For example, the *trace relation* would be the actual *trace links* that associate the instances of requirements *artifacts* with the instances of test case *artifacts* on a project. The *trace relation* is commonly recorded within a *traceability matrix*.
>
> **Traceability matrix** – A matrix recording the *traces* comprising a *trace relation*, showing which pairs of *trace artifacts* are associated via *trace links*.

2.3 Trace

Use of the term *trace* has led to some misunderstanding in the traceability community since it has two distinct meanings dependent upon whether the term is being used as a noun (i.e., "a mark remaining" (OED, 2007)) or as a verb, (i.e., "tracking or following" (OED, 2007)). When used in a software and systems engineering context, the meanings are often used interchangeably whereas they need to be distinguished. "Trace" can, therefore, be defined in two ways.

Trace (Noun) – A specified triplet of *elements* comprising: a *source artifact*, a *target artifact* and a *trace link* associating the two *artifacts*. Where more than two *artifacts* are associated by a *trace link*, such as the aggregation of two *artifacts* linked to a third *artifact*, the aggregated *artifacts* are treated as a single *trace artifact*. The term applies, more generally, to both *traces* that are *atomic* in nature (i.e., singular) or *chained* in some way (i.e., plural).

Trace (Verb) – The act of following a *trace link* from a *source artifact* to a *target artifact* (*primary trace link direction*) or vice-versa (*reverse trace link direction*).

When used as a noun, the term "trace" refers to the complete triplet of *trace elements* that enable the juxtaposition of two pieces of data: the source artifact, the target artifact and the trace link. Additional information, in the form of *trace attributes*, may qualify properties of the overall trace or of each of the three elements. Such traces can either be *atomic* or *chained* (see Fig. 2). Where chained, the trace links are strung together by the source and the target trace artifacts that they connect, the target artifact for one trace becoming the source artifact for the subsequent trace, to form a series of data juxtapositions.

Atomic trace – A *trace* (noun sense) comprising a single *source artifact*, a single *target artifact* and a single *trace link*.

Chained trace – A *trace* (noun sense) comprising multiple *atomic traces* strung in sequence, such that a *target artifact* for one *atomic trace* becomes the *source artifact* for the next *atomic trace*.

Trace element – Used to refer to either one of the triplets comprising a *trace*: a *source artifact*, a *target artifact* or a *trace link*.

Trace attribute – Additional information (i.e., meta-data) that characterizes properties of the *trace* or of its individual *trace elements*, such as a date and time stamp of the *trace's creation* or the *trace link type*.

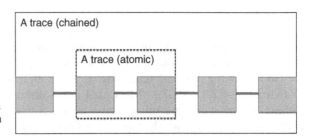

Fig. 2 A trace provided via a single trace link or via a chain of trace links

When used as a verb, the term "trace" (i.e., to trace) is associated with the activity of tracing (see Section 2.5).

2.4 Traceability

Traceability is the potential for traces (as defined above in the noun sense) to be established (i.e., created and maintained) and used. The challenge for traceability is that each of the component elements (i.e., the trace artifacts and trace links) needs to be acquired, represented and stored, and then subsequently retrieved as a trace to enable software and systems engineering activities and tasks. Both the time and the manner in which traces are established and brought together for use will depend upon the purposes to which the traceability is put. Consequently, traces exist within their own life cycles and can (ideally) be reused in different contexts. The type and the granularity of the trace artifacts, and the semantics of the trace link, are therefore details that are best determined on a project-by-project basis. They could perhaps even be determined on a moment-to-moment basis in relation to an overarching traceability strategy. It is this process through which traces come into existence and eventually expire that influences the definition of a generic traceability process model in Section 3.

> **Traceability** – The potential for *traces* to be established and used. *Traceability* (i.e., *trace* "ability") is thereby an *attribute* of an *artifact* or of a collection of *artifacts*. Where there is *traceability, tracing* can be undertaken and the specified *artifacts* should be *traceable*.

Frequently used terms include requirements traceability, software traceability and systems traceability. These all delineate the artifact types that are the primary objects of interest for tracing purposes. For example, in the case of requirements traceability, this focuses explicitly on the potential to establish and use traces that associate requirements-related artifacts in some way or another. Other more specific traceability terms are defined in the glossary that accompanies this book.

> **Requirements traceability** – "The ability to describe and follow the life of a requirement in both a forwards and backwards direction (i.e., from its origins, through its development and specification, to its subsequent deployment and use, and through periods of ongoing refinement and iteration in any of these phases)." (Gotel and Finkelstein, 1994.)

2.5 Tracing

Tracing implies undertaking all those activities required to put traceability in place, in addition to all those activities that exploit the results.

> **Tracing** – The activity of either *establishing* or *using traces*.

Tracing activities demand some form of agency, and leads to the three associated terms of *manual, automated* and *semi-automated tracing* when referring to the nature of the activity that puts the traceability in place.

> **Manual tracing** – When *traceability* is established by the activities of a human *tracer*. This includes *traceability creation* and *maintenance* using the drag and drop methods that are commonly found in current *requirements management tools*.
>
> **Automated tracing** – When *traceability* is established via automated techniques, methods and tools. Currently, it is the decision as to among which *artifacts* to create and maintain *trace links* that is automated.
>
> **Semi-automated tracing** – When *traceability* is established via a combination of automated techniques, methods, tools and human activities. For example, automated techniques may suggest *candidate trace links* or *suspect trace links* and then the human *tracer* may be prompted to verify them.

3 A Generic Traceability Process Model

Figure 3 depicts a generic *traceability process model*. It shows the essential activities that are required to bring traces into existence and to take them through to eventual retirement. Traces are created, maintained and used, all within the context of a broader traceability strategy. This strategy provides the detail of stakeholders' needs, decisions regarding mechanism and automation, and also chains atomic traces in some agreed way to enable required activities and tasks. Continuous feedback is a critical aspect of the entire process to enable the traceability strategy to evolve over time. The four key activities of this generic traceability process model are described in the following sub-sections.

> **Traceability process model** – An abstract description of the series of activities that serve to establish *traceability* and render it usable, along with a

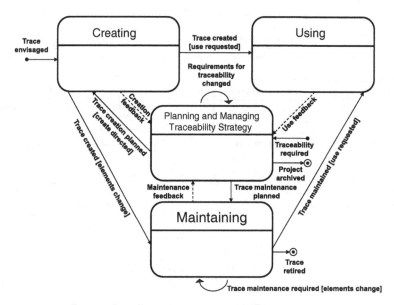

Fig. 3 A generic traceability process model

description of the typical responsibilities and resourcing required to undertake them, as well as their inputs and outputs. Distinctive steps of the process
comprise *traceability strategy, traceability creation, traceability maintenance*
and *traceability use*.

3.1 Traceability Strategy

Effective traceability rarely happens by chance or through ad hoc efforts. Minimally,
it requires having retained the artifacts to be traced, having the capacity to establish meaningful links between these artifacts and having procedures to interrogate
the resulting traces in a goal-oriented manner. Such simple requirements conceal
complex decisions as to the granularity, categorisation and storage of assorted
multi-media artifacts. It also conceals choices as to the approach for generating,
classifying, representing and then maintaining their inter-artifact and intra-artifact
linkages. Additional questions need to be answered, such as: Which of these tracing activities should be manual? Which should be automated? Where should the
responsibilities for these activities lie? When should they be undertaken? There are
many decisions that need to be made and, therefore, an enabling traceability strategy
needs to be built into the engineering and management practices from day one on
a software and systems engineering project. Figure 4 outlines the typical high-level
activities associated with planning and managing a traceability strategy.

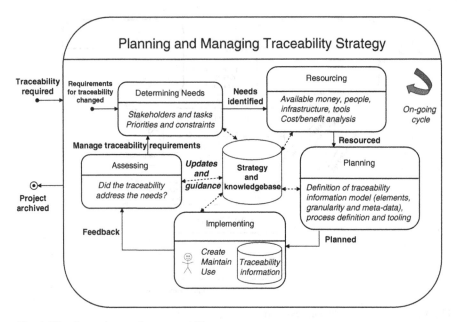

Fig. 4 Planning and managing a traceability strategy

Traceability strategy – Those decisions made in order to determine the *stakeholder* and *system requirements for traceability* and to design a suitable *traceability solution*, and for providing the control necessary to keep these requirements and solutions relevant and effective during the life of a project. *Traceability strategy* comprises *traceability planning* and *traceability management* activities.

Traceability is concerned with the provisioning of information to help in answering project-specific questions and in undertaking project-directed activities and tasks; it is thus a supporting system rather than a goal in its own right. This perspective demands understanding those stakeholders who may need the potential for traceability, what for and when? Acquiring clear-cut answers to these questions at the start of a project is not straightforward, as both stakeholders and their task needs will change. Even if these could be articulated exhaustively, building a *traceability solution* to service all needs is unlikely to be cost-effective, as resources are generally limited in some finite way. Determining whose needs to satisfy, and so which *traceability-enabled activities and tasks* to facilitate, is a value decision that lies at the heart of a traceability strategy; determining needs and resourcing constraints is a precursor to any discussion about trace artifacts, trace links and mechanism.

Traceability solution – The *traceability information model (TIM)* and *traceability process*, as defined, designed and implemented for a particular project situation, along with any associated *traceability tooling*. The *traceability solution* is determined as a core part of the *traceability strategy*.

Traceability information model (TIM) – A graph defining the permissible *trace artifact types*, the permissible *trace link types* and the permissible *trace relationships* on a project, in order to address the anticipated *traceability-related queries* and *traceability-enabled activities and tasks*. The *TIM* is an abstract expression of the intended *traceability* for a project. The *TIM* may also capture additional information such as: the cardinality of the *trace artifacts* associated through a *trace link*, the *primary trace link direction*, the purpose of the *trace link* (i.e., the *link semantics*), the location of the *trace artifacts*, the *tracer* responsible for creating and maintaining the *trace link*, etc. (See (Mäder et al., 2009a) for more detail.)

Traceability process – An instance of a *traceability process model* defining the particular series of activities to be employed to establish *traceability* and render it usable for a particular project, along with a description of the responsibilities and resourcing required to undertake them, as well as their inputs and outputs. The *traceability process* defines how to undertake *traceability strategy*, *traceability creation*, *traceability maintenance* and *traceability use*.

Traceability tool – Any instrument or device that serves to assist or automate any part of the *traceability process*.

Traceability-enabled activities and tasks – Those software and systems engineering activities and tasks that *traceability* supports, such as verification and validation, impact analysis and change management.

Ensuring that the traceability is then established as planned, and yet can adapt to remain effective as needs evolve and as a project's artifacts change, is also the province of traceability strategy. Determining how the traceability will be provisioned such that the requisite quality can be continuously assured further demands analysis, assessment and potential modification of the current traceability solution. Assessing the quality and the execution of the traceability solution, and implementing a feedback loop to improve it, is a critical part of the traceability strategy for a project; it needs to develop and leverage historical *traceability information*.

Traceability information – Any *traceability*-related data, such as *traceability information models*, *trace artifacts*, *trace links* and other *traceability work products*.

Within the context of a broader traceability strategy, the creation, maintenance and use of individual traces and their constituent elements all need to be defined and managed. Given that atomic traces comprise source, target and relational elements, these data requirements need to be identified. This includes decisions as to meta-data to associate, dependent upon what kinds of traceability-enabled activities and tasks the trace is anticipated to participate in and support. Resourcing, planning and implementation decisions may hence vary on a trace-by-trace basis; for instance, it is quite possible that a particular trace is not created or maintained until its use is actually required. Traces thereby inhabit independent life cycles, the constituent activities of which are examined in the following sections.

3.2 Traceability Creation

When creating a trace, the elements of the trace have to be acquired, represented and then stored in some way, as illustrated in Fig. 5. Reference models and classification schemes characterising different types of trace link and trace artifacts drive the *traceability creation* process, as usually defined within the traceability information model of the overarching traceability strategy.

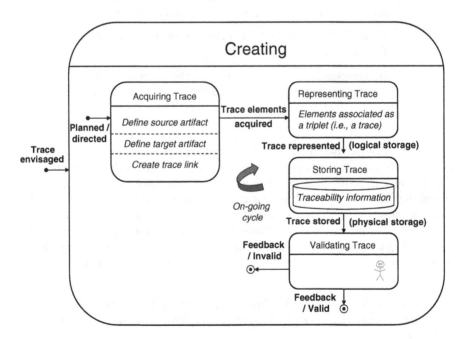

Fig. 5 Traceability creation

Traceability creation – The general activity of associating two (or more) *artifacts*, by providing *trace links* between them, for *tracing* purposes. Note that this could be done manually, automatically or semi-automatically, and additional annotations can be provided as desired to characterize *attributes* of the *traces*.

While project artifacts are generally pre-existing on a project, the links between them may not yet be defined. Techniques to support the creation of trace links can range from manual to automated approaches, each with differing degrees of efficiency and effectiveness. The differentiating factor is often whether the trace links are created concurrently with the forward engineering process (i.e., *trace capture*) or at some point later (i.e., *trace recovery*). Validation is therefore critical to the viability of the traceability creation process, regardless of how trace links are initially created, as it is concerned with determining and assuring the credibility of the trace as a whole.

Trace capture – A particular approach to *trace creation* that implies the creation of *trace links* concurrently with the creation of the *artifacts* that they associate. These *trace links* may be created automatically or semi-automatically using tools.

Trace recovery – A particular approach to *trace creation* that implies the creation of *trace links* after the *artifacts* that they associate have been generated and manipulated. These *trace links* may be created automatically or semi-automatically using tools. The term can be construed to infer that the *trace link* previously existed but now is lost.

3.3 Traceability Maintenance

An association made between two artifacts at a moment in time to serve a particular purpose does not automatically mean that the resulting trace will have a persistent, useful life. The need for maintenance on a trace can be triggered by changes to any of the trace's elements that, in turn, can be triggered by changes to elements within a chain. *Traceability maintenance* can also be required following changes to the requirements and constraints that drive the overarching traceability strategy.

Traceability maintenance – Those activities associated with updating pre-existing *traces* as changes are made to the *traced artifacts* and the *traceability* evolves, *creating* new *traces* where needed to keep the *traceability* relevant and up to date.

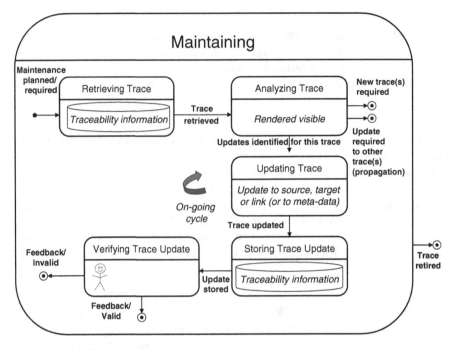

Fig. 6 Traceability maintenance

To maintain a trace, it needs to be retrieved and the nature of the change analysed to determine what update is necessary, as illustrated in Fig. 6. This may necessitate the propagation of changes and/or the creation of entirely new traces. Updates need to be performed, where applicable, recorded and verified. Feedback on the maintenance process is also essential for evolving the overarching traceability strategy. As per traceability creation, traces can be maintained continuously or on-demand.

> **Continuous traceability maintenance** – The update of impacted *trace links* immediately following changes to *traced artifacts*.
>
> **On-demand traceability maintenance** – A dedicated and overall update of the *trace set* (in whole or in part), generally in response to some explicit trigger and in preparation for an upcoming *traceability use*.

3.4 Traceability Use

The availability and usefulness of traces has to be ensured to allow for their ongoing use throughout the software and systems development life cycle, potentially in a myriad of configurable ways. Here, it is helpful to distinguish between short-term *traceability use* during initial product development and long-term traceability use during subsequent product maintenance. Typical short-term uses for traceability include requirements completeness analysis, requirements trade-off analysis or requirements-to-acceptance-test mapping for final acceptance testing. Typical examples of long-term uses for traceability include the determination of effects of changes to a software system or the propagation of changes during its evolution.

> **Traceability use** – Those activities associated with putting *traces* to use to support various software and systems engineering activities and tasks, such as verification and validation, impact analysis and change management.

Any atomic trace is likely to play a role in the context of many use contexts. To use a trace in isolation, or as a constituent part of a chain, it needs to be retrieved and rendered visible in some task-specific way, as suggested in Fig. 7. An important component of the use process is assessing the quality of the traceability that is provided in terms of the fitness for purpose with respect to the task or activity for which the traceability is required. Such information provides a feedback loop to improve the overall traceability strategy.

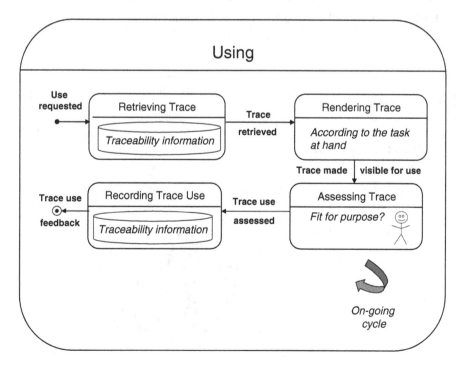

Fig. 7 Traceability use

4 Basic Types of Traceability and Associated Concepts

Additional terms that delineate different basic types of traceability are highlighted in the context of Fig. 8 and defined below.

The traceability of Fig. 8 is bidirectional. *Forward traceability* offers the potential to link a single requirement statement to those methods of the class designed to implement it, and subsequently to follow this trace link to reveal the forward engineering process. *Backward traceability* offers the potential to link the class methods back to the requirement that they help to satisfy, and subsequently to follow this trace link to reveal the reverse engineering process. The forward and the backward direction pertain to the logical flow of the software and systems development process. These are the fundamental and primitive types of tracing.

Forward traceability – The potential for *forward tracing*.

Forward tracing – In software and systems engineering contexts, the term is commonly used when the *tracing* follows subsequent steps in a developmental path, which is not necessarily a chronological path, such as forward from requirements through design to code. Note that the *trace links* themselves could be used in either a *primary* or *reverse trace link direction*, dependent upon the specification of the participating *traces*.

Backward traceability – The potential for *backward tracing*.

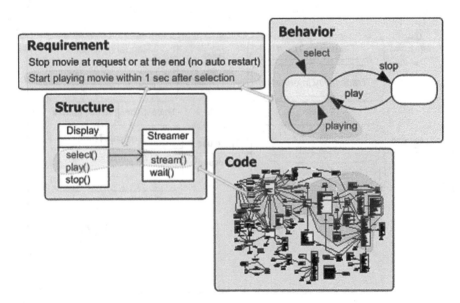

Fig. 8 A simplified, but typical, tracing context

Backward tracing – In software and systems engineering contexts, the term is commonly used when the *tracing* follows antecedent steps in a developmental path, which is not necessarily a chronological path, such as backward from code through design to requirements. Note that the *trace links* themselves could be used in either a *primary* or *reverse trace link direction*, dependent upon the specification of the participating *traces*.

In Fig. 8, the potential to trace from the requirement through to the code is *vertical traceability*, linking artifacts at differing levels of abstraction to accommodate life cycle-wide or end-to-end traceability. Any potential to trace between versions of the requirement or versions of the code is *horizontal traceability*, linking artifacts at the same level of abstraction at different moments in time to accommodate versioning and rollback. These two types of tracing, vertical and horizontal, employ both forward and backward tracing.

Vertical traceability – The potential for *vertical tracing*.

Vertical tracing – In software and systems engineering contexts, the term is commonly used when *tracing artifacts* at differing levels of abstraction so as to accommodate life cycle-wide or end-to-end *traceability*, such as from requirements to code. *Vertical tracing* may employ both *forward tracing* and *backward tracing*.

Horizontal traceability – The potential for *horizontal tracing*.

Horizontal tracing – In software and systems engineering contexts, the term is commonly used when *tracing artifacts* at the same level of abstraction, such as: (i) *traces* between all the requirements created by "Mary", (ii) *traces* between requirements that are concerned with the performance of the system, or (iii) *traces* between versions of a particular requirement at different moments in time. *Horizontal tracing* may employ both *forward tracing* and *backward tracing*.

Two additional types of traceability are more conceptual in nature, and these can employ each of the above tracing types in some combination. *Post-requirements (specification) traceability* comprises those traces derived from or grounded in the requirements, and hence explicates the requirements' deployment process. *Pre-requirements (specification) traceability* comprises all those traces that show the derivation of the requirements from their sources, and hence explicates the requirements' production process. Only post-requirements traceability is evident in Fig. 8 since the requirement is the earliest development artifact available; this is the most common form of traceability in practice.

Post-requirements (specification) traceability – The potential for *post-requirements (specification) tracing*.

Post-requirements (specification) tracing – In software and systems engineering contexts, the term is commonly used to refer to those *traces* derived from or grounded in the requirements, and hence the *traceability* explicates the requirements' deployment process. The *tracing* is, therefore, forward from requirements and back to requirements. *Post-requirements (specification) tracing* may employ *forward tracing, backward tracing, horizontal tracing* and *vertical tracing*.

Pre-requirements (specification) traceability – The potential for *pre-requirements (specification) tracing*.

Pre-requirements (specification) tracing – In software and systems engineering contexts, the term is commonly used to refer to those *traces* that show the derivation of the requirements from their original sources, and hence the *traceability* explicates the requirements' production process. The *tracing* is, therefore, forward to requirements and back from requirements. *Pre-requirements (specification) tracing* may employ *forward tracing, backward tracing, horizontal tracing* and *vertical tracing*.

Figure 8 also serves to highlight some basic complexities surrounding traceability and so lends itself to the definition of a number of associated traceability concepts:

- Do we create an atomic trace for each class method or for the cluster of methods within a class? This is an issue of *trace granularity*.

Trace granularity – The level of detail at which a *trace* is recorded and performed. The granularity of a *trace* is defined by the granularity of the *source artifact* and the *target artifact*.

- Do the three methods in the Display class fully satisfy the requirement? This is a question related to completeness. Does the trace then lead to the right code? This is a question of correctness. Is the trace up to date? This depends upon whether the traced artifacts reflect the latest project status. All of these questions are associated with the concept of *traceability quality*.

Traceability quality – A measurable property of the overall *traceability* at a particular point in time on a project, such as a confidence score depicting its overall correctness, accuracy, precision, completeness, consistency, timeliness, usefulness, etc.

- As Fig. 8 suggests, traces typically associate artifacts that are semantically very different, so the use of natural language alone to derive a trace link cannot always be trusted. For example, the play transition in the behavioural Statechart of Fig. 8 does not trace to the play method in the class diagram, or does it? Open issues in traceability research and practice have led to the formulation of a set of *traceability challenges* by the *traceability community*, and work is now underway to develop a *Traceability Body of Knowledge (TBOK)*.

Traceability community – Those people who are *establishing* and *using traceability* in practice, or have done so in the past or intend to do so in the future. Also, those people who are active in *traceability* research or in one of its many interrelated areas.

Traceability challenge – A significant problem with *traceability* that members of the international research and industrial communities agree deserves attention in order to achieve advances in *traceability practice*.

Traceability Body of Knowledge (TBOK) – A proposed resource for the *traceability community*, containing *traceability benchmarks*, good *traceability practices*, *traceability* experience reports, etc.

5 Conclusions

This chapter has defined terminology and concepts that are fundamental to the discipline of traceability. This includes the essential terms of trace, trace artifact, trace link, traceability and tracing in Section 2, along with a number of interrelated and dependent terms. The chapter has also described a generic traceability process model in Section 3 and characterised the basic activities involved in the life cycle of a trace. This includes a consideration of the activities comprising traceability strategy, traceability creation, traceability maintenance and traceability use. In Section 4, the chapter distinguishes between basic types of traceability and explains some key associated concepts.

The chapter is supplemented by an extensive glossary that has been developed and endorsed by members of the traceability community. This glossary contains additional terms and can be found as an appendix to this book.

References

Aizenbud-Reshef, N., Nolan, B.T., Rubin, J., Shaham-Gafni, Y.: Model traceability. IBM Syst. J. **45**(3), 515–526 (2006, July)

Boehm, B.W.: Software engineering. IEEE Trans. Comput. **c-25**(12), 1226–1241 (1976, December)

Cleland-Huang, J., Settimi, R., Romanova, E., Berenbach, B., Clark, S.: Best practices for automated traceability. IEEE Comput. **40**(6), 27–35 (2007, June)

Dorfman, M., Flynn, R.F.: ARTS – An automated requirements traceability system. J. Syst. Softw. **4**(1), 63–74 (1984, April)

Dorfman, M., Thayer, R.H.: Standards, Guidelines, and Examples on System and Software Requirements Engineering: IEEE Computer Society Press Tutorial. IEEE Computer Society Press, Los Alamitos, CA (1990)

Galvao, I., Goknil, A.: Survey of traceability approaches in model-driven engineering. In: Proceedings of the 11th IEEE International Enterprise Distributed Object Computing Conference, Annapolis, MD, USA, 15–19 Oct, 2007, pp. 313–324.

Gotel, O., Finkelstein, A.: An analysis of the requirements traceability problem. In: Proceedings of the 1st IEEE International Conference on Requirements Engineering, Colorado Springs, CO, USA, 18–22 Apr, 1994, pp. 94–101.

Huffman Hayes, J., Dekhtyar, A., Sundaram, S.: Advancing candidate link generation for requirements tracing: The study of methods. IEEE Trans. Softw. Eng. **32**(1), pp. 4–19 (2006, January)

Lindvall, M., Sandahl, K.: Practical implications of traceability. Softw. Pract. Exp. **26**(10), 1161–1180 (1996, October)

Mäder, P., Gotel, O., Philippow, I.: Getting back to basics: Promoting the use of a traceability information model in practice. In: Proceedings of the 5th International Workshop on Traceability in Emerging Forms of Software Engineering, Vancouver, BC, Canada, 18 May, 2009a.

Mäder, P., Gotel, O., Philippow, I.: Motivation matters in the traceability trenches. In: Proceedings of 17th IEEE International Requirements Engineering Conference, Atlanta, GA, USA, 31 Aug–4 Sept, 2009b, pp. 143–148.

Naur, P., Randell, B. (eds.): Software engineering: Report of a conference sponsored by the NATO Science Committee, Garmisch, Germany, 7–11 October 1968, Brussels, Scientific Affairs Division, NATO (Published 1969)

The Oxford English Dictionary: Online Version, Oxford University Press, Oxford. http://www.oed.com. Accessed on January 2007

Pierce, R.: A requirements tracing tool. ACM SIGSOFT Softw. Eng. Notes. **3**(5), pp. 53–60 (1978, November)

Ramesh, B., Edwards, M.: Issues in the development of a requirements traceability model. In: Proceedings of the IEEE International Symposium on Requirements Engineering, San Diego, CA, USA, 4–6 Jan 1993, pp. 256–259.

Ramesh B., Jarke M.: Towards reference models for requirements traceability. IEEE Trans. Softw. Eng. **27**(1), 58–93 (2001, January)

Randell, B.: Towards a methodology of computing system design. In: Naur, P., Randell, B. (eds.) NATO Software Engineering Conference, 1968, Report on a Conference Sponsored by the NATO Science Committee, Garmisch, Germany, pp. 204–208 (7–11 October 1968). Brussels, Scientific Affairs Division, NATO (Published 1969)

Winkler, S., von Pilgrim, J.: A survey of traceability in requirements engineering and model-driven development. Softw. Syst. Model. **9**(4), pp. 529–565 (2010, September). Springer (Published on line December 22, 2009)

Cost-Benefits of Traceability

Claire Ingram and Steve Riddle

1 Introduction

Cost has been cited as a key reason why many projects neglect or abandon traceability efforts without reaping the full range of potential rewards. In this chapter we introduce some key issues behind maximising the cost-benefit from a traceability system. Achieving the optimal cost-benefit from traceability is about achieving the maximum return on the investment (ROI), as well ensuring that traceability data is sufficient to meet the project goals.

The ultimate purpose of any traceability strategy is to improve the performance of some future activity. The potential uses of traceability data are discussed elsewhere in this book, but trace data can be useful for: conducting impact analysis for estimating change effort; ensuring sufficient test coverage; supporting safety case or some other third party certification; identifying potential candidates for re-use; tracking project progress; reconstructing earlier decisions to avoid rework; and controlling requirements creep. Most projects will need to carry out at least a subset of these traceability-enabled tasks. If traceability data which adequately supports the task is available (e.g., this could be a list of components relevant to a requirement, a list of the reasons why a design decision was made, or a list of people involved in drafting a requirement), much time can be saved and the task can be completed to a high standard with more confidence. Ramesh et al. cite an extreme example of a project forced to back-hire engineers who had left in order to reconstruct the reasons behind original design rationale (Ramesh et al., 1995); this situation could perhaps have been avoided if the reasons for decisions had been more easily traceable. Although this is an extreme case, trace data can generally ensure that future activities like impact analysis or safety case preparation can be conducted to a sufficiently high standard in less time than otherwise.

C. Ingram (✉)
Newcastle University, NE1 7RU, England, UK
e-mail: claire.ingram@ncl.ac.uk

J. Cleland-Huang et al. (eds.), *Software and Systems Traceability*,
DOI 10.1007/978-1-4471-2239-5_2, © Springer-Verlag London Limited 2012

The availability of appropriate trace data thus reduces the effort required for many activities. But at the same time gathering and maintaining such data increases the initial project cost. There is therefore a trade-off between increasing the cost of collecting traceability data and reducing the later costs of carrying out these traceability-enabled activities. We can calculate the financial savings traceability can bring by estimating the cost of completing tasks such as impact analysis without appropriate traceability data; the cost to complete the same tasks *with* trace data (including the cost of creating and maintaining the data); and taking the difference between the two as the cost-benefit. This is illustrated in Fig. 1, where we represent two scenarios. The optimal scenario occurs when the combined cost of managing trace data and consuming it later to perform some traceability-enabled activity is less than the cost of completing these activities without any traceability data. The worst case scenario arises when managing and using trace data is actually *more* expensive than not using trace data at all. This chapter focuses on strategies for achieving the optimal scenario, which includes a combination of:

- keeping the cost of managing traceability data (including collecting and updating it) to a minimum
- ensuring the quality of data collected is of an acceptable quality to meet all project needs

This chapter addresses issues of controlling costs and trace quality in Sections 2 and 3 before discussing some general issues centering on estimating traceability costs in Section 4. In the discussions below we are working towards selecting the best traceability cost strategies to enable the maximum return on investment.

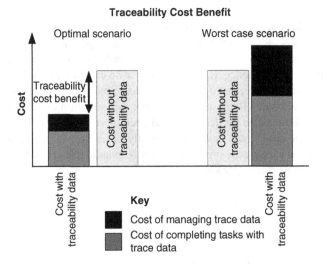

Fig. 1 Bar chart comparing the cost of completing tasks with and without traceability data

We present some possible traceability strategies in Section 5. Finally, in Section 6 we suggest a simple way to conduct a cost analysis during traceability planning.

2 Controlling Traceability Costs

In this section we discuss strategies for minimising the cost of gathering and/or storing trace data. The maximum return on investment is reached by collecting high-quality trace data at a low cost. However, there is a natural tension between these aims, since higher quality data is generally more expensive to collect and to maintain. The first step in controlling the costs of a traceability scheme, therefore, is to ensure that all trace data collected has a definite purpose, and that no effort is wasted on collecting unusable data.

2.1 Establishing Traceability Goals

Capturing, storing and maintaining *all* possible data is prohibitively time-consuming, and likely to result in an unmanageably large dataset. For even a moderately large project, systematically collecting and subsequently maintaining unnecessary data introduces a non-trivial overhead. The resultant mass of data also makes it more difficult to pick out and manage the data which is actually useful. On the other hand, it would be equally undesirable to discover at a later date that the trace data which has been collected is inadequate to support specific activities. Therefore some thought must be given to the subject of traceability at the project outset, and the purpose of the trace data clearly identified. Traceability systems may then be tailored appropriately for the individual project's needs to avoid situations where too much or too little trace data is created. In particular, if trace data is not needed in order to meet a specific goal, then it should not be collected and/or stored (Cleland-Huang et al., 2004).

Any traceability effort should start with the question: what is the main aim/purpose of the traceability data? The main activities which will later be supported by traceability, and the tools that will be used, must be identified beforehand. We outline some key questions to ask in Section 6 in this chapter, which may be helpful in determining the potential use of traceability data.

Egyed et al. introduce the notion of a threshold of usefulness (Egyed et al., 2005). That is, the tools and/or processes which will be used will normally dictate a minimum quality for the trace data. This threshold must be identified for each type of trace data. If the data will not meet this threshold then gathering it is a cost that yields no benefits at all and it should be omitted. In Section 6 of this chapter we discuss some possible pitfalls. It's worth noting, however, that there are some situations in which imperfect traceability data may still be useful – this is discussed further in Section 3.

Once the traceability aims are clear, the actual collection of data can be considered.

2.2 Trace Creation and Evolution

There are two major activities involved in ensuring that trace data is available:

- *Trace creation*, the act of creating links to link two development artifacts
- *Trace maintenance*, activities necessary to keep existing traces up to date

It's generally quicker and more accurate to create trace links between artifacts at the time that those artifacts are created (Heindl and Biffl, 2005). This is when knowledge of artifacts' purposes and interactions is at its most keen. Attempting to create trace links later, after system development has been completed, will most likely take longer because staff who originally worked on the artifacts may have left, or have forgotten (and have to search for) small details regarding linkages. There is also greater chance that useful trace links will be omitted by creating trace data later.

Any data which is captured during trace creation must then be kept up to date carefully. Anecdotal reports and academic research (for example, (Cleland-Huang, 2006; Cleland-Huang et al., 2003)) have indicated that, without active maintenance to evolve the trace links, they will gradually become less and less reliable as the system evolves and the trace links cease to reflect that. Creating more trace data commits the project to a greater maintenance effort in the future, although tools are available to support maintenance of links (Cleland-Huang et al., 2003).

2.3 Using Automated Tools

It has been suggested (Cleland-Huang et al., 2004) that a sensible tracing strategy is to "maximise the usage of dynamic link generation", such as information retrieval technology and heuristic traceability. These types of technology may not apply in all scenarios, however – for example, the precision or recall of a tool may not meet project requirements. A simple optimisation strategy is to use the tool on all requirements, and manually check the links on a subset of prioritised requirements (see Section 3.1). Egyed et al. automated the checking process, optimising an automated trace generator using a filter (Egyed, 2005). Their approach involved measuring the "strength" of each trace link generated; this was calculated as the ratio of the number of methods implementing a requirement and the number of methods that two requirements share as part of their implementation. The filter then determines a threshold of "weak" links, which can be eliminated as they are far more likely to be false positives. The optimisation proved helpful; they found that the weakest 10% of trace links contained only 1% of true traces.

3 Trace Quality

In the introduction to this chapter we said that the cost-benefits of traceability are not reached if data does not reach an acceptable quality for the project's requirements. What is meant by "acceptable quality" varies between different projects.

For example, an avionics system and an online ordering system may have different expectations regarding thoroughness of testing coverage.

We can define the "quality" of traceability data as a function of the following factors:

- the granularity of trace links
- the recall and precision of the links – that is, the number of false positives and/or false negatives that are retrieved
- the level of coverage they achieve for the system as a whole

These attributes are not fixed: the applicable minimum level can be varied for all or any of these factors. In general terms, increasing the quality (by making data more complete, more fine-grained, more accurate or more precise) tends to increase cost. One way, therefore, to control costs is to define carefully the minimum acceptable quality threshold for each type of trace data (bearing in mind that different traceability goals and different areas of the system may have differing requirements) and ensure that data gathered does not exceed it unless there is a clear extra benefit in doing so.

Varying the granularity of trace links is one way to control costs. For example, studies have been completed estimating the effort needed to link requirements variously to packages; to class files; and to individual methods (Egyed, 2005; Egyed et al., 2005, 2007). Increasing the level of granularity of the trace links (e.g., creating trace links that link to class-level as opposed to package-level) tended to increase the effort required by an order of magnitude. However, the researchers detected a decreasing marginal return on investment as the trace links become finer-grained (Egyed et al., 2007). Heindl and Biffl describe a case study where requirements were given one of three priorities (Heindl and Biffl, 2005). Trace links created for level 1 requirements traced from requirements to individual methods, whilst lower-priority requirements were linked to classes or packages. This approach reduced effort required by 30–70%, compared to a fully traced system. In many cases, the reduction in precision was not large, because some classes had few methods, and so the difference between tracing to methods and tracing to classes was small. For requirements where trace data will not be needed frequently, collecting detailed trace links may not yield a good return on investment, because most of the data gathered will never be needed. Storing some granular links initially and improving them on demand later can help to reduce wastefulness. Thus it's important to consider carefully whether a coarse collection of links would be sufficient for some (or all) traceability purposes.

There are other ways to vary the quality of the trace data which is collected. For example:

- The coverage of the system can be varied, so that traceability links do not cover all areas of the system
- The frequency of updates can be varied. Thus the most high-priority trace links may be re-evaluated and updated each time a change is enacted, whilst lower-priority links may not be updated at all after they are created, or only re-evaluated at sparse intervals.

- The use of automated link generation can be varied (discussed in Section 2.3 of this chapter).
- The recall and/or precision of links can be varied. Precision is concerned with achieving a low number of false positives. A false positive is encountered when a trace link is created that is invalid (in reality, no link should exist). Recall is concerned with achieving a low number of false negatives, or "missed" links; a false negative arises where a trace link is not created when a dependency does, in fact, exist.

Varying the recall and precision of trace data is particularly pertinent when using automated tools, as many tools can be calibrated to favour one or the other. Recall and precision frequently exist in a state of mutual tension. For example, 100% recall can be achieved simply by returning all possible links, but this results in a very low level of precision (and is not very useful).

For any traceability strategy, managers should consider whether recall or precision is more important. For safety critical projects, for example, recall will probably be more important. During many traceability-enabled activities on such a project, engineers will not want to run the risk that a link is missed, and are prepared to spend time eliminating false positives. On the other hand, a non-safety critical project with a tight deadline may prefer to favour precision, assuming that an automated tool is likely to return the most important links, and the less important can be detected later.

3.1 Ranking Requirements for Selective Traceability

So, significant cost savings can be made by focussing the higher-quality trace gathering effort on key system areas only. This strategy involves ranking the requirements. Ranking can be conducted using a variety of criteria, for example:

- Ranking on predicted volatility (Heindl and Biffl, 2005). Change-prone components are more likely to be the subject of change impact assessments, which will be much easier to carry out if good quality trace data is available. However, this tactic relies on being able to predict change-prone areas of the system. Some major sources of changes can include: customer expectations; changes to platforms and/or third-party systems; changes to relevant regulations; and market or organisational changes. Informed stakeholders may be able to predict some change-prone requirements if they are aware of these factors. Other approaches for predicting volatility use software metrics which measure complexity or software size to determine which components are more likely to change frequently (Arisholm et al., 2004; Basili et al., 1996; Briand et al., 1999; Chaumun et al., 1999; Han et al., 2008; Ingram and Riddle, 2011; Li and Henry, 1993; Ratzinger et al., 2007; Wilkie and Kitchenham, 2000).
- Ranking on predicted risk. This may be calculated see (Cleland-Huang et al., 2004) as probability multiplied by impact, where *probability* is an estimate of a requirement's likelihood of changing, and *impact* is an estimate of the business impact.

- Ranking on required reliability. Huang and Boehm, for example, assign one of five categories to requirements: loss of human life; high financial loss; moderate recoverable loss; low, easily recoverable loss; and slight inconvenience (Huang and Boehm, 2006). Applying enhanced tracebility to these areas allows critical parts of the system to benefit from better quality traceability, ensuring that later tasks can meet higher expectations of accuracy.
- Asking end users to rank requirements in terms of importance to them (Boehm and Huang, 2006; Heindl and Biffl, 2005). Boehm and Huang suggest using the DMR group's "benefits realisation approach", which provides a framework for estimating the contributions and initiatives of a requirement.

Once requirements have been prioritised, then decisions can be made as to the minimum quality of trace data needed for differently ranked requirements. In some cases, reducing the quality of trace data to be collected results in a reduction in effort but not a commensurate reduction in later cost savings, and these types of compromises may be worth making. We discuss estimations of costs and savings in the next section.

4 Cost Estimation

Estimating the effort needed for a given traceability strategy and scheduling adequate time is an important factor in achieving the maximum return on investment. It's been suggested that traceability is often the first item to be squeezed from a tight project schedule (Jarke, 1998). This could potentially represent the worst case scenario for traceability cost benefit; time spent creating links at the project's outset doesn't result in significantly less effort on later traceability-enabled activities if traceability is abandoned part-way.

As discussed in Section 3.1 of this chapter, the best traceability strategy for a given project may be one in which some compromises are made in order to ensure that other, less acceptable compromises are not necessary. For this reason, estimating the costs of different traceability tactics is important for calculating which compromises bring worthwhile savings, and which compromises are unacceptable. Determining which compromises are likely to be worth making involves:

- a good understanding of the relative importance and impact of different project areas (ranking of requirements is discussed in Section 3.1)
- understanding the cost impacts of various traceability tactics (including the costs of creating trace links and the potential savings in effort later on) compared with the costs of activities without trace data

We briefly introduce some key ideas underpinning cost estimation and traceability in this section. Cost estimation is a major subject in its own right, however, and we don't attempt a full introduction to the subject here.

A number of techniques and models for estimating development effort in general have been proposed, although large scale surveys have shown that no model is likely to be completely accurate all the time (Kemerer, 1987). Most cost estimation models, for maximum effectiveness, require careful calibration to a particular organisation's working culture and problem domain (Kemerer, 1987), since one type of development and business may have substantially different overheads and minimum quality thresholds than another. Data which can be useful for estimating costs includes:

- System size, clearly one of the most important determinants of total effort. This is a basic input used by estimation models such as the COCOMO and SLIM models (Kemerer, 1987). "Size" can be difficult to measure; some models use lines of code (LOC) as a metric. "Function points" was developed as an alternative metric (Kemerer, 1987) by Albrecht (1979); Albrecht and Gaffney (1983). Function points capture features such as the number of input transactions types and the number of reports to be output. This has the advantage over LOC that it is easy to determine at the design stage.
- Expert judgement, which is normally provided by someone with similar previous experience or detailed knowledge of the project at hand. In many cases this may require a mental "rehearsal" of the steps required to complete the task (Hughes, 1996). However, even a competent, experienced and well-informed developer on a project may forget (or be unaware of) small aspects that will need to be investigated.
- Analogy – comparing the new system to be developed to a previous, similar system (Hughes, 1996). Good practice should dictate that estimated and actual costs should be saved from the current project for use in future estimating tasks.
- A selection of "cost drivers" – that is, factors specific to the project that may affect costs. This can include: team size; the productivity/experience of personnel; project complexity; requirements volatility; tools available and so on. Many cost models use this type of data to "calibrate" a model to a particular working environment.

Finally, project "cost" can include the addition of some penalty should a task fail to be carried out to a sufficiently high standard. For example, there are likely to be either direct or indirect financial consequences of failing to ensure some appropriate level of testing coverage.

There's a difference between estimating the effort involved in traceability-related tasks, and estimating the actual costs. We need to understand the effort required to create and evolve trace links so that project schedules can be planned realistically. Traceability *costs*, however, offset the initial cost of that effort against estimated future savings and are useful for selecting appropriate traceability optimisations. We discuss both separately below.

4.1 Estimating Effort for Traceability

Total effort for traceability can be represented by two separate estimates. These can be adjusted independently. There should be an esimate for the time taken to create trace links at the outset, and another estimate for time taken to maintain the links as the system evolves. These two figures will each have an impact on the overall costs, since they will affect positively or negatively the effort required to perform traceeability-enabled activities later. For example, one option is not to perform any updates on links, or to update very infrequently, but this will require more manual checking when the trace data is used to support some activity. Whether this is a worthwhile trade-off will depend on the predicted frequency with which updates will be required.

There are not many studies showing how much time it takes to create or maintain trace links. Heindl and Biffl found that generating trace links from requirements to methods averaged around 45 min per requirement, whilst generating trace links from requirements to classes required a much lower effort, averaging 10 min per requirement (Heindl and Biffl, 2005). They do point out that this data represents time taken to capture trace links after the project's duration, and that estimates may be lower if trace links are generated during the project itself. Cleland-Huang et al. produced some estimates using a guide figure of 15 min to create a trace link (Cleland-Huang et al., 2004), although this is a hypothetical figure produced to illustrate costs for different traceability strategies.

As a more general figure, Heindl and Biffl estimate that tracing effort absorbs around 5% of the total project costs "as part of quality assurance activities" (Heindl and Biffl, 2005). Required documentation standards should already be costed in to the project cost before producing this estimate, as well as project size and duration. In addition, this figure could be refined as follows:

- volatile requirements will tend to increase traceability maintenance costs, whilst very stable requirements will reduce them. Well-informed stakeholders may be able to make some predictions about volatility in requirements to help with this.
- project duration and the estimated length of the maintenance period are likely to affect the cost estimates. A longer project will need to conduct more updates on trace links, so trace maintenance estimates should be increased for longer projects. However, greater savings can potentially be made, as the quantity of traceability-enabled activities tends to increase over time (for example, a longer project will see more change requests), so the effort saved can amalgamate.
- using automated techniques (such as information retrieval tools) is likely to reduce costs for trace creation, but increase costs associated with traceability-enabled activitites, because data may require some manual refinement at point of use. Alternatively, extra time could be spent when generating links ensure that the most important requirements are refined manually at the outset.
- an automated tool which favours recall over precision when creating or searching for trace links is likely to increase the estimate for trace-enabled activities, since more time will be spent on eliminating the false positives from trace queries. However, this will likely result in better overall accuracy, so there will be lower chances of incurring penalties associated with missing any potential links. Conversely, cost estimates for traceability-enabled activities may be lower for tools which favour precision, but there may be extra penalties (such as dissatisfied customers) incurred from dealing with any false negatives ("missed" trace

links) at a later date. This may be a cost-effective strategy, however, for products which require a rapid time-to-market.

- using techniques such as a simple traceability matrix (rather than, for example, adopting automated tools) can increase costs of traceability creation and maintenance (Cleland-Huang et al., 2004).
- more finely-grained trace data will increase trace creation and maintenance costs but is likely to reduce the time taken to complete traceability-enabled activities later. This cost could be altered by selectively varying the granularity of trace data (see Section 3.1). Increasing the granularity of trace data (from package-level to class-level, or from class-level to method-level) has been estimated to raise the required effort by 10% (Egyed, 2005; Egyed et al., 2005, 2007).
- updating trace links more regularly increases the estimate for maintenance but will decrease the estimate for later trace-enabled activities.

Finally, if the requirements are prioritised as suggested in Section 3.1 of this chapter, separate estimates may be needed for the differently-ranked groups of requirements. For example, low-priority requirements may have links auto-generated and not updated, whilst high-priority requirements may be entered manually and updated frequently.

4.2 *Estimating Costs for Traceability*

To come up with an estimate of the *cost* of traceability (as opposed to effort needed for scheduling), we include the cost of creating and maintaining the links, and factor in potential savings made by improving performance on future traceability-enabled activities, as was illustrated in Fig. 1. We can estimate this by looking at:

- the predicted number of times the activities supported by traceability are likely to be repeated. For example, approximately how many change requests can we expect, over what expected duration?
- estimates of the time taken to perform a task both with and without access to updated trace data. For example, a change impact analysis might be expected to take n person-hours when trace data is available, and m person-hours when it is not.

This should lead to two figures for estimated duration of later tasks, representing the effort required when supported and when not supported by trace data. The difference between the two gives the traceability cost benefit, which can be factored in (as a saving) to the final traceability cost.

Graphs produced (Cleland-Huang et al., 2004) make clear that the costs of trace creation and maintenance are generally only repaid after a period of time. This fact underpins a major problem associated with traceability: the cost of traceability is very visible up-front, whilst the financial savings made possible by trace data are not visible until a much later stage in development. However, from the traceability costing described here it should be possible to produce a prediction of when the project can expect to realise benefits from the trace data.

5 Traceability Strategies

Once estimates have been obtained, a traceability strategy can be produced in iterative stages, refining the trace quality as necessary for differently ranked requirements, until an optimal balance of cost and trace quality is achieved. A traceability strategy can make use of any techniques discussed so far, combining tactics such as:

- partitioning or ranking the system for traceability purposes, and selectively applying different traceability rules
- varying the granularity of trace links
- adopting tools where possible to create or search trace links, optimising the recall or precision as appropriate
- varying the coverage of the trace links
- varying the frequency with which trace links are maintained
- varying the application of automated link generation, and/or manual checks of the results

The costs and potential savings of different tactics can be estimated for the project; the tactics that are selected will be those that achieve the best balance between quality and cost. Developing the strategy will therefore be an iterative process (we describe this further in the next section).

Many projects – intentionally or not – adopt a strategy of generating links on an ad-hoc basis as and when required. Superficially, this strategy looks inexpensive, because it does not incur costs on the initial plans, whilst the savings incurred by completing traceability-enabled activities to a high standard are not visible. Several studies have suggested that this is in actuality not a very cost-effective strategy. Heindl and Biffl, for example, determined that, to be viable, the ad-hoc approach relies on infrequent requests for traceability data, a small project, and a high degree of domain and product knowledge among developers (Heindl and Biffl, 2005). In contrast, some studies have found that a strategy that mixes a number of varying approaches tend to produce a good return on investment. Cleland-Huang et al., for example, compared four potential trace strategies (Cleland-Huang et al., 2004), including:

- tracing and maintaining links using a simple matrix
- not maintaining links (it's assumed 15% of requirements change per year) and instead managing changes using "brute force analysis"
- tracing and maintaining links for critical requirements only, and manually tracing others

- the latter but with the addition of tools such as event-based traceability and information retrieval techniques (a "heterogenous" strategy)

The study concluded that the heterogenous strategy produced the lowest costs (for the provided case study).

6 Conducting a Practical Cost Analysis

In the rest of this chapter we suggest a simple method for conducting cost analysis to produce a traceability strategy that best meets project needs. The analysis consists of four steps, designed to fit in with existing traceability and software engineering practices:

1. Establishing traceability goals (this was discussed in Section 2.1 of this chapter)
2. Identifying the minimum data required to achieve the goals (discussed in Section 2.1)
3. Prioritising requirements and implementing traceability optimisations (discussed in Section 3).
4. Estimating effort needed to generate and maintain trace links, and refining choices from step (3) (cost estimation was discussed in Section 4).

The final two steps are envisaged as an iterative process of suggesting possible compromises and estimating which is likely to bring a reduction in traceability costs without significantly reducing traceability benefits.

The cost-analysis process is summarised in Fig. 2. The steps are designed to ensure that the maximum benefit can be achieved from the trace data (that the data is fit for purpose and high quality) whilst the total traceability cost is kept as low as possible. We discuss these steps in detail below, illustrating how the framework can be put to use by referring to the iTrust case study.

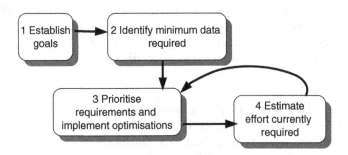

Fig. 2 Steps in a simple traceability cost analysis

6.1 Establish Traceability Goals

Ann is a project manager in charge of a development team working on the iTrust development, tasked with implementing a cost-effective traceability strategy.

She begins by ensuring that appropriate questions are asked of the stakeholders, so that she has enough information to decide what the primary traceability goals must be. Analysis reveals that iTrust is likely to be a highly complex project, with numerous different possible roles users can adopt and potentially a large user base. It's technically challenging, and performance issues are likely to be taxing, given that the system is to support multiple simultaneous connections. Additionally iTrust is affected by strict regulations governing handling of medical data. As a complex and expensive system to develop, iTrust is expected to be in active use for a number of years (i.e., it will have a long maintenance period).

This information leads Ann to conclude that many changes to the system should be expected over its lifespan. These will be prompted by initial performance issues, general complexity, future changes to regulations and varied user demands and expectations. Change management should therefore be a key priority of the project. Strict regulation issues imply that validation and verification activities for both initial development and any future amendments will also be a key issue.

With so many potential sources of requirements and an expected long lifespan, Ann is also keen to record some basic requirements rationale for so that it's clear to customers as well as future development teams exactly why each requirement has been included. This will also help the team to identify and manage situations where users want conflicting features built into the system.

Once identified, the goals will dictate what data will be needed, how it may be managed and which optimisations will be possible. Traceability goals should be considered during requirements elicitation, when stakeholders are available to answer questions on anticipated future use. Some key questions to ask are discussed below. This is not an exhaustive list, but designed to be a practical starting point.

6.1.1 Change

Change management is a major factor underlying many traceability efforts. Answers to these questions are likely to indicate whether methods for improving change management will be a key traceability goal. Key questions here include:

- Do end users or stakeholders anticipate many requirements changes themselves?
- Are there strong expectations that the end system should be adaptable?

- Is this a rapidly developing market?
- Are there external laws or regulations affecting the project and how frequently do they change?
- How many non-functional requirements are there? These can be difficult to "design" and build into the system, and are often approached with iterative improvements to system quality.
- How big is the project/how many requirements does it implement/how long is the project duration? A larger project, or a project with a longer duration, is increasingly likely to see some requirements changes arise.
- How many stakeholders and/or users are involved with the system? Users are a major source of changes, as they discover bugs and make requests. A larger number of users tends to imply that more change requests and/or bug reports can be expected.

6.1.2 Design and Requirements Rationale

Some projects have discovered great benefit can be gained by capturing and storing the rationale behind decisions and deliberations. This type of information can be very helpful for handling major system extensions, refactoring, or preparing safety cases. Projects with high staff turnover are at particularly high risk of knowledge loss; trace data and traceability data structures can present a way to document product knowledge and minimise the loss. Even without staff turnover, developers and designers tend to forget over a period of time the original reasons why key decisions were taken. Taking this on board, Gotel and Finkelstein have suggested a system for recording the people behind major project decisions, particularly requirements rationale (Gotel and Finkelstein, 1995, 1997). Key questions to ask:

- Will the system require any kind of certification (such as a safety case)?
- How experienced are the developers with this type of development?
- Is the system expected to experience a long development/maintenance period?
- How complex is the system?
- What is the expected staff turnover? What is the recent rate of staff turnover in the same organisation?
- How stable (or otherwise) is the project expected to be? (see questions related to change above)

6.1.3 Requirements Management and Testing Coverage

Demonstrating that all requirements are implemented and tested is another very common use of trace data. As with issues relating to change management (above), the presence of many volatile requirements tends to suggest that testing coverage will need to be revisited frequently as requirements change. Key questions to ask include:

- How many requirements does the system implement, and are they stable?
- Are there many sources for requirement – e.g., external regulations or standards?
- Are there conflicts between stakeholders or end users?
- Are there many non-functional requirements? These tend to be cross-cutting (affecting many areas of the system) and are often implemented iteratively, presenting challenges for ensuring testing coverage.
- How many stakeholders and/or users are involved with the system?

6.2 Identifying the Minimum Data Needed

Now that the traceability goals have been identified, Ann can begin to identify the data she needs to capture as part of traceability efforts. Change management is a key issue: for this she will record trace links between requirements, design artifacts, code, test plans and also to requirements sources. These links will allow her to identify areas that will require revisiting should any given requirement be altered. Links to requirements sources (including people) will allow future teams to track down original decision-makers. In some cases, there may be good reasons why a requirement *shouldn't* be modified (e.g., regulations mandate it), so linking to requirements sources and/or rationale will allow developers to identify conflicts quickly and potentially avoid re-work.

Once traceability goals have been identified, subsequent steps become more straightforward, because the data needed is dictated by the goal. As we discussed in Section 2.1 of this chapter, we must aim to store the minimum of information needed. But we should also ensure that all data meets our minimum threshold of usability. Egyed et al. have suggested a list of questions that should be asked when planning a traceability strategy, such as (Egyed et al., 2005):

- is a perfect set of trace links necessary to achieve traceability goals?
- does an increase in quality of trace data justify the cost? (we discussed this point in Section 3)
- are false positives (i.e., the presence of trace links not correct) or false negatives (i.e., the absence of trace links which should be recorded) acceptable?
- what are the implications of errors in trace links?

We discussed in Section 3 how trace quality can be varied, and the potential impact on the ultimate return on investment. Answering the questions suggested by Egyed et al. should help to determine what quality level is an acceptable minimum for each proposed usage. This particular list can also be useful for projects employing automated tools to aid in the creation and/or maintenance of trace links, since tools can be calibrated to produce more complete (probably with more false positives) or more precise (probably with more false negative) sets of trace links.

We provide below a suggested list of link types to be considered. As before, this list is not exhaustive, but intended to be a practical starting point.

- Testing and requirements coverage goals commonly require (at least) trace links between requirements and code/test plans
- Re-use goals require links between requirements and code
- Requirements management also requires links between requirements and code – which can be used to identify where requirements conflict and to control scope creep
- Change management goals will require links between requirements and any other artifact that potentially requires updating as a result of a change. This will almost certainly include requirements, code and test plans. Links to use cases and design data may also be included
- Requirements rationale goals will need links between requirements and their sources
- Design rationale goals will need links between designs, decisions made and rationale behind them, and requirements and/or code affected.

It's tempting to assume that links between requirements and code components (for example) can be implemented by two stages: a link from requirements to design; and a second link from design to code. We might assume that our system could actually conduct two separate searches to find components linked to requirements: firstly, design decisions linked to the requirement; and then components linked to the design decision. This hypothetical set of trace links is illustrated in Fig. 3. However, a collection of links like this can make it impossible to conduct meaningful searches for components linked to requirements if there are many requirements and many components linked to a single design decision. Searching for components linked to Requirement 1 in Fig. 3 is likely to result in a large number of false positives, which will take time to weed out, because the design decision which is an intermediary is linked to many components which are not relevant to Requirement 1.

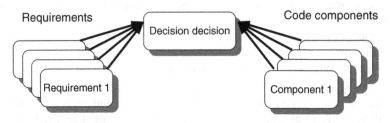

Fig. 3 Hypothetical set of trace links between design decision, requirements and componenets, exhibiting a disparity in granularity

This type of problem can arise anywhere where there is a disparity in granularity between notations used. These scenarios illustrate the need to consider at this stage how trace data will be searched, and to ensure that the quality of the links meets the minimum threshold for usefulness (we discussed this in Section 3 of this chapter).

6.3 Prioritising Requirements and Implementing Optimisations

Before Ann's team begin the task of creating and storing trace links Ann arranges a meeting for key stakeholders to agree a prioritisation of system requirements. This means determining what "value" each requirement has for the system. After discussion the stakeholders agree that, firstly, requirements imposed by medical data regulations are considered to be high priority. Failure to satisfy these requirements will impact on user trust in the system as well as raising the issue of legal penalties.

Responsiveness of the system and ease of use is also high priority; users will not accept the system if it cannot fit into pressured schedules of medical staff, and this is key to its financial success.

Finally, functional requirements are divided by key stakeholders into major (required) and minor (ideal) functions, and accorded different priorities as a result.

Now that the traceability goals, data and priorities are available, Ann can decide whether any optimisations are appropriate. The business impact of failing to meet medical data regulations is appreciated by all stakeholders for iTrust and the cost of assuring that high quality trace data is available for these requirements is accepted. Ann does not therefore need to employ traceability optimisations for tracing test coverage of these requirements. She adopts a finely-grained system here, creating trace links between requirements, individual methods in the code and test cases.

For other areas of functionality, some optimisations can be used. Requirements rationale is stored in free text. For this, Ann asks engineers to generate coarse trace links between requirements rationale and the requirements themselves. Any change to these requirements trigger an alert to the engineer to go and check for changes.

For functional requirements that were not accorded a high priority Ann instructs her team to adopt a coarsely-grained traceability approach, linking requirements to classes instead of methods to reduce the effort expended.

We discussed in Section 3.1 of this chapter some criteria for prioritising areas of the system so that different traceability techniques can be selectively applied.

6.4 Estimating Effort and Refining Choices

Ann's effort estimation overlaps with her work on identifying possible optimisations. She has calculated the effort required in tracing legally-mandated
requirements' testing coverage and justified the cost. However, her estimates
of the effort involved in tracing the rest of the system seem high.

Instead, Ann estimates the cost required to adopt an automated tool to generate links between requirements and documentation for low-priority areas
instead of asking the team to create the links. She re-calculates the estimated
effort needed to generate the links (very low now that a tool is in place) and
to carry out later traceability-enabled activities (a little higher than before,
since tools are not perfect and links will need some filtering from the engineers). The short-term trace creation costs are low when using the tool, but
she estimates that within 18 months she will start to see medium- and long-
term saving in terms of reduced effort for coping with change requests later.
Ann refines her previous choice and adopts the automated tool for generating
low-priority links.

The last two steps – selecting optimisations and estimating effort – are likely to
become an iterative cycle as project planners recalculate the effort required and
select acceptable compromises in order to bring the total costs into acceptable
boundaries. Cost estimations should include both the initial cost of creating trace
links as well as estimating the effort saved on carrying out later traceability-enabled
activities, and a realistic estimate of the expected time-scale before the traceability
system will start to return a saving in effort.

7 Conclusions

In this chapter we have introduced some key issues behind cost-benefits of traceability. In general the return on investment in traceability is maximised by keeping
the quality of the trace data high in areas where it is most needed, and the cost
of generating and maintaining trace data low. By "quality", we mean the recall,
precision, granularity and suitability of the data for its intended purposes. There
are a number of techniques which may be adopted to reduce the cost of traceability with only a minimal impact on quality. A flexible, "heterogeneous" approach
to traceability is likely to achieve the best balance between achieving traceability
benefits and controlling the cost. This strategy involves selecting the best available
technique or strategy to achieve the current goal. Prioritising requirements is an
important step, as it allows a mixture of techniques and optimisations to be selectively applied where they are most appropriate, ensuring the best quality trace data
is applied where needed.

We've suggested a very simple process for analysing the cost benefit of traceability and selecting an appropriate strategy. Any cost analysis of traceability must ensure that the costs of implementing traceability are offset by the cost savings which can be incurred at a later stage when carrying out traceability-enabled activities. Projects with longer durations and/or maintenance periods, for example, might incur relatively high costs for trace creation, but this should be offset by the reduction of effort required for repeated change requests over many years.

References

Albrecht, A.J.: Measuring application development productivity. In: Proceedings, IBM Applications Development Symposium, pp. 14–17. Monterey, CA (1979, October)

Albrecht, A.J., Gaffney, J.E., Jr.: Software function, source lines of code, and development effort prediction: A software science validation. IEEE Trans. Softw. Eng. **SE-9**, 639–648 (1983, November)

Arisholm, E., Briand, L.C., Føyen, A.: Dynamic coupling measurement for object-oriented software. IEEE Trans. Softw. Eng. **30**(8), 491–506 (2004)

Basili, V.R., Briand, L.C., Melo, W.L.: A validation of object-oriented design metrics as quality indicators. IEEE Trans. Softw. Eng. **22**(10), 751–761 (1996)

Boehm, B., Huang, L.G.: Value-based software engineering: A case study. IEEE Softw. **36**(3), 33–41 (2006)

Briand, L.C., Wüst, J., Lounis, H.: Using coupling measurement for impact analysis in object-oriented systems. In: Proceedings. IEEE International Conference on Software Maintenance, (ICSM '99), pp. 475–482. ICSM, Oxford, England (1999)

Chaumun, M. Ajmal, K., Hind, K., Rudolf K., Lustman, F.: Département IRO, and Université De Montréal. A change impact model for changeability assessment in object-oriented software systems. In: Proceedings of the Third Euromicro Working Conference on Software Maintenance and Reengineering, pp. 130–138 (1999)

Cleland-Huang, J.: Just enough requirements traceability. In: 30th Annual International Computer Software and Applications Conference (COMPSAC 2006), pp. 41–42 (2006, September)

Cleland-Huang, J., Change, C.K., Christensen, M.: Event-based traceability for managing evolutionary change. IEEE Trans. Softw. Eng. **29**(9), 796–810 (2003)

Cleland-Huang, J., Zemont, G., Lukasik, W.: A heterogeneous solution for improving the return on investment of requirements traceability. In: 12th IEEE International Conference on Requirements Engineering (RE 2004), pp. 230–239 (2004, September)

Egyed, A.: Determining the cost-quality trade-off for automated software traceability. ASE 2005:360–363 (2005)

Egyed, A., Biffl, S., Heindl, M., Grünbacher, P.: A value-based approach for understanding cost-benefit trade-offs during automated software traceability. In: Proceedings of the 3rd International Workshop on Traceability in Emerging Forms of Software Engineering, TEFSE '05, pp. 2–7. ACM, New York, NY. ISBN 1-59593-243-7 (2005)

Egyed, A., Grünbacher, P., Heindl, M., Biffl, S.: Value-based requirements traceability: Lessons learned. In: 15th IEEE International Requirements Engineering Conference, RE 2007, pp. 115–118 (2007)

Gotel, O., Finkelstein, A.: Contribution structures. In: Proceedings of the Second IEEE International Symposium on Requirements Engineering, pp. 100–107 (1995, March)

Gotel, O., Finkelstein, A.: Extended requirements traceability: Results of an industrial case study. In: International Symposium on Requirements Engineering (RE97), pp. 169–178. Society Press, Annapolis, MD (1997)

Han, Ah.-R., Jeon, S.-Uk., Bae, D.-H., Hong, J.-E.: Behavioral dependency measurement for change-proneness prediction in UML 2.0 design models. In: COMPSAC '08: Proceedings of the 2008 32nd Annual IEEE International Computer Software and Applications Conference, pp. 76–83. IEEE Computer Society, Washington, DC. ISBN 978-0-7695-3262-2 (2008)

Heindl, M., Biffl, S.. A case study on value-based requirements tracing. In: Proceedings of the 10th European Software Engineering Conference Held Jointly with 13th ACM SIGSOFT International Symposium on Foundations of Software Engineering, pp. 60–69. ISBN 1-59593-014-0 (2005)

Huang, L., Boehm, B.: How much software quality investment is enough: A value-based approach. IEEE Softw. **23**(5), 88–95 (2006, September/October)

Hughes, R.T.: Expert judgement as an estimating method. Inform. Softw. Technol. **28**, 67–75 (1996)

Ingram, C., Riddle, S.: Linking software design metrics to component change-proneness. In: WeTSOM 2011 – 2nd International Workshop on Emerging Trends in Software Metrics (WeTSOM 2011). Honolulu, Hawaii (2011)

Jarke, M.: Requirements tracing. Commun. ACM **41**(12), 32–36 (1998, December)

Kemerer, C.F:. An empirical validation of software cost estimation models. Commun. ACM **30**(5), 416–429 (1987)

Li, W., Henry, S.: Object Oriented Metrics Which Predict Maintainability. Technical Report, Department of Computer Science, Virginia Polytechnic Institute and State University, Blacksburg, Virginia (1993, February)

Ramesh, B., Powers, T., Stubbs, C.: Implementing requirements traceability: A case study. In: Proceedings of the 2nd IEEE International Symposium on Requirements Engineering, pp. 89–95 (1995, March).

Ratzinger, J., Sigmund, T., Vorburger, P., Gall, H.C.: Mining software evolution to predict refactoring. In: Proceedings of the International Symposium on Empirical Software Engineering and Measurement (ESEM 2007), pp. 354–363. IEEE Computer Society, Madrid, Spain (2007)

Wilkie, F.G., Kitchenham, B.A.: Coupling measures and change ripples in C++ application software. J. Syst. Softw. **52**(2–3), 157–164 (2000)

Acquiring Tool Support for Traceability

Orlena Gotel and Patrick Mäder

1 Introduction

There are an abundance of commercial tools that claim to support traceability (INCOSE, 2010). The marketing material for the majority of these tools can entice the practitioner into believing that they offer a silver bullet when it comes to traceability. The reality is that such tools can both enable and impede traceability in equal measure. The acquisition of tool support for traceability can have cost ramifications that go well beyond the initial monetary expense — trace artifacts and trace links, once painstakingly crafted into traces, may not integrate across tool and organisational boundaries, so anticipated traceability-related queries may be left unanswerable.

When faced with the task of buying a laundry detergent, the consumer can usually afford to ask friends for opinions, and then take a trial and error approach to finding the perfect detergent for their particular needs. A glossy label may lead to a first purchase, but rarely to a second purchase if the detergent does not clean as well as expected. It is rarely a costly mistake. When faced with the task of buying a car, the consumer may seek a more objective perspective, given the escalation in cost and the risk of a poor decision. Therefore, the consumer may seek advice from consumer reports, those product reviews and comparisons that have been compiled as a result of car ownership and use over time. A specific car is predominantly selected because it fulfils the needs of the future owner and it fits within their price range; however, features that have been prioritised and compared across models may act as the differentiating factor. Importantly, there is a huge used car market that can lessen the pain of a poor decision.

When faced with the task of acquiring tool support for traceability, several immediate challenges confront the consumer: (i) the lack of stand-alone traceability tools

---

The material in this chapter was the basis for a mini-tutorial presented by the authors at RE'09 (Gotel and Mäder, 2009).

O. Gotel (✉)
New York, NY 10014, USA
e-mail: olly@gotel.net

J. Cleland-Huang et al. (eds.), *Software and Systems Traceability*,
DOI 10.1007/978-1-4471-2239-5_3, © Springer-Verlag London Limited 2012

to select from; (ii) selecting between the broader categories of tooling that actually are available, that manage the requirements and other artifacts of the software and systems development life cycle, and provide for traceability in the process; (iii) the intangible nature of what is being acquired; (iv) the lack of a used tool market to compensate for a poor decision; and (v) the deceptively inexpensive alternative of either configuring a general-purpose tool or developing a custom tool to support needs. Given these challenges, undertaking a trial and error approach in this procurement arena is rarely viable. Not only does it require an investment in time to find a solution, it also takes time to realise the benefits. Moreover, one organisation's rationale for a solution may not fit another's, so there is also limited value in simply copying the tool acquisition decisions of others without conducting a more in-depth enquiry.

Reviews of commercial and open-source tools that purport to support traceability have been provided by a number of leading consultants, including (Alexander, 2010; Atlantic Systems Guild, 2010; Wiegers, 1999a), and a feature table through which to compare tools has been populated by tool vendors themselves (INCOSE, 2010). However, there is little objective material that has been obtained over time, and from a wealth of independent consumer use and testing with regard to these tools. A number of useful resources do exist that are directed towards the practitioner, such as (Ebert, 2005; Kress et al., 2007; Rupp, 2002, 2007), but these are currently only provided in German. These resources discuss the traceability functionality and selection of requirements management tools. While the use of reviews and feature comparisons can be a starting point for exploring the support offered by potential tools, tools come and go, and the names of tools and their vendors also change. Consequently, care needs to be taken when relying upon such material to make decisions. What really needs to be examined is how well these features can work together to deliver a required capability or service within a specified context. The task of acquiring tool support for traceability thus necessitates a systematic enquiry.

This chapter presents a seven-step guide for practitioners to work through to conduct such an enquiry. It does not claim to provide a turnkey solution to decision making; rather, it aims to provide a pragmatic framework through which to arrive at a more informed tooling decision. Instead of proceeding directly to selecting from among tool offerings, it recommends that the practitioner first understand the wider requirements management system in which the traceability is likely to play a critical role within their organisation, and then to design or redesign (hereafter [re]design) the process as necessary; any tool decisions need to be made to fit squarely within this context. It offers a more general and complementary approach to those that delineate the required features of requirements management tools based upon roles (Hoffman et al., 2004) or rate a tool's support for requirements management based upon the value contribution of its features (Heindl et al., 2006).

Since the question of traceability support inevitably becomes one of requirements management tooling at present, Section 2 explains the distinction between traceability and requirements management. These two terms are frequently used inconsistently and interchangeably. Section 3 outlines the general categories and capabilities of tool support that is available in this space. The acquisition guide is then described in Section 4, where the objectives and results of each step are explained, along with warning signs to attend to. Section 5 concludes the chapter.

2 Traceability and Requirements Management

Many problems with the acquisition and subsequent introduction of tool support for traceability originate from poor expectation management. The term *requirements traceability* is often used in place of traceability and, thereafter, used synonymously with *requirements management* (Young, 2004). Equally, traceability is often regarded as one of the enabling mechanisms for the various requirements management activities (Berenbach et al., 2009). Not only are traceability and requirements management different things, the term requirements management is itself frequently used in multiple ways, which can confuse matters. For some practitioners, requirements management encompasses all the requirements engineering activities (Davis, 2005), such as the initial requirements elicitation tasks and the specification activities, while for others it is distinct from developing the requirements in the first place (Wiegers, 1999b). How practitioners use the different terms obviously influences what is expected from the associated tool support. Therefore, an important starting point in any tooling discussion is to agree upon the terminology to be used. This will determine what is within the scope of the tool support to be acquired and will help to manage expectations.

2.1 Traceability

In software and systems engineering, a *trace* is "a specified triplet of elements comprising: a source artifact, a target artifact and a link associating the two artifacts" (as defined in this book's glossary). In turn, *traceability* is "the potential for such traces to be established and used" (also defined in this book's glossary). The concept of traceability is, therefore, very simple. However, it is the nature and location of the artifacts to be linked, the mechanics of creating and maintaining this linkage, and the kinds of usage that are ultimately required of the resulting traces that presents the complexity.

Requirements traceability focuses on tracing requirements-related artifacts (Gotel and Finkelstein, 1994), using links that expose both requirements derivation and coverage, to enable tasks such as requirements validation and verification. *Software traceability* extends the definition to encompass and interrelate any uniquely identifiable software engineering artifact to any other, extending the life cycle coverage of the validation and verification activities accordingly. *Systems traceability* goes further and interrelates systems engineering artifacts to a broad range of systems-level components, such as people, processes and hardware models. This chapter uses the more general term "traceability" throughout and assumes that it deals with any artifact of the software and systems development life cycle.

2.2 Requirements Management

Requirements management is "the activity concerned with the effective control of information related to stakeholder, system and software requirements and, in particular, the preservation of the integrity of that information for the life of the system and with respect to changes in the system and its environment" (see this book's glossary).

In practice, the engineering assets to be managed within the scope of requirements management may extend to any software and systems development artifact. In addition, the management of these assets may not simply comprise a set of coordinated activities or processes, but may also refer to the people who have the power and the responsibility to manage them. This chapter, therefore, regards requirements management as a wider socio-technical system that depends upon traceability as its enabling mechanism to interrelate all the artifacts under its control. The requirements management system comprises people, assuming roles and undertaking responsibilities, process and tooling. It is rarely a traceability tool that is desired; rather, it is a tool for managing the artifacts of the software and systems development process with its embedded support for traceability.

2.3 Where Traceability Fits in Requirements Management

To manage the artifacts of the software and systems development life cycle, it is necessary to first gain access to these artifacts and then to define the various dependencies that will facilitate their subsequent control. To preserve the integrity of these artifacts and their dependencies in the face of change, these henceforth need to be accessible, navigable and modifiable. Requirements management comprises five fundamental activities that work together to achieve all these capabilities. In the process, they serve to create, maintain and use the enabling traceability. These activities are:

1. *Obtain and Store* – Obtaining and storing the artifacts to be managed, usually in a shared physical or virtual repository, so as to place them under control.
2. *Augment* – Augmenting these artifacts with meta-data, such as unique identifiers and source information, so as to facilitate their subsequent organisation and retrieval.
3. *Organise* – Structuring and relating these artifacts, effectively establishing their traceability.
4. *Retrieve* – Accessing and reporting on these artifacts, their meta-data and their inter/intra relationships, effectively using the traceability to create views on to all these data in response to traceability-related queries.
5. *Update* – Updating these artifacts, their meta-data and their inter/intra relationships to preserve the integrity of both the traceable artifacts and their actual traces following change, effectively using the traceability to understand, manage and propagate change.

These five activities are fundamental to the general control of data and the maintenance of data dependencies over time. Irrespective of the target software and systems development artifacts being managed, this chapter refers to tool support for such activities as *requirements management capability* given the prevailing use of the term in industry and by tool vendors.

3 Tool Support for Requirements Management and Traceability

All the fundamental activities of requirements management can be undertaken manually and using paper, but this can be tedious and error-prone, particularly as the number of artifacts and stakeholders grows. One area in which the complexity can grow exponentially is in creating and maintaining the underlying traces upon which the requirements management depends. It is therefore worth considering using a tool to support requirements management and traceability when there is a need to:

- *Scale* – When the project has many requirements and other engineering artifacts that need to be managed and traced.
- *Distribute* – When more than one person, site or organisation is doing the engineering and requirements management work, and where there is a need to share and align artifacts and traces.
- *Associate* – When more than one engineering step is necessary to transform the requirements into the desired product and where there is a need to interrelate all these interim artifacts.
- *Reuse* – When requirements and other engineering artifacts, including their traces, are being used and reused in multiple ways, such as within other projects and within product families.
- *Improve* – When there is a desire to learn about and improve the quality of the requirements management and wider engineering process, based upon gathered data and metrics.
- *Alleviate* – When the engineering personnel are under-utilised, such as when they are performing repetitive and administrative tasks to enable requirements management; these are tasks that could easily be supported in some way.
- *Demonstrate* – When there are contractual or legal reasons to use tools to demonstrate traceability, as often mandated by regulators or when working within supply chain arrangements.
- *Maintain* – When a long project or product life is expected, or when there are many customers with likely change requests to manage.

If one or more of the above are drivers in a particular project and organisational context, then tools can offer invaluable support for requirements management and traceability activities. While there are many options on tooling, these fall into three basic categories:

1. *Dedicated Requirements Management Tools* – These tools concentrate specifically on supporting the fundamental activities of requirements management and
   are frequently referred to as traceability tools due to their focused support in
   this area. The traceability provided could be quite sophisticated, particularly
   with respect to those artifacts generated in the life cycle phases associated
   with requirements development. Dedicated requirements management tools are
   traditionally used as a component within a wider tool chain.
2. *Life Cycle Tools* – These tools characteristically support a wide span of the software and systems development life cycle and manage its broader artifact types.
   Such tools provide for varying levels of capability with respect to the fundamental requirements management activities and enable traceability between all the
   supported artifact types. The traceability provided can be more generic in nature
   than with the dedicated tools, though more encompassing of life cycle phases,
   and a single life cycle tool may provide for a total tooling solution.
3. *General-Purpose Tools and Proprietary Development* – Everyday applications
   can be configured to support tailored solutions to requirements management and
   traceability. There is also the option to develop a proprietary tool completely
   from scratch. The nature of the traceability provided, the degree of support
   offered and how the result fits into a wider tool chain will all differ from case
   to case.

The benefits and limitations associated with each category of tooling are summarised in the following sections.

3.1 Dedicated Requirements Management Tools

Dedicated requirements management tools, such as Borland's CaliberRM (Borland,
2010), IBM's Rational DOORS (IBM, 2010a) and IBM's Rational RequisitePro
(IBM, 2010b), typically support the fundamental activities of requirements management in the following ways:

1. *Obtain and Store* – The heart of a dedicated requirements management tool
   is its underlying repository. This is usually provided via a database management system, so it comes with all the associated functionality. A differentiating
   factor will be the diversity of artifact types that the database can handle and
   then subsequently trace (e.g., textual requirements, Unified Modeling Language
   (UML) diagrams, test plans, change requests, etc.). The artifacts may need to be
   imported from third-party tools, requiring data import facilities within the tool.
   Alternatively, an editor may be provided to facilitate the artifact creation process directly within the tool, supplemented by templates and wizards. Capability
   may be provided to perform parsing and linguistic analyses on text-based input
   documents to extract requirements and their traces.
2. *Augment* – Data attributes that are associated with artifacts are regularly used for
   organisation and tracing purposes within dedicated requirements management

tools. These are normally specified within an artifact or trace editor and implemented as database fields. The tools may provide varying capability to manually or automatically capture and validate the attribute values once specified.

3. *Organise* – Dedicated requirements management tools provide the capability for either the manual or automated linking of the stored artifacts to create traces. Manual capability is typically provided via interactive drag and drop interfaces within editors, directly manipulating and interrelating the artifacts concerned, or by textual or graphical specification of the traces. Automated capability is emerging in some tools, using linguistic analyses and information retrieval algorithms to recover trace links from artifact sets automatically. The particular traceability to be used on a project can often be defined with some form of traceability planning facility within these tools. This may take the form of a traceability information model (TIM), or similar concept, providing a specification of the permissible traces for a project. The ability to assess levels of conformance with respect to a TIM as the traceability is created may also be provided. There is also, usually, the capability to structure the stored artifacts as needed into groups, partitions, hierarchies, decompositions, etc.

4. *Retrieve* – Dedicated requirements management tools generally provide the capability to create reports about the managed artifacts and their traces. Visualisation capabilities may augment the reporting in some tools. The kinds of analyses and reports required should help to define the initial TIM for a project, so some facility to define the typical traceability-related queries that are to be supported and their data needs may be provided. To perform the subsequent traceability-enabled analyses requires basic capabilities for searching, sorting and filtering the artifacts, their meta-data and their inter/intra relationships, so these are typically standard within such tools. Data export facilities are also commonly provided to disseminate the reports, as well as to exchange artifacts and traces with third-party tools.

5. *Update* – Security for editing the managed artifacts and their traces is commonly provided via the capabilities of the underlying database management system within dedicated requirements management tools (e.g., via multiple user access control, the ability to define baselines, version and configuration control, update notification mechanisms, etc.). The ongoing maintenance of the artifacts and traces over time depends upon the traceability already implemented, so varying degrees of support for analysing the quality of the traceability may be provided, along with analytical or graphical support to explore impact analysis and change propagation.

In supporting the fundamental activities of requirements management, dedicated requirements management tools tend to have a distinctive architecture comprising a database, an editor, a report generator, an import facility and an export facility, as per Fig. 1. The particular offerings in this space can be differentiated by their graphical user interface and their modes of interaction for creating, maintaining and using traces. They may provide different levels of support for the definition of the requirements management process and TIM that is to be enabled by the tool,

Fig. 1 Typical architecture of a dedicated requirements management tool

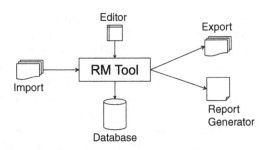

and the ability to monitor or enforce compliance with these. This may extend to workflow definition and team working facilities for the collaboration, coordination and communication of the activities.

The advantage of using a dedicated requirements management tool is that it focuses exclusively on the fundamental requirements management activities and on the enabling traceability. The support for traceability can be extensive and comprehensive. The traceability is either created as a by-product of using the tool, according to the defined requirements management process, and any accompanying TIM if supported, which may or may not be configurable; else, the traces are created manually in an explicit and interactive manner. There is often committed vendor support for designing the wider requirements management system that is needed to capitalise upon the full potential of the tool in use, and for configuring the tool to particular organisational processes and settings.

The use of multiple dedicated tools in a tool chain means that the practitioner can use very specific solutions for different phases of development and gain dedicated support in each area. However, this comes at the potential difficulty and expense of establishing traceability across the tool boundaries to manage the artifacts over time. The key issue with dedicated requirements management tools is that full end-to-end traceability throughout the entire software and systems development life cycle can be problematic. Overcoming this limitation either requires the tool to be truly open for integration with other tools and their data, or for the integration of the traceability work products to have been planned for carefully within the wider tooling environment.

3.2 Life Cycle Tools

Life cycle tools provide support for all or many phases of the software and systems development life cycle (i.e., analysis, design, coding, testing, management, etc.). Such tools are not usually specialised for requirements management per se, but can offer differing levels of support for the fundamental requirements management activities, and so provide support for creating, maintaining and using traceability in the process. This category of tool includes, but is not limited to, full application life cycle management tools such as MKS Integrity (MKS, 2010), UML and SysML (the Systems Modeling Language) modelling tools such as Enterprise Architect (Sparx, 2010), and bug/issue/project tracking tools such as JIRA (Atlassian, 2010).

The advantage of using a single life cycle tool in which all the development artifacts are created and managed is that end-to-end traceability is possible, in theory. It can offer the ultimate promise for achieving ubiquitous traceability (see the chapter "The Grand Challenge of Traceability (v1.0)"). There can also be benefits from having fewer tools to learn to use and to handle. However, it may be necessary to buy into the full paradigm of the development approach supported within the life cycle tool, such as model-driven development using the UML, to gain the anticipated traceability. The other potential compromise is having more generic support for the individual development activities and the traceability, with fewer configuration options.

Using multiple tools that support a span of the software and systems development life cycle, but provide for requirements management and traceability therein, requires the same caution as with integrating a dedicated requirements management tool into a tool chain. The wider tool integration needs to be addressed if the traceability is to be both bidirectional and sustained across any tool boundaries. Where there is no obvious focal tool for the requirements management in a tool chain, different approaches to the underlying activities and its traceability may need to be reconciled.

3.3 General-Purpose Tools and Proprietary Development

At the opposite end of the spectrum, text editors, graphic editors, spreadsheet tools, databases and wikis are all general-purpose tools that can all be configured to allow previously manual and paper-based requirements management activities to be carried out with some form of tool support. A traditional approach to traceability is to create a requirements traceability matrix within a spreadsheet application to link requirements to other derived artifacts or to configure a small database application to do similar. While this may require explicit data entry to populate the requirements artifacts and their trace links, and manual checking of their validity, this solution may be adequate for a number of projects; it may be sufficient to assess the traceability and to undertake impact analysis of the requirements if they change.

More recently, it has become standard practice to build a project wiki to gather software and systems development artifacts together in one place, capitalising upon a wiki's multi-user editing and versioning facilities to manage requirements and their traceability. This is the approach that has been adopted in the iTrust case study of this book (see Appendix B). Traceability matrices have been created manually on the wiki to map each use case in the iTrust requirements to the Java Server Pages in which the requirements have been implemented within the system. The iTrust wiki does not support the user in navigating directly between the artifacts that have been traced. It has also not been configured to provide full requirements management and traceability support, such as the automatic notification on change and the assessment of change impact. The iTrust wiki is mainly communicative in its traceability support. The sophistication and support offered by a wiki can obviously vary quite widely.

The advantages of configuring a general-purpose tool for requirements management and traceability is that such tools are widely available, and many people already know how to use them. A solution can often be configured that is suitable for small and short-lived projects with ease. However, what initially may appear to be an inexpensive proposition could incur a high cost once configured and populated, particularly if the demands on the requirements management, traceability or the context changes. Moreover, it is common to focus on particular aspects of requirements management, such as creating and communicating the traceability (as with iTrust), as opposed to providing support for the full range of activities that may be required to sustain this traceability over time. In the iTrust case, the wider requirements management system that creates and maintains the traceability is a manual system.

The ability to configure a general-purpose tool for requirements management support, or even to develop a tool from scratch, affords the utmost flexibility when it comes to support for traceability. However, the use of general-purpose tools is probably best avoided on unpredictable, sizable, distributed or long-term projects, unless requisite care is given to the wider requirements management system (i.e., the people and their process) in both their configuration and use. Moreover, building a fully functioning tool to support software and systems development is rarely an organisation's primary business priority or domain specialty. There are benefits in leveraging the expertise of those organisations that have made requirements management and traceability their core business, and also an integral part of their products.

4 Guidelines for Acquiring Tool Support for Traceability

Any decision regarding tool support for traceability will depend upon the requirements management system that an organisation employs, as well as its wider software and systems development life cycle environment. A number of experience reports provide for a cautionary perspective when undertaking tooling decisions. For example: (i) how the effort involved in evaluating tools can be somewhat underestimated when attempting to introduce an improved requirements management process into an organisation (Tvete, 1999); (ii) how it is ineffective to introduce a tool without a process, but likewise difficult to implement a process without a supporting tool (Higgins et al., 2002); and (iii) the risks to a project of using a tool incorrectly and the need to bring the various stakeholders together to define tool use before setting off (Hammer and Huffman, 1998).

Based upon a number of such observations, the following seven steps are suggested to help guide a systematic enquiry for making tool acquisition decisions:

1. *Agree on the Problem and Terminology* – Agree there is a traceability-related problem to be tackled and agree on how this fits within the organisation's requirements management system.
2. *Understand the Problem and Commit to Tackling it* – Understand the particular requirements management and traceability-related problem(s) to be tackled, define their success criteria and secure top-level commitment to tackle them.
3. *Identify Stakeholders* – Identify the various stakeholders for requirements management and traceability, and secure their buy-in.
4. *Determine Requirements and Constraints* – Ensure the requirements for requirements management and traceability are stakeholder-driven and sensitive to the context of the organisation.
5. *Design the Wider Requirements Management System* – [Re]design the requirements management process, and clarify both where and how traceability and potential tooling fits in.
6. *Assess and Select Tools* – Assess the value of tooling for this new or improved requirements management system, gather and evaluate data on tooling options, and select a particular tooling solution if it fits the desired scope and adds value.
7. *Plan for Tool Introduction, Adoption and Ongoing Use* – Enact the tooling decision as part of a wider process improvement initiative. Not only does a tool have to be installed and used, the surrounding process has to be adopted by people if the requirements management system as a whole is to succeed.

The majority of these steps do not involve a tooling decision per se. The decision to select a tool needs to arise from a broader analysis of the problem to be tackled and from within the design of either a new or improved system that tackles the problem.

4.1 Step 1: Agree on the Problem and Terminology

- *Objective* – To discuss and agree on the core problem that the organisation hopes to address by introducing a tool to support traceability.
- *Result* – The primary business driver is agreed and the stakeholders pursuing the tool acquisition recognise that they are not simply acquiring a tool to support traceability, but acquiring a tool to support the wider requirements management system.
- *Warning* – When there is the perception that a tool is going to solve all the requirements and traceability-related problems of an organisation.

Many tool acquisitions fail because there is no clear business driver for the tool, no unambiguous statement of either the problem to be fixed or the value to be gained. Together, requirements management and traceability are usually desired to help maintain agreement on requirements throughout the development process, so as to increase the probability of delivering a software system that meets these requirements. While this can be a partial business driver, the current status with regard to requirements conformance within an organisation, and the anticipated business opportunity to be gained from changing the current way of working, also need to be discussed and captured in some tangible way. There is a concomitant need to visualise the improved system concept, assuming process changes and tool introduction.

Step 1 of the enquiry requires understanding the current requirements management system in an organisation, and exploring any associated problems with it and its enabling traceability, albeit at a high-level. This requires consulting any existing process documentation and the process owners. It also requires gathering data from those who currently participate in the requirements management process to gain some preliminary general knowledge. This is necessary to begin to express the process improvement opportunities and to determine whether tool support is even worth investigating. Is there actually a traceability problem that demands a tooling solution?

If the decision is made to proceed with a process improvement initiative and a potential tool acquisition during this step, then it is critical to ensure that agreement is reached on the terms requirements management and traceability. This is necessary to manage expectations before proceeding to further steps, as discussed in Section 2.

4.2 Step 2: Understand the Problem and Commit to Tackling it

- *Objective* – To explore and define the underlying nature of the problem to be tackled and to quantify the anticipated improvements that are sought from a new or improved requirements management system.
- *Result* – An approved business case for a process improvement initiative that will [re]design the requirements management process and investigate a potential tool acquisition, with management sponsorship, leadership and the buy-in of the project team.
- *Warning* – When no measurable business goals for a new or improved requirements management system are articulated.

While there may be agreement on the key business driver following Step 1, there are often as many lower-level expectations surrounding requirements management and traceability as there are stakeholders. These arise from different perceptions of the problems that stakeholders perceive requirements management and traceability should assist them with, and the full extent of these expectations needs to be explored in Step 2 to continue to manage expectations. For example, it is common to assume that improved requirements management and traceability will lead to: better quality requirements; better planning ability; better estimation, allocation and control of work; better management of changing requirements; better ability to reuse work; and better ability to meet contracts demonstrably. However, some expectations may not be the remit of improved requirements management and traceability, and these limitations need to be highlighted before escalating the expectations for tool support. For example, improved requirements management and traceability cannot help the practitioner to gain unambiguous, complete and correct requirements and, if this is what is perceived by better quality requirements, an expectation gap will be created; rather, this is the remit of learning to write better quality requirements and performing more effective reviews.

To explore the underlying nature of the actual problem that will be tackled requires asking a number of questions in an organisation: What activities and tasks are the practitioners attempting to undertake that depend upon traceability? What issues do they currently face in attempting to undertake these activities and tasks? What issues do they face in creating and maintaining traceability if they actually undertake traceability at present? Where no requirements management system currently exists in an organisation, these latter questions still need to be asked of a projected future system.

It is recommended that a business case (or similar) be developed in Step 2 to define the nature of the underlying problem in more detail, and to delineate what is and what is not considered within scope. Metrics for assessing the anticipated improvement to be gained should also be defined, along with success criteria. The business case should further articulate what needs to be spent on tackling the problem, in terms of money, effort and resources, and estimate the projected return on investment. In addition, a plan for the process improvement initiative and potential tool acquisition should be formed, identifying the project owner or sponsor, the project leader and team, the resources that will be available to it, how progress with the problem is going to be measured and the likely risks. It is the process of considering all the questions that inform a typical business case that is important during this step, not the creation of an unwieldy business case document. A one-page project charter could be wholly sufficient for communication and to secure commitment within many organisational contexts.

4.3 Step 3: Identify Stakeholders

- *Objective* – To conduct a systematic analysis of those who have something to gain or something to lose from a new or improved requirements management system.
- *Result* – A prioritised list of stakeholders to guide the subsequent requirements determination and decision-making process.
- *Warning* – When key stakeholders are not identified and whole stakeholder constituencies are overlooked.

One of the first areas of exploration in a general requirements engineering process is the identification of the stakeholders for a proposed system. This is a prerequisite to discovering their various goals, tasks, contexts of use and constraints in a methodical manner. Differing business value will be gained from satisfying the various stakeholder needs, so it is important to identify the key stakeholders in a particular organisational context early on so as to ensure that their needs drive the subsequent requirements gathering. For example, a business analyst may require support for impact analysis, a developer may require support for derivation analysis, a designer may require support for completeness analysis, a customer may require the ability to assess contract fulfilment and a quality administrator may want to determine unimplemented requirements. While it might be ideal to address all these stakeholders' needs, these need to be prioritised unless the business case has agreed an infinite budget. Focusing on the root problems to be tackled and the key stakeholders to be supported can facilitate this. Stakeholder identification and prioritisation is the role of Step 3.

One way to identify all the potential stakeholders in a systematic manner is to use the Onion Model of Stakeholders, as described in (Alexander and Beus-Dukic, 2009). The approach considers the various stakeholder roles that would fill generic slots when the target system is placed at the centre of the model. An example set of stakeholders for a requirements management system is given in Fig. 2.

Fig. 2 Example stakeholder roles for a requirements management system

Figure 2 shows: the normal operators of a requirements management system (i.e., the business analysts and engineers); the beneficiaries of the functionality that the requirements management system provides (i.e., other engineers, the managers, the quality administrators (QA) and customers); the operational support (i.e., the mentors, the software process improvement (SPI) team and potential tool vendors); the wider systems that the requirements management system will need to interface with (i.e., the other processes and tools that support the software and systems development life cycle (SDLC), both within and external to the organisation); the financial beneficiary of the requirements management system (i.e., a potential tool vendor and the organisation itself if there is an attractive business case); the negative stakeholders (i.e., those who neither want change nor want a new requirements management system); etc. These roles need to be instantiated and then prioritised in a particular organisational context, in the light of the goals and constraints of the business case, and then used to help direct the requirements determination in Step 4.

4.4 Step 4: Determine Requirements and Constraints

- *Objective* – To specify the requirements and constraints of those (key) stakeholders involved with establishing and using the products of requirements management and traceability.
- *Result* – A set of detailed scenarios of use for the (key) stakeholders, which highlight the artifacts that need to be managed and traced, the nature of the traceability required, the workflow that needs to be supported and the uses to which the traces need to be put.
- *Warning* – When only the desirable features of a requirements management system have been explored in the requirements gathering process.

Step 4 is to determine what the stakeholders identified in Step 3 need to be able to do that requirements management and traceability can assist them with, and what the subset of stakeholders (i.e., the normal operators) need to be able to do to allow for this potential. This is an analysis of stakeholder goals, supporting tasks and workflow. The artifacts to be managed and traced during these tasks need to be highlighted during this step, and the nature of the traceability that is required to enable these tasks needs to be defined. Data need to be gathered to understand the causes of the current problems and to elicit the requirements for the new or improved requirements management system. For instance: How is the traceability currently created and maintained, and by whom? What techniques, methods and tools are currently employed to do this, when and where?

One recommendation for conducting Step 4 is to first develop use cases for the (key) stakeholder roles – the most frequent or the most important tasks that these stakeholders need to undertake that involve the requirements management system – and to examine the demands for undertaking these tasks on traceability. Example use cases for some of the potential functional beneficiaries of a requirements

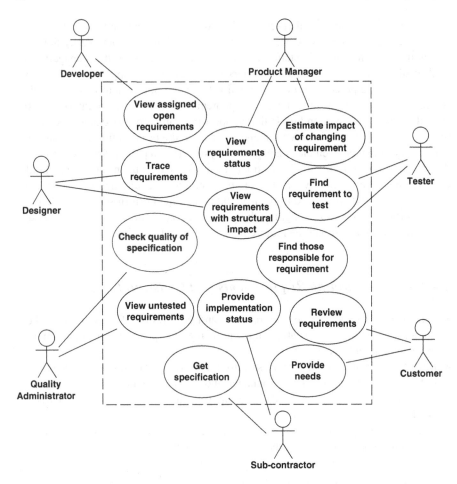

Fig. 3 Example use cases for the functional beneficiary stakeholders

management system are given in Fig. 3. Here: the developer may need to determine which requirements are not yet coded, which requires forward tracing at the identifier level from requirements through to code; the quality administrator may need to identify which requirements are not yet tested, which requires forward tracing from requirements to test cases; and the customer may need to review and provide feedback on the requirements to be developed, which requires backward tracing of the requirements to their sources and traceability between the requirements themselves to understand their dependencies. The primary tasks in an organisational context and their associated traceability needs should be investigated systematically in this way.

The use cases can then be detailed via typical and atypical scenarios to uncover the sequence of activities and artifacts that they involve, and so uncover the further requirements or constraints they impose on traceability. Figure 4 shows a potential sequence of activities in a scenario of use for the customer's review requirements

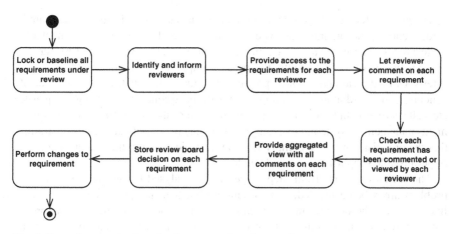

Fig. 4 Example scenario of use for the customer's review requirements use case

use case. If there is a need to trace back to the origin of a requirement when accessing the requirements for review, the third activity shown in Fig. 4, then this will place demands on the types of artifact and the types of traceability that will need to be supported (i.e., pre-requirements traceability back to the requirements sources). Most requirements management tools will claim to provide support for the baselining and notification that is indicated in the scenario of use, so it is important to examine potential tool support in the context of how the stakeholders would want to use these features to deliver a required capability or service. There is little point in having all the requisite features present in a tool if they are unable to work together to support a specific scenario of use that is required. Generating the scenarios of use, systematically, for (key) stakeholders and their tasks can help to produce a prioritised feature list for tool support in an organisational context; but, the added value comes from providing an explicit set of test cases for tool evaluation in Step 6.

4.5 Step 5: Design the Wider Requirements Management System

- *Objective* – To design the new or improved requirements management system and to establish the scope of any potential tool support within it.
- *Result* – A systemic solution to requirements management and traceability is created that weaves together people, process and tools.
- *Warning* – When the encompassing software and systems development life cycle, with its supporting tools, is not taken into account in the design process.

To design a new or improved requirements management system, it is important to understand the organisational setting that the system will be exercised within, as well as the prevailing motivation underlying the drive for process improvement and tool acquisition (Mäder et al., 2009). These data are likely to have been uncovered as a by-product of the previous steps, but need to be examined more thoroughly in Step 5 as the system requirements and candidate designs are explored. Understanding the organisation type, the software and systems development life cycle process, the hardware platforms used, the available systems and resources, the existing processes and tools, the process improvement culture, and the characteristics of typical and atypical projects (i.e., team size, distribution, number of concurrent users, domain, requirements volatility, frequency of change requests, etc.) all serve as data to inform the potential scope of the new or improved requirements management system. For example, there may be security and legal constraints that the organisation has to comply with on its projects that influence the selection of permissible supporting tools and vendors.

The scenarios of use from Step 4 need to be analysed in this step to study the problem areas being tackled, and to demonstrate that any proposed changes are likely to gain the desired improvements and not introduce significant new problems. Only once the requirements of the wider requirements management system have been clarified, and the design options have been specified, can the remit and nature of the tool support be proposed. If projects are typically distributed across regional and organisational boundaries, then support for this workflow needs to be re-examined in the scenarios of use to check for the ramifications on the traceability and need for support. If artifacts and traces need to be exchanged between organisations and tools, then the encryption and alignment of databases may be a prevailing system requirement and design constraint. Therefore, it is necessary to analyse and design the integral components of a new or improved system in Step 5, comprising:

- *People* – What roles and responsibilities will be a part of the new or improved requirements management system? Which stakeholders will assume these roles? Any changes proposed from the current resourcing and workflow will need capturing and examining.
- *Process* – How will each of the fundamental activities of requirements management be undertaken in the new or improved system? In particular, how will the traceability be created, maintained and used? Here it is necessary to define the intended techniques and methods to use, the roles responsible, and to also delineate any planned changes from the current process. Before and after scenarios of use may need examining to plan for training, introduction and adoption of the process changes.
- *Tools* – Which tasks will be undertaken manually in the new or improved system and which tasks will be tool supported, or even completely automated? Where there is a satisfactory role for tool support, the artifact types to be managed and traced will place demands on its database management system. The manner in which the artifacts will be created, retrieved and used will place demands on its import, export, editing and reporting capabilities. The traceability-related queries to be supported will place demands on the types of TIM that will need to be specified and implemented. The portfolio of tools used to support the broader software and systems development life cycle within an organisation will dictate tooling integration needs and this wider solution architecture should be defined to clarify where requirements management tooling fits in.

The available resourcing and projected return on investment for tool support may need to be re-examined during this step. One important question is obviously whether to buy or to build a tool, or whether to forego a tool acquisition altogether.

4.6 Step 6: Assess and Select Tools

- *Objective* – To assess which category of tool best supports the new or improved requirements management system and its organisational context, if any, and to evaluate and select from among options.
- *Result* – A decision with respect to tool support for the new or improved requirements management system.
- *Warning* – When a tool is selected based on it having the most plentiful or the most attractive features, or simply because it is open-source and misconstrued as free.

The driving force for final tooling decisions should be an investigation of their support for the important scenarios of use in the new or improved requirements management system and within the wider context of use. The portfolio of tools used to support software and systems development in an organisation will generally inform as to the most viable category of tool support for requirements management, unless the entire process is under [re]design. Data gathering on potential tool support can and should proceed in parallel with Steps 3 through 5; and, it is worth making a list of such questions during the earlier steps. Typical traceability questions that can be asked about candidate tools at any stage in the enquiry are listed below:

1. What priority does the tool give to traceability?
2. What mechanical and analytical support does the tool provide for creating and maintaining traceability?
3. What kinds of requirements-related information and other artifacts can be made traceable by the tool? Where and how is this obtained and stored?
4. What types of meta-data can the tool accommodate and use for traceability? Where and how is this defined?
5. What support is provided for defining the nature of the traceability that is to be enabled by the tool (i.e., a TIM) and what levels of compliance can be ascertained with respect to this?
6. To what levels of granularity can traceability be provided within the tool (i.e., coarsest through finest that is possible)?
7. What kinds of traceability can be established within the tool (i.e., forward, backward, vertical, horizontal, pre-requirements, post-requirements, etc.)?
8. Who has to create and maintain the traceability when using the tool?
9. What is the process it demands for both establishing and using the traceability? (See the generic traceability process model in the chapter "Traceability Fundamentals".) Is this configurable?
10. Which parts of the traceability process can be automated by the tool?

11. What degree of skill and training is required to establish and use the traceability in the tool?
12. What are the main goals and tasks supported by the traceability that the tool provides in eventual use?
13. What traceability analyses can be facilitated and reported upon by the tool (e.g., traceability completeness and quality assessment)?
14. What is the breadth and longevity of the traceability provided by the tool?
15. Can the traces be extracted and reused outside of the tool?

The quality of a dedicated requirements management tool or life cycle tool can be perceived, initially, from its marketing literature. If a tool's website communicates and is up to date, it is a promising first sign. However, a structured Request For Information (RFI) process should be considered for any short-listed tools to investigate some of the pertinent topics listed in Fig. 5. For example, the longevity of the tool and the track record of the tool vendor need to be taken into account, as these can provide for levels of business confidence in a company and its product (Schwaber and Sterpe, 2007). If the tool is not a perfect match at present, what is the longer-term view? Is the tool vendor evolving the product in a promising direction? Is the tool near end of life? Will support be provided into the future? How easy will it be to migrate the data if use of the tool is discontinued for any reason? An important and often overlooked factor is the total cost of ownership of a tool. There is not only an initial investment, but costs can be incurred in training, both in the tool and in the process to be supported, along with ongoing consulting and maintenance

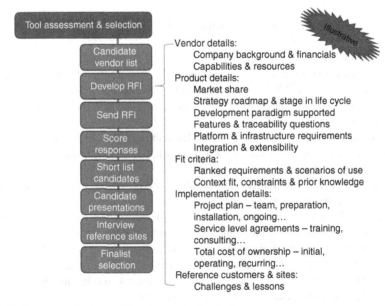

Fig. 5 Common topics to consider when evaluating tools

contracts. There may be a particular licensing model per seat when acquiring a tool and recurring costs to accommodate. Any RFI should include samples of the scenarios of use to be supported, along with details of the wider organisational context that lends constraints, in order for the vendor to demonstrate the tool's potential support (or not). Furthermore, it is important to evaluate whether the skills exist, within or external to the organisation, to configure and customise the tool, if this is potentially needed, along with whether this is even possible to do within the tool.

It is difficult to fully evaluate a tool from its marketing material and from a vendor's response to an RFI alone. Exercising a tool is the best way to examine the actual support it provides for the required scenarios of use and to uncover the process assumptions embedded within the tool. Getting an evaluation license for tools, and the limited duration of such licenses, can be a compounding problem for evaluation though. Getting the various tools installed in a timely fashion can also be problematic. This lead-time needs to be factored into the planning in Step 2. The perception of a tool's quality can be influenced by multiple additional factors while in trial. Does the documentation reflect the latest version of the tool? How often do major and minor updates appear? Is a concrete change log available for each version, showing what was added, fixed or omitted? How reactive and useful is the vendor support? Are there traceable tickets for discovered problems and how long do they normally take to close? Does an active user community exist for the tool? Such a checklist to support both tool and vendor assessment should be developed by an organisation undergoing an evaluation process. Moreover, an examination of the traceability practices of the vendor with respect to their own tool development may prove telling.

Where there is not a good fit between the available tool offerings, or where the cost is prohibitive, the option to configure a general-purpose tool or to build a custom tool from scratch may be a viable option for an organisation. Much of the systems analysis and design work that is essential to undertake this in an informed manner has already been accomplished in Steps 1 through 5. The advantages and disadvantages of taking such a course of action were summarised in Section 2.

4.7 Step 7: Plan for Tool Introduction, Adoption and Ongoing Use

- *Objective* – To plan and manage a tool's introduction, adoption and ongoing viability as a central part of a new or improved requirements management system.
- *Result* – The wider environment for tool introduction, adoption and ongoing use is prepared. People are trained in the process and tool, roles and responsibilities are defined, mentors are assigned, and the stakeholders are motivated and incentivised.
- *Warning* – When a tool is introduced on a high-profile project without sufficient attention paid to preparing the people in the process that is needed to make it succeed.

Fig. 6 Example considerations when introducing tool support

If a tool has been selected as an integral component of the new or improved requirements management system, then this impacts the conduct of the ensuing process improvement initiative. Focus now needs to turn to a tool's introduction and adoption as an enabler of the improvements. The way in which to sustain the value of the tool acquisition over time also needs to be planned for. Example considerations to attend to in Step 7 are highlighted in Fig. 6 and summarised below.

- *Installation* – Install the database that will manage the artifacts to be traced, the server application, the client application, any existing plug-ins and the facilities required to ensure the integration with other tools. Keep a record of the installation details and parameters to aid later trouble-shooting.
- *Configuration* – Configure the tool according to the stakeholders and scenarios of use, as identified in Steps 3 and 4, and the requirements management system components as defined in Step 5. This includes: (i) defining the types of artifact to be managed and traced, the identification system to use, the required meta-data, the default values for these meta-data, etc.; (ii) defining the TIM, or similar, which specifies the types of trace artifact, trace link and permitted traces in the project according to the intended usage; (iii) configuring the usage properties for the tool, such as the roles, the views and the access rights, the versioning and baselining principles, the reports to be produced, the exports to be supported, etc.; and (iv) configuring the tool to enable its integration with the other tools used and their data. Keep a record of the entire configuration undertaken for its tailoring across organisational projects.

- *Customisation* – Tool customisation only becomes necessary if the configuration does not allow all the desired support for the stakeholders and their scenarios of use. Customisation should be used cautiously, however, because of the effort and cost incurred, so it is important to find out whether the needed functionality is really not available in the tool before taking this route. Document any customisation undertaken, as it might need evolution, especially following any updates of the main tool.

- *Data Migration* – Migrating artifacts and pre-existing traces into a tool can be difficult, especially where different concepts for traceability have been used in legacy tools. These data may need transforming into a standard form for tool use. This needs to be determined during tool assessment in Step 6 as it can either be awkward to do or incur unforeseen expense.

- *Training* – Plan not only for training on the tool, but also for training on the [re]designed requirements management process to be used with the tool. An inevitable performance dip needs to be navigated (Nikula et al., 2010), something that can lead to tool abandonment if not anticipated and planned for, so it is ill advised to leave the training entirely until the practitioners are on-the-job. The training required for successful adoption of a tool is often overlooked, so it is emphasised here.

- *Pilot* – The goal of a pilot project is to gain evaluation and training in the field with the tool using real data. Pilot projects require clear objectives, careful design, support, feedback mechanisms and reviews, and they are likely to trigger further configuration changes and additional customisations. Evaluate, remediate and phase the roll out of the tool when the results are acceptable.

- *Maintenance* – Continuously measure, sustain and evolve the effectiveness of the tool in use with regard to the business case of Step 2. Provide detailed and up-to-date information about the organisation's requirements management system, with the process, roles and responsibilities, and the tool set-up for new team members. Provide examples, project templates and support for new projects and personnel. Conduct regular reviews of the wider requirements management system and its tool support, and get feedback from its stakeholders on a regular basis. Analyse completed projects to get information about the success of the system and its tool. Plan for obsolescence and future migration also – a terminal solution is rarely found, and the entire tool acquisition process will eventually start over as novel traceability-related problems begin to emerge, as innovative tools appear in the marketplace and as new business opportunities become envisaged.

5 Conclusions

Exactly which traceability tool to invest in is not a question that this chapter can answer definitively. It is rarely a traceability tool that an organisation actually seeks, but a system to support a wider process in which the development process is controlled and through which its artifacts are managed over time, a process that is enabled by traceability. Support for traceability therefore comes in different forms and the idiosyncrasies of diverse organisational contexts makes tooling decisions both difficult and somewhat unique. The most appropriate tool is clearly the one that is adopted and used by all the required stakeholders in an organisation, in the way that is intended, yielding the benefits that are anticipated, at an acceptable cost. These are the driving factors that need to be uncovered first and foremost in any tool acquisition process.

This chapter has, therefore, cautioned against deciding upon traceability support without first understanding and designing the wider requirements management system in an organisation, and accounting for its more encompassing software and systems development environment. A problem-oriented stakeholder and requirements-driven enquiry is encouraged, and this chapter has outlined a seven-step guide to help practitioners to undertake this:

1. *Agree on the Problem and Terminology* – Agree there is a traceability-related problem to be tackled and agree on how this fits within the organisation's requirements management system.
2. *Understand the Problem and Commit to Tackling it* – Understand the particular requirements management and traceability-related problem(s) to be tackled, define their success criteria and secure top-level commitment to tackle them.
3. *Identify Stakeholders* – Identify the various stakeholders for requirements management and traceability, and secure their buy-in.
4. *Determine Requirements and Constraints* – Ensure the requirements for requirements management and traceability are stakeholder-driven and sensitive to the context of the organisation.
5. *Design the Wider Requirements Management System* – [Re]design the requirements management process, and clarify both where and how traceability and potential tooling fits in.
6. *Assess and Select Tools* – Assess the value of tooling for this new or improved requirements management system, gather and evaluate data on tooling options, and select a particular tooling solution if it fits the desired scope and adds value.
7. *Plan for Tool Introduction, Adoption and Ongoing Use* – Enact the tooling decision as part of a wider process improvement initiative. Not only does a tool have to be installed and used, the surrounding process has to be adopted by people if the requirements management system as a whole is to succeed.

Please note that the steps are not intended to be strictly sequential and the process is not intended to be document intensive; the guide needs to be used pragmatically and more as an aid to thinking throughout the acquisition process.

The acquisition of tool support for traceability demands an open and systematic process of broader enquiry, balancing well-understood needs with the available options. While it could lead to a highly automated tooling solution it could equally lead to a pencil and paper tooling solution; either solution could be optimal for the organisation and problem at hand. Conducting such an enquiry is also advised when a tooling solution is imposed upon an organisation; it can highlight potential problem areas ahead of time and thereby inform the design of mitigating strategies before they have become irreconcilable problems that have led to a tool's rejection.

References

Alexander, I.: Requirements tools listing and synopsis. http://easyweb.easynet.co.uk/~iany/other/vendors.htm. Accessed Dec 2010

Alexander, I., Beus-Dukic, L.: Discovering Requirements: How to Specify Products and Services. Wiley, Chichester, England (2009)

Atlantic Systems Guild Ltd.: Volere requirements resources: Requirements tools. http://www.volere.co.uk/tools.htm. Accessed Dec 2010

Atlassian Pty Ltd.: JIRA. http://www.atlassian.com/software/jira/. Accessed Dec 2010

Berenbach, B., Paulish, D.J., Kazmeier, J., Rudorfer, A.: Software and Systems Requirements Engineering: In Practice, p. 200. Mc-Graw-Hill, New York, NY (2009)

Borland Software Corporation.: CaliberRM^{TM}: Enterprise software requirements management system. http://www.borland.com/us/products/caliber/. Accessed Dec 2010

Davis, A.M.: Just Enough Requirements Management: Where Software Developing Meets Marketing, p. 6. Dorset House Publishing, New York, NY (2005)

Ebert, C.: Systematisches Requirements Management. Dpunkt verlag, Heidelberg (2005)

Gotel, O., Finkelstein, A.: An analysis of the requirements traceability problem. In: Proceedings of the 1st International Conference on Requirements Engineering (ICRE'94), pp. 94–101. IEEE Computer Society, Colorado Springs, CO (1994, April)

Gotel, O., Mäder, P.: How to select a requirements management tool: Initial steps. In: Proceedings of the 17th IEEE International Requirements Engineering Conference (RE'09), pp. 365–367. IEEE Computer Society, Atlanta, GA (2009, August–September)

Hammer, T., Huffman, L.: Automated requirements management – beware HOW you use tools: An experience report. In: Proceedings of the 3rd International Conference on Requirements Engineering (ICRE'98), pp. 34–40. IEEE Computer Society, Los Alamitos, CA (1998)

Heindl, M., Reinisch, F., Biffl, S., Egyed, A.: Value-based selection of requirements engineering tool support. In: EUROMICRO-SEAA, pp. 266–273 (2006)

Higgins, S.A., de Laat, M., Gieles, P.M.C., Geurts, E.M.: Managing product requirements for medical IT products. In: Proceedings of the 10th IEEE International Requirements Engineering Conference (RE'02), pp. 341–349, IEEE Computer Society, Los Alamitos, CA (2002)

Hoffmann, M., Kuhn, N., Weber, M., Bittner, M.: Requirements for requirements management tools. In: Proceedings of the 12th IEEE International Requirements Engineering Conference (RE'04), pp. 301–308. IEEE Computer Society, Washington, DC (2004)

IBM. IBM Rational DOORS. http://www-01.ibm.com/software/awdtools/doors/. Accessed Dec 2010a

IBM. IBM Rational RequisitePro. http://www-01.ibm.com/software/awdtools/reqpro/. Accessed Dec 2010b

International Council on Systems Engineering (INCOSE): Tools Database Working Group (TDWG). INCOSE Requirements Management Tools Survey. http://www.incose.org/ProductsPubs/products/rmsurvey.aspx. Accessed Dec 2010

Kress, A., Stevenson, R., Wiebel, R., Hood, C., Versteegen, G.: Requirements Engineering Methoden und Techniken, Einführungsszenarien und Werkzeuge im Vergleich. iX Studie Anforderungsmanagement, 2nd edn. Heise Verlag, Leipzig, Germany (2007). ISBN: 9783936931198

Mäder, P., Gotel, O., Philippow, I.: Motivation matters in the traceability trenches. In: Proceedings of the 17th IEEE International Requirements Engineering Conference (RE'09), pp. 143–148. IEEE Computer Society, Atlanta, GA (2009, August–September)

MKS Inc.: MKS integrity. http://www.mks.com/platform/our-product. Accessed Dec 2010

Nikula, U., Jurvanen, C., Gotel, O., Gause, D.: Empirical validation of the classic change curve on a software technology change project. J. Inform. Softw. Technol. **52**(6) (2010, June)

Rupp, C.: Requirements-Engineering und -Management, 2nd edn. Hanser Fachbuch-Verlag, Leipzig, Germany (2002)

Rupp, C.: Requirements-Engineering und -Management: Professionelle, iterative Anforderungsanalyse für die Praxis, 4th edn. Carl Hanser Verlag, Leipzig, Germany (2007)

Schwaber, C., Sterpe, P.: Selecting The Right Requirements Management Tool – Or Maybe None Whatsoever. Forrester Research, Inc., (2007, 28th September)

Sparx Systems Pty Ltd.: Sparx systems enterprise architect. http://www.sparxsystems.com.au/. Accessed Dec 2010

Tvete, B.: Introducing efficient requirements management. In: Proceedings International Workshop on Database and Expert Systems Applications. IEEE Computer Society, Los Alamitos, CA (1999)

Young, R.R.: The Requirements Engineering Handbook, pp. 222–223. Artech House, Norwood, MA (2004)

Wiegers, K.E.: Automating requirements management. Softw. Develop. **7**(7), S1–S5 (1999a, July)

Wiegers, K.E.: Software Requirements: Practical Techniques for Gathering and Managing Requirements Throughout the Product Development Cycle, p. 19. Microsoft Press, Redmond, WA (1999b)

Part II
Traceability Creation

Creating traceability links in a project may appear to be a simple task, but it can be quite difficult to accomplish in practice. The difficulty arises in large projects where there may be tens of thousands of regulatory codes, requirements, design components, classes and test cases. Under these circumstances, the traceability effort can be overwhelming in terms of cost and effort, and the resulting traceability links are often incomplete and inaccurate. To address these challenges, numerous research teams have been working to automate the process of traceability creation.

This part of the book presents a variety of techniques that are representative of the state of art with respect to traceability creation. The chapter by De Lucia et al. presents an overview of "Information Retrieval Methods for Automated Traceability Recovery" while the chapter by Ali et al. looks at some of the specific "Factors Impacting the Inputs of Traceability Recovery Approaches". The chapter by Asuncion and Taylor presents an alternate approach to instrument a software development environment and capture traceability links in situ as developers perform their tasks, "Automated Techniques for Capturing Custom Traceability Links Across Heterogeneous Artifacts". Finally, the chapter on "Using Rules for Traceability Creation" describes a rule-based approach for automatically creating trace relationships and for identifying missing elements according to previously defined rules.

Information Retrieval Methods for Automated Traceability Recovery

Andrea De Lucia, Andrian Marcus, Rocco Oliveto, and Denys Poshyvanyk

1 Introduction

Today's software systems are extremely large and include a multitude of artifacts, in addition to the source code. A software system includes artifacts such as: source code, design documents, requirement documents, test cases, bug reports, communications between stakeholders, etc. These are created and maintained over long periods of time by different people. Establishing and maintaining explicit connections between software artifacts is recognized to be a difficult yet important problem. This problem is being addressed from multiple angles. Development processes, such as, model driven or test driven development, address this issue partially. New integrated development environment, such as IBM's Jazz[1] also aim at simplifying this task. Defect tracking systems, such as, Bugzilla,[2] also provide support for this problem. The few cases, usually in mission critical software or certain companies, where explicit traceability between artifacts exists, are the exception rather than the norm. In such cases, this is achieved with very high costs that are prohibitive in commercial settings. In consequence, due to the absence of integrated solutions and cost effective commonly accepted practices, the reality is that most of the existing software systems lack explicit representations of traceability links between artifacts. Legacy systems suffer even more of this problem. Even in cases where efforts were made to establish traceability links among artifacts, they are often obsolete, as different artifacts evolve at different speeds and there are no widespread solutions to maintain existing traceability links. The need for tools and techniques to recover traceability links between artifacts in legacy systems is particularly important for a variety of software evolution tasks. These include general maintenance tasks, impact analysis, program comprehension, and more encompassing tasks such as reverse engineering for redevelopment and systematic reuse.

---

[1] http://www-01.ibm.com/software/rational/jazz/

[2] http://www.bugzilla.org/

R. Oliveto (✉)
University of Molise, Pesche (IS), Italy
e-mail: rocco.oliveto@unimol.it

J. Cleland-Huang et al. (eds.), *Software and Systems Traceability*,
DOI 10.1007/978-1-4471-2239-5_4, © Springer-Verlag London Limited 2012

A major challenge in the recovery of traceability links between software artifacts is the fact that these artifacts are in different formats and at different abstraction levels. More than that, sometimes the semantics of such links is interpreted differently by various people. For example, the main() function of a C++ program can be considered as relevant to all test cases or to none of them, as it will be executed in all scenarios. An added challenge is the fact that there is no defined data format for software engineering data and artifacts, so database and data analysis centered approaches are impractical. However, there is one type of data present in all software artifacts: textual data. Extracting and analyzing this data is essential to the development of traceability link recovery tools and techniques. In most artifacts the textual parts are descriptive in nature, that is, they describe the informal semantics of the artifacts. The assumption is that if the textual content of two artifacts refer to similar concepts, then the two artifacts are conceptually related and a traceability link between them could be established.

One solution adopted by researchers and practitioners to extract and analyze the textual data embedded in software artifacts is the use of Information Retrieval (IR) techniques (Baeza-Yates and Ribeiro-Neto, 1999; Harman, 1993). IR-based methods recover traceability links on the basis of the similarity between the text contained in the software artifacts. The higher the textual similarity between two artifacts, the higher the likelihood that a link exists between them. A distinct advantage of using IR techniques is that they do not rely on a predefined vocabulary or grammar. This allows the method to be applied without large amounts of preprocessing or manipulation of the input, which drastically reduces the costs of link recovery.

This chapter introduces a generic process for the use of IR techniques for the recovery of traceability links between software artifacts. It also describes in details the most common IR techniques used in this process and the main technical challenges with such applications and their evaluations.

2 Using IR Methods for Traceability Recovery

The foundation for applying IR-based methods to traceability link recovery is based on the similarity between the words in the text, which are contained in various software artifacts. The conjecture is that if two artifacts have high textual similarity then they are likely to refer to the same or similar concepts and they are good candidates to be linked with each other. The underlying principle behind this is that many artifacts, such as software documentation, or even source code, contain ample textual descriptions (Antoniol et al., 2002; Dekhtyar et al., 2004) and most programmers use meaningful words from the problem domain to name source code entities, such as identifiers and comments (Antoniol et al., 2002, 2007; Haiduc and Marcus, 2008).

The process for traceability link recovery using IR methods (a.k.a. trace retrieval) consists of several key steps:

1. document parsing, extraction, and pre-processing;
2. corpus indexing with an IR method;

3. ranked list generation;
4. analysis of candidate links.

Taken as a whole, the process is organized in a pipeline architecture, where the output from each step constitutes the input for the next step. In the first step, the software artifacts are extracted at the given granularity level (e.g., class, method, or paragraphs), then they are pre-processed and represented as a set of documents in the resulting corpus. In the second step, the traceability recovery technique uses an IR method (e.g., Latent Semantic Indexing (Deerwester et al., 1990)) to index diverse software artifacts and represent them in a homogeneous document space by extracting information about the occurrences of terms (or words) within them. This information is used to define similarity measures between various documents (i.e., software artifacts). In the third step the IR-based traceability recovery method compares a set of source artifacts (represented as documents) against another set of target artifacts and uses the defined similarity measure to rank all possible pairs by their similarities (*candidate traceability links*). Once these candidate links are generated, they are provided as a result to software engineers for examination. The software engineer reviews the candidate links, determines those that are actual links (*confirmed links*), and discards the *false positives*. In order to do this, the software engineer examines the text of the software artifacts having a candidate link, determines the purpose of these artifacts (e.g., the meanings of the requirements or the functionality of source code), compares the meanings, and makes the decision based on whether she determines that the meanings of these artifacts are adequately related. The process of candidate link evaluation is based on human judgment and thus has all the advantages and disadvantages associated with such activities. The results (confirmed links and false positives) from the candidate link evaluation step may also be used to provide feedback to the IR tool to improve the tracing accuracy (De Lucia et al., 2006b; Di Penta et al., 2002; Hayes et al., 2006). The next subsections describe in details the first three steps of an IR-based traceability recovery process, while the approaches exploited to analyze the candidate links are presented in a separate section (Section 4).

2.1 Document Parsing, Extraction and Pre-processing

The majority of IR-based traceability recovery approaches have been applied to software artifacts, such as requirements,[3] source code,[4] external documentation,[5]

---

[3] See e.g., (Antoniol et al., 2000a; 2000b, 2002; Capobianco et al., 2009a, 2009b; Cleland-Huang et al., 2005, De Lucia et al., 2004, 2006a, 2006b, 2007; Di Penta et al., 2002; Hayes et al., 2003, 2006; Lormans and Van Deursen, 2005, 2006; Lormans et al., 2006, 2008; Marcus and Maletic, 2003; Marcus et al., 2005; Oliveto et al., 2010; Settimi et al., 2004; Zou et al. 2007).

[4] See e.g., (Antoniol et al., 1999, 2000a, 2000b, 2002; De Lucia et al., 2004, 2006a, 2006b, 2007; Capobianco et al., 2009a, 2009b; Di Penta et al., 2002; Marcus and Maletic, 2003; Marcus et al., 2005; Oliveto et al., 2010; Settimi et al., 2004).

[5] See e.g., (Antoniol et al., 1999, 2000a, 2002; Marcus and Maletic, 2003; Marcus et al., 2005).

design documentation,[6] test cases[7], defect or bug reports (Yadla et al., 2005), and emails (Bacchelli et al., 2010).

IR-based traceability recovery approaches extract and represent information from textual software artifacts using different granularities depending on the type of software artifact. Techniques operating on source code artifacts parse these artifacts using a developer-defined granularity (that is, methods, classes, function, or files). While several granularities are applicable to source code artifacts, the majority of recovery methods parse and represent the artifacts at a class level granularity (see e.g., (Antoniol et al., 2002; De Lucia et al., 2007; Marcus and Maletic, 2003)). This makes sense in Object-Oriented software systems, as clases are the primary decomposition unit supported by the programming languages. Traceability recovery methods using other types of artifacts (e.g., requirements, external documentation, design documents, bug reports) represent these artifacts using a user-defined granularity level, which varies from application to application and depends on the physical and logical representation of these artifacts. In such cases, a decision is required on how to partition these artifacts into atomic documents.

Traceability recovery techniques apply different pre-processing strategies on textual documents represented in the corpus, before indexing them with a specific IR method. The frequently used preprocessing steps are:

- *text normalization*: prunes out white spaces and most non-textual tokens from the text (i.e., operators, special symbols, some numerals, etc.);
- *identifier splitting*: splits into separate words terms composed of two or more words. IR techniques may miss occurrences of concepts if identifiers are not split. Similarly, incorrect splitting can cause a decrease of the accuracy of program search techniques (Enslen et al., 2009). To split multi-word identifiers, most existing automatic software analysis tools that use natural language information rely on coding conventions (Antoniol et al., 2002). When simple coding conventions, such as camel casing and non-alphabetic characters (e.g., "_" and numbers), are used to separate words and abbreviations, automatically splitting multi-word identifiers into their constituent words is straightforward. However, there are cases where existing coding conventions break down (e.g., SIMPLETYPENAME). In these cases more sophisticated approaches have to be used (see e.g., (Enslen et al., 2009; Lawrie et al., 2010; Madani et al., 2010)).
- *stop word removal*: an artifact generally contains common words (i.e., articles, adverbs, etc.) that are not useful to capture the semantics of the artifact content. A stop word function and/or a stop word list are applied to discard such words. The stop word function prunes out all the words having a length less than a fixed

---

[6] See e.g., (Capobianco et al., 2009; De Lucia et al., 2004, 2006a, 2006b, 2007; 2009b; Lormans and Van Deursen, 2005; 2006; Lormans et al., 2006, 2008; Settimi et al., 2004).

[7] See e.g., (Capobianco et al., 2009a, 2009b; De Lucia et al., 2004, 2006a, 2006b, 2007; Lormans and Van Deursen, 2005, 2006; Lormans et al., 2006, 2008).

threshold, while the stop word list is used to remove all the words contained in a given word list. Generally, good results are achieved using both the stop word function and the stop word list (Baeza-Yates and Ribeiro-Neto, 1999; Harman, 1993). Stop word lists are language specific, for example, English has different stop words than Italian.

A more complicated document pre-processing is represented by morphological analysis, like stemming. Stemming is the process of reducing inflected (or sometimes derived) words to their stem, base or root form. The stem need not be identical to the morphological root of the word. It is usually sufficient that related words map to the same stem, even if this stem itself is not in a valid root. A stemmer for English, for example, should identify the string "cats" (and possibly "catlike", "catty", etc.) as based on the root "cat", and "stemmer", "stemming", "stemmed" as based on "stem". A stemming algorithm reduces the words "fishing", "fished", "fish", and "fisher" to the root word, "fish". There are several existing stemming algorithms, one of the most popular stemmers for the English language is the Porter stemmer (Porter, 1980). Not all stemmers work the same. Some stemmers are more conservative than others and may generate more false positives or false negatives. However, IR-based traceability link recovery techniques are not very sensitive to the subtle differences between such algorithms. It is important that the same stemmer is used when processing all artifacts.

Some of the pre-processing strategies depend upon which IR model is used to index the artifact corpus. For example, stemming is regularly an optional step while using LSI, but constantly required when using a VSM (Antoniol et al., 2002; Hayes et al., 2006; Marcus and Maletic, 2003). An alternative approach, based on searching for n-grams rather than stems, may be used instead. In (Hollink et al., 2004) the authors investigate the effectiveness of language-dependent (e.g., stemming) and language-independent (e.g., character n-gramming) approaches to cross-lingual text retrieval. They show that morphological normalization improves retrieval effectiveness, especially for languages that have a more complex morphology than English. The authors also showed that n-gram-base can be a viable option in the absence of linguistic resources to support a deep morphological normalization (Hollink et al., 2004). In the context of traceability link recovery the use of 2-grams to compare the content of software artifacts (phrasing) helps improving the overall recovery accuracy, especially in the top part of the ranked list (Zou et al., 2006, 2008, 2010).

The terms extracted from the documents are stored in a $m \times n$ matrix (called *term-by-document matrix* (Baeza-Yates and Ribeiro-Neto, 1999)), where m is the number of all unique terms that occur within the documents, and n is the number of documents in the repository. A generic entry $w_{i,j}$ of this matrix denotes a measure of the weight (i.e., relevance) of the ith term in the jth document (Baeza-Yates and Ribeiro-Neto, 1999). Various methods for weighting terms have been developed in the IR field. However, three main factors come into play in the final term weighting formulation:

1. *Term Frequency* (or *tf*): words that repeat multiple times in a document are considered salient. Term weights based on *tf* have been used in the vector space model since the 1960s.
2. *Document Frequency*: words that appear in many documents are considered common and are not very indicative of document content. A weighting method based on this, called inverse document frequency (or *idf*) weighting, was proposed by Sparck-Jones in the early 1970s (Sparck Jones, 1972).
3. *Document Length*: when collections have documents of varying lengths, longer documents tend to score higher since they contain more words and word repetitions. This effect is usually compensated by normalizing for document lengths in the term weighting method. In the context of traceability recovery, interesting results have been achieved using the pivot normalization term weighting approach that allows to specify the normalization factor depending on the specific collection of artifacts (Settimi et al., 2004).

All these factors can be taken into account while applying both a local and a global weighting to increase/decrease the importance of terms within or among documents. Specifically, a generic entry $a_{i,j}$ of the term-by-document matrix can be calculated as follows:

$$a_{i,j} = L(i,j) \cdot G(i) \tag{1}$$

where $L(i, j)$ is the local weight of the ith term in the jth document and $G(i)$ is the global weight of the ith term in the whole document collection. In general, the local weight increases with the frequency of the ith term in the jth document, while the global weight decreases as much as the ith term is spread across the documents of the document space. For example, each term can be weighted using the *tf-idf* indexing mechanism (Baeza-Yates and Ribeiro-Neto, 1999):

$$a_{i,j} = tf_{i,j} \cdot idf_i$$

where $tf_{i,j}$ and idf_i are the term frequency and the inverse document frequency of the term i, respectively. The term frequency is computed as

$$tf_{i,j} = \frac{n_{i,j}}{\sum_k n_{k,j}}$$

where $n_{i,j}$ represents the occurrences of term i in the document j. The inverse document frequency is computed as

$$idf_i = log\left(\frac{n}{doc_i}\right)$$

where doc_i is the number of documents where the term i appears.

To better understand the tf-idf weighting schema consider an artifact containing 50 words wherein the word "doctor" appears 5 times while the word "system" appears 10 times. Following the previously defined formulas, the term frequency (*tf*) for "doctor" is $(5/50) = 0.1$, while for "system" is $(10/50) = 0.2$. Since the number of occurrences of "system" are higher than those of "doctor" the local weight of the former word is higher. Now, assume we have 100 artifacts and "doctor" appears only in 10 of these, while "system" appears in 90 artifacts. Then, the inverse document frequency for "doctor" is calculated as $log(100/10) = 1$ while for "system" is $log(100/90) = 0.05$. The $tf - idf$ score is the product of these quantities, i.e., $0.2 \cdot 0.05 = 0.01$ for "system" and $0.1 \cdot 1 = 0.1$ for "doctor". As we can see, the schema gives a higher weight to "doctor" as it is a more discriminating word compared to "system".

A more sophisticated weighting schema has been proposed by Dumais (Dumais, 1991). In this schema the local weight is represented by the term frequency scaled by a logarithmic factor, while the entropy of the term within the document collection is used for the global weight:

$$L(i,j) = log(tf_{ij} + 1) \qquad\qquad G(i) = \sum_{j=1}^{n} \frac{p_{ij} log(p_{ij})}{log(n)} \qquad (2)$$

where tf_{ij} is the frequency of the ith term in the jth document and p_{ij} is defined as:

$$p_{ij} = \frac{tf_{ij}}{\sum_{k=1}^{n} tf_{ik}} \qquad (3)$$

An advantage of using the entropy of a term to define its global weight is the fact that it takes into account the distribution of the term within the document space.

The weight of the term could also take into account the importance of the term for the specific domain. In particular, artifacts could contain critical terms and phrases that should be weighted more heavily than others, as they can be regarded as more meaningful in identifying traceability links. These terms can be extracted from the project glossary (Zou et al., 2006, 2008, 2010) or external dictionaries (Hayes et al., 2003). The importance of the terms can be derived also from the analysis of their grammatical nature (Capobianco et al., 2009a). Such an approach is based on the observation that the language used in software documents can be classified as sectorial language,[8] where the terms that provide more indication on the semantics of a document are the nouns, while the verbs tend to play a connection role and have a generic semantics (Jurafsky and Martin, 2000; Keenan, 1975). Thus, the artifact content can be pre-processed to filter out all the terms that are not nouns.

---

[8] The language used by people who work in a particular area or who have a common interest (Jurafsky and Martin, 2000; Keenan, 1975).

2.2 *Corpus Indexing and Ranked List Generation*

Based on the *term-by-document matrix* representation, different IR methods can be used to rank pairs of source and target artifacts based on their similarities. A survey of available research papers reveals that probabilistic models (Abadi et al., 2008; Antoniol et al., 1999; Cleland-Huang et al., 2005), VSM (Baeza-Yates and Ribeiro-Neto, 1999; Harman, 1993; Salton et al., 1975), and LSI (Deerwester et al., 1990) are the three most frequently used IR methods for traceability recovery. In particular, only in few cases different methods have been used to recover traceability links between different types of artifacts (Asuncion et al., 2010; Capobianco et al., 2009b). In (Asuncion et al., 2010) a topic modeling technique, namely Latent Dirichlet Allocation (LDA) (Blei et al., 2003) is used for traceability link recovery between text-based artifacts (such as requirements and design documents). The authors monitor the operations (e.g., opening a requirements specification or visiting a Wiki page) performed by the software engineers during software development identifying a list of potentially related artifacts. Such relationships are then used to extract a set of topics that can be subsequently used to infer other relationships between code and documentation. In (Capobianco et al., 2009b) the proposed traceability recovery method models the information contained in a software artifact by particular interpolation curves of plots mapping terms and their frequency on the artifact. Then, the similarity between artifacts is computed by calculating the distance of the corresponding interpolation curves. It is worth noting that a recent empirical study highlighted that none of these techniques sensibly outperforms the others (Oliveto et al., 2010).

The most used IR methods for traceability link recovery, i.e., the probabilistic models and the vector space-based models (VSM and LSI), are described in the following subsections. In the probabilistic model, a source artifact is ranked according to the probability of being relevant to a particular target artifact. In vector space-based models, artifacts are represented by vectors of terms. Thus, source artifacts are ranked against target artifacts by computing a distance function between the corresponding vectors.

2.2.1 Probabilistic Models

Three different probabilistic models have been proposed to recover links between software artifacts (Abadi et al., 2008; Antoniol et al., 1999; Cleland-Huang et al., 2005). The approaches proposed in (Antoniol et al., 1999; Cleland-Huang et al., 2005) are based on conditioned probability. In particular, this model computes the ranking scores as the probability that a document D_i (target artifact) is related to the query Q (source artifact):

$$sim(D_i, Q) = Pr(D_i|Q) \tag{4}$$

Applying Bayes' rule (Bain and Engelhardt, 1992), the conditioned probability above can be transformed in:

$$Pr(D_i|Q) = \frac{Pr(Q|D_i)Pr(D_i)}{Pr(Q)} \tag{5}$$

For a given query component, $Pr(Q)$ is a constant and it is possible to further simplify the model by assuming that all documents have the same probability. Therefore, for a given query Q, all documents D_i are ranked by the conditioned probabilities $Pr(Q|D_i)$.

These conditioned probabilities are computed by estimating a stochastic language model (De Mori, 1998) for each document D_i. Indeed, due to the hypothesis that the query and the documents insist on the same vocabulary V, a query Q can be represented by a sequence of m words $w_1; w_2; \cdots; w_m$ (the words composing the query) of the vocabulary V and the conditioned probability:

$$Pr(Q|D_i) = Pr(w_1; w_2; \cdots; w_m|D_i) \tag{6}$$

can be estimated on a statistical basis by exploiting a stochastic language model for the document D_i. This model collects statistics about the frequency of the occurrences of sequences of words of V in D_i that allow to estimate $Pr(w_1; w_2; \cdots; w_m|D_i)$ for any sequence of words $w_1; w_2; \cdots; w_m$ of V. However, the probability above can be written as:

$$Pr(w_1; w_2; \cdots; w_m|D_i) = Pr(w_1|D_i) \prod_{k=2}^{m} Pr(w_k|w_1; \cdots; w_{k-1}, D_i) \tag{7}$$

and when m increases the conditioned probabilities involved in the above product quickly become difficult to estimate for any possible sequence of m words in the vocabulary. A simplification can be introduced by conditioning the dependence of each word to the last $n - 1$ words (with $n < m$):

$$Pr(w_1; w_2; \cdots; w_m|D_i) \approx \; \approx Pr(w_1; \cdots; w_{n-1}|D_i) \prod_{k=n}^{m} Pr(w_k|w_{k-n+1}; \cdots; w_{k-1}, D_i)$$

$$\tag{8}$$

This n-gram approximation, which formally assumes a time-invariant Markov process (Cover and Thomas, 1991), greatly reduces the statistics to be collected in order to compute $Pr(Q|D_i)$. Clearly, this also introduces an imprecision. However, n-gram models are still difficult to estimate because, if $|V|$ is the size of the vocabulary, all possible $|V|^n$ sequences of words in the vocabulary have to be considered. Indeed, the estimation can be very demanding even for a 2-gram (bigram) model.[9] Moreover, the occurrence of any sequence of words in a document D_i is a rare event, as it generally occurs only a few times and most of the sequences will never occur due to the sparseness of data. Therefore, in this approach, it is possible to considered a unigram approximation ($n = 1$) that corresponds to consider all words w_k to

---

[9] In a bigram model, $Pr(w_1; w_2; \cdots; w_m|D_i) \approx Pr(w_1|D_i \prod_{k=2}^{m} Pr(w_k|w_{k-1}D_i)$.

be independent. Therefore, each document D_i is represented by a language model where unigram probabilities are estimated for all words in the vocabulary and:

$$sim(D_i, Q) = Pr(Q|D_i) = Pr(w_1; w_2; \cdots; w_m|D_i \approx \prod_{k=1}^{m} Pr(w_k|D_i) \quad (9)$$

Unigram estimation is based on the term frequency of each word in a document. However, using the simple term frequency would turn the product $\prod_{k=1}^{m} Pr(w_k|D_i)$ to zero, whenever any word w_k is not present in the document D_i. This problem, known as the zero-frequency problem (Witten and Bell, 1991), can be avoided using different approaches (see (De Mori, 1998)). A possible approach consists of smoothing the unigram probability distribution by computing the probabilities as follows (Antoniol et al., 2002):

$$Pr(w_k|D_i) \quad (10)$$

where N is the total number of words in the document D_i and c_k is the number of occurrences of words w_k in the document Di. The interpolation term is:

$$\lambda = \frac{n}{(N * |V|)}\beta \quad (11)$$

where n is the number of different words of the vocabulary V occurring in the document D_i. The value of the parameter is computed according to Ney and Essen (1991) as follows:

$$\beta = \frac{n(1)}{(n(1) + 2 * n(2))} \quad (12)$$

where $n(j)$ is the number of words occurring j times in the document D_i.

In the context of traceability link recovery, the probabilistic model based on conditioned probability has been used to recover links among requirements (Gibiec et al., 2010; Cleland-Huang et al., 2010), requirements and UML diagrams (Cleland-Huang et al., 2005), requirements and source code (Abadi et al., 2008; Antoniol et al., 2000a, 2000b, 2000c, 2002; Di Penta et al., 2002), and manual pages and source code (Antoniol et al., 1999, 2000a). In these studies different enhancing strategies have been also proposed in order to improve recovery accuracy. The first strategy exploits partial knowledge of a subset of traceability links (Antoniol et al., 2000b). In particular, a set of previously identified links can be supplied to the probabilistic network to improve the recovery accuracy.

Knowledge about the structure of the artifacts can also be exploited to improve the performances of a probabilistic recovery method. In particular, different enhancing strategies, namely hierarchical modeling, logical clustering of artifacts, and semi-automated pruning of the probabilistic network, have been proposed to incorporate supporting information into a probabilistic retrieval algorithm and improve the retrieval accuracy (Cleland-Huang et al., 2005). The first enhancing strategy (that is, hierarchical modeling) is based on the observation that artifacts are generally arranged in a hierarchical format. This hierarchical structure could be exploited to better identify the context of each artifacts, since, in general, the words used to name and describe the higher level artifacts capture the meaning (i.e., context) of their lower-level components. The hierarchical links are then exploited when computing the probabilities that a target artifact is relevant for a given source artifact. The second strategy is based on the conjecture that links tend to occur in clusters. Thus, if a link exists between a source artifact and a target artifact, and if that target artifact is a part of a logical cluster of artifacts, then there would be a higher probability that additional links should exist between the same source artifact and other target artifacts in the cluster. It is worth noting that this approach differs from the previous ones because the enhancement is based on sibling artifacts rather than on ancestral information. The last enhancing strategy, i.e., pruning of the probabilistic network, aims at attenuating the synonym problem. In particular, a set of constraints can be automatically added to the probabilistic network exploiting previous identified links (used as training set). The proposed enhancing strategies are able to improve the recovery accuracy of a canonical probabilistic recovery method. An analysis of the improvements provided by each enhancement strategy indicates significant overlap between the hierarchical and clustering techniques. Instead, the pruning technique seems to improve different aspects of the probabilistic model. In particular, while the first two approaches tend to generally improve the precision, the third strategies tends to specifically attenuate a particular problem, i.e., the synonym problem (Cleland-Huang et al., 2005). Such a result suggests that the pruning technique could be combined with hierarchical modeling or logical clustering of artifacts.

Recently, another enhancement strategy has been proposed to improve the recovery accuracy of probabilistic retrieval methods. Such a strategy, called Query Term Coverage, increases the relevance ranking of links between artifacts that have more than one unique word in common (Zou et al., 2007, 2010). This approach tends to reduce the number of incorrectly retrieved links between unrelated pairs of artifacts that contain only a single matching word, which co-occurs multiple times.

Another probabilistic model has been proposed by Abadi et al. (2008). The proposed approach, referred as JS model, is driven by a probabilistic approach and hypothesis testing techniques. As well as other probabilistic models, it represents each document through a probability distribution. This means that an artifact is represented by a random variable where the probability of its states is given by the empirical distribution of the terms occurring in the artifact (i.e., columns of the term-by-document matrix). It is worth noting that the empirical distribution of a term is based on the weight assigned to the term for the specific artifact (Abadi et al., 2008). In the JS method the similarity between two artifacts is given by a "distance" of their probability distributions measured by using the Jensen-Shannon (JS) Divergence (Cover and Thomas, 1991).

2.2.2 Vector Space-Based Models

In the VSM, an artifact is represented by a vector of terms (Baeza-Yates and Ribeiro-Neto, 1999; Harman, 1993; Salton et al., 1975). The definition of a term is not inherent in the model, but terms in the context of traceability recovery are typically words. Note that, for example, identifiers are often made of words that are not from a natural language, yet they are considered valid in his context. If words are chosen as terms, then every word in the vocabulary becomes an independent dimension in a very high dimensional vector space. Since any artifact contains a limited set of terms (the vocabulary can be millions of terms), most artifact vectors are very sparse and they generally operate in a positive quadrant of the vector space, i.e., no term is assigned a negative value.

To assign a numeric score to a document (target artifact) for a query (source artifact), the model measures the similarity between the query vector and the document vector. The similarity between two vectors is once again not inherent in the model. Typically, the angle between two vectors is used as a measure of divergence between the vectors, and the cosine of the angle is used as the numeric similarity.[10] If $\vec{D}$ is the document vector and $\vec{Q}$ is the query vector, then the similarity of document to query (or score of for) can be calculated as follows (Baeza-Yates and Ribeiro-Neto, 1999; Harman, 1993):

$$sim(D, Q) = \frac{\vec{D} \cdot \vec{Q}}{\|\vec{D}\| \cdot \|\vec{Q}\|} = \frac{\sum_{t_i \in D, Q} w_{t_i D} \cdot w_{t_i Q}}{\sqrt{\sum_{t_i \in D} w_{t_i D}^2} \cdot \sqrt{\sum_{t_i \in Q} w_{t_i Q}^2}} \tag{13}$$

where $w_{t_i Q}$ is the value of the ith component in the query vector $\vec{Q}$, and $w_{t_i D}$ is the ith component in the document vector $\vec{D}$. Since any word not present in either the query or the document has a $w_{t_i Q}$ or $w_{t_i D}$ equals to 0, respectively, it is possible to sum only over the terms common in the query and the document. As an alternative, the inner-product (or dot-product) between two vectors is often used as a similarity measure. If all the vectors are forced to be unit length, then the cosine of the angle between two vectors is the same as their dot-product (Baeza-Yates and Ribeiro-Neto, 1999; Harman, 1993).

In the context of traceability recovery, the VSM has been used to recover traceability links among requirements (De Lucia et al., 2006b; Hayes et al., 2003, 2006), requirements and source code (Abadi et al., 2008, Antoniol et al., 2000a, 2002, De Lucia et al., 2006b; Marcus and Maletic, 2003; Marcus et al., 2005), manual pages and source code (Antoniol et al., 2000a, 2002; Marcus and Maletic, 2003, Marcus et al., 2005), UML diagrams and source code (De Lucia et al., 2006b, Settimi et al., 2004), test cases and source code (De Lucia et al., 2006b), and defect reports and source code (Yadla et al., 2005).

A common criticism of VSM is that it does not take into account relations between terms (Deerwester et al., 1990). For instance, having an "automobile" in one document and a "car" in another document does not contribute to the similarity measure between these two documents. LSI (Deerwester et al., 1990) was developed to overcome the synonymy and polysemy problems, which occur with the

---

[10] The cosine has a property indicating 1.0 for identical vectors and 0.0 for orthogonal vectors.

VSM model. In LSI the dependencies between terms and documents, in addition to the associations between terms and documents, are explicitly taken into account. LSI assumes that there is an underlying or "latent structure" in word usage that is partially obscured by variability in word choice, and uses statistical techniques to estimate this latent structure. For example, both "car" and "automobile" are likely to co-occur in different documents with related terms, such as "motor", "wheel", etc. LSI exploits information about co-occurrence of terms (i.e., latent structure) to automatically discover synonymy between different terms.

LSI defines a term-by-document matrix A as well as VSM. Then it applies the Singular Value Decomposition (SVD) (Cullum and Willoughby, 1998) to decompose the term-by-document matrix into the product of three other matrices:

$$A = T_0 \cdot S_0 \cdot D_0 \tag{14}$$

where T_0 is the $m \times r$ matrix of the terms containing the left singular vectors (rows of the matrix), D_0 is the $r \times n$ matrix of the documents containing the right singular vectors (columns of the matrix), S_0 is an $r \times r$ diagonal matrix of singular values, and r is the rank of A. T_0 and D_0 have orthogonal columns, such that:

$$T_0^T \cdot T_0 = D_0^T \cdot D_0 = I_r \tag{15}$$

SVD can be viewed as a technique for deriving a set of uncorrelated indexing factors or concepts (Deerwester et al., 1990), whose number is given by the rank r of the matrix A and whose relevance is given by the singular values in the matrix S_0. Concepts "represent extracted common meaning components of many different words and documents" (Deerwester et al., 1990). In other words, concepts are a way to cluster related terms with respect to documents and related documents with respect to terms. Each term and document is represented by a vector in the r-space of concepts, using elements of the left or right singular vectors. The product $S_0 \cdot D_0$ ($T_0 \cdot S_0$, respectively) is a matrix whose columns (rows, respectively) are the document vectors (term vectors, respectively) in the r-space of the concepts. The cosine of the angle between two vectors in this space represents the similarity of the two documents (terms, respectively) with respect to the concepts they share. In this way, SVD captures the underlying structure in the association of terms and documents. Terms that occur in similar documents, for example, will be near each other in the r-space of concepts, even if they never co-occur in the same document. This also means that some documents that do not share any word, but share similar words may nonetheless be near in the r-space.

SVD allows a simple strategy for optimal approximate fit using smaller matrices (Deerwester et al., 1990). If the singular values in S_0 are ordered by size, the first k largest values may be kept and the remaining smaller ones set to zero. Since zeros were introduced into S_0, the representation can be simplified by deleting the zero rows and columns of S_0 to obtain a new diagonal matrix S, and deleting the corresponding columns of T_0 and rows of D_0 to obtain T and D respectively. The result is a reduced model:

$$A \approx A_k = T \cdot S \cdot D \tag{16}$$

where the matrix A_k is only approximately equal to A and is of rank $k < r$. The truncated SVD captures most of the important underlying structure in the association of terms and documents, yet at the same time it removes the noise or variability in word usage that plagues word-based retrieval methods. Intuitively, since the number of dimensions k is much smaller than the number of unique terms m, minor differences in terminology will be ignored.

The choice of k is critical: ideally, it is desirable to have a value of k that is large enough to fit all the real structure in the data, but small enough not to fit the sampling error or unimportant details. The proper way to make such a choice is an open issue in the factor analysis literature (Deerwester et al., 1990; Dumais, 1991). In the application of LSI to information retrieval, good performances have been achieved using about 100 concepts on a document space of about 1,000 documents and a vocabulary of about 6,000 terms (Deerwester et al., 1990). With much larger repositories (between 20,000 and 220,000 documents and between 40,000 and 80,000 terms), good results have been achieved using between 235 and 250 concepts (Dumais, 1991; Poshyvanyk et al., 2007; Revelle et al., 2010). It is worth noting that software repositories are not comparable with document collection generally used in the text retrieval field. This implies that in the context of traceability recovery the size of the LSI subspace does not significantly influence the recovery accuracy (De Lucia et al., 2007) and values between 100 and 250 provides acceptable results (De Lucia et al., 2007; Hayes et al., 2006; Marcus and Maletic, 2003). Nonetheless, the choice of k in this application is still an open issue.

In the context of traceability recovery, LSI has been used to recover traceability links between requirements (De Lucia et al., 2006b; Hayes et al., 2006), requirements and source code (Abadi et al., 2008; De Lucia et al., 2004; De Lucia et al., 2006a, 2006b, 2007; Marcus and Maletic, 2003; Marcus et al., 2005), manual pages and source code (Antoniol et al., 2000a, 2002; Marcus and Maletic, 2003; Marcus et al., 2005), UML diagrams and source code (De Lucia et al., 2004; 2006a, 2006b, 2007, Settimi et al., 2004), test cases and source code (De Lucia et al., 2004; De Lucia et al., 2006a, 2006b, 2007; Lormans and Van Deursen, 2005, 2006; Lormans et al., 2006, 2008).

3 Measuring the Performance of IR-Based Traceability Recovery Methods

The performances–in terms of retrieval accuracy–of an IR-based traceability recovery method is generally evaluated through a set of retrieved links over a set of relevant links. The set of retrieved links is obtained by cutting the ranked list provided by an IR method at a given point and considering only the top links in the ranked list. The set of relevant links is generally derived by a traceability matrix provided by original developers of the system at the end of the process (this matrix is intended to contain the correct links). Clearly, the set of retrieved traceability links, in general, does not match exactly the set of relevant links between the artifacts in the repository. In fact, any IR methods will fail to retrieve some of the relevant links while, on the other hand, it will also retrieve links that are not relevant (false positives). This is one of the key reasons why IR-based traceability recovery methods are semi-automatic and require some degree of interaction between software developers and a traceability link recovery tool.

By and large, the retrieval performance of IR methods is measured using two metrics, namely recall and precision (Baeza-Yates and Ribeiro-Neto, 1999). Recall is the ratio between the number of links that are successfully retrieved and the number of links that are relevant (Baeza-Yates and Ribeiro-Neto, 1999):

$$recall = \frac{|\{relevant\_links\} \cap \{retrieved\_links\}|}{|\{relevant\_links\}|} \tag{17}$$

It is easy to note that it is trivial to achieve 100% of recall by returning all links in response to any query. Therefore, recall alone, is not enough, but one needs to measure the number of non-relevant links as well. Precision is the fraction of the links retrieved that are relevant to the source artifact (Baeza-Yates and Ribeiro-Neto, 1999):

$$precision = \frac{|\{relevant\_links\} \cap \{retrieved\_links\}|}{|\{retrieved\_links\}|} \tag{18}$$

Differently from the recall, precision takes all retrieved links into account. It can also be evaluated at a given cut-off rank, considering only the topmost results returned by the system. This measure is called *precision at n* or *P@n*. Note that the meaning and usage of "precision" in the field of IR differs from the definition of accuracy and precision within other branches of science and technology. In particular, in the fields of science, engineering, industry and statistics, accuracy is a degree of conformity of a measured or calculated quantity to its actual (true) value, while precision, also called reproducibility or repeatability, is the degree to which further measurements or calculations show the same or similar results (Baeza-Yates and Ribeiro-Neto, 1999).

Both measures have values in the interval of [0, 1]. If the recall value is 1, it means that all relevant links have been recovered, though there could be recovered links that are not relevant. If the precision is 1, it implies that all recovered links are relevant, though there could be relevant links that were not recovered. In general, retrieving a lower number of links results in higher precision, while a higher number of retrieved links increases the recall.

The recall and precision are orthogonal metrics and measure two different concepts. Often, an aggregate measure, namely F-measure, is used to obtain a balance between them. The F-measure or balanced F-score is the weighted harmonic mean of precision and recall:

$$F = 2 \cdot \frac{(\text{precision} \cdot \text{recall})}{(\text{precision} + \text{recall})} \qquad (19)$$

This is also known as the F_1 measure, because recall and precision are evenly weighted. The general formula for non-negative real α is:

$$F_\alpha = (1 + \alpha) \cdot \frac{(\text{precision} \cdot \text{recall})}{(\alpha \cdot \text{precision} + \text{recall})} \qquad (20)$$

Two other commonly used F-measures are the F_2 measure, which weights recall twice as much as precision, and the $F_{0.5}$ measure, which weights precision twice as much as recall.

Another metric used to measure the performances of an IR-based traceability recovery method is represented by average precision that is defined as the mean of the precision scores obtained after each correct link is retrieved, using zero as the precision for correct links that are not retrieved (Cleland-Huang et al., 2010; Gibiec et al., 2010).

The main role of IR tools consists of reducing the document space, while recovering all the relevant links between artifacts. Without tool support, one must analyze all artifacts in order to identify the dependencies between them. With a reduced document space the number of artifacts to analyze is generally much smaller. This means that high recall values (possibly 100%) should be pursued. Of course, in this case higher precision values reduce the effort required to discard false positives (documents that are retrieved, but not relevant to a given query).

To achieve an indication of the benefits of using an IR approach in a traceability link recovery process, it is possible to use the Recovery Effort Index (REI), defined as the ratio between the number of documents retrieved and the total number of documents available (Antoniol et al., 2002):

$$REI_i = \frac{|\text{retrieved\_artifacts}|}{|\text{target\_artifacts}|} \%$$

This metric can be used to estimate the percentage of the effort required to manually analyze the results achieved by an IR tool (and discard false positive), when the recall is 100%, with respect to a completely manual analysis. For a given software system, the quantity 1 - REI can be used to estimate the effort savings due to the use of an IR method to recover traceability links, with respect a completely manual analysis (Antoniol et al., 2002). The lower the REI, the higher the benefits of the IR approach.

4 Analysis of Candidate Links

The similarity measures obtained by applying a particular IR method are used to build a ranked list of candidate links. This list contains all possible pairs of source and target artifacts ranked according to textual similarities among source and target artifacts. This means that the list of candidate links inevitably contains links that are not correct and have to be discarded by the software engineer. Two different approaches have been proposed to analyze the ranked list. The first approach is based on the analysis of the full ranked list of candidate links (Capobianco et al., 2009b; Cleland-Huang et al., 2005; De Lucia et al., 2006b, 2007; Hayes et al., 2003; Yadla et al., 2005). However, the list of candidate links contains a higher density of correct traceability links in the upper part of the list and a much lower density of such links in the bottom part of the list (De Lucia et al., 2007, 2009a). This means that in the lower part of the ranked list the effort required to discard false positives becomes much higher than the effort to validate correct links.

The above considerations suggest the use of some method to cut the ranked list (e.g., a threshold on the similarity value), thus presenting the software engineer only the subset of top links in the ranked list (ranked list filtering) (Abadi et al., 2008; Antoniol et al., 2002; De Lucia et al., 2007; Hayes et al., 2006; Lormans et al., 2008; Marcus and Maletic, 2003; Settimi et al., 2004; Zou et al., 2007). Different strategies have been proposed to filter ranked lists. Broadly, these methods can be classified into *cut-point* and *threshold* based strategies. The first category of methods cut the ranked list regardless of the values of the similarity measure (cut point based strategy):

1. *Constant cut point*: this method consists of imposing a threshold on the number of recovered links (Antoniol et al., 2002; Marcus and Maletic, 2003). In this way, the top μ links of the ranked list are selected.
2. *Variable cut point*: this is an extension of the previous method that consists of specifying the percentage of the links of the ranked list that have to be retrieved (cut percentage). In this way the cut point depends on the size of the ranked list.

The second category (threshold based strategy) use a threshold ε on a similarity measure and only the pairs of artifacts having a similarity measure greater than or equal to ε will be retrieved:

1. *Constant threshold*: this is the standard method used in the literature. A widely adopted threshold is $\varepsilon = 0.70$, that for the vector space model (and LSI) approximately corresponds to a 45° angle between the corresponding vectors (Marcus and Maletic, 2003).
2. *Scale threshold*: a threshold ε is computed as the percentage of the best similarity value between two artifacts, i.e., $\varepsilon = c \cdot MaxSimilarity$, where $0 \leq c \leq 1$ (Antoniol et al., 2002). In this case, the higher the value of the parameter c, the smaller the set of links returned by a query.
3. *Variable threshold*: this is an extension of the constant threshold approach. The constant threshold is projected from the interval [0, 1] into the interval [min similarity, max similarity], where min similarity and max similarity are the minimum and maximum similarity values in the ranked list (De Lucia et al., 2004, 2006a, 2007).

It is worth noting that the lower the similarity threshold used, the higher the number of correct links as well as the number of false positives retrieved and the relative effort to discard them. Such a limitation of IR-based traceability recovery methods have encouraged researchers to identify an "optimal" threshold enabling the retrieval of as many correct links as possible, while keeping low the effort required to analyze and discard false positives. However, this ideal threshold is not easy to identify, as it can change together with the type of artifacts and projects (De Lucia et al., 2007). For this reason, an incremental traceability recovery process has been proposed (De Lucia et al., 2007) where the similarity threshold is incrementally decreased to provide the software engineer with the control on the number of correct links validated and false positives discarded at each iteration. In this way, starting with a high threshold, the links suggested by the tool can be analyzed and classified step-by-step and the process can be stopped when the effort of discarding false positives is becoming much higher than the effort of identifying new correct links. Clearly, the traceability recovery tool maintains knowledge about the classification actions performed by the software engineer, thus showing at each iteration only the new traceability links retrieved.

User studies highlighted that the threshold used to stop the recovery process plays an important role (De Lucia et al., 2009a). In particular, when the software engineer stops the traceability recovery process using a low threshold, she increases the number of correct links compared to software engineers stopping the process with a higher threshold. This situation suggests that a higher number of correct links could be traced by providing the software engineer with the full ranked list of possible links ordered by decreasing similarity values (full ranked list contrasted to the incremental approach). A recent study compared the two approaches through a controlled experiment (De Lucia et al., 2008). The achieved results demonstrated that the number of correct links retrieved with two different processes is comparable and that the incremental process significantly reduces tracing errors. Moreover, the number of links analyzed showing the full ranked list is significantly larger than the number of links analyzed adopting the incremental process. All these results suggest that the incremental process reduces the effort required to identify traceability links using an IR-based traceability recovery tool (De Lucia et al., 2008). This means that analyzing the lower part of the ranked list only results in a small improvement of the number of correct links retrieved. Indeed, while in the upper part of the ranked list the density of correct links is quite good, in the bottom part of the list such a density decreases in a way that the prioritization made by the IR method does not help anymore.

The use of the link coverage analysis has been proposed to enrich the set of correct links identified with one of the approaches described above (De Lucia et al., 2009b). In particular, after preliminary traceability link recovery sessions performed using canonical approaches, the software engineer can exploit the information provided by a link coverage analysis to identify source artifacts poorly traced on the set of target artifacts. In particular, for a generic artifact a, it is possible to define a traceability coverage index as follow:

$$traceabilityCoverage_a = \frac{|links_a(targets)|}{|targets|}$$

where *targets* represents the set of target artifacts and $links_a(targets)$ represents the set of links traced between the artifact a and the artifacts in the set *target*. Then, all the source artifacts are ranked (in an increasing order) according to their traceability coverage index.

The ranked list of source artifacts computed according to the link coverage analysis can be exploited to guide traceability recovery sessions focusing attention only on source artifacts with a low traceability coverage index. The conjecture is that the probability of identifying new correct links is higher when focusing on poorly traced artifacts. It is worth noting that after the identification of poorly traced artifacts the software engineer can recover the links using one of the approaches described above.

Once a traceability recovery tool produces a ranked list of candidate links, developers need to examine all these suggestions starting with the documents having highest similarity values. For every candidate link, a decision is required as to whether the link is a correct traceability link between two artifacts. If it is not the correct link, the user discards that and proceeds to the next suggestion in the ranked list. The process is continued until all the links in the ranked list are examined. The size of the ranked list is determined according to one of the strategies (threshold, cut point or combination) described above. The classification performed by the software engineer can be provided to the tool as a feedback for improving tracing performances (Antoniol et al., 2000c; Di Penta et al., 2002; De Lucia et al., 2006b; Hayes et al., 2003, 2006). In general, the user is asked to judge the relevance of the top few links retrieved by the system. If the user judges a retrieved link as correct, different strategies can be used to alter the source artifact in order to "move" it towards relevant artifacts and away from irrelevant artifacts, in the expectation of retrieving more relevant links and less irrelevant links in next iterations. It is worth noting that the first adjustment is designed to potentially increase the recall, while the second adjustment can potentially increase the precision.

5 Trace Retrieval in Action: Recovering Traceability Links in the iTrust System

This section describes the application of different IR methods to recover links between software artifacts of the iTrust system. iTrust is a medical application that provides patients with a means to keep up with their medical history and records as well as communicate with their doctors, including selecting which doctors to be their primary caregiver, seeing and sharing satisfaction results, and other tasks. iTrust is also an interface for medical staff from various locations. It allows the staff to keep track of their patients through messaging capabilities, scheduling of office visits, diagnoses, prescribing medication, ordering and viewing lab results, among other functions. The iTrust artifacts include use cases, source code, test cases, and trace matrices. The source code of the iTrust project is available[11] on sourceforge and is accessible through the project's webpage.

The goals of this empirical study are:

- providing empirical evidence of the accuracy of IR methods when used to recover links between software artifacts;
- analyzing the accuracy improvement achieved by performing a morphological analysis on the software artifacts;
- comparing the accuracy of different IR methods.

In the context of the study we employed three widely used IR methods for traceability recovery, namely JS (a probabistic model), VSM (a vector space based model), and LSI (a space reduction based model). These methods have been applied to recover links between 33 use cases and 47 JSP pages. We focus on this type of artifacts since the trace matrix of the latest version of the system only include mapping between these types of artifacts.[12] The matrix is used as an oracle to evaluate the accuracy of the employed IR-based recovery methods.

For each method, the term-by-document matrix is extracted following the steps of the process described in Section 2.1, i.e., term normalization, identifier splitting, and term filtering and weighting. As for the splitting of composite identifiers, a camel case splitting heuristic was used. For the term filtering process, a canonical English stop word list[13] augmented with HTML keywords is used in combination with a stop list function aimed at pruning out all the terms with a length less than 3. Finally, a *tf-idf* weighting schema is applied on the term-by-document matrix.

To evaluate the accuracy of each recovery method for each traceability recovery activity we automatically collected the number of correct links and false positives by using a tool that takes as an input the ranked list of candidate links produced by the IR method (e.g., VSM) and classifies each link as correct link or false positive until all the correct links in the original traceability matrix have been recovered.

A first analysis and comparison of the different IR methods is performed by recall and precision. Figures 1, 2, and 3 show the precision/recall curves achieved by using the employed IR methods with and without the use of stemming. As we can see, while the precision of all the methods are acceptable for lower values of recall (especially for the JS method), when the goal is to recover all the correct links (100% of recall) the list of candidate links contains a huge number of false positive resulting in a very low precision (lower than 10%). As mentioned before, this is one of the main limitation of IR-based traceability recovery methods. Unfortunately, such a limitation cannot be completely mitigated by using enhancing strategies, such

---

[11] http://agile.csc.ncsu.edu/iTrust/wiki/doku.php

[12] http://agile.csc.ncsu.edu/iTrust/wiki/doku.php?id=tracing

[13] http://www.ranks.nl/resources/stopwords.html

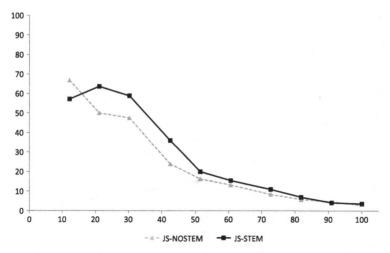

Fig. 1 Using JS to recover links between JSP pages and use cases of iTrust. Precision – vertical axis. Recall – horizontal axis

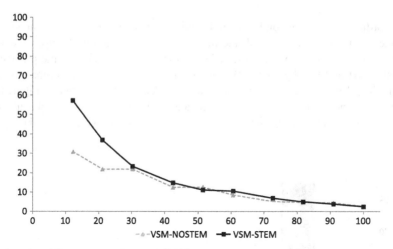

Fig. 2 Using VSM to recover links between JSP pages and use cases of iTrust. Precision – vertical axis. Recall – horizontal axis

as stemming and user feedback analysis (De Lucia et al., 2006b). In our experimentation, it looks like there is an upper bound to the performance improvements that cannot be overcome, even if an advanced artifact pre-processing, like stemming, is used. This means that IR-based traceability recovery tools should be used to trace as many as possible correct links keeping low the effort to discard false positives. Then, focused traceability recovery sessions should be performed to identify links between untraced artifacts (De Lucia et al., 2009b). Alternatively, manual tracing activities could be conducted to enrich the set of traced links.

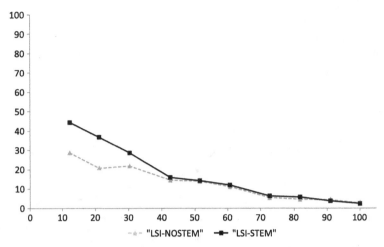

Fig. 3 Using LSI to recover links between JSP pages and use cases of iTrust. Precision – vertical axis. Recall – horizontal axis

Regarding the comparison between the employed IR methods, Fig. 4 shows the average precision achieved by all the methods with and without the use of stemming. As we can seen, the precision of the JS method is better than the precision of both VSM and LSI by about 10% on average. A more detailed comparison of the employed method can be obtained through recall/precision curves. Figures 5 and 6 show the comparison of JS, VSM, and LSI with and without the use of stemming, respectively, through precision/recall curves. As we can see the three

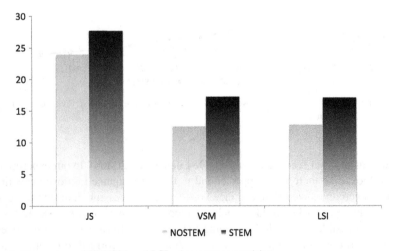

Fig. 4 Comparison of JS, VSM, and LSI using average precision

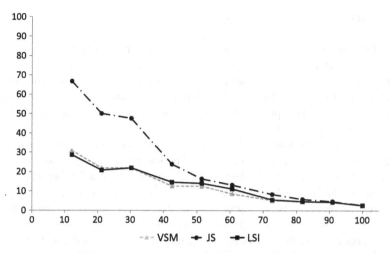

Fig. 5 Comparison of JS, VSM, and LSI without stemming tracing use cases onto JSP pages of iTrust. Precision – vertical axis. Recall – horizontal axis

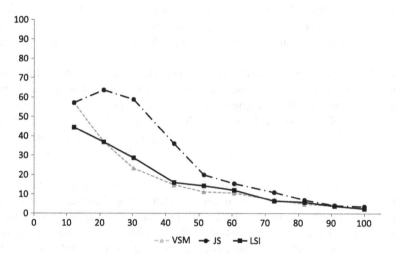

Fig. 6 Comparison of JS, VSM, and LSI with stemming tracing use cases onto JSP pages of iTrust. Precision – vertical axis. Recall – horizontal axis

IR methods exhibit almost the same behavior in the two scenarios, i.e., with and without stemming. The JS method seems to be the more accurate method as compared to VSM and LSI (this confirm the differences in terms of average precision) on this particular data set. It is impossible to generalize this result to other data sets. Interestingly, when recall is higher than 50% the three methods provide almost the same precision.

6 Conclusion

Traceability links between software artifacts represent an important source of information, if available, for different stakeholders, e.g., project managers, analysts, designers, maintainers, and end users, and provides important insights during different phases of software development. Traceability information can also be used when certifying a safety-critical product to show that all requirements were implemented and covered by specific tests.

Unfortunately, establishing and maintaining traceability links between software artifacts is a time consuming, error prone, and person-power intensive task (Ramesh and Jarke, 2001). Consequently, despite the advantages that can be gained, explicit traceability is rarely established unless there is a regulatory reason for doing so. Extensive effort in the software engineering community (both research and commercial) has been brought forth to improve the explicit connection of software artifacts. Promising results have been achieved using Information Retrieval (IR) techniques (Baeza-Yates and Ribeiro-Neto, 1999; Deerwester et al., 1990) to recover links between different types of artifacts (see e.g., (Antoniol et al., 2002; De Lucia et al., 2007; Hayes et al., 2006; Marcus et al., 2005)). IR-based methods propose a list of candidate traceability links on the basis of the similarity between the text contained in the software artifacts. The conjecture is that two artifacts having high textual similarity share similar concepts, thus they are good candidates to be traced on each other.

This chapter presented a general process of using IR-based methods for traceability link recovery and presented some of them in a greater detail: probabilistic, vector space, and Latent Semantic Indexing models. Common approaches to measuring the performance of IR-based traceability methods as well as the latest advances in techniques for analysis of candidate links were also analyzed and presented. An example on using three IR models to retrieve traceability links between artifacts of the iTrust system was also presented.

IR based techniques for traceability link recovery among artifacts proved to be quite successful so far, but the current research and applications also revealed many areas where improvement is needed and expected. Virtually, all IR techniques include a series of parameters that influence their performance, as presented in this chapter. The optimal values for these parameters are usually derived based on the data model at hand. The IR techniques most commonly used in traceability link recovery operate with parameters established in natural text retrieval applications. As mentioned before, the textual data in software artifacts is not the same as in natural text documents. More than that, there is little evidence that the data in one software systems has the same characteristics as in another. Future work will have to address a generic model that can be used for parameter tuning in IR based traceability link recovery application. There is one precondition to this future work: the creation and dissemination of benchmarks for software artifact traceability link recovery. These are not only necessary for parameter tuning, but they are also essential for the investigation of other IR techniques to be used in such applications. Based on current research, it is unclear which IR technique is best suited for this task and whether that depends on the specifics of the software or not. Benchmarks will help us answer this question. They will also help in the development of new techniques that address traceability link recovery. Such techniques should improve on the state of the art results, as established using the future benchmarks.

Acknowledgments We would like to thank the anonymous reviewers for their detailed, constructive, and thoughtful comments that helped us to improve the presentation of the results in this chapter.

References

Abadi, A., Nisenson, M., Simionovici, Y.: A traceability technique for specifications. In: Proceedings of 16th IEEE International Conference on Program Comprehension, pp. 103–112. IEEE CS Press, Amsterdam, The Netherlands (2008)

Antoniol, G., Canfora, G., Casazza, G., De Lucia, A.: Information retrieval models for recovering traceability links between code and documentation. In: Proceedings of 16th IEEE International Conference on SoftwareMaintenance, pp. 40–51. IEEE CS Press, San Jose, CA (2000a)

Antoniol, G., Canfora, G., Casazza, G., De Lucia, A., Merlo, E.: Tracing object-oriented code into functional requirements. In: Proceedings of 8th IEEE International Workshop on Program Comprehension, pp. 79–87. IEEE CS Press, Limerick, Ireland (2000b)

Antoniol, G., Canfora, G., Casazza, G., De Lucia, A., Merlo, E.: Recovering traceability links between code and documentation. IEEE Trans. Softw. Eng. **28**(10), 970–983 (2002)

Antoniol, G., Canfora, G., De Lucia, A., Merlo, E.: Recovering code to documentation links in OO systems. In: Proceedings of 6th Working Conference on Reverse Engineering, pp. 136–144. IEEE CS Press, Atlanta, GA (1999)

Antoniol, G., Casazza, G., Cimitile, A.: Traceability recovery by modelling programmer behaviour. In: Proceedings of 7th Working Conference on Reverse Engineering, vol. 240–247. IEEE CS Press, Brisbane, QLD (2000c)

Antoniol, G., Guéhéneuc, Y.-G., Merlo, E., Tonella, P.: Mining the Lexicon used by programmers during sofware evolution. In: Proceedings of the 23rd IEEE International Conference on Software Maintenance, pp. 14–23. IEEE Press, Paris, France (2007)

Asuncion, Hazeline U., Asuncion, A., Taylor, Richard N.: Software traceability with topic modeling. In: Proceedings of the 32nd ACM/IEEE International Conference on Software Engineering, pp. 95–104. ACM Press, Cape Town, South Africa (2010)

Bacchelli, A., Lanza, M., Robbes, R.: Linking e-mails and source code artifacts. In: Proceedings of the 32nd ACM/IEEE International Conference on Software Engineering, vol. 1, pp. 375–384. ICSE, Cape Town, South Africa (2010)

Baeza-Yates, R., Ribeiro-Neto, B.: Modern Information Retrieval. Addison-Wesley, Reading, MA (1999)

Bain, L., Engelhardt, M.: Introduction to Probability and Mathematical Statistics. Duxbury Press, Pacific Grove, CA (1992)

Blei, D.M., Ng, A.Y., Jordan, M.I.: Latent dirichlet allocation. J. Mach. Learn. Res. **3**, 993–1022 (2003)

Capobianco, G., De Lucia, A., Oliveto, R., Panichella, A., Panichella, S.: On the role of the nouns in IR-based traceability recovery. In: Proceedings of 17th IEEE International Conference on Program Comprehension. Vancouver, British Columbia, Canada (2009a)

Capobianco, G., De Lucia, A., Oliveto, R., Panichella, A., Panichella, S.: Traceability recovery using numerical analysis. In: Proceedings of 16th Working Conference on Reverse Engineering. IEEE CS Press, Lille, France (2009b)

Cleland-Huang, J., Czauderna, A., Gibiec, M., Emenecker, J.: A machine learning approach for tracing regulatory codes to product specific requirements. In: Proceedings of the 32nd

ACM/IEEE International Conference on Software Engineering, pp. 155–164. ICSE, Cape Town, South Africa (2010)

Cleland-Huang, J., Settimi, R., Duan, C., Zou, X.: Utilizing supporting evidence to improve dynamic requirements traceability. In: Proceedings of 13th IEEE International Requirements Engineering Conference, pp. 135–144. IEEE CS Press, Paris, France (2005)

Cover, T.M., Thomas, J.A.: Elements of Information Theory. Wiley-Interscience, New York, NY (1991)

Cullum, J.K., Willoughby, R.A.: Lanczos Algorithms for Large Symmetric Eigenvalue Computations, vol. 1, chapter Real rectangular matrices. Birkhauser, Boston, MA (1998)

De Lucia, A., Fasano, F., Oliveto, R., Tortora, G.: Enhancing an Artifact management system with traceability recovery features. In: Proceedings of 20th IEEE International Conference on Software Maintenance, pp. 306–315. IEEE CS Press, Chicago, IL (2004)

De Lucia, A., Fasano, F., Oliveto, R., Tortora, G.: Can information retrieval effectively support traceability link recovery? In: Proceedings of 14th IEEE International Conference on Program Comprehension, pp. 307–316. IEEE CS Press, Athens, Greece (2006a)

De Lucia, A., Fasano, F., Oliveto, R., Tortora, G.: Recovering traceability link in software Artifacts management systems using information retrieval methods. ACM Trans. Softw. Eng. Methodol. **16**(4), Article 13 (2007)

De Lucia, A., Oliveto, R., Sgueglia, P.: Incremental approach and user feedbacks: A Silver Bullet for traceability recovery. In: Proceedings of 22nd IEEE International Conference on Software Maintenance, pp. 299–309. Sheraton Society Hill, Philadelphia, PA. IEEE CS Press (2006b)

De Lucia, A., Oliveto, R., Tortora, G.: IR-based traceability recovery processes: An empirical comparison of "One-Shot" and incremental processes. In: Proceedings of 23rd International Conference Automated Software Engineering, pp. 39–48. ACM Press, L'Aquila, Italy (2008)

De Lucia, A., Oliveto, R., Tortora, G.: Assessing IR-based traceability recovery tools through controlled experiments. Empirical Softw. Eng. **14**(1), 57–93 (2009a)

De Lucia, A., Oliveto, R., Tortora, G.: The role of the coverage analysis in traceability recovery process: A controlled experiment. In: Proceedings of 25th International Conference on Software Maintenance. IEEE Press, Edmonton, Canada (2009b)

De Mori, R.: Spoken Dialogues with Computers. Academic, London (1998)

Deerwester, S., Dumais, S.T., Furnas, G.W., Landauer, T.K., Harshman, R.: Indexing by latent semantic analysis. J. Amer. Soc. Informat. Sci. **41**(6), 391–407 (1990)

Dekhtyar, A., Hayes, J.H., Menzies, T.: Text is software too. In: Proceedings of Mining of Software Repositories Workshop, pp. 22–26. Edinburgh, Scotland (2004)

Di Penta, M., Gradara, S., Antoniol, G.: Traceability recovery in RAD software systems. In: Proceedings of 10th International Workshop in Program Comprehension, pp. 207–216. IEEE CS Press, Paris, France (2002)

Dumais, S.T.: Improving the retrieval of information from external sources. Behav. Res. Meth. Instrum. Comput. **23**, 229–236 (1991)

Enslen, E., Hill, E., Pollock, L.L., Vijay-Shanker, K.: Mining source code to automatically split identifiers for software analysis. In: Proceedings of the 6th International Working Conference on Mining Software Repositories, pp. 71–80. Vancouver, British Columbia, Canada (2009)

Gibiec, M., Czauderna, A., Cleland-Huang, J.: Towards mining replacement queries for hard-to-retrieve traces. In: Proceedings of the 25th IEEE/ACM International Conference on Automated Software Engineering, pp. 245–254. ACM Press, Antwerp, Belgium (2010)

Haiduc, S., Marcus, A.: On the use of domain terms in source code. In: Proceedings of 16th IEEE International Conference on Program Comprehension, pp. 113–122. IEEE CS Press, Amsterdam, The Netherlands (2008)

Harman, D.K.: Overview of the first Text REtrieval Conference (TREC-1). In: Proceedings of the First Text REtrieval Conference (TREC-1), pp. 1–20. NIST Special Publication, Gaithersburg, MD (1993)

Hayes, J.H., Dekhtyar, A., Osborne, J.: Improving requirements tracing via information retrieval. In: Proceedings of 11th IEEE International Requirements Engineering Conference, pp. 138–147. IEEE CS Press, Monterey, CA (2003)

Hayes, J.H., Dekhtyar, A., Sundaram, S.K.: Advancing candidate link generation for requirements tracing: The study of methods. IEEE Trans. Softw. Eng. **32**(1), 4–19 (2006)

Hollink, V., Kamps, J., Monz, C., de Rijke, M.: Monolingual document retrieval for European languages. Inform. Retriev. **7**(1–2), 33–52 (2004)

Jurafsky, D., Martin, J.: Speech and Language Processing. Prentice Hall, Englewood Cliffs, NJ (2000)

Keenan, E.L.: Formal Semantics of Natural Language. Cambridge University Press, Cambridge (1975)

Lawrie, D.J., Binkley, D., Morrell, C.: Normalizing source code vocabulary. In: Proceedings of the 17th Working Conference on Reverse Engineering, pp. 3–12. IEEE CS Press, Beverly, MA (2010)

Lormans, M., Deursen, A., Gross, H.-G.: An industrial case study in reconstructing requirements views. Empirical Softw. Eng. **13**(6), 727–760 (2008)

Lormans, M., Gross, H., van Deursen, A., van Solingen, R., Stehouwer, A.: Monitoring requirements coverage using reconstructed views: An industrial case study. In: Proceedings of 13th Working Conference on Reverse Engineering, pp. 275–284. IEEE CS Press, Benevento, Italy (2006)

Lormans, M., Van Deursen, A.: Reconstructing requirements coverage views from design and test using traceability recovery via LSI. In: Proceedings of 3rd International Workshop on Traceability in Emerging Forms of Software Engineering, pp. 37–42. ACM Press, Long Beach, CA (2005)

Lormans, M., van Deursen, A.: Can LSI help reconstructing requirements traceability in design and test? In: Proceedings of 10th European Conference on Software Maintenance and Reengineering, pp. 45–54. IEEE CS Press, Bari, Italy (2006)

Madani, N., Guerrouj, L., Di Penta, M., Guéhéneuc, Y.-G., Antoniol, G.: Recognizing words from source code identifiers using speech recognition techniques. In: Proceedings of the 14th European Conference on Software Maintenance and Reengineering. CSMR, Madrid, Spain (2010)

Marcus, A., Maletic, J.I.: Recovering documentation-to-source-code traceability links using latent semantic indexing. In: Proceedings of 25th International Conference on Software Engineering, pp. 125–135. IEEE CS Press, Portland, Oregon (2003)

Marcus, A., Maletic, J.I., Sergeyev, A.: Recovery of traceability links between software documentation and source code. Int. J. Softw. Eng. Knowl. Eng. **15**(5), 811–836 (2005)

Ney, H., Essen, U.: On smoothing techniques for bigrambases natural language modelling. In: Proceedings of IEEE International Conference on Acoustics, Speech, and Signal Processing, pp. 825–828. IEEE CS Press, Toronto, ON (1991)

Oliveto, R., Gethers, M., Poshyvanyk, D., De Lucia, A.: On the equivalence of information retrieval methods for automated traceability link recovery. In: Proceedings of the 18th IEEE International Conference on Program Comprehension, pp. 68–71. Braga, Portugal (2010)

Porter, M.F.: An algorithm for suffix stripping. Program **14**(3):130–137 (1980)

Poshyvanyk, D., Gael-Gueheneuc, Y., Marcus, A., Antoniol, G., Rajlich, V.: Feature location using probabilistic ranking of methods based on execution scenarios and information retrieval. IEEE Trans. Softw. Eng., **33**(6), 420–432 (2007)

Ramesh, B., Jarke, M.: Toward reference models for requirements traceability. IEEE Trans. Softw. Eng. **27**:58–93 (2001)

Revelle, M., Dit, B., Poshyvanyk, D.: Using data fusion and web mining to support feature location in software. In: Proceedings of the 18th IEEE International Conference on Program Comprehension, pp. 14–23. Braga, Portugal (2010)

Salton, G., Wong, A., Yang, C.S.: A vector space model for information retrieval. Commun. ACM **18**(11), 613–620 (1975)

Settimi, R., Cleland-Huang, J., Ben Khadra, O., Mody, J., Lukasik, W., De Palma, C.: Supporting software evolution through dynamically retrieving traces to UML Artifacts. In: Proceedings of 7th IEEE International Workshop on Principles of Software Evolution, pp. 49–54. IEEE CS Press, Kyoto, Japan (2004)

Sparck Jones, K.: A statistical interpretation of term specificity and its application in retrieval. J. Document. **28**, 11–21 (1972)

Witten, I.H., Bell, T.C.: The zero-frequency problem: Estimating the probabilities of novel events in adaptive text compression. IEEE Trans. Inform. Theory **37**(4), 1085–1094 (1991)

Yadla, S., Huffman Hayes, J., Dekhtyar, A.: Tracing requirements to defect reports: an application of information retrieval techniques. Innov. Syst. Softw. Eng.: A NASA J. **1**(2), 116–124 (2005)

Zou, X., Settimi, R., Cleland-Huang, J.: Phrasing in dynamic requirements trace retrieval. In: Proceedings of the 30th Annual International Computer Software and Application Conference, pp. 265–272. Chicago, IL (2006)

Zou, X., Settimi, R., Cleland-Huang, J.: Term-based enhancement factors for improving automated requirement trace retrieval. In: Proceedings of International Symposium on Grand Challenges in Traceability, pp. 40–45. ACM Press, Lexington, Kentuky (2007)

Zou, X., Settimi, R., Cleland-Huang, J.: Evaluating the use of project glossaries in automated trace retrieval. In: Proceedings of the International Conference on Software Engineering Research and Practice, pp. 157–163. Las Vegas, NV (2008)

Zou, X., Settimi, R., Cleland-Huang, J.: Improving automated requirements trace retrieval: A study of term-based enhancement methods. Empir. Softw. Eng. **15**(2), 119–146 (2010)

Factors Impacting the Inputs of Traceability Recovery Approaches

Nasir Ali, Yann-Gaël Guéhéneuc, and Giuliano Antoniol

1 Introduction

Researchers have proposed many approaches based on several techniques: information retrieval Antoniol et al. (2002), events Cleland-Huang et al. (2003), hypertext Maletic et al. (2003); Sherba (2005), scenarios Egyed and Grünbacher (2002), and rules Spanoudakis et al. (2004), to recover traces among software artifacts. These proposed approaches use mainly three inputs for traceability recovery (TR): source documents, target documents, and experts' opinion. To the best of our knowledge, all the proposed traceability recovery approaches (TRA) have low recall and precision.

Our main claim in this chapter is that improving traceability recovery approaches only in themselves cannot help in improving precision and recall; we must also control the factors that impact the inputs of these approaches. To support this claim, we report in Table 1 the precision and recall values of some TRA described in the literature based on the following techniques: Vector Space Model (VSM), Latent Semantic Indexing (LSI), Rule-based, and Jensen-Shannon similarity (JS). It shows that, depending on the data sets, precision values vary from 0.9 to 95.9% and recall values vary from 3 to 99.8%.

Thus, Table 1 sustains our main claim by showing that different approaches using the same techniques report precision/recall values that vary a lot across data sets. For example, Sundaram et al. (2005) achieved 1.5–7.9% precision with VSM whereas Abadi et al. (2008) achieved 50–80% precision with the same techniques. Both groups of researchers used simple VSM to obtain their results and, therefore, factors other than the technique, VSM, are causing the variations in precision and recall.

Abadi et al. (2008) and Sundaram et al. (2005) used three different inputs: (1) source documents, (2) target documents, and (3) experts' opinion, who manually created oracles to calculate precision and recall and vetted the automatically-created

N. Ali (✉)
DGIGL, École Polytechnique de Montréal, Montréal, QC, Canada
e-mail: nasir.ali@polymtl.ca

J. Cleland-Huang et al. (eds.), *Software and Systems Traceability*,
DOI 10.1007/978-1-4471-2239-5_5, © Springer-Verlag London Limited 2012

Table 1 Average precision and recall range of TRAs, bold values represent the example presented in 1

Data sets	VSM		LSI		JS		Rule-based	
	Precision	Recall	Precision	Recall	Precision	Recall	Precision	Recall
SCA Abadi et al. (2008)	20–43	51–76	14–26	41–78	23–41	57–78	–	–
CORBA Abadi et al. (2008)	50–**80**	68–89	11–50	14–61	43–65	55–81	–	–
MODIS Sundaram et al. (2005)	**7.9**	75.6	4.2–6.3	63.4–92.6	–	–	–	–
CM-1 Sundaram et al. (2005)	**1.5**	97.7	**0.9**	98.6–**98.8**	–	–	–	–
Easy Clinic Oliveto et al. (2010)	17–80	4–90	17–60	3–90	17–80	4–91	–	–
eTour Oliveto et al. (2010)	17–68	5–47	17–64	4–46	17–76	5–47	–	–
Mobile Phone Jirapanthong and Zisman (2007)	–	–	–	–	–	–	81–95.9	65.4–97.2
UCMS, TV Software Spanoudakis et al. (2004)	–	–	–	–	–	–	60–81	68–85

links. Our main claim is that it is the variation in the three different inputs that mainly caused the observed variations in precision and recall.

Some researchers, e.g., Ali (2011); Antoniol (2003); Hayes and Dekhtyar (2005), have mentioned factors that impact TRA inputs. However, these factors and their impact on TRA have not received enough attention so far. Even given a TRA uses a technique that can return links with high precision and recall, if its inputs have poor quality, then this approach will produce poor links. Thus, it is important to survey the factors impacting TRA inputs and report metric/tools to measure these factors and precautions to control them.

Typical Problematic Scenario. To understand how some factors impact TRA inputs further, let us consider a scenario where a project manager receives a verification and validation task. To complete her task, she needs up-to-date traceability links between requirements and source code. She uses a TRA that produces results with high precision and recall. She collects TRA inputs, such as experts' opinion, requirement specification document (RSD), and source code and asks the help of the best available resources, i.e., a senior developer of the company with 10 years of Java and C++ programming experience. The senior developer can understand source code written in different programming languages; the updated requirements and latest source code provide traces that represent the actual system.

Let us now further assume that source code is in Perl, source code identifiers' quality is poor, a non-professional person wrote/updated the RSD. Then, it is likely that the expert would miss some links and retains erroneous links, because Perl has a different syntax and structure than Java and C++. The non-professional person would have probably written vague and ambiguous requirements in RSD that creates confusion while verifying links. The developers have used meaningless abbreviations for identifiers, thus complexifying the program comprehension activity. Therefore, the automatically-generated traceability links would be numerous and the expert would get frustrated and tired while verifying each and every one of them.

This scenario highlights the importance of TRA inputs in the TR process and of their analysis to help researchers and practitioners understand the outputs of TRAs.

Objectives and Overall Methodology. Given the importance of TRA inputs, project managers need guidelines to analyse TRA inputs and their impacting factors as well as metrics/tools to measure/improve the TRA inputs quality and preventive measures that must be taken to control the inputs quality. Thus, we define four objectives for this chapter. Objective 1 is to define and document the factors impacting TRA inputs. Objective 2 is to report metrics/tools to measure/improve the quality of the inputs by acting on the factors. Objective 3 is to provide preventive measures to control the factors. Objective 4 is to illustrate our main claim empirically using one of the identified factors: experts' programming knowledge.

To achieve our objectives, we follow the methodology depicted in Fig. 1. In Step 1, we use our own traceability expertise Antoniol et al. (2002, 2008); Hayes et al. (2008) to define preliminary factors that, to the best of our knowledge,

Fig. 1 Main objectives of the chapter and methodology to achieve these objectives

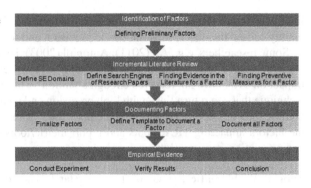

could impact TRA inputs. In Step 2, we perform an *incremental literature review* (ILR), using these first factors as seeds, to identify and define all the factors impacting TRA inputs and find evidence of their impact. We analyse experimental results reported in the literature that provide metrics/tools to measure/improve the quality of TRA inputs. In addition, we also identify and report precautions for the identified factors found in the literature. In Step 3, we document and report all the gathered data using a consistent template. The output of this step is reported in Section 3, which thus achieves our Objectives 1, 2 and 3. In Step 4, we perform an experiment on one factor that impact experts' opinion: experts' programming knowledge. Our empirical findings support our claim that factors impacting TRA inputs cause low precision and recall in state-of-the-art TRAs. This last step helps us achieving our Objective 4.

Assumption, Limitations, and Organisation. Table 2 shows the compulsory and complementary inputs for various TRAs gathered from the literature. These approaches considered, as compulsory inputs, requirements, use-cases, and UML artifacts as source documents and source code and test-cases as target documents.

Table 2 Compulsory and complementary inputs of TRAs

Approach	Compulsory inputs	Complementary inputs
Scenario-based	Requirements, source code	Hypothesized traces Execution traces (scenarios)
Rule-based	RSD, UCD	Requirement-to-object-model traceability rule Analysis object model Inter-requirement traceability rule
Event-based	Requirements, UML artifacts, and test cases	
Hypertext-based	Requirements, source code	Conformance analysis
IR-based	Requirements, UML artifacts, and test cases	Thesaurus, temporal information (SVN, Bug reports, mailing lists) System dynamic information Experts' feedback

Table 3 Template to document TRA inputs, factors, and preventive measures

Attributes	Descriptions
TRA input	Brief introduction to the TRA input
Factor name	Name of the factor impacting the TRA input
Definition	Definition of the factor
Scenario	A scenario illustrating the impact of the factor
Literature review	Literature evidence of the impact of the factor
Preventive measures	Metrics, tools, and precautions to measure and control the factor

They also used complementary inputs as well that may vary for every TRA and have impact on the TRAs results. In the following, we only concentrate on compulsory inputs, because they are the same for all TRAs.

Thus, in this chapter and without loss of generality, we consider requirements as source documents and source code as target documents, to make it easier to describe the factors' impact on TRA inputs. This choice does not change the fact that these factors will impact any TRA inputs, if experts are recovering tractability links among requirements, between test cases and requirements, between scenarios and source code, and so on. For example, if experts are recovering traceability links among requirements then requirements would be both source and target documents, in this kind of situations same factors will impact source and target documents that impact requirements.

We do not report a systematic literature review but choose to rather perform an incremental literature review for reason of form and content. A systematic literature review would have required more space than available to report on all the papers related to the identified factors. Moreover, a systematic literature would have also required a set of predefined factors impacting TRA inputs and of formal criteria to assess these factors, both agreed-upon by the community Kitchenham et al. (2009). Such factors and criteria, to the best of our knowledge, are not yet available in the literature and, thus, our incremental literature review of more than 60 papers is a first step towards identifying such factors and criteria.

The rest of the chapter is organised as follows: Section 2 describes our incremental literature review and summarises the retained factors that impact TRA inputs. Section 3 documents the factors, metrics/tools, and precautions for the retained factors. Section 4 describes our empirical study of the impact of experts' programming language knowledge on TRAs, its results, and threats to its validity. Section 5 discusses the findings in this chapter. Finally, Section 6 concludes with future work.

2 Identification of Factors and Preventive Measures

In the following, we first define an incremental literature review (ILR). Second, we perform a first ILR to identify and retain important factors according to our criteria. Third, we used these factors as input to a second ILR to identify preventive measures. Fourth, we document in Section 3 all the identified factors and preventive measures to measure/improve the quality of TRA inputs using a consistent template, described in Table 3.

2.1 Incremental Literature Review

We define an *incremental literature review* (ILR) to find factors impacting TRA inputs and evidence supporting their impact as well as preventive measures (metrics, tools, and precautions). Figure 2 shows the process that we followed in our ILR.

An ILR is a recursive process. It starts from a pool of eleven possible factors: Ambiguous Requirement, Vague Requirement, Conflicting Requirement, Granularity Level, Identifiers' Quality, Domain Knowledge, Programming knowledge, Document Type, Document Language, Work Environment, Project Size, and Dead Code. We provide the definitions of seven of these factors in Section 4. We seed one factor to find evidence in the literature of its relevance and identify related research papers through queries in six software engineering sub-domains: information retrieval, program comprehension, requirements engineering, reverse engineering, software artifact traceability, and software maintenance. We use the same list of search engines for research papers for both ILRs, i.e., IEEExplore,[1]

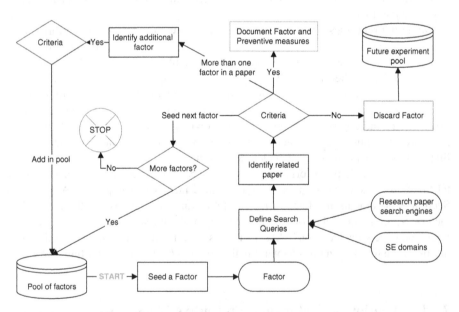

Fig. 2 Incremental literature review process

---

[1] http://ieeexplore.ieee.org/Xplore/guesthome.jsp

ACM Digital Library,[2] Springer,[3] and Google Scholar.[4] We verify if the identified paper provides evidence for the current factor or not. If the paper discusses more than one factor, we verify if the other factors also impact TRA inputs and, if they do, we add them to the pool for the next iteration.

We use two sets of criteria to retain or put aside a factor. In the first iteration of our ILR, we put aside a factor from our study when we cannot find any evidence in the literature for that specific factor and–or when we can find only one paper that is not cited more than one time. In the second iteration of our ILR, we keep all the factors, even though we may not find papers describing related metrics/tools and–or precautions to highlight future research directions in Section 5.

We review and apply a set of criteria on the identified papers to answer two questions: (1) does any paper support the seeded factor? and (2) do the identified papers mention factors not already in the pool? From decision (1), we document or put aside the seeded factor for future experiments on their impact. From decision (2), we add to the pool of factors any missing factor. The process then iterates until there are no more factors to process. In the following two sub-sections, we perform and report the results of the two ILRs.

2.2 Identification of Factors

We listed (recall Section 2.1) of eleven factors that, to the best of our knowledge, could impact TRA inputs. We identified these factors based on our own traceability recovery expertise Antoniol et al. (2002, 2008); Hayes et al. (2008) and past professional experiences performing traceability recovery with private companies.

We performed an ILR for all the eleven factors to find out evidence that these factors impact TRA inputs. We seeded each factor in our ILR process to discover evidence in the literature supporting that the factor impact some TRA inputs. We defined search queries and looked for the papers in the chosen sub-domains using the chosen search engines. For example, we used the query *"identifiers quality"* in Google Scholar to identify the paper "What's in a Name? A Study of Identifiers" Lawrie et al. (2006) supporting the factor "Identifiers' Quality".

After performing this first ILR, we could not find any research papers that clearly state that *Document Type, Document language, Work Environment, Project size*, and *Dead Code* and impact TRA inputs. Therefore, following our criteria, we remove these five factors from our study. Interestingly, we found one more factor during our ILR, i.e., Granularity Level, which impacts TRA inputs as well as the overall economical aspect of traceability. We included this newly-found factor in our identified factors list. Figure 3 presents the final seven $(11 - 5 + 1 = 7)$ factors.

---

[2] http://portal.acm.org

[3] http://www.springer.com

[4] http://scholar.google.ca

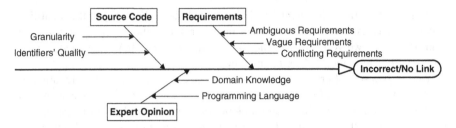

Fig. 3 Inputs of traceability approach and impacting factors

Figure 3 shows the three TRA inputs and the seven factors impacting these inputs. Rectangles represent TRA inputs and arrows represent the factors that impact these inputs. The last rounded rectangle represents the consequences of the factors on the TR process: incorrect/missed traceability links. We document each factor in Section 3.

2.3 Identification of Preventive Measures

Each factor can impact the TRA input negatively, yielding low precision and–or recall. We wanted to identify *metrics/tools* that can measure/improve the quality of TRA inputs. We associated some positive properties with each factor. For example, for Identifiers' Quality, identifiers must be understandable, complete, and unambiguous. Then, we searched for metrics/tools that are useful to measure/improve the quality of TRA inputs and factor with respect to their properties.

We seeded each retained factor in the ILR process. We followed the same steps as in the previous ILR. We analysed the *metrics/tools* reported in the literature for the measurement/improvement of the identified factors. We combined literature review and our own expertise to describe precautions for the factors. We discuss all the identified factors detail with their preventive *metrics/tools* in Section 3.

Figure 4 summarises the output of this ILR. It shows, for each factor, its five main characteristics: input name; factor name, type, property; and, preventive measures (metrics, tools, and precautions). For example, Source code is a TRA input and Identifiers' Quality impact source code. Good quality identifiers must be understandable, complete, and unambiguous. To obtain these properties, expert may use *splitting/expansion* Madani et al. (2010) approach to split identifiers such as `cmdpntr` into `cmd pntr` and then expand the resulting words into `command pointer`. The results of the *splitting/expansion* approach have all the above-mentioned properties of good identifiers. Now, let us assume that an expert is using an IR-based approach to recover traceability links between requirements and source code, the split and expanded identifiers would link to `command pointer`-related requirements more likely than the `cmdpntr` identifier would.

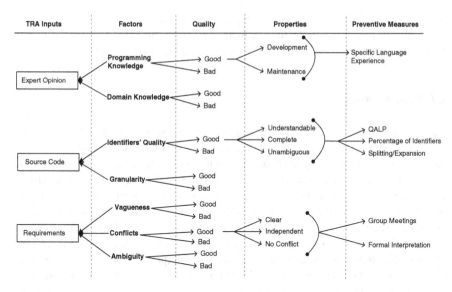

Fig. 4 Inputs of TRAs; factors, their types, properties, and preventive measures

3 Factors Impacting the Inputs of TRAs

Researchers have proposed various TRA, e.g., Antoniol et al. (2002); Cleland-Huang et al. (2003); Egyed and Grünbacher (2002); Sherba (2005); Spanoudakis et al. (2004). To the best of our knowledge, all of these approaches have low recall and precision. Recall is defined as the *number of relevant documents retrieved* divided by the *total number of relevant documents*:

$$Recall = \frac{|\{relevant\ documents\} \cap \{retrieved\ documents\}|}{|\{relevant\ documents\}|}$$

while precision is defined as the *number of relevant documents retrieved* divided by the *total number of retrieved documents*:

$$Precision = \frac{|\{relevant\ documents\} \cap \{retrieved\ documents\}|}{|\{retrieved\ documents\}|}$$

The low precision and recall of the retrieved links impact the usefulness of the TRAs. Low precision requires experts to deal with numerous spurious traceability links while low recall casts doubt in the experts' minds about missing links and requires them to analyse by hand artifacts to possibly identify these missing links.

Researchers proposed various methods Gervasi and Zowghi (2010); Ghazarian (2009); Lawrie et al. (2007a) to improve the precision and recall of TRAs. However, to the best of our knowledge, there has been little work Antoniol (2003); Hayes and Dekhtyar (2005); Ali (2011) on the factors that impact TRA inputs. We now document three types of TRA inputs (requirements, source code, and experts' opinions), factors impacting these inputs, metrics/tools to measure/improve the input quality, and precautions to control the factors, using the template shown in Table 3.

3.1 Requirements

The precise capture, understanding, and representation of requirements is a crucial step in the development of effective and usable information systems Gibson and Conheeney (1995). Requirements are often error-prone due to misinterpretation of natural languages Fabbrini et al. (2001). Requirements are often characterised as complete and correct. For example, if a requirement is incomplete, such as *change time*, it may trace to session time, patient wait-time, or system time; it would be difficult for an expert to verify its corresponding traceability links. In general, completeness and correctness depend on several factors. Hayes (2003a) reports 13 factors, including ambiguous and non-verifiable requirements. In the following, we only report three factors for which, using our ILR, we could find definitions, experimental results, and precautions.

3.1.1 Ambiguous Requirements

Definition: Ambiguous requirement are requirements of which two different experts may have different interpretation Chantree et al. (2006).

Scenario: Ambiguous requirements may result into different interpretation and implementation. They lead to perplexity and waste of effort during their understanding. They also impact the TRAs by leading to the creation of ambiguous links that are complicated to verify. For example, in the requirement *"each new user shall be part of a group"*, the concept of *group* could be ambiguous and an expert could interpret this group to manage access privileges, whereas another expert may interpret it as a group of common, shared interests.

Literature Review: Ambiguity has long been pictured as one of the worst enemy of experts writing requirements, especially with reference to ambiguity in natural language requirements Gervasi and Zowghi (2010). Zisman et al. (2002) mentioned that the main shortcoming of TRAs is their inability to automatically identify and maintain traceability relations involving natural-language artifacts with ambiguous meanings.

Hayes et al. (2003) showed in their paper that senior analysts at Science Applications International Corporation missed 17 links during a manual traceability link recovery activity. The authors' observations on the missing links was: (1) it was difficult to do some of the tracing because the documents/requirements were incomplete, ambiguous and (2) unknown acronyms hindered the trace recovery process.

Haiduc and Marcus (2008) studied several open-source systems and found that about 40% of the domain terms are being used in the source code by developers. If the domain terms are ambiguous, it will also impact source code as well.

Hayes (2003a) presented a methodology for requirement-based fault analysis and its application to NASA software projects. She examined requirements faults for the International Space Station (ISS) software systems. She showed that 6.1% of the faults were caused by ambiguity in the requirements of the ISS.

Preventive Measures: Some approaches Chantree et al. (2006); Gleich et al. (2010); Kamsties et al. (2001) have been proposed by researchers to identify ambiguity in and remove them from requirements. Gleich et al. (2010) presented a tool to detect ambiguities and to explain the sources of these ambiguities. They claimed that their ambiguity-detection tool yields a significant improvement in time and cost and in quality in industrial contexts. Kamsties et al. (2001) presented an inspection technique for detecting ambiguities in informal requirements. Their results showed that inspection techniques yield better results than formal methods in term of the number of identified ambiguous requirements.

3.1.2 Vague Requirements

Definition: Vague requirements are imprecise natural language statements. If the statements of the requirements fail to draw an image or bring an understanding of what is desired, then they are vague because difficult to interpret correctly Joseph (2000).

Scenario: For example, the requirement "*maintaining patients' records shall be good*" is vague. The word "good" is not defined. An expert cannot trace the implementation of "good" patient records into any source code.

Literature Review: Kamsties et al. (1998) conducted case studies with ten different small and medium enterprises (SMEs). They mentioned that SMEs do not document requirements properly, which cause problems such as (1) requirements are too vague or prosaic to be testable, (2) requirements are not traceable, and (3) the domain knowledge implicitly contained in requirements makes the requirements difficult to understand by developers.

Kasser (2004) stated that vague requirements cause expensive cost and delay in project schedule. They mentioned that vague requirements are unverifiable and contain multiple requirements in a single paragraph, which complicate the traceability of tests to requirements.

Ghazarian (2009) showed that 57.5% of bug reports are due to incorrect implementations of requirements in the source code. Vague requirements cause this kind of reports.

Hall et al. (2002) studied the problems experienced by 12 software companies in their requirement process and showed that 48% of their problems stem from requirements and that vague requirements cause 25% of these problems.

Preventive Measures: Kasser (2004) presented a tool, FRED, to detect vague requirements and allow an expert to remove the vagueness from the requirements. FRED also helps to make requirements traceable by splitting two combined requirements.

Lee and Kuo (2002) proposed the Requirements Trade-off Analysis technique to formalise vague requirements. They analysed trade-off among vague requirements by identifying the relationship between requirements, which could be either conflicting, irrelevant, cooperative, counterbalance, or independent. Fabbrini et al. (2001) proposed a tool, QuARS (Quality Analyzer of Requirement Specification), based on their natural-language quality model to detect vague requirements.

3.1.3 Conflicting Requirements

Definition: Conflicting requirements are requirements that are incompatible in a same or different artifacts Hayes (2003a).

Scenario: During the requirement elicitation process, each stake-holder gives her wish list without considering conflicts with other stake-holders' requirements Joseph (2000). For example, one stake-holder could ask that the system shall allow giving bonuses after six months while another stakeholder could ask that the system gives bonuses every three months. Such conflict could result into two separate implementations of the requirements that may then conflict and must be maintained separately. It will also create problems for the experts verifying whether the system allows bonuses.

Literature Review: It is risky to ignore or stifle conflicting requirements because they may have serious negative consequences on the software development process Grünbacher and Briggs (2001). Many researchers have highlighted the significance of identifying and analysing conflicting requirements for the success of system development Grünbacher and Briggs (2001); Hayes (2003b); Hausmann et al. (2005); Joseph (2000).

Egyed and Grünbacher (2004); Egyed and Grünbacher (2002) conducted requirements traceability studies on a video-on-demand system. They found that some requirements have dependencies with other requirements and that these dependencies cause conflicts. For example, in order to start playing a movie, one needs to load the textual information about the movie, which is allowed to take up to three seconds while 1 second is the required maximum duration before starting playing a movie. Egyed et al. recommended that conflicts and dependencies be removed before performing traceability tasks.

Hayes (2003a) divided conflicting requirements into internal and external conflicts Hayes (2003a). She showed that 4.7% of the faults in the ISS software systems are due to conflicting requirements.

Preventive Measures: Stake-holders must discuss and resolve conflicting requirements Grünbacher and Briggs (2001); Joseph (2000); Hayes (2003b).

They can negotiate the conflicting requirements. Egyed (2001); Egyed and Grünbacher (2002) proposed a tool-supported approach, Trace Analyser, to analyse dependency among requirements and detect conflicts. Trace Analyser cannot automatically derive conflicts but, by finding all possible requirement dependencies, it makes it easier to identify potential inconsistencies and conflicts.

Hausmann et al. (2005) presented a formal interpretation of use-case models, which is based on concepts from the theory of graph transformation. Use-case models allow to define precisely the notions of conflict and dependency between functional requirements. Then, use-case models can be statically analysed to identify conflicts and dependencies, which can then be communicated to the stake-holders by annotating the model. They also provided an implementation of the static analysis within a graph transformation tool.

3.2 Source Code

Source code is a common input for of traceability approaches Antoniol et al. (2002); Marcus and Maletic (2003). The quality of the results of a TRA highly depends on the quality of the source code Antoniol (2003). For example, if a developer uses meaningless abbreviations for identifiers, thus use causes low similarity between requirements and source code Lawrie et al. (2006, 2007b) and creates ambiguity for an expert when verifying recovered links. Moreover, some techniques, such as information-retrieval techniques Antoniol et al. (2002); Hayes et al. (2003); Lucia et al. (2005, 2006), require high-textual similarity to recover traceability links.

Developers normally use identifiers Butler et al. (2009) that are easy to remember. However, these identifiers possibly do not represent concepts in the source code and–or system domain. For example, developers usually use i, m, n, and k as variable names for integer values, but these do not represent any concept. Such identifiers can result into low textual similarity and poor links. Appropriate use of identifiers does not only help to improve TR, it also helps in improving the overall software quality Lawrie et al. (2007a).

Developers also often mix different concepts in the same classes and implement as much functionality as possible in a single class under time pressure to implement as quickly as possible new functionalities Marcus and Poshyvanyk (2005); Moha et al. (2010). This "design choice" or, rater, lack thereof, creates overlapped links Egyed and Grünbacher (2004) that are difficult for experts to sort and verify manually.

3.2.1 Granularity Level

Definition: Level of detail considered in the TR. Granularity is generally divided into three levels: coarse, middle, and fine-grained. As the level of granularity increases, a TRA would provide more detailed and numerous links.

Scenario: Let us assume that a developer implements different concepts in the functions of one object-oriented class. Typically, a developer creates one Patient class and implements all patient-related concepts in that class in the form of methods, such as adding walk-in patient, adding emergency patient, and so on. Let us now assume that an expert is recovering links between the requirements and classes of this system. Then, several requirements may link to that one Patient class, which would impede the experts' verification of the links if the requirements are at the class level.

Literature Review: Egyed et al. (2010) showed that tracing requirements to method level requires 3–6 times more effort than tracing requirements to classes. They showed that links at the method-level have no advantage over links at the class-level in terms of quality.

Bianchi et al. (2000) conducted an exploratory case study to evaluate the relationship between the granularity of a traceability model and the effectiveness of the maintenance process. Their case-study results showed that fine-grained traceability requires greater effort to satisfy maintenance requests but also provides better accuracy. Therefore, experts must trade effort for accuracy.

It is equally important to consider the return on investment (ROI) Egyed et al. (2010) of traceability Egyed et al. (2005) while choosing a granularity level. Egyed et al. (2005) evaluated the ROI of tracing at lower levels of granularity. They measured the ROI by the effort needed to recover the links against the value returned through tracing at different levels of precision. Their case study showed that a tenfold increase in cost/effort only produces twofold improvement in precision.

Preventive Measures: It is important to choose the "right" granularity level Bianchi et al. (2000); Cleland-Huang et al. (2007) before starting a TR process. If developers used switches to handle different requirements then it is important to choose a finer-grain granularity. If the ROI is not high then the experts may perform refactoring tasks to separate different implementations of requirements at class level to reduce the number of traceability links. Developers should implement different requirements in different classes, if they are working with an object-oriented programming languages, or in different functions and modules, if they are working with a procedural programming language.

3.2.2 Identifiers' Quality

Definition: An identifier is the name of a token in the source code. Software quality depends on identifiers' quality Butler et al. (2009) because the majority of the source code of a software system consists of identifiers Deissenboeck and Pizka (2006).

Scenario: If a developer used meaningless abbreviations to name identifiers, it will create problem for any automated or manual TR process. For example, if the developer has named a method "*cd*" in a *file management system*, then an expert verifying a traceability link for the *create directory* requirement, would not be able to easily distinguish between *change directory* and *create directory*. The expert must consequently have to read the whole source code to keep or reject the traceability links.

Literature Review: Several studies showed that poor identifiers' quality impacts TR Lucia et al. (2010, 2007); De Lucia et al. (2009). Lucia et al. (2010) used traceability to identify poor quality identifiers. They used a IR-based traceability approach to build links between source code and high-level documents. Their approach highlights the identifiers whose understandability is decreasing due to continuous software maintenance and evolution. Their studies showed that using meaningless identifiers could result into poor quality traces.

Butler et al. (2009) analysed the impact of naming conventions on maintenance effort, i.e., on code quality. They evaluated the quality of identifiers in eight open-source Java libraries using twelve naming conventions. They showed that a statistically-significant relation exists between identifiers and software quality.

Takang et al. (1996) compared abbreviated identifiers with full-word identifiers and uncommented code with commented code and empirically analysed the role played by identifiers and comments on source code understandability. They showed that (1) commented systems are more understandable than non-commented systems and, similarly, that (2) systems containing full-word identifiers are more understandable than those with abbreviated identifiers.

Lucia et al. (2007) stored poor links during traceability recovery experiments to analyse them. They found that poor links helped to identify quality problems in the textual descriptions of the traced artifacts; mainly a poor description of the artifacts. The expert used these poor links to improve the textual description of the artifacts. As a result of these changes, over 60% of the poor links highlighted by the tool improved with a similarity value above the quality threshold at the end of the project.

Preventive Measures: Improving identifiers' quality yields an increase in precision and recall of TRAs. For example, if two concepts are merged in one identifier, it is important to split this identifier to avoid ambiguity among identifiers. Researchers have proposed different approaches Binkley et al. (2007, 2009); Madani et al. (2010) to improve the identifiers' quality. Madani et al. (2010) proposed a speech recognition-based approach to split identifiers and expand them; their approach out-performs the Camel Case splitter.

QALP Binkley et al. (2009) metrics calculate scores between source code identifiers' and comments. High scores highlight a strong relationship between source code and comments. QALP helps to identify any ambiguity among different identifiers and comments. Binkley et al. (2007) proposed an approach based on the percentage of identifiers that violate syntactic conciseness and consistency rules. Their approach helps to avoid confusing identifiers.

3.3 Experts' Opinion

The field of human factors research is large and diverse. As of today, no large-scale study involving human experts has been conducted in TR Cuddeback (2010). Different studies show the importance of experts' opinion in TR D. Cuddeback (2010); Dekhtyar et al. (2007); Eder et al. (1999); Soloway and Ehrlich (1989). Ghazarian (2009) showed that developers cause 82% of the problems of missed implementation in some software systems. Hayes et al. (2005) conducted a case study on experts' feedback. They asked three experts to perform some traceability tasks on three different data sets. They give the experts traceability links with low precision, with high recall, and with high precision and low recall. They showed that experts were not able to provide better results than the tool. They mentioned that there may be other factors, such as domain knowledge, impacting the experts' results.

Expert may analyse false positive links generated by tools but would need lots of efforts to create missing links by analysing the software artifacts manually. In addition, if an expert generates incorrect links, there are usually no second verification; therefore, it is important to analyse the human factors impacting TR. Below are some of the main factors that impact an expert's opinion.

3.3.1 Domain Knowledge

Definition: Domain knowledge characterises an expert's understanding of the field in which the analysed software system is being developed.

Scenario: Experts use their domain knowledge to query the software artifacts for specific concepts. For example, an expert, who does not have Web development experience and wants to search for a function that return all the variable values from a URL, may use keywords such as "*URL*", "*value*", "*get values from URL*", "*URL variable values*", and so on. Thus, the expert wastes effort, making inaccurate queries; whereas, with appropriate domain knowledge, she would simply use the query "*query string*" to search the relevant function.

Literature Review: Hayes et al. (2005) reported that several factors impact the quality of experts' opinion, including their domain knowledge.

Taira (2008) conducted an empirical study to identify the impact of domain knowledge when learning with the help of a search engine. Their results showed that confusion in Web surfing was caused by a lack of knowledge in the domain of interest. They observed that domain knowledge may assist an expert in avoiding being confused and in finding suitable Web pages.

Park and Black (2007) performed an experiment to investigate the impact of domain knowledge on search activities. Their results showed that domain knowledge impacts the precision of search results.

Preventive Measures: Domain knowledge improves the experts' opinion during traceability tasks. Thus, an expert must acquire adequate domain knowledge before exploring source code and other artifacts. An expert can obtain domain knowledge by using the software system Rajlich and Wilde (2002). An expert must also have enough time to learn and understand the overall functionality of the system to consequently be able to recover/verify traceability links adequately.

3.3.2 Programming Knowledge

Definition: Programming Knowledge relates to an expert's ability to solve programming problems and write quality software in a particular programming language.

Scenario: An expert in Java may not be able to understand Smalltalk source code adequately. Indeed, if an expert does not have Smalltalk programming knowledge, she may find concept in source code that she cannot readily understand or could misunderstand. For example, if an expert, with Java programming experience, queries some Smalltalk source code for "*add patient*", she may find the string "*add patient*" and think that it has something to do with the corresponding functionality while quoted strings in Smalltalk are comments.

Literature Review: Studies Hayes et al. (2003, 2005) showed that experts can recover false links and skip correct links during TR. However, to the best of our knowledge, these studies did not consider the experts' programming knowledge. It is quite possible that experts who vet the final traceability links have good programming knowledge experience Soloway and Ehrlich (1989) but not of the specific language that the current system uses.

Chan (2008) performed an empirical study with 100 undergraduate students to measure the effect of domain-specific knowledge and programming knowledge for software maintenance tasks. Their study showed that both programming and domain-specific knowledge have a significant impact on software maintenance productivity. They also discussed that hiring fresh graduates for maintenance tasks can increase the effort and cost.

Lau and Yuen (2009) conducted an empirical study on 217 secondary students to measure the effects of gender and learning styles on computer programming performance. Their results showed that there is no significant effect of gender on programming performance, but academic ability had a differential effect on programming knowledge. Sequential learners Gregorc (1982) in general performed better than random learners Gregorc (1982).

Preventive Measures: Domain knowledge is important to understand a system internal workings. Yet, we cannot ignore that general and specific programming knowledge also matter. It is important that the experts must be knowledgeable of the programming language that the analysed software system uses when performing TR. An expert with one-year Smalltalk programming experience can understand Smalltalk source code better than an expert who has 10 years of Java experience, as discussed in Section 4.4. Expert must be selected based on specific programming language experience if possible.

4 Empirical Study for a Factor Impacting the Inputs of TRAs

Goal. We want to quantify the impact of one identified factor on TRA input. Quantifying one of the factor's impact on TRA inputs is one more step towards improving TR process. We select experts' programming knowledge because if other factors impact TRA to create wrong links or miss correct links, then expert could create/recover that links. However, if experts create wrong links or miss correct links then these links are likely to be so forever.

Study. We study whether experts without the programming knowledge of a system under analysis can perform different traceability tasks, such as creating links missed by TRAs and verifying links recovered by TRAs. We use Java and PHP as programming languages. We use 40 subjects from both industry and academia, divided in two *groups*; the *first group* with good Java knowledge and the *second group* with good PHP knowledge. We ask all the subjects to create and verify traceability links for Java and PHP systems. We measure the subjects' performance with: (1) the NASA task load index for their effort; (2) the time that they spent performing their tasks; and, (3) their percentage of correct answers.

Results. Collected data shows that, in the first group, Java experts' programming knowledge positively impacted their results when they performed TR tasks for a Java system and negatively when they performed TR tasks on a PHP system. In the second group, for PHP experts and Java and PHP systems, collected data show the inverse results.

Relevance. Understanding the impact of the factors is important from the point of view of both researchers and practitioners. For researchers, our results bring further evidence to support our claim of the impact of the identified factors on TRA inputs. For practitioners, our results provide concrete evidence that they should pay attention to the identified factors to improve their TR process and use the reported preventive measures to handle these factors. Our results support our claim that it is also important to control TRA impacting factors to improve precision and recall.

4.1 Experimental Design

Our experiment uses two groups, the subjects in the *first group* have expertise in Java but not in PHP whereas those in the *second group* have expertise in PHP but not in Java. We use a within-subject design Sheskin (2007) in this experiment. An advantage of the within-subject experimental design is that confounding variables due to differences in subjects' skills are reduced Wake (2003).

4.1.1 Research Question

The goal of our experiment is to analyse how experts' programming knowledge supports or hinders experts' opinion during TR tasks. The experiment addresses the following research question: **RQ – Experts' Programming Knowledge**: *Will experts with specific programming language experience provide better traceability results than others?*

We try to reject the following null-hypothesis: *The presence or absence of experts' specific programming language knowledge has **no** statistically significant effect on average performance while performing requirement traceability tasks.*

4.1.2 Subjects Selection

The subjects are volunteers. Subjects have guaranteed anonymity and all data has been anonymised. We received the agreement from the Ethical Review Board of École Polytechnique de Montréal to perform and publish this study. The subjects were aware that they were going to perform requirement traceability tasks, but do not know the particular experimental research question.

We recruited subjects from academia and industry to make sure that academic or industry experience has little impact on our experiment. There are 26 subjects from academia and 14 from industry. Industrial subjects have between 11 months and 5 years industrial experience whereas academic subjects are M.Sc. and Ph.D. students at École Polytechnique de Montréal (ÉPM). Industrial subjects are currently working in industry and academia subjects are currently enrolled at ÉPM. Table 4 shows the subjects programming experience statistics. We only consider a subject expert in Java or PHP, if she has more than four months experience in Java or PHP.

In the first group, the subjects have expertise in Java, Eclipse, basic domain knowledge of content management systems and medical systems, and no expertise in PHP, to qualify for the experiment whereas in the second group, they have expertise in PHP, Eclipse, basic domain knowledge of content management systems and medical systems and no expertise in Java.

4.1.3 Source Code Selection

We used several criteria to select the systems used in our experiment. First, we selected open-source software systems, so that other researchers can replicate our experiment. Second, we avoided small systems that do not represent systems handled by most developers. Finally, we conducted a pre-experiment survey about the subjects' known systems. We selected the systems that subjects did not know to avoid any learning bias. For the experiment, we used iTrust[5] and Joomla.[6] iTrust is developed in Java. It is an online medical record system with 19,604 KLOC, 526 classes, and 3,404 functions. Joomla is a content management system developed in PHP with 203 KLOC, 737 classes, and 4,834 methods.

---

[5] http://agile.csc.ncsu.edu/iTrust/wiki/doku.php

[6] http://www.joomla.org

Table 4 Average precision and recall range of TRAs

| | Industry | Academia | Industry | | Academia | |
	General programming	General programming	Java	PHP	Java	PHP
Group I	1.038461538	4.75	0.503846154	0.038461538	2.280769231	0.307692308
Group II	2.122142857	3.857142857	0.042857143	1.550714286	0.492857143	0.635714286

4.1.4 Links, Tasks, and Questionnaires

The first author created traceability links manually between source code and requirements for Joomla and the second author verified these links to avoid bias. For iTrust, we used the links that iTrust developers provided us. The manually-created links help to evaluate subjects' answers. (One of the subject performed a pilot-study to validate that the requirements used in the experiment are clear and simple. We excluded this subject and pilot-study from our final results.)

In any traceability task, an expert must verify traceability links created by a TRA and create new links that the TRA missed. We designed our questionnaire to address both these tasks. We asked two set of questions to the subjects, in two categories. In the first category, we asked subjects to create missing traceability links among requirements and source code. This category contains two questions for each system. We used vector space model (VSM) Antoniol et al. (2002) to automatically create traceability links between requirements and source code. VSM provided true and false traceability links. In the second category, we asked subjects to verify requirement traceability links recovered by VSM as true or false. This category contains three questions for each system. In the second category, the first system contains 2 true and 1 false traceability links, whereas the second system contains 1 true and 2 false traceability links. Table 5 shows the experimental categories and questions, the text in bold is a placeholder that we replace by appropriate required behaviour of the systems.

For example, with Joomla, we replace *"this functionality"* in Question 1, Category 1, by *"update any article's contents"* and the question reads as: *system shall allow **updating any article's contents***. In Question 3(a), Category 2, we replace *"this functionality"* and *"class"* by *"administrator to add different sections in website"* and administrator.components.com_sections.admin. sections.php and the question reads: *"System shall allow **administrator to add different sections in website"*** links to administrator.components. com_sections.admin.sections.php.

4.2 Procedure

We divide the experiment into three steps. In the first step, subjects are explained the systems. We provide basic details of the systems on the answer sheets. In the second step, we ask the subjects to provide their general Java or PHP industrial and

Table 5 Experimental questionnaire format

Category 1: *Recover traceability links* **Question 1 & 2** System shall allow ***this functionality***
Category 2: *Verify traceability links* **Question 3 (a,b,c)** System shall allow ***this functionality***, links to ***this class or method***

academic programming experience in years. To confirm the subjects' experience, we ask them the maximum source code size that they have developed in the past. We consider that a subject has expertise in a programming language, if she has more than four months experience and has written more than 5,000 LOCs. We use four months because in academia a semester duration is four to six months and in industry it is considered as probation period. Therefore, considering a subject who is currently studying a programming language subject or industry subject who is in probation period could bias the results. In the third step, we ask the subjects to recover and verify traceability links.

For each system, we ask subjects to spend adequate time to explore the code and perform their traceability tasks. We prepare each of the target system in an Eclipse Workspace. We provide the subjects with a timer, developed in Java to record the time that they take to answer a question. We ask subjects to start the timer when they begin looking for an answer and stop when they find the answer. We ask subjects not to start the timer when they are reading and understanding a question or writing an answer.

We measure the subjects' effort using the NASA Task Load Index (TLX) Hart and Stavenland (1988). The TLX assesses the subjective workload of subjects. It is a multi-dimensional measure that provides an overall workload index based on a weighted average of ratings on six sub-scales, i.e., mental demands, physical demands, temporal demands, own performance, effort, and frustration. NASA provides a computer program to collect weights and ratings for the six sub-scales. We combine all workload factors to compute an average workload for each subject. To combine all workload factors, each rating is multiplied by the weight given to that rating by the subject. The sum of the weighted ratings for each task are divided by 15 to get the average workload Hart and Stavenland (1988).

4.3 Analysis Method

We perform the following analysis to answer our research question and attempt rejecting our null hypothesis. We use programming language knowledge as an independent variable whereas time, percentage of correct answers, and effort are dependent variables. We divide the total number of correct answers by the total number of questions to obtain an average of correct answers for each subject.

We use the Mann-Whitney test to compare the two sets of dependent variables and assess whether their difference is statistically significant. The two sets are the subjects' data that we collected when they answered traceability questions with or without specific programming expertise. For example, we compute the Mann-Whitney test to compare the set of average correct answers of Java experts with non-Java expert for the Java system. Mann-Whitney is a non-parametric test; therefore, it does not make any assumption about the distribution of the data.

We compute the Cohen's d impact size Sheskin (2007), which indicates the magnitude of the effect of a treatment on the dependent variables. The effect size is considered small for $0.2 < d < 0.5$, medium for $0.5 < d < 0.8$ and large for $d > 0.8$. It is defined as the difference between the means $(\mu_1 - \mu_2)$, divided by the pooled standard deviation $\sqrt{\left(\sigma_1^2 - \sigma_2^2\right)/2}$ of both variables: $d = (\mu_1 - \mu_2)/\sigma$.

4.4 Experimental Results

After collecting the answer sheets, we compared subjects' responses with the predetermined correct answers to compute the average correct answers for each subject. Table 6 shows the statistics of the results, all the results' values are average values. For example, in the first group with Java expertise, the subjects took an average of 186.04 s to answer a question for the Java system while they took on average 379 s to answer questions for the PHP system. Table 7 shows the p-values and Cohen's d values calculated by comparing the differences between the data collected for each experiment.

There is statistical significant evidence to reject the null hypothesis. Table 7 shows that the p-values are below the standard significant value, $\alpha = 0.05$. Moreover, the Cohen's d values are also high (> 0.8). Subjects with expertise in Java were able to create/verify more correct links in less time and with less effort than the subjects who did not have expertise in Java for the Java system and vice-versa for the PHP experts and the PHP system. We also find some interesting observations. In both groups, there are 3 subjects who are good in both PHP and Java. They performed better than other subjects on both systems by spending less effort and time to find the correct answers.

Thus, we answer the RQ as follows: programming knowledge does impact experts' opinion. It is important for an expert to have good knowledge of the specific programming language in which the system under analysis is written.

Table 6 Experiment result's statistics

Factor: Expert programming knowledge					
Systems	Knowledge	# of subjects	Correct answers	Times	Efforts
iTrust (Java)	Good	26	69.23	186.04s	30.12
Joomla (PHP)	Bad	26	30.00	379.00s	60.02
iTrust (Java)	Bad	14	44.29	205.93s	39.33
Joomla (PHP)	Good	14	80.00	87.57s	49.07

Table 7 Mann Whitney p-values, precision, recall, and Cohen's d effect size for each experiment

	Time		Answers		Efforts	
	M.-W. p	Cohen d	M.-W. p	Cohen d	M.-W. p	Cohen d
Group I	0.000009	2.38	0.000015	2.40	0.000001	2.79
Group II	0.001094	1.89	0.001453	2.43	0.003052	1.62

4.5 *Threats to Validity*

Several threats potentially impact the validity of our experimental results. We discuss below these threats and how we alleviate or accept them.

Construct validity: The construct validity concerns the relation between theory and observations. In this experiment, it could be due to measurement errors. The average correct traceability links created and time spent by a subject, are the main measure in our study. As the correct answers are predetermined before conducting the experiment, measuring individual subject's performance is simply a matter of comparing each subject's answers with the expected correct answers.

Internal validity: The internal validity of a study is the extent to which a treatment effects change in the dependent variable. There can be learning threat in our experiment. We used two different systems and different kinds of requirements' links to avoid this learning threat. We give subjects an opportunity to ask any questions that they may have about the material. While answering their question, we were careful not to reveal any information that could help them to find the correct answers. We only explained what was already available in the training material. We also instruct subjects not to discuss the experiment among themselves. The source code of both systems was not same and we used two groups with different expertises to avoid source code size effect on our results.

External validity: The external validity of a study relates to the extent to which we can generalize the results of our studies. To avoid any external validity threat, we engaged subjects from academic and industry to help generalising our findings to both contexts. Moreover, we performed our study with 40 (26 for first group and 14 for second) and we used two different systems in different languages, Java and PHP. Yet, we cannot claim to generalise our results to other programming languages.

There were only five links (two links to recover and three links to verify) in our experiment, while the traceability links that experts recover or verify in practice are numerous. One major reason to use few traceability links was experimental control. Table 7 shows that the results are significant and that, moreover, the magnitude of the observed effects is large and thus cannot be ignored. Our preliminary study support the claim that it is important to control the factors that impact traceability approaches inputs.

Conclusion validity: Conclusion validity threats deals with the relation between the treatment and the outcome. We paid attention not to violate assumptions made by statistical tests. Therefore, we used a non-parametric test that does not make any assumptions about the distribution of data.

5 Discussions

We now discuss four questions related to the discussed factors and our methodology.

How much does controlling all the factors increase an experts' workload. Using poor quality TRA inputs will result in large number of false positive and missing links. It could be easier for an expert to improve TRA inputs quality than to manually recover missing links and verify large amount of false positive links. Improving TRA inputs may also help during program comprehension, maintenance, and reuse. In future work, we will perform empirical studies to see how much time and effort can be saved if we control these factors' effect on TRA inputs.

Is it possible to control all the factors. It might not be possible for an expert to control all these factors, but controlling the maximum possible number of factors could still yield better results than using poor quality inputs. Future work includes developing and assessing the cost model to compute the ROI of controlling the various factors and combination thereof.

What are the most critical factors. We have not performed a systematic literature review due to space limitations. However, we performed an ILR and found more than 60 papers related to our study. The provided list of factors is a starting point towards traceability improvement by controlling these factors. We will perform in future work a systematic literature review to attempt identifying all factors and their impact on TRA inputs.

Are there more factors then these seven identified factors. We excluded five factors from our study: document type, document language, work environment, project size, and dead code because we could not find significant evidence in the literature that these factors impact TRA inputs. Yet, these excluded factors may impact TRA inputs. For example, if a TRA takes as input some source code and requirement documents and computes their textual similarity, it is possible that many requirements would link to dead code and an expert would have to verify these links even though they are useless. We add these excluded factors in our list of future experiments to quantify their impact on TRA inputs.

6 Conclusion and Future Work

It is important to develop new and improve existing traceability approaches, but it is also important to gain a better understanding of and support for the factors that impact TRA inputs. We claimed in this chapter that some factors impact TRA inputs, in particular, source code, requirements, and experts' opinion.

We defined a methodology to identify in the literature factors impacting TRA inputs as well as their definitions and associated preventive measures. Our methodology is based on two incremental literature reviews (ILRs) to identify critical factors that impact TRA inputs and tools/metrics to measure/improve the quality of the TRA inputs. We also used the ILRs to collect precautions to control the effect of the factors. We documented seven factors using a consistent template and rejected five factors for which we could not find enough supporting evidence.

To empirically support our claim, we conducted an empirical study to measure the experts' programming knowledge impact on experts' opinion. We showed that a group of Java experts could not perform well traceability-related tasks on a PHP system, while PHP experts could, and vice-versa for PHP and Java experts on a Java systems. These results support our claim that expert's programming language knowledge impacts TRA inputs. Thus, the expert must be knowledgeable about the programming language(s) that the system under analysis uses.

In future work, we will perform a systematic literature review to identify more factors and their effect on TRA inputs. We will perform more experiments on all other remaining factors to assess their impact on TRA inputs. We will provide a priority list for project managers so that they can find which factors can impact their inputs more. We also want to provide a TR process that automatically handles potential factors impacting any TRA inputs.

References

Abadi, A., Nisenson, M., Simionovici, Y.: A traceability technique for specifications. In: The 16th IEEE International Conference on Program Comprehension (ICPC'08), pp. 103–112. Amsterdam, The Netherlands (2008)

Ali, N.: Trustrace: Improving automated trace retrieval through resource trust analysis. In: ICPC '11: Proceedings of the International Conference on Program Comprehension (ICPC'11), p. 4. IEEE Computer Society, Washington, DC (2011)

Antoniol, G.: Recovery of traceability links in software artifacts and systems. PhD Thesis, Montreal, QC (2003)

Antoniol, G., Canfora, G., Casazza, G., De Lucia, A., Merlo, E.: Recovering traceability links between code and documentation. IEEE Trans. Softw. Eng. 28(10), 970–983. Piscataway, NJ (2002). ISSN:0098-5589

Antoniol, G., Hayes, J., Guéhéneuc, Y.G., di Penta, M.: Reuse or rewrite: Combining textual, static, and dynamic analyses to assess the cost of keeping a system up-to-date. In: IEEE International Conference on Software Maintenance (ICSM'08), Beijing, China (2008)

Bianchi, A., Fasolino, A., Visaggio, G.: An exploratory case study of the maintenance effectiveness of traceability models. In: Proceedings of the 8th International Workshop on Program Comprehension (IWPC 2000), pp. 149–158. IEEE Computer Society, Los Alamitos, CA (2000)

Binkley, D., Feild, H., Lawrie, D., Pighin, M.: Software fault prediction using language processing. In: Testing: Academic and Industrial Conference Practice and Research Techniques-MUTATION, 2007. TAICPART-MUTATION 2007, IEEE, pp. 99–110. Windsor, UK (2007)

Binkley, D., Feild, H., Lawrie, D., Pighin, M.: Increasing diversity: Natural language measures for software fault prediction. J. Syst. Softw. 82(11), 1793–1803 (2009)

Butler, S., Wermelinger, M., Yu, Y., Sharp, H.: Relating identifier naming flaws and code quality: An empirical study. IEEE Comput. Soc. 0, pp. 31–35, Los Alamitos, CA (2009)

Chan, T.: Impact of programming and application-specific knowledge on maintenance effort: A hazard rate model. In: IEEE International Conference on Software Maintenance (ICSM'08), pp. 47–56. IEEE, Orlando, FL (2008)

Chantree, F., Nuseibeh, B., de Roeck, A., Willis, A.: Identifying nocuous ambiguities in natural language requirements. In: 14th IEEE International Conference Requirements Engineering, pp. 59–68. Minneapolis, MN (2006)

Cleland-Huang, J., Chang, C.K., Christensen, M.: Event-based traceability for managing evolutionary change. IEEE Trans. Softw. Eng. 29(9), 796–810 (2003)

Cleland-Huang, J., Berenbach, B., Clark, S., Settimi, R., Romanova, E.: Best practices for automated traceability. Computer 40, 27–35 (2007)

Cuddeback, D., JHH, Dekhtyar, A.: Automated Requirements Traceability: The Study of Human Analysts. IEEE Computer Society, Los Alamitos, CA (2010)

De Lucia, A., Oliveto, R., Tortora, G.: Assessing IR-based traceability recovery tools through controlled experiments. Empirical Softw. Eng. **14**, 57–92 (2009)

Deissenboeck, F., Pizka, M.: Concise and consistent naming. Softw. Qual. J. **14**, 261–282 (2006)

Dekhtyar, A., Hayes, J., Larsen, J.: Make the most of your time: How should the analyst work with automated traceability tools? In: International Workshop on Predictor Models in Software Engineering (PROMISE'07: ICSE Workshops 2007), pp. 1–4. Minneapolis, MN (2007)

Eder, J., Panagos, E., Rabinovich, M.: Time constraints in workflow systems. In: Proceedings of the 11th International Conference on Advanced Information Systems Engineering, pp. 286–300. Springer, London, CAiSE '99 (1999)

Egyed, A.: A scenario-driven approach to traceability. In: Proceedings of the 23rd International Conference on Software Engineering (ICSE'01), pp. 123–132. Toronto, ON (2001)

Egyed, A., Grünbacher, P.: Automating requirements traceability: Beyond the record & replay paradigm. In: ASE'02: Proceedings of the 17th IEEE international conference on Automated software engineering, p. 163. IEEE Computer Society, Washington, DC (2002)

Egyed, A., Grünbacher, P.: Identifying requirements conflicts and cooperation: How quality attributes and automated traceability can help. Softw. IEEE **21**(6), 50–58 (2004)

Egyed, A., Biffl, S., Heindl, M., Grünbacher, P.: A value-based approach for understanding costbenefit trade-offs during automated software traceability. In: Proceedings of the 3rd International Workshop on Traceability in Emerging Forms of Software Engineering, pp. 2–7. ACM, New York, NY, TEFSE '05 (2005)

Egyed, A., Graf, F., Grünbacher, P.: Effort and quality of recovering requirements-to-code traces: Two exploratory experiments. In: IEEE International Conference on Requirements Engineering, pp. 221–230. IEEE Computer Society, Los Alamitos, CA (2010)

Fabbrini, F., Fusani, M., Gnesi, S., Lami, G.: The linguistic approach to the natural language requirements quality: Benefit of the use of an automatic tool. In: Proceedings of the 26th Annual NASA Goddard, Software Engineering Workshop, pp. 97–105. IEEE Computer Society, Los Alamitos, CA (2001)

Gervasi, V., Zowghi, D.: On the role of ambiguity in requirement engineering. In: REFSQ, pp. 248–254.Springer, Berlin/Heidelberg (2010)

Ghazarian, A.: A design-rule-based constructive approach to building traceable software. PhD Thesis, Toronto, ON (2009)

Gibson, M.D., Conheeney, K.: Domain knowledge reuse during requirements engineering. In: Proceedings of the 7th International Conference on Advanced Information Systems Engineering, pp. 283–296. Springer, London (1995)

Gleich, B., Creighton, O., Kof, L.: Ambiguity Detection: Towards a Tool Explaining Ambiguity Sources. Requirements Engineering: Foundation for Software Quality, pp. 218–232. Essen, Germany (2010)

Gregorc, A.: An Adultâs Guide to Style. Gregorc Associates, Inc., Columbia, CT (1982)

Grünbacher, P., Briggs, R.: Surfacing tacit knowledge in requirements negotiation: Experiences using easywinwin. In: Proceedings of the 34th Annual Hawaii International Conference on System Sciences, 2001, p. 8 (2001)

Haiduc, S., Marcus, A.: On the use of domain terms in source code. In: The 16th IEEE International Conference on Program Comprehension (ICPC'08), pp. 113–122 (2008)

Hall, T., Beecham, S., Rainer, A.: Requirements problems in twelve software companies: an empirical analysis. Softw. IEE Proc. **149**(5), 153–160 (2002)

Hart, S.G., Stavenland, L.E.: Development of NASA-TLX (Task Load Index): Results of empirical and theoretical research. In: Hancock, P.A., Meshkati, N. (eds) Human Mental Workload, chap. 7, pp. 139–183. Elsevier, Amsterdam (1988)

Hausmann, J., Heckel, R., Taentzer, G.: Detection of conflicting functional requirements in a use case-driven approach. In: Proceedings of the 24rd International Conference on Software Engineering (ICSE'02), pp. 105–115. IEEE, Washington, DC (2005)

Hayes, J.: Building a requirement fault taxonomy: Experiences from a NASA verification and validation research project. In: 14th International Symposium on Software Reliability Engineering, (ISSRE'03). pp. 49–59. Denver, CO (2003a)

Hayes, J.H.: Building a requirement fault taxonomy: Experiences from a NASA verification and validation research project. In: Proceedings of the 14th International Symposium on Software Reliability Engineering. IEEE Computer Society, Washington, DC, ISSRE '03 (2003b)

Hayes, J.H., Dekhtyar, A.: Humans in the traceability loop: Can't live with 'em, can't live without 'em. In: Proceedings of the 3rd International Workshop on Traceability in Emerging Forms of Software Engineering, pp. 20–23. ACM, New York, NY. TEFSE '05, doi: http://doi.acm.org/10.1145/1107656.1107661 (2005)

Hayes, J.H., Dekhtyar, A., Osborne, J.: Improving requirements tracing via information retrieval. In: RE '03: Proceedings of the 11th IEEE International Conference on Requirements Engineering, p. 138. IEEE Computer Society, Washington, DC (2003)

Hayes, J.H., Dekhtyar, A., Sundaram, S.: Text mining for software engineering: how analyst feedback impacts final results. In: Proceedings of the 2005 International Workshop on Mining Software Repositories, pp. 1–5. ACM, New York, NY, MSR '05 (2005)

Hayes, J.H., Antoniol, G., Guéhéneuc, Y.G.: Prereqir: Recovering pre-requirements via cluster analysis, vol. 0, pp. 165–174. IEEE Computer Society, Los Alamitos, CA (2008)

Jirapanthong, W., Zisman, A.: Xtraque: Traceability for product line systems. Softw. Syst. Model. 8(1), 117–144 (2007)

Joseph, J.C.: Requirements engineering and management: The key to designing quality complex systems. In: The TQM Magazine, vol. 12, pp. 400–407. MCB UP Ltd., Bradford, West Yorkshire (2000)

Kamsties, E., Hormann, K., Schlich, M.: Requirements engineering in small and medium enterprises. Req. Eng. 3(2), 84–90 (1998)

Kamsties, E., Berry, D., Paech, B.: Detecting ambiguities in requirements documents using inspections. In: Workshop on Inspections in Software Engineering, pp. 68–80. Paris, France (2001)

Kasser, J.: The first requirements elucidator demonstration (FRED) Tool. Syst. Eng. 7(3), 243–256 (2004)

Kitchenham, B., Brereton, O., Budgen, D., Turner, M., Bailey, J., Linkman, S.: Systematic literature reviews in software engineering – A systematic literature review. Inform. Softw. Technol. 51, 7–15 (2009)

Lau, W., Yuen, A.: Exploring the effects of gender and learning styles on computer programming performance: Implications for programming pedagogy. Brit. J. Educat. Technol. 40(4), 696–712 (2009)

Lawrie, D., Feild, H., Binkley, D.: Quantifying identifier quality: An analysis of trends. Empirical Softw. Eng. 12, 359–388 (2007a)

Lawrie, D., Morrell, C., Feild, H., Binkley, D. : What's in a name? A study of identifiers. In: Proceedings of the 14th IEEE International Conference on Program Comprehension, pp. 3–12. IEEE Computer Society, Washington, DC (2006)

Lawrie, D., Morrell, C., Feild, H., Binkley, D.: Effective identifier names for comprehension and memory. Innov. Syst. Softw. Eng. 3, 303–318 (2007b)

Lee, J., Kuo, J.: New approach to requirements trade-off analysis for complex systems. Knowl. Data Eng. IEEE Trans. 10(4), 551–562 (2002)

Lucia, A.D., Fasano, F., Oliveto, R., Tortora, G.: Adams Re-Trace: A Traceability Recovery Tool, vol. 0, pp. 32–41. IEEE Computer Society, Los Alamitos, CA (2005)

Lucia, A.D., Fasano, F., Oliveto, R., Tortora, G.: Recovering traceability links in software artifact management systems using information retrieval methods. ACM Trans. Softw. Eng. Methodol. 16, 1301–1350 (2007)

Lucia, A.D., Penta, M.D., Oliveto, R.: Improving source code lexicon via traceability and information retrieval. IEEE Trans. Softw. Eng. 99, 205–227 (2010)

Lucia, A.D., Penta, M.D., Oliveto, R., Zurolo, F.: Coconut: Code Comprehension Nurturant Using Traceability, pp. 274–275. IEEE Computer Society, Los Alamitos, CA (2006)

Madani, N., Guerrouj, L., Di Penta, M., Guéhéneuc, Y.G., Antoniol, G.: Recognizing words from source code identifiers using speech recognition techniques. In: Proceeding of the Conference on Software Maintenance and Reengineering, pp. 69–78. IEEE, Madrid, Spain (2010)

Maletic, J., Munson, E., Marcus, A., Nguyen, T.: Using a hypertext model for traceability link conformance analysis. In: Proceedings of the 2nd International Workshop on Traceability in Emerging Forms of Software Engineering, pp. 47–54. Montreal, Canada (2003)

Marcus, A., Maletic, J.I.: Recovering documentation-to-source-code traceability links using latent semantic indexing. In: ICSE '03: Proceedings of the 25th International Conference on Software Engineering, pp. 125–135. IEEE Computer Society, Washington, DC (2003)

Marcus, A., Poshyvanyk, D.: The conceptual cohesion of classes. In: Proceedings of the 21st IEEE International Conference on Software Maintenance, pp. 133–142. IEEE Computer Society, Washington, DC (2005)

Moha, N., Guéhéneuc, Y.G., Duchien, L., Le Meur, A.F.: Decor: A method for the specification and detection of code and design smells. Softw. Eng. IEEE Trans. 36(1), 20–36 (2010)

Oliveto, R., Gethers, M., Poshyvanyk, D., De Lucia, A.: On the equivalence of information retrieval methods for automated traceability link recovery. In: Proceedings of the 2010 IEEE 18th International Conference on Program Comprehension, pp. 68–71. IEEE Computer Society, Washington, DC, ICPC '10 (2010)

Park, Y., Black, J.: Identifying the impact of domain knowledge and cognitive style on webbased information search behavior. J. Educat. Comput. Res. 36(1), 15–37 (2007)

Rajlich, V., Wilde, N.: The role of concepts in program comprehension. In: Proceedings of the 10th International Workshop on Program Comprehension, p. 271. IEEE Computer Society, Washington, DC, IWPC '02 (2002)

Sherba, S.A.: Towards automating traceability: An incremental and scalable approach. PhD Thesis, Boulder, CO (2005)

Sheskin, D.J.: Handbook of Parametric and Nonparametric Statistical Procedures, 4th edn. Chapman & Hall/CRC, London (2007)

Soloway, E., Ehrlich, K.: Empirical Studies of Programming Knowledge, pp. 235–267. ACM, New York, NY (1989)

Spanoudakis, G., Zisman, A., Pérez-Minana, E., Krause, P.: Rule-based generation of requirements traceability relations. J. Syst. Softw. 72(2), 105–127 (2004)

Sundaram, S.K., Hayes, J.H., Dekhtyar, A.: Baselines in requirements tracing. In: Proceedings of the 2005 Workshop on Predictor Models in Software Engineering, pp. 1–6, ACM, New York, NY (2005)

Taira, M.: The influence of domain knowledge and task requirement on the selection of learning strategies in the internet. Int. J. Creativ. Probl. Solv. 18(1), 45–53 (2008)

Takang, A.A., Grubb, P.A., Macredie, R.D.: The effects of comments and identifier names on program comprehensibility: An experimental investigation. J. Program. Lang. 4(3), 143–167 (1996)

Wake, W.C.: Refactoring Workbook. Addison-Wesley Longman Publishing Co. Inc., Boston, MA (2003)

Zisman, A., Spanoudakis, G., Pérez-Miñana, E., Krause, P.: Towards a traceability approach for product families requirements. In: Proceedings of 3rd ICSE Workshop on Software Product Lines: Economics, Architectures, and Implications, Orlando, FL (2002)

Automated Techniques for Capturing Custom Traceability Links Across Heterogeneous Artifacts

Hazeline U. Asuncion and Richard N. Taylor

1 Motivation

The goal of software traceability is to identify relevant relationships between artifacts produced in a software life cycle. When fully realized, traceability enables the efficient retrieval of related artifacts, which is useful in a variety of software engineering tasks such as software maintenance, system comprehension and system debugging (Anderson et al., 2002; Ramesh et al., 1995; Richardson and Green 2004). Meanwhile, software development projects are increasingly becoming more distributed, decentralized, and dependent on third party software, motivating the need for effective traceability techniques.

Ideally, we are interested in providing traceability support for a wide range of scenarios. For instance, an architect may want to capture links between the system design and the rationale embedded in different artifacts (e.g., requirements documents, screen mockups, use cases). A developer may then need to navigate from code to its rationale to better understand how to implement the system. As another example, a QA engineer may need to capture verification traceability links from test cases and test reports to requirements. However, current automated traceability approaches (Marcus and Maletic, 2003; Spanoudakis et al., 2004) fall short of supporting these scenarios. For example, difficulties exist in tracing across tool boundaries (Ramesh et al., 1995); moreover, the automated capture of traceability link information is often limited to text-based artifacts (Spanoudakis et al., 2004). Varied stakeholder interests in traceability (Gotel and Finkelstein, 1994) also require customization support, such as tailoring the granularity of trace capture and the types of artifacts to trace.

In this chapter, we present our set of trace capture techniques and our tool support for these usage scenarios. The techniques presented in this chapter are part of our Architecture-Centric Traceability for Stakeholders (ACTS) framework (Asuncion and Taylor, 2011). We capture traceability links prospectively by analyzing user

---

H.U. Asuncion (✉)
Computing and Software Systems, University of Washington, Bothell, WA, USA
e-mail: hazeline@u.washington.edu

J. Cleland-Huang et al. (eds.), *Software and Systems Traceability*,
DOI 10.1007/978-1-4471-2239-5_6, © Springer-Verlag London Limited 2012

interactions with the artifact within the context of a particular development task, such as analyzing requirements, creating or editing design documents, or writing code. Thus, we capture traceability links in situ, while artifacts are generated or modified. It is different from (but complementary with) trace recovery techniques that identify candidate traceability links retrospectively from existing artifacts, by using information retrieval or machine learning techniques to analyze text-based documents (De Lucia et al., 2011; Grechanik et al., 2007; Kagdi et al., 2007; Marcus and Maletic, 2003). In addition, since we can capture temporal or contextual relationships between artifacts, we can use this information to link together heterogeneous artifacts. Moreover, our set of techniques can be combined with other methods, such as those used in trace recovery. We show later in the chapter how we combine our trace capture technique with third party search tools. In previous work, we have also combined prospective trace capture with a machine learning technique known as topic modeling, to guide trace capture and to semi-automate the post-analysis of captured traceability links (Asuncion et al., 2010).

Our techniques use open hypermedia concepts (Anderson et al., 2000) and customizable rules as the underlying mechanisms. Open hypermedia concepts support capturing traceability links across tool boundaries and rendering artifacts at different levels of granularity. In addition, customizable rules enable users to choose the artifacts to trace and to specify traceability link information, such as the trace relationship.

This chapter is organized as follows. In the next section, we discuss our techniques using the mobile phone case study in Appendix C. Section 3 covers the limitations of our techniques. In Section 4, we compare our techniques to related traceability approaches.

2 Techniques for Automating the Trace Capture

In this section, we illustrate how our traceability techniques can be incorporated into a software development context. Our tool support, referred to as the ACTS traceability system, or simply ACTS, is implemented on top of ArchStudio (Dashofy et al., 2007), a mature environment for architecture-centric development that is integrated with Eclipse. ACTS is designed to focus all the traceability links to one central artifact, which we refer to as the primary artifact. The primary artifact used in ACTS is the structural architecture, although it is also possible to relate artifacts to other primary artifacts such as requirements or test cases.

Using the mobile phone case study, we illustrate the main features of our techniques: trace capture across heterogeneous artifacts, easy access to these traced artifacts, maintenance of captured links, and usage of off-the-shelf search tools to guide the trace capture. This case study consists of artifacts of various file types, such as Word documents, PDF files, PowerPoint files, Excel spreadsheets, web pages, and structural designs of the mobile phone. We also show how trace capture can be performed at different levels of granularity.

The following subsections are organized as follows. We first present a usage scenario and we explain how the ACTS tool can support the scenario. We cover the usage scenarios of integrating third-party tools into a traceability system, incorporating custom rules, capturing traceability links, combining trace capture with third-party search tools, and maintaining traceability links over time. We then provide a "behind the scenes" look into how our techniques perform these traceability tasks. An in-depth technical discussion of our techniques can be found in (Asuncion and Taylor, 2011).

2.1 Integrating Third-Party Tools

In this scenario, we will examine how we can cross tool boundaries in capturing traceability links.

2.1.1 Usage Scenario

Let us follow the scenario of a maintenance engineer trying to understand the mobile phone product line in order to modify the Messaging Subsystem of the phone. The maintenance engineer would like to capture traceability links to artifacts that are generated by different tools. This is a common scenario in software development, since a development team often uses different tools to generate various artifacts over the course of a development life cycle.

We can support such a scenario by integrating third-party tools into the ACTS tool through open hypermedia adapters (discussed in the next section). The adapters can be used to capture possible traceability links, display traced artifacts within the third-party tool, or check for link updates. Once the adapters are built, they can be integrated into the ACTS tool through the Preferences user interface. The current implementation of ACTS has tool-specific adapters for MS Word 2007, MS Excel 2007, MS PowerPoint 2007, Mozilla Firefox 3, Adobe Acrobat 9, and ArchStudio 4 running on Eclipse 3.4.2.

2.1.2 Techniques Behind the Scenes

The field of open hypermedia provides techniques for managing relationships between heterogeneous artifacts and tools (Anderson et al., 2000). Third-party tools can be incorporated into the ACTS traceability system by building open hypermedia adapters for these tools. These adapters, referred to as viewers in hypermedia systems (Anderson et al., 2000), are used to render, or display, the traced information at a specified location within a specified tool (e.g., display a specific page in Adobe Acrobat). In addition to the concept of rendering adapters, we created recording and notification adapters. Recording adapters capture user interactions and notification adapters detect changes to traced artifacts. We will discuss these specialized adapters in more detail in the next sections.

Tool-specific adapters are built independently of the ACTS traceability system. These adapters use the third-party tool's public application programming interfaces (APIs) to perform their various functions. While an adapter is an executable invoked by the ACTS traceability system, it has no awareness of the ACTS tool. This design

```
<action>
<event>Text</event>
<resource>C:\Users\Hazel\.archstudio4\otherFiles\MobilePhone_PL.pdf#6
</resource>
<timestamp>1290381999000</timestamp></action>

<action>
<event>Popup</event>
<resource>C:\Users\Hazel\.archstudio4\otherFiles\MobilePhone_PL.pdf#6
</resource>
<timestamp>1290381954000</timestamp></action>
```

Fig. 1 Recorded events when a comment is added in Adobe Acrobat

simplifies the construction of adapters—they do not need to know anything about how the ACTS tool is implemented or how it functions. They simply need to capture user interactions, record the interactions using a uniform event model (discussed below), render a traced artifact, and detect changes to traced artifacts. Because of this loose-coupling, control flow always goes from ACTS to the adapters. Once the adapters finish execution, ACTS resumes execution. Any data that is passed back to ACTS is through a shared location that can be specified in the Preferences user interface of the ACTS tool.

To facilitate linking across tool boundaries, the recorded user interactions must follow a uniform event model (see Fig. 1). The event model, which is independent of the third party tool and is represented in XML, contains a log of actions, with each action containing the type of event, the resource, and a timestamp of the event. The partial event log in Fig. 1 shows the recorded user actions of adding a popup comment and typing a comment. The resource provides the full path to the traced artifact, including a specific location within the artifact as indicated by the "#". In this case, the "#" sign indicates the page number of the artifact.

2.2 Incorporating Custom Rules

In the previous section, we showed how third-party tools can be integrated into a traceability system. In this section, we will show how to create custom rules, represented as XSL Transformations (XSLT), to analyze the recorded events and to transform them into traceability links.

2.2.1 Usage Scenario

Let us suppose that our maintenance engineer wants to tailor the granularity of the traceability link capture as well as to automatically assign a relationship to the captured traceability link.

With regards to the granularity of trace capture, our engineer is only interested in capturing traceability links at the granularity of cells for spreadsheet artifacts. To

```
33:    <xsl:choose>
34:     <xsl:when test="contains($curElement,'.xls') and
       not(contains($curElement,'$'))">
35:        <xsl:call-template name = "nextObject">
36:        </xsl:call-template>
37:     </xsl:when>
38:     <xsl:otherwise>
39:        <xsl:call-template name = "curObject">
40:        </xsl:call-template>
41:     </xsl:otherwise>
42:    </xsl:choose>
```

Fig. 2 Record rule that filters Excel events occurring in non-cell locations

support this scenario, we can create a record rule that discards all potential links to a spreadsheet file, indicated by a .xls file, that do not link to a cell or group of cells. Line 34 in Fig. 2 shows the check for this condition: if the artifact being examined is an Excel spreadsheet, check if it also points to cell(s), which is indicated by a "$"; however, if this latter condition is not met, filter out the current artifact and proceed to examine the next artifact, as indicated by the call to the nextObject template; otherwise create a traceability link to this artifact.

With regard to specifying the traceability link relationship, we can support this scenario by creating an add relationship rule. One example is to assign a relationship type based on the artifact that will be traced. This rule will first extract specific words from the path of the artifact and then it will assign a relationship based on the extracted words. For instance, if a resource path contains the keyword "process", then assign the relationship as "behavior". Figure 3 shows some of the relationships assigned based on keywords.

2.2.2 Techniques Behind the Scenes

Rules are used to process captured user interactions and transform them into traceability links. Because these rules are external to the ACTS tool, users can apply their

```
173:   <xsl:choose>
174:
175:       <xsl:when test="contains($curFileType, 'process')">
176:          <xsl:value-of select="string('behavior')"/>
177:       </xsl:when>
178:
179:       <xsl:when test="contains($curFileType, 'MobilePhone')">
180:          <xsl:value-of select="string('description')"/>
181:       </xsl:when>
182:
183:       <xsl:when test="contains($curFileType, 'func')">
184:          <xsl:value-of select="string('functionality')"/>
185:       </xsl:when>
```

Fig. 3 Partial add relationship rule based on keywords on the artifact's path

own heuristics in determining valid traceability links. Rules may also be used to automatically assign traceability link information, such as traceability relationship type.

As you saw, rules are expressed as XSLT and we use Xalan as our rule engine. An XSLT specifies how to transform a portion of an event log in XML (see Fig. 1) that matches a given pattern. The current implementation includes a set of sample rules that users may take and customize for their use. To start using a newly created rule, users simply specify the rule's path in the ACTS Preferences user interface. In our scenarios, we showed you examples of two types of rules: record rules and add relationship rules.

Record rules are rules that determine valid traceability links. Record rules analyze user events for a matching pattern of interaction to create traceability links between accessed artifacts. Record rules are also used to minimize noise by filtering unnecessary user interactions (such as jitters (Singer et al., 2005) and duplicate pointers to the same artifact). Since traceability links can have multiple endpoints, rules are also used to determine which set of endpoints can be grouped together as one traceability link.

Add relationship rules are used to assign traceability relationship based on the context in which the artifacts are traced. In our scenario, the relationship was based on the presence of words on the artifact path. Relationships may also be assigned based on a pattern of access. For example, if a requirements document is concurrently accessed with the software architecture, traceability links captured may automatically be assigned a "rationale" relationship.

2.3 Capturing Traceability Links

The previous sections covered how to incorporate tool adapters and custom rules into the ACTS tool. This section will illustrate the process of capturing traceability links across different artifacts.

2.3.1 Usage Scenario

Let us follow the scenario of a maintenance engineer going through various documents for the purpose of understanding the mobile phone product line. These documents include structural designs in ArchStudio, descriptions of the messaging subsystem in Adobe Acrobat, process models in PowerPoint, and a list of processes in Excel. Since the maintenance engineer wants to refer back to these visited artifacts, the engineer captures traceability links using the ACTS tool.

Prior to a recording session, the engineer indicates whether to apply the rules interactively or in the background. In interactive rule application, the tool will prompt the user for the rules to apply after each recording session. After a rule is applied, a dialog box shows the status of the transformation. Background rule application enables users to pre-specify a set of rules to apply after each recording session. While interactive rule application may require more time from users, this mode is useful when determining if the rules are correctly specified. When the users are comfortable with the rules, they can then switch to background application. We found that some users prefer the control that interactive rule application provides over the background rule application (Asuncion and Taylor, 2011). In this scenario, the engineer uses the interactive rule application.

Figure 4 shows ArchStudio with the ACTS tool on the right side of the screen. The Outline View on the left shows the various structural designs created for the mobile phone system. The current selection, SubsystemModules, shows the top level structure of the modules in the mobile phone product line. The Mobile Internet Subsystem and the Messaging Subsystem both have substructures or subarchitectures and one can focus on these structures by selecting the MobileInternet_Module or the SMS_Module. Elements of the substructures are also selectable and viewable (by zooming in) within the top level view. Because ArchStudio can model many levels of substructure design, artifacts can be traced to these different levels.

After the engineer specifies how to apply the rules, in this case interactively, the engineer starts recording via the Start Record button. The status indicator then shows that the tool is in record mode (highlighted in Fig. 4). Links to the Messaging Subsystem and its internal components are captured first. To capture links to artifacts, they are opened through the browse button next to the Stop Recording button. After the recording session, the tool displays the captured user interaction events

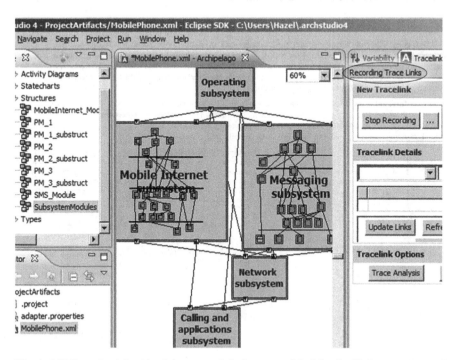

Fig. 4 ACTS, on the right side of the screen, is built on top of ArchStudio. Various structures of the mobile phone are listed in the outline view on the left

and checks with the user whether to transform these events into traceability links. If the user indicates yes, the tool prompts the user to select a rule to apply.

The engineer can verify whether a rule behaves as expected by examining the transformed event logs displayed in ACTS. After applying the record rule, the engineer can see that pointers to spreadsheets are limited to cell locations. Applying the add relationship rule also assigned the traceability relationships "behavior" to the artifacts that contain the word "process" and "description" to artifacts that contain the words "MobilePhone".

After the events are transformed into traceability links, they are then added to the linkbase and displayed in a table in ACTS (see the highlighted table in Fig. 5). The figure shows that the rules are indeed working properly. Other traceability link information, such as capture mode, timestamp, and author of the link, are also shown in the table.

Once the traceability links are shown in the table, they may be deleted or navigated. Traceability links may be deleted by selecting "Delete Link" in the context menu.

2.3.2 Techniques Behind the Scenes

We now discuss the techniques used in this scenario: recording adapters, first-class traceability links, and independent linkbase.

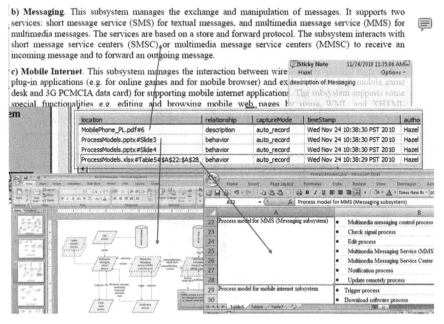

Fig. 5 Navigating the traceability links renders the artifacts within their native editor and at the appropriate location within the artifact

Recording adapters. We capture potential traceability links via recording adapters. Recording adapters detect user's interactions with artifacts within the context of the tool editor. Recording adapters use either the tool's public APIs or the tool's built-in history log (e.g. web browser) to extract the user interaction. Recording adapters may also selectively listen to specific events, instead of capturing all user interactions, to reduce noise. The recorded user interactions, such as those recorded in our first scenario (Fig. 1), are processed by rules to determine valid traceability links.

In order to minimize noise, recording adapters are invoked explicitly by the user when the user switches to the record mode and opens artifacts through the ACTS interface. For instance, if an .xls file is selected, the recording adapter for MS Excel is invoked and will capture user interaction events until the user decides to close the file. To further minimize the noise, traceability links can only be captured across tools with built adapters.

First-class traceability links. Traceability links are first class objects, i.e., they are represented as separate and independent entities from the artifacts they connect (Anderson et al., 2000). This first class representation enables capturing additional information, such as the user who captured the traceability link (referred to as author), timestamp of trace capture, traceability relationship, capture mode, link status, and action(s) to take when navigating a traceability link. Relationship indicates the traceability relationship type. Capture mode indicates whether the traceability link was recorded, recovered (via third party search tools), or manually specified by the user, since the trace tool integrates various means of generating traceability links. Link status indicates whether the traced artifact changed (see Section 2.6). An action is another operation that the tool may perform when a traceability link is navigated. Thus, an action may point to scripts or executables that will be invoked when accessing a traced artifact. An example of an action is highlighting a traced paragraph when it is rendered. Raising the status of traceability links as first class objects also facilitates modeling, querying and visualizing traceability link information.

Traceability links are n-ary, that is they can have multiple endpoints. Consequently, artifacts that have a point of commonality can be grouped together into one traceability link. In addition, the endpoints can themselves be traceability links, enabling hierarchical modeling of traceability links and the composition of multiple traceability links. Hierarchical representation of traceability links can be useful when tracing course-grained to fine-grained artifacts (e.g. high level to low level requirements).

Independent linkbase. Traceability links are also stored outside the artifacts they connect, in an independent traceability linkbase, in contrast to the link representation used by the WWW. There are several advantages to managing traceability links through this model. It is possible to link together read-only third-party artifacts. Traceability links may also be accessed and manipulated by a variety of tools (i.e., not tied to a particular technology) while maintaining a consistent data model. Additionally, traceability link maintenance is possible. If an anchor is removed, all the pointers to that anchor will also be removed.

2.4 Accessing Captured Traceability Links

In this section, we show how the captured traceability links can be accessed.

2.4.1 Usage Scenario

Let us suppose that our maintenance engineer wants to revisit the artifacts that were traced by the ACTS tool. Once the traceability links are shown in the table, they may be accessed by double-clicking each traceability link. Doing so opens the files at the specified location within their native editors. Figure 5 shows that we can access artifacts at different levels of granularity, a page in an Adobe Acrobat file, a slide in a PowerPoint file, and a group of cells in an Excel file.

2.4.2 Technique Behind the Scenes

We facilitate access to artifacts via rendering adapters. Rendering adapters display the captured traceability links within its default tool. Thus, when a user navigates a traceability link, the ACTS traceability system invokes the appropriate adapter. The rendering adapter receives the full path of the artifact to display, invokes the default tool, and directs the tool to open the artifact. If a specific location within the artifact has been included in the path, the adapter will direct the tool to render at the specified location. Depending on the artifact, this location might be an anchor in a web page, a cell within a worksheet within a spreadsheet, or a page within a document. Because the rendering adapters are tool-specific, they understand the level of granularity being specified by the "#". In the example, the PDF rendering adapters understand that "#6" means page 7 because the Adobe Acrobat API starts page numbers with "0". Thus, the granularity of the traceability link endpoints can be flexibly specified. This flexibility is useful when linking to course-grained artifacts, such as a voluminous document, and it is unclear which portion of the artifact is traced.

2.5 Combining Trace Capture with Integrated Search Tools

In this section, we show how our trace capture technique can leverage the features of search tools in identifying traceability links.

2.5.1 Usage Scenario

Let us suppose that our maintenance engineer wants to capture traceability links to online documentation, but is unable to recall the URL of the documentation. Our engineer decides to use a search engine, which happens to be Google, to help find the online documentation. In Fig. 6, for example, Google is used to look for possible web resources related to the Camera module in Product Member 1 (Step 1).

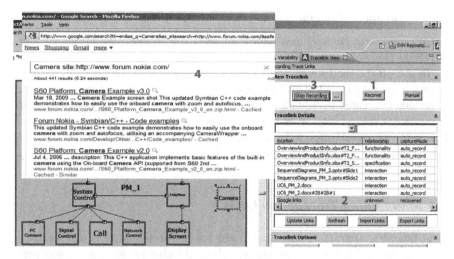

Fig. 6 Steps in combining a search tool with our traceability capture

Once Google's search results are obtained (Step 2), record mode is engaged (Step 3), certain Google links are traversed (Step 4), and sites that the user selects from the search results and navigates to are captured (Steps 5 & 6 in Fig. 7). After recording, ACTS adds the traceability links to these web resources in the table (Step 7). Thus, recording user selections from a set of possible traceability links provided by a search tool can be used to capture traceability links.

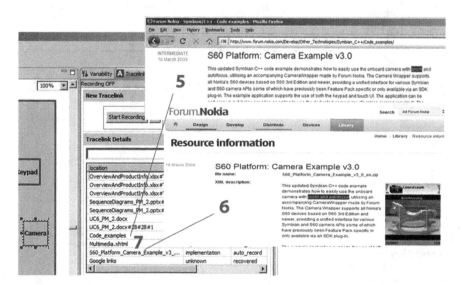

Fig. 7 Continuation of steps in combining a search tool with our traceability capture

2.5.2 Technique Behind the Scenes

Trace capture can be combined with third party search tools. We integrated into ACTS the Google search engine.

To use off-the-shelf search tools like Google, the recover functionality simply creates a traceability link with an endpoint to the Google site and the parameters to include the search term, which is automatically assigned to the component that is selected. Once we start recording, our browser adapter simply tracks the pages that were visited and includes them in the event log. After the recording session, the rules transform the visited sites into traceability links.

2.6 Maintaining Traceability Links

Over time, traced artifacts may change and pointers to the artifacts may become obsolete. In ACTS, notification adapters check for changes to artifacts and perform appropriate updates to traceability link locations and-or to traceability link status.

2.6.1 Usage Scenario

Let us suppose that our maintenance engineer modifies the traced artifacts. Figure 8 (highlighted box) shows the status of Messaging Controller's traceability link to cell

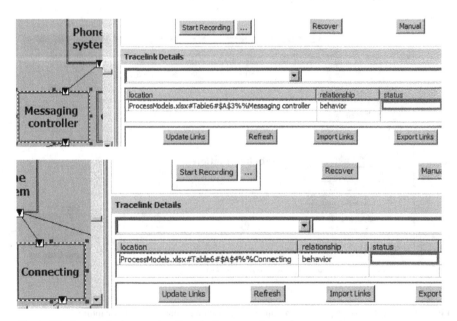

Fig. 8 Blank status in the traced artifacts indicates no change has occured

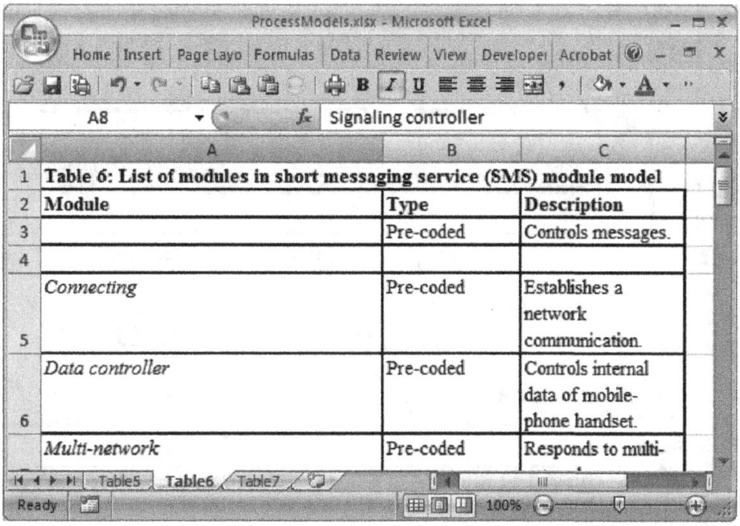

Fig. 9 The modified traced artifact, ProcessModels

location, A3, in the ProcessModels.xlsx Table 6 Worksheet. It shows that the status is blank, indicating that the traceability link has not been changed. Similarly, the module Connecting has a link to another cell location, A4, in the same worksheet. Now suppose the ProcessModels file is modified such that the contents of cell A3 are deleted and a row is inserted between rows 3 and 4. The modified artifact is shown in Fig. 9. These changes result in deleted and moved traceability links.

At some later time, our maintenance engineer can check and update the status of the traceability links. By invoking "Update Links" and "Refresh," the status of Messaging Controller's traceability link to A3 is changed to "deleted." In addition, the status of Connecting's traceability link to A4 is changed to "moved" and the link now points to cell A5 (see Fig. 10).

2.6.2 Technique Behind the Scenes

We maintain traceability links using notification adapters. Notification adapters check whether the traced artifact has been deleted, moved, or revised. Notification adapters run heuristics to determine which of these updates has been performed. For instance, if a traced file is no longer found in the current location, the adapter will run a search for the file within a specified scope, such as within a directory in a file server. If the file is still not found within this scope, the status of the traceability link will be specified as "deleted". If the file is found, the status of the traceability link will be notated as "moved" and the traceability link will be updated to the first found location. On the other hand, if the file is found in the original location, the adapter will run heuristics to determine whether the file has been modified. If so, the status will be updated to "revised". If the file has not been modified, the status

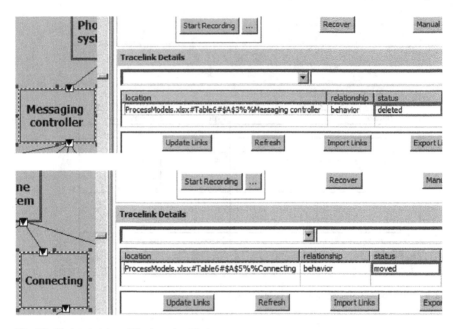

Fig. 10 Updated status of the traced artifacts

is left blank to indicate that no change has occurred. Moreover, since we capture traceability links at different levels of granularity, we use different types of heuristics to determine updates at these different levels. For example, if a traceability link is specified at the slide level in PowerPoint, the search for the slide will only be limited within the context of the PowerPoint file.

In our scenario, the tool was able to find the new location of the traceability link by searching through the file for a cell that contains the string "Connecting". If the content of the cell was not captured, the traceability link would continue to point to the same location, cell A4, since the tool could not determine whether the traceability link had actually moved. In essence, the captured *content* of the cell acts as a traceability link anchor. While this example is quite simplistic, the idea is applicable to other artifacts, such as documents.

When handling updates at the file level, the space in which to search for the file (e.g., local machine, local server, local network) must be specified. Determining if the artifact has changed may also require techniques other than string matching, such as comparing the artifact's previous snapshot with the current version or checking the logs of a configuration management system.

Notification adapters are invoked explicitly by users. When "Update Links" has been invoked, ACTS will go through each traceability link, invoking the appropriate adapters. For example, if the tool encounters a Word document file, it invokes the notification adapter for MS Word. The adapter runs its heuristics and determines the status of the traced artifact.

3 Limitations

To integrate third party tools into the ACTS traceability system, each tool must provide a means for detecting user interactions, in the form of public APIs or built-in history logs. If a tool does not have these capabilities, then the technique cannot capture traceability links to the artifact created by that tool. While this problem exists for some proprietary tools, more tools are now providing open APIs that enable user customization (Eclipse Foundation, 2011; Microsoft Corporation, 2011; Mozilla, 2011). The growing usage of open source tools also indicates that our approach is feasible in many development contexts (Alspaugh et al., 2009).

The current implementation of rules requires an expert technical user who is responsible for creating and modifying rules for other users. This is perhaps not an unreasonable expectation, since current off-the-shelf traceability tools also require a tool administrator (Asuncion et al., 2007). More work is needed to make the rules more accessible to a broader audience.

Scaling the approach to large-scale software development projects is another interesting avenue for future work. The current implementation of rules and notification adapters may incur performance overhead when processing large numbers of user interaction events and traceability links. To address this, more sophisticated rule engines may be used and processing may be scheduled offline.

4 Rationale and Related Work

Manually capturing traceability links is a labor intensive and time consuming task. Without any automated support, capturing traceability links is typically infeasible in practice, especially for large-scale projects. Consequently, various automated approaches have been proposed to minimize human intervention in generating traceability links. Trace recovery techniques (De Lucia et al., 2011; Grechanik et al., 2007; Kagdi et al., 2007; Marcus and Maletic, 2003) often use data mining or machine learning techniques to generate candidate traceability links among an existing set of software artifacts that are textually represented.

Our trace capture technique, in contrast, automatically captures traceability links while a stakeholder interacts with the various artifacts. This technique offers the following features: in situ trace capture, trace capture across heterogeneously represented artifacts, and trace capture across different levels of granularity. Our technique also facilitates traceability link maintenance.

In situ trace capture. Since traceability links are created in the background while users are performing their usual development tasks, effort in trace capture is minimized. One reason important information is often left untraced is the lack of time and resources for capturing traces (Gotel and Finkelstein, 1994); thus, tracing in an online fashion is desirable, but current tool support has been lacking (von Knethen and Paech, 2002). Some trace capture techniques are heavyweight, requiring explicit modeling of the development process (Pohl, 1996) or formal specification of relations between objects (Pinheiro and Goguen, 1996) prior to recording traceability links. Our technique does require some setup overhead, such as creating tool-specific adapters and rules prior to recording traceability links. However, once these adapters and rules are in place, users can continue to work with their usual development tools and follow their development process. The development of adapters and rules are limited to tools and heuristics users choose to employ.

Another set of prospective trace capture techniques are transformation and translation techniques. Transformation techniques, which are often used in model-driven development, generate traceability links based on the transformations of two adjacent models (Richardson and Green, 2004). This technique is limited to tracing between structured or semi-structured artifacts. Translation techniques meanwhile translate heterogeneous artifacts into a homogeneous format (Anderson et al., 2002). Traceability links can then be automatically generated. This technique is also limited to text-based artifacts.

Trace capture across heterogeneous artifacts. Current automated techniques also have difficulties with tracing across large unstructured documents as well as tracing artifacts with different formats (Hayes and Dekhtyar, 2006). Our technique can capture traceability links across heterogeneously represented artifacts with tool-specific recorders, provided that third-party tools have public application programming interfaces to detect user interactions or have history logs.

Trace capture across different levels of granularity. Since the level of granularity of linking varies from one situation to another (Hayes and Dekhtyar, 2007), it is important to flexibly link at different levels of granularity. Existing tools support linking across predefined levels of granularity: between concerns in the architecture and source code (Nistor, 2009) and between tasks and source code (Kersten and Murphy, 2005). Our approach captures traceability links at different levels of granularity, e.g. page level, or element level. Moreover, users can choose the granularity of trace capture by tailoring the recording adapter to only record events at a specified granularity or by creating rules to filter the linked artifacts.

Trace maintenance. Current techniques to maintaining traceability links include using events to notify traced artifacts of changes (Cleland-Huang et al., 2003), analyzing source code commits (Ratanotayanon et al., 2009), and using rules to analyze transformations from one model to another (Mäder et al., 2008). Our approach uses notification adapters, which encapsulates heuristics specific to an artifact type, to determine whether traced artifacts have changed.

5 Conclusion

This chapter presented a set of general automated techniques for linking together heterogeneous software artifacts at various levels of granularity. With our set of techniques, traceability links can be captured in situ and can be effectively maintained over time. Moreover, third party tools can be incorporated into our approach and custom heuristics can be represented as rules, enhancing accessibility and customizability. While several areas of future work remain, such as improving scalability, and incorporating more sophisticated maintenance techniques, our techniques provide a practical step towards effectively managing distributed and heterogeneous information found in many software development projects.

Acknowledgments The authors would like to thank S. Cutler, D. Kwok, C. Leu, A. Marron, J. Meevasin, H. Pham, D. Purpura, and A. Rahnemoon for tool development. This research has been supported by grants from the National Science Foundation IIS-0808783 and CCF-0917129.

References

Alspaugh, T.A., Asuncion, H.U., Scacchi, W.: Intellectual property rights requirements for heterogeneously-licensed systems. In: Proceedings of the International Requirements Engineering Conference (2009)

Anderson, K.M., Sherba, S.A., Lepthien, W.V.: Towards large-scale information integration. In: Proceedings of the International Conference on Software Engineering (2002)

Anderson, K.M., Taylor, R.N., Whitehead, E.J.Jr.: Chimera: Hypermedia for heterogeneous software development environments. ACM Trans. Inf. Syst. **18**(3), 211–245 (2000)

Asuncion, H., François, F., Taylor, R.N.: An end-to-end industrial software traceability tool. In: Proceedings of the Joint Meeting of the European Software Engineering Conference and the SIGSOFT International Symposium on the Foundations of Software Engineering. (2007)

Asuncion, H.U., Asuncion, A.U., Taylor, R.N.: Software traceability with topic modeling. In: Proceedings of the International Conference on Software Engineering (2010)

Asuncion, H.U., Taylor, R.N.: Architecture-Centric Traceability for Stakeholders: Technical Foundations. Technical Report UCI-ISR-11-2, University of California, Irvine, CA (2011)

Cleland-Huang, J., Chang, C.K., Christensen, M.: Event-based traceability for managing evolutionary change. Trans. Softw. Eng. **29**(9), 796–810 (2003)

Dashofy, E.M., Asuncion, H., Hendrickson, S.A., Suryanarayana, G., Georgas, J.C., Taylor, R.N.: ArchStudio 4: An architecture-based meta-modeling environment. In: Proceedings of the International Conference on Software Engineering, volume Informal Research Demonstrations (2007)

De Lucia, A., Di Penta, M., Oliveto, R.: Improving source code lexicon via traceability and information retrieval. Trans. Softw. Eng. **37**(2), 205 –227 (2011)

Eclipse Foundation: Eclipse. http://www.eclipse.org (2011)

Gotel, O., Finkelstein, A.: An analysis of the requirements traceability problem. In: Proceedings of the International Conference on Requirements Engineering (1994)

Grechanik, M., McKinley, K.S., Perry, D.E.: Recovering and using use-case-diagram-to-source-code traceability links. In: Proceedings of the Joint Meeting of the European Software Engineering Conference and the SIGSOFT International Symposium on the Foundations of Software Engineering (2007)

Hayes, J., Dekhtyar, A.: Grand challenges for traceability. Technical Report COET-GCT-06-01-0.9, Center of Excellence for Traceability, http://www.coest.org (2006)

Kagdi, H., Maletic, J.I., Sharif, B.: Mining software repositories for traceability links. In: Proceedings of the International Conference on Program Comprehension (2007)

Kersten, M., Murphy, G.C.: Mylar: A degree-of-interest model for IDEs. In: Proceedings of International Conference on Aspect-oriented Software Development (2005)

Mäder, P., Gotel, O., Philippow, I.: Rule-based maintenance of post-requirements traceability relations. In: Proceedings of the International Requirements Engineering Conference (2008)

Marcus, A., Maletic, J.I.: Recovering documentation-to-source-code traceability links using latent semantic indexing. In: Proceedings of the International Conference on Software Engineering (2003)

Microsoft Corporation: Microsoft Office. http://office.microsoft.com (2011)

Mozilla: Firefox. http://www.mozilla.com/en-US/firefox/ (2011)

Nistor, E.: Concern-driven software evolution. Ph.D. Thesis. (Info & Computer Science), UC, Irvine (2009)

Pinheiro, F.A.C., Goguen, J.A.: An object-oriented tool for tracing requirements. Software **13**(2), 52–64 (1996)

Pohl, K.: PRO-ART: Enabling requirements pre-traceability. In: Proceedings of the International Conference on Requirements Engineering (1996)

Ramesh, B., Powers, T., Stubbs, C., Edwards, M.: Implementing requirements traceability: A case study. In: Proceedings of the International Symposium on Requirements Engineering (1995)

Ratanotayanon, S., Sim, S.E., Raycraft, D.J.: Cross-artifact traceability using lightweight links. In: Proceedings of the Workshop on Traceability in Emerging Forms of Software Engineering (2009)

Richardson, J., Green, J.: Automating traceability for generated software artifacts. In: Proceedings of the International Conference on Automated Software Engineering (2004)

Singer, J., Elves, R., Storey, M.-A.: NavTracks: Supporting navigation in software maintenance. In: Proceedings of the International Conference on Software Maintenance (2005)

Spanoudakis, G., Zisman, A., Pérez-Miñana, E., and Krause, P.: Rule-based generation of requirements traceability relations. J. Syst. Softw. **72**(2), 105–27 (2004)

von Knethen, A., Paech, B.: A survey on tracing approaches in practice and research. Technical Report IESE-Report Nr. 095.01/E, Fraunhofer Institut Experimentelles Software Engineering, Fraunhofer Gesellschaft (2002)

Using Rules for Traceability Creation

Andrea Zisman

1 Introduction

Several approaches have been proposed to support traceability creation. These approaches can be classified as manual (DOORS; Kaindl, 1992; Rational Rose, 2010; RTM), semi-automatic or fully-automatic (Antoniol et al., 2002; Cleland-Huang et al., 2002, 2005; Egyed and Grünbacher, 2002; Egyed, 2003; Marcus et al., 2005; Pohl, 1996b; Pinheiro, 2000; Ramesh and Dhar, 1992; RTM) approaches. One group of approaches advocates the use of rules to support automatic creation of trace relationships between artifacts generated during the development life cycle of software systems. We call these approaches as *rule-based traceability approaches.*

The main motivation for the rule-based traceability approaches is to support automatic traceability creation in various types of documents generated during different phases of the software development life cycle. Manual establishment of traceability is error-prone, difficult, time-consuming, expensive, and complex. Moreover, existing manual approaches are limited on expressiveness given the fact that the relationships are mainly hyperlinks without semantic meanings. Other motivations are concerned with (a) the need to support creation of different types of trace relationships with semantic meanings instead of plain hyperlinks; and (b) the existence of large number of heterogeneous artifacts representing different aspects of a software system, specified with different levels of abstraction and granularity, produced by different stakeholders, and created independently by non-interoperable tools.

In this chapter, we describe a summary of the rule-based traceability creation framework. The framework has been used in three different contexts: object-oriented software systems (Spanoudakis et al., 2004), product line systems (Jirapanthong and Zisman, 2005, 2007), and multi-agent systems (Cysneiros and Zisman 2004, 2007a, 2007b, 2008). The framework assumes the documents represented in XML and different types of trace relationships. The trace relationships are identified based on pre-defined traceability rules expressed in XQuery (2010). The

A. Zisman (✉)

School of Informatics, City University London, London, EC1V 0HB, UK

e-mail: a.zisman@soi.city.ac.uk

J. Cleland-Huang et al. (eds.), *Software and Systems Traceability,*   147

DOI 10.1007/978-1-4471-2239-5_7, © Springer-Verlag London Limited 2012

traceability rules are created based on different aspects, namely (a) the semantic of artifacts being traced, (b) the types of trace relationships concerned with the artifacts, (c) the grammatical roles of words in textual artifacts, and (d) synonyms and other associations of the words in the textual artifacts. We have developed prototype tools to demonstrate the framework. The framework was evaluated in terms of recall and precision measures in various case studies.

The remaining of this chapter is structured as follows. In Section 2 we describe the rule-based traceability creation framework using object-oriented and product line system contexts. In Section 3 we discuss the application of the framework for multi-agent systems. In Section 4 we discuss implementation aspects and results of the evaluation of the framework. Finally, in Section 5 we discuss directions for future work.

2 Rule-Based Traceability Framework

We propose a rule-base traceability framework to support automatic creation of trace relationships and identification of missing elements in heterogeneous software documents created during the development life cycle of software systems. The generated trace relationships have different semantics depending on the types of related artifacts (source and target). In order to support the heterogeneity of documents and various tools that may be used during the software development life cycle, we assume documents represented in XML format.

The framework uses an extended version of XQuery (2010) to represent traceability rules. XQuery is an XML-based query language that has been widely used for manipulating, retrieving, and interpreting information from XML documents. Apart from the embedded functions offered by XQuery, it is possible to add new functions and commands. We have extended XQuery to support representation of the consequence part of the rules, i.e, the actions to be taken when the conditions are satisfied; and to support extra functions to cover some of the trace relationship types and identification of missing elements in the artifacts.

The framework also uses part-of-speech assignments to specify grammatical roles of textual parts of the artifacts to be traced. The textual sentences in the XML documents are annotated with part-of-speech assignments by using general-purpose grammatical taggers like CLAWS (2010).

Figure 1 presents an overview of the architecture of our rule-base traceability framework. As shown in the figure, the framework has three main components: *Grammatical Tagger*, *Document Translator*, and *Traceability Engine*.

The *Grammatical Tagger* is responsible for annotating textual sentences in software artifacts with part-of-speech (POS) assignments by using a general-purpose grammatical tagger. It is important to consider the grammatical roles of the words in the textual parts of the artifacts because of the names given by software engineers for the main elements in certain artifacts. For example, it is a common approach to avoid the use of articles, co-ordinating and subordinating conjunctions,

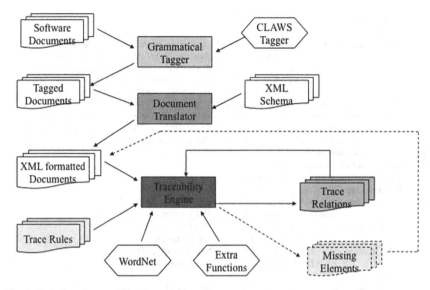

Fig. 1 Rule-based traceability framework architecture

or comparative and superlative adjectives, for the main elements in class, sequence, and statechart diagrams. Therefore, these part-of-speech elements are not considered when trying to relate a requirement statement with a class that represents the requirements.

The *Document Translator* is responsible for generating the documents in XML format based on XML schemas for the specific types of documents and the POS tags generated by CLAWS tagger. The generated POS tags are converted into XML POS-tags. In order to illustrate, consider Fig. 2 with part of the Feature Model of the mobile phone case study in XML format with POS-tags. As shown in the figure, the name of the feature *Text Message* is composed of two nouns represented by POS-tags <NN1> and <NN2>. The description text of the feature is also composed of articles (<ATTO>), nouns (<NN1>, <NN2>), verbs in different tenses (<VVI> <VMO>), adjectives (<AJO>), punctuation marks (<SC>), and conjunctions (<CJC>).

The *Traceability Engine* is responsible for (a) creating trace relationships between the artifacts, and (b) identifying missing elements in the documents based on traceability rules. It uses WordNet (2010) to support the identification of synonyms between the names of artifacts, and extra functions to support the traceability rules. As shown in Fig. 1, the created trace relationships are also used by the *Traceability Engine* to generate other trace relationships; i.e., the trace relationships that depend on the existence of other relationships. Information about identified missing elements is used to amend the documents and new versions of the documents can be used to support creation of trace relationships involving the added elements.

```
<Feature_Model>
<Feature>
<Feature_name> <NN1> Text </NN1> <NN2> Messages </NN2> </Feature_name>
  <Description>  <AT0> The </AT0> <NN1> phone </NN1> <VM0> can </VM0>
                 <VVI> edit </VVI> <SC>,</SC> <VVI> send </VVI> <SC>,</SC>
                 <CJC> and </CJC> <VVI> receive </VVI> <AT0> a </AT0>
                 <AJ0> short </AJ0> <NN1> text </NN1> <NN1> message </NN1>
                 <SC>.</SC> </Description>
  <Issue_and_decision> <NN1> Text </NN1> <NN1> message </NN1> <II> over </II>
                 <JJ> mobile </JJ> <NN1> phone </NN1> <VBZ> is </VBZ> <AT1> a</AT1>
                 <NN1> way </NN1> <IO> of </IO> <NN1> communication </NN1>
  </Issue_and_decision>
  <Type>Application capability</Type>
  <Existential>Mandatory</Existential>
  <Relationship Type="composed_of">
    <Rel_feature> <VVG> Sending </VVG> <NN1> Text </NN1>
                  <NN2> Messages </NN2> </Rel_feature>
    <Rel_feature> <VVG> Receiving </VVG> <NN1> Text </NN1>
                  <NN2> Messages </NN2> </Rel_feature>
    <Rel_feature> <VVG> Editing </VVG> <NN1> Text </NN1>
                  <NN2> Messages </NN2> </Rel_feature>
    </Relationship>
    <Allocated_to_subsystem><NN1> Messaging </NN1>
    </Allocated_to_subsystem>
</Feature> ... </Feature_Model>
```

Fig. 2 Extract of feature model in XML format with POS-Tags

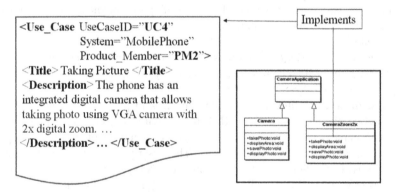

Fig. 3 Example of trace relationship

As an example consider the mobile phone case study with a use case UC4: *Taking Picture* and a class diagram with class *CameraZoom2X* with operation *takePhoto()*, as shown in Fig. 3. A trace relationship of type *implements* is created between use case UC4 and operation takePhoto() because the operation allows for the execution of the use case. In this situation, a traceability rule stating that words that appear in the description of a use case and match the names (or their synonyms) of an operation and the class containing the operation, would cause a relationship of type implements to be created between the use case and the operation.

2.1 Traceability Information Model

The rule-based traceability framework supports traceability creation between different types of software artifacts and different types of trace relationships. The different types of trace relationships were identified based on our study and experience with software traceability (Spanoudakis and Zisman, 2003), the types of trace relationships proposed in the literature (Bayer and Widen 2002; Marcus et al., 2005; Pohl, 1996a; Ramesh and Jarke, 2001), and the semantics of the documents and their artifacts in various contexts.

In the context of object-oriented systems, the rule-based traceability framework supports trace creation for (a) requirements artifacts including requirements statement documents and use case documents, and (b) analysis object models. The types of trace relationships identified for the above artifacts are *overlaps, requires_execution_of, requires_ feature_in,* and *can_partially_realise* relationships. Table 1 shows a summary of the Traceability Information Model (TIM) for object-oriented systems supported by the framework, and Table 2 describes the meaning of each of the relationship types in an informal way. A more detailed definition of the relationship types can be found in (Spanoudakis et al., 2004). In Table 1, the cells contain the different types of relationships between the artifacts represented in the row and column of that cell. The direction of the relationship is represented from a column *[i]* to a row *[j]*. Thus, a relationship type *rel_type* in a cell *[i][j]* signifies that "*[i] is related to [j] though rel_type*".

As an example of a *Requires_execution_of* relationship consider the mobile phone case study. This relationship holds between the sequence of terms "function for taking a photo" in the pre-condition of use case UC4: *Taking a Picture* and the operation *takePhoto()* in class *Camera* in the case study.

For the development of product line systems, the framework assumes a feature-based object-oriented engineering and uses an extension of the FORM (Feature-Oriented Reuse Method) methology (Kang et al., 1998), due to its simplicity, maturity, practicality, and extensibility characteristics. More specifically, the framework

Table 1 TIM for object-oriented systems

	Requirement	Use case
Requirements	Requires_feature_in	Requires_feature_in Can_partially_realise
Use case	Overlaps Requires_feature_in	–
Class	Overlaps	Overlaps
Attribute	Overlaps	Overlaps
Association	Overlaps	Overlaps
Association End	Overlaps	Overlaps
Operation	Requires_execution_of	Requires_execution_of

Table 2 Types of trace relationships for object-oriented systems

Relationship type	Description
Requires_feature_in	It denotes that parts of use cases cannot be realized without the existence of requirement statements, or that requirement statements refer to other requirement statements
Requires_execution_of	It denotes that sequence of terms requires the execution of associated operations
Overlaps	It denotes that connected elements refer to common features of the system or its domain
Can_partially_realise	It denotes that the execution of use cases can realise part of requirement statements

uses artifacts generated by the FORM methodology such as feature, subsystem, process, and module models for the product line level; and object-oriented artifacts such as use case specifications, class, statechart, and sequence diagrams for the product members, as defined in the chapter of the mobile phone product line case study.

The framework supports nine different types of trace relationships, namely *satisfiability, dependency, overlaps, evolution, implements, refinement, containment, similar*, and *different*. Table 3 presents a summary of the Traceability Information Model for product line systems and Table 4 summarises the meaning of the different types of trace relationships. A more formal definition for the relationship types can be found in (Jirapanthong and Zisman, 2007; Lamb et al., 2011).

In Table 3, the cells contain the different types of trace relationships that may exist between the documents described in the row and column of that cell. In the table, we do not represent the exact artifacts that are related in the different documents, but instead we represent the types of the documents. The direction of the relationships is represented from a row *[i]* to a column *[j]*. Thus, a relationship type *rel_type* in a cell *[i][j]* signifies that "*[i] is related to [j] though rel_type*" (e.g. "subsystem model *satisfies* feature model"). The trace relationships that are bidirectional appear in two correspondent cells for that relationship (e.g., "subsystem model overlaps feature model" and "feature model overlaps subsystem model").

As an example of a *similar* relationship type, consider the mobile phone case study. As shown in Fig. 4, a similar relationship holds between use case UC4: *Sending Message* and use case UC2: *Transmitting Messages*, given that both use cases hold a *containment* relationship with feature *Text Messages*. A containment relationship is created between use case UC1 and the feature by a rule since a synonym (send) of verb <VVG> Sending </VVG> and noun <NN1> Message </NN1> appear in the description of the feature in the same sentence; i.e., a sequence of a conjunction of verbs (<VVI> send </VVI> <SC>,</SC>, <CJC>and</CJC>, <VVI> receive</VVI>), followed by a qualifier of the noun *message* (<AT0> a</AT0> <AJ0>short</AJ0> <NN1> text </NN1>), separate the words *send* and *message*. Similarly, a *containment* relationship also exists between use case UC2 and the feature.

Table 3 TIM for product line systems

	Feature model	Subsystem model	Process model	Module model
Feature model		*Overlaps*	*Overlaps*	*Overlaps*
Subsystem model	*Satisfies* *Depends_on* *Refines* *Overlaps*			
Process model	*Satisfies* *Depends_on* *Refines* *Overlaps*	*Refines*		
Module model	*Satisfies* *Depends_on* *Refines* *Overlaps*		*Refines*	
Use case	*Contains* *Depends_on*			
Class diagram	*Satisfies* *Depends_on* *Overlaps* *Implements*	*Refines* *Depends_on*	*Refines* *Depends_on*	*Refines* *Depends_on*
Statechart diagram	*Satisfies* *Depends_on* *Overlaps* *Implements*		*Refines* *Depends_on*	*Refines* *Depends_on*
Sequence diagram	*Satisfies* *Depends_on* *Overlaps* *Implements*		*Refines* *Depends_on*	*Refines* *Depends_on*

	Use case	Class diagram	Statechart diagram	Sequence diagram
Feature model		*Overlaps*	*Overlaps*	*Overlaps*
Subsystem model		*Contains*		
Process model		*Contains*	*Contains*	*Contains*
Module model		*Contains*		
Use case	*Similar* *Different* *Evolves*	*Overlaps*	*Overlaps*	*Overlaps*
Class diagram	*Satisfies* *Depends_on* *Overlaps* *Implements* *Refines*	*Similar* *Different* *Evolves*	*Overlaps*	*Overlaps*
Statechart diagram	*Satisfies* *Depends_on* *Overlaps* *Implements* *Refines*	*Depends_on* *Overlaps* *Contains*	*Similar* *Different* *Evolves*	*Overlaps* *Refines*
Sequence diagram	*Satisfies* *Depends_on* *Overlaps* *Implements* *Refines*	*Depends_on* *Overlaps* *Refines* *Contains*	*Overlaps*	*Similar* *Different* *Evolves*

Table 4 Types of trace relationships for product line systems

Relationship type	Description
Satisfiability	An element e1 *satisfies* an element e2 if e1 meets the expectation and needs of e2
Dependency	An element e1 *depends on* an element e2 if the existence of e1 *relies on* the existence of e2, or if changes in e2 have to be reflected in e1
Overlaps	An element e1 *overlaps* with an element e2 (and an element e2 *overlaps* with an element e1) if e1 and e2 refer to common aspects of a system or its domain
Evolution	An element e1 *evolves to* an element e2 if e1 has been replaced by e2 during the development, maintenance, or evolution of the system
Implements	An element e1 *implements* an element e2 if e1 *executes* or *allows* for the achievement of e2
Refinement	An element e1 *refines* an element e2 when e1 specifies more details about e2
Containment	An element e1 *contains* an element e2 when e1 is a document, or an element in a document, that uses an element e2, or a set of elements from a different document
Similar	A *similar* relationship between elements e1 and e2 depends on the existence of a relationship between e1 and another element e3 and a relation between e2 and element e3. For example, a use case uc1 is *similar* to a use case uc2 if both uc1 and uc2 hold a *containment* relationship with a feature f1
Different	A *different* relationship between an element e1 and e2 depends on the existence of a relationship between e1 and another element e3, and a relationship between e2 and another element e4, where e3 and e4 are variants of the same variability point (e.g. subclasses of the same superclass, sibling features of the same parent feature). For example, a use case uc1 is *different* from a use case uc2 when there are two subclasses c1 and c2 of the same parent class c, where c1 *implements* uc1 and c2 *implements* uc2

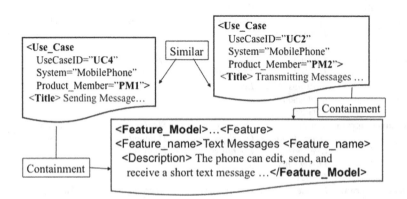

Fig. 4 Example of a similar relationship

2.2 Traceability Rules and Traceability Creation Process

The trace relationship types can be automatically created by the framework based on the use of traceability rules. In general, rules assist and automate decision making, allow for standard ways of representing knowledge that can be used to infer data, facilitate the construction of traceability creators for large data sets, and support representation of dependencies between elements in the documents. In addition, the use of rules allows for the creation of new relationships based on the existence of other relationships, supports the heterogeneity of artifacts being compared, and supports data inference in similar applications.

In the framework, the rules take into consideration several aspects:

(a) The semantics of the artifacts being compared: for example, in the case of feature and use cases, it may be necessary to traverse a feature hierarchy to identify the specific feature.
(b) The various types of trace relationships: for example, evolution relationships exist for artifacts in documents of the same type for the same product member in the case of product line systems.
(c) The grammatical roles of the words in the textual parts of the artifacts: for example the lack of articles, conjunctions, and adjectives in certain artifacts.
(d) Synonyms and distance of words in a text: for example, the existence of two or more words in a paragraph does not imply that the text in the paragraph is concerned with these words, in particular if the words appear in different sentences in the paragraph.

The traceability rules can be *direct*, when they support the generation of trace relationships that do not depend on the existence of other relationships; or *indirect*, when they support the generation of trace relationships that depend on the existence of other relationships. Examples of direct relationships for product line systems are *satisfiability, dependency, overlaps, evolution, implements, refinement,* and *containment*; and examples of indirect relationships for product line systems are *similar* and *different*.

Figure 5 shows a general template for direct and indirect traceability rules for product line systems. In the template in Fig. 5, elements between square brackets ("[" ,"]") are optional, and fi(fi+1...(fi+j(•))...) are embedded XQuery functions or extra functions that we have developed. The rules are composed of three parts as described below.

RULE_IDENTICATION: It is concerned with the identification of the rule and the documents to be compared by the rule. It contains a unique RuleID, a description of the type of the rule (RuleType), and descriptions of the types of documents associated with the rule (DocType1, DocType2). The rule type is the same as the type of the trace relationship to be generated by the rule.

QUERY: It is concerned with the conditions of the rule. It is represented by element <Query> and consists of XQuery statements. It is composed of three other subparts,

```
TRACE_RULE RuleID  = R_ID
      RuleType = R_Type
      DocType1 = DocTypeName
      DocType2 = DocTypeName
  QUERY
  [DECLARE Namespace]
  [DECLARE Function]
  [DECLARE Variable]
  for $variable_name1 in doc(DocType1Placeholder)//XPathExpression
      $variable_name2 in doc(DocType1Placeholder)//XPathExpression
  where fi(fi+1…(fi+j(.))…)
  QUERY_END
  ACTION
    RELATION RuleID  = R_ID
          RelType = R_Type
          DocType1 = DocTypeName
          DocType2 = DocTypeName
    ELEMENT Document = DocName [ElementType1]$variable_name1
              [/XpathExpression] [ElementType2]
    ELEMENT Document = DocName [ElementType1]$variable_name2
              [/XpathExpression] [ElementType2]
    [RelationType {XpathExpression}{XpathExpression}]
    [RelationType {XpathExpression}{XpathExpression}]
  ACTION_END
  TRACE_RULE_END
```

Fig. 5 Template for traceability rules

namely: (i) *declare*, which is optional and contains declarations of namespaces, variables, or extra functions used by the rule; (ii) *for*, which identifies elements of the documents (*DocType1* and *DocType2*) to be compared and binds these elements to variables; and (iii) *where*, which describes the *condition* part of the rule that should be satisfied in order to create a trace relationship. The condition part can use a sequence, conjunction, or disjunction of XQuery in-built functions (e.g., *some*, *contains*, *satisfies*), or of the extra XQuery or Java functions that we have implemented. Depending on the rule, the condition part also takes into consideration the XML POS-tags in the textual parts of the documents.

ACTION: This part describes the *consequence* of the rule and is represented by element (<Action>). It specifies the action(s) to be taken if the conditions in the QUERY part are satisfied. The consequence part describes the type of trace relationship to be created (attribute Type) and the elements that should be related through it in the documents described in the *for-part* of the rule (element <Element>). The content of element <Action> is used to compose the return part of XQuery. The implementation of an action consists of writing the information in the <Action> part in a separated document in XML format.

An example of a traceability rule for a *containment* trace relationship between use cases and feature models is shown in Fig. 6. As shown in Fig. 6, the rule verifies if the words, or their set of synonyms, in the title of a use case appear in the same sentence in the description of a feature, by using the function *checkDistanceControl*. The *checkDistanceControl* function identifies if two words are associated in a

```
<TraceRule RuleID="R1" RuleType="containment"
        DocType1="Use Case" DocType2="Feature Model">
<Query>
  declare namespace s="java:synonym.s";
  declare namespace d="java:distanceControl.d";
  for $item1 in doc("file:///c:/UseCase_UC1.xml")//Use_Case,
    $item2 in doc("file:///c:/Feature_MP.xml")//Feature_Model/Feature
  where
  d:checkDistanceControl($item2/Description,
    s:setof(s:findSynonym($item1/Title/VVI),
        s:findSynonym($item1/title/VVB),
        s:findSynonym($item1/Title/VV0),
        s:findSynonym($item1/Title/VVG)),
    s:setof(s:findSynonym($item1/Title/NN0),
        s:findSynonym($item1/Title/NN1),
        s:findSynonym($item1/Title/NP0),
        s:findSynonym($item1/Title/NN2)))</Query>
<Action>
  <Relation RuleID="R1" RelType="containment"
        DocType1="Use Case" DocType2="Feature Model">
    <Element Document="file:///c:/UseCase_UC1.xml"{$item1/Title}
    </Element>
    <Element Document="file:///c:/Feature_MP.xml">{$item2/Feature_name}
        <Description/> </Element>
  </Relation> </Action>
</TraceRule>
```

Fig. 6 Example of a containment traceability rule

```
<TraceRule RulID="R2" RuleType="similar"
        DocType1="XML-Based-Rel" DocType2="XML-Based-Rel">
<Query>
  for $item1 in doc("file:///c:/Direct_TraceRel.xml")//
        Relation[@type="containment"],
    $item2 in doc("file:///c:/Direct_TraceRel.xml")//
        Relation[@type="containment"]
  where
    $item1/@DocType1="Use Case" and $item1/@DocType2="Feature Model"
  and $item2/@DocType1="Use Case" and $item2/@DocType2="Feature Model"
  and string($item1/Element[2]) = string($item2/Element[2])
  and $item1/Element[1]/@Document != $item2/Element[1]/@Document
  </Query>
<Action>
  <Relation RuleID="R2" RelType = "similar"
    <Element>{$item1/Element[1]/@Document} {$item1/Element[1]/Title}
    </Element>
    <Element>{$item2/Element[1]/@Document} {$item2/Element[1]/Title}
    </Element>
    <Containment>{$item1/Element[2]/@Document}
            {$item1/Element[2]/Feature_name} </Containment>
  </Relation> </Action>
</TraceRule>
```

Fig. 7 Example of similar traceability rule

```
<Relation_Document>
 <Relation RuleID="R1" Type ="containment"
        DocType1 ="Use Case" DocType2 ="Feature Model">
  <Element Document="file:///c:/UseCase_UC1.xml">
        <Title> <VVG>Sending</VVG> <NN1>Message</NN1> </Title>
  </Element>
  <Element Document="file:///c:/Feature_MP.xml">
        <Feature_name> <NN1>Text</NN1> <NN2>Messages</NN2>
        </Feature_name> /Element> </Relation>
 <Relation RuleID="R1" Type ="containment"
        DocType1 ="Use Case" DocType2 ="Feature Model">
  <Element Document="file:///c:/UseCase_UC2.xml">
        <Title> <VVG>Transmitting</VVG> <NN2>Messages</NN2> </Title>
  </Element>
  <Element Document="file:///c:/Feature_MP.xml">
        <Feature_name> <NN1>Text</NN1> <NN2>Messages</NN2>
        </Feature_name> </Element> </Relation>
 <Relation RuleID = "R2" Type ="similar">
  <Element Document="file:///c:/UseCase_UC1.xml">
        <Title> <VVG>Sending</VVG> <NN1>Message</NN1> </Title>
  </Element>
  <Element Document="file:///c:/UseCase_UC2.xml">
        <Title> <VVG>Transmitting</VVG> <N N2>Messages</NN2> </Title>
  </Element>
  <Containment Document="file:///c:/Feature_MP.xml">
   <Feature_name><NN1>Text</NN1><NN2>Messages</NN2>
   </Feature_name> ... </Relation> ...
 <Relation_Document>
```

Fig. 8 Example of results for traceability rule

textual paragraph, depending on how distant the words are in a sentence. The rule checks for synonyms by using WordNet (2010). It also checks for any possible form of the main verb and the noun of the verb-phrase in the title of a user case.

An example of a traceability rule for a *similar* trace relationship is shown in Fig. 7. In this case, the rule verifies if there are two relationships of type *containment* in the results document between a use case and a feature model such that the feature names are the same and the use cases are different. The elements representing feature names and use cases are identified by using XPath (2010) expressions. The rules in Figs. 6 and 7 exist for the use case and feature model shown in Fig. 4. The results of these traceability rules is shown in Fig. 8.

3 Multi-Agent Systems

The rule-based traceability framework has also been used in the context of multi-agent systems to support the creation of trace relationships and identification of missing elements in documents generated during the development life cycle of these systems. In this context, the framework concentrates on documents generated when using Prometheus methodology (Padgham and Winikoff, 2004), goals and business models represented in i* (Yu, 1995), and code specified in JACK (Winikoff, 2005).

The Prometheus methodology provides several diagrams and descriptors to represent the design of multi-agent systems such as goal diagram, role diagram, use cases, system overview diagram, agent overview diagram, capability diagram, process diagram, and protocol diagram. The rationale for using the Prometheus methodology is due to its large acceptance in both academia and industrial settings and its support for the majority of the phases in the software engineering development life cycle. The rationale for using i* is to complement Prometheus methodology and to provide support for early requirements phase. The use of JACK is also due to its large acceptance in industrial settings and the fact that it includes all components of Java programming language.

The framework supports seven different types of trace relationships for multi-agent systems, namely *overlaps, contribution, dependency, usability, satisfiability, creation*, and *composition*. Tables 5 and 6 present a summary of the traceability information model for multi-agent systems, while Table 7 summarises the meaning of the different types of trace relationships. In Tables 5 and 6, the cells contain the trace relationship types that may exist between the artifacts. The direction of a relationship is represented from a row *[i]* to a column *[j]*. Some of these relationship types are common for product line systems.

Table 5   TIM for multi-agent systems

i*\Prometheus	SD goal	SD resources	SD tasks	Actor
Goal	Overlaps	–	Overlaps	Depends
Role	Contributes	Uses	Contributes	Contributes
Agent	Satisfies	Uses	Satisfies	Contributes
Capability	Contributes	Uses	Contributes	Contributes
Plan	Contributes	Uses	Contributes	Creates
Percept	–	Overlaps	–	–
Data	Contributes	–	Contributes	Contributes
Scenario	Depends	Composes	Depends	Depends

i*\Prometheus	SD goal	SD resources	SD tasks
Goal	Overlaps	–	Overlaps
Role	Satisfies	Uses	Overlaps
		Creates	Satisfies
Agent	Satisfies	Uses	Satisfies
		Creates	
Capability	Satisfies	Uses	Satisfies
		Creates	
Plan	Satisfies	Uses	Overlaps
		Creates	
Action	–	–	Overlaps
Data	Uses	Overlaps	Uses
Scenario	Composes	Uses	Composes
		Creates	

Table 6 TIM for multi-agent systems

Jack\ Prometheus	Method	Agent	Plan	Belief Set	Capability	BDI goal event	BDI MSG event
Goal	Contributes	Satisfies	Satisfies	Uses Creates	Satisfies	Overlaps	–
Role	Contributes	Uses	Uses	Uses	Contributes	Satisfies	–
Agent	Contributes	Overlaps	Uses	Uses	Uses	Satisfies	Uses Creates
Capability	Contributes	Uses	Uses	Uses	Overlaps	Satisfies	Uses Creates
Plan	Depends	Uses	Overlaps	Uses	Uses	Satisfies	–
Percept	Depends	Uses	Uses	–	Uses	Depends	–
Action	Overlaps	Creates	Creates	–	Uses	–	–
Message	–	Uses Creates	Uses Creates	Uses	–	–	Overlaps
Data	–	Uses Creates	Uses Creates	Overlaps	Uses	–	Uses

Table 7 Types of trace relationships for agent-oriented systems

Relationship type	Description
Overlaps	An element e1 *overlaps* with an element e2 (and an element e2 *overlaps* with an element e1) if e1 and e2 refer to common aspects of a system or its domain
Contribution	An element e1 *contributes to* an element e2 if e1 assists with the achievement or accomplishment of another element e2
Dependency	An element e1 *depends on* an element e2 if the existence of e1 relies on the existence of and e2, or if changes in e2 have to be reflected in e1
Usability	An element e1 *uses* an element e2 if e1 requires the existence of e2 in order to achieve its objectives
Satisfiability	An element e1 *satisfies* an element e2 if e1 meets the expectation and needs of e2
Creation	An element e1 *creates* an element e2 if e1 generates element e2
Composition	An element e1 *is composed of* an element e2 if e1 is a complex element formed by element e2

As an example of a *satisfiability* relationship, consider an electronic BookStore multi-agent system, which supports the main tasks of buying and delivering books. Figure 9 shows part of the i* SR model and Prometheus role diagram for the electronic BookStore system. As shown in Fig. 9, a *satisfiability* relationship holds between a task in the i* SR model (Organise Delivery) and a role in the Prometheus role diagram (Delivery Handling). This relationship exists because there is an *overlaps* relationship between task Organise Delivery in the SR model and goal Arrange delivery associated with the role.

A general template for traceability rules for multi-agent systems in shown in Fig. 10. In this case, the template is different from the one for traceability rules

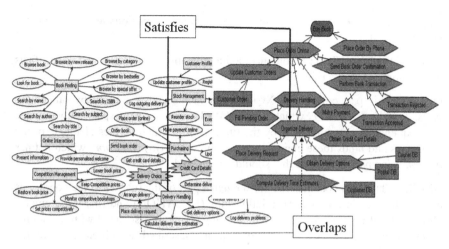

Fig. 9 Example of a satisfiability relationship

```
TRACE_RULE RuleID   = R_ID
     RuleType  = R_Type
     ETypeA    = ElementTypeName
     ETypeB    = ElementTypeName
QUERY
[DECLARE Namespace][DECLARE Documents][DECLARE Sequences]
for $elem_a in $seq_a ... $elem_n in $seq_n
 CONDITION fi(fi+1...(fi+j(.))...)
 ACTION
  RELATION RuleID  = R_ID
       RelType   = Relation_Type
       DegreeOfCompleteness = DegreeOfCompleteness
  [ELEMENT Document = DocumentPath
       ElemType = ElementType
       ElemName = ElementName
       ElemID   = ElementID
   MISSING ELEMENT
       DocSource   = DocumentPath
       TypeSource  = ElementType
       NameSource  = ElementName
       IDSource    = ElementID
       TypeTarget  = ElementType
    [MISSING ELEMENT ...]
   ACTION_END
QUERY_END
TRACE_RULE_END
```

Fig. 10 Template for multi-agent traceability rules

for product line systems (see Section 2.2) in order to provide support not only to the identification of trace relationships, but also to the identification of missing elements in the documents being compared. As in the case of product line systems, in the template in Fig. 10, elements between square brackets ("[", "]") are optional, and

$f_i \left(f_{i+1} \ldots \left(f_{i+j} \left(\bullet \right) \right) \ldots \right)$ represents a composition of functions and if statements used in the rules.

RULE_IDENTICATION: It contains the identification of the rules and the artifacts to be compared by the rule.

QUERY: This part consists of XQuery statements and is formed by other sub-parts, namely: (i) *declare*, which contains declarations of namespaces, documents, and sequence of elements used by the rule; (ii) *for*, which iterates elements of the sequences and binds these elements to variables; and (iii) *condition*, which defines the *condition* part of the rule that should be satisfied.

ACTION: This part specifies the *consequence* part of the rule when the conditions are satisfied. It describes trace relationships (RELATION) and missing elements (MISSING ELEMENTS), if any. The missing elements associated with the source or target elements in a trace relationship are described as sub-elements of the respective element.

An example of a traceability rule for *overlaps* relationships between SR tasks in i* and goals in Prometheus, and for identifying missing SR tasks and goals elements is shown in Fig. 11. In this example, a nested if-statement is used in the condition part. The more external if-expression checks if the name of the task in the SR model

```
<TraceRule      RuleID="R3"      RuleType="overlaps"      ETypeA="SRTask"
ETypeB="Goal">
<Query> <![CDATA[
  declare namespace sin="java:synonymous";
  declare namespace cc="java:completenesschecking";...
  let $istarDoc:=doc("file://C:/users//ElectronicBookStore.tropos")
  let $prometheusDoc:=doc("file://C:/workspace/ElectronicBookshop.pd") ...
    for $SRTask in $SRTasks, $prometheusGoal in $prometheusGoals
    return
      if(syn:isSynonym($SRTask/@name,$prometheusGoal/base/field
      [@name='name']/text())) then
          if (sim:clr() and sim:isPositiveSimilar(sim:getPrometheusSubEl
          ($prometheusGoal,"subGoals"), sim:getSubGoalsAndTask
          ($SRTask), 50.0,"elemB")) then
            <Trace Relationship ruleID="R3" type="overlaps"
          degreeOfCompleteness="{cc:getDegreeOfCompletenessB()}">
              <Element doc="c:/users/by916/ElectronicBookshop.tropos"
            type="SRTask" name="{ $SRTask/@name}"
            id="{$SRTask/@xmi:id}"> {
              for $i in (0 to cc:getNumberOfMissingElementsA())
                    return <MissingElement
                    typeSource="{cc:getTypeOfMissingElementA($i)}"
                    idSource="{cc:getIDMissingElementA($i)}"
                    nameSource="{cc:getNameMissingElementA($i)}"
                    docSource="{cc:getDocSourceMissingElementA($i)}"
typeTarget="{cc:getTypeTargetMissingElementA($i)}"
                    docTarget="{cc:getDocTargetMissingElementA($i)}">
              </MissingElement> } </Element>...</TraceRelationship>else ....]]>
</Query> </TraceRule>
```

Fig. 11 Example on an overlaps traceability rule

is a synonym of the name of the goal in Prometheus (function *isSynonym*). If the condition is satisfied, the next internal if-statement checks if a goal G in Prometheus is *similar* to a task T in i*. Here, the notion of *similar* is given by the situation in which the number of the names of sub-tasks of T and sub-goals of G are greater than a certain threshold. For this case, we assume a threshold of 50%. As shown in Fig. 11, this is verified by function *isPositiveSimilar*. In this case, an overlaps relationship will be created for G and T.

In the case were the names of G and T are not synonyms, although the elements refer to common aspects of the system, the trace relationship can be used by the designer to indicate this situation so that the designer may decide to change the names of these elements to more consistent names.

The result of executing the traceability rule in Fig. 11 for the artifacts in Fig. 9 is shown in Fig. 13. In this case, an overlaps trace relationship is created between elements "Organise Delivery" and "Arrange Delivery" with a degree of completeness of 66.7%. The degree of completeness is identified by function *getDegreeofCompletenessB* in Fig. 11. In this example, the degree of completeness is 66.7% since "Arrange Delivery" has three sub-goals (i.e., Get delivery options, Log outgoing delivery and Calculate delivery), while "Organise Delivery" has two sub-tasks (i.e., Delivery Options and Compute Delivery Time Estimates) and these sub-tasks are related to two of the three sub-goals of "Arrange Delivery" (i.e., Get delivery options and Calculate delivery, respectively), as shown in Fig. 12. A sub-task concerned with sub-goal Log Outgoing Delivery is missing and the degree of completeness in this case is 2/3 = 66.7% (two out of three sub-goals are related to the sub-tasks). The identified missing artifacts are represented in Fig. 13.

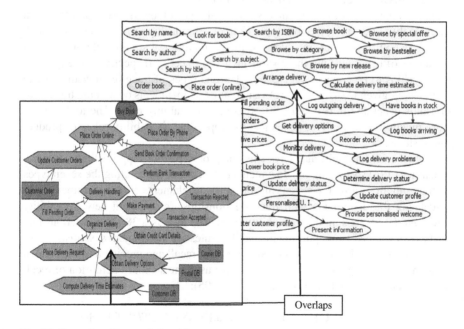

Fig. 12 Examples of trace relationship

```
<TraceRelationship ruleID="R3 type="overlaps"
            degreeOfCompleteness="66,7">
<Element doc="c:/users/ElectronicBookshop.tropos"
     type="SR Task" name="Organize Delivery" id="_103">
<MissingElement
      docSource=="c:/users/ElectronicBookStore.pd"
      typeSource="Goal"
      nameSource="Log Outgoing Delivery"
      idSource="98 "
      typeTarget="SR Task or SR Goal"/>
</Element>
<Element doc="c:/users/ElectronicBookStore.pd"
     type="Goal" name="Arrange delivery" id="104">
<MissingElement
      docSource=="c:/users/by916/ElectronicBookshop.tropos"
      typeSource="Task"
      nameSource="Place Delivery Request"
      idSource="78 "
      typeTarget="SubGoal"/>
</Element>   </TraceRelationship>
```

Fig. 13 Examples of overlaps relationship

4 Implementation and Evaluation

We have developed prototype tools to support the creation of trace relationships between artifacts generated during the development life cycle of object-oriented, product line, and multi-agent systems. The tools have been implemented in Java and uses SAXON (2010) to evaluate XQuery (2010).

In the context of object-oriented systems, the prototype tool supports the main functionality of creating the four types of trace relationships described in Section 2. In the context of product-line systems, the prototype tool supports the main functionalities of (a) specifying the documents to be traced; (b) specifying the types of relationships to be created; (c) creating the nine types of trace relationships based on the input given in (a) and (b); (c) visualising the documents containing trace relationships generated in (c); and (d) testing new traceability rules. The tool uses 21 extra functions that we have developed to support the traceability rules for product line systems.

In the context of multi-agent systems, the prototype tool supports the main functionalities of (a) specifying the documents to be traced; (b) creating the seven types of trace relationships; (c) specifying the missing elements in the documents; (d) visualising the documents with trace relationships, (e) creating new traceability rules; and (f) visualising the traceability rules. The tool uses 38 extra functions that we have developed to support the traceability rules for multi-agent systems.

The framework has been evaluated in terms of recall and precision of the created relationship types. More specifically, we have used the standard definition of recall and precision given in (Faloutsos and Oard, 1995):

$$\text{Precision} = |ST \cap UT| / |ST| \qquad \text{Recall} = |ST \cap UT/ |UT||, \text{ where}$$

- ST is the set of trace relationships detected by XTraQue;
- UT is the set of trace relationships which are identified by the user, and
- |X| denotes the cardinality of a set X (viz. $|ST \cap UT|$, $|ST|$, and $|UT|$).

The evaluation of the object-oriented artifacts was conducted for two systems, namely (i) TV-System: a family of software intensive TV systems, and (ii) UCM-System: a university course management system. In both of these systems we used requirements documents and analysis object models. The evaluation used 26 traceability rules in five different cases, as summarised in Table 8, and compared trace relationships created by the rules with trace relationships manually created by three different users with substantial experience in object-oriented modelling. Table 9 describes the number of artifacts used for the evaluation and Table 10 shows the results of recall and precision for each of the five cases and users that participated in the evaluation. More details of this evaluation can be found in (Spanoudakis et al., 2004).

Table 8   Summary of evaluation cases

Case	Description
Case1	Requirements of audio function of TV-System
Case2	Use cases for audio function and analysis object model of TV-System
Case3	Requirements of video function and analysis object model of TV-System
Case4	Use cases for video function and analysis object model of TV-System
Case5	Requirements and analysis object models for UCM-System

Table 9   Summary of Artifacts used in the evaluation of OO systems

Artifact types	Number of Artifacts	
	TV-System	UCM- System
Requirements statements	178	31
Use cases	113	–
Classes	108	47
Attributes	70	90
Associations	191	58
Operations	277	128

Table 10   Results of recall and precision measurements

		Recall	Precision
Case1	User1	0.81	0.68
	User2	0.81	0.74
Case2	User2	0.95	0.94
	User3	0.79	0.67
Case3	User1	0.51	0.86
Case 4	User1	0.64	0.92
	User3	0.46	0.52
Case 5	User1	0.60	0.85

The evaluation of the product line artifacts was conducted for the mobile phone case study. We conducted five sets of experiments related to five different scenarios concerned with product line engineering. More specifically, these scenarios include (S1) the creation of a new product member for an existing product line, (S2) the creation of a product line system from already existing product members, (S3) changes to a product member in a product line system, (S4) changes at the product line level, and (S5) impact of changes at the product line level to a product member. More details of these scenarios can be found in (Jirapanthong and Zisman, 2007). For each of these scenarios we have identified the stakeholders involved in the process, the types of documents and trace relationships that are related to the scenarios, and evaluated the scenarios in terms of recall and precision measurements. The evaluation used 63 traceability rule templates that were instantiated depending on the artifacts used in each scenario and the types of trace relationships to be identified. Table 11 shows a summary of the number of artifacts and traceability rules used in each scenario. Table 12 presents the results of recall and precision for each of the five scenarios used in the evaluation.

The evaluation of the multi-agent artifacts was conducted for two different case studies, namely (i) air-traffic control system (ATC) and (ii) electronic bookstore system (e-BookStore). Both systems are composed of i* (Yu, 1995), Prometheus (Padgham and Winikoff, 2004), and JACK (Winikoff, 2005) artifacts. The ATC system controls arrival schedules at an airport. More specifically, it attempts to find the best landing time for an aircraft in order to alleviate congestion and its associated delays. The e-Bookstore system supports the main tasks of buying and delivering books. For both systems, the main objectives of the evaluation was to (a) measure recall and precision, (b) identify missing elements in the documents, (c) amend the documents and measure new recall and precision for the new amended documents. More details of the evaluation can be found in (Cysneiros and Zisman 2007a, 2007b, 2008). Table 13 shows the results of recall and precision for the evaluation of ATC and e-BookStore systems, and the number of traceability rules.

Overall, the average precision and recall results in our experiments for the different types of systems are encouraging. Although the data sets used in our work are different from the data sets used in other approaches that support automatic trace creation (Antoniol et al., 2002; Hayes et al., 2006; Marcus and Maletic, 2003), our precision results are better than the results achieved in those approaches, while our

Table 11 Summary of Artifacts and traceability rules

	S1	S2	S3	S4	S5
N. of documents	15	20	12	6	2
N. of direct traceability rule templates	17	15	11	7	2
N. of indirect traceability rule templates	8	11	5	0	0
N. of instantiated direct traceability rule templates	100	192	80	11	2
N. of instantiated indirect traceability rule templates	8	11	5	0	0
Total number of instantiated traceability rules	108	203	85	11	5

Table 12 Results of recall and precision measurements

		S1	S2	S3	S4	S5	Average
No. of direct	*By the users* |UT|	519	1076	128	26	6	–
trace relationships detected	*By XTraQue* |ST|	525	1090	136	21	6	–
No. of indirect	*By the users* |UT|	333	1412	126	0	0	–
trace relationships detected	*By XTraQue* |ST|	341	1418	130	0	0	–
Total no. of trace	*By the users* |UT|	852	2488	254	26	6	–
relationships detected	*By XTraQue* |ST|	866	2508	266	21	6	–
Precision	*Direct relations*	0.956	0.959	0.823	0.81	0.834	0.876
	Indirect relations	0.827	0.852	0.807	–	–	0.828
	All relations	0.905	0.898	0.816	0.81	0.834	0.853
Recall	*Direct relations*	0.967	0.972	0.875	0.654	0.834	0.860
	Indirect relations	0.847	0.855	0.834	–	–	0.845
	All relations	0.920	0.906	0.854	0.654	0.834	0.833

Table 13 Results of recall and precision measurements

System	Document type	Number of traceability rules	Precision	Recall
ATC	i* vs. Prometheus	58	78.2	94.36
	Prometheus & JACK	63	94.9	73.8
	Average		86.55	84.08
e-BookStore	i* vs. Prometheus	23	89.41	86.38
	Prometheus & JACK	63	78.03	72.77
	Average		83.72	79.56

recall results are comparable to the results achieved in those approaches. In order to increase the results of recall in our work, new traceability rules need to be created to support the identification of missing relationships.

Although our framework relies on the use of XML documents, our experience has demonstrated that the creation of these documents is not an issue since many application tools use XML as a standard export format to support data interchange among heterogeneous tools and applications. A possible drawback of our work is concerned with the extra effort to mark-up textual parts of the documents with XML POS-tag elements, when necessary. However, this is alleviated by the use of tools like CLAWS (2010) and our converter that transforms the POS-tags identified by CLAWS into XML elements representing these tags. Another issue of the work is concerned with the creation of traceability rules. However, once a set of rules is created, these rules can be used in different applications with the same types of documents. To alleviate this issue, we have also proposed a machine learning algorithm to support the creation of new traceability rules to generate trace relationships that

existing rules failed to identify, between requirements and object-oriented specifications (Spanoudakis et al., 2003). We plan to extend this work to support the
generation of new traceability rules in the scope of product line and multi-agent
systems.

Our experience has also demonstrated that a large number of trace relationships
can be created. Therefore, it is necessary to develop ways to manage and visualise
these large number of relationships or to develop processes in which only necessary
trace relationships for specific tasks are created. This is also a topic of extension
work of the framework.

5 Conclusions and Future Work

In this paper we describe a rule-based traceability framework that supports automatic traceability creation and identification of missing artifacts for documents
generated during the development of object-oriented, product-line, and multi-agent
systems. We have presented a traceability information model for the documents of
our concerned with different types of trace relationships. The framework assumes
documents represented in XML format and uses traceability rules specified in
XQuery with some extended functions that we have created. Prototype tools have
been implemented to evaluate and demonstrate the framework. The framework has
been evaluated in terms of recall and precision for different case studies. The results
of the evaluation are comparable to other approaches to support automatic creation
of trace relationships.

Currently we are extending the framework to support visualisation of the large
number of trace relationships that are created and to support automatic amendment
of the documents after the missing elements are identified. We are also expanding
the framework to allow traceability creation and identification of missing artifacts
for other types of documents (e.g., documents for domain implementation phase in
product line systems). Another topic that we are investigating is how to optimise the
creation of trace relationships when the documents evolve.

References

Antoniol, G., Canfora, G., Casazza, G., De Lucia, A., Merlo, E.: Recovering traceability
    links between code and documentation. IEEE Trans. Softw. Eng. **28**(10), 970–983 (2002).
    doi:10.1109/TSE.2002.1041053
Bayer, J., Widen, T.: Introducing traceability to product lines. In: Software Product-Family
    Engineering, 4th International Workshop, PFE 2001, Spain, October 3–5, 2001. Appeared in
    Lecture Notes in Computer Science, vol. 2290, Springer, Berlin/Heidelberg (2002)
CLAWS. http://www.comp.lancs.ac.uk/ucrel/claws. Accessed 13 June 2010
Cleland-Huang, J., Chang, C.K, Sethi, G., Javvaji, K., Hu, H., Xia, J.: Automating spec-
    ulative queries through event-based requirements traceability. In: Proceedings of the
    IEEE Joint International Requirements Engineering Conference, Essen, Germany (2002).
    doi:10.1109/ICRE.2002.1048540

Cleland-Huang, J., Settimi, R., BenKhadra, O.: Goal-Centric Traceability for Managing Non-Functional Requirements, International Conference on Software Engineering, USA (2005). doi:10.1109/ICSE.2005.1553579

Cysneiros, G., Zisman, A.: Refining Prometheus Methodology with i*. Third International Workshop on Agent-Oriented Methodologies, OOPSLA, Canada (2004)

Cysneiros, G., Zisman, A.: Traceability for Agent-Oriented Design Models and Code, 19th International Conference on Software Engineering and Knowledge Engineering, SEKE, MA (2007a)

Cysneiros, G., Zisman, A.: Tracing agent-oriented systems. International Symposium of the Grand Challenges for Traceability, Kentucky (2007b)

Cysneiros, G., Zisman, A.: Traceability and completeness checking for agent-oriented systems. 23rd Annual ACM Symposium on Applied Computing, New York, NY (2008). doi:10.1145/1363686.1363706

DOORS: http://www-01.ibm.com/software/awdtools/doors/

Egyed, A.: A scenario-driven approach to trace dependency analysis. IEEE Trans. Softw. Eng. 9(2), 116–132 (2003). doi:10.1109/TSE.2003.1178051

Egyed, A., Grünbacher, P.: Automatic requirements traceability: Beyond the record and replay paradigm. Proceedings of the 17th IEEE International Conference on Automated Software Engineering (ASE), Edinburgh, UK (2002). doi:10.1109/ASE.2002.1115010

Faloutsos, C., Oard, D.: A survey of information retrieval and filtering methods. Technical Report CS-TR3514, Department of Computer Science, University of Maryland (1995)

Hayes, J.H., Dekhtyar, A., Sundaram, S.K.: Advancing candidate link generation for requirements tracing: The study of methods. IEEE Trans. Softw. Eng. 32(1), 4–19 (2006). doi:10.1109/TSE.2006.3

Jirapanthong, W., Zisman, A.: Supporting product line development through traceability. In: Proceedings of the 12th Asia-Pacific Software Engineering Conference, APSEC, Taiwan (2005). doi:10.1109/APSEC.2005.101

Jirapanthong, W., Zisman, A.: XTraQue: Traceability for product line systems. Softw. Syst. Model. J. 8(1), 1619–1374 (2007). doi:10.1007/S10270-007-0066-8

Kaindl, H.: The missing link in requirements engineering. Softw. Eng. Notes. ACM SIGSOFT Softw. Eng. Notes 18(2), 30–39 (1992). doi:10.1145/159420.155836

Kang, K., Kim, S., Lee, J., Kim, K., Shin, E., Huh, M.: FORM: A feature-oriented reuse method with domain-specific reference architectures. Ann. Softw. Eng. 5(1), 143–168 (1998). doi:10.1023/A:1018980625587

Lamb, L., Jirapanthong, W., Zisman, A.: Formalizing traceability relations for product lines. In: Proceedings of the 6th International Workshop on Traceability for Emerging Forms of Software Engineering, Honolulu, Hawaii (2011). doi:10.1145/1987856.1987866

Marcus, A., Maletic, I.: Recovering Documentation-to-Source-Code Traceability Links Using Latent Semantic Indexing. ICSE, Washington, DC (2003). doi:10.1109/ICSE.2003.1201194

Marcus, A., Maletic, I., Sergeyev, A.: Recovery of traceability links between software documentation and source code. Int. J. Softw. Eng. Knowl. Eng. 15(4), 811–836 (2005). doi:10.1142/S0218194005002543

Padgham, L., Winikoff, W.: Developing Intelligent Agent Systems–A Practical Guide. Wiley, West Sussex, England (2004)

Pohl, K.: Process-Centered Requirements Engineering. Wiley West Sussex, England (1996a)

Pohl, K.: PRO-ART: Enabling requirements pre-traceability. In: Proceedings of the IEEE International Conference on Requirements Engineering, ICRE, pp. 76–84 (1996b). doi:10.1109/ICRE.1996.491432

Pinheiro, F.: Formal and informal aspects of requirements tracing. Position Paper in Proceedings of 3rd Workshop on Requirements Engineering (III WER), Rio de Janeiro, Brazil (2000)

Ramesh, B., Dhar, V.: Supporting systems development using knowledge captured during requirements engineering. IEEE Trans. Softw. Eng. 9(2), 498–510 (1992)

Ramesh, B., Jarke, M.: Towards Reference Models for Requirements Traceability. IEEE Transactions on Software Engineering, Germany (2001). doi: 10.1109/32.895989

Rational Rose.: http://www-01.ibm.com/software/awdtools/developer/rose. Accessed 14 June 2010

RDT: http://www.incose.org/productspubs/products/setools/survey/RDT.htm

RTM: Integrated chipware. www.chipware.com

SAXON: http://saxon.sourceforge.net. Accessed 14 June 2010

Spanoudakis, G., Garcez, A., Zisman, A.: Revising rules to capture requirements traceability relations. In: 15th International Conference on Software Engineering and Knowledge Engineering, SEKE, San Francisco, CA (2003)

Spanoudakis, G., Zisman, A.: Software traceability: A roadmap. Handbook of software engineering and knowledge engineering, (V. 3) S.K. Chang, World Scientific Publishing Co. (2003)

Spanoudakis, G., Zisman, A., Pérez-Miñana, E., Krause, P.: Rule-based generation of requirements traceability relations. J. Syst. Softw. **72**(2), 105–127 (2004). doi:10.1016/S0164-1212(03)00242-5

XPath: http://www.w3.org/TR/xpath. Accessed 14 June 2010

XTraQue: XTraQue Project. http://www.soi.city.ac.uk/~zisman/XTraQue. Accessed 14 June 2010

XQuery: http://www.w3.org/TR/xquery. Accessed 14 June 2010

Yu, E.: Modelling Strategic relationships for process reengineering. Dissertation, University of Toronto, Toronto, ON (1995)

Winikoff, M.: Jack^{TM} Intelligent Agents: An Industrial Strength Platform. Springer, USA (2005)

WordNet: http://wordnet.princeton.edu. Accessed 14 June 2010

Part III
Traceability Maintenance

For traceability links to be trusted by developers, they need to not only be created correctly, but also maintained so that they remain consistent and accurate. This is no mean feat in a typical software development project where it is the norm for requirements, design, code and test cases to constantly evolve to meet the changing needs of a project.

The first three chapters of this part of the book describe various approaches for dealing with traceability on evolving projects. The chapter by Mäder and Gotel focuses on maintaining "Ready-to-Use Traceability on Evolving Projects". It promotes the use of a simple traceability information model, explores the requirements for automated maintenance and highlights a semi-automated approach. The chapter by Heider et al. details an event-based approach for acquiring and maintaining traceability links based on tracking changes to artifacts, "Evolution-Driven Trace Acquisition in Eclipse-Based Product Line Workspaces", while the chapter by Seibel et al. discusses a rule-based approach to maintain model-to-model traceability, "Traceability in Model-Driven Engineering: Efficient and Scalable Traceability Maintenance". In a slightly different vein, and pertinent given the plethora of research on semi and automated techniques, the chapter by Dekhtyar and Hayes examines the role of the human to cast light on future directions for in-life cycle tracing research, "Studying the Role of Humans in the Traceability Loop".

Ready-to-Use Traceability on Evolving Projects

Patrick Mäder and Orlena Gotel

1 Introduction

While complete and correct traceability is a common goal for development projects, the quality of the traceability can only be ascertained by an "informed" developer and cannot yet be assessed automatically within industrial applications. A more realistic goal is, therefore, to keep the traceability compliant with a defined traceability information model (TIM) (Mäder et al., 2009a). Compliance with a TIM, a definition of the permissible trace links between artifact types, means that the traceability on a project would always be ready-to-use according to the intentions for a project. While a TIM cannot be used to answer the question of whether a particular instance of a trace is correct or not, it can be examined to answer questions such as: (a) which traces are not required in order to fulfill the current traceability strategy and (b) between which artifact types are trace links intended. A TIM, therefore, provides a guide for where traceability should be created and maintained, and compliance of existing traces with the TIM can be checked and enforced automatically as a project evolves.

This chapter focuses on two of the activities that are part of the traceability life cycle (see Fig. 1) and that work together to provide for ready-to-use traceability on evolving projects: (1) defining the traceability that is required on a project and (2) keeping the traceability ready-to-use by maintaining previously established trace links as the project evolves.

Activity 1 refers to the practice of defining a project-specific traceability information model (TIM) tailored to the goals for traceability in a given project. Such a TIM should be defined according to the intended usage of traceability within the project, but is also dependent upon the structure of the project and the development process used, as these define the artifacts that are actually available for tracing. This means that the evolution of a project's scope (e.g., adding additional models or artifact types) should also trigger the validation of a project's TIM and its customisation

P. Mäder (✉)
Institute for Systems Engineering and Automation (SEA), Johannes Kepler University,
Linz, Austria
e-mail: patrick.maeder@jku.at

J. Cleland-Huang et al. (eds.), *Software and Systems Traceability*,
DOI 10.1007/978-1-4471-2239-5_8, © Springer-Verlag London Limited 2012

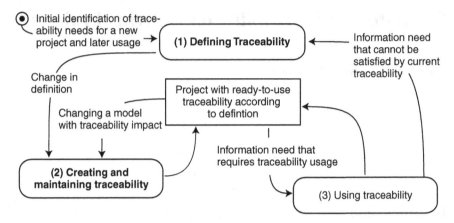

Fig. 1 The traceability life cycle for a development project (Mäder, 2009)

if necessary. This chapter outlines best practices on setting up a TIM according to project-specific needs.

Activity 2 refers to the impact that evolution and change has on previously established traceability. While much attention has been directed towards approaches for establishing traceability among artifacts initially, less attention has been paid to ensuring that this traceability remains correct over time. This chapter discusses the problem of traceability decay and highlights the state of the art in traceability maintenance to address it. It describes the requirements for an automated approach to the problem, and then describes a novel approach for reducing the manual effort and associated costs when maintaining traceability.

The remainder of the chapter is structured as follows. Section 2 discusses the role of a defined traceability strategy and describes a usage-centered process for creating a TIM. Section 3 describes model-based development and traceability in this particular context. While the chapter focuses on model-based development for description and illustration purposes, the theoretical considerations are more broadly applicable to evolving projects in general. Section 4 explains the problem of traceability decay, while Section 5 reviews existing approaches to traceability maintenance and outlines the requirements for an automated approach to support this task. Section 6 discusses a particular approach for the (semi-) automated maintenance of traceability. Finally, Section 7 summarises the chapter and discusses future challenges in the area. Where appropriate, the chapter employs the iTrust case study of Appendix B to exemplify the points discussed.

2 Defining a Project-Specific Traceability Strategy

The most effective way to establish traceability within a software systems development project may be to provide each stakeholder with the opportunity to create traces where and when she/he believes they are required. Although such a naive approach to traceability might be plausible, researchers and practitioners (e.g., Letelier, 2002; Mäder et al., 2009a; Pinheiro, 2004; Ramesh and Jarke, 2001) do not envisage that this would be a viable strategy within industrial projects. Instead, for traceability to provide high development support at minimal costs, a traceability strategy should be defined, followed and updated as an integral part of a project's planning and management. A goal-oriented approach to inform the traceability strategy comprises the following three steps.

2.1 Step 1: Identify Development Tasks that Require Traceability

Specific development tasks that are dependent upon traceability should be identified. For example, the testing engineer of the iTrust project might want to find out about those Java Server Pages implementing a use case that is tested by a failed black box test. In addition, the project manager of the iTrust project might want to find out about all the use cases that are not currently tested by a black box test. Such traceability-enabled tasks can be identified systematically by identifying project goals, and then by analysing the project roles and their related tasks.

For the iTrust project, two general project goals have been identified that require traceability:

Goal 1: Ensure a high quality product through equal test coverage.
Goal 2: Ensure compliance to HIPAA regulations through regular code inspections.

2.2 Step 2: Identify Traceability-Related Queries

Once the traceability-enabled tasks have been identified (Step 1), a set of supporting traceability-related queries should be defined. The queries should provide for an efficient way of supporting the identified development tasks. This step is largely ignored by current tools, which assume that the queries will either be overly simplistic or that high-end users will export data and write customised scripts to support their more advanced queries. Recent work proposes a generic Visual Traceability Modeling Language (VTML) that could fill this gap (Mäder and Cleland-Huang, 2010).

For the iTrust project, three traceability-related queries have been identified for the first project goal, test coverage, and one traceability-related query has been identified for the second project goal, code inspection:

Query 1.1: Return all use cases without acceptance test cases (Test developer).
Query 1.2: Return a count of test cases per use case (Project leader).
Query 1.3: Return all JSPs with failed acceptance tests (Interface designer).

Query 2.1: Find all source code methods that contribute to satisfying a given HIPAA regulation (Code inspector).

2.3 Step 3: Define Traceability

After the traceability-related queries have been identified (Step 2), a project level traceability strategy can be defined to ensure that the necessary trace links are created and maintained. This definition can be provided via a TIM and is commonly represented as a UML (Unified Modeling Language) class diagram. Figure 2 shows an example of a TIM for the iTrust project. Once new or changed project goals and traceability-related queries arise, the defined traceability strategy would need to be updated accordingly.

A TIM is composed of two basic types of entity: trace artifact types, represented as classes; and permitted trace link types between the trace artifact types, represented as associations. Trace artifact types serve as the abstractions supporting the traceability perspective of a project, but they do not necessarily reflect concrete artifact types that exist in the traced models. A trace artifact type might represent an abstraction of several different concrete artifact types existing in the related models or, conversely, it could refer to a single artifact type in a tool. Figure 2 shows the mapping of trace artifact types to their source documents, each one stereotyped as a «toolArtifact». A tool artifact provides information about how a certain trace artifact type is represented within a concrete tool or model. A more in-depth discussion on TIMs is given in (Mäder et al., 2009a).

For the iTrust project (see Fig. 2), a *Use Case* shall be traced to related *Acceptance Tests*, to *HIPAA Regulations* that impact its implementation, and to *Methods* and *Server Pages* implementing it. These trace links were found sufficient to support the four traceability-related queries identified in Step 2. Mäder and Cleland-Huang propose a visual way of defining the identified traceability-related queries and Fig. 3 shows how iTrust Query 1.2 would be defined using this VTML approach (Mäder and Cleland-Huang, 2010). The benefits of VTML are its generic nature, independent from the representation of the queried artifacts, and its more intuitive application compared to standard query languages like SQL.

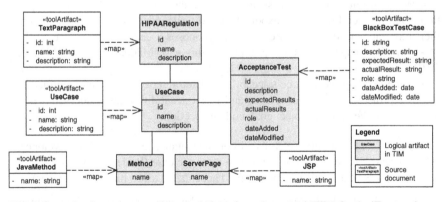

Fig. 2 Example of a project-specific traceability information model (TIM) for the iTrust project

Fig. 3 iTrust Query 1.2,
Return a count of test cases
per use case, in VTML
notation

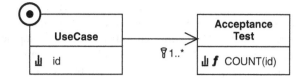

A VTML query is read by starting from the scope element (represented by an encircled dot in the upper left corner of a classifier) and following the direction of the relations. In Fig. 3, the *UseCase* classifier is the scope element, meaning that the query applies to use cases. Before executing a query, the user can decide whether to perform the query on all existing use cases of a development project or on a subset. The query will return the id (see bar graph symbol and *id* attribute in the *UseCase* classifier) of all use cases that are tested by at least one acceptance test (see filter symbol and cardinality at the relation between both classifiers). The query also retrieves the count of related acceptance tests per use case (see bar graph symbol and *COUNT* function defined in the *AcceptanceTest* classifier).

3 Traceability in the Context of Model-Based Development

The engineering of a software system can be a complex task. A common way to manage this complexity is by modelling the product to be developed through different levels of abstraction and from different perspectives. Within this chapter, such a model-based development process is assumed in order to scope the discussion.

3.1 Evolution of Software and System Development Models

A model can be defined as an abstraction of some real world object. In the context of software systems development, a model describes a software product, its structure, functionality, behaviour or code, which is collectively maintained by the many stakeholders that participate during the development life cycle (OMG, 2003, 2007). During software and systems engineering, models are used to represent the requirements, the design and the implementation. As all models of one development project describe different aspects of the same product, they are interrelated by many dependencies. For example, the design of a software system depends upon its requirements, while the implementation depends upon its design. The UML (OMG, 2007) provides a set of structural and behavioural diagrams that allow for the modelling of such related yet separately described facets of a software development process. It is supported by many modelling tools and is the quasi-standard in object-oriented development. The extension, the Systems Modeling Language (SysML) (OMG, 2008), provides additional diagrams and options particular to systems development.

Software systems development may be viewed as a multiphase transformation process from the initial problem statement to the final solution (Jacobson et al., 1999). The transformations are carried out as development activities. Each of these activities is applied to or influenced by various input artifacts and creates new or improved output artifacts. Most current problems are too complex to be solved in a one-time transformation process from the problem to the solution, so state of the art development processes are iterative and incremental (e.g., the Unified Process (Jacobson et al., 1999)). In an iterative process, activities are executed repeatedly until the goals of development are reached. Despite its benefits, creating a solution to a problem in such a manner is not without its difficulties. Almost all of the artifacts created during the development process are subject to changes in a later iteration. Many of these changing artifacts influenced the creation of other dependent artifacts in an earlier iteration, which are now either obsolete or need to be changed also. This requires identifying, managing and resolving inconsistencies between related models and their artifacts. The basis for change impact analysis is knowledge about the dependencies between the changed artifact and other artifacts that may now need changing. These dependencies are only available if they have been created and maintained earlier in the form of trace links.

3.2 Traceability Between Model Elements

Creating a trace link between two artifacts is an expression of their dependence. The representation of such trace links can, therefore, be considered as a type of dependency relationship with a given directionality, as defined within the UML meta-model (OMG, 2004). The graphical representation of the direction points from the dependent model element towards the independent model element (e.g., from a method of the source code to the implemented requirement). This directionality is intended to convey semantics, but it does not prevent bi-directional use or navigation of the trace link. Arlow and Neustadt state that a change to the independent element (i. e., supplier) may effect or supply information needed by the dependent element (i. e., client) and that the client in some way depends upon the supplier (Arlow and Neustadt, 2005). Within the UML, a stereotype *trace* distinguishes trace links from other dependencies that are part of the models (Arlow and Neustadt, 2005; Weilkiens, 2006).

A major problem that arises in model-based development is ensuring that related models, referring to similar aspects of a system, evolve consistently while the development process proceeds (Egyed, 2011; Huzar et al., 2004). Finkelstein et al. state that checking consistency between perspectives and the handling of inconsistency creates many interesting and difficult research problems (Finkelstein et al., 1994). If traceability reflects all the required dependencies correctly, then it can support this complex task by propagating changes in one model to all the related models (Aizenbud-Reshef et al., 2006; Egyed, 2011). Where this is not the case, the traceability inevitably decays.

4 The Problem of Traceability Decay

A change to one model in a setting of multiple related models is likely to cause inconsistencies with respect to one or more of those related models (see Section 3.2). Changes to related models can also require maintaining the existing trace links to reflect all the dependencies between the evolved model elements after the change. In theory, there are three types of impact that a change to a model element can have on a related element and the trace link. Figure 4 illustrates these three types of impact with examples from the iTrust project:

(I)   The change can be solely corrective with no impact on the related element. For example, correcting the name of a use case to align it with other names.
(II) The change can have impact on the related element, but no impact on the traceability. For example, a new method within a class is required due to an enhanced use case. This change to the original model element also requires evolving the related element.
(III) The change can have impact on the related element and, due to changes in the model structure, also on the traceability. For example, a new class is required due to an evolved use case. This change to the original model element not only requires evolving the related element, but also maintaining the traceability between both models.

These types of impact apply separately for each trace link and related element of any one changing element. Since a changed element can have more than one trace link to other elements, the impact can further differ among the three types for each linked element. In addition, each related element may have its own related elements to subsequent models. If a related element has been changed (impact types II or III above), then the three types of impact apply to its related elements as well via the ripple effect. It is also possible that the change to the original element (see

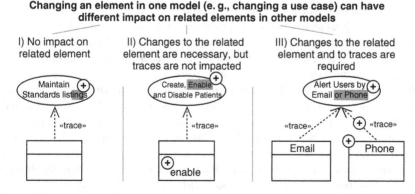

Fig. 4 Different types of impact that a change to a model element can have on related model elements

the use case in Fig. 4) requires a change to its structure (e.g., to split into two use cases in the figure). This change is similar to impact type III and can eventually require updating trace links on the original element as well. Such a step by step degradation of trace links has been called traceability decay (Mäder et al., 2008).

Definition 1 (Traceability decay) The gradual disintegration and break down of the traceability on a project. This tends to result following ongoing traceability evolution.

Traceability decay can be prevented by continuous or on-demand traceability maintenance. Continuous maintenance refers to the update of impacted trace links after changes to traced artifacts. On-demand maintenance refers to a dedicated and overall update of the traceability, generally in response to some explicit trigger and in preparation for an upcoming usage. While the maintenance of traceability is a challenging problem within a model's evolution, the problem is compounded when dealing with related models; traceability information is needed to ensure the consistency of models, but consistency is necessary to compute the correct impact of changes with respect to the traceability.

5 Traceability Maintenance

Researchers have been working on the "Traceability Problem" for almost two decades (Gotel and Finkelstein, 1994) and part of the outcome of that work has been a range of techniques for recovering trace links (e.g., Alexander, 2002; Antoniol et al., 2002; Hayes et al., 2003; Lucia et al., 2008; Marcus and Maletic, 2003). In order to preserve the investment made while creating traceability manually, or with the support of automated recovery techniques such as those referenced, it is necessary to maintain the traceability while the development process proceeds. In contrast, there has been relatively little work focusing on the maintenance of these trace links. The automated solutions to traceability creation are only partially trustworthy and more reliable solutions require expensive, manual feedback from a user. Under these circumstances, it is not feasible to recover trace links anew every time a model changes. Traceability maintenance is, therefore, an expensive and error-prone activity at present (Aizenbud-Reshef et al., 2006).

Murta et al. characterise the problem of traceability maintenance between architectural elements and source code as follows: "given an initial set of established traceability links, and given that both an architecture and its implementation can evolve independently, how can traceability links be updated with the addition of new links, removal of existing links, and changes in existing links to ensure that each architectural element is at all times accurately linked to its corresponding source code configuration items, and vice versa?" (Murta et al., 2006). A more general definition of traceability maintenance is provided in this chapter.

Definition 2 (Traceability Maintenance) Those activities associated with updating pre-existing traces as changes are made to the traced artifacts and the traceability evolves, creating new traces where needed to keep the traceability relevant and up to date.

The ultimate goal of traceability automation is the creation and update of traces without the need for manual intervention. This section reviews work towards this goal, discusses the recognition of change and evolution as a key enabler for automated traceability maintenance, and lists the requirements for an automated traceability maintenance solution.

5.1 Research on the Maintenance of Traceability

Spanoudakis et al. present a rule-based approach for the automatic generation of trace links between documents (Spanoudakis et al., 2004). A requirement-to-object-model rule and a technique based upon information retrieval are used together to automatically establish trace links between requirements and analysis models. A second kind of rule analyses the relations between requirements and object models to recognise intra-requirements dependencies and establishes these trace links automatically. The approach requires the export of all supported artifacts into the XML (Extensible Markup Language) and the rules generate trace links for the exported state of the models. Due to the use of information retrieval, there is uncertainty in the recognition of traces and the automated application of tracing rules does not include the possibility for pruning any false candidate trace links that will be created. The approach, in its current form, does not appear to support the maintenance of traceability following artifact evolution, but the approach proposes interesting ideas that could be configured to support maintenance, such as the idea of organising rules in the style of *event, condition, action*, further stored in the open XML format to facilitate their customisation by the user.

Maletic et al. describe an XML-based approach to support the evolution of trace links between models expressed in the XML (Maletic et al., 2005). The authors also describe a traceability graph and its representation in the XML, independent of specific models or tools. They propose to evolve traceability along with the models by detecting syntactic changes at the same level and type as the trace links (e.g., textual links require textual change detection). The authors do not discuss how to detect these changes nor how to update the impacted trace links, but refer to their own work on the analysis of fine-grained source code differences and mention that this work could be applied to artifacts in the XML format. The idea of converting models into the XML format and applying differencing techniques in order to recognise small incremental changes could be burdensome and slow. The authors do not provide sufficient information to draw conclusions about the practicality of the proposed approach.

Murta et al. describe an approach called ArchTrace that supports the evolution of trace links between architecture and implementation (Murta et al., 2006). The use of the Extensible Architecture Description Language (xADL) for the description of software architectures and Subversion for the versioning of source code is required in the current form of the approach. The authors trigger a set of eight policies on committing a new version of an artifact (e.g., suggest a trace link to a more recent configuration item version if the user creates a trace link to an older version). These policies mostly ensure the update of existing traceability on artifacts to new versions within the version control system and further restrict the creation of new trace links on old artifacts (see also (Murta et al., 2008)). While the approach is an important contribution for evolving projects working with version control systems, it does not offer policies that would allow for the recognition of structural changes to models as the main trigger for traceability maintenance (e.g., the replacing, splitting and merging of related elements).

5.2 Recognising Evolution to Support Traceability Maintenance

An approach that supports traceability maintenance needs to recognise relevant changes to related model elements. There is work on categorising and identifying changes to models that is discussed below.

Cleland-Huang et al. describe a concept for the recognition of change types applied to requirements as part of their event-based traceability approach (Cleland-Huang et al., 2002). These change types are used for the description of a recognised change during change propagation. The authors distinguish and capture seven types of changes to a requirements model as change events: create a new requirement, inactivate a requirement, modify an attribute value, merge two or more requirements, refine a requirement by adding additional parts, decompose a requirement into two or more parts, and replace one requirement with another. All seven change types are composed of a sequence of four different change actions (i.e., create requirement, set requirement attribute, create link and set link attribute). The recognition of complex change types (i.e., merge, refine, decompose and replace) depends upon the manual creation of trace links with a certain type between the original requirement and the newly created requirement(s) and, in certain cases, on setting an attribute of the initial requirement to the state *inactive*. The authors provide an algorithm that identifies the seven change types within a sequence of captured change actions. Furthermore, the authors suggest triggering the actual recognition process only for a completed user-defined session in order to minimise the risk of false recognition due to inclusions between the change types (e.g., a decompose change type consists of a refine change type and an inactivate change type). Since the focus of the approach is on recognising types of requirements changes, it does not deal with the more complex task of recognising multi-step change activities to models comprising different element types.

Engels et al. present a classification of UML model refinements to preserve consistency during the evolution of UML-RT models (a UML enhancement for real-time systems) (Engels et al., 2002). The authors identify three kinds of atomic modification: creation, deletion and update. The focus is limited to four model elements: capsules, ports, connectors and protocols. The focus of this work lies on preserving and maintaining consistency after incremental evolution. The work does not show how atomic changes can be combined into the recognition of composite change activities with development intent and how to maintain consistency in these cases.

Hnatkowska et al. specify behavioral refinements in UML collaboration diagrams and describe how these relate to structural refinements (Hnatkowska et al., 2003). The purpose is to establish refinement relationships between different abstraction layers. The authors provide a classification of nine simple class diagram refinements: adding a class, modifying an attribute, modifying a method, adding an attribute to a class, splitting a class into two classes with an association, introducing a successor of a class, adding an association, modifying an association and introducing an intermediate class. The authors do not discuss how these refinements can be detected and, accordingly, require the developer to establish the relationships manually at present.

Mens et al. describe an extension to the UML meta-model to support the versioning and evolution of UML models (Mens et al., 2005). The authors classify possible inconsistencies of UML design models and provide rules, expressed in the Object Constraint Language (OCL), to detect and resolve these. They transform the models into a supported format, apply their rules and suggest model refactorings based upon the results. While the authors discuss the necessity for traceability management and change propagation during the evolution of UML models, they provide no support for this scenario.

Many researchers discuss the recognition and the classification of changes to development models, especially in the context of consistency management between models after their evolution. However, the necessity to maintain traceability, along with changing a related model, has been little emphasised. To date, there is no approach that recognises structural changes to related model elements as a main trigger of traceability decay, in turn necessitating the maintenance of traceability.

5.3 Requirements for Automated Traceability Maintenance

Addressing this shortcoming, this section provides a list of requirements for a (semi-)automated approach to traceability maintenance, an approach that would support the recognition of changes to related model elements with impact on traceability as well as the propagation of these changes between related models. It refers to the chapter "Grand Challenge of Traceability" and to related work to show how these contributed to the requirements. The aim of an approach that meets these requirements is to reduce the effort for traceability maintenance significantly, in turn reducing the overall costs for a traceable development project (see the section Traceability Challenge 2: Traceability that is cost-effective in the chapter "The Grand Challenge of Traceability (v1.0)"). While an automated solution to traceability maintenance would be the ultimate vision (see the chapter "The Grand Challenge of Traceability (v1.0)": Ubiquitous Research Theme RT 2), there is no statistic available to inform the necessary reduction of manual effort that would be required to get acceptance from the user community; this would also probably vary among users and projects.

Requirement 1 (Recognise Model Changes with Traceability Impact) *Develop a technique to recognise changes with impact on traceability, the changes that make trace links obsolete, the changes that require new trace links and the changes that require modifications to existing trace links (see the chapter "The Grand Challenge of Traceability (v1.0)": Trusted Requirement Req 9) and (Murta et al., 2006). This needs to support complex models with different types of related artifacts and multiple possible development activities to evolve these artifacts (see the chapter "The Grand Challenge of Traceability (v1.0)": Scalable Requirement Req 8 and Portable Requirement Req 7). Information will need to be gathered on the intention of a change to decide about the necessary traceability maintenance.*

Requirement 2 (Maintain Trace Links to Prevent Traceability Decay) *Prevent traceability decay by maintaining trace links in a way that is comparable to the effectiveness of manual maintenance (see the chapter "The Grand Challenge of Traceability (v1.0)": Cost-effective Requirement Req 6). This will require performing all traceability updates in accordance to the project's TIM (Pinheiro, 2004), (see the chapter "The Grand Challenge of Traceability (v1.0)": Configurable Requirement Req 5).*

Requirement 3 (Reduce Effort) *The high effort for handling traceability manually has been reported as one of the major reasons for its rare usage in the past (Arkley et al., 2002; Gotel and Finkelstein, 1994; Ramesh and Jarke, 2001). It is necessary to significantly reduce the effort necessary for the manual maintenance of traceability by converting it into computational effort (see the chapter "The Grand Challenge of Traceability (v1.0)": Ubiquitous Requirement Req 4). Algorithms need to perform the required computations without recognisable delays for the user to accept such an approach (see the chapter "The Grand Challenge of Traceability (v1.0)": Purposed Requirements Req 10 and Req 11).*

Requirement 4 (Operate Incrementally) *A technique for supporting the maintenance of traceability can operate incrementally at run-time rather or batch-wise (see the chapter "The Grand Challenge of Traceability (v1.0)": Cost-effective Goal G 3 and (Maletic et al., 2005)). In batch-wise operation, two states of a model can be compared and the differences can be computed. While the identification of small differences might allow for the reasoning about those development activities that transformed the earlier state of the model into the later state, that reasoning becomes very uncertain for larger differences. Without knowledge about the performed development activities, and therefore about the intent behind a change, an automated update of traceability is seldom possible. With incremental operation, the traces are updated and propagated as they become impacted, and so they are always ready-to-use (see the chapter "The Grand Challenge of Traceability (v1.0)": Cost-effective Requirement Req 7).*

Requirement 5 (Propagate Changes to Related Artifacts) *Propagate changes to related artifacts as they occur (Grundy et al., 1998). The change to a model element might have impact on related elements and the traces between those elements (see Section 4). Change propagation captures the information about a change and* *reminds stakeholders to fix the resulting inconsistencies whenever convenient. It is necessary to inform the developer about inconsistencies and provide support for resolving these (Cleland-Huang et al., 2003). Such a change propagation is required in those situations where one stakeholder causes inconsistencies in models she/he is not responsible for (see the chapter "The Grand Challenge of Traceability (v1.0)": Portable Requirement Req 7). The whole mechanism should be tightly integrated with the modelling tool and the development process in order to get acceptance from users and to operate efficiently (see the chapter "The Grand Challenge of Traceability (v1.0)": Ubiquitous Requirement Req 4).*

Requirement 6 (Transparency of Integration) *The approach needs to be transparent for the user and the interactions need to be reduced to a minimum. The underlying implementation of the approach needs to be general enough to allow for its use within different tools, model types and development paradigms. User interfaces should be integrated seamlessly into any tool in order to minimise the learning period for the user. (see the chapter "The Grand Challenge of Traceability (v1.0)": Purposed Requirements Req 7, Req 9 and Req 12.)*

6 A (Semi-)Automated Approach to Traceability Maintenance

This section introduces an approach, emerging from a multi-year research project, that demonstrates one way to meet the requirements introduced in the previous section. The objective is to show how the challenging and effort-intensive task of traceability maintenance can be (semi-)automated and to discuss what can be gained or lost with such a solution.

The fundamental idea of the approach is the recognition of semantically meaningful development activities applied to model elements and the (semi-)automated update of impacted traceability if needed. The approach consists of three stages:

Stage 1: Capturing elementary changes to model elements and generating events.
Stage 2: Recognising the wider development activity applied to the model element, as comprised of several elementary changes.
Stage 3: Updating the trace links associated with the changed model element.

The first stage consists of issuing a change event to each elementary change that is applied to a model element. This assumes that development is taking place within a tool that supports model-based development. During the second stage, these change events are compared with abstract, pre-defined sequences of changes (called development activities) that require traceability maintenance. In order to reduce the effort for the definition of change sequences, while at the same time being able to handle the high variability in the ways in which development activities can be performed, a sophisticated method for comparing change events and change sequences has been developed. This is described fully in (Mäder, 2009). The third stage consists of performing an update action for the impacted traceability. A set of traceability update rules contains signatures of development activities and the corresponding traceability update that is necessary. The captured elementary changes are compared with these rules and, in the case of a match, the necessary traceability update is performed.

The current set of traceability update rules comprise 21 rules and is able to recognise 37 different development activities. Among these rules are, for example, one to recognise the extraction of an attribute into a separate class, one to recognise the replacement of a class with a component and one to recognise the splitting of a class. The definition of these rules is founded on an in-depth analysis of development methodologies and observations of developers creating and updating software models during their daily work. In order to estimate the completeness of the rule set, six basic types of development activities are accounted for: create an element, delete an element, split an element, merge an element, replace an element and move parts between elements.

6.1 Illustrative Example

A simple scenario, again based upon the iTrust project, is provided to illustrate the approach. In Fig. 5, a change to a requirement impacts a realised use case and it becomes necessary for the developer to convert an existing attribute within one class into its own class.

Step 1 of Fig. 5 shows the initial situation and the trace link between class *LOINCbean* and use case *Maintain Standards Lists*. Steps 2 to 5 show one way for the developer to carry out the development activity based upon a sequence of elementary changes. With the last elementary change, deleting the original attribute,

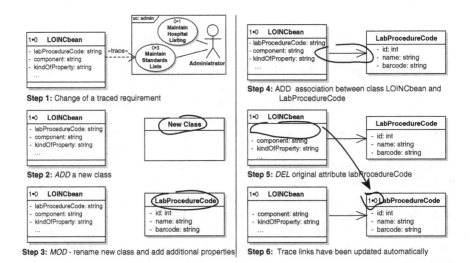

Fig. 5 Development activity with automated traceability maintenance

the development activity is recognised by the approach and the necessary update of the trace links is performed automatically. Step 6 shows the automatically created trace link between class *LabProcedureCode* and use case *Maintain Standards Lists* (depicted by the number "1" placed in the upper left corner of the class). The scenario is representative of many regular development activities. Nevertheless, there are activities that do not lead to clear directives for a traceability update. In such situations, a dialog is required for the user to decide upon the update. This makes the approach (semi-)automated.

6.2 Prototype and Evaluation

In order to evaluate the approach, a prototype called *traceMaintainer* (short: *tM*) was developed (Mäder et al., 2009b). traceMaintainer not only implements the recognition of development activities and the update of impacted trace links, but also supports the customisation and definition of new traceability update rules. The prototype has been used in industrial projects at Siemens and its integration with software modelling tools is under discussion.

Several pilot studies of the approach were undertaken to inform a controlled experiment to explore the following research questions:

1. Does use of the approach reduce the manual effort necessary for maintaining trace links significantly?
2. Do the traceability updates performed by the approach result in a set of trace links of comparable quality to those that result when maintained purely manually?

The experiment was conducted on freely available models for a mail-order system described with UML diagrams. The project artifacts included models on three levels of abstraction: requirements, analysis and design. These models consisted of 33 diagrams, 15 of which were structural diagrams supported by the developed approach. They further consisted of 104 classes, 223 attributes and 404 methods. The initial model had been annotated with 214 trace links according to a pre-defined TIM. This set of trace links provided a baseline for the later analysis of the results.

Sixteen students participated in the experiment, all of whom were in the 8th and 9th semester of their computer science studies. They were assigned equally to an experimental group (*tM*) and a control group (*notM*), according to their experience in the area of model-based development. The participants had to perform three tasks to evolve the project over a three hour period. Since they were permitted to perform the tasks according to their own ideas and experiences, a realistic spread of different solutions to the same problem was captured.

While the experiment is described fully in (Mäder, 2009), the salient points are provided here. To determine the effort spent on maintaining traceability, the number of manual and automated changes to trace links n_m and n_a, as well as the number of user interactions n_{UI}, were counted. To determine the quality of the performed traceability updates, the number of correct, incorrect and missing trace link changes were captured. These data were then used to compute the commonly used metrics of precision Q_P and recall Q_R. Precision refers to the percentage of performed changes that were correct and recall refers to the percentage of necessary changes that were actually performed.

6.3 Evaluation Results

Tables 1(a) and 1(b) summarise the results of the experiment per task and across all tasks (see the task column). The remaining columns, from left to right, refer to the dependent variable (var), the treatment (treat), the mean of the measured values (mean), the standard deviation of the measured values (sd) and the difference of the mean value of both treatments as a percentage (%-diff). The t-test column of Tables 1(a) and 1(b) shows the computed p-values as the result of two-sample t-tests for the dependent variables n_m, Q_P, and Q_R. The significance threshold for the tests was set to $\alpha = 0.05$.

Table 1(a) additionally shows the difference in relative effort between both treatments per task and across all tasks. The computation of that value weights the number of created trace links and the number of removed trace links differently in order to reflect that deleting a trace link requires less effort than creating a new one on average. The relative effort further takes into account the effort for user interaction during semi-automated traceability updates. A detailed discussion of the relative effort and its computation is given in (Mäder, 2009).

Regarding research question 1, Table 1(a) shows that the subjects of the tM-treatment working with support of the approach spent between 48 and 82% less time per task and 71% less time across all tasks for maintaining traceability. All

Table 1 Experiment statistics

(a) Number of changes and interactions   (b) Precision and recall of changes

task	var	treat	mean	sd	%-diff	t-test	var	treat	mean	sd	%-diff	t-test
1	n_m	notM	18.6	9.5	−87%	0.00	Q_P	notM	78.9	36.5	21%	0.34
		tM	2.4	1.8				tM	95.7	6.0		
	n_a	tM	36.2	23.9	rel. effort		Q_R	notM	78.0	36.3	−6%	0.82
	n_{ui}	tM	2.0	2.0	−82%			tM	73.3	32.7		
2	n_m	notM	7.7	4.9	−90%	0.01	Q_P	notM	83.3	31.0	19%	0.29
		tM	0.8	1.8				tM	98.9	2.5		
	n_a	tM	13.0	3.3	rel. effort		Q_R	notM	59.5	35.3	51%	0.10
	n_{ui}	tM	6.2	4.9	−48%			tM	90.0	14.1		
3	n_m	notM	10.0	4.7	−66%	0.04	Q_P	notM	81.6	37.5	17%	0.44
		tM	3.4	4.7				tM	95.6	6.5		
	n_a	tM	12.4	14	rel. effort		Q_R	notM	76.2	35.8	−11%	0.67
	n_{ui}	tM	0.8	0.8	−67%			tM	67.8	27.3		
All	n_m	notM	36.3	12.8	−82%	0.00	Q_P	notM	79.5	25.7	21%	0.19
		tM	6.6	3.8				tM	95.9	4.3		
	n_a	tM	59.6	34.7	rel. effort		Q_R	notM	71.3	27.6	11%	0.61
	n_{ui}	tM	9.0	4.1	−71%			tM	78.8	19.0		

the discovered differences between the treatments were statistically significant. These figures demonstrate that the approach affords a reduction of manual effort for maintaining traceability.

Regarding research question 2, Table 1(b) shows that the precision of the changes across all tasks in the tM-treatment were 95.9% on average. This means that the precision of the changes across all tasks in the experimental group was 21% higher than that of the control group on average. The computed recall metric for the performed changes shows that members of the *tM* treatment performed 11% more of the required changes on average. Nevertheless, all the computed quality measures for recall and precision possess a high standard deviation, especially for the control group, thus all the differences between both treatments regarding quality are not statistically significant. This means that the approach delivers a maintenance quality comparable to manually performed traceability maintenance, though the results also show a tendency for the precision to be better than if the developer worked manually.

6.4 Discussion

While trying to find partners to evaluate the approach, two perspectives materialised. After an explanation of the approach with employees responsible for traceability within development projects at Siemens, one employee replied: "I do not think that I like an automated solution for this sensible task. I want people to think about their changes again while maintaining traceability." A second employee replied: "That is exactly the solution I was waiting for; it can save us a lot of work." The decision for or against a (semi-)automated approach to traceability maintenance is individual. The approach can save tedious and error-prone work, but it should not be seen as a solution that makes the maintenance of traceability something the developer does not have to think about anymore. With respect to the particular approach outlined in this chapter, the following critique is provided.

Development Methodology The approach assumes model-based development, using a UML modelling tool, establishing traceability in accordance to a TIM. Except for the use of a TIM, this is exactly the scenario that was reported by nine of the ten companies profiled in (Mäder et al., 2009). While the scenario is common in industry, there are other domains with different settings. The extension of the approach to additional types of diagrams and models remains a future task. Regarding the use of a TIM, a major problem is the missing support for such definitions within the most commonly used commercial CASE (Computer-Aided Software Engineering) tools.

Predefined Rule Catalogue A limitation of the approach is that only predefined development activities can be recognised and these are unlikely to be exhaustive. It will be necessary to customise and extend the rule catalogue. In order to address this issue, a rule editor is provided by the prototype with checks to validate changes to rules. Nevertheless, the task remains a manual one.

Semantic Correctness of Trace Links The approach maintains existing trace links irrespective of whether they are semantically correct or not. It is not possible to find out about the correctness of these trace links, or even to improve their quality, so a reasonable pre-existing set is required to make the approach useful. For projects where this initial quality cannot be guaranteed, the manual maintenance of traceability might be the better choice, allowing the developer to correct problems when recognised.

Uncertainty in the Recognition Process There are several points of uncertainty in the process of recognising development activities that might lead to incorrect or missing traceability updates. Missing rules and missing alternatives within rules can lead to unrecognised development activities and missing updates, while insufficiently defined rules can lead to the recognition of development activities that have not been performed and so, in turn, lead to incorrect traceability updates. The validation functionality within the rule editor supports the identification of certain problems within a rule definition. Nevertheless, large parts of ensuring the correctness and completeness of the rule catalogue remains manual work. While no concrete figures regarding the quality of the current rule catalogue can be given, the fact that all (semi-)automated updates were performed without mistakes during the discussed experiment indicates a high effectiveness of the current rule catalogue.

Scope of and Threats to Empirical Studies More statistical data need to be gathered on the cost/benefit trade-off of the approach, costs in terms of customising and extending the rules, and benefits in terms of the time saved on manual maintenance across all projects using the rules. The discussed experiment showed a saving in effort while using the existing rule catalogue. Unfortunately, no data are available on the work related to evolving related models and triggering the necessity for traceability maintenance within development projects. Without this information it is difficult to calculate how much effort is really saved on a project.

7 Conclusions and Future Challenges

This chapter has focused on the traceability-related challenges of evolving projects. It discussed two of the core activities of the traceability life cycle: (1) defining the traceability that is required on a project and (2) keeping the traceability ready-to-use by maintaining previously established trace links as the project evolves. It also described a (semi-)automated approach that can reduce the effort of maintaining traceability within a model-based development context.

TIMs are an essential component of any traceability process. Unfortunately, they are not widely adopted in industrial projects. CASE tool vendors are encouraged to provide better support for TIMs and the benefits of having a defined traceability strategy, including a TIM, should be further promoted by consultants and researchers.

The motivation for the development of the approach described in this chapter was to reduce the manual effort involved in the maintenance of traceability as much as possible. Nevertheless, there are two points that still require manual work to keep traceability ready-to-use: (1) selecting impacted trace links during a semi-automated update and (2) customising and extending the rules that guide the update. To address the first point, the visualisation and animation of the impacted element, along with all related elements before and after the update, could support the user in her/his decision. To address the second point, the existing rule editor could be extended by functionality that allows new rules to be determined semi-automatically, by observing a developer performing change activities in situ using a rule recorder.

While the approach supports structural UML diagrams, it would be desirable to extend it to other kinds of development model. The necessary preconditions would be models described in a semi-formal language with a defined meta-model and sufficient element properties to allow for the identification of meaningful development activities. The following types of diagrams would meet these preconditions: behavioural UML diagrams, feature diagrams, Mathworks Simulink^{TM} diagrams and NI LabView^{TM} diagrams.

The described approach has a local perspective on the traceability maintenance problem, meaning that traces connecting to elements of a changed model will be maintained. There is also a global perspective on the traceability maintenance problem, where changes to one model often have an impact on related models and their traces (see Section 3). A common solution is the propagation of information about a change on to related models via existing trace links. While such a change propagation approach has been used in commercial development, the problem lies in the classification of the impact a change to one model has on a related model (see Fig. 4). The state of the practice is the propagation of any change, leaving the developer with the decision as to whether the propagated change has an impact on the artifact she/he is responsible for or not. A more sophisticated and selective procedure would be desirable, based upon the available information about the change and its type, following the work of (Cleland-Huang et al., 2003). The knowledge of recognised development activities could facilitate this goal.

The requirements traceability problem (Gotel and Finkelstein, 1994) has many facets and it is unlikely that there will ever be one single approach that solves the whole problem, but much has been achieved over the past decade providing promising approaches to partial aspects. A major goal for the traceability community should clearly be the integration of promising techniques in order to provide a solution for the whole traceability life cycle of a project. The integration of automated approaches that support the initial creation of traceability with the approach described in this chapter would give stakeholders the opportunity to retain their investment through ongoing (semi-)automated traceability maintenance. Another more technical issue of integration refers to the tooling environment within larger projects. Different artifacts of the development process are often held in a variety of tools and the support for traceability between these tools is, in many cases, not sufficient (Mäder et al., 2009). This integration seems to be a precondition for the extended usage and ongoing maintenance of traceability in larger distributed industrial projects.

References

Aizenbud-Reshef, N., Nolan, B.T., Rubin, J., Shaham-Gafni, Y.: Model traceability. IBM Syst. J. **45**(3), 515–526 (2006). ISSN 0018-8670

Alexander, I.: Toward automatic traceability in industrial practice. In: Proceedings of 1st International Workshop on Traceability in Emerging Forms of Software Engineering (TEFSE02). In Conjunction with the 17th IEEE International Conference on Automated Software Engineering (ASE02), Edinburgh, UK, pp. 26–31 (2002, September)

Antoniol, G., Canfora, G., Casazza, G., Lucia, A.D., Merlo, E.: Recovering traceability links between code and documentation. IEEE Trans. Softw. Eng. **28**(10), 970–983 (2002, October). ISSN 0098-5589

Arkley, P., Mason, P., Riddle, S.: Position paper: Enabling traceability. In: Proceedings of 1st International Workshop on Traceability in Emerging Forms of Software Engineering (TEFSE02). In Conjunction with the 17th IEEE International Conference on Automated Software Engineering (ASE02), Edinburgh, UK, pp. 61–65 (2002, September)

Arlow, J., Neustadt, I.: UML 2 and the Unified Process: Practical Object-Oriented Analysis and Design, 2nd edn. Addison-Wesley, Boston, MA (2005). ISBN 0-321-32127-8

Cleland-Huang, J., Chang, C.K., Christensen, M.J.: Event-based traceability for managing evolutionary change. IEEE Trans. Softw. Eng. **29**(9), 796–810 (2003). ISSN 0098-5589

Cleland-Huang, J., Chang, C.K., Ge, Y.: Supporting event based traceability through high-level recognition of change events. In: Annual International Computer Software and Applications Conference (COMPSAC02), pp. 595–602. IEEE Computer Society, Los Alamitos, CA (2002). ISBN 0-7695-1727-7

Egyed, A.: Automatically detecting and tracking inconsistencies in software design models. IEEE Trans. Softw Eng. **37**(2), 188–204 (2011, March). ISSN 0098-5589

Engels, G., Heckel, R., Küster, J.M., Groenewegen, L.: Consistency-preserving model evolution through transformations. In: Proceedings 5th International Conference UML 2002 – The Unified Modeling Language. Model Engineering, Languages, Concepts, and Tools. Lecture Notes in Computer Science, vol. 2460, pp. 212–226. Springer, Berlin (2002). ISSN 3-540-44254-5

Finkelstein, A.C.W., Gabbay, D.M., Hunter, A., Kramer, J., Nuseibeh, B.: Inconsistency handling in multiperspective specifications. IEEE Trans. Softw. Eng. **20**(8), 569–578 (1994, August). ISSN 0098-5589

Gotel, O.C.Z., Finkelstein, A.C.W.: An analysis of the requirements traceability problem. In: Proceedings of the First International Conference on Requirements Engineering (ICRE94), pp. 94–101. IEEE Computer Society, Colorado Springs, CO (1994, April). ISBN 0-8186-5480-5, 0-8186-5481-3

Grundy, J.C., Hosking, J.G., Mugridge, W.B.: Inconsistency management for multiple-view software development environments. IEEE Trans. Softw. Eng. **24**(11), 960–981 (1998). ISSN 0098-5589

Hayes, J.H., Dekhtyar, A., Osborne, J.: Improving requirements tracing via information retrieval. In: Procerdings of 11th IEEE International Requierments Engineering Conference (RE03), pp. 138–148. IEEE Computer Society, Los Alamitos, CA (2003, September). ISBN 0-7695-1980-6

Hnatkowska, B., Huzar, Z., Kuzniarz, L., Tuzinkiewicz, L.: Refinement relationship between collaborations. In: Proceedings Workshop on Consistency Problems in UML-Based Software Development, UML'03, pp. 51–57. IEEE Computer Society, San Francisco, CA (2003)

Huzar, Z., Kuzniarz, L., Reggio, G., Sourrouille, J.-L.: Consistency problems in UML-based software development. In Nunes, N.J., Selic, B., da Silva, A.R., Álvarez, J.A.T. (eds.) UML Satellite Activities. Lecture Notes in Computer Science, vol. 3297, pp. 1–12. Springer, Heidelberg (2004). ISBN 3-540-25081-6

Jacobson, I., Rumbaugh, J., Booch, G.: The Unified Software Development Process. Object Technology Series. Addison-Wesley, Reading, MA (1999). ISBN 0-201-57169-2

Letelier, P.: A framework for requirements traceability in UML-based projects. In: Proceedings of 1st International Workshop on Traceability in Emerging Forms of Software Engineering (TEFSE02). In Conjunction with the 17th IEEE International Conference on Automated Software Engineering (ASE02), pp. 32–41. Edinburgh, UK (2002, September)

Lucia, A.D., Oliveto, R., Tortora, G.: IR-based traceability recovery processes: an empirical comparison of one-shot and incremental processes. In: 23rd IEEE/ACM International Conference on Automated Software Engineering (ASE 2008), 15–19 September 2008, L'Aquila, Italy, pp. 39–48. IEEE Computer Society, Los Alamitos, CA (2008). ISBN 978-1-4244-2776-5

Mäder, P.: Rule-based maintenance of post-requirements traceability. PhD Thesis. MV-Verlag, Münster (2009, October). ISBN 978-3-86991-093-2

Mäder, P., Cleland-Huang, J.: A visual traceability modeling language. In Petriu, D., Rouquette, N., Haugen, Ø. (eds.), Model Driven Engineering Languages and Systems. Lecture Notes in Computer Science, vol. 6394, pp. 226–240. Springer, Berlin/Heidelberg (2010)

Mäder, P., Gotel, O., Philippow, I.: Rule-based maintenance of post-requirements traceability relations. In: Proceedings of 16th International Requirements Engineering Conference (RE'08), Barcelona, Spain, pp. 23–32 (2008, September). ISSN 1090-705X

Mäder, P., Gotel, O., Philippow, I.: Getting back to basics: Promoting the use of a traceability information model in practice. In: Proceedings of 5th International Workshop on Traceability in Emerging Forms of Software Engineering (TEFSE2009). In conjunction with the 31st International Conference on Software Engineering (ICSE09), pp. 21–25. Vancouver, Canada (2009a, May)

Mäder, P., Gotel, O., Philippow, I.: Semi-automated traceability maintenance: An architectural overview of trace MAINTAINER. In: Proceedings 5th ECMDA Traceability Workshop (ECMDA-TW 2009). In conjunction with the 5th European Conference on Model-Driven Architecture Foundations and Applications (ECMDA2009), pp. 7–16. Enschede, The Netherlands (2009b, June)

Mäder, P., Gotel, O., Philippow, I.: Motivation matters in the traceability trenches. In: Proceedings of 17th International Requirements Engineering Conference (RE'09), pp. 143–148. Atlanta, GA (2009, August)

Maletic, J.I., Collard, M.L., Simoes, B.: An XML based approach to support the evolution of model-to-model traceability links. In Proceedings of 3rd International Workshop on Traceability in Emerging Forms of Software Engineering TEFSE'05, pp. 67–72. ACM, New York, NY (2005). ISBN 1-59593-243-7

Marcus, A., Maletic, J.I.: Recovering documentation-to-source-code traceability links using latent semantic indexing. In: Proceedings of the 25th International Conference on Software Engineering (ICSE03), pp. 125–137. IEEE Computer Society, Piscataway, NJ (2003, May 3–10)

Mens, T., van der Straeten, R., Simmonds, J.: A framework for managing consistency of evolving UML models. In Yang, H. (ed.) Software Evolution with UML and XML, pp. 1–30. Hershey, PA: IGI Publishing (2005). ISBN 1-59140462-2

Murta, L.G.P., van der Hoek, A., Werner, C.M.L.: Archtrace: Policy-based support for managing evolving architecture-to-implementation traceability links. In: 21st IEEE/ACM International Conference on Automated Software Engineering, 2006 (ASE'06), pp. 135–144 (2006, September). ISSN 1527-1366

Murta, L.G.P., van der Hoek, A., Werner, C.M.L.: Continuous and automated evolution of architecture-to-implementation traceability links. Automat. Softw. Eng. J. 15(1), 75–107 (2008). ISSN 0928-8910

OMG: MDA Guide Version 1.0.1. Object Management Group (OMG), Framingham, MA. omg/2003-06-01 (2003, June)

OMG.: UML 2.0 Superstructure. OMG Final Adopted Specification. Ptc/04-10-02. Object Management Group (OMG), Framingham, MA (2004, June)

OMG.: OMG Unified Modeling Language Specification (OMG UML) Version 2.1.2. Object Management Group (OMG), Framingham, MA formal/2007-11-02 (2007, November)

OMG.: OMG System Modeling Language (OMG SysML) Version 1.1. Object Management Group OMG, Framingham, MA. formal/2008-11-01 (2008, November)

Pinheiro, F.A.C.: Requirements traceability. In: Leite, J.C.S.P., Doorn, J. (eds.), Perspectives on Software Requirements, pp. 91–113. Kluwer, The Netherlands (2004). ISBN 1-402-07625-8

Ramesh, B., Jarke, M.: Toward reference models of requirements traceability. IEEE Trans. Softw. Eng. 27(1), 58–93 (2001). ISSN 0098-5589

Spanoudakis, G., Zisman, A., Pérez-Miñana, E., Krause, P.: Rule-based generation of requirements traceability relations. J. Syst. Softw. 72(2), 105–127 (2004, Juli). ISSN 0164-1212

Weilkiens, T.: Systems Engineering mit SysML/UML. dpunkt.verlag (2006). ISBN 3-8986-4409-X

Evolution-Driven Trace Acquisition in Eclipse-Based Product Line Workspaces

Wolfgang Heider, Paul Grünbacher, Rick Rabiser, and Martin Lehofer

1 Introduction

Practitioners and researchers generally agree that trace links are vital for understanding software systems and for supporting mission-critical engineering tasks. Trace links can be used for determining the impact of changes during maintenance, they allow performing coverage analyses, and they support checking consistency among arbitrary artifacts. Traceability is nowadays mandated by standards and prescribed in development methods in many domains. Despite significant advances in traceability research, acquiring trace links remains challenging and requires high efforts of developers and domain experts (Egyed et al., 2010).

Traceability represents a major challenge in software product line engineering (PLE) as variability has to be addressed at multiple levels of abstraction (Anquetil et al., 2010). PLE distinguishes two life cycles (Pohl et al., 2005): development for reuse (also called domain engineering) and development with reuse (also called application engineering). Domain engineering covers the development of reusable artifacts such as code, models, or documents and defining their variability. Application engineering deals with deriving products from the product line by exploiting its variability. In PLE traceability is relevant to understand dependencies among the diverse reusable artifacts as well as between the product line and the derived products which often include additional developments and customizations. Traceability in PLE thus helps understanding variability and ensuring the consistency of products. Engineers need traceability support in IDEs when modifying product line artifacts.

There are basically two ways for acquiring trace links (Asuncion, 2010). In *retrospective trace acquisition*, trace links are identified ex post by statically analyzing artifacts, for example, by parsing existing product line models to find trace links among model elements. In *prospective approaches* trace links are created

W. Heider (✉)
Christian Doppler Laboratory for Automated Software Engineering, Johannes Kepler University, Linz, Austria
e-mail: heider@ase.jku.at

J. Cleland-Huang et al. (eds.), *Software and Systems Traceability*,
DOI 10.1007/978-1-4471-2239-5_9, © Springer-Verlag London Limited 2012

"on the fly" by observing artifacts as they are created and modified by users during development. Researchers have proposed various techniques and heuristics to support the acquisition and evolution of traces. Examples include event-based approaches (Cleland-Huang et al., 2003), information retrieval (Cleland-Huang et al., 2007), feature location techniques (Koschke and Quante, 2005), process-oriented approaches (Pohl, 1996), scenario-based techniques (Egyed, 2001), or rule-based methods (Mäder et al., 2008; Spanoudakis et al., 2004).

This chapter presents an event-based approach that allows acquiring trace links in a standard IDE used for model-based product line development. There are two contributions: *we discuss challenges of traceability in PLE and illustrate these challenges* in the context of the tool-supported DOPLER approach. Furthermore, *we present a trace acquisition approach for PLE that is based on tracking changes in an IDE*. Our EvoKing tool uses a meta-model that defines artifacts, evolution events and trace links. Traces are identified based on evolution events which are created based on tracking changes or analyzing files in the workspace. The tool uses information about the artifact structure defined as extensions to the EvoKing framework. These extensions include mappings of change notifications and facts (i.e., analyzed data of stored models and files) with evolution events and trace links. Our model-based approach supports both retrospective and prospective tracing and can deal with arbitrary types of artifacts.

Throughout the chapter we use the mobile phone product line case study (see Appendix C) to illustrate our approach. We regard our approach as interesting to both researchers in the area of tool-supported trace acquisition as well as practitioners that need to provide support for traceability in their development environment.

2 Product Line Engineering and Traceability

A software product line is a "a set of software-intensive systems sharing a common, managed set of features that satisfy the needs of a particular market segment or mission and that are developed from a common set of core assets in a prescribed way" (Clements and Northrop, 2001). Product lines aim at increasing the degree of reuse in software engineering to reduce cost and time-to-market and to increase software quality and reliability (Pohl et al., 2005). Reports show that product lines are successfully used in many business environments (Clements and Northrop, 2001; Pohl et al., 2005; van der Linden et al., 2007). Many product line approaches are based on models that define the variability of the reusable artifacts. For instance, researchers and practitioners use feature models (Czarnecki and Eisenecker, 2000; Kang et al., 1990) or decision models (Schmid et al., 2011) to define product line variability.

PLE involves modeling the problem space (the variability of the product line's features and capabilities) and the solution space (the architecture and the components of the technical solution). It is fundamental to understand the relationship between the problem and solution space. It is however also critical to establish trace links among the elements within both spaces (Vierhauser et al., 2010). Trace links are needed in PLE when configuring and assembling products. Traceability is thus a prerequisite for automation in PLE.

Several authors have presented research on traceability in product lines. For instance, Jirapanthong and Zisman (2009) describe support for rule-based trace link generation between different artifacts and discuss scenarios of how trace links can help in PLE. Berg et al. (2005) discuss tracing of variability in product lines at different levels and present a variability modeling approach with support for traceability. Mohan and Ramesh (2007) argue that "high-end traceability practices significantly improve the performance of product family developers in maintenance tasks." However, existing research does not provide sufficient traceability support for the evolution of product line artifacts in specific development environments.

Commercial product line tools provide basic traceability support. For instance, the pure::variants synchronizer (pure systems GmbH, 2006) for CaliberRM and DOORS allows developers to benefit from the functionalities of these requirements management tools. Similarly, GEARS (Krueger, 2008) integrates with DOORS, UGS TeamCenter, and IBM/Rational RequisitePro to support requirements management. However, despite these basic mechanisms the tools lack full life cycle support for traceability in PLE. According to Anquetil et al. (2010) existing commercial tools for requirements management and traceability do not provide proper built-in support for product line evolution and there is also only little progress regarding traceability support in existing PLE tool suites.

Compared to traditional single systems engineering traceability in PLE is challenged by the interconnected life cycles of domain and application engineering. More specifically, the traceability challenges shown in Fig. 1 are relevant in PLE:

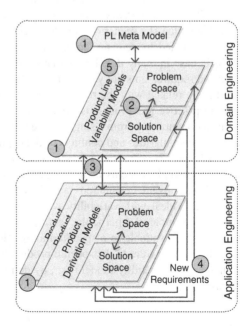

Fig. 1 Traceability challenges in the two product line life cycles. The *arrows* indicate common types of trace links in product line engineering. The *numbers* indicate traceability challenges

Challenge (1) – Dealing with the diversity of product line artifacts and tools.
Product lines comprise different types of artifacts, e.g., variability models, software components, or documents. The artifacts are created and maintained with different tools. Traceability is required among the artifacts as well as between specific elements within the artifacts, e.g., the model elements. Meta-models are often used to define the artifact types and their granularity. They allow establishing vertical trace links between different types of artifacts and between artifacts at different levels of granularity.

Challenge (2) – Ensuring traceability during product line development. During product line development it is essential to establish trace links among problem space elements representing variability from the perspective of users, for example, between different choices about the functionality of a mobile phone camera. Similarly, trace links are needed among solution space elements representing reusable and interdependent assets, e.g., between components, test cases, or documents implementing or describing the mobile phone camera. Furthermore, solution space models have to be mapped to the actual reusable artifacts like code or test cases. Establishing such trace links is essential for keeping the product line consistent (Vierhauser et al., 2010).

Challenge (3) – Establishing traceability from the product line to the products.
The ultimate goal of PLE is to turn out products. Trace links between domain engineering artifacts and application engineering artifacts support maintenance activities and help determining the impact of a change on existing products, e.g., when trying to find out whether an existing mobile phone software can be updated after a change to the product line. Managing such horizontal traces can become very challenging as many products are derived from a product line over time. Also, as the product line evolves products are typically derived from different releases.

Challenge (4) – Relating new product requirements with the product line. The unrealistic blue-sky scenario in product derivation is that all customer requirements can be satisfied by reusing and composing existing product line assets. A more realistic case in many domains is that customers articulate additional, often unanticipated requirements not yet covered by the product line. These new requirements need to be related with the reusable assets to support the evolution of the product line. In practice this process is often further complicated as multiple products are derived concurrently from a single product line. In this case trace links are essential to analyze similarities and conflicts of the captured requirements.

Challenge (5) – Treating variability as a first class citizen in traceability. Models describing single systems do not regard variability as a first class citizen and all model elements are considered part of the system. In product lines modelers need to explicitly deal with variability which makes managing traceability more difficult. For example, if a particular feature is not included in a derived product (e.g., no camera is available in a specific mobile phone) one still needs to capture trace links from the feature to the specific product to avoid possible inconsistencies after changing the variability model (e.g., by defining the camera as mandatory in later releases).

3 Traceability in the DOPLER Product Line Approach

We further illustrate the presented traceability challenges in the context of the DOPLER approach (Dhungana et al., 2011; Grünbacher et al., 2009; Rabiser et al., 2009). DOPLER uses decision models to define variability. The DOPLER tools allow defining a product line meta-model and support product derivation involving different types of product line artifacts (cf. challenge 1).

From a traceability perspective the relevant types of artifacts in DOPLER are product line meta-models, variability models, derivation models, and specific model elements in these models. Figure 2 depicts these key artifact types together with relevant relations. It also shows examples of change events that can result in the creation or update of trace links.

Product line meta-models specify the types of reusable assets, their attributes, and dependencies for a given domain. In the mobile phone example, the asset type Implementation Technique represents components providing capabilities like the Bluetooth connectivity of a mobile phone. This asset type consists of the attributes name, description, and version. Implementation Technique also defines a possible dependency implements to assets of type Operating Environment.

Variability models in DOPLER describe the problem space with decision models and the solution space with asset models that are based on the asset types predefined in the product line meta-model (Dhungana et al., 2011). Decisions represent the assets' variability. Decisions have a name (e.g., "connectivity") and a type (Boolean, String, Double, or Enumeration). They are represented as questions, e.g., "Which connections for transferring data?" Decisions can depend on each other hierarchically (e.g., a decision needs to be taken before another one) and/or logically (e.g.,

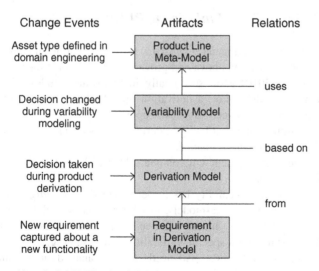

Fig. 2 Key artifacts in DOPLER with high-level relations and examples of change events (Heider et al., 2009)

taking a decision changes the value of another one). The decision dependencies determine the order of taking decisions but do not define configuration constraints. Assets are related with decisions via explicit inclusion conditions to establish traceability between the solution space and the problem space of the product line (cf. challenge 5) and define for an asset under which condition it is part of a product. For example, the asset Bluetooth Stack is part of the product if the option Bluetooth is selected for the decision on data transfer connections. Assets without an explicit mapping to the problem space can be included for a derived product through functional relations from other assets (cf. challenge 2) that are included because of a decision.

A *derivation model* (Rabiser et al., 2007) is a product-specific instance of a variability model and establishes trace links between the product line and concrete products (cf. challenge 3). It further defines additional elements such as tasks, roles, and users. Tasks are groups of decisions, which result in trace links from product derivation tasks to decisions, and guide product derivation by providing multiple views on the problem space. Roles define responsibilities for tasks, e.g., sales, project management, or engineering. Roles can be assigned to concrete users resulting in user-role-task relations. Derivation models are furthermore used to define guidance on decisions, e.g., to provide documentation useful for resolving variability. Derivation models also store the actual values of decisions. They can also contain requirements that represent new customer wishes (Rabiser and Dhungana, 2007) captured during product derivation, e.g., requested functionalities such as "bookmark synchronization" of a mobile phone browser. These requirements are also related with product line variability models through trace links (cf. challenge 4).

3.1 Granularity of Trace Links in DOPLER

The DOPLER tool suite (Dhungana et al., 2011) supports creating and managing the models and artifacts described above and provides initial support for model evolution (Dhungana et al., 2010). More specifically the tool suite includes a meta-model editor, a variability model editor, a derivation model editor, and a configuration wizard supporting end users such as sales people or project managers in deriving products. The configuration wizard utilizes derivation models and guides the user in resolving variability by taking decisions.

Similar to other development environments DOPLER distinguishes between coarse- and fine-grain traces:

Coarse-grain traces. Traceability has to be managed *in the large*, i.e., among the diverse types of models (meta-models, variability models, and derivation models). For instance, a variability model is based on a particular meta-model and a derivation model instantiates a specific variability model (see Fig. 2).

Fine-grain traces. Traceability also needs to be managed *in the small*, i.e., between model elements such as decisions, assets, or requirements. These elements are often not part of the same model. For example, requirements are captured in different derivation models but can be related with individual decisions or assets in arbitrary variability models.

4 EvoKing Traceability Support

To address traceability at different levels of granularity and for arbitrary artifacts we have been developing the EvoKing approach and tool (Heider et al., 2009). EvoKing is based on a generic meta-model similar to existing approaches for software evolution analysis (Girba and Ducasse, 2006) and traceability frameworks (Anquetil et al., 2010). This generic meta-model has to be extended to define the elements that are to be tracked. EvoKing monitors changes to artifacts and derives trace links by analyzing these changes. EvoKing saves data about changes right in the moment the elements are modified (live prospective tracing) but also allows restoring traceability information from already existing workspace artifacts (ex post retrospective tracing).

The tool is realized as a set of Eclipse plug-ins monitoring low-level change events in Eclipse and creating trace links between arbitrary artifacts such as code, documents, or models stored in Eclipse workspaces. EvoKing thereby complements the existing file-level change tracking feature of Eclipse and can easily be adapted to any Eclipse-based IDE. Our testbed for developing EvoKing has been the DOPLER tool suite.

4.1 Tracking Changes to Acquire Trace Links

Our approach establishes trace links while product line artifacts evolve and thus relies on tracking changes to diverse artifacts during product line modeling and maintenance. Examples of changes in model-based PLE are the creation of models (e.g., new product derivation model) or modifications of models (e.g., adding a new feature to a variability model).

Our approach focuses on establishing trace links on the fly to provide as much information as possible to the modeler in product line maintenance. However, trace links are not just based on prospective tracing by observing model changes. Upon activating EvoKing the first time, a retrospective analysis of the artifacts is performed automatically to extract trace information by utilizing the APIs of the integrated tools. For instance, we instrumented DOPLER to track all changes to variability models in the IDE and to find all derivation models using a specific variability model.

Extensions to our tool define how events map to relations between the involved artifacts and how trace links can be found within a file or a model. We do not apply heuristics or statistical data as other retrospective analysis methods. We use facts to recover artifact-specific trace links. For example, we check model equality to find the variability model that is used for a derivation model. However, in artifact definitions one could also implement heuristics to recover trace links if desired.

4.2 Evolution Meta-Model

When adapting EvoKing to a particular product line development environment one needs to define the artifacts to be tracked, the events to be captured and the trace link types as relations among them. The generic EvoKing meta-model for tracking evolution comprises the elements Artifact, Event, and Relation (cf. Fig. 3). We use a layered approach: our generic meta-model defines just the basic elements for the evolution and traceability data structure. These elements are then refined to specific domains and technologies using custom artifact definitions.

An **artifact** represents an element of interest for establishing traceability and tracking changes. Examples of artifacts in product lines are meta-models, variability models, model elements (e.g., decisions, assets), documents (Rabiser et al., 2010), or new product requirements captured during product derivation (Rabiser and Dhungana, 2007). Artifacts can have arbitrary attributes, e.g., the URL of the related resource and a flag whether it has been deleted or still exists in the workspace. A change event fired by the IDE (e.g., a derivation model file was created) or by model editors (e.g., a decision was added) indicates changes to artifacts and might lead to the creation of trace links (e.g., if a derivation model is instantiated from a variability model).

Based on the generic evolution meta-model, arbitrary **events** can be defined and are instantiated with the specified artifact definitions. Relevant events can be derived from existing process models and workflows in product line engineering (cf. Fig. 2). For example, modifying a decision to add a new network option to the mobile phone product line constitutes an event with information about a new version of this decision.

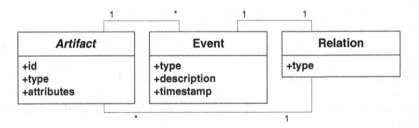

Fig. 3 Generic EvoKing meta-model for evolution tracking of arbitrary artifacts. Artifact is an abstract class and has to be extended for defining concrete artifacts. Implementing an artifact also requires instantiating events and relations as reactions to change notifications

A **relation** among artifacts is established by an event tracked for a specific artifact. Such links can be spatial or temporal. Spatial relations between artifacts describe how the artifacts are organized, e.g., a derivation model is an *instance of* a variability model or a decision is *defined in* a variability model. Temporal relationships are created to track the evolution history of artifacts, for instance, each modification of a decision is stored in events related to the variability model containing that decision. When refining our evolution meta-model to a particular development environment, users can define different types of trace links with different semantics in their definitions of artifacts. For example, the artifact definition of a derivation model covers decisions taken during product derivation. In this case trace links are created from decisions to derived products, e.g., to determine how a particular decision has been made in already derived products.

4.3 Capturing Notifications and Establishing Traceability

Software engineers customize EvoKing for tracking evolution and generating trace links in arbitrary Eclipse-based environments. Our evolution meta-model defines a data structure for storing evolution and trace data. It can be refined for arbitrary elements and represents the core of our tool-supported approach. EvoKing allows adding extensions for resolving domain-specific relations. It supports interpreting notifications from Eclipse for specific models or model elements and therefore add semantic information to change events.

As depicted in Fig. 4, EvoKing works as a consumer and recipient of primitive change notifications coming from Eclipse or other tools (e.g., a variability model editor) involved in modifying the artifacts. Based on the incoming notifications evolution events with more detailed information regarding changed content and new or changed trace links are generated as implemented in the domain-specific artifact

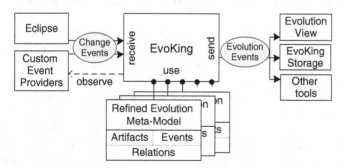

Fig. 4 EvoKing receives change events and adds information through artifact/event/relation definitions from refined evolution meta-models and stores evolution and trace information

definitions. Evolution events are stored for each artifact. EvoKing receives change events based on information from two sources:

(i) EvoKing receives and analyzes *Eclipse* resource *change events* such as "file added" or "file modified". Using the model-specific APIs the tool then retrospectively parses the models stored in the files to recognize internal changes. Such changes are mapped to artifacts, events, and trace links as defined in the refined evolution meta-model. EvoKing thus complements the existing notification mechanisms of Eclipse by adding explicit semantics to events. For example, users can define in the artifact definitions of their refined EvoKing meta-model that the meaning of adding a new file of type derivation model to the workspace represents the start of a new product derivation based on a related variability model. In this case a trace link can be established to the originating variability model (cf. Fig. 2).

(ii) *Custom event providers* for specific artifact types (e.g., variability models) can send custom events (e.g., "decision added") to EvoKing to enable live, prospective tracking. A listener can be generated semi-automatically using Java Reflection for a particular type of model to receive and store change notifications. EvoKing can then track internal changes made to a model. Notifications are automatically transformed to evolution events according to the artifact definitions.

The *evolution events* are stored in a local file if working offline or in the online *EvoKing storage* accessible by other product line stakeholders to synchronize engineering activities. *Other tools* can implement EvoKing's notification interfaces to be informed about relevant evolution events. For instance, EvoKing's storage can be visualized in a tree-based *evolution view* (cf. Fig. 7) depicting all tracked artifacts, the evolution events as well as trace links to affected artifacts.

4.4 Evolution Tracking in the DOPLER Eclipse Workspace

The predefined Eclipse artifacts automatically tracked by EvoKing are the workspace entities file and project (cf. Fig. 5). Users can specify the Eclipse projects and specific file types they want to be tracked by activating EvoKing for Eclipse projects and by providing the proper artifact definitions for the file extensions as Java classes. For tracking DOPLER models we defined the file extensions .meta (*Product Line Meta-Model*), .var (*Variability Model*) and .gen (*Product Derivation Model*). These artifact definitions include implementations to utilize the DOPLER model APIs for extracting and observing internal changes and to find references to extract trace links. The implementer of an artifact definition is responsible to create the events and to add the trace links for the change notifications.

When EvoKing is activated for a specific project a full scan of the project workspace is performed to determine trace links in the defined artifacts

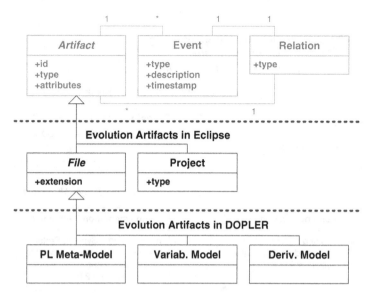

Fig. 5 Basic evolution meta-model for the Eclipse workspace and examples of DOPLER artifacts. The abstract definition of an artifact is extended for specific artifacts in Eclipse and DOPLER. Events and relations are defined within the specific artifact implementations according to the change notifications relevant for trace links

(retrospective tracing). From then on, live prospective tracing is active and EvoKing also tracks internal changes to models.

5 Application Example: Evolving the Mobile Phone Product Line

We provide examples of evolving DOPLER artifacts to illustrate EvoKing's capabilities for tracking changes and acquiring trace links. We created DOPLER product line models based on the data of the mobile phone product line case study. We used the existing feature models, descriptions of mobile phone functionalities, module models and the technical specifications of three product members given to define an initial DOPLER product line model.

Figure 6 shows examples of decisions and assets of the mobile phone product line defined in the product line model. The decision conn offers the three options Bluetooth, Infrared, and USB. According to the cardinality one to three options can be chosen. If at least one connectivity option is selected, the decision syncML becomes available to the user. The inclusion condition for the operating environment asset Bluetooth defines that it is included for a product if the selected options of the conn decision comprise Bluetooth. The relationship implemented by leads to the inclusion of the implementation technique asset named Bluetooth

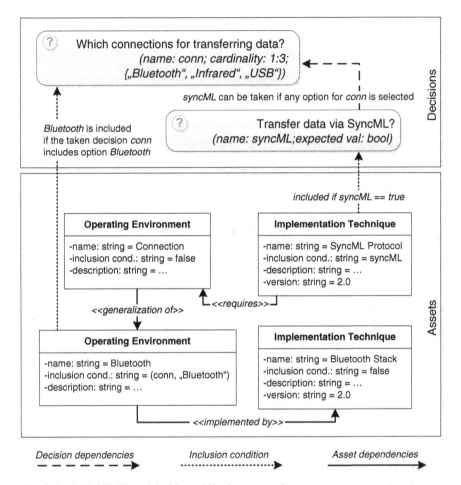

Fig. 6 Partial DOPLER model of the mobile phone example

stack. The asset SyncML Protocoll is added if the syncML decision is set to true. This asset requires the operating environment Connection, which in turn generalizes the Bluetooth operating environment and also all other available connection assets.

We performed multiple changes to the mobile phone product line model (cf. Table 1) to simulate realistic product line evolution (Heider et al., 2010). For example, we added decisions and assets about more advanced mobile phone features such as touch screens.

Using the mobile phone example, we show how EvoKing and its evolution view can assist in coping with the five challenges we described earlier.

Challenge 1 – Dealing with the diversity of product line artifacts and tools. The DOPLER meta-model for the mobile phone example defines all possible asset types in the solution space of the product line. More specifically, we defined

Table 1 Examples of product line evolution

Change activity	Description
Remove decision	We removed the decision on Java support from the variability model as it was decided that Java support should be a part of all products from now on
Change assets	After the "remove decision" change we defined the related assets as mandatory to include full Java support for all future products. We had to change the inclusion conditions of the assets related to the decision on Java support
Capture new requirements	While answering decisions to derive a mobile phone we captured the requests for touch screen and WiFi support. This simulates the situation of mobile phone configuration performed by a product manager defining the new generation of a mobile phone device series
Add decision	We added a Boolean decision "Touch sensitive screen?" to offer the requested support for touch screen
Change decision	We added the option "Wireless LAN" to the decision on connectivity options to offer the requested WiFi connectivity
Add assets	According to the new options for screen and connectivity we added the assets "Touch Screen" and "WiFi" of asset type "Operating Environment"
Add asset relationships	We added generalization relations from the assets "Input Method" and "Screen" to the new asset "Touch Screen"

implementation technique, domain technology and operating environment as asset types. The DOPLER asset model of the mobile phone example (cf. Fig. 6) comprises elements found in the feature model and the module model of the mobile phone case study, for example, Bluetooth and SyncML. The decision model defines questions that need to be asked to resolve variability. We have modeled several decisions (e.g., "Which connections for transferring data?") based on the described product members and their functionalities and based on the variability that is described in the existing feature model.

EvoKing supports tracking changes to these diverse artifacts. Fig. 7 (left pane) shows the unstructured default view of folders and files in the workspace: the Eclipse project explorer contains different files (models) related to the mobile phone product line. Without EvoKing, traceability relations would not be accessible to developers without manually inspecting the involved files. The right pane in Fig. 7 depicts a tree outline of the relevant content (requirement Req_VT100 is expanded), trace links among the different artifacts (Req_VT100 is stored in derivation model mobile_v02.gen, which uses variability model mobile_v02.var), and internal changes (decision changes in variability model mobile_v02.var). EvoKing provides this outline for all artifacts tracked as defined in the EvoKing meta-model. The tree structure represents the trace links among artifacts.

Challenge 2 – Ensuring traceability during product line development. Product line development not just means evolving the reusable components but also requires maintaining the variability models. This ensures that the models reflect the actual functionality that can be offered. After a change to a variability model we need

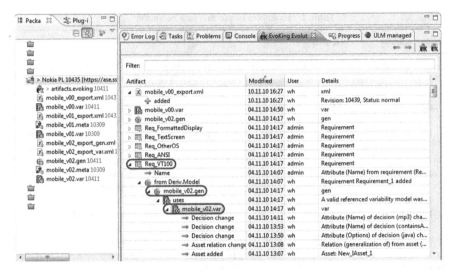

Fig. 7 The unstructured list of product line files in the Eclipse project viewer (*left*) shows no trace links. The EvoKing evolution view (*right*) provides a structured visualization of vertical (e.g., "uses" relation between .gen and .var file) and horizontal trace links between the DOPLER artifacts (e.g., changes to decision attributes in mobile_v02.var)

to find model elements and product line artifacts that are potentially affected to consider them for revision. The dependencies in a specific version of the product line model may be insufficient to determine the backward compatibility of the product line to the products. EvoKing thus allows inspecting the model elements' history to reveal more details about earlier changes and dependencies no longer present in the current product line model.

For example, a modeler intending to update the decision "Touch sensitive screen?" will be interested in related screen functionalities such as Graphic Screen (cf. Fig. 8). The change history reveals possible side effects to other decisions like camera. The figure depicts the change history of model elements related to a search term "screen". We see that in variability model mobile_v02.var the inclusion condition (IncludedIF attribute) of the Graphic Screen asset refers to the camera decision and in variability model mobile_v03.var a new screen option "Touch Screen" was added. This suggests that the modeler should consider possible conflicts or necessary changes regarding the camera option, the graphic screen, and the touch screen option.

Challenge 3 – Establishing traceability from the product line to the products. Changes to the product line models potentially have an impact on already derived products and ongoing product derivation projects. If we want to "replay" a product derivation that was performed with an earlier version of the product line, we need to understand the impact of all changes made in the variability model. For example, when removing a decision from the variability model to thereby define Java support as mandatory feature in future products we need to know the decision values of past

Artifact	Modified	User	Details
▲ 📋 mobile_v03.var	11.11.10 16:28	wh	var
⇒ Asset relation change	11.11.10 16:28	wh	Relation (generalization of) from asset (Screen) to asset (Touch Screen) added
⇒ Asset change	11.11.10 16:26	wh	Attribute (IncludedIF) of asset (Touch Screen) changed from "touch" to "touchscreen"
⇒ Decision change	11.11.10 16:26	wh	Attribute (Name) of decision (touchscreen) changed: "touch" -> "touchscreen"
⇒ Asset change	11.11.10 16:26	wh	Attribute (IncludedIF) of asset (Touch Screen) changed from "true" to "touch"
⇒ Decision change	11.11.10 15:18	wh	Attribute (Question) of decision (touch) changed: "" -> "Touch sensitive screen?"
⇒ Asset relation change	11.11.10 15:16	wh	Relation (generalization of) from asset (Input Method) to asset (Touch Screen) added
⇒ Asset relation change	11.11.10 15:15	wh	Relation (requires) from asset (Touch Screen) to asset (Graphic Screen) added
⇒ Asset change	11.11.10 15:15	wh	Attribute (Name) of asset (Touch Screen) changed from "New_IAsset_1" to "Touch Screen"
▲ 📋 mobile_v02.var	11.11.10 14:59	wh	var
⇒ Asset change	04.11.10 14:11	wh	Attribute (IncludedIF) of asset (Graphic Screen) changed from "camera || videos" to "cam..."
⇒ Asset change	04.11.10 13:55	wh	Attribute (IncludedIF) of asset (Graphic Screen) changed from "camera" to "camera || vid..."
⇒ Asset change	04.11.10 13:03	wh	Attribute (IncludedIF) of asset (Graphic Screen) changed from "true" to "camera"

Fig. 8 Evolution view showing changes to trace links between different model elements (e.g., asset relation change) and temporal trace links showing the history of individual model elements (e.g., asset change)

product derivations. This helps the modeler to assess whether existing products can be derived again with a newer version of the product line.

In Fig. 9 we see mobile phone product line evolution data stored by EvoKing related to the search term "java". In the variability model mobile_v03.var the decision java was removed. In two product derivation projects (represented by derivation models mobile_v03.gen and Product_NKE2311.gen) this decision was set to ["Mobile Media API, Wireless Messaging API"]. A developer can infer maintenance tasks to avoid compatibility issues. For example, she has to make at least these two functionalities and related assets mandatory to avoid reducing the functionality of the products when deriving them again from the product line models, i.e., mobile_v03.gen and Product_NKE2311.gen.

Challenge 4 – Relating new product requirements with the product line. New requirements captured during product derivation are triggers for product line evolution. Engineers incorporate required changes in the product line as early as

Artifact	Modified	User	Details
▲ 📋 mobile_v03.var	16.11.10 15:12	wh	var
⇒ Decision removed	16.11.10 15:12	wh	Decision java removed
▲ 🔩 mobile_v03.gen	16.11.10 15:12	wh	gen
⇒ Decision taken	11.11.10 17:18	wh	Decision java set to value: [Mobile Media API, Wireless Messaging API]
▷ 📋 mobile_v02.var	16.11.10 15:12	wh	var
▷ 🔩 mobile_v02.gen	16.11.10 15:12	?	gen
▲ 🔩 Product_NKE2311.gen	16.11.10 15:12	wh	gen
⇒ Decision taken	11.11.10 17:19	wh	Decision java set to value: [Mobile Media API, Wireless Messaging API]

Fig. 9 EvoKing Evolution view. The events are filtered using the name of a model element (e.g., "java"). The view shows that changes to that model element (e.g., removing decision "java") has an impact on two existing products represented by derivation models NKE2311.gen and mobile_v03.gen

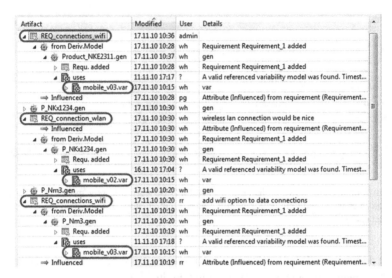

Artifact	Modified	User	Details
⊿ 🔲 REQ_connections_wifi	17.11.10 10:36	admin	
⊿ 🔘 from Deriv.Model	17.11.10 10:28	wh	Requirement Requirement_1 added
⊿ 🔘 Product_NKE2311.gen	17.11.10 10:37	wh	gen
▷ 🖼 Requ. added	17.11.10 10:28	wh	Requirement Requirement_1 added
⊿ 📇 uses	11.11.10 17:17	?	A valid referenced variability model was found. Timest...
▷ 📇 mobile_v03.var	17.11.10 10:15	wh	var
⇒ Influenced	17.11.10 10:28	pg	Attribute (Influenced) from requirement (Requirement...
▷ 🔘 P_NKx1234.gen	17.11.10 10:30	wh	gen
⊿ 🔲 REQ_connection_wlan	17.11.10 10:30	wh	wireless lan connection would be nice
⇒ Influenced	17.11.10 10:30	wh	Attribute (Influenced) from requirement (Requirement...
⊿ 🔘 from Deriv.Model	17.11.10 10:30	wh	Requirement Requirement_1 added
⊿ 🔘 P_NKx1234.gen	17.11.10 10:30	wh	gen
▷ 🖼 Requ. added	17.11.10 10:30	wh	Requirement Requirement_1 added
⊿ 📇 uses	16.11.10 17:04	?	A valid referenced variability model was found. Timest...
▷ 📇 mobile_v02.var	17.11.10 10:15	wh	var
▷ 🔘 P_Nm3.gen	17.11.10 10:20	wh	gen
⊿ 🔲 REQ_connections_wifi	17.11.10 10:20	rr	add wifi option to data connections
⊿ 🔘 from Deriv.Model	17.11.10 10:19	wh	Requirement Requirement_1 added
⊿ 🔘 P_Nm3.gen	17.11.10 10:20	wh	gen
▷ 🖼 Requ. added	17.11.10 10:19	wh	Requirement Requirement_1 added
⊿ 📇 uses	11.11.10 17:18	?	A valid referenced variability model was found. Timest...
▷ 📇 mobile_v03.var	17.11.10 10:15	wh	var
⇒ Influenced	17.11.10 10:19	rr	Attribute (Influenced) from requirement (Requirement...

Fig. 10 Trace links from new requirements to the derivation model which is related to the variability model (e.g., *REQ_connection_wifi* – from Deriv. Model – *Product NKE2311.gen* – uses – *mobile_v03.var*)

possible to avoid duplicate product-specific developments. We thus need to collect all new requirements captured in concurrent product derivations and analyze the requests with respect to similarities and affected variability models. Figure 10 shows data provided by EvoKing including new requirements (REQ_connections_wifi, REQ_connection_wlan). These can be also processed by other tools, for example, when using an issue tracker to plan product line maintenance. The requirements originate from the derivation models Product_NKE2311.gen, P_NKx1234.gen and P_Nm3.gen which are related to the variability models mobile_v02.var and mobile v03.var as shown by the trace links presented to the user (cf. Fig. 10, "uses" trace link). Additionally, references to related model elements (i.e., via the influenced attribute) that are captured with new requirements are presented by EvoKing. This enables a modeler to quickly find the models (e.g., mobile_v03.var) and model elements that need to be adapted to address a specific requirement.

Challenge 5 – Treating variability as a first class citizen in traceability. To ensure traceability in product line evolution we have to treat decisions as first class citizens and track them throughout product line modeling and product derivation. Figure 8 shows modifications and usage of the mobile phone product line decision touch. The product line modeler can see in which version of the product line (variability model file mobile_v03.var with a certain timestamp) this decision was introduced and when, by whom or in what respect it was changed or deleted. Taking decisions during product derivation is also tracked as shown in Fig. 9. This enables identifying the impact of changing decisions.

6 Summary and Conclusion

This chapter gave an overview of traceability in product line engineering and discussed five key challenges of tracing in PLE arising from: (1) diverse artifacts with interrelations at different levels of granularity; (2) inter- and intra-model relations; (3) multiple, concurrent product derivations; (4) feedback from product derivation projects; and (5) variability as a first class citizen regarding traceability and evolution. We presented the decision-oriented variability modeling approach DOPLER with its specific traceability requirements to illustrate the five challenges. We described tool support to cope with these challenges. Using scenarios from the mobile phone product line we showed how EvoKing facilitates model maintenance and product line evolution.

The EvoKing framework is flexible and can be adapted to track arbitrary artifacts. However, there is also a limitation of the approach as the artifacts, evolution events, and trace link types need to be defined in advance through implementation. Also, the framework is currently only available for the Eclipse IDE. For future work we plan to extend the EvoKing framework to provide the user with more visualizations and guidance for easier utilization of the trace links and evolution data.

References

Anquetil, N., Kulesza, U., Mitschke, R., Moreira, A., Royer, J.C., Rummler, A., Sousa, A.: A model-driven traceability framework for software product lines. Softw. Syst. Model 9(4), 427–451 (2010)

Asuncion, H.U., Asuncion, A.U.: Taylor RN software traceability with topic modeling. In: 32nd International Conference on Software Engineering (ICSE '10), pp. 95–104. ACM, Cape Town, South Africa (2010)

Berg, K., Bishop, J., Muthig, D.: Tracing software product line variability – from problem to solution space. In: 2005 Annual Research Conference of the South African Institute of Computer Scientists and Information Technologists on IT Research in Developing Countries, pp. 182–191. South African Institute for Computer Scientists and Information Technologists, White River, South Africa (2005)

Cleland-Huang, J., Berenbach, B., Clark, S., Settimi, R., Romanova, E.: Best practices for automated traceability. IEEE Comp. 40(6), 27–35 (2007)

Cleland-Huang, J., Chang, C.K., Christensen, M.J.: Event-based traceability for managing evolutionary change. IEEE TSE 29(9), 796–810 (2003)

Clements, P., Northrop, L.: Software Product Lines: Practices and Patterns. SEI Series in Software Engineering, Addison-Wesley, Boston, MA (2001)

Czarnecki, K., Eisenecker, U.W.: Generative Programming: Methods, Techniques, and Applications. Addison-Wesley, Boston, MA (2000)

Dhungana, D., Grünbacher, P., Rabiser, R.: The DOPLER meta-tool for decision-oriented variability modeling: A multiple case study. Automat. Softw. Eng. 18(1), 77–114 (2011)

Dhungana, D., Grünbacher, P., Rabiser, R., Neumayer, T.: Structuring the modeling space and supporting evolution in software product line engineering. J. Syst. Softw. 83(7), 1108–1122 (2010)

Egyed, A. A scenario-driven approach to traceability. In: 23rd International Conference on Software Engineering (ICSE 2001), pp. 123–132. Toronto, ON (2001)

Egyed, A., Graf, F., Grünbacher, P.: Effort and quality of recovering requirements-to-code traces: Two exploratory experiments. In: 18th International Requirements Engineering Conference, IEEE, pp. 221–230. Sydney, Australia (September 27–October 1, 2010)

Girba, T., Ducasse, S.: Modeling history to analyze software evolution. J. Softw. Maint. Evol.: Res. Pract. **18**, 207– 236 (2006)

Grünbacher, P., Rabiser, R., Dhungana, D., Lehofer, M.: Model-based customization and deployment of eclipse-based tools: Industrial experiences. In: 24th IEEE/ACM International Conference on Automated Software Engineering (ASE 2009), pp. 247–256. IEEE/ACM, Auckland, New Zealand (2009)

Heider, W., Froschauer, R., Grünbacher, P., Rabiser, R., Dhungana, D.: Simulating evolution in model-based product line engineering. Inform. Softw. Technol. **52**(7), 758–769 (2010)

Heider, W., Rabiser, R., Dhungana, D., Grünbacher, P.: Tracking evolution in model-based product lines. In: 1st International Workshop on Model-driven Approaches in Software Product Line Engineering (MAPLE 2009), Collocated with the 13th International Software Product Line Conference (SPLC 2009), pp. 59–63. Software Engineering Institute, Carnegie Mellon, San Francisco, CA (2009)

Jirapanthong, W., Zisman, A.: (2009) XTraQue: Traceability for product line systems. Softw. Syst. Model. **8**(1), 117–144

Kang, K.C., Cohen, S., Hess, J., Nowak, W., Peterson, S.: Feature-Oriented Domain Analysis (FODA) Feasibility Study. Technical Report CMU/SEI-90TR-21, Software Engineering Institute, Carnegie Mellon University, Pittsburgh, PA (1990)

Koschke, R., Quante, J.: On dynamic feature location. In: 20th IEEE/ACM International Conference on Automated Software Engineering (ASE 2005), pp. 86–95. Long Beach, CA (2005, November 7–11)

Krueger, C.: The BigLever software gears unified software product line engineering framework. In: 12th International Software Product Line Conference (SPLC 2008), vol. 2, p. 353. Lero, Limerick, Ireland (2008)

Mäder, P., Gotel, O., Philippow, I.: Enabling automated traceability maintenance by recognizing development activities applied to models. In: 23rd IEEE/ACM International Conference on Automated Software Engineering (ASE 2008), pp. 49–58. L'Aquila, Italy (2008)

Mohan, K., Ramesh, B.: (2007) Tracing variations in software product families. Commun. ACM **50**(12), 68–73

Pohl, K.: PRO-ART: Enabling requirements pretraceability. In: 2nd International Conference on Requirements Engineering (ICRE '96), pp. 76–85. IEEE Computer Society, Springs, Colorado (1996, April 15–18)

Pohl, K., Böckle, G., van der Linden, F.: Software Product Line Engineering: Foundations, Principles, and Techniques. Springer, Berlin Heidelberg (2005)

pure systems GmbH: Variant Management with pure::variants, Technical Whitepaper. http://www. pure-systems.com/fileadmin/downloads/pv-whitepaper-en-04.pdf (2006). Last checked on 22 April 2008

Rabiser, R., Dhungana, D.: Integrated support for product configuration and requirements engineering in product derivation. In: 33rd EUROMICRO Conference on Software Engineering and Advanced Applications (SEAA'07), pp. 219–228. IEEE Computer Society, Lübeck, Germany (2007)

Rabiser, R., Dhungana, D., Heider, W., Grünbacher, P.: Flexibility and end-user support in model-based product line tools. In: 35th EUROMICRO Conference on Software Engineering and Advanced Applications (SEAA 2009), pp. 508–511. IEEE CS, Patras, Greece (2009)

Rabiser, R., Grünbacher, P., Dhungana, D.: Supporting product derivation by adapting and augmenting variability models. In: 11th International Software Product Line Conference (SPLC 2007), pp. 141–150. IEEE Computer Society, Kyoto, Japan (2007)

Rabiser, R., Heider, W., Elsner, C., Lehofer, M., Grünbacher, P., Schwanninger, C.: A flexible approach for generating product-specific documents in product lines. In: Bosch, J., Lee, J. (eds)

14th International Software Product Line Conference, Jeju Island, South Korea, pp. 47–61. Springer, Berlin/Heidelberg (2010)

Schmid, K., Rabiser, R., Grünbacher, P.: A comparison of decision modeling approaches in product lines. In: 5th International Workshop on Variability Modelling of Software-intensive Systems (VaMoS 2011), pp. 119–126. ACM, Namur, Belgium (2011)

Spanoudakis, G., Zisman, A., Pérez-Minana, E., Krause, P.: Rule-based generation of requirements traceability relations. J. Syst. Softw. **72**(2), 105–127 (2004)

van der Linden, F., Schmid, K., Rommes, E.: Software Product Lines in Action – The Best Industrial Practice in Product Line Engineering. Springer, Berlin/Heidelberg (2007)

Vierhauser, M., Grünbacher, P., Egyed, A., Rabiser, R., Heider, W.: Flexible and scalable consistency checking on product line variability models. In: 25th IEEE/ACM International Conference on Automated Software Engineering (ASE 2010), pp. 63–72. ACM, Antwerp, Belgium (2010)

Traceability in Model-Driven Engineering: Efficient and Scalable Traceability Maintenance

Andreas Seibel, Regina Hebig, and Holger Giese

1 Introduction

Developing a software system is a complex endeavor. A software development project is conducted throughout several development life cycles. Each life cycle considers the specification of a certain level of abstraction of the software system. Thus, in each life cycle different software artifacts have to be developed and maintained, e.g.; business processes (environment of the software system), stakeholder requirements, use cases, software architectures, implementation code, etc. *Model-Driven Engineering* (MDE) addresses the increased complexity in software development by employing models and model transformations as first-class citizens (cf. (Kent, 2002)).

In MDE various types of software artifacts have to be considered because MDE is always part of a software development process. We classify software artifacts into *informal* (text intensive), *semi-formal* and *formal* (structure intensive). Informal software artifacts are prominent in early life cycles, e.g., unstructured requirements specifications. Formal software artifacts are primarily present in later life cycles, which make the application of MDE more attractive that life cycles.

Software artifacts directly or indirectly represent specific concerns of the developed software system, but at different levels of abstraction or from different perspectives. Thus, software artifacts do not exist in isolation, but rather have inherent dependencies between each other. The types of dependencies are versatile. In most requirements traceability approaches (cf. (Antoniol et al., 2001)), dependencies exist because software artifacts have textual similarities (e.g., the name of a class in a UML class diagram is related to a term within a requirements specification). In MDE, we can distinguish between three types of dependencies: *hard references*, *soft references* and *semantic connections* (cf. (Lochmann and Hessellund, 2009)). Hard and soft references are syntactic relationships between arbitrary software artifacts. A hard reference is an explicit reference between

A. Seibel (✉)
Hasso-Plattner-Institute, The University of Potsdam, 14482 Potsdam, Germany
e-mail: andreas.seibel@hpi.uni-potsdam.de

J. Cleland-Huang et al. (eds.), *Software and Systems Traceability*,
DOI 10.1007/978-1-4471-2239-5_10, © Springer-Verlag London Limited 2012

software artifacts whereas a soft reference is an implicit reference between software artifacts encoded by means of name equivalence of certain attributes. A semantic connection is a complex connection between software artifacts, which may involve other software artifacts to describe this connection.

In any case, it is important to the software development process that these dependencies are explicitly captured. Ignoring these dependencies may endanger the success of the whole development project because inconsistencies, due to missed change propagation, may find their way into the final software system. In addition, traceability approaches are beneficial because they enable impact analysis, change propagation or just ease the understanding of software artifacts.

Automated establishment of traceability links is necessary because thousands of dependencies between all kinds of software artifacts may exist implicitly. Various approaches to automatically establish traceability links exist. Generally, we can distinguish between *prospective* and *retrospective* approaches (cf. (Asuncion et al., 2010)). A prospective approach generates traceability links in situ, e.g., by directly analyzing actions (e.g., (Asuncion et al., 2010) or (Mäder et al., 2009)). In MDE, a common way of realizing prospective traceability is generating traceability links as by-product of model transformations (e.g., (Jouault, 2005)). An inherent benefit of prospective approaches is that they are efficient and scalable because they are incremental by nature. However, they either require a tight integration into existing environments or technologies (e.g., model transformations) or are restricted to capture traceability links from behavioral information only.

A retrospective approach infers traceability links ex post facto from a set of software artifacts. Classical traceability approaches are retrospective and rely on *information retrieval* methods to automate traceability link establishment. In contrast to prospective approaches, retrospective approaches are applicable in settings where no behavioral information is available.

In information retrieval, dependencies between software artifacts cannot be formally specified. Thus, *heuristic* methods, e.g., *latent semantic indexing* (LSI) (e.g., (Jiang et al., 2008)) are employed to determine the similarity between software artifacts by means of textual similarity. The inherent benefit is that traceability links between informal as well as formal software artifacts could be established with only one common/pre-defined heuristic. However, using a heuristic always requires manual post-processing because required traceability links may be not automatically established or traceability links are falsely established (false positives). Thus, the quality information retrieval approaches is rather "low" (measured by means of *precision* and *recall*). On the contrary, formal methods, i.e. pattern matching, can also be employed to establish traceability links (e.g., (Seibel et al., 2010)). A formal method basically does not require any post-processing because the dependencies are precisely specified and not contain any vague statements as in case of information retrieval. Because of their preciseness, formal methods are best applicable to establish traceability links between formal software artifacts and, to some extent, between semi-formal software artifacts.

Another important challenge to prospective and retrospective traceability approaches is *traceability maintenance*. Changes to software artifacts occur frequently, which leads to the question whether new traceability links have to be established or existing and potentially invalidated traceability links have to be de-established because related software artifacts have changed. Rejecting all existing traceability links first and subsequently establishing all traceability links again is a naïve solution toward retrospective traceability maintenance. However, this strategy does not scale because the computational effort such approaches depend on the number of considered software artifacts.

The approach we present in this chapter is an efficient and scalable retrospective traceability maintenance approach in the MDE domain, which is a successive development of a previous traceability approach we presented in (Seibel et al., 2010). Our traceability maintenance approach relies on formal rules to automatically maintain traceability links, which represent dependencies primarily between formal software artifacts.[1] The formal rules are encoded by means of *Story Diagrams*[2]) to specify a precise semantic for specific types of traceability links. In the past, we have developed an interpreter (Giese et al., 2009a, b) for Story Diagrams that we apply in this approach. We specify rules for the establishment (*creation rules*) and de-establishment (*deletion rules*) of traceability links.

A drawback of our previous approach is that the constitution of the rules is considerably complex, which makes the specification of our rules tedious. Thus, we extended our approach to simplify the constitution of the creation and deletion rules. Furthermore, our previous approach does only provide a naïve solution toward traceability maintenance and, thus, does not scale with increasing number of software artifacts. In this chapter, we introduce an incremental traceability maintenance approach that leverages change information to specifically establish new traceability links and de-establish invalidated traceability links efficiently. The approach scales because it does not rely on the number of software artifacts but on the number of changes.

This chapter is structured as follows: first particular characteristics of the employed case study are outlined in Section 2. In Section 3, our approach is completely outlined on an informal level including technical implementation details. In Section 4, we provide a rigorous formal definition of our approach and a detailed description of our traceability maintenance strategies. In Section 5, we evaluate the envisioned efficiency and scalability and further discuss our approach concerning applicability and accuracy. The paper finally concludes with a discussion of related work in Section 6 and a conclusion and outlook on future work in Section 7.

---

[1] Our approach is technically not restricted to formal software artifacts, but it develops its full potential in that domain. We evaluate our approach in a slightly different domain than proposed because the software artifacts of the applied case study are primarily semi-formal.

[2] A Story Diagram is a combination of UML activity diagrams and graph-rewriting rules (Fischer et al., 2000).

2 Case Study

In this chapter, we apply the mobile phone product line software system case study as introduced in Appendix C. We employ all software artifacts provided in that case study except the shown state diagrams. We use the case study to exemplarily illustrate as well as to evaluate the runtime complexity of our traceability approach. The dependencies that we are going to trace in this chapter are informally explained in the following.

- SubsystemDependsOnFeature: a subsystem depends on a feature. The condition for tracing this dependency is that a feature is allocated to a subsystem.
- ProcessModelRefinesSubsystem: a process model refines a subsystem model. It holds between a process model and individual subsystems of a subsystem model. It should be traced if a feature has a soft reference to a subsystem (equivalent names).
- ModuleModelRefinesProcess: a module model refines a process. It should be traced if a process in the module model has a soft reference to a process in a process model (equivalent names).
- UseCaseDependsOnFeatureModel: a use case depends on a feature model. It should be traced if the system of a use case has a soft reference to a feature model (equivalent names).
- UseCaseDependsOnFeature: a use case depends on a feature of a feature model. It should be traced if the use case depends on a feature model and if the description of the use case is somehow similar to the description of the feature in a feature model.[3]
- UMLDiagramImplementsUseCase: a class diagram or a sequence diagram implements a use case. It should be traced if a package of a UML diagram has a soft reference to a family member of a use case (equivalent names).
- ClassDiagramRelatedToSequenceDiagram: a sequence diagram relates to a class diagram. It should be traced whenever both reside in the same package (semantic connection).
- MessageOverlapsAssociation should be traced if the message uses an association (semantic connection). In addition, it should be only traced if their related sequence and class diagrams are related.
- LifelineOverlapsClass should be traced if a lifeline has a soft reference to a class (equivalent names). This traceability link type should be only traced if their related sequence and class diagrams are related.
- MessageOverlapsOperation should be traced if a message has a soft reference to an operation (equivalent names) and the related class of the operation overlaps with the lifeline of the message.

---

[3] We can only trace this dependency if the descriptions are completely similar.

Because of the focus on models in the context of MDE, we mainly consider traceability between sequence diagrams and class diagrams in the following sections.

3 Traceability Approach

Our traceability approach is implemented as a set of plugins within *Eclipse*.[4] Currently, it supports all kinds of software artifacts that are conform to *Ecore*.[5] The integration of our traceability approach into Eclipse and EMF works seamlessly. This means that a developer is able to modify, create or delete any software artifact without recognizing that traceability links are automatically maintained in the background. A condition for a seamless integration is an efficient and scalable traceability maintenance approach, which we introduce in this chapter.

3.1 Traceability Information Model

The foundation of our traceability approach is a *traceability information model*, which is combined of a *traceability model* and a *traceability reference model*. The traceability model is responsible for storing existing traceability links while the traceability reference model is responsible for providing the semantics of traceability links by means of traceability link types. We already informally introduced ten traceability link types in the pervious section. The Ecore conform metamodel of the traceability information model is shown in Fig. 1. The major constituents of our traceability model are:

- SoftwareArtifact: a software artifact acts as a proxy for models (Model) and model elements (ModelElement). Thus, both represent EObject instances by means of the root and rep reference, respectively. Software artifacts act as source and targets of traceability links. In addition, a software artifact can contain other software artifacts realized by the inherited *contains* reference. We use this reference to reflect the containment structure of EMF models. Thus, we have a flexible *trace granularity* at model level as well as model element level.
- TraceabilityLink: a traceability link manifests a dependency between software artifacts. A traceability link has a read direction encoded by the source and target reference. As software artifacts, traceability links can also contain other traceability links realized by the same inherited contains reference. We use this reference to encode that a traceability link exists in the context of another traceability link (hierarchy), which is an important concept for our traceability maintenance approach.

---

[4] http://www.eclipse.org/

[5] Ecore is the metametamodel of *Eclipse Modeling Framework* (EMF). http://www.eclipse.org/modeling/emf/

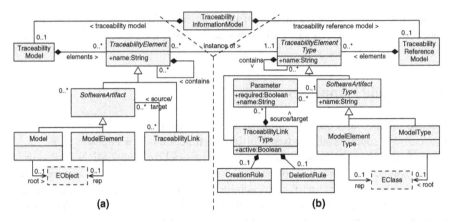

Fig. 1 Ecore metamodel of the traceability information model. **a**. Metamodel of the traceability model. **b**. Metamodel of the traceability reference model

The major constituents of our traceability reference model are:

- SoftwareArtifactType: a software artifact type acts as a proxy for metamodels (ModelType) and metamodel elements (ModelElementType). We further call metamodels and metamodel elements to be software artifact types. Thus, both kinds of software artifact types represent EClass instances because the type of an EObject is an instance of EClass. Our model reflects this dependency by means of the inherited instance of reference. This reference permits reflection without needing Java's reflection mechanism. Software artifact types act as source and targets of traceability link types. Furthermore, as software artifacts, software artifact types also reflect the containment structure of EMF metamodels by means of the inherited contains reference.
- TraceabilityLinkType: a traceability link type defines the dependency between software artifacts at type level by interrelating software artifact types via the source and target references. However, software artifact types are only indirectly referenced through Parameter instances. A parameter is related to exactly one software artifact type. Parameters are required to technically realize the application of our rules. A traceability link type can be related to a *creation rule* (CreationRule) and a *deletion rule* (DeletionRule), which represent the rules. A traceability link type can contain further traceability link types via the inherited contains reference, which is used to define additional context that is required for the existence of traceability links.

Software artifacts and software artifact types are automatically synchronized with software artifacts in the workspace of the modeling environment because in our implementation software artifacts and software artifact types are only proxies. A developer just needs to initially register the software artifacts and software artifact types, which should considered for traceability. The semantic of traceability

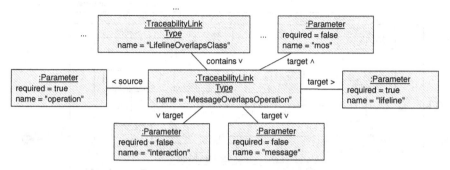

Fig. 2 Abstract syntax showing the traceability link type MessageOverlapsOperation

links is defined by means of traceability link types, which implies the specification of creation and deletion rules. This is previously obtained by a designer of the environment. Figure 2 is an excerpt of the case studies' traceability reference model showing the MessageOverlapsOperation traceability link type. It shows the source and target parameters and that it is contained by the LifelineOverlapsClass traceability link type. The contains reference is set because we have defined that traceability links of type MessageOverlapsOperation should only exist in the context of a traceability link of type LifelineOverlapsClass.

3.2 Traceability Maintenance Rules

Traceability maintenance rules are the building blocks for our traceability maintenance approach. We distinguish between deletion rules and creation rules. These rules are responsible for creating and deleting instances of the related traceability link type. Thus, the maintenance rules can be interpreted as a *condition* for the existence of traceability links. A creation rule checks if the condition holds and, thus, whether a traceability link should be created. A deletion rule checks if the condition is violated and, thus, whether a traceability link should be deleted. Nevertheless, we do not expect that traceability link types always have a creation or a deletion rule related. Sometimes, it is necessary to automatically create traceability links but not to automatically delete them, e.g., when subsequently applying change propagation or conformance analysis. These maintenance rules are currently implemented by means of Story Diagrams. We have developed an interpreter for Story Diagrams that is employed for applying these maintenance rules (see (Giese et al., 2009a, b)).

The application of maintenance rules always needs a *context* where to apply them. In case of deletion rules, the context (*deletion context*) is always a traceability link that already exists between software artifacts.

Figure 3 shows a deletion rule of the MessageOverlapsOperation traceability link type shown in Fig. 2. The structure of this deletion rule is representative for all other

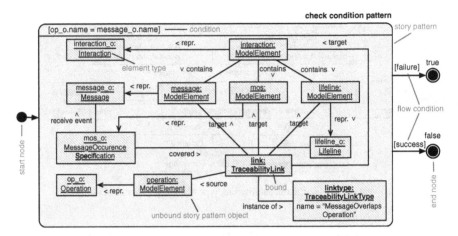

Fig. 3 Deletion rule from the case study (MessageOverlapsOperation)

deletion rules. The deletion rule is defined by a single Story Pattern. It encodes the condition of the related traceability link type. The deletion context for applying this rule is the traceability link that should be checked for deletion (link). The Story Pattern expects that this traceability link is already bound in the beginning. If the condition is violated, the deletion rule will terminate and return true, which indicates that the traceability link should be deleted subsequently. Else, the deletion rule will return false, which indicates that nothing should happen.

In case of creation rules, reasoning about the context (*creation context*) for application is not that trivial, because the considered traceability link does not yet exists. In this case, we only have the traceability link type as some kind of blueprint for the creation. A simple approach could be finding all possible creation contexts that reflect all possible combinations of software artifacts, which are required for applying the creation rule.

As explained in Section 2, we expect to trace the overlap of messages and operations only if they are in the context of overlapping lifelines and classes, which themselves are in the context of related sequence and class diagrams. Thus, we do not expect traceability links to be created between class diagrams and sequence diagrams defined in different product members, because they do not relate to each other. Thus, if the creation rules do not explicitly consider this context in their condition, this strategy would lead to traceability links in places where they should not exist (false positives).

We could define the necessary condition (message and operation belongs to lifelines and classes, which are in sequence and class diagrams of the same product member) explicitly in creation rules, which results in an increased complexity of the creation rules and an increased size of creation context. This also leads to redundancy, since parts of creation rules might have been defined in other creation rules, too. For example, a creation rule of a traceability link type between classes and lifelines also requires that sequence and class diagrams belong to the same product member.

In our previous approach, we explicitly encoded the existence of traceability links as parts of the condition of creation rules, which reduces the complexity of creation rules. However, they are still too complex. Furthermore, creation rules are indirectly coupled to others because they refer to the existence of traceability links of a specific type. This decreases reusability of creation rules and still leads to re-occurring patterns in creation rules that have the same traceability link type as additional context. In this approach, we do not require to explicitly define the existence of other traceability links in the creation rules. This dependency is explicitly defined within the definition of traceability link types only. Figure 2 shows that the traceability link type MessageOverlapsOperation can only exist in the context of a traceability link that is an instance of the type LifelineOverlapsClass. In this case, the creation contexts are not all possible combinations of software artifacts but only all combinations of software artifacts that are in the context of an existing traceability link. For example, the creation contexts for applying the creation rule of MessageOverlapsOperation does only consider messages and operations that are in the context of lifelines and classes that are related via a traceability link of the type LifelineOverlapsClass. Thus, the creation rules are less complex and can be reused in different contexts. Furthermore, we avoid redundancy in creation rules that have to be applied in the same context.

Figure 4 shows the creation rule related to the LifelineOverlapsClass traceability link type. The structure of this creation rule is representative for all creation rules where the required context is equal to the sources and targets of the related traceability link type. All parameters of the traceability link type have required set to true. A creation context of this creation rule consists of a *lifeline* and a *class* software artifact (already bound). Technically, we always require the traceability link type as part of the creation context, too. For a given creation context, the first Story Pattern checks whether there already exists a traceability link of the considered traceability link type that is connected to software artifacts in the creation context. If this is the

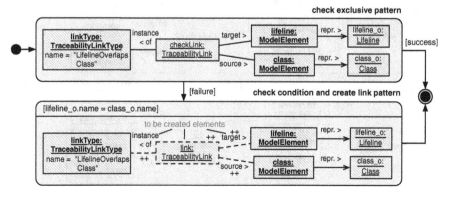

Fig. 4 Creation rule from the case study (LifelineOverlapsClass)

case, the creation rule will terminate because another traceability link of that type should not be created in the same creation context. If there is no such traceability link yet, the subsequent Story Pattern is executed. It first checks the condition of the traceability link type (lifeline_o.name = class_o.name). If the condition is fulfilled, a traceability link is created into that creation context and is set as instance of the given traceability link type.

All creation rules, which related traceability link type has at least one parameter that is not set to required, are defined differently. In this case, creation rules start from creation contexts that only contain matchings for required parameters. From this creation context, the creation context is subsequently complemented. An example of such a creation rule from the case study is shown in Fig. 5.

The shown creation rule is related to the MessageOverlapsOperation traceability link type. The structure of this creation rule is representative for all creation rules where the required context is only a subset of the sources and targets of the related traceability link type. The traceability link type has five parameters (see Fig. 2). However, because only lifeline and operation are set as required, we can apply the creation rule from a creation context that only contains two software artifacts

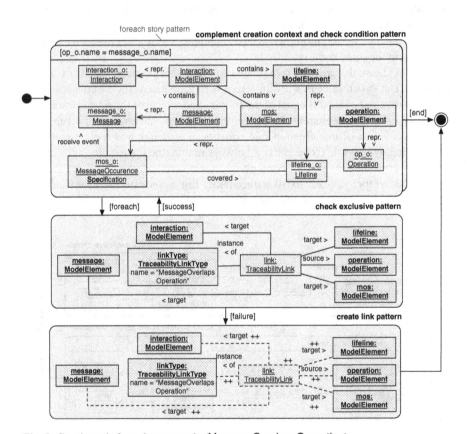

Fig. 5 Creation rule from the case study (MessageOverlapsOperation)

of these types. One should keep the number of software artifacts in the creation context low because with increasing number of software artifacts in creation context, the number of possible combinations and, therefore, the number of necessary applications is increasing drastically. The first Story Pattern is a combination of complementing the creation context and subsequently checking the condition. If a match that fulfills the condition is found, the second Story Pattern checks if there is already a traceability link of the considered type in between these software artifacts. If so, the first Story Pattern is triggered again to find another possible complement. This is done until no more matches can be found. However, if the second Story Pattern cannot find a traceability link between a given extended creation context, the third Story Pattern is executed which actually creates the traceability link. If the traceability link is created, the Story Diagram terminates execution.

3.3 Traceability Maintenance

Existing traceability links become out of date resulting in suspect or even obsolete traceability links because software artifacts are subject to constant change. In order to keep traceability links up to date, traceability maintenance is required.

Our traceability approach supports two traceability maintenance strategies, which both rely on the previously shown maintenance rules: a *batch strategy* and an *incremental strategy*. The batch strategy is a *reactive* traceability maintenance strategy. It can be triggered by a developer on demand and reasons on the current state of the software artifacts only. Thus, it can be employed in situations where no information about changes is available. For example, if our approach is initially applied to a set of software artifacts (initial situation). In contrast, the incremental strategy is *proactive*. This strategy is triggered automatically when changes occur. Thus, it only creates and deletes traceability links in the direct context of actual changes. This approach is efficient and further scales with increasing number of software artifacts. In both approaches, we cover the automatic maintenance of traceability links that are related to deletion and creation rules.

The incremental strategy facilitates changes that are currently coming from the Eclipse workspace (in case that coarse granular software artifacts have been changed) and from EMF or GMF[6] editors (in case that fine granular software artifacts have changed). Changes are stored in a changed record, which is created by the following schema. If a software artifact has been created or changed (e.g., if the value of an attribute has changed or a related reference has been added or deleted), it is added to a change record. If a software artifact has been deleted, all software artifacts that reference the deleted software artifact are added to the change record. In addition, existing traceability links that are connected to deleted software artifacts are added to the change record, too.

---

[6] *Graphical Modeling Framework*; www.eclipse.org/gmf/

4 Rigorous Formal Definition of the Traceability Approach

In this section, the foundations of our traceability approach are defined in a rigorous formal way. The formalisms relate to the terminology introduced in Section 3. However, technical aspects are not mentioned here or are simplified to stay focused on the essence of our approach.

4.1 Formal Definition of the Traceability Information Model

A formal definition of the traceability reference model is shown in Definition 1.

Definition 1 (Traceability Reference Model) A traceability reference model m_t is a 7-tuple $(A_t, L_t, R_c, R_d, C_t, S_t, T_t)$ with A_t is a finite set of software artifact types, $L_t \subseteq R_c \times R_d$ is a finite set of traceability link types, R_c is a finite set of creation rules, R_d is a finite set of deletion rules, $S_t \subseteq A_t \times L_t$ is a finite set of tuples defining the sources of traceability link types, $T_t \subseteq A_t \times L_t$ is a finite set of tuples defining the targets of traceability link types, $C_t \subseteq (A_t \cup L_t) \times (A_t \cup L_t)$ is a finite set of tuples defining the containments of software artifact types and traceability link types with $\forall (x, y) \in C_t, (x', y') \in C_t : (x \in A_t \implies y \in A_t) \wedge (x \in L_t \implies y \in L_t) \wedge (y = y' \implies x = x')$ defines that software artifact types only contain software artifact types and traceability link types only contain traceability link types and that a software artifact type or a traceability link type can only have a single container, and $\forall (l_t^1, l_t^2) \in C_t, (a_t', l_t^2) \in S_t \cup T_t, \exists (a_t, l_t^1) \in S_t \cup T_t : a_t' \in containedBy(a_t)$ defines that any software artifact type in the source or target of a contained traceability link type l_t^2 must be contained by a software artifact type that is source or target of the container traceability link type l_t^1 with $containedBy : A_t \to 2^{A_t}$ thus that $\forall a_t' \in containedBy(a_t) : (a_t, a_t') \in C_t \vee (\exists a_t'' \in containedBy(a_t) : (a_t'', a_t') \in C_t)$, which defines that all a_t' are directly or indirectly contained by a_t.

Concerning the traceability reference model shown in Fig. 1, the set C_t is related to the contains reference between traceability link types, the sets S_t and T_t are related to the source and target references. The traceability model is formally defined as shown in Definition 2.

Definition 2 (Traceability Model) A traceability model m is a 5-tuple (A, L, C, S, T) with A is a finite set of software artifacts with $\forall a \in A, \exists a_t \in A_t : \phi(a) = a_t$ defines that any software artifact a is an instance of a software artifact type a_t, L is a finite set of traceability links with $\forall l \in L, \exists l_t \in L_t : \rho(l) = l_t$ defines that any traceability link l is an instance of a traceability link type l_t, $S \subseteq A \times L$ is a finite set of tuples defining the sources of traceability links, $T \subseteq A \times L$ is a finite set of tuples defining the targets of traceability links, $C \subseteq (A \cup L) \times (A \cup L)$ is a finite set of tuples defining the containments of software artifacts and traceability links with $\forall (x, y) \in C, (x', y') \in C : (x \in A \implies y \in A) \wedge (x \in L \implies y \in L) \wedge (y = y' \implies x = x')$ defines that software artifacts only contain software artifacts and traceability links only contain traceability links and that a software artifact or a traceability link can only have a single container, and $\forall (l^1, l^2) \in C, (a', l^2) \in S \cup T, \exists (a, l^1) \in S \cup T : a' \in containedBy(a) \wedge (\rho(l^1), \rho(l^2)) \in C_t)$ defines that any software artifact in the source or target of a contained traceability link l^2 must be contained by a software artifact that is source or target of the container traceability link l^1 and there must be a containment of the instantiated traceability link types too with $containedBy : A \rightarrow 2^A$ thus that $\forall a' \in containedBy(a) : (a, a') \in C \vee (\exists a'' \in containedBy(a) : (a'', a') \in C)$ which defines that all a' are directly or indirectly contained by a.

When mapping this definition to the metamodel of the traceability model shown in Fig. 1, C is mapped to the contains reference between traceability links, and S and T is mapped to the source and target references.

4.2 Formal Definition of Traceability Maintenance

Applying deletion rules is much simpler than applying creation rules. In this case, we only need a traceability link that should be potentially deleted. Thus, the deletion context is always a single traceability link. The application of a deletion rule for a given deletion context is defined as show in the following.

Defintion 3 (Deletion Rule Application) Given a traceability link type $l_t = (r_c, r_d) \in L_t$ and a traceability link l with $\rho(l) = l_t$, the application of the deletion rule $r_d \in R_d$ for a traceability link l as deletion context is defined as $app_D : L \rightarrow L' \cup \{\emptyset\}$. Calling $app_D(l)$ applies the deletion rule r_d on l as deletion context. If the deletion rule decides that l should not be deleted, $app_D(l) = \{\emptyset\}$ else $app_D(l) = \{l\}$.

Before defining how to apply creation rules, we have to define the creation context that is required for the application. A formal definition of the creation context is given in Definition 4.

Definition 4 (Creation Context) For a given traceability link type $l_t \in L_t$, a creation context $CC_{l_t} \subseteq req(l_t) \times A$ is a finite set of tuples of required sources and targets of l_t and software artifacts A. Each $c \in CC_{l_t}$ is a mapping of a software artifact $a \in A$ to a required source or target software artifact type $a_t \in A_t$ with $\forall ((a_t, l_t), a) \in CC_{l_t} : \phi(a) = a_t$ defines that the type of the mapped software artifact is equal to the software artifact type of the required source or target of l_t, $\forall (a'_t, l'_t) \in req(l_t), \exists ((a''_t, l''_t), a'') \in CC_{l_t} : (a'_t, l'_t) = (a''_t, l''_t)$ defines that the creation context is always complete, $\forall ((a_t, l_t), a) \in CC_{l_t}, ((a'_t, l_t)', b) \in CC_{l_t} : (a'_t, l_t)' = (a_t, l_t) \implies a = b$ and $\forall ((a_t, l_t), a) \in CC_{l_t}, ((a'_t, l_t)', b) \in CC_{l_t} : a = b \implies (a'_t, l_t)' = (a_t, l_t)$ defines that a software artifact can only be mapped once. The required context $req : L_t \rightarrow 2^{S_t \cup T_t}$ is a function that provides a subset of sources S_t and targets T_t for a given traceability link type $l_t \in L_t$ with $\forall (a'_t, l''_t) \in req(l'_t) : l''_t = l'_t$ and $\forall (a'_t, l'_t) \in req(l'_t), \exists (a_t, l_t) \in (S_t \cup T_t) : l'_t = l_t \wedge a''_t = a_t$ defines that any element returned by the function is related to l_t and is in $S_t \cup T_t$.

Thus, the creation context for applying a creation rule is basically a set of software artifacts, with the type of each software artifact maps to a source or target of the related traceability link type. Nevertheless, in some cases it is sufficient to only provide a subset of these types as creation context (required) because the creation rule can complement the creation context on its own from a given creation context. Thus, the creation context provides a minimal set of software artifacts that is required for applying a creation rule as defined in the following.

Defintion 5 (Creation Rule Application) Given a traceability link type $l_t = (r_c, r_d) \in L_t$ and a set of all possible creation contexts $CC^*_{l_t}$ with $CC_{l_t} \in CC^*_{l_t}$, the application of the creation rule r_c is defined as $app_C : L_t \times CC^*_{l_t} \to 2^{L'} \times 2^{S'} \times 2^{T'}$ with $\forall l' \in L' : \rho(l') \in L_t$ is the set of created traceability links, $S' \subseteq A \times L'$ is the set of created source tuples and $T' \subseteq A \times L'$ is the set of created target tuples. We further assume that the traceability links that are created do not exist before defined by $L' \cap L = \emptyset$. Additionally, $\forall (L'', S'', T'') \in app_C(l_t, CC_{l_t}), l' \in L'', (a, l''') \in S'' \cup T'', \exists l \in L'' : \rho(l') = l_t \wedge l = l'''$ holds, which defines that each created traceability link l' must be of type l_t and that created source and target tuples must be related to a created traceability link l.

4.2.1 Batch Traceability Maintenance

The batch strategy is completely state-based and, thus, needs to analyze all software artifacts whether existing traceability links have to be deleted or new traceability links have to be created. The main procedure of the batch strategy is shown in Listing 1.

```
1   procedure batchMaintenance(m, m_t) {
2     // m = (A, L, C, S, T); m_t = (A_t, L_t, R_c, R_d, C_t, S_t, T_t)
3     forall (l ∈ L) {
4       L' := app_D(l); // apply deletion rule on l
5       L' := L' ∪ getAllSubLinks(L');
6       forall (l' ∈ L') {
7         C := C \ {(l'', l')|(l'', l') ∈ C}; // remove containments
8         S := S \ {(a, l')|(a, l') ∈ S}; // remove sources of l'
9         T := T \ {(a, l')|(a, l') ∈ T}; // remove targets of l'
10        L := L \ {l'}; // remove l' from L
11      }
12    }
13    forall (l ∈ L) { createNonRootBatch(l, m, m_t); }
14    forall ({l_t| ∄(l'_t, l_t) ∈ C_t : l'_t ≠ l_t}) {
15      createRootBatch(l_t, m, m_t);
16    }
17  }
```

Listing 1 Main procedure of the batch strategy

In Line 3–12 each existing traceability link l is removed from the traceability model if it got obsolete. In Line 4 the deletion rule of the traceability link type $\rho(l)$

is applied to l. If the traceability link l should be deleted, Line 5 first estimates all directly and indirectly contained traceability links of l because they must be deleted, too. Else they would exist without a container, which is not allowed due to the nature of the containment. Thus, for each $l' \in L'$, Line 7–10 removes these traceability links appropriately. When all necessary traceability links have been deleted, each existing traceability link is taken as additional context for establishing new traceability links (Line 13) by calling *createNonRootBatch* (see Listing 2). Afterwards, it has to be ensured that also traceability links are created which do not require another traceability link as container (Line 14–16) by calling *createRootBatch* (see Listing 3).

```
1   procedure  createNonRootBatch(l,m,mₜ)  {
2       // m = (A,L,C,S,T);  mₜ = (Aₜ,Lₜ,R_c,R_d,Cₜ,Sₜ,Tₜ);  l ∈ L
3       lₜ := ρ(l);
4       forall  (l'ₜ ∈ {l''ₜ|∃(l^a_t,l^b_t) ∈ Cₜ : l^a_t = lₜ ∧ l^b_t = l''ₜ})  { // sub types of lₜ
5           A' := filterArtifacts(l,l'ₜ,A);
6           CC*_{l'ₜ} := generateCreationContexts(l'ₜ,A');
7           forall  (CC_{l'ₜ} ∈ CC*_{l'ₜ})  {
8               (L',S',T') := app_C(l'ₜ,CC_{l'ₜ});
9               L := L ∪ L';  S := S ∪ S';  T := T ∪ T';  // add links to L
10              forall  (l' ∈ L')  {
11                  C := C ∪ (l,l');  // add l' as child of l
12                  createNonRootBatch(l',m,mₜ);
13              }
14          }
15      }
16  }
```

Listing 2 Batch procedure of creating a non root traceability link

```
1   procedure  createRootBatch(lₜ,m,mₜ)  {
2       // m = (A,L,C,S,T);  mₜ = (Aₜ,Lₜ,R_c,R_d,Cₜ,Sₜ,Tₜ);  lₜ ∈ Lₜ
3       A' := filterArtifacts(lₜ,A);
4       CC*_{lₜ} := generateCreationContexts(lₜ,A');
5       forall  (CC_{lₜ} ∈ CC*_{lₜ})  {
6           (L',S',T') := app_C(lₜ,CC_{lₜ});  // apply creation rule from lₜ
7           L := L ∪ L';  S := S ∪ S';  T := T ∪ T';
8           forall  (l' ∈ L')  { createNonRootBatch(l',m,mₜ); }
9       }
10  }
```

Listing 3 Batch procedure of creating a root traceability link

The algorithm for *createNonRootBatch* iterates over all traceability link types l'_t, which are directly contained by the traceability link type $l_t = \rho(l)$ (Line 3). For each traceability link type l'_t, it first estimates a set of software artifacts $A' \subseteq A$ (Line 5) by calling *filterArtifacts*. This procedure is responsible for filtering software artifacts that have to be considered when generating the creation context. For each software artifact $a' \in A'$ holds that it is in the direct context of l defined by $(a',l) \in$

$(S \cup T)$ or that it is in the indirect context of l defined by $\exists (a'', l) \in S \cup T : a' = containedBy(a'')$. Furthermore, for each $a' \in A'$ holds that $\exists (a'_t, l'_t) \in req(l'_t) : a'_t = \phi(a')$, which means that only software artifacts are in A' which type is required source or target of l'_t. This filtered set of software artifacts is then used to generate all possible creation contexts (Line 6) by calling *generateCreationContexts*. This procedure generates all possible creation contexts for a given set of software artifacts created by the filter. For each creation context $CC_{l'_t}$, the creation rule related to l'_t is applied (Line 8). Subsequently, the resulting triple (L', S', T') is added to the traceability model (Line 9). Each traceability link l' that has been created is then set as contained by l (Line 11) and *createNonRootBatch* is called recursively for each newly created traceability link l'. The algorithm terminates as soon as no more traceability link types are contained by $\rho(l)$.

The algorithm for *createRootBatch* first estimates a set of software artifacts $A' \subseteq A$ (Line 3). This filter differs from the one in Listing 2 because it does not consider a traceability link as context for filtering. Thus, the type of each software artifact $a' \in A'$ is only a required source or target of l_t defined by $\exists (a'_t, l_t) \in req(l_t) : a'_t = \phi(a')$. This set is used to generate all possible creation contexts by calling *generateCreationContexts* (Line 4), which is similar to the procedure called in Listing 2. For each creation context $CC_{l'_t}$, the creation rule related to l_t is applied (Line 6). Afterwards, the resulting triple (L', S', T') is added to the traceability model (Line 7). Each newly created traceability link l' is then set as then further processed by calling *createNonRootBatch* (Line 8) in order to create links in context of l'.

4.2.2 Incremental Traceability Maintenance

In comparison to the batch strategy, the incremental strategy starts analyzing from a given set of changes $Ch \subseteq A \cup L$, which contains created and changed software artifacts as well as changed traceability links due to deleted software artifacts. The main algorithm is shown in Listing 4. First, it applies deletion rules to any traceability link that is suspect (Line 4–17). The deletion rules are applied to traceability links only if they have changed (Line 5) or if they are indirectly changed (Line 6). Then for all $l \in L'$, the related deletion rule is applied (Line 8). If a traceability link l is declared to be obsolete, l and all its directly and indirectly contained traceability links, estimated by *getAllSubLinks*, are deleted appropriately (Line 9–15). Afterwards, L should only contain traceability links that are neither suspect nor obsolete.

Now, the algorithm checks if new traceability links have to be created based on given changes (Line 18–27). For each ch, which is a changed or created software artifact ($ch \in A$), a set of affected traceability link types L'_t is estimated by calling *getAffectedTraceabilityLinkTypes* (Line 19) with $\forall l'_t \in L'_t, \exists (ch, l'_t) \in (S_t \cup T_t)$ holds. For all traceability link types $l'_t \in L'_t$, which are contained by another traceability link type $(\exists (l''_t, l'_t) \in C_t)$, a set of traceability links L' is derived by calling *getContextLinks* (Line 22). The procedure retrieves only traceability links that are potential containers for the instantiation of l'_t. A potential container is a traceability link l' that

```
1   procedure incrementalMaintenance(m,mₜ,Ch) {
2     //m = (A,L,C,S,T);  mₜ = (Aₜ,Lₜ,Rc,Rd,Cₜ,Sₜ,Tₜ)
3     //Ch ⊆ A∪L is a set of changes (change record)
4     forall (ch ∈ Ch) {
5       L' := {ch}∩L; //traceability link directly changed
6       L' := L'∪{l|∃(ch,l) ∈ (S∪T)}; // indirectly changed
7       forall (l ∈ L') {
8         L'' := appD(l); //apply deletion rule on l
9         L'' := L'' ∪ getAllSubLinks(L'');
10        forall (l' ∈ L'') {
11          C := C\{(l'',l')|(l'',l') ∈ C}; // remove containments
12          S := S\{(a,l')|(a,l') ∈ S}; // remove sources of l'
13          T := T\{(a,l')|(a,l') ∈ T}; // remove targets of l'
14          L := L\{l'}; // remove l' from L
15        }
16      }
17    }
18    forall ({ch|ch ∈ Ch∩A}) {
19      L'ₜ := getAffectedTraceabilityLinkTypes(ch);
20      forall (l'ₜ ∈ L'ₜ) {
21        if (∃(l''ₜ,l'ₜ) ∈ Cₜ) { //the link type l'ₜ is a non root
22          L' := getContextLinks(ch,l'ₜ);
23          forall (l' ∈ L') { createNonRootInc(ch,l'ₜ,l',m,mₜ); }
24        }
25        else { createRootInc(ch,l'ₜ,m,mₜ); }
26      }
27    }
28  }
```

Listing 4 Main procedure of incremental strategy

has a as source or target with $ch \in containedBy(a)$ and whose type $\rho(l')$ contains l'_t $((\rho(l'),l'_t) \in C)$. For all these potential containers l' of a traceability link type l'_t, *createNonRootInc* is called (Line 23), which is shown in Listing 5. If the traceability link type $l'_t \in L'_t$ is not contained by another traceability link type, *createRootInc* is called (Line 25), which is shown in Listing 6.

```
1   procedure createNonRootInc(ch,lₜ,l,m,mₜ) {
2     //m = (A,L,C,S,T); mₜ = (Aₜ,Lₜ,Rc,Rd,Cₜ,Sₜ,Tₜ); lₜ ∈ Lₜ; ch ∈ Ch∩A; l ∈ L
3     A' := filterArtifacts(l,lₜ,ch,A);
4     CC*ₗₜ := generateCreationContexts(lₜ,ch,A');
5     forall (CCₗₜ ∈ CC*ₗₜ) {
6       (L',S',T') := appC(CCₗₜ,lₜ);
7       L := L ∪ L'; S := S ∪ S'; T := T ∪ T'; //add links to L
8       forall (l' ∈ L') {
9         C := C ∪ (l,l'); // add l' as child of l
10        createNonRootBatch(l',m,mₜ);
11      }
12    }
13  }
```

Listing 5 Incremental procedure of creating a non root traceability link

```
1    procedure createRootInc(ch,lₜ,m,mₜ) {
2       // m = (A,L,C,S,T) ;  mₜ = (Aₜ,Lₜ,Rc,Rd,Cₜ,Sₜ,Tₜ) ;  lₜ ∈ Lₜ ;  ch ∈ Ch∩A
3       A' := filterArtifacts(lₜ,ch,A) ;
4       CC*_lₜ := generateCreationContexts(lₜ,ch,A') ;
5       forall  (CC_lₜ ∈ CC*_lₜ)  {
6          (L',S',T') := appc(CC_lₜ,lₜ) ;
7          L := L ∪ L';  S := S ∪ S';  T := T ∪ T';  //add  links  to  L
8          forall  (l' ∈ L')  {  createNonRootBatch(l',m,mₜ) ;  }
9       }
10   }
```

Listing 6 Incremental procedure of creating a root traceability link

The procedure *createNonRootInc* starts with estimating a subset of software artifacts A' by calling *filterArtifacts*. This procedure is similar to the *filterArtifacts* procedure used in Listing 2 but there is only one software artifact of type $\phi(ch)$ in A', which is ch. This further reduces the size of A'. However, it is equal to *filterArtifacts* in Listing 2 if the considered traceability link type l_t has more than one source or target of the same software artifact type (e.g., $\exists (ch_t, l_t) \in (S_t \cup T_t), (a_t, l'_t) \in (S_t \cup T_t) : (ch_t = a_t) \wedge (l_t = l'_t) \wedge (ch_t, l_t) \neq (a_t, l'_t)$). In that case, we would not find all required software artifacts for creating the necessary creation contexts. Based on the filtered software artifacts A', all possible creation contexts $CC^*_{l_t}$ are generated by calling *generateCreationContexts*. This procedure is a variation of the procedure in Listing 2 and 3. It returns only creation contexts that also include ch. From this point, this procedure works like *createNonRootBatch* in Lines 7–14.

The procedure *createRootInc* also starts with estimating a subset of software artifacts A' by calling *filterArtifacts*. This procedure is similar to the *filterArtifacts* procedure used in Listing 3 but there is only one software artifact of type $\phi(ch)$ in A', which is ch. It is equal to *filterArtifacts* in Listing 3 if the considered traceability link type l_t has more than one source or target of the same software artifact type. By means of A', all possible creation contexts $CC^*_{l_t}$ are estimated by calling *generateCreationContexts*, which is similar to the equally named procedure in Listing 5. From this point, this procedure works like *createRootBatch* in Lines 5–10.

5 Evaluation

The purpose of our evaluation is to validate our implicitly stated hypothesis that our traceability filter maintenance approach is efficient and scales with increasing number of software artifacts. We expect that hypothesis is satisfied if 1) the time for maintaining traceability links for a realistic number of changes is less than one second (efficiency) and 2) the performance is not directly affected by the number of software artifacts (scalability).

To validate our hypothesis, we perform a performance evaluation by means of a subset of software artifacts from the given case study. We conduct two separate

	2,508 modeling artifacts (28 models)	4,454 modeling artifacts (46 models)	6,400 modeling artifacts (64 models)	8,346 modeling artifacts (82 models)	10,292 modeling artifacts (100 models)
Product Line Models	1x	1x	1x	1x	1x
Product Member 1 Models	1x	2x	3x	4x	5x
Product Member 2 Models	1x	2x	3x	4x	5x
Product Member 3 Models	1x	1x	1x	1x	1x

Fig. 6 Evaluation scenarios

evaluations because our approach is a combination of initial establishment of traceability links (batch strategy) and a subsequent incremental maintenance of traceability links (incremental strategy). The first evaluation shows the performance of the batch strategy whereas the second shows the performance of the incremental strategy. In both evaluations, we apply ten traceability link types, as informally explained in Section 2. Beside the given case study scenario, we have generated four additional scenarios that vary in the number of software artifacts only. The scenarios are artificially generated by multiplying the software artifacts systematically as shown in Fig. 6.[7]

5.1 Batch Traceability Maintenance Evaluation

In the first evaluation, we have conducted a measurement for each scenario. In each scenario, we have initially not traceability links established. Thus, the number of traceability links that are created are the number of traceability links that exist in the scenario. For each measurement, we recoded the execution time in seconds (s) and the number of created traceability links (#) by applying the batch strategy. The results are shown in Fig. 7.

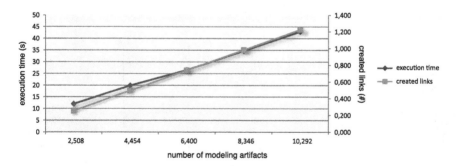

Fig. 7 Evaluation of batch strategy

---

[7] The performance evaluation is conducted on a Apple MacBook Pro 2.4 GHz, 4 GB main memory, Mac OS X 10.6.5, Java 1.6.0, and Eclipse 3.5.2 with EMF 2.5.0.

As expected, applying the batch strategy results in a linear increase of the execution time. The execution time varies from 11 s in the first scenario up to 42.9 s in the last scenario. Thus, only applying the batch strategy is not sufficient to satisfy our hypothesis.

5.2 Incremental Traceability Maintenance Evaluation

In the second evaluation, we have conducted the same measurements on the same scenarios. The only difference is that in these scenarios we also take the previously established traceability links into account. Beside the five scenarios, another important parameter for the second evaluation is the number of changes to software artifacts. For each scenario, we conduct four measurements with each has a different number of changes (5, 60, 120 and 200 changes). We assume that 200 changes is realistic size. For this measurement, we only took updates of software artifacts into account. Thus, each measurement contains the execution time of finding impacted traceability links and applying the related deletion rule.

Because we randomly generated these changes, we have applied 20 measurements on each combination of scenario and set of changes. The results are shown as the average of the execution time in seconds in Fig. 8. The chart also contains the confidence interval with a confidence level of 95%.

We can see that for each scenario, and even for a realistic number of changes, the execution times are less then one second. We can also observe that the execution time does not correlate to the number of software artifacts but rather correlate to the number of changes. Thus, we conclude that our incremental strategy satisfies our hypothesis. It is efficient because the execution times are considerable low (less than one second) and it scales with increasing number of software artifacts.

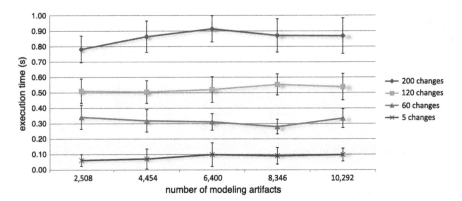

Fig. 8 Execution time of incremental strategy

5.3 Threats to Validity

Now, our evaluation is discussed by means of *internal* and *external validity*.

5.3.1 Internal Validity

In our evaluation, we have not considered all correlating variables exhaustively. Concerning the changes, we only considered updates and, furthermore, these updates do not result in actual de-establishment of traceability links. This has impact on the efficiency because de-establishing a traceability link would cause an impact on other traceability links, which also might have to be de-established. Concerning the type of changes, deleting a software artifact is basically similar to updating software artifacts. Creating a software artifact will result in new traceability links. Both cases have impact on the efficiency but do not impact the scalability because it does not increase the number of software artifacts afterwards.

The number of software artifacts in all five scenarios may be too small. Huge application examples have about 100,000 software artifacts (cf. (Egyed, 2007)). However, because the incremental strategy only relies on the number of changes, the scalability is not endangered.

In our evaluation, we completely neglected the variation of the number of traceability link types. Concerning deletions and updates, the number of traceability link types does not matter but only the number of actually established traceability links that are impacted by the change. The creation of new software artifacts requires checking whether there are any traceability link types that have to be established. Thus, the number of traceability link types impacts the efficiency but it does not affect scalability.

The constellation of the scenarios and the kind of traceability link types can affect the efficiency and scalability. For example, if a traceability link type is defined to hold between any pair software artifact, the number of established traceability links would be greater than the number of software artifacts. In such case, an arbitrary change would have impact to the number of traceability links that is greater than the number of software artifacts. However, we think that this scenario is unrealistic because traceability link types refer to more specific software artifacts and changes occur locally and not distributed over all software artifacts.

5.3.2 External Validity

Our approach is best suited in the MDE domain because the software artifacts are primarily formal. In that domain, we cover three kinds of dependencies between software artifacts that are hard references, soft references and semantic connections (cf. (Lochmann and Hessellund, 2009)). A hard reference is an explicit reference between software artifacts encoded in the language of the software artifacts. Our approach translates these explicit references into our traceability model. Thus, techniques like impact analysis can be applied also for those relationships. A soft reference is an implicit reference between software artifacts encoded by means of name equivalence of certain attributes. Such soft references occur in heterogeneous MDE environments working with loosely coupled DSLs. Our approach can make these relationships explicit by creating traceability links. A semantic connection is any overlap between software artifacts, which basically means the same but have different syntactical representations. Semantic connections are covered by the pattern capability of our employed formal specification method.

Our approach is a retrospective traceability approach. Thus, it only reasons about the existence of traceability links by means of software artifacts. Prospective and retrospective traceability approaches are complementary because both are disjunctive concerning their ability to establish traceability links. Because both have their advantages and disadvantages, we agree Lucia et al. as they argue that those approaches should complement each other (Lucia et al., 2007).

Because the automated establishment of traceability links bases on a formal method, we expect that all established traceability links are of highest precision. However, we assume that a designer of the creation and deletion rules does only define correct and complete rules. Whenever a rule may be incorrect or incomplete, the precision of our established traceability links is questionable. Nevertheless, we cannot validate the correctness or completeness of creation and deletion rules because it always depends on the specific intention of each individual traceability link type.

A similar situation holds for the question about recall. Currently, we assume that all necessary traceability link types are formally underpinned by means of creation and deletion rules. However, we might miss the establishment of certain traceability links if the creation and deletion rules are specified incorrectly or if whole traceability link types are missing.

Nevertheless, we may support the designer in specifying creation and deletion rules. There are approaches that focus on the automated establishment of mappings between metamodels (cf. (Del Fabro and Valduriez, 2007)). These approaches may use the same heuristics as in information retrieval. Because of applying heuristics, the established mappings underlie the same accuracy issues than usual traceability approaches. However, employing such approaches can be used to automatically synthesize executable creation and deletion rules or guide a designer in specifying them.

6 Related Work

Many traceability approaches are retrospective. There are approaches that only rely on information retrieval methods to automatically establish traceability links (Antoniol et al., 2001, 2002; Asuncion et al., 2010; Cleland-Huang et al., 2003; De Lucia et al., 2008; Lucia et al., 2007). These approaches only focus on the initial establishment of traceability links and the reached quality of their outcome concerning precision and recall.

In (Nguyen et al., 2002), Nguyen et al. introduce an approach called *Software Concordance* to manage versions of software documents and traceability links (relations) in between. Their focus is on the invalidation of traceability links whenever anchor (connected) software artifacts are created, deleted or updated. Each time a traceability link is invalidated, a new version is created. Furthermore, they employ a *timestamp strategy* to heuristically reason about the conformance of software artifacts connected to these invalidated traceability links. In (Maletic et al., 2003) they argue that only relying on a timestamp strategy is not sufficient. Thus, the semantic of the underlying change should also be taken into account. However, our notion of maintenance is different because we reason about the existence of traceability links (invalidation) and not the effect to conformance of connected software artifacts. If a deletion rule is triggered on a traceability link, the context of the impacted traceability link has changed in a way that the condition for the existence of the impact traceability links may not hold anymore. We agree that in certain situations, the deletion of invalidated traceability links is too restrictive. However, it is not clear whether their approach operates incrementally nor the efficiency and scalability is evaluated.

In (Jirapanthong and Zisman, 2009), Jirapanthong and Zisman have shown a comprehensive work on automated traceability establishment in the context of software product lines. It is a semi-formal method to establish traceability links based on a combination of XML-based rules and LSI. However, they do not focus on the incremental maintenance of traceability links.

Salay et al. show a traceability approach in the context of model management (Salay et al., 2009). They use a formal method to establish traceability links (relationships) based on metamodel morphisms, which they call a macromodel. This macromodel is used to automatically establish traceability links. Furthermore, they guide the user to complete the models in a way that traceability link get inferred. However, they do not consider maintenance questions.

Ivkovic and Kontogiannis show another traceability approach toward automatic establishment of traceability links (model dependencies) in (Ivkovic and Kontogiannis, 2006). They show a combination of heuristic and formal methods to establish traceability links (using type-based, spatial and text-based association rules). However, their approach does not provide the notion of incremental traceability maintenance and, thus, scalability is questionable.

Maletic et al. show an XML-based approach toward traceability in (Maletic et al., 2005). In their paper, evolution of traceability in the domain of MDE is discussed. However, they only discuss that traceability links should evolve whenever software artifacts change. They do not give any detailed insight of how to actually maintain traceability links in case of changes.

Another idea toward a retrospective traceability approach is discussed in (Aizenbud-Reshef et al., 2005). It advocates that traceability links should be maintained by means of formal operational semantics. Furthermore, they propose to use the event-condition-action (ECA) method to realize the maintenance of traceability links. However, they do not show how these operational semantics look like nor how to actually realize the maintenance of traceability links by means of ECA.

Jiang et al. show in (Jiang et al., 2008) the only retrospective and incremental traceability maintenance approach. They have developed an incremental version of LSI called iLSI. They also evaluated time complexity and showed that their approach is efficient and indeed scalable. Because their approach relies on LSI, established traceability links still need to be post-processed manually. Nevertheless, our approach presents a good complement to their approach because we focus on formal methods in the domain of MDE.

The prospective traceability approaches are incremental by nature, if they establish and de-establish traceability links by means of changes or change records.

Mäder et al. have shown in (Mäder et al., 2009) a prospective approach to incrementally maintain traceability links in the UML context. They employ rules that are used to specify development activities. In addition, they define in detail how elementary changes affect existing traceability links and whether new traceability link have to be established. Thus, their notion of incremental traceability maintenance is similar to ours. The only difference is that they do not consider the initial establishment of traceability links because their approach is not retrospective. Therefore, their approach does only function in environments that provide change information. However, their approach can be considered as another complement to ours.

Common prospective traceability approaches in the context of MDE are the approaches that automatically establish traceability links as by-products of the application of model transformations (Aleksy et al., 2008; Boronat et al., 2005; Falleri et al., 2006; Jouault, 2005; Jouault et al., 2010; Walderhaug et al., 2006). However, these approaches are restricted to establish traceability links only in combination with applying model transformations. Furthermore, whenever software artifacts change, the model transformations have to be re-applied completely.

Prospective approaches can be considered as complementary to retrospective approaches. However, prospective approaches are not sufficient in case that inferring traceability links is required because no change information is available.

7 Conclusions and Future Work

The presented traceability approach supports the specification of maintenance rules for automated maintenance (delete and create) of traceability links between software artifacts in an MDE setting. We have explained our foundational traceability information model, the nature of our maintenance rules, and how they are employed when it comes to automate traceability maintenance. Furthermore, we have given a rigorous formal definition of the traceability information model, the application of maintenance rules and, finally, a detailed strategy for batch and incremental traceability maintenance. An evaluation, using the mobile phone product line case study, demonstrates that our approach is efficient and scales with increasing complexity due to the incremental strategy.

As ongoing work, it is planned to integrated model management into our traceability approach by considering traceability links as the application of model transformations and not only as any kind of overlaps between software artifacts. This would enable us to coordinate the application of model transformations. The linguistic components of our maintenance rules are currently integrated via additional conditions encoded in OCL, which is somehow similar to the integration like in (Jirapanthong and Zisman, 2009) but not that powerful. We currently think about ways to better link both concepts by also support not exact structural rules like in (Niere, 2002).

References

Aizenbud-Reshef, N., Paige, R.F., Rubin, J., Shaham-Gafni, Y., Kolovos, D.S.: Operational semantics for traceability. In: ECMDA-TW'05: Proceedings of 1st Workshop on Traceability, pp. 7–14. Nurnberg, Germany, SINTEF (2005)

Aleksy, M., Hildenbrand, T., Obergfell, C., Schwind, M.: A pragmatic approach to traceability in model-driven development. In: Heinzl, A., Appelrath, H.J., Sinz, E.J. (eds.) PRIMIUM, CEUR Workshop Proceedings, vol. 328. CEUR-WS.org (2008)

Antoniol, G., Canfora, G., Casazza, G., De Lucia, A.: Maintaining traceability links during object-oriented software evolution. Softw. Pract. Exper. **31**, 331–355 (2001)

Antoniol, G., Canfora, G., Casazza, G., De Lucia, A., Merlo, E.: Recovering traceability links between code and documentation. IEEE Trans. Softw. Eng. **28**, 970–983 (2002)

Asuncion, H.U., Asuncion, A.U., Taylor, R.N.: Software traceability with topic modeling. In: Proceedings of the 32nd ACM/IEEE International Conference on Software Engineering – Volume 1, ICSE '10, pp. 95–104. ACM, New York, NY (2010)

Boronat, A., Carsí, J.A., Ramos, I.: Automatic support for traceability in a generic model management framework. In: First European Conference ECMDA-FA 2005, pp. 316–330. Nuremberg, Germany (2005)

Cleland-Huang, J., Chang, C.K., Christensen, M.: Event-Based traceability for managing evolutionary change. IEEE Trans. Softw. Eng. **29**, 796–810 (2003)

De Lucia, A., Oliveto, R., Tortora, G.: Adams re-trace: Traceability link recovery via latent semantic indexing. In: ICSE '08: Proceedings of the 30th International Conference on Software Engineering, pp. 839–842. ACM, New York, NY (2008)

Del Fabro, M.D., Valduriez, P.: Semi-automatic model integration using matching transformations and weaving models. In: Proceedings of the 2007 ACM Symposium on Applied Computing, SAC '07, pp. 963–970. ACM, New York, NY (2007)

Egyed, A.: Fixing inconsistencies in UML design models. In: Proceedings of the 29th International Conference on Software Engineering, ICSE '07, pp. 292–301. IEEE Computer Society, Washington, DC (2007)

Falleri, J.R., Huchard, M., Nebut, C.: Towards a traceability framework for model transformations in Kermeta. In: ECMDA-TW'06: Proceedings of 2nd Workshop on Traceability, Bilbao, Spain. SINTEF (2006)

Fischer, T., Niere, J., Torunski, L., Zündorf, A.: Story diagrams: A new graph rewrite language based on the Unified Modeling Language and Java. In: TAGT'98: Selected Papers from the 6th International Workshop on Theory and Application of Graph Transformations, LNCS, vol. 1764/2000, pp. 296–309. Springer, London (2000)

Giese, H., Hildebrandt, S., Seibel, A.: Feature report: Modeling and interpreting EMF-based story diagrams. In: Van Gorp, P. (ed.) Proceedings of the 7th International Fujaba Days, Eindhoven, The Netherlands, pp. 5–9. Technische Universiteit, Eindhoven (2009a). http://alexandria.tue.nl/repository/books/656886.pdf

Giese, H., Hildebrandt, S., Seibel, A.: Improved flexibility and scalability by interpreting story diagrams. In: Magaria, T., Padberg, J., Taentzer, G. (eds.) Proceedings of the 8th International Workshop on Graph Transformation and Visual Modeling Techniques (GT-VMT 2009), York, UK, vol. 18. Electronic Communications of the EASST (2009b)

Ivkovic, I., Kontogiannis, K.: Towards automatic establishment of model dependencies using formal concept analysis. Int. J. Softw. Eng. Knowl. Eng. **16**(4), 499–522 (2006)

Jiang, H.Y., Nguyen, T.N., Chen, I.X., Jaygarl, H., Chang, C.K.: Incremental latent semantic indexing for automatic traceability link evolution management. In: Proceedings of the 2008 23rd IEEE/ACM International Conference on Automated Software Engineering, ASE'08, pp. 59–68. IEEE Computer Society, Washington, DC (2008)

Jirapanthong, W., Zisman, A.: Xtraque: Traceability for product line systems. Softw. Syst. Model. **8**, 117–144 (2009). doi: 10.1007/s10270-007-0066-8

Jouault, F.: Loosely coupled traceability for atl. In: Proceedings of the European Conference on Model Driven Architecture (ECMDA) Workshop on Traceability, pp. 29–37 (2005)

Jouault, F., Vanhooff, B., Bruneliere, H., Doux, G., Berbers, Y., Bezivin, J.: Inter-DSL traceability and navigability support by combining megamodeling and model weaving. In: Proceedings of Special Track on the Coordination Models, Languages and Applications at the 25th Symposium on Applied Computing (SAC 2010), Sierre, Switzerland, March 22–26, 2010

Kent, S.: Model driven engineering. In: Butler, M., Petre, L., Sere, K. (eds.) Proceedings of the Third International Conference on Integrated Formal Methods (IFM 2002), Turku, Finland. Lecture Notes in Computer Science (LNCS), vol. 2335, pp. 286–298. Springer, Berlin/Heidelberg (2002)

Lochmann, H., Hessellund, A.: An integrated view on modeling with multiple domain-specific languages. In: Proceedings of the IASTED International Conference Software Engineering (SE 2009), pp. 1–10. ACTA Press, Chamonix, France (2009)

Lucia, A.D., Fasano, F., Oliveto, R., Tortora, G.: Recovering traceability links in software artifact management systems using information retrieval methods. ACM Trans. Softw. Eng. Methodol. **16**(4), 13 (2007)

Mäder, P., Gotel, O., Philippow, I.: Enabling automated traceability maintenance through the upkeep of traceability relations. In: Proceedings 5th European Conference on Model-Driven Architecture Foundations and Applications (ECMDA2009) – LNCS5562, pp. 174–189. Enschede, The Netherlands (2009)

Maletic, J.I., Collard, M.L., Simoes, B.: An XML based approach to support the evolution of model-to-model traceability links. In: Proceedings of the 3rd International Workshop on Traceability in Emerging Forms of Software Engineering, TEFSE '05, pp. 67–72. ACM, New York, NY (2005)

Maletic, J.I., Munson, E.V., Marcus, A., Nguyen, T.N.: Using a hypertext model for traceability link conformance analysis. In: Proceedings of the 2nd International Workshop on Traceability in Emerging Forms of Software Engineering (TEFSE), pp. 47–54. Montreal, Canada (2003)

Nguyen, T., Gupta, S.C., Munson, E.V.: Versioned hypermedia can improve software document management. In: Proceedings of the Thirteenth ACM Conference on Hypertext and Hypermedia, HYPERTEXT '02, pp. 192–193. ACM, New York, NY (2002)

Niere, J.: Fuzzy logic based Interactive Recovery of Software Design. In: Proceedings of the 24th International Conference on Software Engineering (ICSE), pp. 727–728. Orlando, FL (2002)

Salay, R., Mylopoulos, J., Easterbrook, S.: Using macromodels to manage collections of related models. In: Proceedings of 21st International Conference on Advanced Information Systems Engineering (CAiSE'09), LNCS, vol. 5565/2009, pp. 141–155. Springer, Amsterdam, The Netherlands (2009)

Seibel, A., Neumann, S., Giese, H.: Dynamic hierarchical mega models: Comprehensive traceability and its efficient maintenance. Softw. Syst. Model. **9**(4), 493–528 (2010). doi: 10.1007/s10270-009-0146-z

Walderhaug, S., Johansen, U., Stav, E., Aagedal, J.: Towards a generic solution for traceability in MDD. In: Neple, T., Oldevik, J. , Aagedal, J. (eds.) ECMDA Traceability Workshop (ECMDA-TW'06). Bilbao, Spain, SINTEF (2006)

Winkler, S., von Pilgrim, J.: A survey of traceability in requirements engineering and model-driven development. Softw. Syst. Model. **9**(4), 529–565 (2010). doi: 10.1007/s10270-009-0145-0

Studying the Role of Humans in the Traceability Loop

Alex Dekhtyar and Jane Huffman Hayes

1 Introduction

Traceability information has been captured and used to perform value-added activities as part of a "good" software engineering process since the coining of the phrase "software engineering." Often, this information has been captured after the fact, possibly not to the proper level of detail, and probably has not been kept up to date. Yet when traceability information is available early, it becomes the underlying foundation of vital activities throughout the life cycle, such as change impact analysis and regression testing, and has been an acknowledged part of the software engineering process for decades.

Traceability information can be generated as the life cycle proceeds or after the fact. Of the two, after-the-fact tracing is more straightforward: the analyst has access to the entire collection of artifacts and usually does not have as tight a delivery schedule. Tracing "as you go" is, unfortunately, a rare activity. It is often viewed as taking software engineers away from development and other "core" life cycle activities. Even when done, it is often *not* performed to the level of detail required (e.g., tracing sections to sections instead of tracing requirements to test cases) and/or is not kept current. It has also been noted in the Grand Challenges chapter that some organizations do not bother to trace until they have a need for the traceability matrix. After-the-fact tracing, thus, is often the default approach.

> **Definition.** We formally define **in-life cycle tracing** as any tracing activity or activities that happen *before the software is deployed*. Similarly, **after-the-fact tracing** is any tracing activity or activities that happen *after the initial deployment of the software*.

In practice, *in-life cycle tracing* is usually performed on projects where traceability information is either very important for the later stages of the life cycle or its presence is mandated by laws and/or regulations. The software produced

A. Dekhtyar (✉)
Cal Poly State University, San Luis Obispo, CA, USA
e-mail: dekhtyar@calpoly.edu

J. Cleland-Huang et al. (eds.), *Software and Systems Traceability*,
DOI 10.1007/978-1-4471-2239-5_11, © Springer-Verlag London Limited 2012

by such a project is usually mission- and/or safety-critical in nature. Federal regulations require that mission- and safety-critical software deployed by the federal government undergo pre-deployment *independent verification and validation* (IV&V), a quality assurance process performed by an authorized third party. Tracing is one of the key components of IV&V, supplying requisite information to other IV&V processes such as requirements satisfaction assessment and criticality analysis. Third-party analysts performing IV&V must certify that the software product conforms to all requirements and specifications before the software is deployed.

Regardless of when it is performed, the tracing process, in its traditional *manual form*, is commonly considered to be unpleasant and is often described as boring and repetitive. To alleviate this, much focus has been placed on the automation of tracing. Other chapters in this book describe a variety of techniques that have been used to automatically generate traceability links between various software engineering artifacts as well as the methods used to evaluate such techniques (generally involving running an experiment or study on a dataset and capturing various standard accuracy measures). All of these techniques take as input the artifacts to be traced and output candidate traceability matrices (deemed "candidate" until a human approves them).

As we define it, a *manual tracing process* is one in which *all tracing activities are performed and all tracing decisions are rendered* by a human analyst or a group of human analysts. We define a *fully automated tracing process* as one in which human analysts *do not perform any tracing activities* and where *all tracing decisions* are rendered by software.

A fully automated tracing process stops when the software generates a candidate traceability matrix. This matrix is then used in the subsequent activities as the source document for the traceability relation between the artifacts considered. In theory, full automation is beneficial as it is much faster than a manual tracing process, and thus it frees up analyst time. In practice though, automated methods still fall short of consistently capturing the exact traceability relationships between pairs of artifacts.

Herein lies the key distinction between after-the-fact tracing and in-life cycle tracing. Typical goals of after-the-fact tracing are such that "good enough" but not perfectly recovered traces are still very useful, and the ability to obtain them quickly and with little human effort is appreciated. However, *use of the results of fully automated tracing processes is not appropriate for the majority of in-life cycle tracing activities.*

Essentially, for in-life cycle tracing scenarios, *manual tracing* is highly undesirable due to its time-consuming and arduous nature. At the same time, *fully automated tracing* cannot be used in most situations, as the nature of the tracing process requires human analysts to accept responsibility for the traceability relationships that they produce (and at present, the automated methods come with no accuracy guarantees).

The main question that this chapter addresses is ***how to design in-life cycle tracing processes that are both accurate and cost-effective***. To address this problem, we propose a third category of tracing processes, *semi-automated tracing*, a.k.a.

assisted tracing, defined as a tracing process in which tracing activities can be performed by both human analysts and tracing software. In the *semi-automated tracing* processes that we consider in this chapter, human analysts render final traceability decisions.

When performing *semi-automated tracing*, human analysts, at a minimum, *need to examine* the results produced by the automated methods. Additionally, analysts may *interact with the tracing software, provide tracing feedback to the software*, and *ask the tracing software to retrace*. It is therefore important to study how human analysts make decisions when performing tracing tasks, how they interact with the automated tracing methods and the tracing software, and what factors lead to the analysts (hopefully) being able to construct accurate traceability relations. This chapter attempts to shed light on how to approach the study of these questions.

The chapter is organized as follows. Section 2 presents a motivating example. Section 3 discusses the semi-automated process in detail. Section 4 provides an overview of the research questions under consideration for semi-automated tracing. Section 5 provides concluding thoughts.

2 Semi-Automated Tracing by Example

Let us examine the case of MedComp. They are developing a software system, iTrust, in order to provide their patient customers with: (a) a way to maintain their personal medical history/records, (b) a way to select a doctor, and (c) a way to communicate with their doctors (iTrust, 2011). In addition, iTrust can support a medical office: it provides an interface for medical staff from various locations, allows the staff to keep track of their patients through messaging capabilities, allows the scheduling of office visits, the prescribing of medication, etc. (iTrust, 2011). Of particular interest to MedComp is the assurance that prescriptions are ordered properly and patients are not given the wrong medication (drug interactions, allergies, illegal narcotics, etc.). To ensure that this requirement is satisfied, MedComp has decided to develop a traceability matrix from requirements (represented in the use cases document) to code. We assume that there are M requirements and N individual code elements (e.g., classes or methods). We consider three possible tracing scenarios.

Scenario 1. Manual tracing. In a traditional manual tracing process, the analyst reads all M of the requirements and finds matches for each within the N code elements. The analyst can approach the task in many ways, perhaps reading all the requirements and then reading through the code elements to find matches. If the analyst is highly fortunate, the matches might be found with only one reading of each artifact, meaning that the analyst would read M + N elements. In the worst case though, the analyst must examine every code element as a possible match each time that a requirement is read, meaning that the analyst must examine M * N elements.

Manual tracing allows the analyst to examine as many or as few candidate links as the analyst sees fit. It gives the analyst the opportunity to render the correct decision on each candidate link. It also ensures that the process continues until the analyst is satisfied and thus stops.

At the same time, manual tracing suffers from a number of clear drawbacks. While in practice examining the full M^*N candidate links is unlikely, the most popular way to trace still remains a scan of a low-level artifact for each high-level element to be traced. The expected number of candidate links that will be checked thus is more likely to be quadratic in M and N rather than linear. For large datasets with hundreds of requirements and thousands of code elements (e.g., individual methods), this quickly becomes either outright infeasible or extremely time-consuming. Additionally, while manual tracing gives the analyst the opportunity to render correct decisions, it is not a given that analysts will do this every time. Studies show that the boring nature of the task makes the process error-prone (Egyed et al., 2010).

Scenario 2. Fully automated tracing. Automated tracing starts with the analyst starting up the automated tracing software, setting up the tracing task by selecting the high- and low-level artifacts, a specific tracing technique to apply along with any required settings. The software tool then generates a traceability matrix (TM) which is submitted by the analyst as the discovered traceability relationship. In this process, the analyst may study the output of the tracing software, but she does not modify the results of the automated tracing process.

The fully automated process gives the analyst the control of initial settings, but excludes the analyst from any further decision-making. Tracing tools are fast – even large datasets can be traced in a matter of minutes if not seconds. However, iTrust requires accountability: the analyst performing the tracing task *certifies* the correctness of the established traceability relationship. Fully automated tracing **does not ensure accountability**, which disqualifies it as a possibility for tracing the iTrust requirements to code.

Scenario 3. Semi-automated tracing. Initially, this process follows the same steps as the automated process – all the way until a candidate matrix is generated by a software tool. At this point, the analyst starts examining the candidate TM, making any needed changes to it by either (a) adding links missed by the tracing tool or (b) removing candidate links suggested by the tool but deemed incorrect. When satisfied, the analyst certifies and submits the resulting TM as the established traceability relation.

As mentioned above, the manual process provides accountability and potentially high accuracy, but at the cost of high effort. The fully automated process is fast, but is not accountable and may not be accurate. The semi-automated process, *at least in theory*, can be the *"best of both worlds"* by combining the efficiency of the automated methods in vetting a large number of candidate links with the accountability of the manual process. On the other hand, it can potentially combine *"the worst of both worlds,"* if the automated method produces very poor results and requires the analyst to apply an inordinate amount of time and effort to fix. In the next section, we examine the semi-automated tracing process in more detail.

3 Semi-Automated Tracing Process

The semi-automated tracing process can be viewed as consisting of two main actors: a human analyst and an automated tracing tool. The process has a number of inputs: the artifacts to be traced to each other and a selection of tracing techniques and settings for the techniques. The outputs are candidate traceability matrices and final traceability matrices. We examine each in turn.

Inputs

Artifacts – Artifacts may be textual, graphical, even multi-media. Most research has focused on textual artifacts. The artifacts can strongly impact the semi-automated tracing task. If the two textual artifacts were written by different people or using different terminology, the automated tool may miss many links.

Techniques – Automated tracing techniques available for use in the tracing tool. Some techniques are better suited to certain artifacts than others. We defer to earlier chapters which have covered this topic in detail.

Settings for techniques – Choices that the human analyst can make regarding the specifics of using automated tracing techniques. Settings vary from technique to technique. Examples of settings include selection of the vocabulary base (high-level artifact, low-level artifact, both artifacts) for LSI, selection of a stop word list for any technique or use of feedback processing to interact with the software tool and cause it to retrace portions of candidate traceability matrix.

Actors

Human analyst – The analyst is truly the lynch pin in the process. The analyst may be highly knowledgeable about the system/domain and may have many years of tracing experience, the analyst may be very new to the project and have never traced before, or possess experience that is in between these two extremes. The analyst may spend a tremendous amount of time performing tracing, examining each possible link in great detail; the analyst may only glance at each link (or only a subset of them); or may apply some level of effort that falls between the extremes. The analyst may review links in the order in which they appear, or may jump around. The analyst may provide feedback on every candidate link, may not provide any feedback, or may provide some feedback. The analyst may search for links that do not appear in the candidate TM, may not search at all, or may search for a small or large number of missing links. The analyst may use the relevance weights to guide the process, or may not. Last but not least, the analyst may be prone to human error at any point of the tracing process. There is a high degree of variability regarding this actor.

Tool – To qualify as an actor in a tracing process, a software tool must, at a minimum, possess the ability to produce a qualitative or quantitative "relationship" assessment for each pair of elements from the artifacts being traced. The tool will largely be a collection of techniques. The tool must provide the human analyst the ability to set up a tracing task and output the results that the analyst can peruse. The tool may have an interactive user interface (UI). The UI design can impact the work performed by the analyst.

Candidate TM – Any traceability matrix/traceability relation generated or updated by an automated method.[1] The accuracy of the candidate TM can influence the final results. It seems intuitive that a high quality candidate TM might make work easier for the analyst.

Final TM – The traceability matrix/traceability relationship produced by the analyst as the result of the tracing process and **explicitly** declared as a "ready-for-submission" artifact. The accuracy of this TM is of paramount importance, especially if "upstream" decisions in the life cycle will be made based upon it.

Semi-automated tracing generates two results, a candidate TM produced by the tool, and a final TM delivered by the analyst. We can measure the accuracy of these TMs using the standard information retrieval (IR) measures of recall, precision, and f-measure (or f2-measure). These measures were defined earlier, as a reminder *recall* evaluates how well the tool or analyst retrieved true links, *precision* looks at how many false links were retrieved by the tool or analyst, and *f-measure* is the harmonic mean of recall and precision (*f2-measure* favors recall over precision). Now that we are able to evaluate the semi-automated tracing process, we can examine some important questions.

4 Directions for the Evaluation of Semi-Automated Tracing

The success of the semi-automated tracing process will be judged based on the accuracy (we desire 100% recall, 100% precision) of the final TM which is passed on for other "upstream" software engineering activities. Thus in assessing the success of a semi-automated tracing process, we are measuring the quality of human performance.

What factors can affect the analyst performance when tracing? In a semi-automated process, the analyst obtains the initial candidate TM from an automated method, uses tracing software (or some other process), and relies on her expertise to validate candidate links and search for the ones missing from the candidate TM. As such, we can separate the key factors that can have effect on the analyst performance into three broad categories: (a) *task-related*, (b) *tool-related*, and (c) *analyst-related*. We discuss each group of factors in turn.

Task-related factors. These factors quantify the properties of the tracing task at hand: the input artifacts and the traceability matrices constructed. Among the specific parameters (or factors) we can identify:

---

[1] As well as any "work-in-progress" traceability matrix observed throughout the process.

1. *Size of high- and low-level artifacts*: usually measured in terms of numbers of elements.
2. *"Quality"* of high- and low-level artifacts: measured in terms of reading level, size/verbosity of individual elements, size of corpus, difference in language between the high- and the low-level documents, etc.
3. *Size of true traceability relationship*: in real tracing tasks, this information is usually not available, but it is available for staged experiments.
4. *Accuracy of the initial candidate trace*: measured using recall, precision, f/f 2-measure, selectivity, etc. Note that this factor can both be considered domain- and software-tool-dependent.

Tool-related factors. These factors describe how the software tool used in the process makes tracing decisions (tracing method), what parameters guide the work of the tracing algorithm, and how users are expected to interact with the software tool and observe/react to the produced results. Among the key factors in this category are:

1. *Automated tracing method* used to produce candidate TMs.
2. *Use of feedback*: whether it is used at all, and specific feedback processing method if used.
3. *Use of filtering* and specifics of a filtering method: which candidate links are shown to the analyst and which are not?
4. *Tool functionality and UI*: what features are available for the analyst to use when tracing with the tool? What are the steps necessary for the analyst to use these features?

Analyst-related factors. These factors cover the analyst's tracing expertise and domain knowledge. Some of the analyst-related factors we identify are:

1. *General expertise* working in the field of software engineering (measured in years, number of projects, etc.)
2. *Expertise with tracing*: which can be measured on the "Not expert" – to – "Expert" ordinal scale, or in terms of the number of tracing tasks completed/undertaken to date and/or hours spent performing tracing tasks.
3. *Domain expertise*: level of analyst's familiarity with the application domain.
4. *Personal qualities*: while hard to objectively measure, personal qualities (such as attention to detail, attention span, whether the language of the artifacts is the native language of the analyst, etc.) can potentially influence how an analyst engages in trace validation.
5. *Effort*: how much time the analyst puts into performing the actual tracing. It can be measured in total time to trace or time to trace per observed candidate link.

Whenever empirical studies of semi-automated tracing are performed, a fourth category of factors is also present:

Empirical study-specific factors. This category encompasses a variety of factors that are present in the empirical study design. Examples of such factors are:

1. *Experiment location/cohort*: in a repeated/replicated experiment, the cohort and/or location of the analyst (site A of the experiment vs. site B) may play a role in the observations of analyst behavior. Generally speaking, when conducting multi-site/multi-cohort experiments, the researchers want to eliminate the effects of these factors on the results.
2. *Analyst opinions*: Empirical studies allow researchers to collect information about the opinions of the analysts on a variety of issues related to the experiment: their level of comfort, their self-assessment, their tracing preferences. While these factors might not have *causal* effect on the accuracy of the analyst-submitted TM, they might have *predictive* effect.

The large number of factors that can influence analyst performance in semi-automated traceability tasks present a clear challenge for traceability study design. In deciding which specific factors to consider, we can propose a somewhat different ontology:

1. *Factors that can be controlled by study designers.* These are the factors whose values can be altered by the study designers at will. They are the key candidates for becoming the control/independent variables in the study design. Examples include initial TM accuracy, tracing software behavior, cohort/location.
2. *Factors that can be observed/measured by study designers.* These are the factors that either cannot be controlled at all (e.g., analyst effort), or are hard to control given the realities of the empirical studies[2] (e.g., analyst experience with tracing).

Initial studies of semi-automated tracing, out of necessity, must concentrate on studying the influence of the factors from the former category, while collecting and analyzing any correlations and/or predictive effects of the factors from the latter category. As such, we put forth three key research questions which need to be addressed.

> **[RQ1].** *What is the influence of the accuracy of the candidate TM on the accuracy of the final TM submitted by the analyst?*
> **[RQ2].** *Is analyst behavior when performing semi-automated tracing tasks predictable and reliable?*
> **[RQ3].** *What makes the best automated tracing tool for the semi-automated tracing process?*

---

[2] Key to such reality is the scarcity of potential participants in experimental studies. This makes any analyst-specific control (e.g., by education level, experience with tracing, etc.) harder to implement in practice.

In the sections that follow, we discuss approaches to studying these questions, the studies already undertaken, and their results.

4.1 Accuracy of the Candidate Traceability Matrix

What to study. Accuracy of the candidate traceability matrix produced by an automated method is the key feature of the candidate TM. *In theory*, the more accurate the initial TM is, the less effort the analyst needs to spend to validate it.

How to study. Given an initial traceability matrix, there are two ways to assess the performance of an analyst on the task. First, we can look at the absolute accuracy of the final TM submitted by the analyst. Second, we can look at the change in the accuracy from the initial to the final TM. The accuracy of the final TM is measured in terms of *precision, recall* and, through them, the *f2-measure*. By the same token, the change in the accuracy can be measured in terms of difference in *recall*, difference in *precision*, and difference *in f2-measure* between the initial and the analyst-submitted TM. It is important to consider both groups of measures. The former tell us how close the final TM is to the true trace (golden standard). The latter tell us how well the analysts made their decisions.

Visualization of results. One of the most straightforward ways of visualizing the results of the analyst's work is illustrated in Fig. 1. The initial and the final TMs are represented as points in the *recall* (X-axis) – *precision* (Y-axis) space. We can draw a vector from the point representing the initial TM to the point representing the final TM. The length of the vector illustrates the difference in *recall* (horizontal component) and *precision* (vertical component). In the recall-precision space, vectors directed towards the (1,1) (a.k.a. 100% recall and 100% precision) point exhibit the desired behavior – *the analyst has improved the accuracy of the candidate TM*, while the proximity of the heads of the vectors to the point (1,1) indicates the desirability of the final outcome – *the analyst came close to identifying the correct TM*.

Studies to date. Research on this topic, addressing **RQ1**, began in 2005 with an anecdotal study (Hayes et al., 2005b) of four industry analysts working on NASA's IV&V projects. The idea was to ask each analyst to complete a trace of a small subset of requirements taken from NASA's MODIS (MODIS, 1997) project. Analysts were assigned candidate TMs of varying quality to see if this impacted the quality of the final TM. The results of the pilot study are shown in Fig. 2. The findings were a bit astonishing: all of the analysts decreased the accuracy of the TMs. Also, they tended to move the TMs toward the recall = precision line. It was not until 2010–2011 that this anecdotal evidence was examined further, with a large study conducted at two universities by Cuddeback et al. (Cuddeback et al., 2010), and later replicated and extended by Dekhtyar et al. (Dekhtyar et al., 2011). We use the experimental framework of Hayes and Dekhtyar (Hayes and Dekhtyar, 2005) to examine the two studies.

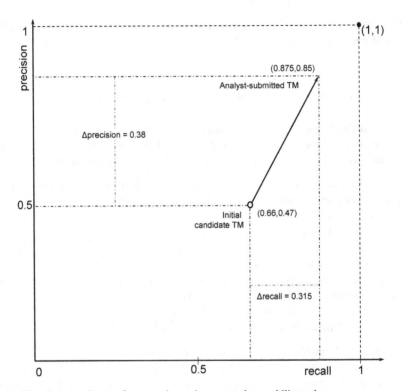

Fig. 1 Visualizing analyst performance in semi-automated traceability tasks

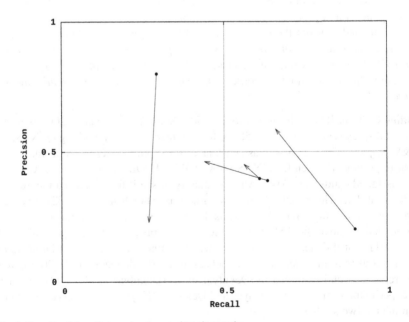

Fig. 2 Results of the pilot semi-automated tracing study

The *motivation* for the original study (Cuddeback et al., 2010) was to understand the behavior of analysts and the impact of accuracy of the candidate TM on the accuracy of the final TM. For the second study (Dekhtyar et al., 2011), the original motivation was expanded to add *confirmation* of findings.

The *purpose* of both studies was to evaluate the impact of starting candidate TM quality on final TM quality from the *perspective* of a researcher. The *null* and *alternate hypotheses* were not stated, instead, three *research questions* were asked:

1. How do human analysts transform the requirements traceability information produced by automated methods?
2. How does the accuracy change in that process?
3. Does the amount of time an analyst spends on trace validation impact the quality (accuracy) of the results?

The second study added a fourth research question:

4. Are there any factors that serve as statistically significant predictors of the accuracy of the final TM?

For the first experiment, the automated tracing tool Requirements Tracing On target (RETRO) (Hayes et al., 2007) was modified to deliver a pre-calculated candidate TM to an analyst as opposed to computing the TM "on the fly." Candidate TMs of varying recall and precision were constructed for a dataset and then were assigned to various study participants based on their experience (determined by their responses to a pre-study questionnaire). In the second experiment, two more processes were added. A group of participants was asked to perform manual trace validation: participants received hardcopies of the two artifacts being traced to each other and a hardcopy of a candidate TM and were asked to validate it. The third process used in the experiments involved using an updated version of RETRO called RETRO.NET (Dekhtyar et al., 2007), which included a significantly modified UI. The back end of RETRO.NET was instrumented to automatically log information about user activity (Kong et al., 2011).

In both experiments, the *scope* was a single project whose *importance* level was convenience. The *project* examined was ChangeStyle, a BlueJ plugin that formats Java programs. The project came out of a junior-level Software Engineering two-course sequence at Cal Poly. The ChangeStyle dataset used in the experiments consisted of 32 requirements and 17 test cases (Cuddeback et al., 2010). The project, when acquired by researchers, had a traceability relationship associated with it. The research team examined and extended the traceability relation to produce the *"golden standard"* TM used in the experiments against which to validate. The golden standard, a.k.a. the true TM, contained 24 links between the requirements and the test cases.

Both studies collected the same information. The *independent variables* were broken into two categories: *baseline independent variables* and *observed independent variables*. Tables 1 and 2 list the variables.

Table 1 Baseline
independent variables

Variable	Abbreviation	Scale
Precision of initial TM	SPrec	[0,1]
Recall of initial TM	SRec	[0,1]
F 2-measure of initial TM	SF 2	[0,1]
Quadrant of initial TM	SQuadrant	{Q1, Q2, Q3, Q4}
Size of initial TM	SSize	# links (1 --- 544)

Table 2 Observed independent variables

Variable	Abbreviation	Scale	Type
Procedure used	Procedure	{RETRO, Manual, RETRO.NET}	Tool-related
Location	Location	{CalPoly, UK}	Experiment-related
Software engineering experience	SEExp	{0,1,2}	Analyst-related
Tracing experience	TRExp	{0,1}	Analyst-related
Time to perform task	Time	# minutes	Analyst-related
Grade level	Grade	{F, Soph, J, S, G}	Analyst-related
Confidence w/tracing	TrConf	1 – 5	Analyst-related
Opinion on Tool vs. Manual	Opinion	{Manual, Software}	Experiment-related
Effort searching for omitted links	MissingEff	0---5	Analyst-related
Effort validating offered links	ValidEff	0---5	Analyst-related
Level of preparedness	Prepared	1---5	Analyst-related

The *baseline independent variables* are the variables whose values were directly or indirectly controlled in the study. The experiments assigned each participant a starting (initial) TM with a predefined accuracy, controlled by *precision* and *recall* numbers. *Precision* and *recall* of the initial TM uniquely determine the values of the other three baseline variables: *F 2-measure* of the initial TM, a convenient single-value surrogate for the precision/recall pair, the *quadrant* of the initial TM (the *precision, recall* pair discretized into four values: {*low precision/low recall, low precision/high recall, high precision/low recall, high precision/high recall}*), and *size* of the initial TM.

The *observed independent variables* were collected as follows. Prior to tracing, participants took a preliminary survey designed to gauge their level of expertise with tracing. During the tracing process, we collected information about the time it took the participants to complete the task. After the task, participants took a short post-study survey which measured their impressions of the process. From these three sources, information about 11 variables (factors) was collected. Most of the variables collected represent *analyst-related* factors, as seen in Table 2. Only one tool-related and one experiment-related variable were collected. We briefly describe each variable below.

Procedure used (Procedure). The experiments were run in three cohorts, each cohort being offered a different tracing experience. Two cohorts used software tools (RETRO and RETRO.NET), one cohort traced manually.

Location (Location). The experiments took place at two locations: on the campuses of California Polytechnic State University (Cal Poly) and University of Kentucky (UK). All participants in the manual tracing cohort were from one location. The other two cohorts had participants from both locations.

Software Engineering experience (of the participant). (SEExp). This was determined from participant answers to questions about the software engineering courses they took and their industry experience.

Tracing experience (of the participant) (TExp). The pre-study survey asked a number of questions about prior experience the analysts had with tracing, both in industry and in coursework, and the circumstances of the prior experience. This variable is the composite of the answers.

Time to perform task (Time). The amount of time spent by the participant on performing the assigned task was collected in each experiment.

Grade level (Grade). The grade level (freshman, sophomore, junior, senior, graduate student) of the experiment participants.

Confidence with tracing (TRConf). The post-study survey asked the participants to evaluate their level of confidence when performing tracing tasks.

Opinion on tool vs. manual tracing (Opinion). The post-study survey asked every participant if they would prefer tracing manually or using a software tool (regardless of how they were asked to trace in the experiment).

Effort searching for omitted links (MissingEff). Each participant was asked a post-study question about the amount of effort they spent searching for missing links.

Effort validating offered links (ValidEff). Each participant was asked a post-study question about the amount of effort they spent validating/vetting candidate links from the initial TM presented to them.

Level of preparedness (Prepared). The participant's response to the post-study survey question asking how prepared they felt for the tracing task.

Table 3 lists the *dependent variables* that were collected in the experiments. Two groups of dependent variables were collected: (a) recall, precision, and f2-measure of each participant's final TM, and (b) the "deltas": the differences in the recall, precision, and f2-measure between the initial and the final TM.

No *pilot study* was discussed. The participants traced the 32 requirements to the 17 test cases using the candidate TMs assigned to them. The *samples* used were representative with respect to content to what is used in industry, but were small. The first experiment did not *replicate* any prior studies. The second experiment *replicated* the first experiment using two different tracing procedures: one using a different software tool, and the other using manual trace validation.

Table 3 Dependent (response) variables

Variable	Abbreviation	Scale
Precision of the final TM	FinPrec	[0,1]
Recall of the final TM	FinRec	[0,1]
F 2-measure of the final TM	FinF 2	[0,1]
Difference in precision	ΔPrec	[-1.1]
Difference in recall	ΔRec	[-1,1]
Difference in f 2-measure	ΔF 2	[-1,1]

Table 4 A summary of two experiments (Cuddeback et al., 2010, Dekhtyar et al., 2011)

Cohort	Date	Tracing process	University A	University B	Total
1	11/2009	RETRO	16	10	26
1	04/2010	RETRO	0	7	7
2	11/2010	Manual	38	0	38
3	12/2010	RETRO.NET	8	5	13
All		All	62	22	84

The results of the studies are documented in the graphs and tables below. Table 4 shows the basic information about the experiments. The experiments were performed at two sites (University of Kentucky and Cal Poly, referred to as «University A» and «University B» in the table) over a period of approximately one year. The experiment participants were students enrolled in upper-division or graduate software engineering courses. The first procedure, trace validation using the front-end of the requirements tracing tool RETRO, was used on two occasions, and a total of 33 participants completed this task. Thirteen participants performed trace validation using the UI of RETRO.NET, a newer, more streamlined, user-friendly version of RETRO. Thirty eight participants validated presented hardcopy candidate TMs by hand.

Prior to the tracing task, each participant completed a pre-study survey. For cohorts involving software tools, a tool demonstration introduced the appropriate tool (RETRO or RETRO.net) and allowed participants to learn its UI. Participants in the manual tracing cohort instead received a brief overview of tracing and traceability. Each participant was assigned a unique *userID*, tied to a specific accuracy (precision, recall) of a candidate TM the participant was asked to trace.

To simplify observation and highlight trends, the results of both studies are combined and presented in the graphs in Fig. 3 broken down by the *quadrant* of the initial TM. Based on the results, the following observations about analyst behavior were made.

Low-precision, low-recall TMs. Analysts who validated candidate TMs with **low precision and low recall**, for the most part, showed *significant improvement* of both recall and precision of the final TMs that they submitted. Low precision and low recall TMs have moderate size averaging about the size of the true TM (i.e., 24 links). Analysts removed false positives from the candidate TM, noticed that it became too small and went looking (and found!) for omitted true links.

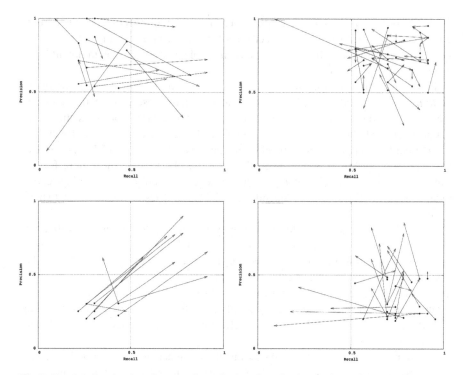

Fig. 3 Results of assisted tracing experiment broken down by the quadrant of the initial TM

Low-precision, high-recall TMs are very large, containing many true links and even more false positives. With a few notable exceptions, analysts presented these TMs *tended to concentrate on removing false positive links* from the candidate TM, thus improving precision. At the same time, they occasionally removed a true link, decreasing recall. They tended to submit TMs that were smaller in size than the ones given to them, although not every submitted TM had close to 24 links.

High-precision, low-recall TMs presented a different challenge to the analysts. These TMs are very small in size – some containing as few as 5–7 candidate links. Analysts correctly *determined that many true links were missing* and went searching for them. Except for a few outliers, most analysts successfully discovered a significant number of true links, improving, sometimes quite significantly, recall. At the same time, most added a number of false positive links, decreasing precision. Most analysts in this group submitted TMs that were similar or somewhat larger in size than the true TM.

High-precision, high-recall TMs. Analysts working with **high-precision, high-recall** TMs were less predictable. Most of the analysts correctly recognized that their initial TMs have relatively high accuracy, and therefore *did not affect too many changes*. What changes they made, however, had small but diverse and, *often negative*, effects. Analysts tended to slightly decrease the overall accuracy of the TM, while still supplying some of the most accurate final TMs.

True TM not recovered. Not a single experiment participant recovered the correct trace or at least discovered all correct links (finished with recall of 100%). At the same time, every correct link was found by multiple analysts, although not all links were uniformly easy for them to discover.

Following our experimental framework (Hayes and Dekhtyar, 2007), the *interpretation context* for this work is the field of tracing research. In this context, these observations shed some light onto the first two research questions studied in (Cuddeback et al., 2010) and (Dekhtyar et al., 2011): analyst behavior and accuracy of the final trace appeared to depend on the accuracy of the initial TM. To address the remaining questions and confirm the informal observations in a more formal way, (Dekhtyar et al., 2011) analyzed the influences of both baseline and observed independent variables on the dependent variables and tested them for statistical significance.

Tables 5 and 6 detail the results of the analysis. Table 5(a) examines the influence of the independent variables *Initial Precision* and *Initial Recall* on the response variables using multiple regression, bolded items are statistically significant. The first column reports the adjusted R-square value, R^2_{adj}, column two lists the F-value, and column three reports the significance level (*pvalue*) for each model. The initial accuracy of the TM has a statistically significant effect on the precision of the final TM. It also has a statistically significant effect on changes in precision, recall, and F 2-measure.

Linear regression was applied to examine the influence of the *Initial F 2-measure* on our response variables. Table 5(b) summarizes the results: initial F 2-measure statistically significantly influences final precision, final F 2-measure, the change in recall, and the change in F 2-measure.

Next, we examined how our observed independent variables related to the response variables. We controlled for two baseline independent variables, initial precision and initial recall, to prevent systematic bias and reduce error variance within groups. Of the eleven variables, only *time to complete the tracing task* (Time) is continuous, thus multiple linear regression analysis was used for it. We used one-way ANCOVA to analyze the remaining 10 (categorical) variables. Table 6 shows

Table 5 (a) Influence of initial precision and initial recall on response variables (degrees of freedom: 2,81); (b) Influence of initial F 2-measure on response variables (degrees of freedom: 1,82)

(a)				(b)			
Response Variable	R^2_{adj}	F-value	Sig. (pval)	Response Variable	R^2_{adj}	F-value	Sig. (pval)
FinPrec	**0.12**	**6.659**	**0.002**	**FinPrec**	**0.056**	**5.913**	**0.017**
FinRec	−0.004	0.842	0.434	FinRec	0.037	3.117	0.081
FinF 2	0.0	1.012	0.368	**FinF 2**	**0.053**	**4.604**	**0.035**
ΔPrec	**0.454**	**35.548**	**0.0001**	ΔPrec	0.036	3.02	0.086
ΔRec	**0.444**	**34.115**	**0.0001**	**ΔRec**	**0.312**	**37.227**	**0.0001**
ΔF 2	**0.288**	**17.761**	**0.0001**	**ΔF 2**	**0.238**	**25.672**	**0.0001**

Table 6 Analysis for observed independent variables controlling for initial TM precision and recall

Response		Location	Procedure	SEExp	TRExp	Time	Grade	TrConf	Opinion	MissingEff	ValidEff	Prepared
FinPrec	R^2_{adj}	0.12	0.109	0.107	0.121	0.127	0.148	0.083	0.129	0.049	0.126	0.102
$R^2_{adj} = 0.120$	F	1.012	0.510	0.876	2.034	1.025	1.668	0.045	1.111	0.091	1.02	1.003
	P	0.318	0.602	0.421	0.158	0.315	0.166	0.833	0.335	0.965	0.413	0.423
FinRec	R^2_{adj}	0.006	0.001	−0.001	0.002	−0.012	0.017	−0.022	−0.017	−0.016	0.115	−0.053
$R^2_{adj} = -0.004$	F	1.789	1.180	1.028	1.306	0.126	1.423	0.001	0.373	0.847	2.810	0.340
	P	0.185	0.313	0.362	0.257	0.724	0.234	0.978	0.690	0.522	0.023	0.887
FinF2	R^2_{adj}	−0.006	0.01	0.019	0.016	−0.008	−0.025	−0.022	0.0	−0.024	0.153	−0.022
$R^2_{adj} = 0.0$	F	0.496	1.383	1.765	2.284	0.013	0.503	0.077	0.784	0.717	3.428	0.741
	P	0.483	0.257	0.178	0.135	0.910	0.734	0.782	0.46	0.613	0.008	0.595
ΔPrec	R^2_{adj}	0.461	0.448	0.466	0.475	0.475	0.472	0.460	0.462	0.427	0.465	0.459
$R^2_{adj} = 0.454$	F	1.012	0.510	0.876	2.034	1.025	1.668	0.045	1.111	0.191	1.02	1.003
	P	0.318	0.602	0.421	0.158	0.315	0.166	0.833	0.335	0.965	0.413	0.423
ΔRec	R^2_{adj}	0.449	0.446	0.443	0.445	0.416	0.455	0.445	0.413	0.444	0.493	0.424
$R^2_{adj} = 0.444$	F	1.789	1.180	1.028	1.306	0.126	1.423	0.001	0.373	0.847	2.810	0.34
	P	0.185	0.313	0.362	0.257	0.724	0.234	0.978	0.69	0.522	0.023	0.887
ΔF2	R^2_{adj}	0.284	0.297	0.322	0.297	0.243	0.270	0.291	0.245	0.265	0.326	0.268
$R^2_{adj} = 0.288$	F	0.541	1.565	2.530	1.17	0.021	0.521	0.001	0.571	0.598	2.582	0.653
	P	0.464	0.216	0.086	0.283	0.885	0.721	0.980	0.568	0.702	0.034	0.66

the results of the analyses. We report the R^2_{adj}, the F-value, and the p-value as well as the baseline R^2_{adj} value for each response variable's effect with initial precision and initial recall. As can be seen from the table, **only one variable**, ValidEff has statistically significant effect on any response variables.

ValidEff quantifies the amount of effort participants put into evaluating candidate links from the initial TM as collected in the post-experiment survey (on a $0 - 5$ scale, where 0 meant *"never performed this type of activity"* and 5 meant *"performed this type of activity for every single link."*). The key reason for the statistically significant influence on final recall and change in recall of ValidEff was interesting. Of 84 participants, 62 specified values of 0, 1, 2, or 3 in response to the question. Thirteen participants gave a response of 4 and one participant gave a response of 5. The average recall for those responding 4 or 5 was 20.5% less than the average recall of those whose responded 0 through 3. Those who responded 4 or 5 were the only group of participants whose mean change in recall was negative, at an alarming -24.22%. Therefore, it appears that those participants who "overthought" the problem of validating the given TM performed significantly worse than everyone else.

Based on the obtained results, the accuracy of the initial TM was the *best predictor* for the *change in the TM accuracy*. Initial precision and initial recall together account for over 40% of variability of $\Delta Prec$ and ΔRec response variables. Of the 11 observed independent variables, only ValidEff had statistically significant effect on ΔRec and $\Delta F2$, explaining an additional 7–8% of variability. This was much less than the baseline variables.

From these two studies we draw two important conclusions which have overarching consequences for the overall study of traceability. First, **accurate automated methods do not necessarily guarantee accurate final traces:** human analysts, surprisingly, do not perform well when given fairly accurate candidate TMs. Second, **human analysts are predictably fallible.** To be successful, semi-automated procedures **must take this into account!**

4.2 Studying Reliability

In the context of semi-automated tracing, *analyst consistency*, a.k.a. *analyst predictability*, is the degree to which analysts tend to produce similar final results when given similar initial candidate TMs. *Analyst reliability* is the degree to which the analysts improve the initial TMs (i.e., can be relied on to deliver the correct TM). Semi-automated tracing procedures should allow analysts to behave **both** consistently and reliably – i.e., being able to predictably improve the initial candidate TMs and to reach the true TM. This behavior should not depend on the accuracy and/or other parameters guiding the specifics of the initial candidate TMs. Failing that, we would like to observe that *there is a certain region of parameter/factor values* for the initial TM which leads to both consistent and reliable behavior.

Consistency. Current results, described in the sections above, suggest a certain degree of predictability of analyst behavior. The second study described above

(Dekhtyar et al., 2011) shows that the accuracy of the initial TM (precision, recall) is a significant predictor for the accuracy of the final TM and for the change in accuracy. In fact, this was the factor with the *highest* predictive power of all the factors, both controlled and observed in the experiment. While it can be seen from Fig. 3 that the accuracy of the initial TM is not a perfect predictor – analysts shown similar TMs do not always behave in exactly the same manner – the overall behavior of the analysts is affected by the initial TMs they are getting.

- Analysts receiving *low-recall, low-precision* intial TMs show consistent and significant improvement in accuracy. They tend to keep the size of the final TMs close to the size of the candidate TMs they received and spend time both validating existing links (and rejecting false positives) and searching for missing links and including them into their final TM.
- Analysts receiving *high-recall, low-precision* initial TMs (i.e., TM has a large number of candidate links) spend most of their time vetting candidate links from the TM. They have shown the ability to improve (sometimes significantly) the *precision* of the TM. That is, they are able to recognize and reject false positive candidate links, for the most part. However, together with removing false positives, the analysts tend to remove small numbers of true links, thus somewhat decreasing recall.
- Analysts receiving *low-recall, high-precision* initial TMs exhibit the opposite behavior. Low-recall, high-precision TMs contain very few links, so the analysts tend to vet them quickly. After vetting provided links, most analysts conclude that their TM is not complete and start searching for missing links. They wind up adding a number of links (sometimes a significant number of links) to the TM before submitting. In doing so, most of them succeed in finding more true links. However, they also tend to introduce non-trivial numbers of false positives into the TM. As a result, analysts achieve improved recall, but at the price of decreased precision.
- Analysts receiving *high-recall, high-precision* initial TMs show the least agreement in behavior. Generally speaking, these analysts tend to correctly recognize that their TMs are already "pretty good" and require only a few "tweaks." Some tweak the TM by adding a few links, some tweak it by removing links, some do a bit of both. Interestingly enough, on average the tweaks have negative effects on the accuracy of the final analyst-submitted TMs, i.e., most of the tweaks to the candidate TM are introduced in error. As a result, the final TMs tend to have a slightly lower overall accuracy than the candidate TMs, although without a specific discernable pattern of what (recall, precision) improves and what deteriorates.

The studies essentially show that the analysts are *predictably unreliable.* Indeed, while some analysts show consistent improvement in TM accuracy, *no analyst in the studies* has ever been able to recover the true TM, or even to reach a TM with 100% recall. Something in the studies made analysts unreliable.

5 Conclusions

The study of the role of the analyst in semi-automated tracing scenarios has serious implications for both traceability researchers and industry practitioners engaged in *in-life cycle tracing*. There are a number of important implications for traceability research:

Semi-automated procedures. Semi-automated tracing scenarios change our understanding of what the "best" automated tracing methods and techniques are/should be. For automated tracing research, the choice of a better tracing method is straightforward: it's the one producing more accurate candidate RTMs. In semi-automated tracing settings, the accuracy of the final, analyst-submitted TM trumps the accuracy of the automatically generated candidate TM. As seen from the semi-automated tracing studies, higher accuracy TMs *do not lead to better analyst performance* in semi-automated tracing tasks and do not *always lead to better results*.

> As such, in the context of semi-automated tracing, there is a second notion of "goodness" of automated methods: a better automated method is one which induces better analyst performance and higher accuracy of the *final, analyst-submitted TM*.

> **Importance of HCI.** Human-computer interaction in semi-automated tracing scenarios can play an important role as analysts who work with software tools with poor UI capabilities may be more error prone. This introduces a new direction in traceability research: determining how to construct the *right* front-end for a special-purpose tracing tool in order to improve analyst performance. Measuring analyst performance in response to small design changes to such a front-end will also challenge researchers.

There are some key implications for industry as well.

- Manual tracing processes currently employed for in-life cycle tracing tasks require much effort and are prone to error, i.e., are not reliable. Semi-automated tracing can decrease required effort. Thus the challenge to making semi-automated tracing reliable is as much of an industry imperative as it is a research endeavor.
- Because full automation of tracing in-life cycle is infeasible, training analytical personnel to trace requirements and to do so using *imperfect tracing tools* (i.e., tools that do not produce 100% accurate traceability matrices) is an important direction in academia-to-industry technology transfer.
- It seems intuitive that these findings could more broadly pertain to any setting where an automated tool provides "advice" or intermediate results from which a human must make a final decision. As semi-automated tracing is studied further, transferrable/adaptable findings should be pursued and disseminated.

References

Cuddeback, D., Dekhtyar, A., Hayes, J. H.: Automated requirements traceability: The study of human analysts. In: Proceedings of IEEE International Conference on Requirements Engineering (RE), Sydney, Australia (2010, September)

Dekhtyar, A., Dekhtyar, O., Holden, J., Hayes, J.H., Cuddeback, D., Kong, W.-K.: On human analyst performance in assisted requirements tracing: Statistical analysis. In: Proceedings of IEEE International Requirements Engineering Conference, Sydney, Australia (2011)

Dekhtyar, A., Hayes, J.H., Larsen, J.: Make the most of your time: How should the analyst work with automated traceability tools? Predictor Models in Software Engineering, International Workshop on, p. 4, Third International Workshop on Predictor Models in Software Engineering (PROMISE'07: ICSE Workshops 2007)

Egyed, A., Graf, F., Grünbacher, P.: Effort and quality of recovering requirements-to-code traces: Two exploratory experiments. Requirements Engineering, IEEE International Conference on, pp. 221–230, 2010 18th IEEE International Requirements Engineering Conference (2010)

Hayes, J.H., Dekhtyar, A.: A framework for comparing requirements tracing experiments. Int. J. Softw. Eng. Knowl. Eng. (IJSEKE) 15(5), 751–781 (2005, October)

Hayes, J.H., Dekhtyar, A., Sundaram, S.: Text mining for software engineering: How analyst feedback impacts final results. In: Proceedings of Workshop on Mining of Software Repositories (MSR), Associated with ICSE 2005b, pp. 58–62. St. Louis, MO (2005b, May)

Hayes, J.H., Dekhtyar, A., Sundaram, S.K., Holbrook, E.A., Vadlamudi, S., April, A.: REquirements TRacing on target (RETRO): Improving software maintenance through traceability recovery. Innov. Syst. Softw. Eng.: A NASA J. (ISSE) 3(3), 193–202 (2007)

iTrust: http://agile.csc.ncsu.edu/iTrust/wiki/doku.php. Last accessed 10 May 2011

Kong, W.-K., Hayes, J.H., Dekhtyar, A., Holden, J.: How do we trace requirements? An initial study of analyst behavior in trace validation tasks. In: Proceedings of 4th International Workshop on Cooperative and Human Aspects of Software Engineering (CHASE 2011), an ICSE workshop, pp. 32–39. ACM, New York, NY, USA

MODIS Science Data Processing Software Requirements Specification Version 2, SDST-089, GSFC SBRS (1997, 10 November)

Part IV
Traceability Use

Traceability can be used to check that specified requirements have been satisfied in design and code, and help to assess and manage the impact of changing requirements, among many other things. The demands that are placed upon the traceability for end use, and thus the ability to use traceability effectively in practice, obviously varies dependent upon the context in which software systems are engineered and used.

This part of the book describes some typical development contexts and pinpoints their particular concerns. The chapter by Cleland-Huang, "Traceability in Agile Projects", reminds us that while successful traceability is always needs driven, there are sometimes leaner ways to achieve traceability goals in certain contexts. The chapter by De Borger et al. examines aspect-oriented software development, a context within which "Traceability Between Run-Time and Development Time Abstractions" becomes the all-important focus. The chapter by Mirakhorli and Cleland-Huang considers the benefits that can arise from "Tracing Non-Functional Requirements" and explains the associated complexity. Architectural centric traceability is proposed as an approach for those contexts in which the quality of service is the foremost concern. Finally, the chapter by Mc Caffery et al. on "Medical Device Software Traceability" explains the special demands of tracing regulatory requirements in the medical device industry and illustrates a medical device traceability software process assessment method.

Traceability in Agile Projects

Jane Cleland-Huang

1 Introduction

Agile methodologies represent a set of development processes in which both the requirements and the delivered solution evolve incrementally through a series of short iterations. Such projects are characterized by an emphasis on human interactions and collaborations, lightweight development processes, frequent deliverables, and minimal documentation (Ambler, 2004; Beck and Andres, 2004; Cockburn, 2000; Schwaber, 2004; Warden and Shore, 2007), Not surprisingly, traceability is generally perceived by agile developers as a heavy-weight and burdensome activity which returns little value to the project (Appleton, B. ACME Blog, 2005; Cleland-Huang 2006). On the other hand, agile practices are increasingly adopted in larger, distributed, and sometimes safety-critical projects, and it is often in these environments that the benefits of traceability outweigh its costs. For example, if agile methods are used to build a healthcare device, then the approval process for that device will require a demonstration that the device is safe. The Federal Drug Administration (FDA), which is responsible for approving such devices in the USA, specifically requires traceability between requirements, design, code, and test cases (USA Food and Drug Administration, 2005). For such projects, the burden is therefore placed on developers to create a project environment that establishes the necessary traceability relationships (Gotel and Finkelstein, 1994; Pinheiro FAC, 2003; Ramesh and Jarke, 2001).

As explained in the chapter "Traceability Fundamentals" of this book, the traceability efforts for a project must be fit for purpose. This means that there is no "one-size-fits-all" option where traceability is concerned, and traceability decisions will vary widely across different kinds of agile projects. In this chapter we therefore explore the issues, challenges, and goals for tracing in an agile environment, and propose specific solutions that we believe balance the spirit of agility with the increasingly common challenges of scale, complexity, and compliance.

J. Cleland-Huang (✉)
DePaul University, School of Computing, 60604 Chicago, USA
e-mail: jhuang@cs.depaul.edu

J. Cleland-Huang et al. (eds.), *Software and Systems Traceability*,
DOI 10.1007/978-1-4471-2239-5_12, © Springer-Verlag London Limited 2012

2 A Quick Look at Agility

Although a thorough discussion of agile methods is outside the scope of this book, we briefly present the philosophies and practices of agile development in order to provide the context for the remainder of this chapter. In general, agile practices share a set of fundamental philosophies, documented in the Agile Manifesto.[1] These philosophies stress the importance of people and their interactions over a strict adherence to processes and tools and the delivery of executable code over masses of documentation. They also emphasize the need to work closely with customers to shape the product and to resolve issues as they emerge instead of relying upon rigidly defined contracts. Finally they stress the importance of embracing changing requirements instead of rigidly following a pre-set development plan (Beck and Andres, 2004; Warden and Shore, 2007).

One of the most popular and well adopted agile approaches is eXtreme Programming (Beck and Andres, 2004), introduced by Kent Beck in 2004. XP includes several different practices which Beck found to be a particularly effective mix in the projects he had worked on. These practices are summarized in Table 1 and discussed below.

Requirements in XP projects are first captured as user stories and then later transformed by the customer into user acceptance tests. We illustrate this using an example taken from the healthcare domain. CCHIT (Certification Commission for Health Information Technology) certification standards requires all healthcare related systems, such as iTrust, to use ISO-8601 compatible timestamps. In an XP project, this might be documented as the following user story:

User story
Export all time stamps using ISO-8601 format.

which could be transformed into an acceptance test as follows:

Acceptance Test
Given a system timestamp of "November 5, 1994, 8:15:30 am, US Eastern Standard Time", when the system exports the timestamp as part of a patient's visit log, then the timestamp shall appear as "1994-11-05T13:15:30-05:00"

In most XP projects, it is the test cases, rather than the user stories, which are considered to categorically document the user requirements. When the test cases are executed and the tests are passed, the system is considered to meet its requirements. A pure XP project will therefore have little in terms of documentation beyond some

---

[1] Agile Manifesto: http://agilemanifesto.org

Table 1 Practices of extreme programming (Beck and Andres, 2004)

XP practice	Brief description
1. Customer team member	Include a customer in the core team who can define & prioritize features, write test scripts, and work closely with developers
2. User stories	Capture initial requirements as user stories i.e. brief and informal descriptions of features, each of which typically takes 1-3 weeks of work
3. Short cycles	Build and deliver the product in a series of short iterations
4. Acceptance tests	Transform user stories into scripted acceptance tests
5. Pair programming	Developers work in pairs. One thinks and assesses while the other writes code
6. Test-driven development	Write test cases first before writing the code. Automate all test cases
7. Collective ownership	All developers are responsible for all of the code
8. Continuous integration	Integrate new code frequently, and rerun all automated tests following each integration. When tests fail, roll-back, fix code, resubmit, and rerun tests
9. Sustainable pace	Keep a maintainable pace throughout the project
10. Open workspace	Work in an environment which is conducive to collaboration and which emphasizes the use of informal shared work spaces for tracking progress, agile modeling etc
11. The planning game	Developers and customers work together to plan iterations and releases
12. Simple design	Choose the design option which is the simplest solution for meeting the current needs of the project. Don't engage in big upfront designs or design solutions which look too far into the future of "what if" scenarios
13. Refactoring	Keep the design clean. A clean design is more poised to accommodate change
14. Metaphor	Provide meaningful and well-understood names to elements of the project

possibly throw-away user stories, user acceptance tests, and code (including unit test cases).

Although, not part of eXtreme Programming per se, Agile Modeling (AM), as proposed by Scott Ambler (Ambler, 2004) uses basic models from the unified modeling language (UML) and other approaches to shape the overall design of the system. However, in AM, the architectural and design models are more likely to be sketched on white boards or flipcharts than in more formal modeling tools. Furthermore, many agile models are considered throw-away, i.e. they are used to help sketch important elements of the design, but are not retained as permanent documentation. As a result of these practices, agile projects tend to travel quite "light" and have few traceable artifacts.

As depicted in Table 1, eXtreme Programming also follows the three practices of simple design, refactoring, and continuous integration (Beck and Andres, 2004). Together, these three practices serve the primary purpose of keeping the system flexible and maintainable, so that it is poised to embrace change. The constantly evolving nature of an agile project introduces additional challenges, and as a result, traditional approaches in which significant effort is needed to manually create and maintain traceability links are very unlikely to be adopted. Any viable traceability solution must therefore be light-weight, highly adaptable, and sufficiently robust to be effective in the continually changing environment of an agile project.

This discussion highlights an interesting facet of the traceability problem. While software engineers place significant emphasis on building maintainable systems in which classes or other kinds of modules are loosely coupled and highly cohesive, they have generally failed to extend these same practices to traceability. As a result, most traceability processes create a brittle and rigid layer over an otherwise relatively flexible software system. Given the environment and goals of an agile project, a brittle traceability solution is simply not a viable option. In the following sections we therefore explore some viable options for tracing in agile projects.

3 The Benefits of Tracing in Agile Projects

In many respects the traceability needs in agile projects are not that different from other project environments (Gotel and Finkelstein, 1994; Pinheiro FAC, 2003). Brad Appleton identified several reasons for tracing in an agile project (Appleton, B. ACME Blog, 2005), of which the most important ones are listed below:

- **Change impact analysis** – to assess how a proposed change will impact the existing system, in order to accommodate tasks such as communication, team coordination, and effort estimation.
- **Product conformance** – to ensure that the delivered product meets the customers' needs i.e. realizes their requirements. This is commonly referred to as requirements validation.
- **Process compliance** – to ensure that any procedural processes such as reviews and tests have been conducted.
- **Project accountability** – to provide assurance that the solution does not include gold-plating (i.e. excess functionality), and that all changes match a requested feature request.
- **Baseline reproducibility** – to support configuration of baselines, so that different versions can be reproduced.
- **Organizational learning** – to document rationales behind critical decisions in order to transfer knowledge to new team members.

Agile traceability goals are similar to those found in non-agile projects (Cleland-Huang et al., 2007; Gotel and Finkelstein, 1994), but differ in the way in which they are achieved. Appleton points out that if we look beyond the limitations of traditional traceability techniques, many tracing goals can be satisfied through trust and communication in a project. For example, if team members intrinsically hold the knowledge for how a modification will impact a system, then there is no need to capture that kind of information in the form of traceability links, or if developers trust each other not to gold-plate the system, then there is no need to create traceability links to demonstrate that all sections of the code trace back to requirements. However, while many agile projects, successfully follow such approaches, the practices become increasingly inadequate in larger and more complex projects.

4 Tracing in Agile Projects

4.1 Basic Traceability

The most common tracing scenario for an agile project is depicted in the Traceability Information Model (TIM) shown in Fig. 1. It is interesting to note that this TIM emerged as a result of forum discussions with agile developers[2] and therefore reflects their perception of common practice. This TIM shows how traceability is first established between acceptance tests and user stories through inserting a cross-reference to one or more user story into each of the acceptance tests. This is very simple, and is currently supported by a number of agile management tools such as Rally Software[TM]. When test cases are executed and passed, we are assured that the code implements the test case, and we can therefore implicitly establish an "implements" trace from the test case to the code. This means however, that the code is treated as a single high-level target artifact, and there is no visibility as to which classes are related to which test cases.

This raises the interesting question of whether traceability at this level of granularity supports the primary traceability goals of impact analysis and product

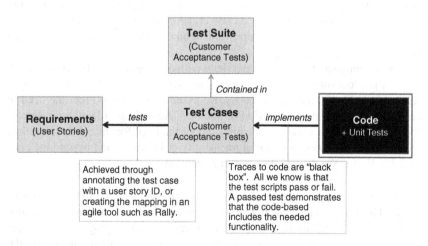

Fig. 1 A traceability information model for a basic agile project

---

[2] Agile Project Management Forum hosted on Yahoo – Discussion thread "Agile Traceability"

conformance. Clearly, it can demonstrate product conformance because for any given user story we can identify the related acceptance tests and determine if they are satisfied by the code (Richardson and Green, 2004). What it does not do, is to support traditional impact analysis in which traceability links are used to identify potentially impacted sections of the code in order to plan a proposed change, manage risks, or estimate effort. However, this level of support is not necessarily needed in many agile projects, especially if the projects are small or medium sized. In practice developers draw from their own knowledge of the system to plan and execute a change, and then run automated test cases to make sure that the change has been correctly implemented without unwanted side effects. A benefit of this approach is that it provides a highly resilient traceability mechanism anchored around acceptance and user tests, and which does not become brittle over time.

This approach is feasible unless the size of the project is too large, or the longevity of the project and staff turnover mean that communal knowledge is insufficient for the tracing task.

4.2 Beyond the Basics

In his article on "Lean Traceability" (Appleton et al., 2007), Brad Appleton describes several additional techniques for lightweight tracing. One such technique utilizes existing configuration management tools in order to capture traceability links. If changes are implemented at the level of granularity that would be expected in a test-driven environment, then software-level requirements, design, code, and test cases would all be part of the same task, and could easily be tracked to a single transaction ID in the change management system. Implementing simple configuration management, which is a natural part of an agile project, would therefore automatically produce traces into the code at the granularity of the check-in units (Guckenheimer, 2006). This is an improvement on the black-box approach depicted in Fig. 1.

Jacobsson conducted a series of interviews with developers, testers, configuration managers, product owners, scrum masters, and scrum coaches from several agile development projects (Jacobsson, 2009). He asked them "do you feel the need to trace in a project, and if so what kind of tracing?" According to Jacobsson, several of the interviewees were initially skeptical about the need for traceability, but then did identify several potentially useful traceability tasks, above and beyond the ones depicted in Fig. 1. We discuss the most important ones below:

- Stakeholder to requirements – to track who contributed the requirement (or user story). This makes it possible to identify the source of each requirement, and also to create a feedback loop to keep stakeholders notified of progress. The traceability link can be implemented simply by tagging each requirement with the contributing stakeholders' names.
- Requirements (user stories) to versions – to track exactly which requirements have been implemented in a specific revision. This can be accomplished quite

trivially using a source control tool such as Perforce, SVN, or Clear Case by attaching user story IDs to all committed changes. This provides traceability between requirements and code as a natural byproduct of the configuration management process. Trace granularity is at the checkin level. In fact, this process is described in greater detail in the chapter "Evolution-Driven Trace Acquisition in Eclipse-Based Product Line Workspaces" of this book.

- Requirements to requirements – to track dependencies between user stories. Although this could potentially create significant overhead, it is relatively easy to insert identified dependencies into user stories. Furthermore, it is possible to document dependencies as they are observed, or as new stories are introduced. This can be useful during the planning process, and there is no need to retain such traces once stories have been implemented.

4.3 Trace Retrieval

One of the themes pervading the previous sections of this chapter is that in many cases traces can be generated as a byproduct of the normal agile process at only negligible cost. In this section we explore one additional low-cost option, which can be useful in larger projects when developers may not have sufficient intrinsic knowledge of the overall project, and may therefore need automated support to understand the impact of a new user story, or to determine the purpose behind a feature in the code.

Just-in-time Traceability (JITT) addresses this problem through using information retrieval techniques to automatically create candidate traceability links (Cleland-Huang et al., 2007; De Lucia et al., 2007; Hayes et al., 2003; Lin et al., 2006). Although JITT does not produce perfect results, it has been shown to significantly reduce the cost and effort of the tracing process. In this chapter we do not present the theory or algorithms behind JITT, as they have been described in significant detail in the chapter "Automated Techniques for Capturing Custom Traceability Links Across Heterogeneous Artifacts"; however we do discuss its application to agile projects.

Figure 2 shows an example of JITT in action. In this example, the developer wants to find out how a new user story "Display drug-related interactions for each patient at the time a new order is being placed" will impact the code. It may be that the developer is fairly new to the project, or that the system was deployed a while ago and not modified recently, or it could be that the developer has a general idea of which classes might be impacted but wants to augment her existing knowledge with a dynamic trace. Either way, the tool returns a list of candidate classes and shows the likelihood that the retrieved class is related to the user story. Classes exhibiting higher similarity to the user story are returned towards the top of the list as they are more likely to be correct links than those returned further down the list. The developer can explore the details of individual classes, or may interactively improve the trace query through filtering terms or adding additional search words. A JITT tool therefore provides an interactive environment for retrieving potentially relevant

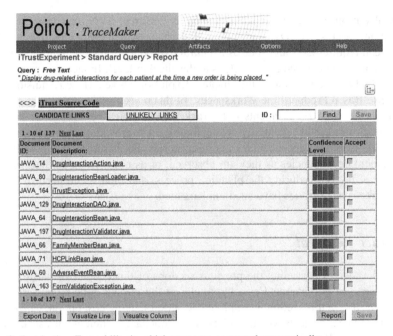

Fig. 2 Just-in-time Traceability in which traces are generated automatically

code. No permanent traces need to be stored or maintained, and the primary cost and effort of the trace is incurred at the time of need, thereby avoiding the problem found in more traditional approaches in which developers must invest significant time creating traceability links which they may or may not ever actually need.

On the other hand utilizing JITT on a project does require initial setup of the JITT tool, and this involves interfacing with the version control system so that queries can be launched against the code base. This is generally quite simple as there are several tools, such as src2ML (Collard et al., 2003) which can quickly convert code into a format parsable by JITT tools.

5 Traceability Across Different Types of Agile Projects

Agile projects come in many different shapes and sizes, and therefore their traceability needs differ quite significantly. This fact was stressed by Espinoza and Garbajosa, who proposed a model-based approach to planning traceability in agile projects (Espinoza and Grabajosa, 2011). This extends Ramesh's previous work on metamodels (Ramesh and Jarke, 2001), and the general practice of using Traceability Information Models (TIMs) as outlined in the chapter "Traceability Fundamentals" of this book. Espinoza advocates making traceability fit for purpose through allowing user-defined traceability links, well defined roles, and linkage rules which specify what kinds of traceability links can and must be created.

In this chapter of the book, we do not attempt to propose specific TIMs for different types of projects, but rather provide some general guidelines for tracing in three different types of agile projects. These can be characterized according to size, longevity, complexity, and criticality.

5.1 Typical Small to Medium Sized Agile Projects

A typical project is characterized primarily by its small to medium size and by the volatility of its requirements. While it may be hard to justify the creation and maintenance of traditional traceability links in such projects, the basic traces from Requirements (user stories) to test cases, and from test cases to (black-box) code, provide sufficient support in many projects. As the project size increases, there is increasing value in extracting traceability information from the check-in transactions of the version control systems to establish more finely grained traceability links from requirements and test cases to code.

5.2 Large Scaled, Distributed, or Long-Lived Projects

The second kind of agile project is characterized by a multi-year development duration, large and potentially distributed teams, and size and complexity of the code-base. In such projects it becomes difficult, if not impossible, to rely on communal memory to understand where specific functions have been implemented in the code, or to recall parts of the code that are sensitive to change because of interrelated trade-offs. This is particularly important to consider, because studies of agile projects have shown that although the cost and effort of change in agile projects, increases far more slowly than in traditional projects, it still does increase over the life of the project.

Furthermore, agile projects often suffer from some of the same ailments as traditional projects in terms of quality degradation. While we are not advocating the need for a heavy-weight traceability solution we suggest a customized mix of three different techniques: (i) basic traces from user stories → test cases → black-box code, (ii) JITT, and (iii) more fine-grained user-stories → code traces achieved through tagging checkin units with associated user stories.

5.3 Safety Critical Project

Finally, we consider the traceability needs of agile projects that incorporate safety-critical components. Such projects are obligated to demonstrate that the devices, including the software that runs on them, are safe for use (Appleton et al., 2007; USA Food and Drug Administration, 2005). Under these circumstances, traceability becomes compulsory, and certification requirements typically require bi-directional traces to be established from requirements to design, design to code, and code to test cases.

When the safety case is not adequately made, the company can be fined, or worse still, any devices running the uncertified software can be forcibly recalled. While a complete discussion of tracing in safety critical systems is outside the scope of this chapter, we do stress that such projects must follow a more rigorous traceability process in which risks are analyzed, hazards are identified, and mitigating requirements are specified (Cleland-Huang et al., 2012). It is then expected that a safety case will be developed which shows full life cycle traceability between hazards, requirements, design, code, and test cases. Such traces are likely to be stored in a more traditional traceability matrix which carries with it all the responsibilities and costs associated with manually creating and maintaining traceability links. These costs are justified due to the certification requirements of such a project.

6 Conclusions

This chapter has presented some basic ideas for effective tracing in agile projects. The guiding principles have been to eradicate the significant overheads of traditional traceability techniques and replace them with techniques that are significantly more cost effective. While many agile developers have a tendency to scoff at the idea of traceability, the increasing size and complexity of agile projects compels us to find ways to achieve the benefits of traceability without the cost and effort of traditional approaches. We are therefore forced to question the purpose of traceability, and look far beyond the confines and problems of traditional traceability techniques to discover new approaches for achieving the same goals.

References

Ambler, S.: The Object Primer: Agile Model-Driven Development with UML 2.0 (2004, 22 March)

Appleton, B. ACME Blog: Traceability and TRUST-ability. http://bradapp.blogspot.com/2005/03/traceability-and-trust-ability.html (2005, Tuesday, 15 March). Accessed June 2011

Appleton, B., Cowham, R., Berczuk, S.: Lean traceability: A smattering of strategies and solutions, CM Crossroads (Configuration Management) (2007, Tuesday, 18 September, 16:57)

Beck, K., Andres, C.: Extreme programming explained:embrace change, 2nd edn. Addison-Wesley, Boston, MA (2004). ISBN:0321278658

Cleland-Huang, J.: Just enough requirements traceability. COMPSAC 1, 41–42 (2006)

Cleland-Huang, J., Berenbach, B., Clark, S., Settimi, R., Romanova, E.: Best practices for automated traceability. IEEE Comp. 40(6), 27–35 (2007). ISSN:0018-9162

Cleland-Huang, J., Heimdahl, M., Hayes, J.H., Lutz, R., Maeder, P.: Trace queries for safety requirements in high assurance systems. In: Working Conference on Requirements Engineering for Quality. Essen, Germany, March 2012

Collard, M., Kagdi, H., Maletic, J.: An XML-based lightweight C++ Fact extractor. IWPC 134–143 (2003)

De Lucia, A., Fasano, F., Oliveto, R., Tortora, G.: Recoveringtraceability links in software artifact management systems using information retrieval methods. ACM Trans. Softw. Eng. Methodol. 16(4), 13 (2007). ISSN:1049-331

Cockburn, A.: Selecting a project's methodology. IEEE Softw. **17**(4), 64–71 (2000). ISSN:0740-7459. doi:10.1109/52.854070

Espinoza, A., Grabajosa, J.: A study to support agile methods more effectively through traceability. Innov. Syst. Softw. Eng. **7**, 53–69 (2011)

Gotel, O., Finkelstein, A.: An analysis of the requirements traceability problem. In: Proceedings of the International Conference on Requirements Engineering (RE), pp. 94–102. IEEE Computer Society, Springs, Colorado (1994)

Guckenheimer, S.: Software Engineering with Microsoft Visual Studio Team System. Adison Wesley, Boston, MA (2006, May)

Hayes, J.H., Dekhtyar, A., Osborne, J.: Improving requirements tracing via information retrieval. In: Proceedings of the IEEE International Conference on Requirements Engineering (RE), p. 138. IEEE Computer Society, Washington, DC (2003). ISBN:0-7695-1980-6

Jacobsson, M.: Implementing traceability in agile software development. Master's Thesis, Lund Institute of Technology (2009, January)

Lin, J., Lin, C.C., Cleland-Huang, J., Settimi, R., Amaya, J., Bedford, G., Berenbach, B., Ben Khadra, O., Duan, C., Zou, X.: Poirot: A distributed tool supporting enterprise-wide automated traceability. In: Proceedings of the 14th IEEE International Requirements Engineering Conference (RE'06). IEEE Computer Society, Washington, DC (2006). ISBN:0-7695-2555-5

Pinheiro, F.A.C.: Requirements traceability. In: Sampaio do Prado Leite, J.C., Doorn J.H. (eds.), Perspectives on Software Requirements, vol. 753, pp. 93–113. Springer, Berlin (2003)

Ramesh, B., Jarke, M.: Toward reference models for requirements traceability. IEEE Trans. Softw. Eng. **27**(1), 58–93 (2001)

Richardson, J., Green, J.: Automating traceability for generated software artifacts. In: Proceedings of the 19th IEEE International Conference on Automated Software Engineering (ASE '04), pp. 24–33. IEEE Computer Society, Washington, DC (2004). ISBN:0-7695-2131-2

Schwaber, K.: Agile Project Management with Scrum. Microsoft Press, Redmond, WA (2004). ISBN:073561993X

Warden, S., Shore, J.: The Art of Agile Development: With Extreme Programming. O'Reilly Media, Inc., Sebastopol, CA (2007). ISBN:0596527675

USA Food and Drug Administration: Guidance for the Content of Premarket Submissions for Software Contained in Medical Devices, May 11, 2005

Traceability Between Run-Time and Development Time Abstractions

A Case Study on AOSD and Debugging

Wouter De Borger, Bert Lagaisse, and Wouter Joosen

1 Introduction

Traceability throughout the software life cycle of requirements, architecture, design, development, testing and maintenance is an important research problem. Being able to relate effects to their causes is fundamental to any software engineering process. However this is still a challenge. Keeping track of all software artifacts, abstractions, relations and transformations throughout this life cycle requires sophisticated relationship management.

The software engineering life cycle is a process of gradual creation, transformation and refinement, where the artifacts of one phase are translated and transformed into those of the next phase (see Fig. 1). In the requirements phase, the functional and non-functional requirements are described. The architecture phase selects tactics to fulfill these requirements and documents the overall structure of the solution in various architectural views. During the design phase, the architecture is further refined into implementable components. Finally in the development phase, the designs are implemented and compiled into an actual system. Each of these phases uses its own abstractions. Many implicit associations exist between these different abstractions, which are vital to relate the actual system to its origins.

At run-time, the higher level abstractions used during development are no longer present. Even the artifacts used in the intermediate phases are no longer present in the actual system. They were lost in the process of translation and transformation. All there is left is a complex, synthetic run-time structure that is optimized for efficient execution and often too complex to understand.

In this chapter we focus on traceability in the final phases of the software life cycle: between the development and run-time phases. Between these phases, an abstraction gap exists: the various high level abstractions used during development are no longer present in the run-time environment. This often makes inspection of the complex, synthetic run-time structure impossible.

W. De Borger (✉)
DistriNet Research Group, K.U. Leuven, B-3001 Heverlee, Belgium
e-mail: wouter.deborger@cs.kuleuven.be

J. Cleland-Huang et al. (eds.), *Software and Systems Traceability*,
DOI 10.1007/978-1-4471-2239-5_13, © Springer-Verlag London Limited 2012

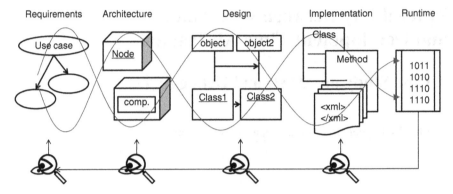

Fig. 1 Creation and transformation of abstractions throughout software life cycle

During the development phase libraries, languages and middlewares provide abstractions that shield the developers from the technical complexity of the underlying system and allow them to focus on core functionality. In the run-time environment, these abstractions have been compiled away. Technical and synthetic artifacts are polluting and replacing the abstraction of the original program. Due to the power and complexity of modern composition techniques, the synthetic execution structure no longer resembles the original program. It is too complex to understand even to the original developers themselves. Trends towards distribution and heterogeneity further widen this abstraction gap.

We propose a methodology for restoring the abstractions. Based on a declarative model that relates the development abstractions to the run-time abstractions, a trace information model is derived. For this case specificaly, this trace information model contains all information lost during compilation. At compile time, this trace is extracted. At run-time, the trace is combined with run-time information to recreate the development abstractions.

Concretely, we present results of our approach applied in the context of the debugging of aspect oriented software. Aspect Oriented Software Development (AOSD) (Filman et al., 2004) addresses the shortcomings of existing modularity techniques by focusing on the systematic identification, modularization, representation and composition of concerns or requirements throughout the software life cycle. The compilation process of aspect oriented programs is inherently complex. Tracing back from the actual run-time state to the development abstractions is not possible without proper tools.

In our previous work (De Borger et al., 2009), we have built a debugger for Aspect Oriented Programming (AOP) languages, capable of presenting AOP programs in terms of AOP abstractions. This debugger, based on the Aspect Oriented Debugging Architecture (AODA), will serve as a specific example of the use of traceability information to inspect the run-time state.

This chapter will first go deeper into what AOSD is and how it poses a challenge to run-time traceability. Section 2 will discuss the AODA approach to solving this problem. Section 3 evaluates the result by comparing the resulting debugger to existing tools. Sections 4 and 5 will give a short overview of future challenges and conclude.

2 Aspect Oriented Software Development and Debugging

This section first introduces the most commonly used AOP programming language, AspectJ. Next the problems of tracing AOP abstractions back to the run-time are discussed. In the third subsection, the existing solutions to this problem are discussed.

2.1 What Is AOSD

AOSD tackles inter-dependency and modularization issues by focusing on the systematic identification, representation and composition of (often crosscutting) concerns throughout the software development process. The core concept is that of an aspect: a coherent entity that addresses one specific concern, and has properties that can be changed independently of other entities.

Aspects allow behavior to be linked to global predicates over the structure of a program. An aspect can for example define: before each method whose name starts with **set**, execute a security check. More concrete, aspects allow us to express *pointcuts*, which are conditional statements selecting a number of events or locations in a program, called *joinpoints*. An aspect can provide a number of *advices*, which provide behavior that is executed before, after or instead of specific joinpoints.

For example: the aspect in Listing 1 logs the entry of every public method whose name starts with get and takes no arguments. This aspect has one advice (lines 2–4). The pointcut [execution(..)] selects all methods that take no arguments, whose name starts with get. The before keyword indicates that this advice must be executed before every joinpoint matched by the pointcut. The advice also use the thisJoinPoint keyword, that gives the advice access to information about the joinpoint the advice is applied to.

This sample demonstrates the power of AOSD: a concern that is usually scattered throughout the code, like logging, can be modularized into a single aspect.

```
1  aspect Logging{
2    before(): execution(public * *.get*()){
3      log(thisJoinPoint.getSignature());
4    }
5  }
```

Listing 1 Logging with AspectJ

Aspects are also applicable to more complex tasks. Consider the software used in hospitals. This software is bound to regulations and laws concerning privacy, security and accountability. To comply to these rules, security checks must be added to the software. These checks are often scattered throughout the software and rely on context information. Take for example the simple rule that sensitive information about a patient can only be viewed by the attending physician. This check must be placed on any possible access path towards this information and it depends on who is requesting the information, about which patient the information is and what their relation is. As such, placing this check poses two problems: where does it have to be placed and how can it find the context information, such as who's files are being requested, who is making the request and what is their relation. On top of that, the laws and rules change with geographic location and time. When they change, all security checks must be reviewed and the software must be modified to make the required context information available.

With AOSD, these security rules can be separated into their own aspects. If we for example take the requirement that every change to the database must be logged, we can write the aspect in Listing 2.

```
1   public aspect LogDataObjects {
2       before(): call(* edu.ncsu.csc.itrust.dao.mysql.*.*(..)) {
3           log(...);
4       }
5   }
```

Listing 2 Logging database access in the iTrust case with AspectJ

This aspect logs any method call [call (..)] towards the data access objects. It can be further refined to capture the current user name and other context information.

The aspect in Listing 3 illustrates scoping. The percflow(..) construct defines the scope of the aspect. Each time the execution control flow passes through a method in the org.apache.jsp package, with as first argument an object of a subclass of HttpServletRequest a new instance of the aspect is created. In practice this means that every web-request handled by the server has its own instance of this aspect and thus a safe place to store context information. This allows multiple concurrent requests to be handled without interference.

```
1   public aspect Security percflow(
2       execution(* org.apache.jsp..*.*(HttpServletRequest +,..))){
3       private Principal user;
4
5       before(HttpServletRequest req):
6           execution(* org.apache.jsp..*.*(HttpServletRequest +,..)) && args(req,..) {
7           user = req.getUserPrincipal();
8       }
```

Listing 3 Capturing context information in the iTrust case with AspectJ

The aspect also has an advice that captures and stores the current user's identity [Principal]. Because the scope of this aspect is bound to the current request, this principal can be used for security checks during the request.

Further reading on the application of AOP for security can be found in the work of De Win et al. (2004) en Verhanneman et al. (2006).

2.2 Traceability and AOSD

Aspect oriented techniques are not limited to the development phase of the life cycle, but they exist for various other life cycle stages. Aspect oriented requirements engineering (Rashid et al., 2002) identifies aspects during the requirements phase. The aspectual requirements are refined and transformed to form an aspect oriented architecture (Pinto and Fuentes, 2007; Tekinerdogan, 2004) and an aspect oriented design (Baniassad and Clark, 2004). At the end of the development phase, the compilation process weaves the various aspects into the base code. Pointcuts are matched to joinpoints and advice calls and aspect instantiation instructions are woven into the code. This weaving process yields a synthetic run-time structure that is often too complex to understand. The complexity of the weaving process makes it difficult to trace between the run-time and the development abstractions.

The transformation between aspect oriented source code and executable code creates two problems: the behavior-traceability problem and the data-abstraction problem.

The behavior-traceability problem arises when it is not clear which source code statement causes which behavior. For example, when a certain behavior is executed, it is often unclear which advice contains this behavior. Advices are often inlined into other parts of the program, making it hard to find their origin. Even if the advice is known, it is often not clear which pointcut triggered this advice, as multiple pointcuts can be bound to a single advice. This problem is called the causal pointcut problem.

The data-abstraction problem arises when a mismatch exists between data-structures at development time and at run-time. Aspect scoping for example suffers from the data-abstraction problem. As the example in listing 3 shows, aspect instances are transparently created. When an advice is applied, the correct aspect instance is selected automatically. How this selection is done and where these instances are stored is not clear. This makes it impossible to find out which instance of an aspect is bound to the current execution context, making contextual information inaccessible.

The stack trace also suffers from the data-abstraction problem: because the structure of the program was transformed, the information present on the stack is no longer meaningful. The stack trace (Fig. 2) of the previous aspect (Listing 2), clearly

≡ AuthDAO.edu$ncsu$csc$itrust$dao$mysql$AuthDAO$getLoginFailures$aop(String) line: 335
≡ JoinPoint_getLoginFailures_N_5777861951194645837_2(AuthDAO$JoinPoint_getLoginFailures_N_5777861951194645837).
  dispatch() line: not available
≡ JoinPoint_getLoginFailures_N_5777861951194645837_2.invokeNext() line: not available
≡ SimpleInterceptor.invoke(Invocation) line: 14
≡ JoinPoint_getLoginFailures_N_5777861951194645837_2.invokeNext() line: not available
≡ JoinPoint_getLoginFailures_N_5777861951194645837_2.invokeJoinpoint(AuthDAO, String) line: not available
≡ AuthDAO$AuthDAOAdvisor.getLoginFailures_N_5777861951194645837(AuthDAO, String) line: not available
≡ AuthDAO.getLoginFailures(String) line: not available
≡ LoginFailureAction.isValidForLogin() line: 66
≡ authenticate.jsp line: 26

Fig. 2 Stack trace of the aspect in Listing 2, when implemented by JBoss AOP

shows this. This example is the simplest possible application of AOP and already it is too complex to understand. When the more advanced features of AOP, such as joinpoints on exception handlers, come in to play, this abstraction gap becomes increasingly wide.

2.2.1 State of the Art

While the abstraction gap is a known issue in the AOSD community, most existing languages offer no extensive traceability support. For debugging, developers have to fall back to the synthetic run-time abstraction. This leads to the two problems mentioned before.

Currently used tools have no actual support for debugging beyond Java debugging. Most tools use the Java debugger (JDI), when inspecting AspectJ programs. JDI can only observe the synthetic run-time structure. Editing and development tools, such as the aspect java development tool (AJDT), attempt to improve behavior-traceability. The AJDT places markers in the source code to indicate where advices can influence the source code. This helps estimating which advices acted where, but it is not sufficient to solve the causal pointcut problem.

Research in this area has produced two solutions to alleviate this problem. Eaddy et al. (2007) have created the Wicca language. Wicca is specifically designed to support source weaving: the weaver no longer produces machine code but synthetic source code. This produces a view of the woven program which is readable as it is expressed in a programming language. The behavior-traceability problem is reduced by a source-to-source mapping, that indicates the origin of each instruction. The causal pointcut problem is not solved, as pointcuts produce no actual instructions and thus leaves no trace in the synthetic source. The data-abstraction problem is not addressed, all information is presented in terms of OO-abstractions. An additional drawback of this approach is that it requires the woven code to be optimized for readability, and not for efficiency. This approach can present a detailed representation, but only in terms of synthetic OO-abstractions.

Pothier and Tanter (2008) created TOD, the omniscient debugger. Omniscient debuggers maintain a complete trace of the execution itself. The result of every instruction is recorded. This makes it possible to replay a program backwards, so that effects (in the program state) can be traced back to their causes. This trace is presented in terms of the byte code instructions. Furthermore each instruction is related to its origin in the source code. Synthetic code is highlighted to make it easily distinguishable from the actual functional code. This alleviates the code-location problem, but leaves the causal pointcut problem unsolved. The data-abstraction problem is not solved as data can only be inspected in terms of low-level abstractions. As such, this approach has similar properties to the previous, but at a much finer level of granularity. This means that the trace is more accurate, but also that it suffers harder from the lack of abstraction. Even with highlighting, byte-code remains very hard to decode. Due to its high level of detail, TOD is a perfect tool for language designers to evaluate the internal workings of their languages. For the average user however, the massive amount of low-level information is not very useful.

Table 1 Comparison of inspection techniques for AspectJ. Comparing the Java debugger (JDI), the Java debugger with the AspectJ development tools (AJDT), TOD (Pothier and Tanter, 2008), Wicca (Eaddy et al., 2007) and our proposed solution (AODA) to the qualities described in Section 1.2

	JDI	AJDT	TOD	Wicca	AODA
Behavior	−	+	+	+	++
Data	−	−	−	−	+

As such, the existing solutions for debugging of aspect based programs make an effort to overcome the aforementioned problems, they are not generally applicable. The abstraction gap is reduced, but not bridged (see Table 1). There exists no explicit representation of the run-time state in terms of the development abstractions.

3 The AODA Approach

To bridge the abstraction gap between the run-time structure and the programming abstractions we propose a methodology that represents the run-time state in terms of the programming abstractions.

The approach encompasses five steps: modeling of the abstractions, modeling of the relations between the abstractions, derivation of the trace model, extraction of the trace, and implementation of the transformation (Fig. 3).

1. In the *abstraction modeling* phase the run-time and language abstractions are modeled according to the principles of mirroring (Bracha and Ungar, 2004). Both these models describe which entities exist in their respective view of the system. Each model also describes the interface by which the system can be debugged. (Sections 2.1 and 2.2)
2. In the *relational modeling* phase the two models are related by a model-to-model transformation. This transformation is an abstract representation of the compilation. It describes how the compiler breaks down the language level entities into run-time structures, in an abstract and declarative way. (Sections 2.3 and 2.4)
3. In the *trace derivation* phase, a trace information model is derived from the transformation. This trace model defines which trace information the compiler must output to make the compilation reversible. In other words, the trace information model contains all information lost during the compilation. (Section 2.4)
3. In the *trace extraction* phase, the compiler is modified to actually output a trace conforming the trace information model. (Section 2.5)
5. In the *transformation implementation* phase, the model-to-model transformation, created in the relational modeling phase is implemented. The result is a component that consumes run-time information through an interface conforming to the run-time model and combines it with trace information emitted by the compiler to create an interface conforming to the language model. (For more detail see De Borger et al. (2009).)

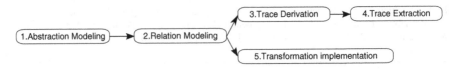

Fig. 3 The AODA approach

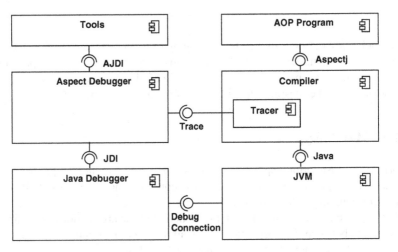

Fig. 4 Principle of run-time tracing

When we apply this approach to AspectJ, this results in Fig. 4. On the right hand side, there is a program, written in AspectJ, which is compiled to JVM-byte-code. The resulting program is executed by the JVM, that can be debugged by a Java debugger. On the left hand side, the information presented by the Java debugger is in terms of Java abstractions, conforming to the run-time model JDI. This model contains no aspect specific entities such as aspects or advices.

The AspectJ abstractions are restored by the aspect debugger. This aspect debugger consumes trace information and combines it with debug information. It provides a debug interface conforming to the AJDI model, which contains all the aspect specific entities such as Aspects and Advices.

In the remainder of this chapter, we explain the first four phases of the process. For the final phase, we refer to De Borger et al. (2009). First the principles of mirroring are discussed. These principles define the JDI and AJDI interfaces. Section 2.2 provides more details on how the AJDI interface is created by applying these principles to AspectJ. Section 2.3 gives a general introduction into model transformations. Section 2.4 describes how we can use model transformations to model the compilation and derive the trace information model from the compilation model. Section 2.5 covers the technical details of recording the trace and the structure of the tracer.

3.1 Mirror Based Reflection

The foundation of this approach is situated in the research domain of computational reflection. Maes (1987) describes reflection as the capability of a system to reason about itself and act upon this information. For this purpose, a reflective system maintains a representation of itself that is causally connected to the underlying system that it describes. In other words, a reflective model is an abstract representation of the run-time state of the system itself.

An important design principle for reflective systems is mirror based reflection. Bracha and Ungar (2004) describe four design principles for mirrors:

1. **"Encapsulation:** [reflective] facilities must encapsulate their implementation.
2. **Stratification:** [reflective] facilities must be separated from base-level functionality.
3. **Structural correspondence:** the structure of [reflective] facilities should correspond to the structure of the language they reflect on.
4. **Temporal correspondence:** [reflective] APIs should be layered in order to distinguish between static and dynamic properties of the system. "

In the context of debugging, encapsulation and stratification are not a problem, as the debugger is a completely separate process.

The combination of structural and temporal correspondence is also named ontological correspondence. To bridge the abstraction gap, ontological correspondence is crucial. If this correspondence is maintained, the abstractions are maintained. Ontological correspondence implies that the trace information must relate a meaningful model of the run-time to a meaningful model of the high-level language.

3.2 The AJDI Model

AJDI is the reflective front-end interface of our AODA debugging solution. It is based on the mirror design principles that have been defined in Section 2.1.

The AspectJ language is an extension of the Java language. In the same way, the AJDI, representing AspectJ, is an extension of the Java Debugging Interface (JDI), representing Java. The AJDI interface extends the JDI by specializing the existing entities with additional aspect related properties as well as by introducing new entities that are specific to AOP. The essential concepts of AJDI are depicted in Fig. 5. The gray part is the JDI model representing Java. The white components are specific to AJDI. They represent AOP-related entities that don't exist in Java.

The virtual machine itself is reified as the *VirtualMachine* mirror. This mirror encapsulates the debug connection between the actual virtual machine under

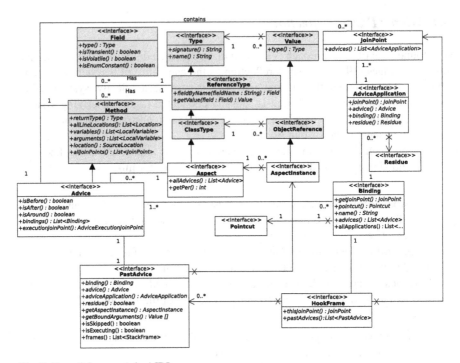

Fig. 5 Essential concepts in AJDI

inspection and the mirroring system. The VM mirror creates and manages all other mirrors. All mirrors provided by the VirtualMachine mirror are interrelated thus allowing exploration of the program structure. For example: to inspect the type of an object, the `referenceType()` method is invoked. This method returns a mirror of the ReferenceType class that represents the type of the object. The ReferenceType can then be queried for its name, methods, fields, super classes, interfaces and other properties.

We now summarize the basic JDI entities and the extensions on these entities that are relevant. These extensions are mainly related to inspecting joinpoints within the context of a JDI entity and where the JDI entity is located in the source.

Type reifies a type. A type can be primitive, void or a `ReferenceType`. Types have a name (`name()`) and a signature (`signature()`).

Value reifies a typed entity. A value can be primitive, void or an `ObjectReference`. Each value has a type (`type()`).

ClassType reifies a class. ClassType extends Type. A ClassType has `Fields`, `Methods`, `Constructors`, `Interfaces`, a `Superclass`, `Subclasses`, etc.

Method reifies a method. A Method can have an `ExecutionJoinPoint` and several other `JoinPoints` in its body (`allJoinPoints()`).

The essential AOP-related mirrors offered by AJDI are defined as follows:

Aspect reifies an aspect. Aspect extends `ClassType`, as an aspect is based on a class. It thus has state (`Fields`) and behavior (`Methods`). However, every attempt to explicitly instantiate an aspect instance with the reflective API, will cause an exception.

Advice reifies an advice. `Advice` extends `Method` as advices are based on methods. However, every attempt to explicitly invoke it through the reflective API will result in an exception.

Binding reifies the relation between an advice and a pointcut. A binding can have a name or can be nameless. In AspectJ each advices is bound to exactly one pointcut by a nameless binding. When an advice is bound to a pointcut, the advice is applied on any joinpoint matched by the pointcut.

AdviceApplication reifies the application of a certain advice under a certain binding on a certain joinpoint.

JoinPoint reifies a joinpoint. A hierarchy of subclasses is offered by AJDI (but not depicted) to represent specific joinpoint types. In this context a joinpoint is a specific location in the program, sometimes called a joinpoint shadow.

HookFrame extends `StackFrame`. HookFrames indicate the presence of joinpoints in the control flow. HookFrames provide information about the joinpoint and the advices that have executed, are executing and will execute on that joinpoint.

PastAdvice encapsulates the state of an advice that has been executed, that is being executed or that could have been executed.

The mirrors of the AO software system are related to the exact locations in the underlying byte code and the underlying source code. `Bindings`, `Fields`, `Methods` and `Advices` are all related to a source code location. `StackFrames` and byte code indices inside a method or advice are related to a byte code location and a source code location. `Joinpoints` are related to a range of byte code indices and source code lines as they can span more than one instruction.

Both JDI and AJDI can be divided in a static and a dynamic part. The static part is know at compile time, the dynamic part is only know at run-time. Aspects and Classes are part of the static part, AspectInstances and Objects are not. Joinpoint matching is somewhat special, as it is done partly at compile time and partly at run-time. The compiler matches as much of the pointcut as possible. All locations matched by the compiler are marked with an AdviceApplication mirror. At run-time, the pointcuts are further evaluated. The result of this evaluation is represented by a PastAdvice mirror.

3.3 QVT Model to Model Transformations

As described at the start of this section, the models presenting the run-time and language structure can be related by a model-to-model transformation (Czarnecki

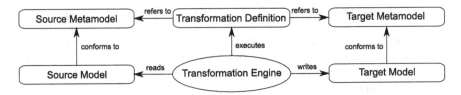

Fig. 6 Overview of model to model transformations (based on Czarnecki and Helsen, 2006)

and Helsen, 2006). In this subsection we will describe the general principles of model transformations, in the context of the Query View Transformer (QVT) (http://www.omg.org/spec/QVT/1.0/) relations language. In the next subsection we will apply this theory to the JDI and AJDI models.

In general, a model-to-model transformation expresses the relations between a source model and a target model (Fig. 6). The model transformation definition defines how entities in the source model are related to entities in the target model and vice versa.

A QVT transformation consists of a set of relations. Each relation models a trace between a specific entity in the source model and its corresponding entity in the target model. In Listing 4 such a relation is depicted, both in an abstract form and a concrete form. Each entity is expressed as a pattern (lines 3 and 18–20). It has the keyword domain followed by the name of the domain it belongs to and the type of the entity. The pattern binds each property of the entity to a variable. If the variables, bound in both patterns, have the same values, the relation holds. Relations can also contain conditions and assertions (lines 8–13 and 28–34). The keyword when indicates all conditions, the keyword where all assertions. If the conditions are not satisfied, the relation doesn't hold. If a relation holds, the assertion must hold. Relations can use other relations as conditions or assertions.

The concrete pattern thus means that each Package in JDI is equivalent to a Package in AJDI when both packages have the same name and are in equivalent VM's. When the packages are equivalent, the classes in this package, in the JDI domain are equivalent to either classes in AJDI domain or to aspects in the AJDI domain.

Model transformations can be executed in two modes: they can either verify whether two models are related according to the transformation, or they can produce a valid target model for a given source model. Even in this second mode, most model transformations can be executed either way: they can not only produce a target model based on a source model, but they can also produce a source model based on a target model.

A model transformation also defines a trace information model: the complete set of variables bound in a relation defines a trace record. By keeping track of all bindings of all relations, a trace of the transformation can be automatically generated.

```
 1   relation <RelationName>{
 2    domain <InputModel> <InputEntity> {
 3     <attribute> = <variable>
 4    }
 5    domain <OutputModel> <OutputEntity>{
 6     <attribute> = <variable>
 7    }
 8    when {
 9     <condition>(<variables>)
10    }
11    where {
12     <assertion>(<variables>)
13    }
14   }
15
16   relation PackageToPackage{
17    domain JDI Package {
18       name = cn,
19       virtualMachine = jvm,
20       classes = jclasses
21    }
22    domain AJDI Package{
23       name = cn,
24       virtualMachine = ajvm,
25       classes = ajclasses ,
26       aspects = aspects
27    }
28    when {
29     VmToVm(jvm,ajvm);
30    }
31    where {
32     ClassToClass(jclasses , ajclasses );
33     ClassToAspect(jclasses , ajclasses );
34    }
35   }
```

Listing 4 Example of a model transformation

3.4 From Transformation Model to Trace Information Model

Consider a QVT transformation with as source meta-model the AJDI and as target meta-model JDI. The part of this transformation relating the static parts of both models represents the compilation. The reverse of this transformation (from JDI to AJDI) is the transformation capable of bridging the abstraction gap.

As was previously described, both Java and AspectJ can be described by mirroring models, (JDI and AJDI). This subsection describes the model transformation that converts AODA into JDI. This model transformation defines the relation between the abstraction in both languages. It can be refined into a trace information model and into a high-level debugger, as described at the start of this section.

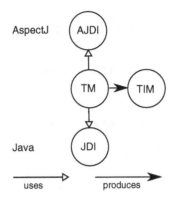

Fig. 7 Inter-model relations

Figure 7 gives an overview of the different models and their meta model. On top is AJDI, representing AspectJ. On the bottom, there is JDI representing Java. In the middle we can see the relations between the models. The complete set of relations between AJDI and JDI is described in the form of a model transformation (MT). This transformation is bi-directional: it describes both the compilation and the debugging. In the direction of the compilation, the input uniquely determines the output: an AJDI model always produces the same JDI model. Due to the loss of abstraction, the reverse is not true: given a JDI model, there can be many possible AJDI programs that caused it. Or, in terms of model transformations: for some JDI entities, multiple relations may hold, other than those that created the JDI entity.

To be able to reconstruct the abstractions, the reverse transformation must be made uniquely determined. To do this, we use the trace information defined by the static part of the transformation. This corresponds to the information that is lost during compilation. Because of the well-typedness of Java, the dynamic part is uniquely determined if the static part is uniquely determined (i.e. if the run-time type is determined, the structure of its instances is determined). As such the trace must capture all information that is lost during compilation, in order to be capable of restoring the abstraction correctly.

In summary, our approach to restoring abstractions is based on this model transformation, applied to run-time structure. Due to the loss of abstraction, this model transformation requires trace information to restore the development abstractions.

An example is in Listing 4. The left relation states that any aspect (in AODA) is equivalent to a class (in JDI) with the same name if [when] they are in the same package. If this pattern matches then [where] all advices (in AODA) are methods (in JDI), as defined by the adviceToMethod relation and all methods and fields respectively become methods and fields. The right pattern shows a nearly identical relation that transforms classes (in AODA) to classes (in JDI).

If we execute this transformation from AODA to JDI, it is uniquely determined. In the other direction, it is not. Any class (in JDI) can be either a class (in AJDI) or an aspect (in AJDI). Therefore we need tracing information that indicates, for each class (in JDI), whether it is an aspect or not.

The tracing information model for this part of the transformation will contain a record to distinguish between these two possible transformations. For each class, the trace must mark it as either a class or an aspect. In the same way, to distinguish between the `methodToMethod` and `adviceToMethod` transformations, each method will have to be marked as being either a method or an advice. This yields a trace information model defines the following records:

1. `ClassRecord(class:jdi.Class, isAspect:boolean, isClass:boolean)`
2. `MethodRecord(method:jdi.Method, isMethod:boolean, isAdvice:boolean)`

This trace information can be reincorporated into the transformation as an extra condition (Listing 6, line 16). Adding such conditions to the entire transformation yields both a complete trace information model and a reversible transformation, capable of restoring the AspectJ abstractions. For entities such as classes, the trace information model is quite simple. For other entities, such as pointcuts, which have no Java counterpart, the trace information model may contain the entire entity.

Also note that the model transformation is not the compilation, but a model of the compilation. If the compiler has to take a complex decision, like the matching of pointcuts to joinpoints, it is not necessary to model the mechanics of this decision. The decision can be represented by a function with no implementation. This makes it clear that tracing information is required to invert the function. As the transformation is not intended to be executed without this tracing information, this model is sufficient.

```
1  relation classToAspect{               22  relation classToClass{
2    domain JDI c:class {                23    domain JDI c:class {
3      package = jp:Package{},           24      package = jp:Package{},
4      name = cn:String ,                25      name = cn:String ,
5      methods = jm:List<Method>{},      26      methods = jm:List<Method>{},
6      fields = jf:List<Fields>{},       27      fields = jf:List<Fields>{}
7    }                                   28    }
8    domain AODA a:aspect{               29    domain AODA a:class{
9      package = ap:Package{},           30      package = ap:Package{},
10     name = cn:String ,                31      name = cn:String ,
11     methods = am:List<Method>{},      32      methods = am:List<Method>{},
12     fields = af:List<Fields>{},       33      fields = af:List<Fields>{}
13     advices = ad:List<Advice>{},      34    }
14   } when {                            35    } when {
15     packageToPackage(jp,ap);          36      packageToPackage(jp,ap);
16   } where {                           37    } where {
17     methodToMethod(jm,am);            38      methodToMethod(jm,am);
18     adviceToMethod(jm,ad);            39      fieldToField(jf,af);
19     fieldToField(jf,af);             40    }
20  }
21
```

Listing 5 Transform relating classes to aspects

```
1    relation classToAspect{
2      domain JDI c:class {
3        package = jp:Package{},
4        name = cn:String,
5        methods = jm:List<Method>{},
6        fields = jf:List<Fields >{},
7      }
8      domain AODA a:aspect{
9        package = ap:Package{},
10       name = cn:String,
11       methods = am:List<Method>{},
12       fields = af:List<Fields >{},
13       advices = ad:List<Advice>{},
14     } when {
15       packageToPackage(jp,ap);
16       trace.isAspect(c);
17     } where {
18       methodToMethod(jm,am);
19       adviceToMethod(jm,ad);
20       fieldToField(jf,af);
21   }
```

Listing 6 Transform relating classes to aspects with tracing information

3.5 Trace Collection

Once the trace information model is known, the required trace information can be collected in the compiler. The AspectJ compiler conceptually consists of three stages: front-end, weaver and back-end. Each stage consists out of several steps. The front-end builds the abstract syntax tree (AST) of the program. During this stage, the source files are parsed into an abstract syntax tree. Types and names are resolved and various validations, such as type checking and exception checking are performed. At the end of the front-end stage, a correct and complete model of the program exists in the form of an AST. The weaving stage transforms the AspectJ AST into a Java AST. Pointcuts are matched to joinpoints, advice calls are inserted at the matched positions. All aspects and advices are transformed into classes and methods. In the back-end stage, the code is optimized and written to disk.

As such, the AJDI AST is present before the start of the weaving stage and the JDI AST is present after the weaving stage. The most complex transformations take place within the weaving stage. In the front-end, only one kind of information is lost and that is the line-numbering. As such, the front-end must only trace line numbers up to the abstract syntax tree. In the back-end, optimizations take place. Instruction sequences are reordered or eliminated. For the back-end, it is important that the collected trace-information is still applicable after instruction reordering.

In general two basic techniques for tracing through compilation exist: generic meta-data passing or maintaining explicit traces. The generic approach attaches meta-data about the origin of entities to these entities. When an entity is transformed, all meta-data of the origin is replicated into the target. If entities are merged, so is their meta-data. The second approach requires modification of each stage of the compiler so that is explicitly outputs a trace.

The advantages of the generic approach is that it requires no modification of the various compiler stages. The disadvantage is that the meta-data signatures can become arbitrarily complex.

In our implementation, we adapted all relevant stages in the weaver, so they explicitly produce trace information. At the end of the weaving phase, the trace information is attached to the relevant AST nodes and carried through all optimizations as meta-data. At the end, the trace is outputted and stored in the class files.

If we apply this extraction to the trace information model part derived in Section 2.4 on the code segment in Listing 3 we get the following trace information:

```
ClassRecord(Security,true,false)
MethodRecord(Security.$before0,false,true)
```

Meaning that the Java class `Security` is an aspect in AspectJ and that the Java method `Security.$before0` is actually an advice in AspectJ.

4 Evaluation

To illustrate the use of AODA, this section will compare the standard AspectJ tools with AODA. We will search for a number of common bugs with both the AspectJ development tools (AJDT) and AODA.

As case study, we use the iTrust application, but with aspect based security (Listing 7). The security system consists of two advices: a first advice captures the session context (line 5–10) and a second advice does a security check before every security sensitive action and logs the action (line 12–18). This second advice is bound to many different pointcuts, for different types of security sensitive actions.

This example contains the following bugs

1. The security checking advice is bound to overlapping pointcuts, which causes some actions to be logged multiple times (line 26 and 30). One of them should be removed or refined.
2. The security checking advice has an incorrect dynamic condition in a pointcut, that causes it to be skipped at run-time (line 14). The first part of the pointcut (`secureAction()`) selects all joinpoints matching `secureAction`. The second part `!cflow(secureAction())` selects all joinpoints not in the control flow in or below the `secureAction` pointcut. This combination is always false, as every point in the control flow is in or below itself. The pointcut should be `cflowbelow`, which selects all points in the control flow not below the secureAction. The combination secureAction() `&&!cflowbelow(secureAction())` makes sure that the security check is only executed once for each operation.
3. The security checking advice doesn't execute the actual behavior, but skips it (line 17). `return null` should be replaced with `return proceed()`

```
1   public abstract aspect Security percflow(servletEntry){
2     pointcut servletEntry():
3       execution(* org.apache.jsp..*.*(javax.servlet.http.HttpServletRequest+,..));
4
5     private Principal user;
6
7     before(HttpServletRequest req): servletEntry() && args(req,..) {
8       if(req != null && req.getUserPrincipal() != null)
9         user = req.getUserPrincipal();
10    }
11
12    abstract pointcut secureAction();
13
14    Object around(): secureAction() &&!cflow(secureAction()){
15      if(!SecurityManager.allowed(user,getActionName()))
16        throw new SecurityException();
17      return null;
18    }
19  }
20
21  public aspect DoaSecurity extends Security {
22    pointcut secureAction(): execution(* edu.ncsu.csc.itrust.dao.mysql.*.*(..));
23  }
24
25  public aspect EditSecurity extends Security {
26    pointcut secureAction(): execution(* edu.ncsu.csc.itrust..*.edit*(..));
27  }
28
29  public aspect ActionSecurity extends Security {
30    pointcut secureAction(): execution(* edu.ncsu.csc.itrust.action.*.*(..));
31  }
```

Listing 7 Security aspects

When we execute the system with these errors, the system no longer displays any information or allows any login. If we use the AJDT and we place a breakpoint on one of the security sensitive methods and step forward, we step into synthetic code, that is visible in the stack trace but of which there is no source (Fig. 8). If we keep on stepping forward long enough, we enter the security check. The stack trace doesn't indicate how the check was reached, as only synthetic code seems to be present. If we step on, we eventually drop out of the synthetic code, without ever executing a single instruction out of the method body of the security sensitive method.

≡ Security.allowed(Principal, String) line:35

≡ Security.ajc$inlineAccessMethod$Security$Security$allowed(Security, Principal, String) line: 1

≡ AuthDAO.getUserName_aroundBody5$advice(AuthDAO, long, JoinPoint, Security, AroundClosure, JoinPoint) line: 18

≡ AuthDAO.getUserName(long) line: 1

≡ authenticate.jsp line: 11

Fig. 8 Stack trace as presented by AJDT

If we use AODA, the stack trace looks like Listing 8. This immediately shows the problem: the target was skipped.

```
1  +—HookFrame: JoinPoint = AuthDao.getUserName
2  | +—X AuthDao.getUserName:          not executed (skipped)
3  | +—V Security.enforcer:            executed
4  +—Authenticate.jsp
```

Listing 8 Stack trace as presented by AODA

If this bug is fixed, the system still acts as if no one is logged in. If we place a breakpoint in the context collection advice, this breakpoint is never reached. The AJDT shows the advice is deployed on the correct location and that it has a run-time condition. With AODA we can place a breakpoint on the broken joinpoint and inspect the run-time condition. This inspection shows the following stack-trace.

```
1  +—HookFrame: JoinPoint = login.jsp
2  | +—V login.jsp:                    executed
3  | +—X Security.context:             not executed (no match)
```

Listing 9 Stack trace as presented by AODA after the first bug is fixed

This stack trace immediately shows that the dynamic condition did not match. When this bug is fixed, the system works normal, but the log of the security actions shows that many actions were logged twice. This points to a bug in the security checking advice. This advice is deployed multiple times, with different pointcuts. The existing tools can show where and when the advice is executed, but they can't show which pointcut caused the application of the advice. With AODA, we can see all advice acting on the stack on any given time and see which pointcut caused which application.

```
1  +—HookFrame: JoinPoint = EditPrescriptionAction.editPrescription
2  | +—V EditPrescriptionAction.editPrescription:      executed
3  | +—V EditSecurity.enforcer:                        executed
4  | +—V ActionSecurity.enforcer:                      executed
5  +—Authenticate.jsp
```

Listing 10 Stack trace as presented by AODA

This example shows the added value of using the correct abstractions for debugging.

5 Ongoing Work and Future Challenges

Representing the run-time structure in terms of development abstractions is still a challenge in many ways. We have outlined the methodology to create debuggers capable of representing the run-time state in terms of development abstractions. While this is an improvement to the current state-of-the-art, it is not well supported, both in terms of theory and practice.

In practice, no design guidelines or tools exist to support development of tools for tracing between the run-time and the development abstractions. The phases trace derivation and transformation implementation could be automated, but no tool support exist.

From a software engineering perspective, debuggers (and other run-time inspection tools) are quite challenging. Most debuggers have been built in an ad-hoc way and are not well modularized. The transformation they execute is only documented in their source, as are the techniques they use to implement the transformation. This lack of modularity makes debuggers very prone to the ripple effect: if the transformation is to be changed, the inspection techniques have to be reimplemented or even reinvented. Vice versa in order to change or optimize the used techniques, the transformation must be redefined. With the structured approach described in this chapter, we make a first step towards separation of concerns, by making the transformation explicit.

The theoretical foundations of debugging are not complete. It is not possible yet to determine the limits of this approach. It is clear that not all run-time effects can be derived directly from compile time artifacts. This is a limiting factor to our approach. Currently there is however no theoretical framework to determine which abstractions can be restored and which can not.

This work can be extended in three dimensions: beyond AOP, beyond debugging and beyond development abstractions.

This work can be extended beyond AOP. Other complex languages (such as Scala) and middlewares (such as JBoss AOP) also suffer from the abstraction gap. Many new languages and domain specific languages would benefit from this approach. Applying this methodology to such languages is our next step in this research.

It can also be extended beyond debugging: the abstraction gap also affects other forms of software inspection, such as profiling, monitoring and auditing. The same models and traces could be reused in these different tools. The automatic implementation of these various tools, based on the declarative specification of the model transformation would allow us to rapidly construct many different tools out of the same model.

And finally, it can be extended beyond development abstractions. The grand challenge is the application of tracing information to restore higher abstractions, used earlier in the software life cycle. This would allow architects to benefit from the abundance of operational data present in the run-time. This would have important consequences for the way we treat software. Features such as drill down debugging may become achievable. This would allow tracing failures through a system, starting from an unfulfilled requirement, through the architecture, into the designs and components, all the way down to machine code.

6 Conclusion

In the software life cycle an abstraction gap exists between development abstractions and run-time abstractions. Software is developed using powerful abstractions, as present in models, languages, middlewares and libraries. In the run-time these abstractions have been compiled into a complex synthetic structure, that is often too complex to understand.

To extract meaningful information out of a running system, the abstractions must be restored. This chapter described a methodology that can restore abstractions, based on a declarative specification of the relations between abstractions. From this specification, we derive a tracing model that captures all information required to bridge the abstraction gap. This approach was validated in an example case study.

In the future, we hope to extend this approach beyond AOP to other languages, beyond debugging to other forms of inspection and beyond programming abstraction. To us, the grand challenge is to relate all software development artifacts to the actual system, to allow different forms of inspection, in terms of different abstractions.

References

Baniassad, E., Clarke, S.: Theme: An approach for aspect-oriented analysis and design. ICSE '04 Proceedings of the 26th International Conference on Software Engineering IEEE Computer Society Washington, DC, USA, pp. 158–167 (2004).

Bracha, G., Ungar, D.: Mirrors: design principles for meta-level facilities of object-oriented programming languages. In: Proceedings of the 19th Annual ACM SIG-PLAN Conference on Object-Oriented Programming, Systems, Languages, and Applications, ACM, New York, NY, USA, pp. 331–344 (2004).

Czarnecki, K., Helsen, S.: Feature-based survey of model transformation approaches. IBM Syst J 45(3):621–645 (2006).

De Borger, W., Lagaisse, B., Joosen, W.: A generic and reflective debugging architecture to support runtime visibility and traceability of aspects. In: Proceedings of the 8th ACM International Conference on Aspect-Oriented Software Development, ACM, New York, NY, USA, pp. 173–184 (2009).

De Win, B., Joosen, W., Piessens, F.: Developing secure applications through aspect-oriented programming. In Aspect-Oriented Software Development. Addison-Wesley, Boston, MA, pp. 633–650 (2004).

Eaddy, M., Aho, A., Hu, W., McDonald, P., Burger, J.: Debugging Aspect-Enabled Programs. Lecture Notes in Computer Science, vol. 4829, p. 200. Springer, Heidelberg (2007).

Filman, R., Elrad, T., Clarke, S.: Aspect-Oriented Software Development. Addison-Wesley Professional, Boston, MA (2004).

Maes, P.: Concepts and experiments in computational reflection. In: OOPSLA '87: Conference Proceedings on Object-Oriented Programming Systems, Languages and Applications, ACM, New York, NY, USA, pp. 147–155 (1987).

OMG. Meta object facility (mof) 2.0 query/view/transformation. http://www.omg.org/spec/QVT/ 1.0/.

Pinto, M., Fuentes, L.: Ao-adl: An adl for describing aspect-oriented architectures. Early Aspects: Current Challenges and Future Directions, pp. 94–114. Springer, Berlin (2007).

Pothier, G., Tanter, É.: Extending omniscient debugging to support aspect-oriented programming. In SAC '08: Proceedings of the 2008 ACM Symposium on Applied Computing, ACM, New York, NY, USA, pp. 266–270 (2008).

Rashid, A., Sawyer, P., Moreira, A., Araújo, J.: Early aspects: A model for aspect-oriented requirements engineering. In International Conference on Requirements Engineering, pp. 199–202. IEEE Computer Society, Essen (2002).

Tekinerdogan, B.: Asaam: Aspectual software architecture analysis method. In: Working IEEE/IFIP Conference on Software Architecture, Oslo (2004), p. 5.

Verhanneman, T., Piessens, F., Win, B. D., Truyen, E., Joosen, W.: A modular access control service for supporting application-specific policies. Distributed Systems Online, IEEE 7, 6 June 2006, p. 1.

Tracing Non-Functional Requirements

Mehdi Mirakhorli and Jane Cleland-Huang

1 Introduction

In this chapter we focus on tracing *non-functional requirements* (NFRs), also referred to as Quality of Service requirements, performance constraints, or "ili-ties". In contrast to *functional requirements*, which define what the system must do in terms of transforming inputs into outputs (Davis, 1993; Sommerville, 2004; Wiegers, 1999), NFRs define non-behavioral attributes of a system which constrain the way in which the system must behave. For example, one NFR might specify the required response times for executing a search, while another might define the degree of availability required for a critical component. Yu et al., identified over 100 different types of NFRs (Chung, 2000) describing qualities such as reliability, main-tainability, safety, usability, portability, and security (Davis, 1993; Antón, 1997). Each type of NFR is satisfied in very unique ways in the architectural design. For example security requirements might be achieved through including authentication and authorization functions, while reliability concerns might be achieved through incorporating redundancy tactics to increase the degree of fault-tolerance.

NFRs play a strategic role in driving the architectural design of a software intensive system, and architects must understand the complex interdependencies and trade-offs that occur between them. From a traceability perspective, NFRs are significantly more difficult to trace than functional requirements as they often exhibit cross-cutting and broad-reaching impacts across the system and are realized through components and behaviors that are visible across various architectural and implementation views at very different abstraction levels. Unfortunately, standard traceability processes do not begin to address this degree of complexity.

This chapter briefly discusses the major benefits of tracing NFRs across the software development life cycle. It presents an overview of the different practices and methods used for NFR traceability, evaluates the challenges and goals, and explores proposed solutions.

M. Mirakhorli (✉)
Depaul University, Chicago, IL, USA
e-mail: m.mirakholi@acm.org

J. Cleland-Huang et al. (eds.), *Software and Systems Traceability*,
DOI 10.1007/978-1-4471-2239-5_14, © Springer-Verlag London Limited 2012

The remainder of this chapter is laid out as follows. Sections 2 and 3 discuss the specific benefits and challenges of tracing NFRs. Sections 4 and 5 describe several common techniques that either produce traceability links as a byproduct of another process, or else create them explicitly. We do not claim a complete analysis of all techniques, but rather a representative sampling of the most common ones. Section 6 describes our pattern-based approach for tracing NFRs, which addresses many of the shortcomings of existing methods by providing reusable, tactic-based traces. All of the examples in this chapter are built around the case study of the Mobile

Table 1 NFRs in the mobile phone case study

NFR description	Design decision
NFR.1.Security: The system shall provide safe browsing of the internet and safe use of internet applications	Restrict access, secure transmission of data, WAP security, SSL
NFR.2.Security: When a malicious application tries to alter sensitive data or access services and devices, the system shall block the malicious access and notify the user	Restrict access
NFR.3.Security: The system shall provide the capability for establishing security settings and associated access policies for installed applications	Access control by security policies
NFR.4.Security: The system shall limit access of the master reset, personal data and the SIM card, to authorized users	Phone protection by authentication
NFR.5.Security: The system shall provide safe connections through using Bluetooth, Infrared, and USB devices	Restrict access, encryption (PGP, DES) User notification of accesses
NFR.6.Performance: The system shall load and display stored images in less than 10 s	Avoid data compression
NFR.7.Performance: The system shall respond to requests for queries against retrieved data in less than 3 s	Larger heap memory (Jar, Shared, Heap)
NFR.8.Reliability: When a software crash occurs, the system shall prevent information loss	Data backup and recovery
NFR.9.Reliability: When the user accidentally deletes data from the address book and requests restoration of the data the system shall recover and restore the information	Autonomous address book backup; and recovery
NFR.10.Reliability: When the cell phone user moves from the range of one base station to another the system will provide reliable handover without loss or interruption of service	Call queuing
NFR.11.Availability: When multiple wireless networks are available, the cell phone shall provide a continuous internet connection	Heartbeat
NFR.12.Security: The system shall only allow connections to secure and trusted service providers	Authentication
NFR.13.Usability: The system shall allow the user to perform common tasks in less than three steps	Short cut key
NFR.14.Usability: The system shall allow the user to switch between a running application and a call in a single step	Short cut key
NFR.15.Extensibility: The system shall provide a simple process for deploying upgrades	Bridge pattern

Phone application and to this end we have augmented the requirements specification and the design solution to include both the NFRs and the design decisions listed in Table 1.

2 Benefits of Tracing NFRs

In many software systems, the success of the system or the safety of the people it serves, are dependent upon the underlying quality concerns. For example, a safety-critical avionics system must guarantee levels of safety through performance and dependability requirements, while a mobile phone service must provide reliable hand-over as a subscriber moves across various towers, deliver high quality voice and data service, and provide fast response times for placing calls and sending text messages. These same systems must also demonstrate compliance to government regulations describing safety, privacy, and other such operational procedures.

In early phases of software development, NFR traceability provides support for software project planning, and control (http://www2.cdc.gov/cdcup/library/practices_guides/CDC_UP_Requirements_Traceability_Practice_Guide.pdf; Ramesh and Edwards, 1993). Forward traces from early quality concerns to candidate architectural solutions can help project stakeholders recognize risks and uncertainties associated with achieving quality goals, estimate their associated costs, and gain a more complete understanding of the total cost of achieving each quality goal (Kazman et al., 2000). Furthermore traceability can help project managers track delivered qualities in each software build and observe the progress with which individual NFRs are satisfied.

During the requirements analysis and software design process, tracing NFRs to design decision can be useful for several reasons. Trace links can help architects determine whether all NFRs have been fully accounted for in the proposed design, and conversely identify unresolved concerns (Tang et al., 2010; Ramesh and Edwards, 1993). Second, trace links can help in identifying conflicting requirements (Antoniol et al., 2002; Egyed and Grünbacher, 2005; Cleland-Huang et al., 2005) or misunderstandings (Antoniol et al., 2002; Egyed and Grünbacher, 2005; Kruchten, 2004; Cleland-Huang et al., 2005). Finally, having the ability to visualize and understand relationships between quality concerns, NFRs, and architectural design decisions, improves the ability to reason about an architectural solution (Tang et al., 2007) and helps architects to discover tradeoffs, risks and sensitivity points (Kazman et al., 2000).

The ability to connect each design and implementation element back to design decisions and its related NFRs can also provide capabilities for verifying and evaluating the completeness of the design, and for understanding the rationale behind each element in the design (Cleland-Huang et al., 2005; Cleland-Huang and Schmelzer, 2003; Mirakhorli and Cleland-Huang, 2011a; Gurp et al., 2005; Tang et al., 2010; Tekinerdogan et al., 2007).

During the maintenance phase, existing traces from NFRs to the design provide support for change impact analysis and also help to mitigate and prevent the tricky and seemingly ubiquitous problem of architectural erosion (Perry and Wolf, 1992; Mirakhorli and Cleland-Huang, 2011a). The erosion problem occurs when developers make a modification without fully understanding the architectural intent behind the design. Such changes can often have negative repercussions upon underlying quality concerns. An effective traceability scheme can help developers more fully understand the consequences of both minor and major modifications to the code or the design artifacts, and therefore can help to maintain architectural quality (Gurp et al., 2005).

Finally NFR traceability is an integral part of documenting the architectural decisions and their relationship to quality goals and NFRs. This is useful for multiple activities such as building a safety case, or simply communicating information to developers and testers (Kruchten, 2004; Mirakhorli and Cleland-Huang, 2011a; Tang et al., 2007; van Vliet, 2008; Tekinerdogan et al., 2007).

3 Challenges of Tracing NFRs

Despite all these benefits, tracing NFRs is not easy to accomplish in practice. Figure 1 presents a traditional metamodel for supporting traceability of NFRs. The model is amalgamated from individual metamodels for requirements management, rationales and contribution structures, design allocation, and compliance verification previously developed by Ramesh and Jarke (2001). The model shows that

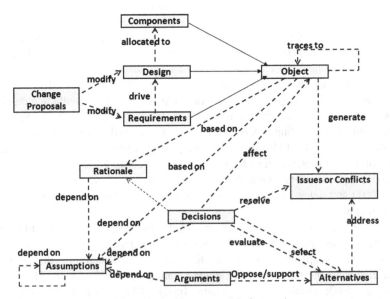

Fig. 1 Components extracted from Ramesh's metamodels for requirements management, rationales and contribution structures, design allocation, and compliance verification (Antón, 1997)

requirements drive design decisions which are supported by rationales, assumptions, and various supporting arguments. Specific design elements are allocated to components. This meta-model is representative of traceability graphs proposed by other researchers, such as Burge (Burge and Brown, 2008) and Kruchten (2004) for documenting and managing design rationales. Unfortunately, using this model to guide the traceability effort would likely produce an excessive number of traceability links, as the full meta-model (only partially shown in Fig. 1) is a relatively complete graph. It is clear that a better approach is needed for tracing NFRs.

To better understand what NFR traces should look like, we conducted an extensive study of architecturally significant requirements and their associated tactical decisions across several high-assurance software systems (Mirakhorli and Cleland-Huang, 2011a) including the Airbus A320/330/340 family, Boeing 777, Boeing 7J7 (Siewiorek and Narasimhan, 2005; Aplin, 1997), NASA robots (http://prime.jsc.nasa.gov/ROV/nlinks.html) and also performance centric systems such as Google Chromium OS (http://www.chromium.org/developers/design-documents). This study provided many concrete examples that illustrated the specific issues involved in tracing NFRs.

An initial analysis of the specification revealed several critical quality concerns for each system. For example reliability, availability, and fault tolerance were identified as concerns for the flight control systems of both the Airbus and Boeing, with the primary reliability requirement defined as *the likelihood of loss of aircraft function or critical failure is required to be less than 10^{-9} per flight hour.* Similarly our investigation of the CHROME browser identified security, portability, reliability, and availability as specific concerns. Security was important for defending against attackers exploiting vulnerabilities in the rendering engine, while portability was important for allowing the browser to run on multiple platforms.

The study first analyzed the tactical decisions that were made to implement these NFRs, and then explored techniques for tracing such decisions. As a result of the study we identified the following fundamental issues related to tracing NFRs.

- *Multi-level*: High-level architectural decisions are often associated with a fairly extensive set of subsequent lower-level decisions which impose constraints on the behavior, structure, and deployment of the system, and which work synergistically to support and shape the higher level decision. Traceability solutions must therefore explicitly link high-level decisions to their related low-level decisions, and then provide the means of tracing lower level decisions into the architectural design.
- *Multi-path*: Different architectural decisions are visible across different architectural views. While traditional Traceability Information Models (TIM) assume standard traceability paths for tracing requirements, our study showed that NFR related traceability links must be established across a wide variety of architectural views. In practice this means that a trace from a specific NFR to the architecture may be established along one or more potential trace paths, and that the

sum of the traces will provide a more complete traceability picture. Furthermore, different NFRs will be traced along different paths.

- *Heterogeneous*: NFRs are realized through a broadly diverse set of architectural decisions, for example an availability requirement might be realized through a decision for 3-way redundancy of a critical component, with diverse development teams and programming languages. In this case it is not sufficient to just trace structural elements of the design, as traces must also be possible (in some form) to less traditional elements such as development processes and organizational structures.

- *Multi-granularity*: Architectural decisions are characterized by a variety of roles and constraints. For example, a tactic such as *ping-echo*, designed to satisfy an availability requirement, includes high-level roles represented by *ping* and *monitor* components, as well as very low-level roles to control the *ping* rate. Traceability links must therefore be created and maintained at various levels of granularity including layers, processors, components, and variables.

- *Tacit traces*: NFRs are often difficult to trace, simply because they are satisfied implicitly through non-documented design decisions representing tacit architectural knowledge. Tacit decisions must therefore be articulated and documented in order to establish traceability.

- *Tradeoffs*: Design decisions exhibit tradeoffs and interdependencies. Relationships between decisions, including both positive contributions and negative trade-offs need to be explicitly modeled as traceability links (Cleland-Huang et al., 2005).

- *Semantically typed*: Ramesh's prior study on traceability high-lighted the need for traceability links to be semantically typed (Ramesh and Jarke, 2001). This is especially important in tracing NFRs because of the varied roles played by different components in realizing architectural decisions.

- *Strategic*: Complex high-assurance and high-performance systems are rich with design decisions (Hofmeister et al., 2000; Tryggeseth and Nytro, 1997). Given the known problems of creating, maintaining, and using traceability links, it is important to develop a minimalistic traceability strategy that removes redundancy, while retaining only those traceability links needed to support critical software engineering tasks such as impact analysis and architectural preservation.

- *Minimalistic*: NFRs tend to have broad-reaching impact across the architectural design and can therefore result in the proliferation of hard-to-use traceability links. An effective NFR traceability solution must therefore minimize the number of traceability links through strategic and cost-effective traceability decisions, while simultaneously scaling up to support traceability in large and complex software systems.

These requirements are used throughout the remainder of this paper to evaluate the potential and effectiveness of the various traceability techniques.

4 Software Architecture Practices that Capture NFR Traces

In practice, many architectural assessment and project scoping techniques rely on project stakeholders to explicitly map out relationships between NFRs and downstream work products. The significant benefits of building traceability techniques on top of such methods is that project stakeholders realize immediate benefits from their traceability efforts. The disadvantage is that NFR traceability links are often embedded in documentation that is specific to a given activity, and it is therefore difficult to extract and use those links to support other unrelated activities. For example, NFR trace links which are created and documented within an architectural analysis document, will likely be available for future architectural analysis activities, but will not be readily available for programmers who may need to understand how a low level code modification impacts an architectural decision.

In this section, we describe four representative software engineering activities that incorporate the creation and utilization of NFR traceability links. These practices are the Architectural Tradeoff Analysis Method (ATAM), Architectural Documentation, Enterprise Architectural Frameworks, and management of architectural knowledge.

4.1 Architecture Tradeoff Analysis Method (ATAM)

The Architecture Tradeoff Analysis Method (ATAM) is a well-known approach for evaluating an architecture with respect to a set of clearly articulated quality scenarios (Kazman et al., 2000).

ATAM uses a utility tree to generate concrete quality scenarios, which can later be transformed into specific NFRs. The utility tree starts with a root node which represents the overall quality of the system. The system is decomposed into intermediate nodes representing quality goals such as reliability, performance and security and low level leaf nodes representing quality scenarios. As such, ATAM uses the utility tree to help stakeholders explore quality concerns in order to clearly define their expectations for the system.

ATAM then implicitly documents traceability relationships among quality scenarios and the architectural elements in which they are realized. For example Fig. 2 shows the output of the analysis for a simple security scenario stating that "*NFR.1 The system shall provide safe browsing of the internet and safe use of internet applications*". It documents the architectural decisions as *restricting access, data encryption* and reliance upon *WAP secure communication and SSL*. These decisions have been analyzed to identify risks, sensitivity points, and trade-off points in the architecture. Each NFR is then mapped to its corresponding architectural decision and the design fragment in which the architectural solution is implemented. These mappings create a de facto traceability matrix, documenting relationships between quality concerns, tactical architectural decisions, and lower level design solutions. Unfortunately, as previously noted, this information is not easily accessible for any purpose other than architectural analysis. However, Mirakhorli and Cleland-Huang

Scenario SC1	The system resists malicious altering			
NFR(s)	Security			
Environment	Under Normal Operation			
Stimulus	Identified user or application tries to modify the data			
Response	Denying them access			
Architectural Decisions	**Sensitivity**	**Trade-off**	**Risk**	**Non-Risk**
Restrict Access				N1
Encryption	S1	T1		
WAP Security, SSL	S2			N2
Reasoning	Access control to sensitive data for internet application and user is simple and effective. Encryption causes a trade-off among performance and security. Choices of encryption algorithm might affect the level of reliability as PGP first compress the data so data movement will be faster. WAP security provide internet security but it might affects transmission speed			
Architecture Diagram	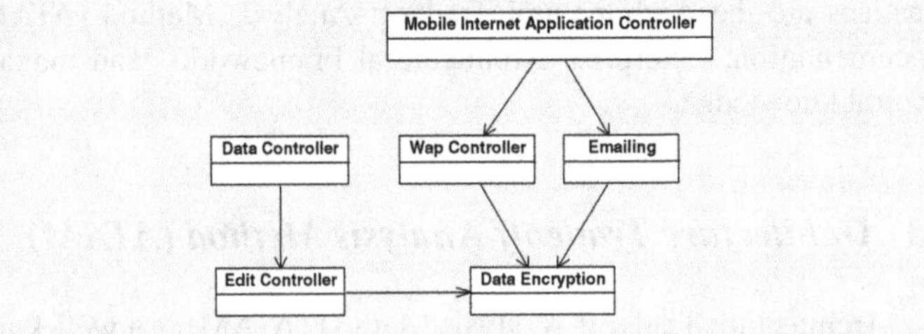			

Fig. 2 A scenario analysis from the mobile phone application

(2011b) have partially addressed this problem through developing a utility for extracting traceability information from ATAM documents and using it to construct a more traditional traceability matrix.

4.2 Architecture Documentation Methods

Architectural documentation approaches such as Views-and-Beyond (Bass et al., 2003), Siemens S4V (Hofmeister et al., 2000), and RUP 4+1 (Kruchten, 1995) provide guidelines and a template for documenting architectural solutions across multiple views. Each view depicts a coherent set of architectural elements from a specific perspective such as hardware resources, runtime behavior, or data usage, and is presented visually with a supporting catalog describing the behavior and property of each element, their interfaces, and the qualities associated with each interface. Architectural decisions and rationales associated with each view are also documented. The catalog of elements implicitly captures traceability relationships among architectural elements and the quality concerns exposed by a component or its interfaces.

In the Siemens architecture documentation approach (Hofmeister et al., 2000), a global analysis is conducted to analyze requirements and goals. Factors influencing any aspect of the architecture are then identified and documented in a factor table. Factors can include budgetary issues, technology factors such as specific development frameworks, and product factors such as functional and quality concerns. Each factor is described in terms of its flexibility, and the potential influence that a change in the factor will have on the system. It is this element of the factor table which provides implicit traceability from the factors to the system design.

To illustrate this, consider Table 2, which depicts a subset of factors for the Mobile Application case study. The first two factors relate to NFR 6 and NFR 15, and are therefore considered product factors, while the third factor is an organizational one. The table shows that the *File loading performance* factor is susceptible to change across different products, and that changes to this factor could affect data communication performance, data processing units, and communication units of the system. This kind of traceability information captured by the factor tables is designed to support long-term system maintenance of the Mobile Phone systems. However, the limitations of tracing NFRs through factor tables are similar to those realized when tracing through ATAM scenarios, as such tables can clearly only be parsed and used in a manual way by a human user, and are unable to support automated trace queries.

4.3 Enterprise Architectural Frameworks

An enterprise architectural framework provides a mechanism for describing and communicating architectural concerns, for comparing different architectural

Table 2 Example of factor table and implicit traceability

Factors	Description	Changeability	Impact
File loading performance	The system shall load and display stored images in less than 10 s	Depending on product families and application types it might vary	Affects data communication performance, data processing units, communication unit
Extensibility in use of different hardware for screen, keypad, and Bluetooth	There might be varieties of hardware to interact with external system, user	Extensibility is not a dominant factor less likely to change	Large impact on components involved in acquisition and input event processing
Minimum marketable features	Features are prioritized based on stakeholders request and market	Negotiable	It might have an impact on meeting milestones

solutions, and for helping to ensure integrity and completeness of a solution. Several architectural frameworks, including the *Command, Control, Computers, Communication, Intelligence, Surveillance, and Reconnaissance* (C4ISR) framework (http://www.afcea.org/education/courses/archfwk2.pdf), have directly addressed issues of tracing quality concerns. C4ISR was developed by the U.S. Department of Defense (DoD) to improve operational capabilities of warrior systems across defense agencies. The C4ISR framework provides three different architectural views. The Operational View (OV) artifacts define operational elements, activities and tasks, as well as the information exchange needed to accomplish an operation. The System View (SV) artifacts describe the physical systems, software services and interconnections needed to support operations. Finally the Technical View (TV) defines technical standards, implementation conventions, rules and criteria governing interaction and interdependences of system parts.

C4ISR utilizes traceability in several different ways. For example the System Interface Description is used to map supporting security and communication requirements to system interfaces, while the Operational Information Exchange Matrix (OV-3) is used to describe operational node connectivity descriptions such as Throughput, Security, Timeliness (e.g., 10/minute), and Required Interoperability Level. In these cases, the traceability matrices are used to map qualities to software elements; however the traces are relatively high level and do not provide detailed mappings from quality concerns to subsystems.

4.4 Knowledge Management Tools

Software architectural knowledge management tools provide support for documenting architecturally significant requirements, the decisions that were made to satisfy those requirements, and the rationale behind those decisions (van Vliet, 2008). Documenting architectural knowledge helps developers and architects maintain existing systems, and can also be used to improve the architectural design of future systems.

Tyree and Akerman (2005) proposed a taxonomy of items needed to effectively document design rationales including issues, decisions, assumptions, arguments, implications, related decisions, related requirements, related artifacts, related principles, and notes. Other researchers, such as Kruchten (2004) and Burge and Brown (2008), have proposed similar ontologies to document architectural decisions. All of these works assume the underlying use of traceability links to relate architectural decisions to external artifacts such as requirements, design documents, and architectural assessments. Several tools have been developed to capture and re-use architectural knowledge. Although the primary focus of these tools is on architectural knowledge, the organization of that knowledge relies upon user-created traceability links.

Most architectural management tools, such as Process-based Architecture Knowledge Management Environment (PAKME) (Dutoit et al., 2006), Archium

(Jansen and Bosch, 2005) and Architecture Design Decision Support System (ADDSS) (Capilla et al., 2006), help architects to create traceability links between the knowledge related items including requirements and design decisions, and external documents. However, the tools we evaluated, support only relatively coarse-grained traceability between documents, and do not support finer grained traceability between NFRs and specific design or code elements in which architectural decisions are realized. Furthermore, the tools have not yet been integrated with architectural modeling tools (Tang et al., 2010), which further limits their ability to support NFR traceability to critical elements of the architecture.

4.5 Summary of Tracing in Architectural Techniques

In summary, while architectural analysis and related knowledge management techniques incorporate tracing into their practices, they tend to suffer from three different problems. In the first case, architectural analysis techniques tend to encapsulate traceability information into proprietary documents which are difficult to use for anything other than the originally intended architectural analysis or project planning process, and therefore can only be parsed and understood manually by a human analyst. In the second case, architectural management tools provide rich environments for tracing between designs decisions, rationales, and other supporting information, but do not provide support for tracing into the architectural design or the code. Finally, architectural management tools which do incorporate traceability practices, tend to support only relatively high level trace links.

5 Custom Processes and Techniques for Tracing NFRs

In addition to software architecture practices which utilize NFR traceability to support their prime objectives, there are several other techniques, some of which are designed specifically for creating and maintaining NFR traces. In this section we describe four techniques including use of UML Profiles, Goal-Centric Traceability, Tracing through Design Patterns, and Decision-Centric Traceability. The benefits of these approaches are that they provide higher degrees of automation for using and understanding traceability links, and in some cases are designed specifically with maintainability in mind; however unlike the methods described in the previous section, these approaches require specific modeling environments or development practices, and, as they are not integrated with a specific task such as architectural analysis, do not necessarily return immediate benefits to the trace creators. This raises practical concerns related to the costs versus benefits of investing in an infrastructure of traceability links, and makes it less likely that such approaches will be broadly adopted in practice.

5.1 Techniques that Embed Traceability Links into UML

The Unified Modeling Language (UML) is used to visualize, specify, and construct elements of an object-oriented system. It models boundaries and interactions
between the system and its users, the communication between objects, the state of
those objects, the static structure of the system, and the physical architecture of
the system (Booch et al., 2000). Standard UML can be customized for a particular
domain through the use of UML Profiles, which allow the semantics of standard
UML elements to be refined through the use of stereotypes, tags, and the object
constraint language (OCL). For example, a <<trace>> stereotype could be created
and associated with a dependency link to depict a traceability relationship.

Several researchers have developed UML profiles for supporting traceability
of NFRs. For example, Salazar-Zárate et al. (2003) modeled NFRs and related
them to functional elements through use of a <<NFR Behaviour>> stereotype,
and then described behavioral attributes using OCL. Figure 3 illustrates the use of
this approach for the Mobile Phone Application. For example "Data Controller"
is related to its corresponding NFRs through the <<Has Behaviour>> dependency.
Furthermore, additional constraints, such as "response time shall be less than 10
seconds" are expressed through OCL statements.

The Architecture Rationale and Element Linkage (AREL) (Tang et al., 2007)
approach provides two new UML profiles for modeling Architectural Entities (AE)
and Architectural Rationales (AR). These profiles, and an associated tool, allow
architects to visualize AEs and their related ARs. AEs can represent functional

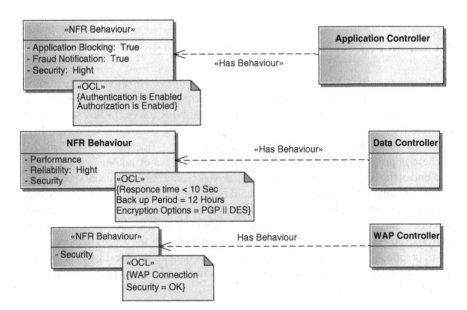

Fig. 3 Using UML profile providing support for NFR traceability

requirements, non-functional requirements, components, processors, or text docu-ments; while ARs describe quantitative rationales such as the costs, benefits, and risks associated with architectural decisions, and the qualitative rationales which document the issues, arguments, alternatives, and trade-offs associated with a design decision. As depicted in Fig. 4, an AREL model is represented as an acyclic graph, in which causal dependencies between design rationales and design objects can be traversed in order to extract traceability links. Figure 5 provides an example of several trace links captured by the AREL tool to establish relationships between

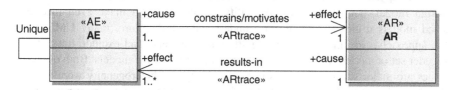

Fig. 4 Trace relationships in AREL

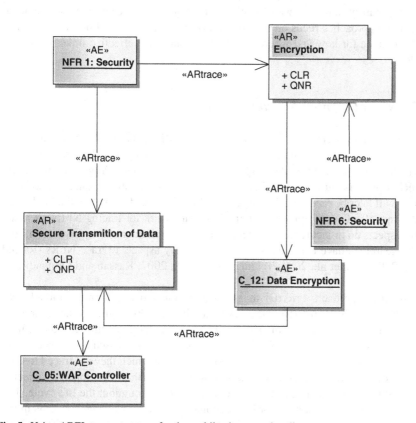

Fig. 5 Using AREL to create traces for the mobile phone product line

security NFRs and specific architectural decisions such as the secure transmission of data, or the use of encryption. In related work Zhu and Gorton (2007) proposed two UML profiles for modeling architectural decisions and NFRs. However, one of the limitations of embedding traceability links into UML diagrams, is the fact that trace links are limited to individual models. Cysneiro et al. addressed this limitation by developing a Language Extended Lexicon (LEL) that facilitated the tracing of goals across multiple UML diagrams. Their approach embedded controlled keywords from the LEL into goals and elements of the UML models (Cysneiros and Leite, 2004).

UML approaches enable traceability relationships to be depicted within the design model, but suffer from scalability problems which make even medium sized models difficult to create and understand. Furthermore, many UML profile approaches are limited to tracing structural elements and exclude traces to a broader set of models such as deployment or implementation models. Both of these issues are major short-comings as both scalability and heterogeneity were identified through our study of safety and performance-critical systems as fundamental requirements for tracing NFRs. Despite these issues, the idea of incorporating traceability into UML models is quite appealing, simply because the UML models are a natural part of many software development projects. However, it should be noted that such approaches focus on the notation of the trace links and provide very limited guidance for how and where to establish useful and effective links for tracing NFRs.

5.2 Aspect Oriented Approach

Aspect Oriented Requirements Engineering (AORE) approaches focus on identifying crosscutting concerns early in the software development life cycle (Rashid et al., 2002; Grundy, 1999). As a precursor to Aspect Oriented Programming (AOP), AORE's primary purpose is to identify candidate cross-cutting concerns, some of which will later be recognized as aspects and implemented as such in the final code. The concepts of AORE provide an enticing framework for tracing NFRs, as many early aspects do in fact represent specific quality requirements. For this reason, several researchers have explored ideas of using early aspects to trace NFRs (Rashid et al., 2003; Gan et al., 2004; Tekinerdoğan et al., 2007; Kassab and Ormandjieva, 2006).

The first approach, referred to as "Aspect-oriented development model with traceability mechanisms" (Kassab and Ormandjieva, 2006) facilitates the separation, composition and traceability of crosscutting *concerns* (both functional and nonfunctional). This approach includes a dynamic view, in which crosscutting concerns are traced to use-cases and scenarios, and a static view in which they are traced to conceptual classes. In related work, Tekinerdoğan et al. (2007) developed a concerns traceability meta-model (CTM) for tracing concerns throughout the life cycle. The meta-model provides support for bidirectional traceability between concerns in the requirements and design, and for traces between concerns and other artifacts. Like

Ramesh's original metamodels, AORE approaches define quite precisely the elements which should be traced. In this case they include concerns, relationships, dependencies, behaviors, compositions, mappings, and user needs, but the literature in this area lacks traceability guidelines, rules, and heuristics for mapping entities and trace information to different artifacts across the entire development life cycle (Rummler et al., 2007). However, the approach is intended to support AOP rather than more general development environments.

5.3 Goal Centric Traceability

Goal-Centric Traceability (GCT) provides traceability support for managing and maintaining NFRs and their related quality concerns over the long-term life of a software intensive system (Cleland-Huang et al., 2005). As its name suggests, GCT is a goal-oriented approach which assumes that quality concerns are modeled in a goal hierarchy such as the NFR framework (Chung, 2000), i* (Yu, 1997), tropos (Castro et al., 2002), or an ATAM utility tree (Kazman et al., 2000). GCT also assumes that during the initial analysis, design, and implementation of the software system, a number of different models are developed to evaluate the quality of the design. These might include ATAM scenarios for evaluating how well a design satisfies critical use cases, a Software Performance Execution (SPE) graph (Salazar-Zárate et al., 2003) to evaluate response time goals, a system execution graph to measure throughput and latency (Lamsweerde and Letier, 2004), an attack graph (Sheyner et al., 2002) to evaluate security attributes, usability metrics to evaluate a graphical user interface, or an executable test-case to evaluate functionality that that is needed to satisfy quality goal. GCT refers to these kinds of models at Quality Assessment Models (QAMs) (Cleland-Huang et al., 2005).

The GCT framework, includes: (i) a goal model that captures stakeholders quality concerns and their tradeoffs, (ii) a set of QAMs that have been designed to evaluate the extent to which the architecture satisfies the stated quality goals, (iii) a traceability infrastructure that is used to link QAMs to goals, (iv) GCT algorithms that manage the automated impact analysis and propagation of change across the goal hierarchy, and finally (v) an impact report which describes the potential impact of a change on the overall quality goals.

GCT supports two specific traceability tasks. The first involves identifying the initial impact of a change upon the GCT model. For example, if a developer changes a section of the code, or an architect makes a change in a UML model, traceability is used to identify potentially related goals or operationalizations (design solutions) in the goal model. Either manually created or automatically generated traces (Cleland-Huang et al., 2005) can be used to perform this initial trace. The second traceability task is triggered once an initial impact point is discovered. This second task is internal to the GCT model, and utilizes the internal structure of the goal model, the executable traceability links between specific goals and QAMs, and the GCT propagation algorithms. In GCT, an executable trace is defined as a trace which carries sufficient semantics to be processed automatically, so that the QAM can be

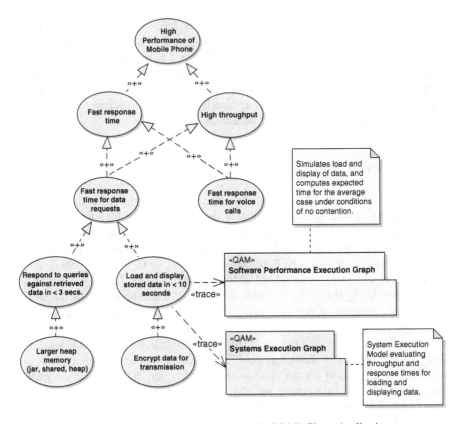

Fig. 6 GCT applied to a performance requirement in the Mobile Phone Application

parameterized and re-executed, and output values are returned to the GCT model for evaluation.

In Fig. 6, GCT is illustrated for a small subset of performance goals for the mobile phone application. In this example, response time and throughput goals are modeled for both voice and data scenarios. One of the goals, to "load and display stored data in < 10 seconds" is evaluated through two simulations (i.e. QAMs). The GCT model establishes traceability links between the response time goal and each of these QAMs, so that the simulations can be automatically re-executed if potentially impacted by a proposed change.

The primary advantage of GCT is that it provides support for maintaining quality concerns over the long-term by making use of QAMs that were already created during the initial development phase; however GCT is only viable if tool support is available to automate the process, and if QAMs, such as simulation models, are created as an integral component of the development process. GCT is therefore best deployed for only a critical set of goals, for which executable QAMs are available, and as such cannot be seen as a holistic solution for tracing all NFRs.

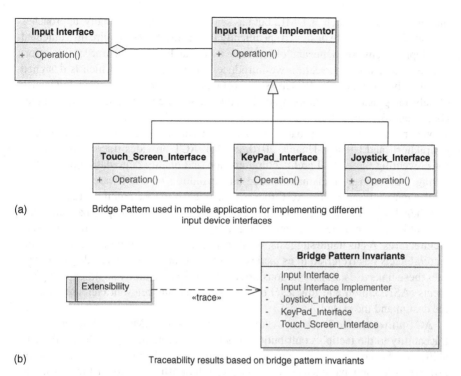

(a)   Bridge Pattern used in mobile application for implementing different
                              input device interfaces

(b)   Traceability results based on bridge pattern invariants

Fig. 7 Pattern based traceability for mobile phone product line software system. **a** Bridge Pattern used in mobile application for implementing different input device interfaces. **b** Traceability results based on bridge pattern invariants

5.4 Design Pattern-Based Approaches

A design pattern represents a reusable solution to a commonly occurring problem in software design (Gamma et al., 1995), and often addresses a specific set of quality concerns such as maintainability, flexibility, or portability. Gross and Yu (2001) and Cleland-Huang and Schmelzer (2003) proposed tracing NFRs to software designs through the use of existing design patterns as intermediaries. This technique supports traceability for any NFR that can be implemented as a design pattern. Figure 7 shows how it can be instantiated for a sample pattern in the mobile application case study used to achieve extensibility.

6 Tracing NFRs Through Architectural Decisions

In the previous two sections of this chapter, we have presented approaches for tracing NFRs. The first approach is integrated with existing architectural analysis and management processes, but produces traceability information that is deeply embedded into the resulting architectural documents. The second incorporates tracing into modeling notations such as UML, but has scalability problems. Finally, approaches such as GCT, which are designed specifically for tracing NFRs, require instrumented development environments and often create a timelag between the traceability effort and its benefits. In this section we introduce a hybrid approach which is designed specifically for tracing NFRs across the software development life cycle, but is also closely integrated into common Architectural assessment and analysis techniques (Burge and Brown, 2008).

We refer to this approach as Architectural Centric Traceability (ACT) (Mirakhorli and Cleland-Huang, 2010, 2011c). ACT provides traceability support for preventing the typical architectural erosion and quality degradation that occurs during long-term system maintenance and evolution of a software system. Like Goal Centric Traceability, ACT focuses on traceability of architectural qualities and their long-term maintenance; however unlike GCT, ACT capitalizes on existing architectural practices that are core concepts in the creation of quality software architectures. As its name suggests, ACT anchors traceability links around the architectural decisions (referred to as tactics) that have shaped the delivered system, and uses these links to establish relationships between architecturally significant requirements (ASRs), high and low level design decisions, and relevant elements in both the design and the code.

ACT utilizes *tactic Traceability Information Models* (tTIMs) to define backwards traceability to the tactic's contribution structures and rationales, and forward traceability to the architectural elements in which it is realized. A tTIM defines the primary roles and parameters of the tactic, relationships between the roles, and proxy elements (i.e. classes, methods, variables, files etc.) which are used to map architectural elements in design models and code to the tTIM. Traceability links between tactics and architecture are therefore established as mappings.

This is illustrated through the example of the heartbeat tactic used in the mobile phone application. The tTIM for the heartbeat tactic and its associated mappings into the mobile phone application are shown in Fig. 8. The tTIM shows that the heartbeat pattern helps satisfy the availability requirement (NFR.11) "*When multiple wireless networks are available, the cell phone shall provide a continuous internet connection.*" It also shows that this tactic contributes towards availability and reliability goals, and that the tactic is implemented through three primary roles of emitter, receiver, and fault monitor, as well as four supporting parameters of *heart beat rate, heart beat message, checking interval*, and *acceptable silence*, all of which are used to parameterize the way the heartbeat tactic is implemented. In this example, we chose to trace only at the coarse-grained level, meaning that we established mappings for the three primary components only. These components were mapped to the network subsystem, Mobile Internet Subsystem::Signaling controller, and "Mobile Internet Subsystem:: Connecting" respectively.

Using tTIMs to establish NFR traceability links reduces the cost and effort of traceability through providing a set of re-usable traceability links. Furthermore, these re-usable links are meaningfully typed to reflect the relationship between the related artifacts. The infrastructure of each tTIM enables visualization of architectural decisions while the proxy elements defined in the tTIM provide guidance for

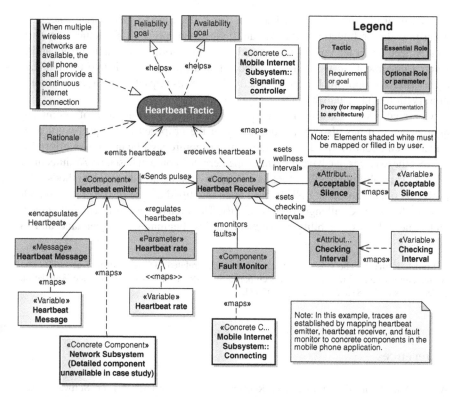

Fig. 8 NFR traceability links established for the mobile phone through mapping emitter, receiver, and monitor components to proxies in the tTIM

establishing both fine-grained and coarse-grained traceability links. This leads to more consistent traces, and reduces the time needed to define strategic traceability plans for a project. It also supports scalability because the number of traces that need to be created to trace each individual tactic are significantly reduced and supplemented by the reusable traces provided by the tTIM. Finally, the tTIMs simplify tracing by transforming it to a basic mapping task. As a result of these benefits, the tTIM approach supports software engineering tasks such as requirements validation, impact analysis, compliance verification, and prevention of architectural degradation.

7 Future Directions and Conclusions

This chapter has discussed the significant benefits that can be realized through tracing NFRs, but also the specific traceability challenges that result from the crosscutting nature and interdependencies of NFRs. Given the well-understood reticence of practitioners to create and maintain traceability links unless there is a clearly defined return on investment, it becomes very appealing to incorporate trace creation into the architectural analysis and assessment process. To achieve this we clearly need better techniques for extracting the traceability information from architectural documents in which it is embedded, and transforming it into formats that are useful for supporting longer-term activities such as impact analysis, architectural preservation, and visualization.

Our analysis of existing techniques has highlighted a number of promising approaches, but has also shown that many of the proposed techniques work only under certain conditions, do not scale well, or require significant human effort. To address these issues, we have presented an alternate approach based on Architectural Centric Traceability (ACT), which builds upon existing architectural methods. The problems related to tracing NFRs have been identified as one of the open research tasks in the Grand Challenges of Traceability. This area represents a critically important issue, which traceability researchers are just beginning to understand and to address.

Acknowledgments The work described in this chapter related to Goal Centric Traceability and Architectural Centric Traceability has been partially funded by the National Science Foundation under grants CCF-0810924 and CCF-0447594.

References

Antón, A.I.: Goal Identification and Refinement in the Specification of Software-Based Information Systems. Georgia Institute of Technology, Atlanta, GA (1997).

Antoniol, G., Canfora, G., Casazza, G., De Lucia, A., Merlo, E.: Recovering traceability links between code and documentation. IEEE Trans. Softw. Eng. **28**(10), 970–983 (2002).

Aplin, J.: Primary flight computers for the Boeing 777. Microprocess. Microsy. **20**(8), 473–478 (1997).

Bass, L., Clements, P., Kazman, R.: Software Architecture in Practice. Addison Wesley, Boston, MA (2003).

Booch, G., Jacobson, I., Rumbaugh, J.: Unified Modelling Language Specification, version 1.3. (2000).

Burge, J.E., Brown, D.C.: Software engineering using RATionale. J. Syst. Softw. **81**(3), 395–413 (2008).

C4ISR Architecture Working Group: C4ISR Architecture Framework, Version 2.0. Washington, DC: Department of Defense, 1997, http://www.afcea.org/education/courses/archfwk2.pdf.

Capilla, R., Nava, F., Pérez, S., Dueñas, J.C.: A web-based tool for managing architectural design decisions. SIGSOFT Softw. Eng. Notes. **31** (2006). http://dl.acm.org/citation.cfm?id=1163514. 1178644.

Castro, J., Kolp, M., Mylopoulos, J.: Towards requirements-driven information systems engineering: The Tropos project. Inf. Syst. **27**(6), 365–389 (2002).

CDC UP | Practices Guides on Requirements Traceability, http://www2.cdc.gov/cdcup/library/practices_guides/CDC_UP_Requirements_Traceability_Practice_Guide.pdf.

Chromium projects, Design documents, http://www.chromium.org/developers/design-documents.

Chung, L.: Non-functional Requirements in Software Engineering. Kluwer Academic, Boston, MA (2000).

Cleland-Huang, J., Schmelzer, D.: Dynamically tracing non-functional requirements through design pattern invariants. In: Workshop on Traceability in Emerging Forms of Software

Engineering in Conjunction with ASE 2003 IEEE International Conference on Automated Software Engineering. Montreal, Canada (2003).

Cleland-Huang, J., Settimi, R., Khadra, O.B., Berezhanskaya, E., Christina, S.: Goal-centric traceability for managing non-functional requirements. In: Roman, G., Griswold, W.G., Nuseibeh, B. (eds.) Proceedings of the 27th International Conference on Software Engineering (ICSE 2005), 15–21 May 2005, St. Louis, MO, USA, pp. 362–371, ACM, New York, NY (2005).

Cysneiros, L.M., Leite, J.C.S.D.P.: Nonfunctional requirements: From elicitation to conceptual models. IEEE Trans. Softw. Eng. **30**(5), 328–350 (2004).

Davis, A.M.: Software Requirements – Objects, Functions, and States. Prentice Hall, Englewood Cliffs, NJ (1993).

Dutoit, A.H., McCall, R., Mistrik, I., Paech, B.: Rationale Management in Software Engineering. Springer-Verlag New York, Inc., Secaucus, NJ (2006).

Egyed, A., Grünbacher, P.: Supporting software understanding with automated requirements traceability. Int. J. Softw. Eng. Know. Eng. **15**(5), 783–810 (2005).

Gamma, E., Helm, R., Johnson, R., Vlissides, J.: Design Patterns: Elements of Reusable Object Oriented Software. Addison Wesley, Reading, MA (1995).

Gan, B.T., Moreira, A., Araújo, J., Clements, P.: Early aspects: Aspect-oriented requirements engineering and architecture design—workshop report. In: Gan, B.T., Clements, P., Moreira, A., Araújo, J. (eds.) Early Aspects: Aspect-Oriented Requirements Engineering and Architecture Design. pp. 3–14. Lancaster, UK (2004). http://doc.utwente.nl/56986/1/00000112.pdf.

Gross, D., Yu, E.S.K.: From non-functional requirements to design through patterns. Requirements Eng. **6**(1), 18–36 (2001).

Grundy, J.C.: Aspect-oriented requirements engineering for component-based software systems. In: Proceedings of the 4th IEEE International Symposium on Requirements Engineering. pp. 84–91. IEEE Computer Society, Washington, DC (1999).

Gurp, J.V., Brinkkemper, S., Bosch, J.: Design preservation over subsequent releases of a software product: a case study of Baan ERP: Practice articles. J. Softw. Maint. Evol. **17**, 277–306 (2005).

Hofmeister, C., Nord, R., Soni, D.: Applied Software Architecture. Addison-Wesley Longman Publishing Co., Inc., Boston, MA (2000).

Jansen, A., Bosch, J.: Software architecture as a set of architectural design decisions. In: Proceedings of the 5th Working IEEE/IFIP Conference on Software Architecture, pp. 109–120. IEEE Computer Society, Washington, DC (2005).

Kassab, M., Ormandjieva, O.: Towards an aspect oriented software development model with tractability mechanism. In: Proceedings of Workshop on Early Aspects: Aspect-Oriented Requirements Engineering and Architecture Design. Bonn, Germany (2006). http://trese.cs.utwente.nl/workshops/early-aspects-Traceability-AOSD2006/.

Kazman, R., Klein, M., Clements, P.: ATAM: A Method for Architecture Evaluation. Software Engineering Institute, Pittsburgh, PA (2000).

Kruchten, P.: An Ontology of Architectural Design Decisions in Software Intensive Systems. In *2nd Groningen Workshop on Software Variability*. Citeseer. pp. 54–61 (2004). http://www.kruchten.com/inside/citations/Kruchten2004_DesignDecisions.pdf.

Kruchten, P.: The 4+1 View Model of Architecture. IEEE Softw. **12**, 42–50 (1995).

Lamsweerde, A.V., Letier, E.: From Object Orientation to Goal Orientation: A Paradigm Shift for Requirements Engineering. Springer, Berlin (2004).

Mirakhorli, M., Cleland-Huang, J.: A decision-centric approach for tracing reliability concerns in embedded software systems. In: Proceedings of the Workshop on Embedded Software Reliability (ESR), ISSRE10. San Jose, CA, USA (2010).

Mirakhorli, M., Cleland-Huang, J.: Tracing architectural concerns in high assurance systems (NIER Track). In: Proceedings of the 33th International Conference on Software Engineering, New Ideas and Emerging Results Track, ICSE. Waikiki, Honolulu, HI, USA (2011a).

Mirakhorli, M., Cleland-Huang, J.: Transforming trace information in architectural documents into re-usable and effective traceability links. In: Proceedings of the 6th Workshop on Sharing and Reusing Architectural Knowledge. Waikiki, Honolulu, HI, USA (2011b).

Mirakhorli, M., Cleland-Huang, J.: Using tactic traceability information models to reduce the risk of architectural degradation during system maintenance. In: Proceedings of the 27th International Conference on Software Maintenance. Williamsburg, VA, USA (ICSM) (2011c).

NASA's Robots, http://prime.jsc.nasa.gov/ROV/nlinks.html.

Perry, D.E., Wolf, A.L.: Foundations for the study of software architecture. SIGSOFT Softw. Eng. Notes. 17(4), 40–52 (1992).

Ramesh, B., Edwards, M.: Issues in the development of a requirements traceability model. In: Proceedings of IEEE International Symposium on Requirements Engineering, pp. 256–259 (1993). http://ieeexplore.ieee.org/xpls/abs_all.jsp?arnumber=324849&tag=1.

Ramesh, B., Jarke, M.: Toward reference models of requirements traceability. IEEE Trans. Softw. Eng. 27(1), 58–93 (2001).

Rashid, A., Moreira, A., Araújo, J.: Modularisation and composition of aspectual requirements. In: Proceedings of the 2nd International Conference on Aspect-Oriented Software Development. pp. 11–20. ACM, New York, NY (2003).

Rashid, A., Sawyer, P., Moreira, A.M.D., Araújo, J.A.: Early aspects: A model for aspect-oriented requirements engineering. In: Proceedings of the 10th Anniversary IEEE Joint International Conference on Requirements Engineering. pp. 199–202. IEEE Computer Society, Washington, DC (2002).

Rummler, A., Pohl, C., Grammel, B.: Improving traceability through AOSD. In: Proceedings of the Third Workshop on Models and Aspects, Handling Crosscutting Concerns in MDSD at the 21st European Conference on Object-Oriented Programming. Berlin, Germany. pp. 9–10 (2007) (Forschungsberichte der Fakultät IV, Elektrotechnik und Informatik, Bericht Nr. 6, 2007).

Salazar-Zárate, G., Botella, P., Dahanayake, A.: Introducing non-functional requirements in UML. In: Favre, L. (ed.) UML and the Unified Process. pp. 116–128. IGI Publishing, Hershey, PA, USA (2003).

Sheyner, O., Haines, J., Jha, S., Lippmann, R., Wing, J.M.: Automated generation and analysis of attack graphs. 2002 IEEE Symposium on Security and Privacy (SSP '02). pp. 273–284. IEEE, Washington – Brussels – Tokyo (2002).

Siewiorek, D.P., Narasimhan, P.: Fault-tolerant architectures for space and avionics applications (2005). http://ic-www.arc.nasa.gov/projects/ishem/Papers/Siewiorek_Fault_Tol.pdf.

Sommerville, I.: Software Engineering, 7th edn. Pearson Addison Wesley, Boston, MA (2004).

Tang, A., Avgeriou, P., Jansen, A., Capilla, R., Babar, M.A.: A comparative study of architecture knowledge management tools. J. Syst. Softw. 83(3), 352–370 (2010).

Tang, A., Jin, Y., Han, J.: A rationale-based architecture model for design traceability and reasoning. J. Syst. Softw. 80(6), 918–934 (2007).

Tekinerdogan, B., Hofmann, C., Aksit, M.: Modeling traceability of concerns for synchronizing architectural views. J. Object Technol. 6(7), 7–25 (2007).

Tekinerdoğan, B., Hofmann, C., Akşit, M., Bakker, J.: Metamodel for tracing concerns across the life cycle. In: Proceedings of the 10th International Conference on Early Aspects: Current Challenges and Future Directions, pp. 175–194. Springer, Berlin, Heidelberg (2007).

Tryggeseth, E., Nytro, I.: Dynamic traceability links supported by a system architecture description. In: Proceedings International Conference on Software Maintenance, pp. 180–187. Bari, Italy (1997).

Tyree, J., Akerman, A.: Architecture decisions: Demystifying architecture. IEEE Softw. 22(2), 19–27 (2005).

van Vliet, H.: Software architecture knowledge management. In: Proceedings of 19th Australian Conference on Software Engineering, 2008, ASWEC 2008, pp. 24–31 (2008).

Wiegers, K.E.: Software Requirements. Microsoft Press, Redmond, WA (1999).

Yu, E.S.K.: Towards modeling and reasoning support for early-phase requirements engineering. In Proceedings of the 3rd IEEE International Symposium on Requirements Engineering (RE'97), pp. 226–235 (1997).

Zhu, L., Gorton, I.: UML profiles for design decisions and non-functional requirements. Proceedings of the 2nd Workshop on SHAring and Reusing Architectural Knowledge Architecture, Rationale, and Design Intent, pp. 8–15. IEEE Computer Society, Washington, DC (2007).

Medical Device Software Traceability

Fergal Mc Caffery, Valentine Casey, M.S. Sivakumar, Gerry Coleman, Peter Donnelly, and John Burton

1 Introduction

Software is becoming an increasingly important component of medical devices, as it enables often complex functional changes to be implemented without having to change the hardware (Lee et al., 2006). With increasing demands for greater functionally within medical devices, the complexity of medical device software development also increases (Rakitin, 2006). This therefore places increased demands for appropriate traceability and risk management processes and tools.

Due to the safety-critical nature of medical device software it is important that highly effective software development practices are in place within medical device companies. Medical device companies must comply with the regulatory requirements of the countries in which they wish to sell their devices (Burton et al., 2006). To tackle these issues, governments have put in place regulatory bodies whose role is to define regulatory systems for medical devices and to ensure that only safe medical devices are placed on the market (Mc Caffery et al., 2010a). Although guidance exists from regulatory bodies on what software activities must be performed, no specific method for performing these activities is outlined or enforced (Mc Caffery et al., 2010b).

To this end, in the USA, the Food and Drug Administration (FDA) Center for Devices and Radiological Health (CDRH) has published guidance papers which include risk-based activities to be performed during software validation (US FDA Center for Devices and Radiological Health, 2002), pre-market submission (US FDA Center for Devices and Radiological Health, 2005) and when using off-the-shelf software in a medical device (US FDA Center for Devices and Radiological Health, 1999). Although the CDRH guidance documents provide information on which software activities should be performed, they do not enforce any specific method for performing these activities. The obvious implication of this is that medical device manufacturers could fail to comply with the expected requirements.

F. Mc Caffery (✉)
Regulated Software Research Group, Lero, Dundalk Institute of Technology, Dundalk, Ireland
e-mail: Fergal.McCaffery@dkit.ie

J. Cleland-Huang et al. (eds.), *Software and Systems Traceability*,
DOI 10.1007/978-1-4471-2239-5_15, © Springer-Verlag London Limited 2012

Therefore, within the medical device industry a decision was made to recognize ISO/IEC 12207 (1995) (a general software engineering life cycle process standard) as being suitable for general medical device software development. However, the Association for the Advancement of Medical Instrumentation (AAMI) software committee carefully reviewed ISO/IEC 12207 and decided that, due to a number of shortfalls, it was necessary to create a new standard specifically for medical device software development. The AAMI used ISO/IEC 12207 as the foundation for their new standard "AAMI SW68, Medical device software – Software life cycle processes" SW68 (2001). In 2006, a new standard AAMI/IEC 62304 (2006) was released that was based on the AAMI SW68 standard.

In 1993, the Council of the European Communities published the Council Directive 93/42/EEC (1993), the "Medical Device Directive" (MDD), on medical devices. The MDD is intended to ensure the safety of medical devices placed on the market in the European Union, and has the backing of national legislation in member states. Amendments to this directive occurred via Directives 2000/70/EC (2000), 2001/104/EC (2001), 2003/32/EC (2003), and 2007/47/EC (2007).

Whenever we mention medical device guidelines within this chapter we refer to the following medical device standards and guidelines: IEC 62304, FDA, the MDD, ISO 14971 (2007), EN 60601-1-4 (2000), TIR 32 (2005), IEC 80002-1 (2009), IEC 62366 (2007), GAMP 5 (2008), IEC/TR 61508 (2005), ISO 13485 (2003) and IEC 60812 (2006).

In this context, we embarked on a study of Software Traceability, which is critical to the requirements and safety aspects of software for medical devices. Within this chapter we include the following sections:

2. Requirements for traceability in the context of software development for medical devices;
3. The development of a software traceability process assessment method (Med-Trace) for determining the capability of a medical device software development organization to perform regulatory compliant and effective traceability;
4. Implementation of Med-Trace within two medical device software development organizations;
5. How each of the two assessed organizations plan to improve traceability;
6. Challenges the medical device software industry is facing in terms of implementing traceability;
7. Foundation for further research in this area and how Med-Trace may be rolled out to assist organizations.

2 Requirements for Medical Device Software Traceability

In order to understand the requirements for traceability in the context of medical device software development we conducted a literature review of generic practices for software traceability and in particular a review of the medical device standards requirements for traceability.

2.1 Traceability Literature Review

The literature review was undertaken in three stages and focused on:

- Generic software development and traceability;
- Safety-critical software development and traceability;
- Medical device software traceability requirements.

2.2 Traceability for Generic Software Development

"Requirements traceability refers to the ability to describe and follow the life of a requirement in both a forwards and backwards direction – i.e. from its origins, through its development and specification, to its subsequent deployment and use, and through periods of on-going refinement and iteration in any of these phases" (Gotel and Finkelstein, 1997). An important focus of requirements traceability is identifying how high level requirements are transformed into low level requirements and how these are subsequently implemented in the software product.

Initially requirements traceability was utilized as an aid in tracing requirements from customer/stakeholder needs to implementation and final verification before delivering the product to the customer. The role traceability plays has expanded and it has become an important tool in the software development activities of project management, change management, and defect management (Nuseibeh and Easterbrook, 2000). This is particularly relevant as software development is increasingly globally distributed across multiple teams and sites (Casey, 2010; Damian and Moitra, 2006). It is therefore essential to have an effective traceability process in place as it provides an essential support for developing high quality software systems (Espinoza and Garbajosa, 2008).

When considering generic software development, two of the most popular process assessment and improvement frameworks are the Capability Maturity Model® Integration (CMMI®) (CMMI Product Team, 2006) and ISO/IEC 15504-5 (2006) and Liao et al. (2005). Both recognize the importance traceability plays and incorporate it in their respective models. Each model was reviewed in detail with regard to the requirement for effective traceability and how this was addressed.

2.3 Traceability for Safety-Critical Development

Software products are increasingly being deployed in complex, potentially dangerous products such as military systems, cars, aircrafts and medical devices. Software products for these areas can be critical because failure can result in loss of life, significant environmental damage, or major financial loss (Kannenberg and Saiedian, 2009).

Traceability is especially vital for critical systems which must satisfy a range of functional and non-functional requirements, including safety, reliability and availability (Mason, 2005).

Within the safety-critical software arena, different standards/certifications are available for different industries. These include DO-178B (1992) for the Aerospace industry, with Automotive SPICE (2005) and ISO 26262 (2009) being required in the Automotive industry. IEC 60880 (2006) describes the European standards for certification of nuclear power generating software and IEC/TR 61508 (2005) describes a general-purpose hierarchy of safety-critical development methodologies that have been applied to a variety of domains ranging from medical instrumentation to electronic switching of passenger railways. Requirements traceability is an important clause in all the above mentioned standards/certifications.

In addition to the software development life cycle, a software safety life cycle has also to be implemented for safety-critical systems. It is crucial to maintain traceability between the software safety requirements, the decisions taken during design, and their actual implementation in the code. This is a complex task and needs to be performed whilst the system is being developed and not after the development has finished (Panesar-Walawege et al., 2010).

2.4 Medical Device Software Traceability Requirements

A detailed review was undertaken of the medical device guidelines with regard to traceability. A key point to emerge from this study is that while requirements traceability is essentially part of risk management, hazard traceability is of equal importance in medical device software development. The most relevant findings regarding traceability are presented here in summary.

2.4.1 ANSI/AAMI/IEC 62304:2006

In 2006, ANSI/AAMI/IEC 62304:2006 (*Medical Device Software – Software Life Cycle Processes*) was released. Traceability plays a key role in this standard and is defined as the "Degree to which a relationship can be established between two or more products of the development process" (ANSI/AAMI/IEC 62304, 2006). It is specifically addressed in the following sections of the standard: Section 5.1 states that "the manufacturer shall establish a software development plan for the development activity". This plan shall address "Traceability between system requirements, software requirements, software system test, and risk control measures implemented in the software". Section 5.2 specifies that "the manufacturer shall verify and document that the software requirements are traceable to the system requirements or other source." Section 5.7 states that "the manufacturers shall verify that the software system test procedures trace to the software requirements". In section 7.3 Verification of Risk Control Measures the standard specifies that "the Manufacturer shall document traceability of software hazards as appropriate: From the hazardous situation to the software item. From the software item to the specific software cause.

From the software cause to the risk control measure and from the risk control measure to the verification of the risk control measure".

As part of the Configuration Management Process in section 8 the standard specifies that "the manufacturer shall create an audit trail whereby each change request, problem reports and approval of change request can be traced".

Traceability is also addressed in B.6 Software Maintenance Process which states "It is especially important to verify through trace or regression analysis that the risk control measures built into the device are not adversely changed or modified by the software change that is being implemented as part of the software maintenance activity".

2.4.2 Medical Device Directive and Amendments

The European Medical Device Directive (MDD) (European Council, 2003) mentions traceability twice, but only in relation to the calibration of test equipment: In 2007, Directive 2007/47/EC added the following amendment to section 8 of the MDD: "For devices which incorporate software or which are medical software in themselves, the software must be validated according to the state of the art taking into account the principles of the development life cycle, risk management, validation and verification" (European Council, 2007). It is in this context that effective software requirements and risk management traceability are essential to achieve state of the art validation.

2.4.3 General Principles of Software Validation

The US FDA CDRH *General Principles of Software Validation; Final Guidance for Industry and FDA Staff* document (US FDA Center for Devices and Radiological Health, 2002) provides guidance on validation and traceability in medical device software development. The scope of the document outlines that traceability is an important activity that provides support to achieve a final conclusion that software is validated. Under section 3.1.2 it states: "the validation of software typically includes evidence that all software requirements have been implemented correctly and completely and are traceable to system requirements". In section 3.2 it specifies that "software validation includes confirmation of conformance to all software specifications and confirmation that all software requirements are traceable to the system specifications". The document goes on to outline in section 5 that traceability is key across almost all of the software development processes and especially in relation to the requirements, design, construction and test processes.

2.4.4 Premarket Submissions for Software Contained in Medical Devices

The FDA CDRH document *Guidance for the Content of Premarket Submissions for Software Contained in Medical Devices* (US FDA Center for Devices and Radiological Health, 2005) provides information to industry regarding the documentation to include in premarket submissions for software devices, including standalone software applications and hardware-based devices that incorporate software. In this document traceability analysis is defined as linking together the product design requirements, design specifications, and testing requirements. It also provides a means of tying together identified hazards with the implementation and testing of the mitigations. It also states that traceability analysis should be included as part of the premarket submission for Moderate and Major level of concern medical devices.

2.4.5 Off-The-Shelf Software Use in Medical Devices

The FDA CDRH *Guidance for Industry, FDA Reviewers and Compliance on Off-The-Shelf Software Use in Medical Devices* (US FDA Center for Devices and Radiological Health, 1999) document was developed to address the many questions asked by medical device manufacturers regarding what they need to provide in a pre-market submission to the FDA when they adopt Off-The-Shelf (OTS) software. With regard to traceability it states: "The introduction of new or modified OTS components to a product baseline may impact the safety of the product. Therefore a safety impact assessment of the medical device must be performed and the associated hazards documented in a Failure Modes and Effects Analysis (FMEA) table. Each hazard's consequence should be provided and expressed qualitatively; e.g., major, moderate, or minor. Traceability between these identified hazards, their design requirements, and test reports must be provided".

2.4.6 ISO 14971:2007

ISO 14971:2007 (*Medical devices – Application of risk management to medical devices*) is the de-facto standard on risk management for medical devices. The FDA recognize the standard (US FDA Center for Devices and Radiological Health, 2002) and agree compliance with it as acceptable for pre-market submissions in the US (US FDA Center for Devices and Radiological Health, 2005). In the EU, conformance with the standard is also acceptable for meeting the requirements of the medical device directives. In section A.2.3.5 the standard defines the risk management file as: "Where the manufacturer can locate or find the locations of all the records and other documents applicable to risk management. This facilitates the risk management process and enables more efficient auditing to the standard. Traceability is necessary to demonstrate that the risk management process has been applied to each identified hazard."

2.4.7 IEC/TR 80002-1:2009

IEC/TR 80002-1:2009 (*Medical Device Software – Part 1: Guidance on the application of ISO 14971 to medical device software*). Though this technical report does not add to, or otherwise change, the requirements of ISO 14971:2007, it does provide direction on how the standard can be implemented specifically for medical device software. The technical report states: "The software process should set up a system that makes traceability possible, starting from the software-related hazards and the software risk control measures and tracing their implementation to the corresponding safety-related software requirements and the software items that satisfy those requirements. All of these should be traceable to their verification".

2.4.8 ISO 13485:2003

ISO 13485:2003 (*Medical devices – Quality management systems – Requirement for regulatory purposes*). The standard specifies requirements for a quality management system that can be used by an organization for the design and development, production, installation and servicing of medical devices, and the design, development, and provision of related services (ISO 13485, 2003). With reference to traceability, the standard states in section 7.5.3.2.1: "The organization shall establish documented procedures for traceability. Such procedures shall define the extent of product traceability and the records required". It goes on in section 7.5.3.2.2 with reference to "Particular requirements for active implantable medical devices and implantable medical devices" to state: "In defining the records required for traceability, the organization shall include records of all components, materials and work environment conditions, if these could cause the medical device not to satisfy its specified requirements. The organization shall require that its agents or distributors maintain records of the distribution of medical devices to allow traceability and that such records are available for inspection. Records of the name and address of the shipping package consignee shall be maintained."

2.4.9 Traceability for Medical Device Software Development

Software development for medical devices can be a difficult and complex endeavour compared to other domains. Safety is a key area which must be successfully addressed given the potential for harm that defective medical device software can cause. An analysis of medical device recalls by the FDA in 1996 (Wallace and Kuhn, 2001) found that software was increasingly responsible for product recalls: In 1996, 10% of product recalls were caused by software-related issues. The standards and guidelines created to overcome this have already been discussed, but problems still persist. In the period the 1st November 2009 to 1st November 2010 the FDA recorded 78 medical device recalls and state software as the cause (Medical & Radiation Emitting Device Recalls, 2010).

Our literature review highlighted there was a limited amount of published material regarding implementation challenges and advances in the field of traceability in medical device software. This was in contrast to other sectors in the same context e.g., automotive and aerospace software development. Another important aspect to emerge from our literature review was that while there is a requirement to address traceability, and undertake traceability analysis, there is limited guidance available to help implement traceability effectively in organizations. This finding is in line with a review of guidance for all aspects of medical device software development which took place in 2009 (Mc Caffery and Dorling, 2009).

3 Development of the Med-Trace Assessment Method

One of the main aims of the Regulated Software Research Group in Dundalk Institute of Technology is to support the growth of a medical device software development industry within Ireland. Therefore, as traceability is central to the development of regulatory compliant software development we decided to develop an assessment method specifically to assist companies to adhere to the traceability aspects of the medical device software standards.

The Adept method (Mc Caffery et al., 2007) was previously developed to provide a lightweight assessment of software processes from CMMI® and ISO/IEC 15504-5 and was not domain specific. The Adept method provides an organization with a choice of 12 process areas that may be assessed using Adept. However, based upon previous research four of these process areas are considered to be important to the success of any software development company and these processes are therefore mandatory – Requirements Management, Configuration Management, Project Planning, Project Monitoring & Control. Therefore, the organization only can select 2 of the process areas to be assessed from the remaining 8 process areas. Adept consists of eight stages, the main stage involves an assessment team conducting process area interviews for each of the 6 selected process areas with appropriate members of the assessed organization. Based upon these interviews a findings report consisting of a set of strengths, issues and recommendations as to how to address the highlighted issues is produced.

Med-Trace is a new lightweight assessment method that provides a means of assessing the capability of an organization in relation to medical device software traceability. Med-Trace is based upon Adept but whereas Adept relates to generic software development processes Med-Trace is specific to the traceability process with medical device software development organizations. Med-Trace enables these software development organizations to gain an appreciation of the fundamental traceability best practices based on the software engineering traceability literature, software engineering process models (CMMI®, ISO/IEC 15504-5), and the medical device software guidelines and standards. Med-Trace may be used to diagnose an organization's strengths and weaknesses in relation to their medical device software development traceability practices.

3.1 Med-Trace Stages

Med-Trace is composed of eight stages (see Fig. 1). The assessment team typically consists of two assessors who conduct the assessment between them. It is essential that the assessors are trained in how to conduct a Med-Trace assessment and have the requisite knowledge of the requirements for medical device software traceability.

The purpose of stage 1 of a Med-Trace assessment is to "Receive Site Briefing and Develop Assessment Schedule". This involves a preliminary meeting between the assessment team and the organization wishing to undergo a Med-Trace

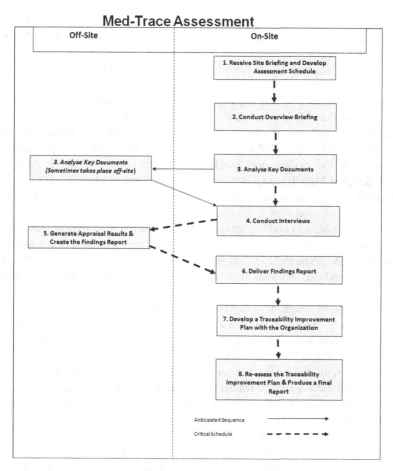

Fig. 1 Stages in a Med-Trace assessment

assessment. The assessment team discuss the main drivers for the organization embarking upon a Med-Trace assessment and what can be achieved. Based on the outcome of that discussion an assessment schedule is prepared and agreed.

The purpose of stage 2 is to "Conduct Overview Briefing" During this stage the lead assessor provides an overview of the Med-Trace assessment to members of the organization who will be involved in the subsequent stages of the assessment. This includes what the assessment will involve and cover. What will be required and expected of the participants will also be outlined.

The purpose of stage 3 is to "Analyse Key Documents". The objective of this stage is to provide insight into relevant process documentation and artifacts which refer or relate to traceability. These are collected, analysed and discussed by the assessors and they record their findings. The first 3 stages are normally performed on the organization's premises, but the documentation collected in stage 3 is sometimes taken off-site as it can then be used to assist with the generation of additional questions for stage 4.

The primary source of data for a Med-Trace assessment is gathered through a series of interviews conducted in stage 4. Therefore the purpose of stage 4 is to "Conduct Interviews". At this stage a set of scripted questions (Appendix: Sample Scripted Med-Trace Questions) are used as the foundation for asking questions that are based upon the software traceability literature search, traceability practices within the CMMI® and ISO/IEC 15504-5 models, and traceability practices that are required by the medical device industry. References are provided in Appendix: Sample Scripted Med-Trace Questions to show the sources of these questions. The assessment team return onsite and key staff members from the organization are interviewed. Each interview is scheduled to last approximately 1.5 hours. At each interview two assessors and one or more representatives from the organization are present. The lead assessor conducts the interview based on the scripted questions and evaluates the responses. The second assessor prepares interview notes based on the responses and may ask additional questions if clarification is required on specific points.

The purpose of stage 5 is to "Generate Assessment Results and Create the Findings Report". This is a collaborative exercise between the assessors to develop the findings report and takes place off-site. The evaluation and interview notes are analysed and discussed in detail from each interview. The findings from all the interviews and from the results from document analysis (undertaken at stage 3) are then considered and the assessment results generated. Based on these results the findings report is prepared and finalised. The resultant findings report consists of a list of strengths, issues and suggested actions for improving traceability.

The purpose of stage 6 is to "Deliver the Findings Report". This stage takes place on-site and involves the lead assessor presenting the findings report to management and participating staff in the organization. Stage 7's purpose is to "Develop a Traceability Improvement Plan with the Organization". This involves the assessors collaborating with management and staff from the organization to collectively develop a pathway towards achieving highly effective and regulatory compliant traceability practices. The findings report provides guidance to the assessed organization and will focus upon practices that will provide the greatest benefit in terms of the organizations business goals with regard to traceability, in addition to quality and compliance. The collaborative aspect of this step is essential as the relevant management and staff take a key part in developing the improvement plan and they ultimately have ownership of it. In these circumstances they are motivated to ensure its successful implementation.

The purpose of stage 8 is to "Re-assess the Traceability Improvement Plan and Produce a Final Report". As part of this stage the assessed organization is revisited approximately 3 months after the completion of stage 7. Progress is reviewed against the recommended improvement path. The outcome of this stage is an updated improvement path and a final report detailing the progress that has been accomplished along with additional recommendations.

4 Implementation of Med-Trace

In this section we discuss how we implemented the Med-Trace assessment method in two medical device organizations. The objective of performing both case studies was to demonstrate how Med-Trace could be used within similar sized and types of organizations (albeit in different countries) to assess the current status of their software traceability processes. We felt that it was important to illustrate the findings from implementing Med-Trace in more than one organization so observations could be made in relation to both the findings and the performance of Med-Trace. Additionally, we wanted to discover what the main issues are that medical device software development organizations face in terms of traceability. We present the process improvement objectives that were collaboratively agreed by both organizations to improve their respective traceability process. We also outline our observations from the findings of undertaking both assessments.

4.1 Implementation in MedSoft

We implemented a Med-Trace assessment in a Small to Medium Size (SME) Irish medical device organization, MedSoft (a pseudonym). MedSoft develop electronic based medical devices that require compliance with both the FDA and the MDD. MedSoft sought a resource-light method to obtain guidance as to how they could improve their software development traceability process, which Med-Trace provided.

4.1.1 Med-Trace Assessment Recommendations Provided to MedSoft

Based on the analysis of the results from the Med-Trace assessment, and in collaboration with MedSoft staff, an improvement plan was developed with the following recommendations:

1. The organization will initiate steps to measure the time spent on traceability and evaluate its effectiveness.
2. The task of performing traceability, in future, will be identified as part of the project plan and adequate time will be allocated to undertake this important task.
3. Good practices which are employed while performing the traceability process will be documented in an efficient format and disseminated to relevant parties as and when required.
4. Project managers will mandate the use of traceability while conducting impact analysis, promoting its usage as a management tool and thus enabling the capture of information for management use.
5. The software development life cycle will contain milestones which will not permit further advancement to other phases/stages of the life cycle until the requirements for traceability are satisfied.

6. A mechanism for tracing the open bugs/known issues to the safety/hazard/risk management system and linking them to the requirements will be made available and utilised.
7. The organization will evaluate tools for the process of automating traceability and requirements management. A tool will then be selected and implemented.

4.2 Implementation in MedNorth

We also undertook a Med-Trace assessment in a UK based medical device organization, MedNorth (a pseudonym). Like MedSoft, MedNorth is an SME and develop electronic-based medical devices that require compliance with both the FDA and the MDD. MedNorth also sought a resource-light method to obtain guidance as to how they could improve their software development traceability process.

4.2.1 Med-Trace Assessment Recommendations Provided to MedNorth

Based on the analysis of the results from the Med-Trace assessment (the MedNorth response to one of the Med-Trace scripted questions is illustrated in Table 1), and in collaboration with MedNorth staff, a pathway was developed as follows:

1. The process for software development traceability and for meetings between the various parties involved will be formalised and documented.
2. A formal training program will be introduced to ensure the adoption of best traceability practices for requirements and risk management.
3. The current Excel-based traceability application will be replaced with an appropriate automated traceability tool.

Table 1 MedNorth response to a Med-Trace scripted question

Question	Response
What kind of resources are provided for the activity of traceability management?	MedNorth developed a dedicated process specifically for traceability that provides coverage of hardware and software. Part of this process involves meetings between parties that are involved in the development of various components that must work together in order to produce the final medical device product. MedNorth feel that the inclusion of these meetings as part of their traceability procedure is a good way of bringing everyone together from the different areas (i.e. software, hardware, mechanical) to ensure that everyone is fully aware of what is required from them and to help ensure that nothing slips within the overall project. The project manager in MedNorth has overall ownership of traceability.

4. Terminology usage with regard to traceability will be standardised and a formal definition of both risk and hazard agreed. A formal method for quantifying probability of harm will also be introduced and deployed.
5. A defined traceability and validation procedure will be developed, implemented and monitored to verify the activities of the staff that perform the traceability and validation function.
6. A formal procedure will be developed and implemented to facilitate mapping from the design documentation to the software code.
7. Resources will be allocated to enable the full implementation of the Ideagen tool. This tool has already been purchased to allow digital signatures to be recorded at each development stage, but it had not been properly implemented in the organization.

4.3 Observations from the 2 Med-Trace Implementations

In both organizations the importance traceability plays in medical device software development was understood and a member of the management team was responsible for its implementation. The dual role of tracing requirements and managing risk and hazards were appreciated, but were recognized as complex and difficult to achieve. The lack of detailed guidance on how best to implement traceability was highlighted as a problem by both organizations. While they both employed a process for software development with regard to traceability this needed to be improved and formalized. The requirement for relevant training and the ability to record and leverage best practice with regard to traceability also emerged.

The serious limitations of utilising manual tools such as Excel, to manage traceability and the need for automated tools was recognized, and required addressing. It was also appreciated that this had to be undertaken with due care and within the financial and temporal constraints of both organizations.

Both organizations welcomed the opportunity to participate in a Med-Trace assessment. The fact that it was lightweight and specifically addressed traceability was considered worthwhile and very relevant. The findings reports addressed key areas where improvements were required and this was confirmed in consultation with the management and staff of both organizations. The adoption of the development pathway provided realistic goals and the collaborative process provided motivation for their achievement. Both organizations are implementing their respective development pathways and have agreed to be reassessed (part of stage 8 of the Med-Trace assessment method).

5 Medical Device Software Industry Traceability Challenges

Due to the critical nature of medical device software and the potential harm failure can cause, the implementation of an effective traceability process is essential. Therefore, to ensure validity, software requirements traceability analysis needs to be conducted to trace software requirements to (and from) system requirements, and to risk analysis results. While this is mandated by the medical device guidelines it is recognized by the industry as a difficult and complex endeavour. This is not helped by the fact that organizations have highlighted the lack of detailed guidance and direction as to how this can be successfully achieved.

A key factor which has been highlighted by the Med-Trace assessments and the literature is the importance of incorporating automated traceability tools into the development process. Especially, considering that many medical device software development organizations employ manual systems like Excel for traceability (Denger et al., 2007). This is a real challenge, which needs to be addressed. There is also a requirement to define and formalise processes which specifically facilitate effective traceability. These need to be supported by resources to provide relevant training and infrastructure.

While the need to provide requirements traceability cannot be underestimated, the necessity to provide traceability for each identified hazard is of equal importance. Risk management is a key activity for medical device software development and hazards have to be traced to risk analysis, risk evaluation and the implementation and verification of the risk control measures.

The number of standards and guidelines which govern medical device software development is also a challenge. To determine the exact requirements of each document with regard to traceability can be time consuming. The information provided can also lack the level of detail required to successfully implement these requirements.

When comparing generic and medical device software development the key difference lies in the mission critical nature and potential for harm which can be inherent in medical device software. Therefore, as risk is a key factor, requirements and hazard traceability both need to be addressed. It is somewhat surprising in these circumstances that tools are used less in medical device software development than in other software development domains (Denger et al., 2007). However, upon closer inspection of the medical device standards there is perhaps a reason in that such tools will also have to be validated in order to achieve regulatory compliance. The use of new automated tools require validation (including Risk and Hazard Analysis/Management) in their own right prior to their use as part of the Quality Management System. This is a very time consuming and costly exercise, especially for a SME. The more complex the tool, the more time, effort and cost associated with the validation and roll-out of the tool.

6 Foundation for Further Research in This Area

The work presented here will be used as the basis for further research in the area of medical device software traceability. It will also be utilized in Medi SPICE (Mc Caffery et al., 2010; Mc Caffery and Dorling, 2009) a software process assessment and improvement model specifically for the medical device industry. The Regulated

Software Research Group is currently developing Medi SPICE in collaboration with international standards bodies and the medical device industry.

Med-Trace will continue to be refined based on the results of ongoing research and feedback from future assessments and practitioners. The goal is to roll out Med-Trace nationally and internationally to assist with traceability. Given the positive response it has received, it is envisaged that research will be undertaken into the development of a tool to automate Med-Trace. The objective of the tool will be to facilitate the international roll out of Med-Trace and encourage its wider use. It is planned that the tool will also collect metrics which will be automatically passed back to the Regulated Software Research Group for analysis. This will assist with the future development of Med-Trace and Medi SPICE.

Acknowledgments This research is supported by the Science Foundation Ireland (SFI) Stokes Lectureship Programme, grant number 07/SK/I1299, the SFI Principal Investigator Programme, grant number 08/IN.1/I2030 (the funding of this project was awarded by Science Foundation Ireland under a co-funding initiative by the Irish Government and European Regional Development Fund), and supported in part by Lero – the Irish Software Engineering Research Centre (http://www.lero.ie) grant 03/CE2/I303-1. The research presented in this chapter was partially funded by the ARTEMIS Joint Undertaking of the European Commission, under grant agreement n° 100022 (CHARTER).

Appendix: Sample Scripted Med-Trace Questions

Question	**Source** – Software Traceability Literature	**Source** – Medical Device Standards
What kind of resources are provided for the activity of traceability management?	Ramesh (1998)[a]	
Is there a documented procedure in place for traceability? Is training provided on traceability and to what extent is explicit knowledge made available on software traceability	Ramesh (1998)[a]	
Implementation of traceability – Forward, Backward Traceability and the Relationship between Requirements (Dependent Requirements), Traceability tracking from the safety perspective and traceability to hazards/risk management	de Leon and Alves-Foss (2006)[a]	

(continued)

Question	Source – Software Traceability Literature	Source – Medical Device Standards
Where does traceability start – market requirements, product roadmap, system specifications? Where does proper requirement tagging start and how is it documented? Does any tool support this? How is safety classification in traceability achieved?		
How is traceability established between System Requirements, Software Requirements, and Software System testing?		Section 5.1.1 (ANSI/AAMI/IEC 62304:2006, 2006)[a]
How are software requirements traceable to system requirements and how is this verified?		Section 5.2.6 (ANSI/AAMI/IEC 62304:2006, 2006)[a]
How is traceability demonstrated between the software requirements and software system testing?		Section 5.7.4 (ANSI/AAMI/IEC 62304:2006, 2006)[a]
What traceability activities are undertaken during the design phase?		Section 3.2 (US FDA Center for Devices and Radiological Health, 2002)[a]
What traceability activities are undertaken during the coding and construction phase?		Section 5.2.4 (US FDA Center for Devices and Radiological Health, 2002)[a]
How are software systems test procedures traced to software and verified? What elements of system test procedures need to be traced? What are the difficulties in tracing? How does updating of results happen and how are they traced?		Section 5.7.4 (ANSI/AAMI/IEC 62304:2006, 2006)[a]
How are risk control measures traced to the software requirements?		Section 7.3.3 (ANSI/AAMI/IEC 62304:2006, 2006)[a]
How is traceability established between the risk control measures implemented in software?		Section 6.3 (ISO 14971:2007, 2007)[a]
The standard IEC 62304 specifies that the manufacturer shall document traceability of software hazards as appropriate: How is such complex traceability achieved? What are the tools available for achieving this?		Section 7.3.3 (ANSI/AAMI/IEC 62304:2006, 2006)[a]
How is traceability undertaken from the software related hazards and the software risk control measures to the corresponding safety-related software requirements and the software items that satisfy those requirements?		Section 3.5 (ISO 14971:2007, 2007)[a]

(continued)

Question	Source – Software Traceability Literature	Source – Medical Device Standards
How is software requirements traceability analysis conducted to trace software requirements to (and from) system requirements to risk analysis results?		Section 5.2.2 (US FDA Center for Devices and Radiological Health, 2002)[a]
What documentation do you use to provide traceability to link together design, implementation, testing, and risk management?		US FDA Center for Devices and Radiological Health (2005)[a]
In a software release, there is usually a process of noting down the known errors/known bugs. Is there a concept of traceability from these known bugs to the requirements or any other technical documentation?		Section 5.1.1 (ANSI/AAMI/IEC 62304:2006, 2006)[a]
How is the process of traceability measured and managed for effectiveness? Is there a way of consolidating feedback periodically on how well this process is performed?	Ramesh (1998)[a]	
To what extent has the organization automated traceability? What kind of tools are available which you think are useful for your organization? Have you evaluated them?	Higgins et al. (2003)[a], Feldmann et al. (2007)[a]	

[a] Denotes the relevant reference from the Software Traceability Literature or Medical Device Standards & Guidelines on which the question is based

References

AAMI TIR32:2004: Medical Device Software Risk Management. AAMI, Arlington (2005)

ANSI/AAMI SW68:2001: Medical Device Software – Software Life Cycle Process. AAMI, Arlington (2001)

ANSI/AAMI/IEC 62304:2006: Medical Device Software—Software Life Cycle Processes. AAMI, Arlington (2006)

Automotive SIG Automotive SPICE Process Assessment Ver. 2.2. August 2005

BS EN 60601-1-4:2000 Medical Electrical Equipment, Part 1 – General Requirements for Safety. BSI, London (2000)

Burton, J., Mc Caffery, F., Richardson, I.: A risk management capability model for use in medical device companies. In: International Workshop on Software Quality (WoSQ '06), Shanghai, China, May 2006. ACM, New York, NY, pp. 3–8

Casey, V.: Virtual software team project management. J. Brazil. Comp. Soc. 16(2), 83–96 (2010)

CMMI Product Team: Capability Maturity Model® Integration for Development Version 1.2. Software Engineering Institute. Pittsburgh, PA (2006)

Damian, D., Moitra, D.: Global software development: How far have we come? IEEE Softw. **23**(5), 17–19 (2006)

de Leon, D., Alves-Foss, J.: Hidden implementation dependencies in high assurance and critical computing systems. IEEE Trans. Softw. Eng. **32**(10), 790–811 (2006)

Denger, C., Feldmann, R., Host, M., Lindholm, C., Shull, F.: A snapshot of the state of practice in software development for medical devices. In: First International Symposium on Empirical Software Engineering and Measurement, Madrid, Spain, 2007, pp. 485–487

DO-178B: Software Considerations in Airborne Systems and Equipment Certification. RTCA, USA, 1st Dec 1992

Espinoza, A., Garbajosa, J.: A proposal for defining a set of basic items for project-specific traceability methodologies. In: Proceedings of the 32nd Annual IEEE Software Engineering Workshop, Kassandra, Greece, pp. 175–184 (2008)

European Council: Council Directive 93/42/EEC Concerning Medical Devices. Official Journal of the European Communities, Luxembourg (1993)

European Council: Council Directive 2000/70/EC (Amendment). Official Journal of the European Union, Luxembourg (2000)

European Council: Council Directive 2001/104/EC (Amendment). Official Journal of the European Union, Luxembourg (2001)

European Council: Council Directive 2003/32/EC (Amendment). Official Journal of the European Union, Luxembourg (2003)

European Council: Council Directive 2007/47/EC (Amendment). Official Journal of the European Union, Luxembourg (2007)

Feldmann, R.L., Shull, F., Denger, C., Host, M., Lindholm, C.: A survey of software engineering techniques in medical device development. In: Joint Workshop on High Confidence Medical Devices, Software, and Systems and Medical Device Plug-and-Play Interoperability, Cambridge, MA, USA, 25th–27th June 2007, pp. 46–54

GAMP 5:2008: A Risk-Based Approach to Compliant GxP Computerized System. ISPE, Florida (2008)

Gotel, O., Finkelstein, A.: Extended Requirements Traceability: Results of an Industrial Case Study. In: Proceedings of the 3rd International Symposium on Requirements Engineering, Annapolis, MD, USA, 6th–10th Jan 1997, pp. 169–178

Higgins, S.A., de Laat, M., Gieles, P.M.C., Geurts, E.M.: Managing requirements for medical IT products. IEEE Softw. **20**(1), 26–33 (2003)

IEC 60812:2006: Analysis Technique for System Reliability – Procedure for Failure Modes and Effects Analysis (FMEA), 2nd edn. IEC, Geneva, Switzerland (2006)

IEC 60880:2006: Nuclear Power Plants – Instrumentation and Control Systems Important to Safety – Software Aspects for Computer-Based Systems Performing Category A Functions. IEC, Geneva, Switzerland (2006)

IEC 62366:2007: Medical Devices – Application of Usability Engineering to Medical Devices. IEC, Geneva, Switzerland (2007)

IEC/TR 61508:2005: Functional Safety of Electrical/Electronic/Programmable Electronic Safety Related Systems. BSI, London (2005)

IEC/TR 80002-1:2009: Medical Device Software Part 1: Guidance on the Application of ISO 14971 to Medical Device Software. BSI, London (2009)

ISO 13485:2003: Medical Devices — Quality Management Systems — Requirements for Regulatory Purposes, 2nd edn. ISO, Geneva, Switzerland (2003)

ISO 14971:2007: Medical Devices — Application of Risk Management to Medical Devices, 2nd edn. ISO, Geneva (2007)

ISO/DIS 26262: Road Vehicles – Functional Safety. ISO, Geneva, Switzerland (2009)

ISO/IEC 12207:1995: Information Technology — Software Life Cycle Processes. ISO, Geneva, Switzerland (1995)

ISO/IEC 15504-5:2006: Information Technology — Process Assessment — Part 5: An Exemplar Process Assessment Model. ISO, Geneva, Switzerland (2006)

Kannenberg, A., Saiedian, H.: Why software requirements traceability remains a challenge. Cross Talk: The Journal of Defense Software Engineering **22**(5), 14–17 (2009)

Lee, I., Pappas, G., Cleaveland, R., Hatcliff, J., Krogh, B., Lee, P., Rubin, H., Sha, L.: High-confidence medical device software and systems. Computer **39**(4), 33–38 (2006)

Liao, L., Qu, Y., Leung, H.: A software process ontology and its application. In: Workshop on Semantic Web Enabled Software Engineering, Galway, Ireland, Nov 2005

Mason, P.: On traceability for safety critical systems engineering. In: Proceedings of the 12th Asia-Pacific Software Engineering Conference, 2005, Taipei, Taiwan, 15th–17th Dec 2005

Mc Caffery, F., Burton, J., Casey, V., Dorling, A.: Software process improvement in the medical device industry. In: Laplante, P. (ed.) Encyclopedia of Software Engineering, vol. 1. CRC Press Francis Taylor Group, New York, NY (2010a)

Mc Caffery, F., Dorling, A.: Medi SPICE: An overview. In: International Conference on Software Process Improvement and Capability Determinations (SPICE), Turku, Finland, 2nd–4th June 2009, pp. 34–41

Mc Caffery, F., Dorling, A., Casey, V.: Medi SPICE: An update. In: International Conference on Software Process Improvement and Capability Determinations (SPICE), Pisa, Italy, 18–20 May 2010. Edizioni ETS, pp. 195–198 (2010b)

Mc Caffery, F., Taylor, P.S., Coleman, G.: Adept: A unified assessment method for small software companies. IEEE Software – Special Issue SE Challenges in Small Software Organization **24**(1), 24–31 (2007)

Medical & Radiation Emitting Device Recalls: FDA. http://www.accessdata.fda.gov/scripts/cdrh/cfdocs/cfres/res.cfm. Accessed 25 Nov 2010 (2010)

Nuseibeh, B., Easterbrook, S.: Requirements engineering: A roadmap. In: International Conference on Software Engineering, Limerick, Ireland (2000), pp. 35–46

Panesar-Walawege, R., Sabetzadeh, M., Briand, L., Coq, T.: Characterizing the chain of evidence for software safety cases: A conceptual model based on the IEC 61508 Standard. In: Third International Conference on Software Testing, Verification and Validation, Paris, 6th–10th Apr 2010, pp. 335–344

Rakitin, R.: Coping with defective software in medical devices. Computer **39**(4), 40–45 (2006)

Ramesh, B.: Factors influencing requirements traceability practice. Communications ACM **41**(12), 37–44 (1998)

US FDA Center for Devices and Radiological Health: General Principles of Software Validation; Final Guidance for Industry and FDA Staff. CDRH, Rockville (2002)

US FDA Center for Devices and Radiological Health: Guidance for the Content of Premarket Submissions for Software Contained in Medical Devices. CDRH, Rockville (2005)

US FDA Center for Devices and Radiological Health: Off-The-Shelf Software Use in Medical Devices; Guidance for Industry, Medical Device Reviewers and Compliance. CDRH, Rockville (1999)

Wallace, D.R., Kuhn, D.R.: Failure modes in medical device software: An analysis of 15 years of recall data. Int. J. Reliability, Quality, Safety Eng. **8**(4) (2001)

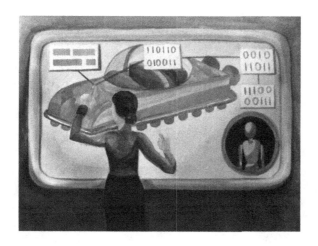

Part V
Traceability Challenges

A workplace in which traceability is ubiquitous means that traceability is built into the engineering process. The traceability is fit for purpose and accommodates the changing needs of stakeholders. The traceability can be exchanged and extended across organisational boundaries. The traceability is valued and depended upon, and its benefits demonstrably exceed its costs.

Members of the traceability community have been exploring the problems and challenges of traceability for a number of years, and this final part of the book describes their vision for traceability in the year 2035 and in the context of a flying solar car project. This vision presents a number of challenges for traceability research and practice, and systematically catalogues the associated research topics that need to be tackled over the intervening years to address them. The chapter by Gotel et al., "The Grand Challenge of Traceability", is reproduced courtesy of the Center of Excellence for Software Traceability. It is offered as a framework through which to motivate and track both research work and industrial experiences in the area of traceability going forwards.

The Grand Challenge of Traceability (v1.0)

Orlena Gotel, Jane Cleland-Huang, Jane Huffman Hayes, Andrea Zisman, Alexander Egyed, Paul Grünbacher, Alex Dekhtyar, Giuliano Antoniol, and Jonathan Maletic

1 Introduction

As software systems permeate our society, we must entrust many of them with the lives of everyday people on a daily basis. For example: a commuter on a train trusts that the switching software correctly routes the trains, an airline passenger trusts that the developers of air traffic control software and aviation flight control software have built the system correctly, the grocery shopper purchases produce that they trust has been found to be safe and can be tracked back to the farm using software developed to U.S. Food and Drug Administration (FDA) standards, and patients in a hospital are monitored remotely by software systems that many parties trust will work as intended. The ability to attain a requisite level of trust in these everyday examples is enabled through some form of traceability.

Requirements traceability, defined as "the ability to describe and follow the life of a requirement, in both a forwards and backwards direction (i.e., from its origins, through its development and specification, to its subsequent deployment and use, and through periods of on-going refinement and iteration in any of these phases)" (Gotel and Finkelstein, 1994) is a critical element of any rigorous software and systems development process. For example, the U.S. FDA states that traceability analysis must be used to verify that the software design implements all of the specified software requirements, that all aspects of the design are traceable to software requirements, and that all code is linked to established specifications and established test procedures (FDA, 2002). Similarly, the U.S. Federal Aviation Administration (FAA) has established DO-178B (FAA, 1992) as the accepted means of certifying all new aviation software, and this standard specifies that at each and every stage of development "software developers must be able to demonstrate traceability

This chapter is reproduced material from Center of Excellence for Software Traceability Technical Report #CoEST-2011-001, with permission. Please direct any feedback on this material via the CoEST website (http://www.coest.org).

O. Gotel (✉)
New York, NY10014, USA
e-mail: olly@gotel.net

J. Cleland-Huang et al. (eds.), *Software and Systems Traceability*,
DOI 10.1007/978-1-4471-2239-5_16, © Springer-Verlag London Limited 2012

of designs against requirements." Software process improvement standards that are being adopted by many organisations, such as the Capability Maturity Model Integration (CMMI Product Team, 2010), require similar traceability practices.

Although there have been significant advances since the early processes and tools to support traceability were introduced in the 1970s (Pierce, 1978), it is unfortunate that there is still almost universal failure across both industry and government projects to implement successful and cost-effective traceability (Egyed et al., 2007). For example, one global corporation working towards achieving CMMI level-three compliance was thwarted in this plan primarily because it was unable to successfully meet the traceability requirements for its legacy software products. In another organisation governed by the U.S. FAA, developers of a software control system for a well-known airplane struggled to trace each line of code back to requirements and were finally able to accomplish this only through reverse engineering a large number of requirements.[1] These difficulties have been broadly attributed to problems associated with creating, maintaining and using requirements traceability matrices and other enabling techniques, and also attributed to the perception by many developers that the effort of establishing traceability exceeds the benefits it returns (Gotel and Finkelstein, 1994; Lindvall and Sandahl, 1996; Bianchi et al., 2000; Ramesh and Jarke, 2001; Arkley and Riddle, 2005).

The challenges of traceability are significant; however, the payoffs for getting it right are also considerable. Over the past two decades, traceability researchers have been systematically addressing the challenges in an attempt to alleviate the traceability problem experienced by practitioners, and to better understand how to create and maintain cost-effective, accurate and meaningful traceability that is fit-for-purpose. Because of the difficulty in accomplishing these goals, a number of international researchers gathered in a series of two workshops funded by NASA and the NSF (respectively held at NASA's IV&V facility in the Summer of 2006, and in Lexington, Kentucky in the Spring of 2007) with the specific intention of determining the state of the practice and research in traceability, and of identifying the significant challenges that need to be addressed. The participants represented academic, government, and industrial researchers and practitioners, and they brought a wealth of experience to the working sessions. This series resulted in the creation of a draft Problem Statement and Grand Challenges (v0.1) document (Cleland-Huang et al., 2006).

This chapter follows on from these workshop discussions and draft document, and it is a community effort among members of the Center of Excellence for Software Traceability. It is a reformulation of the material so as to give grounding, cohesion and structure to the challenges, and to articulate a single grand challenge for traceability as opposed to forty, along with a smaller set of supporting challenges.[2]

---

[1] Both of these accounts were provided first hand to one of the authors of this chapter.

[2] A traceability matrix, one that maps this new reformulation of The Grand Challenge of Traceability (v1.0) to the draft Problem Statement and Grand Challenges (v0.1) document (Cleland-Huang et al., 2006), is provided in Fig. 2 of Section 12 of this chapter.

The chapter first presents a vision of what traceability makes possible 25 years into the future, by describing a hypothetical software and systems development scenario in 2035, and then outlines the assumptions that are necessary to make this vision a reality. These assumptions constitute the revised and updated set of traceability challenges, and they are eight crosscutting concerns – traceability that is purposed, cost-effective, configurable, trusted, scalable, portable, valued and ubiquitous. The last challenge is elevated to the status of the *grand challenge of traceability* since it demands progress with the other seven. The objective of this reformulation is to provide a structured and motivated research agenda for the traceability community, and a basis upon which to classify and track this research going forwards. It therefore highlights eight major research themes to tackle the challenges and delineates their underlying research topics.

The chapter is a complement to existing survey work in the area, notably two comprehensive surveys of the traceability landscape (von Knethen and Paech, 2002; Winkler and von Pilgrim, 2010), as well as more focal surveys on traceability relations (Spanoudakis and Zisman, 2005) and requirements interdependencies (Dahlstedt and Persson, 2005).

The chapter is organised as follows. Section 2 presents a traceability vision for 2035 and summarises the traceability assumptions underlying this vision. These assumptions form the eight traceability challenges. Section 3 describes the framework that was used to explore each of the challenges in more detail, and to derive the major research theme associated with each challenge and its underlying research topics. Sections 4 through 10 present the first seven challenges of traceability in turn – traceability that is purposed, cost-effective, configurable, trusted, scalable, portable and valued. Section 11 presents the eighth and grand challenge of traceability – traceability that is ubiquitous. Section 12 explains the approach to evaluation that is in progress and the intended future use of the traceability challenges by researchers and practitioners. Section 13 concludes the chapter, and reiterates the challenges and major research themes for the traceability community.

2 Traceability Vision

The vision for traceability revolves around the software and systems development practice that traceability will help to make possible in the year 2035: the problems traceability solves, the questions it answers, and the overall software and systems engineering experience it enables. Given that there are likely to be many concomitant advances in the processes and technologies that are used for software and systems development, this vision is grounded in what is envisaged will be a typical working environment in 2035. A Utopian scenario from this future is outlined in Section 2.1, the traceability it demands is summarised in Section 2.2 and the assumptions needed to achieve this traceability are elaborated in Section 2.3.

2.1 Utopian Traceability Scenario – Vestigia Sine Lacrimis[3]

The software systems engineer highlighted the five key stakeholder types that she knew were interested in the new flying solar car for which she was developing the controller software. She dragged their avatars into the requirements task area of her application life cycle tool with a wave of her pointer finger. Three flashing red alerts appeared:

- One potential stakeholder type is missing. The impact of their exclusion or inclusion has been analysed and the results are ready to examine.
- High priority requirement 55 of stakeholder type 'Police officer' conflicts with high priority requirement 33 of stakeholder type 'disabled citizen'. Stakeholder representatives have been identified and the resolution process is ready to proceed.
- The software demands safety certification. Policy regulations have been retrieved and safety requirements have been determined from related systems in the requirements knowledgebase. Confirm to inspect and integrate.

"I overlooked all that," she muttered as she pulled up the impact analyser, conflict resolver and requirements integrator all with a snap of her left hand. A few minutes later, green check marks then appeared with the message:

All identified requirements have been negotiated and validated with relevant parties. There are no current conflicts, inconsistencies or known omissions, and change management procedures have been established for this requirements baseline. Prioritised requirements with associated test cases are now ready for design and initial architectural options have been retrieved.

The engineer said aloud: "Let's see the options then," and the design process engaged. A series of questions then appeared to the engineer:

- Is usability more important than reliability?
- Is reliability more important than maintainability?
- …

The engineer worked through the design goal parameters diligently, pulling up visual design aids and assessing the requirements change impact as needed. Having balanced the design attributes with cost parameters as the requirements evolved further, the engineer shipped off the results to the hardware analyst and other specialists to ensure that there were no lurking issues before proceeding further.

Eventually, working in this manner, the engineer had a fully tested software release ready to integrate into the flying solar car system. With the latest set of requirements verified, the necessary safety certificate was issued. After integration, system testing and launch, the engineer moved on to focus on her next project.

---

[3] *Tracing without tears* – with thanks to Dr. Robert Natelson for the Latin version of this motto (*http://www.umt.edu/law/faculty/natelson.htm*).

A few days later, the flying solar car project appeared on the engineer's pursetop with this note:

> A new stakeholder requirement has been identified for project flying solar car following end user feedback. Please review the impact of this addition and of an inconsistency that has been identified if this is to be accommodated.

The engineer clicked on the warning message and projected a rendering of the relationships between the new requirement request and the existing requirements, design, code and tests. Walking through the virtual project environment, the engineer could see that a similar requirement already existed due to the colour of the requested requirement's visual path and that of an existing requirement. After a discussion with holographic avatars representing the stakeholders affected, the engineer pressed the "dupe requirement" icon with her pinkie finger. Confident that the detailed rationale underlying this decision from the virtual discussion would be assembled and sent to the project manager and requesting end users, and added into the requirement's record for future reference, she moved back to concentrate on her current project.

Eleven months after the deployment of the software and first production run of the flying solar car an alert arrived on the engineer's prototype smart cashmere sweater sleeve:

> ALERT! The license for the navigation software used by the flying solar car project expires in one month. Renew at $22 million per annum or substitute with one of the following new software services: (a) Nav-U-Like at $11.5 million or (b) Never-Get-Lost at $11.75 million. No negative impact of either code substitution has been identified during simulation and a benefit is projected for each option. Option (a) implements a requirement that would address open bug report 686 of priority 2, and requires a small design change estimated to take Bob one working week to fully integrate and test. An analysis of the multimedia materials accompanying option (b) indicates that it satisfies requirements that align with a forthcoming change to world policies on open skies flight that is scheduled to take effect in three months time and negate our current safety certificate. The impacted components will take the full team in Johannesburg two weeks to re-align the software and re-verify the requirements.

"Let's plan ahead and go with Never-Get-Lost," she decides as she taps option (b) on her sweater sleeve.

2.2 Traceability in 2035

In 2035, traceability will be purely in the background and simply expected to be there. It will be accurate and trusted by all project stakeholders. Traceability will be seamless to software and systems engineering tasks, and something that underlies many of the techniques and technologies that engineers use habitually. With the disappearance of traceability as a primary concern, the engineer and other project stakeholders will be free to focus on those activities and decisions that utilise their skills and knowledge fully.

Traceability will facilitate tasks in all phases of the software and systems engineering life cycle, providing for both productivity and quality gains. In particular, it will help with the definition of requirements through reuse at the requirements level, retrieving associated design, code and test cases, along with all the underpinning traceability. It will also help to identify services to satisfy those requirements and to monitor the violations of service-centric systems. It will help to discover discrepancies and inconsistencies in requirements perspectives by identifying connections between disparate requirements, in real-time, by following their trace links to assess the implications. It will also help to assess requirements completeness and satisfaction, and is the mechanism through which certificates of assurance will be issued.

In summary, traceability will be the thread that weaves data together on a project to tell a myriad of stories, from the rationale underlying decisions through to the underlying social network that came together to make these decisions and is, therefore, best able to change them. Traceability will be completely requirements-driven in 2035.

2.3 Assumptions of the Vision -> Traceability Challenges

To achieve this vision of traceability, advances will be required in a number of areas, ranging from everyday communication devices and visual displays through to the manner in which requirements are described and organised. Based upon progress over the past 25 years, it is likely that the technologies mentioned in the Utopian scenario will be historic by 2035, but the changes demanded in software and systems engineering practice will remain ambitious. The assumptions demanded of the traceability practice are highlighted below.

To provide for the level of engineering support envisaged, the results of the traceability must be amenable to use and fully trusted, echoing the theme of the examples provided in the introduction to this chapter. The starting point for securing this trust will be buy-in, accompanied by accurate and up to date underlying data to trace, along with timely and meaningful linkages between these data. Much will depend upon the quality of these data, be they business goals, requirements, design ideas or code, whatever the representation or medium used. In an ideal world, there would be elaborate trace links between all of these differing data, and these would be established on demand and cost-effectively, as needed, to satisfy end user needs. An engineer might adjust some default settings, as far as the type of trace link to generate or when each one should be generated, so that traces would be created at the level of granularity appropriate to support the context and intent of a specific traceability-enabled activity or task. Furthermore, these trace links would be maintained in an accurate state by monitoring changes to the software system, at all locations at which it is distributed around the globe. Provisional traceability updates would be generated automatically as and when the system evolves.

In 2035, the traceability is assumed to be:

1. *Purposed.* Traceability is fit-for-purpose and supports stakeholder needs (i.e., traceability is requirements-driven).
2. *Cost-effective.* The return from using traceability is adequate in relation to the outlay of establishing it.
3. *Configurable.* Traceability is established as specified, moment-to-moment, and accommodates changing stakeholder needs.
4. *Trusted.* All stakeholders have full confidence in the traceability, as it is created and maintained in the face of inconsistency, omissions and change; all stakeholders can and do depend upon the traceability provided.
5. *Scalable.* Varying types of artifact can be traced, at variable levels of granularity and in quantity, as the traceability extends through-life and across organisational and business boundaries.
6. *Portable.* Traceability is exchanged, merged and reused across projects, organisations, domains, product lines and supporting tools.
7. *Valued.* Traceability is a strategic priority and valued by all; every stakeholder has a role to play and actively discharges his or her responsibilities.
8. *Ubiquitous.* Traceability is always there, without ever having to think about getting it there, as it is built into the engineering process; traceability has effectively "disappeared without a trace."

These eight assumptions constitute the eight traceability challenges and are examined in turn in Sections 4 through 11. The framework used to explore and discuss each challenge is described in Section 3.

Note that traceability challenge eight, traceability that is *ubiquitous*, is referred to as the *grand challenge of traceability* because its realisation depends upon having made significant progress with each of the seven other challenges. Traceability challenge eight is longer term and all-encompassing.

3 Challenges Framework

The vision for traceability was created as a result of a brainstorming effort among the authors of this chapter, following on from the Kentucky workshop. The concept was to describe what software and systems development would be like in 2035 if the traceability problem were solved. Based upon the Utopian scenario, the assumptions that would need to hold true of the traceability to realise the vision were then determined, also in an iterative manner. This led to agreement upon eight crosscutting concerns that now form the eight traceability challenges. In the subsequent sections of this chapter, each challenge is elaborated according to the following framework:

- *Link to Vision.* The challenge is anchored in the Utopian scenario of the vision via a short description.

- *Problems Addressed.* The current problems with traceability that realisation of the challenge would help to address are summarised. This provides additional rationale and motivation for prioritising and addressing the challenge.
- *Dream Process.* To explore the traceability process that would be needed to realise each challenge, the authors developed a model of a generic traceability process. This model was developed in an iterative manner and is described fully in the chapter "Traceability Fundamentals". In summary, the model comprises an abstract description of the series of activities that serve to establish traceability and render it usable, along with a description of the typical responsibilities and resourcing required to undertake them, as well as their inputs and outputs. The model considers the various stages in the life of a trace and the overarching process that brings traces into existence. An overview of this model is provided in Fig. 1. The key activities are: traceability planning and management (strategy), traceability creation and maintenance, and traceability use. The dream approach to each traceability process activity is described for the challenge.
- *Goals.* The high-level goals that would need to be satisfied to achieve the challenge are listed. These goals are given a unique identifier in order to track progress towards their satisfaction, using the following format: <challenge name> <goal number> (e.g., Purposed G 1, Purposed G 2, Valued G 1, etc.).

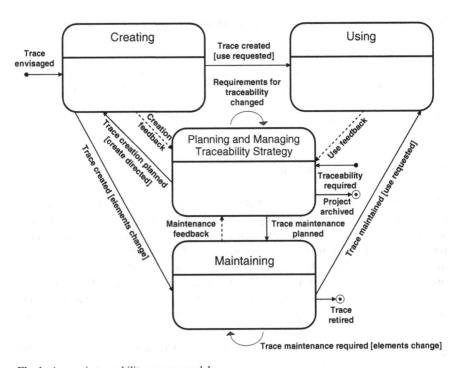

Fig. 1 A generic traceability process model

- *Requirements.* The goals suggest and decompose into a number of requirements. The requirements relevant to each of the traceability process activities (i.e., strategy, creation and maintenance, and use) are examined in turn for each challenge. For each requirement that is defined, a brief review of the current status of the research and practice is provided, and areas of promise are highlighted.[4] These requirements are given a unique identifier in order to track progress towards their satisfaction, using the following format: <challenge name> <requirement number> (e.g., Purposed Req 1, Purposed Req 2, Valued Req 1, etc.). Each requirement is cross-referenced to the goals it supports.
- *Recommended Research.* Based upon the prior analysis, a major research theme was identified for each challenge. This was then decomposed into a number of supporting research topics. These research topics are given a unique identifier in order to track future progress with the research, using the following format: <challenge name> <research topic number> (e.g., Purposed RT 1, Purposed RT 2, Valued RT 1, etc.). Each research topic is cross-referenced to the requirements it addresses.
- *Positive Adoption Practices for Industry.* The framework ends with a list of practices that, if implemented in industrial settings, would facilitate and/or begin to show satisfaction of the requirements, and so progress towards the realisation of the challenge. These industry practices are also given a unique identifier in order to subsequently track the progress, using the following format: <challenge name> <industry practice number> (e.g., Purposed IP 1, Purposed IP 2, Valued IP 1, etc.).

The intention of creating a framework for exploring the challenges was to provide a systematic structure for directing and tracking future traceability research and practice. The details provided in the following sections serve to highlight salient points to assist with this objective, arising from working discussions among the authors of this chapter; they do not provide an exhaustive review of the entire traceability field. The reader is referred to a number of existing surveys for such traceability review material (von Knethen and Paech, 2002; Dahlstedt and Persson, 2005; Spanoudakis and Zisman, 2005; Winkler and von Pilgrim, 2010).

4 Traceability Challenge 1: Traceability that Is Purposed

Traceability is fit-for-purpose and supports stakeholder needs (i.e., traceability is requirements-driven).

---

[4] Please note that this chapter is a result of community workshops and discussions; the objective is to highlight general points about the state of the art and the practice in traceability, not to provide an exhaustive set of references to projects and publications. The reader is referred to the website of the Center of Excellence for Software Traceability for such materials: *http://www.coest.org.*

4.1 Link to Vision (Purposed)

In the vision scenario, traceability helps the engineer to detect those stakeholders to involve during requirements elicitation, to identify missing and conflicting requirements, and to demonstrate compliance to regulatory codes. Traceability also helps the engineer to see the impact of new and modified requirements, and facilitates the requirements negotiation and validation process with appropriate stakeholders. Traces are used to retrieve the context and rationale for decisions, to examine costs and to verify compliance to product requirements. Traceability supports the engineer explicitly in all aspects of her daily work over the course of the project. The traceability is fit-for-purpose.

4.2 Problems Addressed (Purposed)

Traceability will not be implemented and used in practice unless it is perceived as useful or is mandated. Currently, there is poor understanding of what people need traceability for and how people actually use traceability over time. Further, traceability will not be created or maintained effectively if the required tasks to do so are themselves not understood and supported. Currently, there is poor understanding of what individuals and teams need to do to create and maintain traces. This distinction between satisfying the requirements of those stakeholders who establish traceability and those stakeholders who use traceability lies at the heart of many traceability problems, for these roles are not necessarily overlapping. The stakeholder community for establishing and using traceability is potentially vast and dynamic, and the skills and incentives of these stakeholders vary widely. Tools are frequently purchased to enable traceability but, because they are often insufficiently configured to support these specific stakeholder requirements for traceability, they do not support their processes nor adapt to their changing needs; therefore, the tools rarely realise their potential.

4.3 Dream Process (Purposed)

- *Traceability Strategy.* The initial stakeholder requirements for traceability on a project will be selected from profiles and templates, and the integrated development environment used on the project will handle all the details necessary to design and implement a traceability solution to satisfy them. The effectiveness of this solution will be measured over time as the requirements evolve and are accommodated.
- *Traceability Creation and Maintenance.* All traces on a project will be demonstrably created based upon specified stakeholder requirements for establishing traceability, accounting for the nature of the artifacts to be traced in different environments. Once created on a project, the traces will be maintained such that

changing stakeholder requirements for establishing traceability are continuously and demonstrably satisfied.

- *Traceability Use.* The traceability provided will fit the end users' contexts and needs. A feedback-driven learning system will adapt the traceability that is established to fully address its end users' evolving task contexts and needs.

4.4 Goals (Purposed)

Purposed G 1   Prototypical stakeholder requirements for traceability use are understood, defined and shared by the software and systems research and development communities.

Purposed G 2   Prototypical stakeholder requirements for creating and maintaining traceability are understood, defined and shared by the software and systems research and development communities.

Purposed G 3   Stakeholder requirements for traceability drive, and are demonstrably satisfied in, traceability solutions.

Purposed G 4   The effectiveness of the traceability in end use is measured and drives traceability process improvement.

Purposed G 5   The effectiveness of the traceability creation and maintenance process is measured and drives traceability process improvement.

Purposed G 6   Executed trace queries provide value beyond simply retrieving a set of artifacts; they actively support specific software and systems engineering tasks.

4.5 Requirements (Purposed)

4.5.1 Traceability Strategy (Purposed)

Purposed Req 1   To understand and define the full range of stakeholders to be supported in and by a comprehensive traceability solution. [Purposed G 1, G 2]

- *Status*: Little attention has been paid to the full set of stakeholders for traceability. The focus of both research and practice has been on partial views of restricted constituents and their tasks, and this knowledge has not been consolidated in one place for the traceability community. Many traceability stakeholders are typically forgotten about during strategy formulation, such as the downstream consumers of traceability (e.g., subcontractors). Stakeholders also have both near and long-term needs for traceability, and this is rarely distinguished in the strategy.
- *Promise*: Traceability personas are being developed by the Tracy project to explore stakeholder requirements for traceability tools (Cleland-Huang et al., 2011). Characterising personas and their requirements for establishing and using traceability (i.e., standard role models) would be a natural and valuable extension

of this work, and would begin to address the current lack of requirements focus in and by the traceability community.

Purposed Req 2   To understand and characterise the contextual factors that constrain and shape options for traceability solutions, such as the project type, organisational type, regulatory demands, domain, etc. [Purposed G 1, G 2]

- *Status*: The contextual factors shaping the traceability provided in various domains are generally explained in any case study reporting. Various classification schemes also exist to characterise the nature of projects, organisations, etc. However, there is as yet no agreed upon classification scheme and the demands that such factors place on traceability solutions have not yet been examined systematically.
- *Promise*: Such classification material could be consolidated so as to begin to be more methodical about defining the "context" for traceability solutions. Empirical studies could then be framed by comparable expressions of their contexts.

Purposed Req 3   To understand and define the numerous properties required of traceability for it to be considered effective for supporting the various stakeholder tasks and contexts, such as different demands on trace quality, completeness and granularity. [Purposed G 1, G 2, G 4, G 5, G 6]

- *Status*: Given the lack of systematic attention to stakeholder identification and requirements determination for traceability, there has been a corresponding lack of attention to what would be required of a traceability solution to satisfy them; these criteria for assessing the effectiveness of any supporting traceability solutions are rarely articulated.
- *Promise*: Better definition of stakeholder requirements for traceability, along with their contexts and acceptance criteria, will help in designing and assessing potential solution options for traceability more comprehensively.

Purposed Req 4   To design traceability solutions that are driven by, and traceable to, stakeholder requirements and contexts for traceability, providing access to the rationale for strategic decisions. [Purposed G 3]

- *Status*: There are few practical guidelines for practitioners as to good practices for designing and implementing an effective and traceable traceability solution for their project, one that is driven by the stakeholder requirements for traceability and project context. There is much reliance on past experience and informal knowledge sharing at present.

- *Promise*: The creation of a Traceability Body of Knowledge (TBOK), a resource proposed by the traceability community for the community, is essential to disseminate good traceability practices and to advance them. The development of such a resource is part of the impetus behind the formation of the Center of Excellence for Software Traceability (Hayes et al., 2007).

Purposed Req 5 To tailor traceability solutions to accommodate key and potentially changing stakeholder requirements and contexts for traceability, and to evolve the overarching traceability strategy as needed. [Purposed G 3]

- *Status*: Once the traceability solution has been designed for a project context, the strategy is generally to fix this solution for the duration of the project. It can be a non-trivial exercise to reconfigure the entire approach mid-project.
- *Promise*: The growth in the use of agile approaches to software and systems development, coupled with more focus on the use of services to satisfy requirements, is necessitating the development of lightweight, lean and dynamic traceability solutions. Such solutions are emerging.

Purposed Req 6 To agree upon measures of effectiveness with respect to organisational and business needs for a traceability strategy and its component aspects. [Purposed G 4, G 5]

- *Status*: There are no agreed upon measures for assessing the effectiveness of competing traceability strategies in different organisational and business contexts. Reporting on the effectiveness of an overarching traceability strategy, and its underlying models, processes and tools is largely the remit of qualitative industrial case studies at present.
- *Promise*: The number of industrial case studies and traceability experience reports has been growing in recent years and there would be value in more systematic cross-comparison of this work.

4.5.2 Traceability Creation and Maintenance (Purposed)

Purposed Req 7 To understand and define the requirements and constraints of those stakeholders who create and/or maintain traces (i.e., the creators' and maintainers' requirements for traceability). [Purposed G 2]

- *Status*: The goal of research is to simplify the task of traceability creation and maintenance by reducing the human effort required. However, this research has focused more on the study of techniques, methods and tools than on the people creating and maintaining the traceability and their needs. As a consequence, there is little real appreciation as to what may be gained or what may be lost by the move to increasing automation in these processes, such as the tacit role that a manual creator or maintainer plays, and the implicit development and maintenance knowledge gained by humans from doing the work.

- *Promise*: Empirical studies of humans undertaking various traceability tasks are beginning to emerge from research on trace automation, and this will lead to more understanding of the underlying activities and provide baselines for performance comparison.

Purposed Req 8   To develop a model of the general process of traceability creation and maintenance that depicts the generic workflow and component activities of the process and articulates the life cycle of a single trace within this process. [Purposed G 2]

- *Status*: There is no fine-grained description of traceability creation and maintenance processes, along with how these fit into a wider traceability process. The various steps and activities involved in creation and maintenance of a single trace are neither articulated nor agreed.
- *Promise*: Initial work on a generic traceability process model by the traceability community deconstructs the traceability creation and maintenance processes into their fundamental activities, and examines the workflow needed to create and maintain a single trace (see the chapter "Traceability Fundamentals"). Understanding and agreeing upon the underlying specifics of these processes will potentially help to identify process bottlenecks, and then guide and improve the support in these areas.

Purposed Req 9   To use the creators' and maintainers' requirements for traceability, in conjunction with a generic traceability process model, to guide and support the traceability creation and maintenance process. [Purposed G 3]

- *Status*: While there has been focus on the need to define the traceability process to be enabled by traceability techniques, methods and tools, the support to actually define this process on a project and then to implement this process in a team setting is not always readily available to practitioners.
- *Promise*: Guidance for traceability process definition is provided in some leading commercial tools or supported via consulting arrangements. Ideally, creators and maintainers would be provided with the means to define and configure their own working processes.

Purposed Req 10   To agree upon measures of effectiveness with respect to traceability creation and maintenance. [Purposed G 3]

- *Status*: Researchers have conducted some initial studies to compare the effectiveness of fully automated, semi-automated and manual approaches to traceability creation and maintenance, resulting in well-accepted measures of trace recall and trace precision. While these measures focus on the quality of the trace links, they do not account for the quality of their end use by stakeholders. They also do not account for the impact of using various traceability creation and maintenance techniques, methods and tools on the wider development tasks.

- *Promise*: Any discussion on the effectiveness of the traceability creation and maintenance process needs to be tied to the effectiveness of the traces in end use. Even where trace links are well crafted, this does not imply that the creation process was effective. Promise lies in a more sophisticated understanding and analysis of "effectiveness" and its associated measures.

Purposed Req 11   To gather data on and monitor the process of traceability creation and maintenance, using agreed measures of effectiveness, so as to continuously improve the process. [Purposed G 3, G 5]

- *Status*: Researchers have conducted some initial studies to compare the effectiveness of fully automated, semi-automated and manual approaches to traceability creation and maintenance, though this has not yet matured to using these data to then evolve the process of creation and maintenance.
- *Promise*: More comparative studies of manual processes for traceability creation and maintenance with semi and fully automated settings are emerging, along with baselines for comparisons upon which to improve. Benchmark experiments and data sets will shape the future research direction and practical uptake strategies in these areas.

Purposed Req 12   To understand the paradigm used to develop the software or system (e.g., object-oriented, agent-oriented, service-oriented, product line, etc.), the nature of the artifacts involved and the domain specifics, so as to contextualise support for the traceability creation and maintenance processes within the wider software and systems development workflow. [Purposed G 3]

- *Status*: Approaches to traceability vary across development type and domain. However, there has been little systematic effort to articulate those project characteristics that impact the choices made for the approach to traceability creation and maintenance.
- *Promise*: Understanding what approaches to traceability creation and maintenance work best in different situations, and blending approaches as needed.

Purposed Req 13   To collect and use data about traceability evolution, such as intermediate versions of traces, to improve the initial traceability creation process and subsequent maintenance tasks. [Purposed G 5]

- *Status*: Trace maintenance data has been under-utilised to date.
- *Promise*: Historical traceability data may reveal useful insight into both traceability creation and maintenance process improvement areas.

4.5.3 Traceability Use (Purposed)

Purposed Req 14   To understand and define the full range of stakeholders who use the end products of traceability (i.e., its end users), their task needs, their constraints and their contexts of use. [Purposed G 1, G 6]

- *Status*: To date, the focus of the traceability community has been more on the processes and software needed to support the mechanics of traceability than on the needs of the consumers of the traces. Where the needs of the end users is a concern, research has focused mostly on using traceability to support the tasks of a specific subset of stakeholders, such as independent validation and verification analysts, and representatives from regulatory bodies, rather than on the full range of end users.
- *Promise*: End user stakeholder requirements for traceability are discussed in a fragmented way across various publications, often in terms of high-end users and low-end users of traceability. Typical end user requirements for traceability in different projects, organisations and domains could be consolidated and classified as a definitive resource for the traceability community to draw upon.

Purposed Req 15   To provide guidelines to determine and prioritise which traces are needed on a project, by whom, for what purposes, when, how, at what level of granularity, under what constraints, etc. [Purposed G 1]

- *Status*: Actual traceability use in various domains is patchy, as engineering professionals do not always recognise that traceability is needed or could save money or lives. Traceability need assessment is quite coarse and little active support is provided to do this.
- *Promise*: Practitioners are beginning to publish more experience reports of traceability in use to the wider traceability community. However, there is the issue of confidentiality that restricts progress. When organisations implement traceability techniques and methods that do not work as intended, they do not always publish the results. This makes it very hard for the traceability community to find out what does and does not work over time. Better ways to anonymise, sanitise and incentivise such reporting are sorely needed.

Purposed Req 16   To agree upon measures of effectiveness with respect to traceability in end use. [Purposed G 4]

- *Status*: There are no proposed or routinely used measures to assess traceability effectiveness in end use in different organisational and business contexts. Traceability metrics tend to focus on the effectiveness of the actual trace links (i.e., is it a real one?) and so support assessment for traceability creation and maintenance purposes only. Researchers have no hard statistics to confirm whether traceability actually enables what it sets out and purports to do.

- *Promise*: Researchers advocate the use of traceability information models that capture decisions about the anticipated traceability-related queries that the traceability solution should support, and describe the trace artifacts and the trace links needed to support those queries. This requirements and task-directed approach is promoted in researcher-led training sessions and there has been some initial uptake in practice. The obvious next step is to track the effectiveness of the solution in satisfying these queries from an end user perspective. The metrics component now needs more consideration.

Purposed Req 17   To gather data on and monitor traceability end use against stakeholder requirements for traceability, using agreed measures of effectiveness, to evolve the end user requirements and the capacity for their satisfaction in traceability solutions. [Purposed G 3, G 4]

- *Status*: If practitioners have end use effectiveness data, it is rarely shared within the traceability community, for the reasons described above. Practitioners primarily rely upon word of mouth (externally) or tool-generated traceability-related reports (internally) to get feedback about traceability end use for process improvement purposes.

- *Promise*: Anonymous feedback, ranking and rating systems are now common when distributing information on websites. There could be potential in examining similar strategies for evaluating traceability end use, focusing on measures less reliant on the concept of "traffic" or "throughput", to assess whether the results of traceability are used as intended and are actually useful in practice.

4.6 Recommended Research (Purposed)

The major research theme to achieve purposed traceability is *to define and instrument prototypical traceability profiles and patterns*. These would comprise typical stakeholder requirements for traceability, a way to characterise the wider project context, and recognised approaches for their accommodation and satisfaction in traceability solutions. Supporting research topics are listed below.

Research ID	Description	Req ID
Purposed RT 1	Develop a profile of prototypical role, task and context-based stakeholder requirements for traceability, including scenarios of end use for traceability.	Purposed Req 1, 7, 8, 14, 15
Purposed RT 2	Develop a classification scheme to define the context of a traceability need, such as salient properties of projects, organisations and domains.	Purposed Req 2, 12, 15
Purposed RT 3	Develop patterns for traceability implementations associated with traceability profiles and contexts.	Purposed Req 3, 4, 9, 15
Purposed RT 4	Instrument a mechanism to both use and evolve this resource of profiles, contexts and patterns, integrating feedback from practice and experience.	Purposed Req 5, 9, 11, 13, 17
Purposed RT 5	Propose and agree upon metrics to measure effectiveness in all areas of the traceability process.	Purposed Req 3, 6, 10, 16
Purposed RT 6	Perform empirical studies to determine whether the various stakeholder types find traceability techniques, methods and tools fit-for-purpose.	Purposed Req 3, 6, 10, 11, 16, 17
Purposed RT 7	Develop a Traceability Body of Knowledge (TBOK) to define the traceability terminology, profiles, contexts, patterns, practices, techniques, methods and tools, and to include resources on metrics, case studies, lessons, experts, benchmarking, baselines, etc. Careful attention will need to be paid to the contribution process for the credibility and sustainability of such a resource.	Purposed Req 1-17

4.7 Positive Adoption Practices for Industry (Purposed)

Purposed IP 1 Practitioners consult, use and contribute to an evolving Traceability Body of Knowledge (TBOK).

Purposed IP 2 Practitioners draw upon prototypical traceability profiles, contexts and patterns when designing and implementing a traceability solution for their project, organisation and domain.

Purposed IP 3 Practitioners routinely measure the effectiveness of all aspects of their traceability process, evolve their solution accordingly and contribute these data to the Traceability Body of Knowledge (TBOK).

5 Traceability Challenge 2: Traceability that Is Cost-Effective

The return from using traceability is adequate in relation to the outlay of establishing it.

5.1 Link to Vision (Cost-Effective)

By establishing traceability automatically and early in the vision scenario, the engineer is alerted to product requirements that she overlooked in the initial stages of the engineering process, avoiding the need for costly rework later. Such knowledge has been accrued over a myriad of projects thanks to traceability analyses. The engineer is able to focus on her job, and on those analyses that demand her expertise and decision-making skills, and is not distracted by building in traceability support continuously as she works. Moreover, by having the opportunity of creating or maintaining the traceability on-demand later, the engineer does not have to worry now about having a traceability problem in the future; she knows that any missing traceability can always be established cost-effectively if and when needed, based upon tried and tested best-of-breed techniques, methods and tools.

5.2 Problems Addressed (Cost-Effective)

Complete traceability is often impractical, expensive to establish and not always necessary. Too much time can be invested in establishing traceability that may never be used or useful on a project, such as the provision of rich link semantics that are not actually exploited in traceability-related queries or analyses. It is difficult to know what is "just enough" traceability for each project situation because these situations themselves are often poorly expressed. The costs incurred in establishing traceability are also perceived to come too early on in a project, which leads to delays in implementing traceability, or in implementing it only under crisis mode; but traceability is not something that can be retrofitted with ease later. Because there is little sharing of good practices and heuristics for traceability, costs can further escalate as well known mistakes are made. Furthermore, there is inadequate understanding of the costs incurred during the entire traceability life cycle, so the approximate return on investment from traceability is not readily known or knowable at present. Together, these issues give traceability a bad reputation financially and present a real dilemma, as industry is reluctant to take on new approaches emerging from research without more data on the full costs and anticipated returns.

5.3 Dream Process (Cost-Effective)

- *Traceability Strategy.* Interactive and intelligent planning models, decision support tools and return on investment simulators will illustrate the business impact of spend decisions on traceability solution options.
- *Traceability Creation and Maintenance.* Traceability will only be created when it is needed, at exactly the quality needed – no more, no less – and each trace will be created in the most economical way possible to serve its intended purpose. Just enough traceability will always be maintained, and each trace will be maintained

in the most economical way possible to continue to serve its intended purpose. Traces will be archived and discarded once they are no longer needed to avoid unnecessary maintenance costs.

- *Traceability Use.* The end user will always be effectively supported in his or her task. The costs for establishing this traceability will only be incurred at the point of end use, which will be proportional to the benefits obtained, and these data will be known ahead of time for planning purposes.

5.4 Goals (Cost-Effective)

Cost-effective G 1   The total cost of traceability throughout a project's life is computed, along with the projected return on investment, and it is available to assess the potential effectiveness of competing traceability solutions.

Cost-effective G 2   Just enough traceability is provided, balancing the stakeholder requirements for traceability with the resource constraints.

Cost-effective G 3   The perfect middle ground between creating and maintaining traceability early and creating and maintaining traceability on demand is attained, so that the time, effort and money that are expended in establishing traceability are in balance with the resourcing profile of the project and the required quality in end use.

Cost-effective G 4   Lessons learned are captured, shared and capitalised upon, so that the cost and effectiveness of various traceability techniques, methods and tools are known and improved upon.

Cost-effective G 5   Intuitive user interfaces and interaction mechanisms enable process-related cost decisions to be explored and altered at all stages of the traceability process. The factors that influence traceability cost-effectiveness at different stages of the project life cycle are hence monitored and the traceability process can be adapted as needed.

5.5 Requirements (Cost-Effective)

5.5.1 Traceability Strategy (Cost-Effective)

Cost-effective Req 1   To provide support to get the right traceability (how good) at acceptable cost (how much) at the appropriate time (when) during traceability planning. [Cost-effective G 2, G 3, G 5]

- *Status*: There are no traceability-specific planning techniques and tools that help the practitioner to balance stakeholder requirements for traceability against its implementation costs. Practitioners tend to rely upon more traditional project management techniques and tools to assist their traceability planning at present. Furthermore, the resulting strategies are unlikely to vary over time.

- *Promise*: A better understanding and definition of what traces are needed, when and where, at what levels of quality, and for what duration on a project (i.e., progress with traceability challenge one) will assist with progress on this challenge. Research on value-based traceability is already underway and is needed for making strategy decisions on the traceability that is needed, leading to viable and mixed approaches in the future, and to more sophisticated visual planning aids.

Cost-effective Req 2   To agree upon metrics for measuring the traceability return on investment on a project, informing those data to collect, and those mechanisms to put in place to obtain these data and measures. [Cost-effective G 1]

- *Status*: Few agreed upon return on investment metrics are available for traceability, let alone used routinely, when planning and making strategic traceability decisions.
- *Promise*: Value-based approaches could lead to the situation where every trace that is created and maintained, manually, semi-automatically or fully automatically, is routinely tagged with data on both the price to create and maintain the trace, and the expected return in terms of the anticipated need it will satisfy. The cost to achieve this crude metric would itself need to be balanced against the benefits of so doing.

Cost-effective Req 3   To understand the fixed and variable costs for a life cycle-wide traceability solution. [Cost-effective G 1]

- *Status*: Currently, there is little examination as to where the various traceability costs actually lie across the entire software and systems development life cycle. Furthermore, there is little understanding as to the essential costs and the optional costs, such as those specific to particular project characteristics.
- *Promise*: Models of the traceability process are beginning to decompose the underlying activities of traceability, thus providing a structure to investigate and delineate the cost profile. This needs to be superimposed on to development life cycle models and the wider cost profile.

Cost-effective Req 4   To understand the costs and benefits of establishing traceability at different times on a project, and at varying levels of granularity. [Cost-effective G 3]

- *Status*: There are two extreme strategies for establishing traceability: (1) Early, by people who are familiar with the software or system. While this may produce quality traces at little cost per trace, the traces may never be used or useful; (2) On-demand, by people who may lack intricate knowledge of the software or system. While the speed and quality of the traces may be lacking in this approach, the traces that are produced are actually needed and used. No single strategy is perfect and a balance is now being sought.

- *Promise*: Proposals to distribute the cost of traceability across the whole project life cycle, and to mix strategies such as (1) and (2) over this life cycle, have been made and now need to be developed further.

Cost-effective Req 5   To capitalise upon historical return on investment measures and cost-benefit analyses when setting up a traceability strategy. [Cost-effective G 1, G 2, G 4]

- *Status*: Many of the benefits resulting from traceability may be realised only after the delivery of a product. This is hard to factor into fixed budgeting strategies without historical evidence of such. Practitioners share data on traceability practices, and rely upon past experiences when formulating traceability strategies, but this knowledge sharing may be restricted to personal networks or internal to organisations at present.
- *Promise*: There is a growing body of practitioner experience reports that are beginning to disseminate knowledge on traceability results and successful practices among the traceability community. More quantitative data on the costs and benefits now need to be gathered.

5.5.2 Traceability Creation and Maintenance (Cost-Effective)

Cost-effective Req 6   To establish benchmarks to compare and contrast the cost-effectiveness of the various traceability creation and maintenance techniques, methods and tools. [Cost-effective G 4]

- *Status*: There is little comparative data available on the cost-effectiveness of various traceability techniques, methods and tools. Researchers have focused on measuring disparate aspects of individual approaches. There is no simple mechanism for the practitioner to measure the cost-effectiveness of the total trace creation and maintenance effort on a project because the cost-effectiveness of creating and maintaining even a single trace link is not measured at present.
- *Promise*: Benchmarking has become a priority topic within the traceability research community. The Tracy project is developing TraceLab as an environment within which to facilitate the development and use of such benchmarks for experimental studies. This should lead to the availability of more comparative data in the near future.

Cost-effective Req 7   To provide a mix of continuous and on-demand approaches to traceability creation and maintenance to balance the costs throughout a project's life. This may include traces that are discovered, created and maintained only when needed. [Cost-effective G 3]

- *Status*: In practice, traces are often created that are never used, mostly manually, which is costly in terms of the time, effort and money expended. The true costs of this expenditure are rarely measured and known. The research focus on automated traceability creation and maintenance seeks to reduce the costs and errors that occur when this process is performed manually. The emphasis to date has been on exploring continuous versus on-demand approaches to traceability creation and maintenance, and the effectiveness of these techniques and methods, not on their respective costs.
- *Promise*: The promise lies in the potential to mix and match from a portfolio of complementary traceability creation and maintenance approaches, so as to balance needs with the available resources. To do this effectively, the various options will need to have cost profiles.

Cost-effective Req 8   To develop more cost-effective techniques, methods and tools for traceability creation and maintenance. [Cost-effective G 4]

- *Status*: With a research focus on the automated creation of trace links, to save on the costs of initial traceability creation and the costs of ongoing maintenance, the emphasis has been on the effectiveness of these techniques, methods and tools in creating actual trace links. The costs incurred and the savings made in using these, in relation to manual processes, are still under investigation. Moreover, it is the traces that are used in practice that are more likely to be maintained, whereas those that are not used are left to decay. There has been no research to date on whether this is an effective strategy.
- *Promise*: The focus on benchmarks for traceability, establishing frameworks for experimentation and baselines to improve upon, will provide the needed comparative data to assess and improve upon individual techniques, methods and tools.

5.5.3 Traceability Use (Cost-Effective)

Cost-effective Req 9   To reduce the cost and increase the performance of retrieving and displaying traces for end use. [Cost-effective G 1, G 4, G 5]

- *Status*: The costs for undertaking each activity in the traceability process are rarely quantified at present. The assumption is that retrieving and displaying traces can be a performance bottleneck and a deterrent to end use where it distracts the end user from their primary task.
- *Promise*: Ongoing improvements in performance with regard to information retrieval and data visualisation will negate this issue over time, leading to the potential for real-time immersive trace data to facilitate end user tasks more seamlessly.

Cost-effective Req 10   To configure and adapt traces to support end user tasks dynamically, creating new traces on-demand as needed, rather than hardwiring them in upfront just in case they are needed. [Cost-effective G 3]

- *Status*: In practice, many trace links are created and maintained that are either never used or never used effectively, partly because they are not needed and partly because the associated traces required to support a complete end user task are missing. Research has not identified the optimal set of traces, partly because it does not have a thorough understanding of stakeholder needs (traceability challenge one).
- *Promise*: Progress in automated traceability creation could lead to dynamically generating traceability to support end user tasks, if low cost. This would need to be coupled with a greater understanding of task-specific needs, and a way for end users to articulate these needs both dynamically and non-intrusively.

Cost-effective Req 11   To provide visualisations and interaction mechanisms for end users to navigate and access traces, so as to render traces more effective for task-supported end use. [Cost-effective G 5]

- *Status*: The artifacts that are related on a project are generally presented to practitioners in ways that do not always support their end user tasks explicitly, such as via textual lists or traceability matrices. So, while traceability may be present on a project, it is not guaranteed that the practitioner can and will use it. This means that the return from the effort expended may never be realised. Little research attention has been paid to the usability and effectiveness of the results of traceability in end user tasks or to improvement thereof.
- *Promise*: Researchers are beginning to propose interesting visualisations for traceability, but these tend to depict the trace links so as to support their validation rather than to support end user tasks. Human-computer-interface researchers and practitioners, interaction designers and visual artists are enhancing many aspects of software and systems development practice. Their contributions are essential to make traceability end use more intuitive and amenable to task support.

5.6 Recommended Research (Cost-Effective)

The major research theme to achieve cost-effective traceability is *to develop cost-benefit models for analysing stakeholder requirements for traceability and associated solution options at a fine-grained level of detail.* Supporting research topics are listed below.

Research ID	Description	Req ID
Cost-effective RT 1	Agree upon metrics for measuring traceability cost-effectiveness.	Cost-effective Req 2
Cost-effective RT 2	Understand the typical cost profile of traceability outlay on a project.	Cost-effective Req 3, 9
Cost-effective RT 3	Develop the means to associate a cost and a benefit profile with every trace that is brought into existence and maintained.	Cost-effective Req 7, 10
Cost-effective RT 4	Create decision support tools and impact analysis tools for making traceability return on investment decisions, such as a mechanism to globally and locally optimise the traceability solution based upon stakeholder requirements for traceability, the available resources and the return on investment required.	Cost-effective Req 1, 4, 5, 7
Cost-effective RT 5	Gather and disseminate benchmark empirical studies for researchers to demonstrate the cost-effectiveness (or not) of various traceability processes, techniques, methods and tools, as part of the Traceability Body of Knowledge (TBOK).	Cost-effective Req 3, 5, 6
Cost-effective RT 6	Decrease the costs and improve the effectiveness of the techniques, methods and tools supporting all activities of the traceability process.	Cost-effective Req 8, 11

5.7 Positive Adoption Practices for Industry (Cost-Effective)

Cost-effective IP 1   Practitioners consult the Traceability Body of Knowledge (TBOK) to understand the cost-effectiveness of existing and new techniques, methods and tools when making traceability strategy decisions.

Cost-effective IP 2   Practitioners use decision support tools and impact analysis tools to explore the cost-effectiveness of employing various and mixed traceability strategies on a project, and to help adapt the strategy over time.

Cost-effective IP 3   Practitioners track the return on investment from traceability on a project and contribute these data routinely to the Traceability Body of Knowledge (TBOK).

6 Traceability Challenge 3: Traceability that Is Configurable

Traceability is established as specified, moment-to-moment, and accommodates changing stakeholder needs.

6.1 Link to Vision (Configurable)

Traceability is established and used with consistency across the distributed teams in the vision scenario, to suit the particular needs of the engineer's project, organisation and domain. As the engineer walks through a virtual project environment to explore the impact of a new requirement on the project, the paths and discussions that are taken are simultaneously packaged as traceable rationale for any decisions implemented, according to the project's and organisation's potentially changing requirements for traceability. There is a real-time intention for traceability on the project, which is specified and complied with at all times by all team members.

6.2 Problems Addressed (Configurable)

The traceability solution is generally fixed upfront for a project and rigid thereafter. Once a traceability information model and an enabling process have been agreed to on a project (if at all), it can be problematic to change the particulars mid-project. Even when the traceability process is pre-defined and agreed upon, it is often implemented inconsistently in and across teams, irrespective of whether the team is co-located or distributed. Furthermore, when the stakeholder requirements for traceability change or the implementation specifics change, not all of the stakeholders may be notified. With time, the manner in which the traceability is established on a project can drift from the specified intent. A typical concern that is a common barrier to technology transfer of new traceability techniques, methods and tools in industry is whether research-initiated techniques can actually be configured to fit real project needs and circumstances as they emerge.

6.3 Dream Process (Configurable)

- *Traceability Strategy.* A traceability planning and management tool will automatically create a project-specific traceability solution with an underlying traceability information model and process that reflects stakeholder requirements for traceability. It will also provide an interactive traceability dashboard that will allow this all to be re-configured in real-time.
- *Traceability Creation and Maintenance.* Traces will be identified and created based upon a project's traceability information model and its actual artifacts, and they will be compliant with this definition of traceability intent. Traces will then be self-maintained such that they align with what is defined in a project's traceability information model at all times.
- *Traceability Use.* Semantically rich traceability will be personalised to satisfy individual needs for end use at all times, by dynamically reconfiguring and re-purposing existing traces as needed.

6.4 Goals (Configurable)

Configurable G 1   The intended traceability is defined for a project, using rich semantics for trace links, and any changes to these intentions are reflected.

Configurable G 2   The traceability solution on a project complies with the definition of intent, accommodating diverse and potentially changing needs at all times.

Configurable G 3   Proactive prediction provides support for determining and accommodating future stakeholder requirements for traceability, adapting the specification of intended traceability, updating the pre-existing traceability solution and reconfiguring existing traces over time as needed.

Configurable G 4   Levels of compliance are defined so as to either relax or tighten the traceability that is established on a project, thereby configuring the extent to which it is necessary to comply with the intended traceability at different times, for differing artifacts or by differing stakeholders.

6.5 Requirements (Configurable)

6.5.1 Traceability Strategy (Configurable)

Configurable Req 1   To define the intended traceability for a project as an integral part of the traceability solution. [Configurable G 1]

- *Status*: Researchers advocate that the intended traceability for a project be defined within a semantically rich traceability information model or meta-model. Such a model defines the trace artifact types and their associated trace link types based upon the analyses made possible by traversing these traces. The state of the practice is that traceability information models, if built, are typically rudimentary and their trace links are rarely semantically typed. The potential of using rich semantics is thus seldom exploited in traceability-related queries and end use. While there are some domain-specific traceability information models, it appears that many practitioners have yet to be convinced of their value. High-level goals tend to be provided to explain the purpose of traceability information models, rather than actual guidance in their construction and use.

- *Promise*: Research has emphasised simple and pragmatic traceability information models recently, so some flow-through to industry is expected. The Tracy project further proposes to include a downloadable traceability information model tool for practitioners to configure and use, potentially facilitating uptake.

Configurable Req 2   To define variable levels of granularity in the intended traceability, to accommodate different stakeholders and artifacts,
and to account for differing parts of a system at different times in a project's life (i.e., heterogeneous solutions to
heterogeneous needs). [Configurable G 1, G 4]

- *Status*: Traceability solutions are typically designed to be homogeneous (i.e., one
size fits all). Research has not addressed variability in the traceability solution, so
tools rarely support this. Traceability information models, where created, rarely
come in a heterogeneous and partitioned form either.
- *Promise*: Finer-grained and parameterised traceability information models, tailored to different project contexts and needs, may enable variability. Individual
requirements may demand different levels of traceability based upon their value
and volatility, so risk-driven provisioning may be worth investigating.

Configurable Req 3   To use the definition of the intended traceability to provide
traceability process guidance, and to undertake compliance
and consistency checks in the actual implementation of the
traceability process across team members and other project
constituents. [Configurable G 2, G 4]

- *Status*: A number of commercial tools offer assistance to define the intended
traceability on a project and then to enforce compliance and consistency in its
implementation. Process compliance and consistency management is already a
mature topic in other branches of software and systems engineering.
- *Promise*: Process-aware integrated development environments that monitor the
current state of a project and, when coupled with a well-defined traceability
information model, provide guidance and feedback on the traceability that is
implemented in real-time. Using a definition of the intended traceability on a
project more habitually would enable such compliance checking and consistency
management.

Configurable Req 4   To adapt the definition of the intended traceability, and any
associated process, to accommodate changing contexts and
needs. [Configurable G 1, G 2, G 3]

- *Status*: Traceability information models, where defined and used, seldom come
in an evolvable form. They can, therefore, be difficult to change retrospectively.
Research has not addressed subsequent changes to the traceability information
model and process, so tools rarely support this evolution.
- *Promise*: The concepts underpinning self-managing and adaptive systems, along
with techniques from autonomic computing, are likely to play an important role
in the required re-configurability of traceability solutions.

6.5.2 Traceability Creation and Maintenance (Configurable)

Configurable Req 5   To create and maintain traces that comply with the intended traceability for a project, whenever, however and wherever these traces are established. [Configurable G 2, G 4]

- *Status*: Research proposes defining traceability information models to guide the creation of valid traces. Such models help to check the validity of the trace links that have been created, and tools can enforce this checking, but they do not readily help in capturing the trace links in the first place. Semantics may be attached to trace links in practice, by putting attributes on trace links in leading requirements management tools, but these semantics are often minimal, inconsistently applied and not always subsequently exploited in traceability end use.
- *Promise*: Using a definition of the intended traceability on a project, as specified in a semantically rich traceability information model, to guide the actual discovery and creation of trace links, and then to guide ongoing trace maintenance activities.

Configurable Req 6   To assess whether there is a need to remove and re-create existing traces when the definition of the intended traceability changes on a project, as an alternative to maintaining versions of existing traces. [Configurable G 3]

- *Status*: Where the context of a project changes, such as the introduction of new audit requirements in an industry or the reuse of an existing project's artifacts and associated traceability in a completely new project, the traceability remains relevant to the prior context. No research has investigated switches of context mid-project or in reuse situations for its ramifications with respect to trace validity and ongoing trace maintenance.
- *Promise*: In theory, the established traceability can be checked against its traceability information model at any time, where one exists on a project, and any discrepancies can either be noted or rectified. In practice, such models are infrequently used in this way beyond initial trace creation and then for ongoing maintenance, but this support would be a simple and natural progression.

6.5.3 Traceability Use (Configurable)

Configurable Req 7   To use models of the end user, the wider end use process and end user traceability-related queries to guide the fine-grained definition of the intended traceability on a project. [Configurable G 1, G 3]

- *Status*: Researchers advocate that traceability information models be constructed that reflect and enable the answering of end user traceability-related queries. But, because there is an incomplete understanding of the various end users of traceability at present, their task queries are not routinely used to define traceability information models in practice. However, studies of how users use traces and models of the end use process are both emerging.

- *Promise*: Operational profiles indicate where to focus the testing effort in software and systems development. A similar profile of intended end use could lead to defining a profile for the traceability focus on a project, allowing for variation in both its specification and implementation over time and contexts.

Configurable Req 8   To monitor end use to predict future needs and re-configure the definition of the intended traceability as needed. [Configurable G 3]

- *Status*: Since there is seldom a feedback loop from traceability in actual use back to the original intentions, the traceability that is created and maintained is rarely adjusted moment-to-moment. It is not clear whether this would even be a cost-effective approach.
- *Promise*: Data collected on end use, both historical and real-time, may provide insights into likely future needs and enable the development of probabilistic end use models. There may also be some scope for end users to define and manipulate their own traceability needs and models.

Configurable Req 9   To adapt pre-existing traces to address end user requirements for traceability dynamically. [Configurable G 3]

- *Status*: Where implemented, trace links are generally hard-wired to provide support for particular predefined uses in practice and are rarely reconfigurable to support new contexts of traceability use.
- *Promise*: With advances in monitoring, and in autonomic techniques and technologies, traces could be self-aware and adapt to changing demands. Smart traces would assist with the reuse and repurposing of traces for new end uses.

6.6 Recommended Research (Configurable)

The major research theme to achieve configurable traceability is *to use dynamic, heterogeneous and semantically rich traceability information models (or similar specifications of the intended traceability) to guide the definition and provision of traceability.* Supporting research topics are listed below.

Research ID	Description	Req ID
Configurable RT 1	Provide better ways to define the traceability that is required on a project, accommodating varying levels of granularity and rich semantics to account for differing tracing needs, artifacts and stages of the project life cycle. This could be via traceability information models or other specification concepts.	Configurable Req 1, 2, 7

(continued)

Research ID	Description	Req ID
Configurable RT 2	Provide a mapping from the traceability information model (or similar specification concept) to its instantiation on a project, so as to support change and enable compliance checks and consistency management in its implementation.	Configurable Req 3, 4, 5
Configurable RT 3	Investigate techniques to automatically propose traceability information models (or similar specification concept) based upon an analysis of stakeholders' requirements for traceability and the projected project artifacts in various organisations and domains.	Configurable Req 7, 8
Configurable RT 4	Investigate how to reconfigure or re-purpose a pre-existing set of traces to accommodate changes in the definition of the traceability information model (or similar specification concept) – i.e., smart trace links.	Configurable Req 6, 9

6.7 Positive Adoption Practices for Industry (Configurable)

Configurable IP 1 — Practitioners use a traceability information model (or similar specification concept) to define and update their traceability intentions for a project. This definition and use process will be supported and form an integral part of the traceability solution.

Configurable IP 2 — Practitioners work on global and distributed projects establishing traceability consistently and as intended (which may not mean homogeneously) irrespective of locale.

Configurable IP 3 — Practitioners change their particular approach to traceability as their needs and context dictate, yet comply with the traceability of other practitioners.

7 Traceability Challenge 4: Traceability that Is Trusted

All stakeholders have full confidence in the traceability, as it is created and maintained in the face of inconsistency, omissions and change; all stakeholders can and do depend upon the traceability provided.

7.1 Link to Vision (Trusted)

In the vision scenario, the engineer is confident in making decisions based upon the options presented to her. She trusts the results of the traceability and expects the associated analyses it enables to be accurate and up to date at all times. The engineer is alerted to the impact on traceability of potential changes in the requirements and their implementation, and any necessary traceability updates for the changes that are implemented are made proactively, meaning that this confidence in the traceability is retained. The traceability simply self-repairs and evolves at all times without the engineer having to do anything explicit. The engineer is also comfortable in delegating any ensuing tasks that will impact the traceability, as she trusts that the overall traceability will not be jeopardised by others' actions or inactions. The traceability is always dependable; it is "ready-to-use" by the engineer and even "ready-to-wear" on her sweater sleeve.

7.2 Problems Addressed (Trusted)

The traceability that is established on many projects often has a dubious provenance, impacting how much trust can be placed in the analyses it facilitates, as well as its longevity. People establishing traceability make mistakes that go undetected and the impact of such mistakes are rarely known. Traces decay unless they are cultivated, but the useful life and quality of the trace links is usually also unknown. The traced artifacts can themselves expire and this can remain unknown, with unforeseeable consequences. Without effort, there is traceability entropy over time. This is a vicious cycle for both establishing and using traceability – why keep the traceability current if it is already flawed and why use it? Practitioners are not going to invest in something that they do not find trustworthy or that demands inordinate housekeeping effort from them to keep it dependable and credible.

7.3 Dream Process (Trusted)

- *Traceability Strategy.* An up to date quality profile for all the traces established and used on a project will be planned for and made available at any moment in time.
- *Traceability Creation and Maintenance.* Every trace that is created will have associated quality metrics. Once created, every trace will be guaranteed to a defined quality level and strive to retain its own ongoing integrity, despite changes in the system and artifacts, and its quality metrics will be updated accordingly if necessary.
- *Traceability Use.* Only trusted traces will be used to support different traceability-enabled tasks on a project. The end user will trust the traceability and depend upon its analyses.

7.4 Goals (Trusted)

Trusted G 1   The factors that impact the quality of the traceability process and product are known and factored into traceability strategies.

Trusted G 2   The quality of the traceability is measured on a project, at an individual trace level and at a trace set level, and this information is provided to all stakeholders.

Trusted G 3   Degrees of confidence in the analyses provided by the traceability are calculated and this information is provided to all stakeholders.

Trusted G 4   The traceability is self-healing, so its quality is preserved in the face of change, or updated where adjusted.

7.5 Requirements (Trusted)

7.5.1 Traceability Strategy (Trusted)

Trusted Req 1   To agree upon metrics to define the quality, both required and actual, of all aspects of the traceability process and product. [Trusted G 2, G 3]

- *Status*: Research on automated trace recovery and trace capture has made wide use of a number of quality metrics common in the information retrieval discipline, such as for the recall and precision of trace links. Other than these and their associated metrics, there are few agreed upon measures for traceability quality.
- *Promise*: Precision and recall metrics are only a start, and quantitative measures of traceability process and product quality will only take us so far. Qualitative and probabilistic measures of traceability quality will need to be added to provide for a mix of measures.

Trusted Req 2   To account for levels of completeness, correctness, consistency, etc. in the various trace elements when planning and managing a traceability solution. [Trusted G 1, G 2]

- *Status*: The artifacts to be traced are seldom "perfect". Researchers have focused on the quality of the trace links, more so than the quality of the trace artifacts to date, but the quality of the overall traceability is part determined by the quality of those artifacts being linked and traced. There is rarely any discussion on artifact quality and its ramifications on the traceability, and little "cleaning" of the artifacts to be traced takes place in practice.
- *Promise*: If you link garbage you retrieve garbage. Those artifacts being traced need to be of an acceptable quality standard (i.e., accurate, complete, up to date, consistent, etc.). Or, where artifact quality is lacking, their quality attributes need to be understood and taken into account. Improvements in development practices, coupled with agreed upon quality metrics for traceability, will be important here. Advances will come from more focus on writing better requirements and by improving the other engineering artifacts to be traced, and by providing real-time feedback on their potential traceability at the time at which these artifacts are created.

Trusted Req 3   To measure all aspects of the traceability process for completeness, correctness, consistency, etc., based upon agreed metrics. [Trusted G 1, G 2]

- *Status*: The quality of the traceability process itself is even less examined than the quality of the elements forming the traces. Process quality measures are not routinely integrated into the traceability strategy, limiting the potential for informed traceability process improvement.
- *Promise*: The use of process data and quality measures to advance the quality of the trace product, as is common practice in general process improvement, would provide a mechanism for traceability process improvement. Levels for such improvement could also be defined along the lines of the more general capability maturity models.

Trusted Req 4   To understand the nature and impact of human vulnerability on all aspects of the traceability process, and to build in suitable mitigation strategies to address them. [Trusted G 1, G 2, G 3, G 4]

- *Status*: When creating and maintaining traceability manually, humans can err in their decisions, actions and inactions. When traces are created automatically, humans may not always trust the process that was used to create the traces, impacting their likelihood to use them. Furthermore, when performing certain traceability-enabled tasks in practice (such as impact analysis where it is essential to discover each and every impacted component), any incompleteness or error in the traces created (either manually or automatically) may lead the end users to mistrust other traces created in the same manner, especially where they are led to believe that the traces will be complete. Little attention has been paid to the impact of human involvement and trace confidence levels in all aspects of the traceability process.
- *Promise*: Models of human involvement in the traceability process are needed to gain a greater understanding of the potential value humans add to the process and the bottlenecks they present. Researchers are now beginning to look at the "humans in the loop" and more studies of this nature are essential.

Trusted Req 5   To use the traceability itself to understand and strengthen the quality of the traceability on a project (i.e., traceability bootstrapping). [Trusted G 2, G 4]

- *Status*: The traceability that is already established on a project can itself be used to help identify some quality attributes, such as the completeness of the traceability via an examination of missing artifacts. Researchers are also beginning to study what can be learned about the traceability from both the presence and the absence of traces.
- *Promise*: Using traceability analyses to advance traceability quality may present some interesting opportunities for traceability bootstrapping.

7.5.2 Traceability Creation and Maintenance (Trusted)

Trusted Req 6   To define and agree upon standards to create and maintain quality traces. [Trusted G 2, G 4]

- *Status*: Researchers informally agree upon what would be acceptable values for potential traceability quality metrics, such as for the recall and precision associated with automated traceability creation. In an attempt to reach such quality targets, recent research combines automated techniques to identify candidate trace links with voting-based mechanisms to improve and bolster the confidence in the quality of the traces created.
- *Promise*: Reaching agreement upon how the quality of a trace and its component elements are defined, and establishing benchmark experiments and datasets to compare techniques, methods and tools for their creation and maintenance against baselines.

Trusted Req 7   To gather requisite data for both traceability quality assessment and the future upkeep of this quality at the time of a trace's creation. [Trusted G 2, G 4]

- *Status*: Researchers have paid much attention to boosting the confidence levels with automated traceability creation, using the concept of "candidate links" and by setting thresholds for selecting among them.
- *Promise*: Providing suitable semantics and meta-data to clarify the quality attributes of a trace at the point of its initial creation and at every stage in the traceability maintenance process. This relies upon gaining progress, more generally, with agreeing upon quality metrics for traceability.

Trusted Req 8   To understand the impact of the familiarity of the stakeholders who establish the traceability with the artifacts under trace (i.e., where stakeholders are less familiar with the code, there may be less trust in their ability to trace the design to the code). [Trusted G 1]

- *Status*: The quality of the traceability is, in part, determined by the person or the tool doing the tracing, and that topic has received limited attention to date. Equally, with the emergence of more automated approaches, researchers have not yet determined whether people trust automatically created traces more than manually created ones. With automatically created traces, practitioners still need to take the time to approve the candidate trace links to assure confidence in the trace link. This means that automated approaches still necessitate human skills in the loop at present.
- *Promise*: Empirical studies of the role of human involvement in the traceability process are emerging and more such studies are needed.

Trusted Req 9   To monitor for any kind of change that impacts the quality of the traceability. [Trusted G 1, G 4]

- *Status*: In practice, the validity of traces expires and becomes obsolete, and this is not always accounted for in practice. This leads to a degradation of trust in the traceability over time. Research into the automated maintenance of traces assigns a status of "suspect" to previously created trace links that change and in which confidence has been lost. Each suspect trace link demands user confirmation on subsequent actions to perform, while unambiguous updates can only sometimes be performed in the background.
- *Promise*: Techniques that identify potentially obsolete trace links, along with support to update, version and archive these trace links, are needed to retain the traceability quality. This includes the propagation of updates to ensure that the overall traceability remains credible. Initial work based upon event-based and rule-based maintenance is promising.

Trusted Req 10 To understand the process of traceability decay, and to predict and measure the useful life of a trace. [Trusted G 1, G 4]

- *Status*: It is currently a costly proposition to maintain all the traces previously created during a development project. It is also not really known how the quality of each individual trace impacts the overall traceability quality and so it is uncertain as to which trace links really deserve the attention.
- *Promise*: The life expectancies of different traces probably vary and it may not be necessary to maintain and preserve them all. A triage-based approach to traceability maintenance would identify those traces that can be thrown away and those that can maintain themselves satisfactorily, relieving time to focus on those that need to be maintained more explicitly and on a case-by-case basis.

7.5.3 Traceability Use (Trusted)

Trusted Req 11 To define the necessary and acceptable quality for different traceability-enabled end user tasks. [Trusted G 3]

- *Status*: The quality required of the traceability to support the various end users and their tasks is rarely articulated in practice, chiefly because the tasks themselves have not been specified (traceability challenge one).
- *Promise*: The required traceability quality is unlikely to be a fixed value across people, projects, tasks and time, so this needs to be articulated. This depends upon progress with traceability challenge one.

Trusted Req 12 To present confidence levels for the traceability and the analyses it enables to the end users, with respect to its suitability for different tasks. [Trusted G 3]

- *Status*: All trace links are usually presented as equal in practice (i.e., they either exist or they do not exist). It can also be difficult to assess whether a trace link is up to date or not. Some trace visualisations explore the use of colour to suggest the age and likely relevance of trace links to assist in their end use.

- *Promise*: Further visual mechanisms to render the quality of the traceability visible to end users, and to indicate the suitability for various tasks, are needed. Traces are sometimes going to be less than perfect, so the promise also lies in making the best use of such traces and ensuing that the risks of this use is made visible.

Trusted Req 13   To retrieve the most current trace with respect to an end user query, reflecting real-time dependencies between the latest artifacts. [Trusted G 3, G 4]

- *Status*: To boost the quality and credibility of trace analyses, these must be based upon up to date trace artifacts and trace links, unless the analyses are historical in nature. Version control systems allow for such fine-grained control of artifacts and their dependencies.
- *Promise*: Version control systems are mature technologies and improvements in this area will be of continued value to traceability advances.

Trusted Req 14   To accommodate or repair breaks in the traceability record, so that the quality status of the traceability is always made evident to the end user. [Trusted G 2, G 4]

- *Status*: Automated techniques enable traceability to be recovered afresh on end use request if traces are missing or problematic, but the difficulty lies in identifying that either a trace is missing or has been compromised in the first place.
- *Promise*: More attention to monitoring the quality of traces over time is essential. This relies upon quality metrics and knowledge of the quality levels required to support various end user tasks. The quality could be repaired dynamically during end use if any issues are encountered. Requirements monitoring research is already in evidence and could lend insight here.

Trusted Req 15   To provide a link to those people who have contributed traced artifacts or have created trace links, to enable the end user to assess whether they are trusted entities and to do further checks on quality concerns (in person) when needed. [Trusted G 1, G 2, G 3]

- *Status*: Practitioners often infer trust in traced artifacts and trace links based upon who created and who maintained them (i.e., the quality of a product is a reflection of the process and the people undertaking the process). Equally, where the traceability provided at the point of end use is confusing or deficient in some way, sometimes the only resort in practice is to talk to the people who established the traces. Some research has proposed tying in the social production network underlying the traceability network to enable this support, such as by modelling the social network underlying the creation and maintenance of traceability (e.g., contribution structures).

- *Promise*: Further integration of social network modelling approaches and analyses into the traceability process is desirable here.

Trusted Req 16   To provide a way for end users to exchange data about the perceived and actual quality of a trace and of the analyses provided following the end use of a trace. [Trusted G 2, G 3]

- *Status*: There is little research into those mechanisms to help identify and alert end users to mistakes or problems in the traceability (i.e., incorrect or missing traces), in turn to provide experiential quality data to factor into traceability analyses. However, most contemporary development environments now include integrated emailing and chat capabilities, discussion forums, etc. for developers to communicate about the development process, and sometimes these are being used to support traceability in these ways.
- *Promise*: Further exploitation of integrated communication capability within integrated tooling holds promise, to enable all stakeholders to report on quality issues in both establishing and using traceability.

7.6 Recommended Research (Trusted)

The major research theme to achieve trusted traceability is *to perform systematic quality assessment and assurance of the traceability.* Supporting research topics are listed below.

Research ID	Description	Req ID
Trusted RT 1	Develop a model of the vulnerabilities in the traceability process, including human error in both manual and automated approaches, and develop suitable techniques to reinforce their reliability.	Trusted Req 4, 8, 15, 16
Trusted RT 2	Formulate metrics for traceability quality assessment, especially for the traces that are created and maintained.	Trusted Req 1, 3, 6
Trusted RT 3	Gain improvements in the quality of both manual and automatically created and maintained trace links.	Trusted Req 2, 5, 6, 7, 9, 13, 14
Trusted RT 4	Provide ways of inferring trust in the traceability based upon how the trace links are established and used, and by whom, and upon the useful life expectancy of traces.	Trusted Req 4, 8, 10, 15, 16
Trusted RT 5	Create a visual dashboard for displaying and examining traceability quality attributes on a project.	Trusted Req 2, 3, 7, 9, 12, 15, 16
Trusted RT 6	Catalogue the quality required of the traceability for supporting different end user tasks within the Traceability Body of Knowledge (TBOK).	Trusted Req 11

(continued)

Research ID	Description	Req ID
Trusted RT 7	Gather empirical evidence as to the quality of traceability techniques, methods and tools with respect to the quality of the traces they enable within the Traceability Body of Knowledge (TBOK).	Trusted Req 2, 3, 6, 7, 8, 16
Trusted RT 8	Advance the run-time monitoring of traceability quality with validated error detection models for trace links.	Trusted Req 7, 9
Trusted RT 9	Apply concepts from autonomic computing to explore self-healing traceability techniques, methods and tools, covering diagnosis, repair actions and propagation, to apply at both the individual trace and trace set levels.	Trusted Req 5, 14

7.7 Positive Adoption Practices for Industry (Trusted)

Trusted IP 1   Practitioners routinely specify acceptable levels for traceability quality attributes for their end user tasks.

Trusted IP 2   Practitioners are provided with the data they need to determine whether they can trust the traceability techniques, methods and tools that they use and the analyses that are based upon their end use.

Trusted IP 3   Practitioners supply feedback on the quality of the traceability unobtrusively and as part of its creation, maintenance and end use.

8 Traceability Challenge 5: Traceability that Is Scalable

Varying types of artifact can be traced, at variable levels of granularity and in quantity, as the traceability extends through-life and across organisational and business boundaries.

8.1 Link to Vision (Scalable)

The engineer has an enormous quantity of data that is rendered traceable in the vision scenario: eleven months of fine-grain project artifacts, links back to past archives containing other project artifacts, full records of project rationale and context, etc. The traceability that the engineer makes use of accounts for a myriad of artifact types, such as requirements, live links to stakeholders and contributors, test cases and government regulations. The engineer can rely upon the traceability having been established from the onset of her development project, through its transition into a maintenance project, to the eventual project closure and system retirement.

8.2 Problems Addressed (Scalable)

Traceability is often an afterthought on projects and established when it is needed, rather than from the first days in which project artifacts begin to accumulate. Pre-requirements artifacts can therefore be missed and remain untraceable. Likewise, traceability can erode over time unless the transition of traceability from a development project into its maintenance phase is also planned for. It is often difficult to account for the entirety of the artifacts relevant to development in the traceability, notably multimedia and unstructured informal artifacts. The traceability can become complex to depict and hence unusable over time. Some datasets are intrinsically difficult to trace due to inconsistencies in terminology, the nature of the artifact types, the lack of structure and heterogeneous formats. Non-functional requirements that have a global impact on the system are also notoriously difficult to trace. Traceability processes, techniques and methods tend to break down with scale in its various dimensions (e.g., the quantity of traceable artifacts or trace links, and time). Practitioners are reluctant to use new and emerging techniques, methods and tools without evidence of scalability in these multiple dimensions. The issue of scale can be compounded where customers mandate traces without discerning attention to their intended end use.

8.3 Dream Process (Scalable)

- *Traceability Strategy.* Full life cycle and all-embracing traceability will be planned for and managed, and any scale issues will be reduced via auto-completion tools.
- *Traceability Creation and Maintenance.* Trace creation will be as fast in large projects as it is in small ones, linking anything within its scope without a performance hit. Traceability maintenance will also be as fast in large projects as it is in small ones, and the traceability will not entropy over time.
- *Traceability Use.* End users will only see what they need to see from among a mass of project artifacts when they use traceability, and they will switch between coarse-grain and fine-grain traceability routinely.

8.4 Goals (Scalable)

Scalable G 1	There are no practical limits to the quantity of traceable artifacts and trace links that can be created and maintained in a project.
Scalable G 2	All media and artifact types serve as potentially traceable artifacts.
Scalable G 3	Traceable artifacts are "zoomed" into as required, to trace at varying levels of granularity.
Scalable G 4	Full project life cycle traceability coverage and longevity of this coverage is provided throughout a system's life, extending across organisations and business entities.

8.5 Requirements (Scalable)

8.5.1 Traceability Strategy (Scalable)

Scalable Req 1 To plan and manage traceability from the first day of a project until the last day of the project. [Scalable G 1, G 2, G 4]

- *Status*: Traceability is sometimes not implemented in practice until it is needed, or it is truncated to cover a period of a project's life, such as from requirements to design, or from requirements to code. This is often a side effect of the disparate tools being used.
- *Promise*: Late or restricted implementation of traceability is often a consequence of the investment required upfront on a project, coupled with unclear cost-benefit studies. Progress here will depend upon progress with traceability challenge two.

Scalable Req 2 To set up an open system to accommodate multiple types of trace artifacts and trace links. [Scalable G 2, G 4]

- *Status*: Traceability is often planned for in a homogenous manner on projects, irrespective of the project artifacts and project size, so many artifacts can thus be excluded from traceability support. Traceability is primarily planned for and applied on code, textual descriptions (e.g., natural language requirements) and UML (Unified Modeling Language) artifacts at present. Nevertheless, industrial researchers are piloting the traceability of heterogeneous artifacts in very large projects with some success.
- *Promise*: Designing approaches to traceability based upon traceability abstractions, rather than concrete artifacts types, which can accommodate all the artifacts that are likely to arise in the life of a project.

Scalable Req 3 To specify the concept of granularity, formally, to provide a way to define and retrieve the levels of granularity required for traceability on a project. [Scalable G 3]

- *Status*: Researchers have proposed establishing macro and micro levels of traceability to accommodate diverse media types, promoting the concept of granularity layers in the traceability provided, but this has not yet been fully developed or adopted in practice. Granularity remains an informally defined concept, with no real consensus on what is actually meant by fine-grain and coarse-grain, and all the levels in between. At present, a trace artifact accounts for both a full requirements document and an individual word within a requirement statement.
- *Promise*: Trace link semantics have received a great deal of attention by the research community and more use of such will find its way into practice via rich links. A more discerning ontology for specifying trace artifacts is now equally needed.

Scalable Req 4   To understand how traces are needed and used across organisations and business entities (i.e., accounting for subcontractors, etc.) and accommodating broader needs in the traceability strategy. [Scalable G 4]

- *Status*: Stakeholder requirements for traceability are poorly understood at present (see traceability challenge one).
- *Promise*: Progress with traceability challenge one is essential to progress here. However, this needs to take care to examine additional stakeholders beyond the obvious candidates to examine the breath of artifacts to be traced.

Scalable Req 5   To apply traceability practices and processes to large, distributed, multi-person, multi-year projects. [Scalable G 1, G 4]

- *Status*: To support distributed contexts requires that the traceability does not decay as changes are made to interrelated and externally maintained artifacts over time. In practice, a lack of seamless bi-directionality of the traceability across all the possible tools that produce and hold the traced artifacts can compound the update of traceability following changes made to any associated external artifacts. This issue is usually addressed where projects use a single and shared application life cycle tool.
- *Promise*: The growing interoperability of tools and data offers promise here because standardisation on a single tool across a distributed multi-organisational setting may not always be viable. There are also dependencies that can reduce the scalability problem to a smaller, more manageable problem, such as exploiting the transitivity properties among trace links. If one trace can partially or fully imply another trace, then this can be reasoned about and be potentially supported by auto-completion strategies.

Scalable Req 6   To understand the particular scale issues associated with tracing the global properties of systems, such as non-functional requirements, and with tracing in the context of systems of systems. [Scalable G 1, G 4]

- *Status*: The traceability of non-functional requirements is receiving attention in the research community, as the perception is that the traceability of such global properties is more complex and difficult to handle. Differentiating the particular nuances of systems of systems development, for tracing purposes, has received less attention to date.
- *Promise*: Early industry and government adopters of automated trace recovery techniques have made datasets available for research into the issues associated with the scalability of traceability techniques, methods and tools. The issues of local and global traceability could be examined in such contexts to gain a clearer understanding of the different issues with scale in these two increasingly important dimensions.

8.5.2 Traceability Creation and Maintenance (Scalable)

Scalable Req 7   As scale grows, to maximise the use of automated traceability creation and maintenance. [Scalable G 1]

- *Status*: Pilot studies have been conducted in large industrial projects to examine the scalability of automated trace recovery techniques with promising results. The recall measure for trace links recovered via automated techniques is now generally acceptable, even on large datasets. The validation of automated maintenance techniques is still mostly restricted to small datasets at present.
- *Promise*: To provide for a viable approach to completely automated traceability creation and maintenance in large projects over time, the method of automation may need to be differentiated according to the criticality of the artifacts. For example, traces might be created as a by-product of formal specifications for highly critical components, while traces might be created using trace retrieval methods for less critical components.

Scalable Req 8   To create and maintain trace links between artifacts of different types, in terms of their media, formality, level of structure, etc., and at any level of granularity [Scalable G 2, G 3]

- *Status*: The focus of traceability creation has been from requirements through to code to date (i.e., post-requirements traceability). There has been limited research on the indexing and retrieval of informal, unstructured and multimedia artifacts in a software and systems development context, so they are often not included as potential traceable artifacts in traceability solutions that adopt automated traceability creation techniques and methods. Traceability maintenance techniques and methods also deal primarily with structured textual artifacts, UML diagrams and code. In general, there has been less focus on accounting for pre-requirements artifacts in traceability solutions by researchers or practitioners, though some recent industry attention has been on tracing back to regulatory codes.
- *Promise*: In theory, any artifact that can be indexed can be traced, so more attention needs to be paid to developing ontologies for describing different types of traceable artifact. Navigating and presenting the resulting traces also demands rendering these artifacts in some way, so this requires progress with trace visualisation.

Scalable Req 9   To prune the growing mass of traceable artifacts and trace links to keep trace maintenance and trace retrieval manageable. [Scalable G 1]

- *Status*: Research has focused on accumulating trace links rather than on pruning them. Trace links are rarely retired in practice, potentially impeding future traceability as they grow in number. Trace links need versioning and garbage collection if the traceability is to scale, and well-known versioning systems are increasingly a core component of many traceability solutions.

- *Promise*: The versioning and garbage collection techniques common to other areas of software and systems engineering need to be applied more widely within traceability solutions.

8.5.3 Traceability Use (Scalable)

Scalable Req 10   To retrieve and filter trace artifacts, potentially represented as diverse media types, to address traceability-related queries. [Scalable G 1, G 2]

- *Status*: There has been limited analysis on how to exploit artifacts of different media types in trace retrieval algorithms, so presenting traces containing multiple media artifacts is not standard. There can be performance issues associated with using traceability in large datasets in practice, an issue compounded by the presence of rich media artifacts.
- *Promise*: Ongoing improvements in multimedia search, retrieval and filtering will make media-rich traces increasingly feasible in the future. However, the actual need for and value of media-rich traces requires more empirical study.

Scalable Req 11   To provide visual mechanisms to augment large-scale traceability in end use, switching between coarse-grain views of traceability (i.e., broad) and fine-grain views of traceability (i.e., deep) with ease. [Scalable G 1, G 3]

- *Status*: End users often need to untangle a mass of trace links in order to make use of them in practice. Commonly used visual mechanisms, like traceability matrices, while wholly appropriate for many traceability-enabled activities and tasks, do not scale. Researchers are beginning to focus on visualisations for trace links, to overcome their complexity in actual use, mostly appearing in prototype tools at present. However, there are few usability studies on the use of such emerging visuals, particularly for handling the traceability of large datasets.
- *Promise*: The improved visualisation of traces will facilitate their end use and make the resulting analyses more accessible to end users. Layered approaches to traceability, building on similar concepts to those seen in computer-aided design tools, where layers can be turned on or off depending on need, would help to provide filters and so address some of the issues associated with scale.

8.6 Recommended Research (Scalable)

The major research theme to achieve scalable traceability is *to provide for levels of abstraction and granularity in traceability techniques, methods and tools, facilitated by improved trace visualisations, to handle very large datasets and the longevity of these data.* Supporting research topics are listed below.

Research ID	Description	Req ID
Scalable RT 1	Obtain industrial datasets from various domains to enable researchers to investigate scalability issues, and the potential of techniques, methods and tools to address them, both systematically and comparatively.	Scalable Req 5, 6, 7, 9
Scalable RT 2	Develop effective search, filtering and visual mechanisms to navigate and query large numbers of trace artifacts and trace links, of varying media types.	Scalable Req 2, 5, 10, 11
Scalable RT 3	Develop an abstract model of the traceability process and its component activities, to enable pluggable techniques, methods and tools that apply to differing process activities and differing layers of abstraction to be created, located and used.	Scalable Req 1, 2, 3, 5
Scalable RT 4	Develop a cost-benefit model to assess granularity decisions that impact subsequent scale issues with respect to traceability.	Scalable Req 1, 3, 8
Scalable RT 5	Provide techniques to evaluate the traceability potential of various datasets and media assets, and to guide in setting up a suitable traceability strategy to accommodate them.	Scalable Req 1, 8
Scalable RT 6	Gain improvements in performance for the real-time automated recovery and capture of trace links to account for scale.	Scalable Req 5, 7
Scalable RT 7	Gain improvements in performance for the real-time retrieval and rendering of traces to account for scale.	Scalable Req 5, 10, 11
Scalable RT 8	Define ontologies for software and systems development artifacts, and investigate the need for and value of integrating the various artifact types and media into traceability end use.	Scalable Req 2, 8
Scalable RT 9	Explore the unique scalability issues associated with tracing non-functional requirements, and develop effective techniques, methods and tools for this context.	Scalable Req 6
Scalable RT 10	Explore the unique scalability issues associated with tracing within and across systems of systems, and across organisational and business boundaries, and develop effective techniques, methods and tools for this context.	Scalable Req 4, 6

8.7 Positive Adoption Practices for Industry (Scalable)

Scalable IP 1   Practitioners establish traceability from the onset of a project, along with the housekeeping procedures that are needed to keep the traceability use viable through to project completion.

Scalable IP 2   Practitioners take a multi-pronged approach to establish traceability, to account for all project artifacts over time, but the unique details remain hidden behind a simpler and more abstract treatment of the artifacts.

Scalable IP 3   Practitioners switch seamlessly between 2D and 3D visualisations as they walkthrough multimedia-rich traces at varying levels of granularity.

Scalable IP 4   Practitioners contribute datasets to enable researchers to examine scalability issues with emerging traceability techniques, methods and tools.

9 Traceability Challenge 6: Traceability that Is Portable

Traceability is exchanged, merged and reused across projects, organisations, domains, product lines and supporting tools.

9.1 Link to Vision (Portable)

Traceability is merged across all components of the full flying solar car system in the vision scenario, where software is but one component of the system, and requirements from related projects are reused, along with their entire traceability networks. Interrogating the traceability networks of external software systems and services aids the engineer's decision making regarding procurement. The engineer integrates a new service into the existing system with the confidence that the traceability back to the requirements will facilitate both the uncoupling of the expired software and the integration of the new service, and so provide the team in South Africa with all the information that they need to complete the update. The entire traceability history is always available for use and reuse, irrespective of where the actual traces were created and the tools that were used to create them.

9.2 Problems Addressed (Portable)

Traceability is often legacy and locked into projects and tools, so it is rarely extractable and reusable across projects or components therein. It is also typically project, organisation and person-specific, so difficult to reconcile in a timely manner. Standards are rarely used across more than locales and, where they are used, they can be applied somewhat inconsistently such that problems are not recognised until the traceability is needed and found wanting. In reality, it can be tricky to trace to artifacts created by other people and in other organisations, or to use others' trace links; much of the contextual knowledge needed to interpret and understand the traceability is often missing.

9.3 Dream Process (Portable)

- *Traceability Strategy.* Projects and organisations across the globe will use industry agreed upon standards, policies, representations and terminology for traceability, not because of mandate, but due to the obvious benefits and value of so doing.

- *Traceability Creation and Maintenance.* Where traceability is pre-established within a set of artifacts, it will be extracted, reused and integrated with the traceability of other artifacts with ease, irrespective of the tooling. Where traceability is integrated across a set of artifacts with their own traceability networks, this newly created traceability network will be maintained with ease.
- *Traceability Use.* Traceability will be retrieved such that it draws upon wider traceability networks to support any end user traceability-related query or application need.

9.4 Goals (Portable)

Portable G 1   An industry agreed policy for traceability serves to define the minimal conditions under which any traceability solution and any resulting traceability network will integrate with any other.

Portable G 2   Comprehensive traceability information, comprising traceability information models, trace artifacts and trace links, are expressed in a common way, and retained and reused for full projects or for components therein.

Portable G 3   The traceability associated with individual projects and components is reconciled and merged seamlessly when reused across projects, product lines, organisations and domains. The traceability information models, processes and tools supporting the traceability are designed to enable this integration.

Portable G 4   Where traceability is reused or re-purposed for new contexts, multiple traceability networks are maintained as the trace elements change.

Portable G 5   Traceability is established dynamically, reaching out to incorporate previously unconnected artifacts within its scope as the search space for traceability widens.

9.5 Requirements (Portable)

9.5.1 Traceability Strategy (Portable)

Portable Req 1   To standardise key aspects of the traceability process. [Portable G 1]

- *Status*: Traceability policies and standards are few at present, focus mostly on single project or organisational processes, and are rarely used in other than regulated industries and domains (e.g., military and aerospace standards).
- *Promise*: A loose framework of guiding policies, as common in some other industries requiring tracing (e.g., the food industry), supported by defined roles and

responsibilities, may provide for a more flexible and less burdensome way to address the need for wider standardisation in traceability processes.

Portable Req 2   To agree upon and use a common representation to express the intended and actual traceability on a project. [Portable G 2]

- *Status*: While the traceable artifact types and trace link types may be listed in a requirements management plan, there is no agreed upon way to describe a traceability information model in research or practice, or even to describe a single trace that is created and maintained. While there have been numerous proposals as to the semantics of trace links, there is yet to be an agreement upon their classification and use. The traceability information models that show the full traceability intent for a project need to be examinable and the semantic meaning needs to be consistent to assess trace compatibility across projects. Likewise, the traces created and maintained need themselves to be examinable, consistent and extractable if they are to be shared and reused.
- *Promise*: A unified representation for expressing traceability information models, traces and other interchangeable traceability information would offer promise.

Portable Req 3   To monitor and assure compliance to the policies, standards, representations and language used for traceability. [Portable G 1, G 2]

- *Status*: In regulated industries, the compliance of the traceability is generally assessed and assured via third parties. Automated techniques and tools are also beginning to assist in this space. This is less widely practiced in non-regulated industries. A related issue is the fact that the traceability terminology is not yet shared within the traceability community.
- *Promise*: Compliance will become easier to assess when the policies and representations for traceability have themselves have become better defined and their use is integrated into practice. A glossary of traceability terminology accompanies this chapter (see the glossary of this book) and may help to foster future agreement in the use of traceability terms by the community.

Portable Req 4   To examine the integration potential of existing traces when they are to be merged and/or reused from across distributed project settings, and the subsequent potential for their maintainability. [Portable G 3, G 4]

- *Status*: There are no explicit mechanisms to assess the potential integration of traceability that has been pre-established for different artifact sets and is held in different tools, nor of the likely issues for subsequent traceability maintenance. Most of the research focus and practical implementation has been on inner product traceability, so there is no agreed upon standard for extracting and sharing the traceability across products over time. This is often the case even within organisations. Recent attention has been paid to reusing traceability between variants in a product line, and support for this is maturing in practice in some industries (e.g., in the automotive industry). This trace reuse is carefully built into the engineering practice, through an examination of variability, and is not determined post-hoc.

- *Promise*: The traceability work that is emerging from product line engineering contexts may have wider applicability to broader traceability reuse.

Portable Req 5   To develop reconciliation tactics to accommodate specific project and organisational needs when merging and reusing previously disparate or legacy traceability networks. [Portable G 3]

- *Status*: Legacy projects can have their traceability recovered via automated techniques with some success, though research has not yet looked into wider traceability integration and reconciliation of traces across multiple traceability networks. Reconciling traces that have been created by other people in other projects and organisations is a relatively open area, but one that will become increasingly relevant with the service-oriented provisioning of software and systems. The attention to incorporating institutional knowledge about traceability may facilitate such sharing and reuse.
- *Promise*: The provision of appropriate contextual information, alongside the traces that are used or reused, may ease the understanding and merging of myriad trace elements by humans. Useful trace meta-data to support automatic reconciliation also needs to be explored.

9.5.2 Traceability Creation and Maintenance (Portable)

Portable Req 6   To provide supporting mechanisms to facilitate tracing to artifacts created by other people in other projects and organisations, perhaps held in diverse toolsets. [Portable G 1, G 2, G 3]

- *Status*: Dedicated requirements management tools offer varying levels of support for incorporating artifacts created outside of the tool within a traceability network, often via pre-processing, though support for bi-directional traceability to these other tools can be variable and impede future maintenance of the traceability once incorporated. There are prototype tools that have demonstrated the creation of trace links across heterogeneous CASE tools at distributed locations though. A common method for supporting trace portability between artifacts in disparate tools is indirectly via XML (Extensible Markup Language). Such trace links may also be held in one place and as a separate artifact to ease extraction and reuse.
- *Promise*: Decoupling the representation of the trace links from the trace artifacts, irrespective of where the trace elements are physically stored, will further aid trace extraction, portability and reuse.

Portable Req 7   To monitor and identify changes in trace-related artifacts, irrespective of their storage location, and to propagate the necessary traceability updates to those traceability networks in which they participate. [Portable G 4]

- *Status*: It can be problematic to maintain traceability in dedicated requirements management tools if other third party tools have been used for different stages of the software and systems development life cycle. This requires clear protocols for the interchange and interoperability of data between the tools. Application life cycle management tools ameliorate the problem as they are fully integrated tools and, as such, can propagate traceability changes internally. The repurposing of artifacts in multiple traceability networks may happen routinely within a single project and tool, but extending this to their inclusion within additional project and tooling contexts is not routine at present.
- *Promise*: Maintaining reused traces will be less problematic where the reused trace artifacts and trace links are initially created and maintained, and then subsequently reused, within fully integrated and interoperable toolsets. Where this is not the case, differentiating live reuse (i.e., where updates to artifacts impact the traceability) from copied reuse (i.e., where updates to artifacts does not impact the traceability) may be important to investigate here.

9.5.3 Traceability Use (Portable)

Portable Req 8   To understand and use the trace artifacts and trace links established by third parties in traceability-related queries. [Portable G 5]

- *Status*: Traceability-related queries are generally targeted to an associated set of artifacts for which the traceability has been explicitly defined and created. Research has not looked at how this could be extended to incorporate additional artifacts, opportunistically, within its remit, and whether this would even add value as a concept. This may become more important as systems are developed from pre-existing components and services.
- *Promise*: Drawing upon a number of traceability networks or non-traced artifacts in providing support for end user tasks demands standards in the base representation of traces and trace elements. A Google-strength search capability may be incorporated into future traceability solutions to find new traces.

9.6 Recommended Research (Portable)

The major research theme to achieve portable traceability is *to agree upon universal policies, standards, and a unified representation or language for expressing traceability concepts.* Supporting research topics are listed below.

Research ID	Description	Req ID
Portable RT 1	Develop a unified representation or language for expressing traceability information models and for representing traces.	Portable Req 2
Portable RT 2	Define and agree upon the semantic meaning of the various types of trace artifacts and trace links used in different domains.	Portable Req 2
Portable RT 3	Define policies, standards, infrastructure, processes and tools for tracing distributed artifacts in distributed settings, enabling cross-boundary traceability of all forms.	Portable Req 1, 6, 7
Portable RT 4	Examine the likely forms of cross-boundary traceability required in the future.	Portable Req 6, 7
Portable RT 5	Provide a way to examine pre-established traceability and to assess its integration or reuse potential with or within other contexts of use.	Portable Req 4
Portable RT 6	Develop mechanisms to help extract, integrate and reuse traceability work products.	Portable Req 3, 4, 5, 6, 7, 8
Portable RT 7	Learn about traceability representations, policies and standards in other distributed industries (such as the food industry), and the regulatory standards that mandate it, to apply lessons to software and systems contexts.	Portable Req 1, 2
Portable RT 8	Re-conceptualise traceability as a service so that it can be procured and interchanged at will.	Portable Req 8

9.7 Positive Adoption Practices for Industry (Portable)

Portable IP 1   Practitioners actively engage in defining and using policies and standards that enable cross-boundary traceability of multiple forms.

Portable IP 2   Practitioners use a unified representation or language to describe both the intended traceability and the actual traceability on their projects.

Portable IP 3   Practitioners reuse and integrate the traceability from other projects, and from components of other projects and services, with ease.

Portable IP 4   Professional bodies agree upon ways to encourage and enforce the use of industry agreed upon standards, policies, representations and terminology for traceability.

10 Traceability Challenge 7: Traceability that Is Valued

Traceability is a strategic priority and valued by all; every stakeholder has a role to play and actively discharges his or her responsibilities.

10.1 Link to Vision (Valued)

In the vision scenario, all the stakeholders simply expect the traceability to be there in the engineer's project just like computation, electricity and oxygen. Traceability is a commodity that is built into organisations and projects since they have realised that they cannot be agile and competitive without it. Its value is undisputed and has long been institutionalised within the engineer's organisation and the wider industry, supported by top management and workers alike. Every action that the stakeholders take on the project preserves and adds to this valuable traceability asset. The engineer could not do her job without traceability and the flying solar car business of her organisation would not be viable in the longer-term without the value-added support provided by traceability.

10.2 Problems Addressed (Valued)

Traceability is often valued to the extent that organisations may invest in a tool; there is still somewhat of a misconception that tools will do the traceability job once configured. While current tools provide varying levels of support for traceability, they require organisations to define (at a minimum) a traceability process to be used effectively, and many organisations do not invest in this aspect of the tool procurement process sufficiently. Inadequate training in the ensuing traceability process compounds the issue. The required skills for doing a good job at traceability are unclear and so people may be allocated the job without sufficient preparation and training. Such people do not always see the personal reward from doing this job meticulously and there can be little motivation to do the task well if the benefits are perceived to be too few or too distant. This can lead to a lack of total stakeholder buy-in to establishing traceability. Traceability certifications do not exist, so are consequently not expected of people or of organisations, so what you get by way of traceability in practice can be a complete surprise. The granularity at which to trace also remains a value question concerning effort and payback, and getting this wrong can devalue any traceability that is established. To management, the competitive advantage of traceability may therefore end up not being evident. A typical concern that is a barrier to technology transfer is whether any investment in a traceability initiative, including training, is actually worth it; value is questioned, along with its value to whom.

10.3 Dream Process (Valued)

- *Traceability Strategy.* The inherent and added value of traceability will be discussed on day one of a project and everyone, henceforth, will work together to do a good job on it.
- *Traceability Creation and Maintenance.* Practitioners will love the intellectual challenge of creating and maintaining trace links. They will take real pride in

their job because they know that what they do is valued and respected by their peers who will use the resulting traces in the future.

• *Traceability Use.* Everyone will want traceability and expect it, as it is one of the most valued support dimensions of a project, making testing more exacting and helping functioning code to meet its stakeholder requirements.

10.4 Goals (Valued)

Valued G 1   Everyone, from upper management to workers, understands and buys into the value of traceability on a project.

Valued G 2   A return on investment profile for traceability is available to consult and a traceability value proposition is used in strategic project planning.

Valued G 3   Resources are provisioned to match the traceability need for a project, meaning that people are trained in traceability logistics and tools are grounded in traceability processes.

Valued G 4   Traceability use is exploited to add value to many project planning and management tasks.

10.5 Requirements (Valued)

10.5.1 Traceability Strategy (Valued)

Valued Req 1   To develop a value proposition for traceability on a project to help determine and sustain a suitable traceability strategy. [Valued G 2]

• *Status*: Some practitioners may be hard-pushed to articulate the actual value of traceability to them, or even to their projects and organisations, while some project managers still have not even heard of traceability. Traceability is obviously more valued in certain domains than in others at present, such as for safety-critical software systems, which impacts the degree of traceability planning and management undertaken in the various domains. While this should and will continue to be the case, as the value of traceability will differ widely between organisations dependent upon the business environment and domain of the company, there is scope to examine traceability value propositions in varying contexts. A recent follow-up survey of an industry pilot study showed that engineers found trace retrieval methods useful, so awareness of traceability value is emerging. However, there is currently no language as such for describing and discussing traceability value. When costs are cut on a project, traceability can be one of the first things to go, and this is somewhat indicative of how its actual value is construed, measured and managed at present.

• *Promise*: Value-based traceability is a growing area of interest in the traceability community and is leading the way in researching the concept of and measures for traceability value. Such research needs to find its way into strategic planning and management tools for traceability. Progress here will also depend upon advances with traceability challenge two.

Valued Req 2   To provide people with the necessary knowledge and skills that they need to undertake their traceability tasks successfully. Further, to provide the requisite money, time and technology resources for these people to fulfil these tasks. [Valued G 3]

- *Status*: People are often assigned to a traceability task in practice with a vague job description and little prior training. While there are also many experienced traceability practitioners, there is a lack of an established industry-wide apprenticing or a mentoring model to acquire or impart the necessary traceability skills to new personnel. Few educational or training programs exist to impart proficiency in how to plan for and manage traceability, how to create and maintain traces, or even how to educate as to its inherent and wider value.
- *Promise*: There are conferences and workshops that emphasise traceability topics. The reporting on industry case studies can demonstrate value, put new practitioners in contact with seasoned ones, and hence communicate both the value of and skills underlying traceability. The systematic gathering of good practices and benchmark examples will help to foster knowledge sharing further.

Valued Req 3   To define traceability roles and responsibilities on a project, both within and across organisations. [Valued G 3]

- *Status*: It is often unclear as to who is in charge of traceability in an organisation (e.g., is it the requirements engineers, software architects, developers, maintenance team, etc.?) In practice, the responsibilities for traceability tend to lie with one or a few people on a project; traceability is rarely a fully distributed responsibility.
- *Promise*: Visibility is important to accountability and more could be done to make the roles and responsibilities for traceability visible, such as via the creation of traceability development contracts. To accommodate complex settings, traceability tasks really need to be made part of the job description of all software and systems development roles such that some form of traceability is made an integral part of everyday work activities.

Valued Req 4   To make traceability assurance a fundamental part of project management and quality assurance practice, performing regular trace audits to monitor and measure value creation. [Valued G 3, G 4]

- *Status*: Traceability value is implied where it is required by standard process improvement initiatives, such as the Capability Maturity Model Integration (CMMI), or by various regulatory bodies. In such cases, traceability is fundamental to the process, valued as such and assessed. Where organisations have been appraised at certain maturity levels, some assurance of their traceability practices may be assumed.

- *Promise*: If traceability value propositions are defined and integrated into the software and systems development process more routinely, then they can be tracked and measured in the future.

10.5.2 Traceability Creation and Maintenance (Valued)

Valued Req 5   To define value propositions for traces as they are created and to update these value propositions for traces as they are maintained. [Valued G 2]

- *Status*: Researchers have not built a convincing case regarding the value of traceability creation and maintenance, especially to those engaged in the traceability process, let alone the value of the respective strategies for so doing, such as creating traces early or on-demand, and maintaining traces continuously or on demand. There is also little understanding of those decisions that impact value when creating and maintaining traces, such as the specific technique to use and the granularity.
- *Promise*: Measures, baselines and benchmark experiments for examining the value of traces over time are needed here.

Valued Req 6   To reward practitioners for doing a good job at traceability creation and maintenance. [Valued G 1]

- *Status*: What constitutes and defines a "good" job at traceability creation and maintenance is not really a matter of consensus. Few educational or training programs exist to impart proficiency in how to create and maintain traceability as part of regular development training activities, nor convey the standards to which to aspire. Without such baselines it is difficult to set expectations and for practitioners to be held accountable for their work.
- *Promise*: Well-defined job descriptions for traceability creators and maintainers, ones that account for the specifics of organisations, domains and development approaches, and ones that set guidelines for practice, will help to advance the parameters for traceability quality measures. Industry awards for excellence in traceability creation and maintenance may be an option to build up the reputation of practice.

10.5.3 Traceability Use (Valued)

Valued Req 7   To add value to wider project tasks through the use of traceability, to inform business decisions and to measure the resulting value. [Valued G 2, G 4]

- *Status*: Value-based traceability research is examining how traceability can support the global value estimation of a software product, release management, feature prioritisation, etc. Nevertheless, few educational and training programs currently exist to impart proficiency in how to use the results of traceability for development or business strategic advantage. Practitioners and customers in regulated domains are primarily the ones demanding traceability at present, though it is not always clear whether this is due to mandate or due to the perception of value.
- *Promise*: Research in how traceability can be put to wider end use in software and systems engineering, followed by education and training, will promote the value perception of traceability. The promise lies in software tools that use traceability more than today to provide sophisticated support to business stakeholders, as well as to the engineers. More case studies reporting on the risks and impact of not having readily accessible traceability on a project, in addition to positive value case studies, are needed.

10.6 Recommended Research (Valued)

The major research theme to achieve valued traceability is *to raise awareness of the value of traceability, to gain buy-in to education and training, and to get commitment to implementation.* Supporting research topics are listed below.

Research ID	Description	Req ID
Valued RT 1	Develop techniques, methods and tools to support and measure various traceability value propositions on a project.	Valued Req 1, 4, 5, 7
Valued RT 2	Define traceability roles and responsibilities within a traceability development contract, and provide support for instantiating and discharging these in different project and organisational settings.	Valued Req 2, 3, 6
Valued RT 3	Identify the core knowledge areas and associated skills for doing (and using) traceability, and create effective pedagogical materials (e.g., model examples) to integrate competency for traceability into software and systems engineering teaching and training.	Valued Req 2, 5, 7
Valued RT 4	Increase awareness of traceability value by developing software tools that use traces in more interesting and value-added ways than today for wider software and systems engineering and business tasks.	Valued Req 1, 4, 7
Valued RT 5	Gather experimental evidence within the Traceability Body of Knowledge (TBOK) on the role of traceability with respect to software and systems development success rates and longevity.	Valued Req 1, 7

10.7 Positive Adoption Practices for Industry (Valued)

Valued IP 1   Managers are aware of the value of traceability on their project and in their organisation, so they ensure that their employees are trained in the discipline and that they are compensated for doing a good job.

Valued IP 2   Practitioners actively seek training, and potentially certification, in traceability excellence.

Valued IP 3   Practitioners both want and demand traceability of their software and systems engineering work products and processes; customers of software, systems and services expect "traceability inside".

Valued IP 4   Universities and colleges integrate traceability into their software and systems engineering curricula, at all degree levels, and students choose these curricula for their future job prospects.

Valued IP 5   The Traceability Body of Knowledge (TBOK) is consulted to determine and use value propositions to guide traceability strategising and practice.

11 Traceability Challenge 8: Traceability that Is Ubiquitous

The Grand Challenge of Traceability – "Traceability is always there, without ever having to think about getting it there, as it is built into the engineering process; traceability has effectively disappeared without a trace."

11.1 Link to Vision (Ubiquitous)

There is no mention of traceability anywhere in the vision scenario as it is truly behind the scenes. The engineer does not establish traceability explicitly; traceability is established automatically via her actions and via the actions of others. Traceability of the requirements trade-offs and negotiations are automatically captured from the tooling environments that the engineer uses, along with the rationale. Traceability data is presented to the engineer in a ready-to-use and usable manner as a by-product of her engineering process and of using her tools, and is never explicitly sought. Traceability neither disrupts the engineer from her primary tasks nor does she spend a micro second thinking about it. Software components, systems and services are customised by the other engineers while not having to worry about the detailed specifics of the underlying technologies and traceability information.

11.2 Problems Addressed (Ubiquitous)

Traceability is perceived as, or actually is, a burden for practitioners as it is mostly manual and repetitive in nature. Establishing or using traceability often interrupts tasks that are considered more important when it comes to software and systems development. It also often requires engineers to use special-purpose tools and so disrupts their primary working practices. Establishing traceability manually is further open to human error and inconsistency, and its quality is only as good as the efforts of its weakest human link. Traceability should not be the goal of software and systems development, and it certainly should not force a break in an engineer's workflow, but it often ends up being construed that way. If traceability gets in the way, people simply stop doing it with the care and with the rigor that it demands to be successful; and, if traceability is not there when it is needed and expected, people stop using it. It can be a vicious cycle.

11.3 Dream Process (Ubiquitous)

- *Traceability Strategy.* An integrated development environment will be set up and configured to establish the traceability demanded of a project, in the confidence that the approach will be adapted as needed, allowing the people involved to focus on the more creative development work.
- *Traceability Creation and Maintenance.* Trace creation will be completely automated, to specified quality levels, with 100% recall and precision. Trace maintenance will either be completely automated or superseded by automated on-demand trace creation, dependent upon the cost proposition of either strategy.
- *Traceability Use.* Stakeholders will both use and come to depend upon traceability on an everyday basis, without even really knowing it.

11.4 Goals (Ubiquitous)

Ubiquitous G 1   Near zero (or acceptable) stakeholder effort is required to establish and make use of traceability, with no (or minimum) impact on their primary task.

Ubiquitous G 2   Traceability is de facto in software and systems development processes and their supporting integrated development environments.

Ubiquitous G 3   A virtuous cycle is sustained as traceability is established and used both painlessly and effectively.

11.5 Requirements (Ubiquitous)

While there are many dependencies between all the requirements of the seven previously discussed traceability challenges,[5] traceability challenge eight is unique in

---

[5] Expressing these requirements dependencies and determining priorities remain topics for future work (see Section 12).

that it really depends upon having made significant progress with satisfying the requirements of these previous seven challenges. In addition to the status and areas of promise for each requirement, the core dependencies with the previous challenges are also suggested in this section.

11.5.1 Traceability Strategy (Ubiquitous)

Ubiquitous Req 1   To automate routine traceability planning and management tasks. [Ubiquitous G 1]

- *Status*: Traceability has to be planned for on a project, and the implementation of this plan requires ongoing human monitoring and control. This can comprise setting up a traceability solution (i.e., a traceability information model, process and tooling) and ensuring both its use and fitness for use over time. The underlying components of this task are under examination as part of a generic traceability process model to inform as to those areas amenable to automation and to offer more practice guidelines.
- *Promise*: Progress with traceability challenge one (purposed), in the form of profiles and patterns for traceability, will assist with defining and setting up traceability on a project. Progress with traceability challenges three (configurable) and six (portable) will lead to the parameterisation, reuse and adaptation of traceability strategies, while progress with traceability challenge two (cost-effective) will reduce the cost of traceability start-up.
- *Dependencies*: Traceability that is purposed, cost-effective, configurable and portable.

Ubiquitous Req 2   To integrate traceability planning and management processes into the overarching software and systems development planning and management process. [Ubiquitous G 1, G 2]

- *Status*: Traceability is not always an integral part of general project planning and management, so it is often tackled in isolation as and when needed on projects, rather than built into the software and systems development life cycle. Two exceptions are model-driven development and formal development processes where the transformations are essential to the underlying development philosophy and provide for traceability.
- *Promise*: Progress with traceability challenges one (purposed) and seven (valued) will assist with getting traceability integrated into wider development processes, as tighter support for primary development tasks is demanded and provided.
- *Dependencies*: Traceability that is purposed and valued.

Ubiquitous Req 3   To determine where manual intervention is unavoidable in the traceability process, to keep the required human involvement to a minimum, and to provide for better process guidance and tool support when unavoidable. [Ubiquitous G 1, G 2, G 3]

- *Status*: While the ultimate goal may be for total automation of traceability, it is likely that there will always be some cases in which human intervention is required to assess the validity and value of traces, resulting in a more symbiotic system. Work on understanding the component activities of a generic traceability process model, and the potential human interaction points, is underway.
- *Promise*: Three key drivers for the complete automation of traceability are to reduce the cost of traceability, to increase the trust in the results and to allow for scale. Progress with traceability challenges two (cost-effective), four (trusted) and five (scalable) will help to shape the boundaries for what is viable in the way of traceability automation.
- *Dependencies*: Traceability that is cost-effective, trusted and scalable.

11.5.2 Traceability Creation and Maintenance (Ubiquitous)

Ubiquitous Req 4   To create and maintain traces automatically, as a by-product of working in integrated development environments. Where manual intervention is unavoidable, to make traceability creation and maintenance a single "click" process. [Ubiquitous G 1, G 2, G 3]

- *Status*: Traceability creation and maintenance is still mostly manual in practice, and it can become a full time job for some people in some projects. However, the automated recovery and capture of trace links is producing reasonable results in research settings and gaining some acceptance in industrial practice. There is also successful semi-automated maintenance of trace links in certain development contexts, such as in UML-based development, and research on the full automation of trace maintenance is gaining momentum. Leading requirements management and application life cycle management tools provide for some flexibility in defining the traceability that can be enabled through their use and for some automated capturing of the traces (e.g., support for real-time trace capture as a by-product of working in the JAZZ environment). UML-based tools that support model-driven development are also leading the way in this area.
- *Promise*: Automated techniques, methods and tools for traceability creation and maintenance will continue to improve. More variety in the base techniques (e.g., information retrieval based, rule based, event based, etc.), along with options to vote on the results from competing techniques, will lead to improved quality levels in the traces they obtain. Moreover, the ability to automatically recover traces faster than identifying the delta of what has changed would potentially eliminate the need for traceability maintenance altogether (i.e., traces would simply be created on-demand and never maintained). What is lost from having no human involvement and no record of the trace evolution would need to be studied

carefully, and the cost/benefit trade-off of trace creation versus trace maintenance also studied. However, the promise lies not just in performance improvements, but in closing the loop to ensure that the traces that are created and maintained are fit for purpose, account for the entire necessary artifact types and are trusted. This relies upon progress with traceability challenges one (purposed), four (trusted) and five (scalable).

- *Dependencies*: Traceability that is purposed, trusted and scalable.

11.5.3 Traceability Use (Ubiquitous)

Ubiquitous Req 5   To support end user tasks, without any distraction from the underlying traceability that is being retrieved and rendered visible to make this support possible. [Ubiquitous G 1, G 2, G 3]

- *Status*: Traceability is used in a number of wider software and systems engineering activities, such as testing, version control, configuration management and quality assurance. There are some traceability-enhanced tools for these areas that do not make the traceability evident and unwieldy. In general, end users are presented with unintuitive traceability matrices and hierarchical reports at present, to interpret and make use of the traceability to support many other tasks. Their use can be cumbersome and get in the way of the task at hand, so end users are often made very aware of the traceability that they are have to call upon.
- *Promise*: Improved support for end user tasks relies upon progress with traceability challenge one (purposed) and on novel approaches to address issues of scale and complexity in traceability end use, particularly through improved visualisations and task matching, so progress with traceability challenge five (scalable) too. Re-conceptualising traceability as a service for wider software and systems development tasks, integral to all the supporting processes and tools, could also provide for advances here. This relies upon progress with traceability challenges three (configurable) and six (portable).
- *Dependencies*: Traceability that is purposed, configurable, scalable and portable.

11.6 Recommended Research (Ubiquitous)

The major research theme to achieve ubiquitous traceability is *to provide automation such that traceability is encompassed within broader software and systems engineering processes, and is integral to all tool support.* Supporting research topics are listed below.

Research ID	Description	Req ID
Ubiquitous RT 1	Investigate novel ways to define the traceability strategy, such as in an executable way, so that the traceability solution simply follows from the specification of the traceability need, as per model-driven or formal development.	Ubiquitous Req 1, 2
Ubiquitous RT 2	Total automation of (or "one-click") traceability creation and trace maintenance, with quality and performance levels superior to manual efforts.	Ubiquitous Req 3, 4
Ubiquitous RT 3	Embed traceability into all the software and systems engineering techniques and methods for all of the tasks that it facilitates, and provide this traceability support seamlessly from within a total automated tooling solution that is underpinned by a sound traceability process.	Ubiquitous Req 3, 4, 5

11.7 Positive Adoption Practices for Industry (Ubiquitous)

Ubiquitous IP 1   Practitioners choose integrated development environments based upon the traceability-enabled software and systems engineering activities that they provide and enable. They have "traceability inside".

Ubiquitous IP 2   Practitioners configure the traceability parameters that they need on a project in an integrated development environment and then forget about it, as it is henceforth established and evolved as needed and behind the scenes.

Ubiquitous IP 3   Practitioners know that they are establishing and making use of traceability in their everyday tasks, but they do not have to do anything extra to achieve this. They further benefit from this traceability when developing and customising their own applications based upon the composition of building blocks and services.

Ubiquitous IP 4   Practitioners do not talk about the "traceability problem" because it has been solved.

12 Validation, Evolution and Intended Use

This chapter presents a snapshot of a community work in progress, now over five years into the process. The new and updated Grand Challenge of Traceability v1.0 has been cross-referenced to the draft Problem Statement and Grand Challenges (v0.1) document (Cleland-Huang et al., 2006) to maintain continuity. Figure 2 shows the traceability matrix between the two versions, as created by two of the

Traceability Challenges		Purposed	Cost-effective	Configurable	Trusted	Scalable	Portable	Valued	Ubiquitous
A: Traceability Knowledge	A-GC1	■		■			■		
B: Training & Certification	B-GC1							■	
	B-GC2								
	B-GC3							■	
C: Supporting Evolution	C-GC1		■						
	C-GC2				■				■
	C-GC3			■		■	■		
	C-GC4		■	■		■	■		
D: Link Semantics	D-GC1			■					
	D-GC2	■		■	■	■			
	D-GC3	■				■			
E: Scalability	E-GC1					■			
	E-GC2			■					■
	E-GC3			■	■	■			
F: Human Factors	F-GC1	■							
	F-GC2				■				
	F-GC3					■			
	F-GC4					■			
G: Cost Benefit Analysis	G-GC1	■	■						
	G-GC2								
	G-GC3			■			■		
H: Methods & Tools	H-GC1					■			
	H-GC2					■			
	H-GC3					■			■
I: Organizational Boundaries	I-GC1			■			■		
	I-GC2			■			■		
	I-GC3			■					
J: Process	J-GC1					■	■		
	J-GC2					■			
K: Compliance	K-GC1						■		
	K-GC2						■		
	K-GC3				■				
L: Measurement & Benchmarks	L-GC1		■						
	L-GC2					■			
	L-GC3					■			
	L-GC4				■				
M: Technology Transfer	M-GC1							■	■
	M-GC2	■						■	
	M-GC3	■		■				■	
	M-GC4								

Fig. 2 Example traceability matrix mapping the challenges of the draft Problem Statement and Grand Challenges (v0.1) document (Cleland-Huang et al., 2006) to those of The Grand Challenge of Traceability (v1.0)

contributing authors of this chapter. The intended use of the reformulated material, along with the process for gathering feedback from the wider traceability community, is outlined in this section.

12.1 Dissemination and Feedback Process

The core material from this chapter is made publicly available on the website of the Center of Excellence for Software Traceability (Hayes et al., 2007): *http://www. coest.org*. The CoEST website lists all eight traceability challenges and their major research themes. For each challenge, it summarises the underlying goals, requirements, areas of promise, research topics and positive adoption practices for industry.

The website has been set up as a community resource to disseminate traceability good practices, and to gain wider feedback to validate and evolve the work on the traceability challenges.

Feedback is currently being solicited on the individual research topics to gain community input on the likely impact of the research topic, the anticipated research difficulty and the effort required to accomplish the research. Given the internal traceability of the individual research topics to the requirements, goals and challenges within this document, the broader intention is to accumulate these data to ascertain the status of and progress with respect to the individual traceability challenges over time, and so, in turn, with the overarching grand challenge.

Feedback is also being sought from practitioners on the state of the industry practice. This is to assess whether the positive adoption practices are evident in any domains, organisations and projects, and to be in a position to track this status over time. References are also being sought to existing publications and ongoing research projects that address the various research topics. The intention here is to gain data to summarise the state of the art in a more exacting manner, to understand where traceability research efforts are and are not directed at present, and to assess the status of the overarching research theme for each traceability challenge over time.

Such data gathering is going to require a substantial and sustained effort by the traceability community to be both useful and successful. One proposal to ease this effort is to use the research topics and industry practices as a means to classify traceability-related submissions and publications at future conferences and workshops. This would help to track traceability research contributions and industrial reality going forwards. Equally, each new research contribution in the field could be more explicit in documenting the traceability challenges that it tackles.

An environment for traceability experimentation and benchmarking is currently in development under the auspices of the Tracy project (Cleland-Huang et al., 2011). This environment, called TraceLab, intends to provide the traceability community with experiments and datasets to begin to baseline and benchmark traceability techniques, methods and tools. The proposal is to launch traceability contests within TraceLab that serve to contribute progress towards the various research topics. This will provide an additional way to collect data on traceability research efforts with respect to the challenges going forwards.

12.2 Towards a Roadmap for Traceability Research

The material within this chapter forms the basis for a traceability research roadmap that is currently under preparation by the authors. The realisation of the grand challenge of ubiquitous traceability is dependent upon progress with each of the seven other challenges. These traceability challenges are, themselves, crosscutting concerns, so progress on certain research topics will therefore contribute to a number of the other challenges in various ways. The intent of the research roadmap is to highlight these research dependencies and, in conjunction with early feedback from the CoEST website, to delineate priorities for traceability research over the near-term, mid-term and longer-term.

13 Conclusions

The Grand Challenge of Traceability (v1.0) is a major update to a draft document developed by members of the traceability community in 2006 (Cleland-Huang et al., 2006). It reformulates the forty prior grand challenges as seven major traceability challenges and one overarching grand challenge for traceability. Associated with these challenges are seven major themes for traceability research, along with one more dominating and long-term theme.

The Grand Challenge of Traceability is to make traceability ubiquitous:

The Grand Challenge of Traceability – Traceability that is Ubiquitous. Traceability is always there, without ever having to think about getting it there, as it is built into the engineering process; traceability has effectively "disappeared without a trace."

Associated with achieving this grand challenge is the following major long-term research theme:

Long-term Research Theme – To provide automation such that traceability is encompassed within broader software and systems engineering processes, and is integral to all tool support.

To achieve such traceability ubiquity in software and systems engineering practice, seven underlying traceability challenges need to be tackled. Each of these challenges has a major research theme associated with it:

1. *Purposed.* Traceability is fit-for-purpose and supports stakeholder needs (i.e., traceability is requirements-driven).
   Major Research Theme – To define and instrument prototypical traceability profiles and patterns.
2. *Cost-effective.* The return from using traceability is adequate in relation to the outlay of establishing it.
   Major Research Theme – To develop cost-benefit models for analysing stakeholder requirements for traceability and associated solution options at a fine-grained level of detail.
3. *Configurable.* Traceability is established as specified, moment-to-moment, and accommodates changing stakeholder needs.
   Major Research Theme – To use dynamic, heterogeneous and semantically rich traceability information models (or similar specifications of the intended traceability) to guide the definition and provision of traceability.
4. *Trusted.* All stakeholders have full confidence in the traceability, as it is created and maintained in the face of inconsistency, omissions and change; all stakeholders can and do depend upon the traceability provided.

Major Research Theme – To perform systematic quality assessment and assurance of the traceability.

5. *Scalable.* Varying types of artifact can be traced, at variable levels of granularity and in quantity, as the traceability extends through-life and across organisational and business boundaries.

Major Research Theme – To provide for levels of abstraction and granularity in traceability techniques, methods and tools, facilitated by improved trace visualisations, to handle very large datasets and the longevity of these data.

6. *Portable.* Traceability is exchanged, merged and reused across projects, organisations, domains, product lines and supporting tools.

Major Research Theme – To agree upon universal policies, standards, and a unified representation or language for expressing traceability concepts.

7. *Valued.* Traceability is a strategic priority valued by all; every stakeholder has a role to play and actively discharges his or her responsibilities.

Major Research Theme – To raise awareness of the value of traceability, to gain buy-in to education and training, and to get commitment to implementation.

The eight traceability challenges were determined by exploring the assumptions of a community vision for traceability in 2035. The major research themes associated with each challenge were determined by expressing the goals and requirements that would be needed of a generic traceability process to address the challenge, by examining the state of the art and the state of the practice, and by considering areas of promise and necessary topics for research. In conducting this systematic analysis, one challenge and its associated research theme appeared to depend upon progress with all of the others, and so it was labelled as the grand challenge of traceability.

The intention of this new document is to provide a structured framework for directing, classifying and tracking past and future research efforts in the field of traceability.

Acknowledgements The authors would like to thank all the participants of the two initial traceability workshops in which the initial grand challenges for traceability were explored (at NASA's IV&V facility in the Summer of 2006, and in Lexington, Kentucky in the Spring of 2007). They would also like to thank NASA and the NSF for funding these original workshops (NASA grant number NNX06AD02G and NSF grant number 0647443).

References

Arkley, P., Riddle, S.: Overcoming the traceability benefit problem. In Proceedings of the 13th IEEE International Conference on Requirements Engineering, Paris, France, pp. 385–389, 29 Aug–2 Sep 2005.

Bianchi, A., Visaggio, G., Fasolino, A.R.: An exploratory case study of the maintenance effectiveness of traceability models. In Proceedings of the 8th International Workshop on Program Comprehension, Limerick, Ireland, pp. 149–158, 10–11 June 2000.

Cleland-Huang, J., Hayes J.H., Dekhtyar, A. (Eds.): Center of Excellence for Traceability: Problem Statements and Grand Challenges (v0.1). Center of Excellence for Traceability Technical Report COET-GCT-06-01-0.9, 10 Sep 2006.

Cleland-Huang, J., Czauderna, A., Dekhtyar, A., Gotel, O., Huffman Hayes, J., Keenan, E., Leach, G., Maletic, J., Poshyvanyk, D., Shin, Y., Zisman, A., Antoniol, G., Berenbach, B., Egyed, A., Maeder, P.: Grand challenges, benchmarks, and TraceLab: Developing infrastructure for the software traceability research community. In: Proceedings of the 6th International Workshop on Traceability in Emerging Forms of Software Engineering, Honolulu, Hawaii, USA, 23 May 2011.

CMMI Product Team: CMMI for Development, Version 1.3. Technical Report CMU/SEI-2010-TR-033 (ESC-TR-2010-033), Carnegie Mellon University Software Engineering Institute, Nov 2010.

Dahlstedt, A.G., Persson, A.: Requirements interdependencies: State of the art and future challenges. In: Aurum A., Wohlin, C. (Eds.), Engineering and Managing Software Requirements, Springer, Berlin, Heidelberg (2005).

Egyed, A., Grünbacher, P., Heindl, M., Biffl, S.: Value-based requirements traceability: Lessons learned. In: Proceedings of the 15th IEEE International Requirements Engineering Conference, New Delhi, India, pp. 115–118, 15–19 Oct 2007.

Gotel, O., Finkelstein, A.: An analysis of the requirements traceability problem. In: Proceedings of the 1st IEEE International Conference on Requirements Engineering, Colorado Springs, CO, USA, pp. 94–101, 18–22 Apr 1994.

Hayes, J.H., Dekhtyar, A., Cleland-Huang, J.: Charter (Business Plan) for the center of excellence for traceability. COET-CBP-07-02-1.0, 15 Feb 2007. http://www.traceabilitycenter.org/.

Lindvall, M., Sandahl, K.: Practical implications of traceability. Softw. Practice Exper. 26(10), 1161–1180 (Oct, 1996).

Pierce, R.: A requirements tracing tool. ACM SIGSOFT Software Engineering Notes. 3(5), 53–60 (Nov, 1978).

Ramesh, B., Jarke, M.: Towards reference models for requirements traceability. IEEE Trans. Softw. Eng. 27(1), 58–93 (Jan, 2001).

Radio Technical Commission for Aeronautics, Inc. (RTCA). DO-178B: Software considerations in airborne systems and equipment certification, Issued 12-1-92, Prepared by SC-167, Supersedes DO-178A, Errata Issued 3-26-99.

Spanoudakis, G., Zisman, A.: Software traceability: A roadmap. In: Chang, S.K. (ed.) Handbook of Software Engineering and Knowledge Engineering, Volume 3: Recent Advances, World Scientific Publishing Co., ISBN:981-256-273-7, Aug 2005.

U.S. Food and Drug Administration, General Principles of Software Validation; Final Guidance for Industry and FDA Staff, January 11, 2002, http://www.fda.gov/MedicalDevices/deviceregulationandguidance/guidancedocuments/ucm085281.htm.

von Knethen, A., Paech, B.: A survey on tracing approaches in practice and research, Fraunhofer IESE Research Report 095.01/E, Kaiserslautern, Germany, 2002, http://publica.fraunhofer.de/documents/N-9197.html. Accessed Jan 2010.

Winkler, S., von Pilgrim, J.: A survey of traceability in requirements engineering and model-driven development. Softw. Syst. Model. 9(4), 529–565 September 2010, Springer. (Published on line 22 Dec 2009).

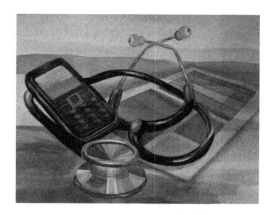

Appendices

The appendices draw together the resources for traceability that have been referred to throughout the book. Appendix A provides a copy of a traceability glossary that has been created by members of the traceability community. This glossary is included in an attempt to promote a greater consistency in the use of traceability terms and concepts, and we have attempted to remain faithful to this glossary where possible in the book. Appendices B and C provide the materials for the two case studies that have been used as exemplars in the various chapters. Appendix B provides a synopsis of the "iTrust Electronic Health Care System" and includes its associated resources. Appendix C does likewise for the "Mobile Phone Product Line Software System". Appendix D provides an overview of "The Center of Excellence for Software Traceability", and provides a link to its resources and membership opportunities. Appendix E lists the objectives of "TraceLab: A Tool for Supporting Traceability Research" and indicates how others can get involved.

J. Cleland-Huang et al. (eds.), *Software and Systems Traceability*,
DOI 10.1007/978-1-4471-2239-5, © Springer-Verlag London Limited 2012

Appendix

Appendix A: Glossary of Traceability Terms (v1.0)

Orlena Gotel, Jane Cleland-Huang, Andrea Zisman, Jane Huffman Hayes, Alex Dekhtyar, Patrick Mäder, Alexander Egyed, Paul Grünbacher, Giuliano Antoniol, and Jonathan Maletic

Answer set – A known set of *trace links* derived prior to a *tracing* experiment, usually prepared by system experts.

Artifact – Something that is created or shaped by humans, either directly or indirectly via automation. In software and systems engineering contexts, the term refers to the products of the engineering process. See *trace artifact*.

Artifact type – See *trace artifact type*.

Assisted traceability – See *semi-automated traceability*.

Assisted tracing – See *semi-automated tracing*.

Association – An as yet unspecified connection between a pair of *artifacts*. Where augmented with semantics providing directionality, the *association* becomes traversable and is referred to as a *trace link*.

Atomic trace – A *trace* (noun sense) comprising a single *source artifact*, a single *target artifact* and a single *trace link*.

Attribute – A characteristic or property inherent in or ascribed to something. In software and systems engineering contexts, the term refers to the properties of *artifacts* and their *trace links*. See *trace attribute*.

Automated traceability – The potential for *automated tracing*.

Automated tracing – When *traceability* is established via automated techniques, methods and tools. Currently, it is the decision as to among which *artifacts* to create and maintain *trace links* that is automated.

Backward traceability – The potential for *backward tracing*.

Backward tracing – In software and systems engineering contexts, the term is commonly used when the *tracing* follows antecedent steps in a developmental path, which is not necessarily a chronological path, such as backward from code through design to requirements. Note that the *trace links* themselves could be used in either a *primary* or *reverse trace link direction*, dependent upon the specification of the participating *traces*.

This glossary is reproduced material from Center of Excellence for Software Traceability Technical Report #CoEST-2011-001, with permission. An up to date version of this glossary is maintained on the CoEST website (*http://www.coest.org*). Please direct any glossary additions or updates to this website. To promote consistency in the use of terms within the *traceability community*, preferred terms are denoted by * and U.S. English spellings are used throughout.

Bidirectional trace link – A term used to refer to the fact that a *trace link* can be used in both a *primary trace link direction* and a *reverse trace link direction*.

Bidirectional traceability – The potential for *bidirectional tracing*.

Bidirectional tracing – When *tracing* can be undertaken in both a *forward* and *backward* direction.

Body of knowledge for traceability – See *Traceability Body of Knowledge (TBOK)*.

Candidate trace link – A potential, as yet unverified, *trace link*.

Center of Excellence for Software Traceability (CoEST) – A *traceability community* initiative. "Our goal is to bring together *traceability* researchers and experts in the field. We hope to encourage research collaborations, assemble a *body of knowledge for traceability*, and develop new technology to meet *tracing* needs." (Hayes et al., 2007.) See: *http://www.coest.org*.

Chained trace – A *trace* (noun sense) comprising multiple *atomic traces* strung in sequence, such that a *target artifact* for one *atomic trace* becomes the *source artifact* for the next *atomic trace*.

Continuous traceability maintenance – The update of impacted *trace links* immediately following changes to *traced artifacts*.

Creating traceability – See *traceability creation*.

Element – A fundamental constituent of a composite entity. In a *traceability* context, the term refers to the fundamental constituents of a *trace* (noun sense). See *trace element*.

Establishing traceability – Enacting those parts of the *traceability process* associated with *traceability creation* and *maintenance*, and in accordance with the *traceability strategy*.

Forward traceability – The potential for *forward tracing*.

Forward tracing – In software and systems engineering contexts, the term is commonly used when the *tracing* follows subsequent steps in a developmental path, which is not necessarily a chronological path, such as forward from requirements through design to code. Note that the *trace links* themselves could be used in either a *primary* or *reverse trace link direction*, dependent upon the specification of the participating *traces*.

Golden standard requirements traceability matrix – See *answer set*.

Grand Challenge of Traceability – A fundamental problem with *traceability* that members of the international research and industrial communities agree deserves attention in order to achieve a revolutionary advance in *traceability practice*. It is a problem with no point solution; its solution involves first understanding and tackling a myriad of underlying challenges, and so will demand the effort of multiple research groups over an extended time period.

Horizontal traceability – The potential for *horizontal tracing*.

Horizontal tracing – In software and systems engineering contexts, the term is commonly used when *tracing artifacts* at the same level of abstraction, such as: (i) *traces* between all the requirements created by "Mary", (ii) *traces* between requirements that are concerned with the performance of the system, or (iii) *traces* between versions of a particular requirement at different moments in time. *Horizontal tracing* may employ both *forward tracing* and *backward tracing*.

Just in time tracing (JITT) – See *reactive tracing*.

Link – See *trace link*.

Link base – See *link set*.

Link semantics – The purpose or meaning of the *trace link*. The *link semantics* are generally specified in the *trace link type*, which is a broader term that may also capture other details regarding the nature of the *trace link*, such as how the *trace link* was created.

Link set – The totality of the *trace links* on a project.

Link type – See *trace link type*.

Maintaining traceability – See *traceability maintenance*.

Manual traceability – The potential for *manual tracing*.

Manual tracing – When *traceability* is established by the activities of a human tracer. This includes *traceability creation* and *maintenance* using the drag and drop methods that are commonly found in current *requirements management tools*.

Obsolete trace link – A pre-existing, and previously verified, *trace link* that is no longer valid.

On-demand traceability maintenance – A dedicated and overall update of the *trace set* (in whole or in part), generally in response to some explicit trigger and in preparation for an upcoming *traceability use*.

Post-requirements (specification) traceability – The potential for *post-requirements (specification) tracing*.

Post-requirements (specification) tracing – In software and systems engineering contexts, the term is commonly used to refer to those *traces* derived from or grounded in the requirements, and hence the *traceability* explicates the requirements' deployment process. The *tracing* is, therefore, forward from requirements and back to requirements. *Post-requirements (specification) tracing* may employ *forward tracing*, *backward tracing*, *horizontal tracing* and *vertical tracing*.

Pre-requirements (specification) tracing – The potential for *pre-requirements (specification) tracing*.

Pre-requirements (specification) traceability – In software and systems engineering contexts, the term is commonly used to refer to those *traces* that show the derivation of the requirements from their original sources, and hence the *traceability* explicates the requirements' production process. The *tracing* is, therefore, forward to requirements and back from requirements. *Pre-requirements (specification) tracing* may employ *forward tracing*, *backward tracing*, *horizontal tracing* and *vertical tracing*.

Primary trace link direction – When a *trace link* is traversed from its specified *source artifact* to its specified *target artifact*, it is being used in the primary direction as specified. Where *link semantics* are provided, they provide for a way to "read" the traversal (e.g., A implements B).

Proactive tracing – Initiating *trace capture* without explicit response to a stimulus to do so (i.e., *traces* are created in the background). Compare with *reactive tracing*.

Prospective tracing – See *trace capture*.

Reactive tracing* – Responding to a stimulus to initiate *trace capture* (i.e., *traces* are created on demand). Compare with *proactive tracing*.

Ready-to-use traceability – Where previously established *trace links* are maintained as a project evolves, generally in compliance with a *traceability information model (TIM)*, so that the *traceability* on a project is always ready to be used according to the intentions for a project. This may combine *continuous* and *on-demand traceability maintenance* as appropriate.

Reference set – See *answer set*.

Requirements management – The activity concerned with the effective control of information related to stakeholder, system and software requirements and, in particular, the preservation of the integrity of that information for the life of the system and with respect to changes in the system and its environment. *Requirements management* depends upon *requirements traceability* as its enabling mechanism.

Requirements management tools – Tools that support *requirements management*.

Requirements traceability – "The ability to describe and follow the life of a requirement in both a forwards and backwards direction (i.e., from its origins, through its development and specification, to its subsequent deployment and use, and through periods of ongoing refinement and iteration in any of these phases)." (Gotel and Finkelstein, 1994.)

Requirements traceability matrix (RTM) – See *traceability matrix*.

Retrospective tracing – See *trace recovery*.

Reverse trace link direction – When a *trace link* is traversed from its specified *target artifact* to its specified *source artifact*, it is being used in the reverse direction to its specification. The *link semantics* may no longer be valid, so a change from active to passive voice (or vice-versa) is generally required (e.g., if A replaces B then B is replaced by A).

Semi-automated traceability* – The potential for *semi-automated tracing*.

Semi-automated tracing* – When *traceability* is established via a combination of automated techniques, methods, tools and human activities. For example, automated techniques may suggest *candidate trace links* or *suspect trace links* and then the human *tracer* may be prompted to verify them.

Software traceability – See *requirements traceability*, extending the definition to encompass and interrelate any uniquely identifiable software engineering *artifact* to any other.

Source artifact* – The *artifact* from which a *trace* originates.

Stakeholder requirements for traceability – *Stakeholder requirements for traceability* comprise two parts: (i) why end users (i.e., people, organizations, etc.) need *traceability*; and (ii) what *tracers* need in order to establish and use this *traceability*. The latter form part of the *system requirements for traceability*.

Suspect trace link – A pre-existing, and previously verified, *trace link* that may no longer be valid.

System requirements for traceability – What the *traceability solution* needs to do to fulfill the *stakeholder requirements for traceability*. Note that the agent (human or automated) that establishes the *traceability* is part of the *traceability solution*.

Systems traceability – See *requirements traceability*, extending the definition to encompass and interrelate any uniquely identifiable systems engineering *artifact* to a broad range of systems-level components, such as people, processes and hardware models.

Target artifact* – The *artifact* at the destination of a *trace*.

Trace (Noun) – A specified triplet of *elements* comprising: a *source artifact*, a *target artifact* and a *trace link* associating the two *artifacts*. Where more than two *artifacts* are associated by a *trace link*, such as the aggregation of two *artifacts* linked to a third *artifact*, the aggregated *artifacts* are treated as a single *trace artifact*. The term applies, more generally, to both *traces* that are *atomic* in nature (i.e., singular) or *chained* in some way (i.e., plural).

Trace (Verb) – The act of following a *trace link* from a *source artifact* to a *target artifact* (*primary trace link direction*) or vice-versa (*reverse trace link direction*). See *tracing*.

Trace acquisition – See *trace creation*.

Trace artifact* – A *traceable* unit of data (e.g., a single requirement, a cluster of requirements, a UML class, a UML class operation, a Java class or even a person). A *trace artifact* is one of the *trace elements* and is qualified as either a *source artifact* or as a *target artifact* when it participates in a *trace*. The size of the *traceable* unit of data defines the *granularity* of the related *trace*.

Trace artifact type* – A label that characterizes those *trace artifacts* that have the same or a similar structure (syntax) and/or purpose (semantics). For example, requirements, design and test cases may be distinct *artifact types*.

Trace asset – See *trace element*.

Trace attribute* – Additional information (i.e., meta-data) that characterizes properties of the *trace* or of its individual *trace elements*, such as a date and time stamp of the *trace's creation* or the *trace link type*.

Trace capture* – A particular approach to *trace creation* that implies the creation of *trace links* concurrently with the creation of the *artifacts* that they associate. These *trace links* may be created automatically or semi-automatically using tools.

Trace creation* – The activity of *creating* a single *trace*, associating two *artifacts* via a *trace link*. The *trace link* may be created manually, automatically using tools or semi-automatically using some combination of tool and manual input. The terms of *trace capture*, *trace recovery* and *trace retrieval* lend connotations as to when a *trace link* is created, along with the technique used to create the *trace link* in the case of *trace retrieval*.

Trace data – See *trace element*.

Trace element* – Used to refer to either one of the triplets comprising a *trace*: a *source artifact*, a *target artifact* or a *trace link*.

Trace generation – A particular approach to *trace creation* that implies that the *trace links* are created automatically or semi-automatically using tools.

Trace granularity – The level of detail at which a *trace* is recorded and performed. The granularity of a *trace* is defined by the granularity of the *source artifact* and the *target artifact*.

Trace life cycle – A conceptual model that describes the series of activities involved in the life of a single *trace*, from initial conception, through creation, maintenance and use, through to eventual retirement. This is the *traceability process* from the perspective of a single *trace* flowing through the *traceability process*.

Trace link* – A specified *association* between a pair of *artifacts*, one comprising the *source artifact* and one comprising the *target artifact*. The *trace link* is one of the *trace elements*. It may or may not be annotated to include information such as the *link type* and other semantic *attributes*. This definition of *trace link* implies that the *link* has a *primary trace link direction* for *tracing*. In practice, every *trace link* can be traversed in two directions (i.e., if A tests B then B is tested by A), so the *link* also has a *reverse trace link direction* for *tracing*. The *trace link* is effectively *bidirectional*. Where no concept of directionality is given or implied, it is referred to solely as an *association*.

Trace link type* – A label that characterizes those *trace links* that have the same or similar structure (syntax) and/or purpose (semantics). For example, "implements", "tests", "refines" and "replaces" may be distinct *trace link types*.

Trace maintenance – Those activities associated with updating a single pre-existing *trace* as changes are made to the *traced artifacts* and the *traceability* evolves, *creating* new *traces* where needed to keep the *traceability* relevant and up to date.

Trace precision – A commonly used metric in *automated tracing* that applies to represent the fraction of retrieved *trace links* that are relevant. It is computed as: Precision = (Relevant *Links* ∩ Retrieved *Links*) / Retrieved *Links*.

Trace quality – A measurable property of a single *trace* at a particular point in time on a project, such as a confidence score depicting its correctness.

Trace query – A term often used in the process of generating or vetting *trace links*, where one high level *element* is regarded as the *trace query* for searching into an *artifact* collection to find *trace links* (as distinguished from *traceability-related queries*).

Trace recall – A commonly used metric in *automated tracing* that applies to represent the fraction of relevant *trace links* that are retrieved. It is computed as: Recall = (Relevant *Links* ∩ Retrieved *Links*) / Relevant *Links*.

Trace record – Persistent information that registers the triplet of *trace elements* constituting a *trace* and is subject to version control. The *trace record* can also refer to the entire *trace set*.

Trace recovery* – A particular approach to *trace creation* that implies the creation of *trace links* after the *artifacts* that they associate have been generated and manipulated. These *trace links* may be created automatically or semi-automatically using tools. The term can be construed to infer that the *trace link* previously existed but now is lost.

Trace relation – All the *trace links* created between two sets of specified *trace artifact types*. The *trace relation* is the instantiation of the *trace relationship* and hence is a collection of *traces*. For example, the *trace relation* would be the actual *trace links* that associate the instances of requirements *artifacts* with the instances of test case *artifacts* on a project. The *trace relation* is commonly recorded within a *traceability matrix*.

Trace relationship – An abstract definition of a permissible *trace relation* on a project (i.e., *source artifact type, target artifact type* and *trace link types*), as typically expressed within a *traceability information model (TIM)*. Note that the *trace links* of the instances of the two *artifact types* may not necessarily have the same *trace link type*.

Trace retrieval – A particular approach to *trace creation* where information retrieval methods are used to dynamically create a *trace link*. This approach can be used for both *trace capture* and *trace recovery*.

Trace set – The totality of the *traces* on a project.

Trace sink artifact – See *target artifact.*

Trace source artifact – See *source artifact.*

Trace target artifact – See *target artifact.*

Trace use – Those activities associated with putting a single *trace* to use to support various software and systems engineering activities and tasks.

Traceability – The potential for *traces* to be established and used. *Traceability* (i.e., *trace* "ability") is thereby an *attribute* of an *artifact* or of a collection of *artifacts*. Where there is *traceability*, *tracing* can be undertaken and the specified *artifacts* should be *traceable*.

Traceability analyses – The analyses that can be undertaken following *traceability-related queries*.

Traceability benchmark – A standard measure or test against which approaches to various aspects of the *traceability process* can be evaluated and compared.

Traceability benchmark data – Datasets that contain two or more *artifact types* and validated *traceability matrices*, the latter serving as *answer sets* (i.e., reference sets), for evaluating experimental results.

Traceability Body of Knowledge (TBOK)* – A proposed resource for the *traceability community*, containing *traceability benchmarks*, good *traceability practices*, *traceability* experience reports, etc.

Traceability challenge – A significant problem with *traceability* that members of the international research and industrial communities agree deserves attention in order to achieve advances in *traceability practice*.

Traceability community – Those people who are *establishing* and *using traceability* in practice, or have done so in the past or intend to do so in the future. Also, those people who are active in *traceability* research or in one of its many interrelated areas.

Traceability configuration management – The process of identifying, defining, recording and reporting on *traces* as configuration items, also controlling both the release of *traces* for *traceability use* and the changes that occur during *traceability maintenance*. *Traceability configuration management* depends upon *traceability version control*.

Traceability creation – The general activity of associating two (or more) *artifacts*, by providing *trace links* between them, for *tracing* purposes. Note that this could be done manually, automatically or semi-automatically, and additional annotations can be provided as desired to characterize *attributes* of the *traces*.

Traceability decay – The gradual disintegration and break down of the *traceability* on a project. This tends to result following ongoing *traceability evolution*.

Traceability-enabled activities and tasks – Those software and systems engineering activities and tasks that *traceability* supports, such as verification and validation, impact analysis and change management.

Traceability-enabled tasks and activities – See *traceability-enabled activities and tasks*.

Traceability end use – See *traceability use*.

Traceability end user – The human or system engaged in *traceability use*.

Traceability entropy – The inevitable and steady deterioration of *traceability* as a result of *traceability decay*.

Traceability evolution – The gradual change of the *traceability* on a project. It generally refers to the tendency for pre-existing *traces* to become outdated and/or obsolete over time as changes are made to the *traced artifacts*, unless the *traceability* is maintained sufficiently. Ongoing deterioration of the *traceability* may lead to *traceability decay*.

Traceability graph – A representation of the *trace set*, with *trace artifacts* depicted as nodes and *trace links* depicted as edges.

Traceability history – A record of the *traceability evolution* and the associated *traceability maintenance* that has taken place on a project.

Traceability information – Any *traceability*-related data, such as *traceability information models*, *trace artifacts*, *trace links* and other *traceability work products*.

Traceability information model (TIM)* – A graph defining the permissible *trace artifact types,* the permissible *trace link types* and the permissible *trace relationships* on a project, in order to address the anticipated *traceability-related queries* and *traceability-enabled activities and tasks*. The *TIM* is an abstract expression of the intended *traceability* for a project. The *TIM* may also capture additional information such as: the cardinality of the *trace artifacts* associated through a *trace link*, the *primary trace link direction*, the purpose of the *trace link* (i.e., the *link semantics*), the location of the *trace artifacts*, the *tracer* responsible for *creating* and *maintaining* the *trace link*, etc. (See Mäder et al. (2009) for more detail.)

Traceability intent – See *traceability information model (TIM)*.

Traceability life cycle – A conceptual model that describes the series of activities associated with a full end-to-end *traceability process*.

Traceability link – A term often used in place of *trace link*. Arguably, while *traceability link* captures the enabling role of the *link* for *traceability* purposes, *trace link* emphasizes the fact that the *link* is a primary *element* of a *trace*.

Traceability link document – A document depicting *traces*, showing which pairs of *trace artifacts* are associated via *trace links*.

Traceability maintenance – Those activities associated with updating pre-existing *traces* as changes are made to the *traced artifacts* and the *traceability* evolves, *creating* new *traces* where needed to keep the *traceability* relevant and up to date.

Traceability management – Those activities associated with providing the control necessary to keep the *stakeholder* and *system requirements for traceability* and the *traceability solution* up to date during the life of a project. *Traceability management* is a fundamental part of *traceability strategy*.

Traceability matrix – A matrix recording the *traces* comprising a *trace relation*, showing which pairs of *trace artifacts* are associated via *trace links*.

Traceability meta-model – Defined constructs and rules related to the *trace artifact types* and *trace link types* for building *traceability information models (TIMs)*.

Traceability method – A prescription of how to perform a collection of *traceability practices*, integrating *traceability techniques* with guidance as to their application and sequencing.

Traceability metric – A measure for some property or aspect of the *traceability process*, either quantitative or qualitative, such as *trace recall* and *trace precision* for *trace recovery*.

Traceability model – See *traceability information model (TIM)*.

Traceability network – A *traceability graph* in which the directionality of the *trace links* is expressed (i.e., the *artifacts* are depicted as ordered pairs) and where the *trace links* are potentially weighted in some manner.

Traceability planning – Those activities associated with determining the *stakeholder* and *system requirements for traceability* and designing a suitable *traceability solution*. *Traceability planning* is a fundamental part of *traceability strategy*.

Traceability policy – Agreed principles and guidelines for *establishing* and *using traceability* in practice.

Traceability practices – Those actions and activities associated with *planning*, *managing*, *creating*, *maintaining* and *using traceability*.

Traceability process – An instance of a *traceability process model* defining the particular series of activities to be employed to establish *traceability* and render it usable for a particular project, along with a description of the responsibilities and resourcing required to undertake them, as well as their inputs and outputs. The *traceability process* defines how to undertake *traceability strategy*, *traceability creation*, *traceability maintenance* and *traceability use*.

Traceability process improvement – The activity of defining, analyzing and improving upon an existing *traceability process*.

Traceability process model – An abstract description of the series of activities that serve to establish *traceability* and render it usable, along with a description of the typical responsibilities and resourcing required to undertake them, as well as their inputs and outputs. Distinctive steps of the process comprise *traceability strategy*, *traceability creation*, *traceability maintenance* and *traceability use*.

Traceability product – See *traceability work products*.

Traceability quality – A measurable property of the overall *traceability* at a particular point in time on a project, such as a confidence score depicting its overall correctness, accuracy, precision, completeness, consistency, timeliness, usefulness, etc.

Traceability quality assessment – The activity of assessing the *traceability quality* on a project.

Traceability quality assurance – The activity of assuring that defined standards and processes for *traceability* are appropriate and applied on a project.

Traceability quality attribute – A measurable property of a single *trace link* or of a group of *trace links*, such as a confidence score depicting the likelihood that a recovered *candidate trace link* is correct or the usefulness of a particular *trace link* over time.

Traceability reference model – See *traceability information model (TIM)*.

Traceability-related queries – Those questions that a software or systems engineer may pose to which *traceability* can help to retrieve answers, such as the percentage of the specified requirements that are *traceable* to test cases and the existence of any requirements that are not *traced* through to design *artifacts*.

Traceability scheme – See *traceability information model (TIM)*.

Traceability solution[*] – The *traceability information model (TIM)* and *traceability process*, as defined, designed and implemented for a particular project situation, along with any associated *traceability tooling*. The *traceability solution* is determined as a core part of the *traceability strategy*.

Traceability stakeholders – Those roles (i.e., people or systems) that have something to gain or something to lose from either having or not having *traceability* on a project.

Traceability standard – Mandatory practices and other conventions employed and enforced to prescribe a disciplined and uniform approach to *traceability*, generally written down and formed by consensus.

Traceability strategy – Those decisions made in order to determine the *stakeholder* and *system requirements for traceability* and to design a suitable *traceability solution*, and for providing the control necessary to keep these requirements and solutions relevant and effective during the life of a project. *Traceability strategy* comprises *traceability planning* and *traceability management* activities.

Traceability system – See *traceability solution*.

Traceability technique – A prescription of how to perform a single *traceability practice*, such as *traceability creation*, along with a description of how to represent its *traceability work products*.

Traceability tool – Any instrument or device that serves to assist or automate any part of the *traceability process*.

Traceability use* – Those activities associated with putting *traces* to use to support various software and systems engineering activities and tasks, such as verification and validation, impact analysis and change management.

Traceability version control – *Tracking* changes to a particular *trace* over time. Each time a *trace* is changed in some way, a new version of the *trace* is effectively generated. This provides for an audit trail, and for parallel development and rollback possibilities.

Traceability work products* – Those *artifacts* produced as a result of *planning, managing, creating, maintaining* and *using traceability*, including the *trace set*.

Traceable – The potential for *artifacts* to be accessed and retrieved by following *trace links* (i.e., by undertaking *tracing*). *Traceable* (i.e., *trace* "able") is thereby an *attribute* of an *artifact* or of a collection of *artifacts*.

Traced – The *artifacts* that have been accessed by *tracing*, and so by having followed *trace links*.

TraceLab – A visual experimental workbench for designing and executing *traceability* experiments, providing *traceability* researchers with access to algorithms, datasets, experimental frameworks and benchmarking tools. *TraceLab* is a major component of the *Tracy project*.

Tracer – The agent engaged in the activity of *tracing*, where the agent can be a human or supporting tool.

Tracing – The activity of either *establishing* or *using traces*.

Tracing activity or task – A discrete and identifiable unit of work associated with the broader activity of *tracing*; an atomic activity of the *traceability process*.

Tracing benchmark – A clearly defined *tracing task*, with associated data sets and metrics that have been agreed upon by the *traceability community*, and which is used to evaluate different *traceability techniques* and *methods* comparatively.

Tracing contest – A clearly defined *tracing task* that has been identified by the *traceability community* as a critical *traceability practice* that warrants *traceability benchmarking*.

Tracing task or activity – See *tracing activity or task*.

Tracking – In software and systems engineering contexts, the term commonly applies to the act or process of following requirements and depends upon *requirements traceability*.

Tracy project – A National Science Foundation funded project designed to instrument the *traceability* research community, and to develop tools for facilitating the transfer of technology to industry and government organizations (Cleland-Huang et al., 2011).

True requirements traceability matrix – See *answer set*.

Using traceability – Enacting those parts of the *traceability process* associated with *traceability use*.

Value-based traceability – An approach to *traceability* that actively seeks to create, manage and measure either the monetary worth or utility worth of *traceability* on a project.

Vertical traceability – The potential for *vertical tracing*.

Vertical tracing – In software and systems engineering contexts, the term is commonly used when *tracing artifacts* at differing levels of abstraction so as to accommodate life cycle-wide or end-to-end *traceability*, such as from requirements to code. *Vertical tracing* may employ both *forward tracing* and *backward tracing*.

References

Cleland-Huang, J., Czauderna, A., Dekhtyar, A., Gotel, O., Huffman Hayes, J., Keenan, E., Leach, G., Maletic, J., Poshyvanyk, D., Shin, Y., Zisman, A., Antoniol, G., Berenbach, B., Egyed, A., Maeder, P.: Grand challenges, benchmarks, and TraceLab: Developing infrastructure for the software traceability research community. In: Proceedings of the 6th International Workshop on Traceability in Emerging Forms of Software Engineering, Honolulu, Hawaii, USA, 23 May 2011.

Gotel, O., Finkelstein, A.: An analysis of the requirements traceability problem. In: Proceedings of the 1st IEEE International Conference on Requirements Engineering, Colorado Springs, CO, USA, 18–22 Apr 1994, pp. 94–101.

Hayes, J.H., Dekhtyar, A., Cleland-Huang, J.: Charter (Business Plan) for the center of excellence for traceability. COET-CBP-07-02-1.0, 15 Feb 2007. (http://www.traceabilitycenter.org/).

Mäder, P., Gotel, O., Philippow, I.: Getting back to basics: Promoting the use of a traceability information model in practice. In: Proceedings of the 5th International Workshop on Traceability in Emerging Forms of Software Engineering, Vancouver, Canada, 18 May 2009.

Appendix B: iTrust Electronic Health Care System Case Study

Andrew Meneely, Ben Smith, and Laurie Williams

1 Introduction

Electronic health record (EHR) systems present a formidable "trustworthiness" challenge because people's health records, which are transmitted and protected by these systems, are just as valuable to a myriad of attackers as they are to health care practitioners. Major initiatives in EHR adoption and increased sharing of health information raise significant challenges for protecting the privacy of patients' health information.

The United States is pursuing the vision of the National Health Information Network (NHIN) in which the electronic health records of the American people are passed between sometimes-competing health care providers. The American Recovery and Reinvestment Act of 2009 (ARRA, 2009) provides $34 billion of incentives to health care providers to deploy a government-approved EHR. The ARRA will, by 2014, impose penalties on those who do not. As a result, the use of EHR systems is likely to proliferate in the US in the next four years.

Dr. Laurie Williams created iTrust in 2005 as a course project for undergraduates in North Carolina State University's Software Engineering course. iTrust is intended as a patient-centric application for maintaining an EHR. An ideal health care system combines medical information from multiple sources to provide a summary or detail view of the history of a particular patient in a way that is useful to the health care practitioner.

iTrust is not intended to fulfill the requirements set forth to be approved by the government, nor is it intended for use by practitioners in the field of medicine. The primary goal for the project is to provide software engineering students with a project with real-world relevance and enough depth and psychological complexity as to mimic industrial systems that students may encounter while working in the software industry. Additionally, iTrust provides an educational testbed for understanding the importance of security and privacy requirements. iTrust is particularly focused with maintaining the privacy standards set forth in the HIPAA Security and Privacy Rules (2002).

The notion that a software developer's role is often to maintain, test, and refine software rather than creating it "from scratch" is a unique learning objective for students at North Carolina State. For the past five years, each semester students in the undergraduate software engineering course enhance the project deemed to be the best from the prior semester. Refactoring of iTrust by graduate students often occurs during the summer. As such, students must learn the code base of more than 10,000 lines of Java Server Page code to make required enhancements.

This chapter highlights the key pieces of iTrust's project artifacts that pertain to traceability and describes the project in detail. The version of iTrust we are describing in this chapter is v10.0, which was released in the August 8th, 2010, and built from requirements specification v18. The source code for this project, as well as all the artifacts we describe in this chapter are available from iTrust's homepage.[1] The iTrust project consists of the following artifacts:

- Source code, including:

  o Production source code (Java, Java Server Pages)
  o Automated test code

- Testing documents, including:

  o Black box test plan
  o Acceptance test plan
  o Test data

- Requirements, including sections describing:

  o System Roles
  o Use cases
  o Non-functional requirements and constraints
  o Data field formats
  o Use case tracing from requirements to JSP pages

- Traceability Matrix

The rest of this chapter is organized as follows. Section 2 focuses on iTrust as a project and how the team develops and maintains it. Section 3 describes an overview of the iTrust functionality. Section 4 describes the architecture and organziation of the iTrust system. Section 5 describes the traceability provided by the project's maintainers, and Section 6 summarizes the chapter.

2 iTrust Project

iTrust is an active team project for undergraduate students in North Carolina State University's Software Engineering course. Dr. Laurie Williams conceived the project in the Fall of 2005 and the project has been released to undergraduate and graduate students at North Carolina State for the following five years (10 semesters).

---

[1] http://realsearchgroup.com/iTrust

Table 1 iTrust project size

Component	Number of files	LOC#
Production classes	226	14,570
Java server pages	135	12,942
Unit tests	244	11,936
HTTP tests	50	4,146

As a part of their homework assignments, students in the undergraduate Software Engineering course as well as the graduate Software Testing course are required to perform maintenance and feature additions to iTrust.

In between semesters, the project administrators (typically graduate students) perform a "housekeeping" procedure. The graduate students spend approximately one to two weeks on housekeeping, and the procedure entails one or more of the following:

- *Updating the automated test plan*, which consists of improving the coverage and accuracy of JUnit and system-level integration testing.
- *Fixing or clarifying the documentation of the iTrust code*, which consists of Javadoc that explains the functionality and use of each Java class.
- *Discussions on the future of the project*, including possible architectural design changes, new decisions on technologies to use for testing, and other high-level decisions that would be infeasible during a semester.
- *Minor features*, which often involve removing or adding functionality that students have complained about but not changed, or functionality that would be required to prepare the system for assignments in the upcoming semester.
- *Cosmetic changes*, primarily involving editing the style sheets and Java Server Pages to improve the user interface of the system.
- *Refactoring*, which has often been major, involving a complete redesign of the system, or sometimes minor, such as implementing and redesigning a component of the system to be more amenable to future changes and development.

Table 1 presents measurements on the source lines of code and number of Java classes or JSP files that make up the iTrust code base.

The iTrust requirements v18 contains 40 functional requirements, six non-functional requirements, and eight constraints. iTrust v11 was released for download from SourceForge on August 8th, 2010. Since students were the primary developers for iTrust, there has been no public feedback on the project, although the install base is rather large. Since this release date, iTrust v11 has been downloaded from SourceForge 394 times.

3 iTrust Functionality

We designed iTrust to be a patient-centric application for maintaining an electronic health record. An ideal health record combines medical information from multiple sources to provide a summary or detail view of the history of a particular patient in a way that is useful to the health care practitioner. iTrust is particularly focused with maintaining the privacy standards set forth in the HIPAA Security and Privacy Rules (2002). In addition to maintaining the patient's personal information and health history, iTrust maintains a comprehensive transaction log. The transaction log, which can be used for repudiation and to track the actual operational profile, contains 53 different high-level transaction types that include viewing patients' information, sending reminders, and adding a prescription. The patient can view a list of which health care professionals have viewed his or her medical information upon login. Also, iTrust has a focus on providing health care providers with dynamically determined information regarding a patient's chronic disease risk factors including diabetes and heart disease. Finally, iTrust allows a health care professional to view trend information about patients' causes of death. Often iTrust requirements are obtained from the US Department of Health and Human Services (HHS) use cases (2006–2009)[2]; those that are obtained from HHS reference the use cases. The remaining requirements are developed in a creative process by the teaching staff, with the intent of covering the software engineering curriculum.

3.1 System Roles

iTrust contains eight roles in its role-based access control system. The role of a user determines their viewing and editing capabilities.

- *Patient*: When an American infant is born or a foreigner requests medical care, each is assigned a medical identification number and password. Then, this person's electronic records are accessible via the iTrust Medical Records system.
- *Administrator*: The administrator assigns medical identification numbers and passwords to LHCPs. (Note: for simplicity of the project, an administrator is added by directly entering the administrator into the database by an administrator that has access to the database.)
- *Licensed Health Care Professional (LHCP)*: A licensed health care professional that is allowed by a particular patient to view all approved medical records. In general, a patient does not know this non-designated health care professional, such as an emergency room doctor, and the set of approved records may be smaller than that granted to a designated licensed health care professional.
- *Designated Licensed Health Care Professional (DLHCP)*: A licensed health care professional that is allowed by a particular patient to view all approved medical records. Any LHCP can be a DLHCP to some patients (with whom he/she has an established relationship) and an LHCP to others (whom he/she has never/rarely seen before).
- *Emergency Responder (ER)*: Police, Fire, Emergency Medical Technicians (EMTs), and other medically trained emergency responders who provide care while at, or in transport from, the site of an emergency (referred to as "on site care

---

[2] http://www.hhs.gov/healthit/usecases/

providers" by Department of Health and Human Services Emergency Responder Electronic Health Record Use Case (2006–2009)).

- *Unlicensed Authorized Personnel (UAP)*: A health care worker such as a medical secretary, laboratory technician, case manager, care coordinator, or other authorized clerical-type personnel. An unlicensed personnel can enter and edit demographic information, diagnosis, office visit notes and other medical information, and can view records.

- *Personal Representative*: A person legally authorized to make health care decisions on an individual's behalf or to act for a deceased individual. When a person logs into iTrust, if he or she is a personal representative, they view their own records or those of the person/people they are representing. (For example, a mother is a personal health representative for her children and could choose herself and any one of her children upon logging into iTrust.)

- *Public Health Agent*: A person legally authorized view and respond to aggregated reports of adverse events.

- *Software Tester*: An information technology worker who tests the iTrust Medical Records system. Of particular interest to the software tester is the operational profile information which informs him/her of the frequency of use of the features of the system.

3.2 Patient-Centered Functionality

One of the unique characteristics of iTrust is its patient-centered functionality where patients can log into the system to view their own records and perform a variety of tasks.

The primary way of tracking care for a given patient is through office visits. An office visit represents a specific consultation with an LHCP on a specific date in a specific location. Various standardized health care codes are linked to office visits, including diagnoses, immunizations, procedures, prescriptions, and general demographics such as height and weight. The LHCP logs the information for a given office visit, and the patient can view the records for of his or her previous office visits. Patients can also take a satisfaction survey on the LHCP, which is aggregated for other patients in search for an LHCP.

In addition to office visit tracking, patients have access to several forms of auditability. iTrust takes data provenance very seriously, so all access and changes to patient records are permanently logged. Patients are presented with an activity feed upon logging in to iTrust, and can configure email alerts when their records have been accessed or changed.

Lastly, iTrust focuses on providing informative feedback to both patients and LHCPs. Patients are shown potential risk factors on their record, such as for diabetes or heart disease. High risk patients who have not had a recent office visit are also alerted. LHCPs can also request biosurveillance to detect potential epidemics. The epidemic detection feature uses statistical modeling to determine an abnormal number of diagnoses for a given location. Additionally, LHCPs can view cause-of-death trends for a given location.

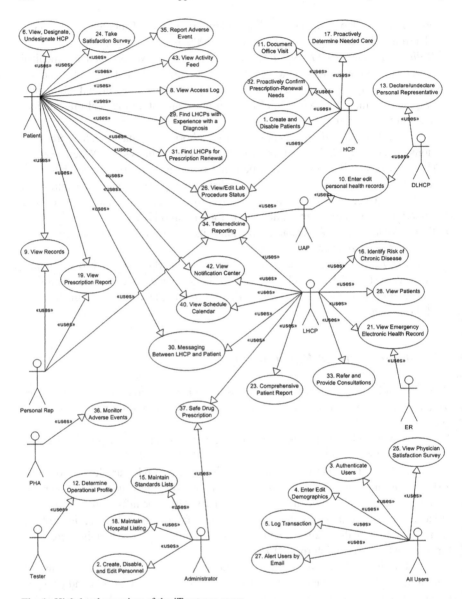

Fig. 1 High-level overview of the iTrust use cases

The requirements document in iTrust is a use-case based specification as shown in Fig. 1.

The requirements specification breaks down into the following sections:

- System Roles (described in Section 3.1)
- Use cases

- Non-functional requirements and constraints
- Data field formats

Each use case represents a small piece of functionality that students implemented in a two week iteration. The project administrators wrote the use cases in terms of the roles to imply the access controls surrounding the feature. Each use case has a precondition describing what conditions need to be met prior to accessing the feature (e.g. authentication). The main flow of the use case provides a high-level overview of the feature from the perspective of what the user does. The main flow of the use case references different sub-flows of the use case that provide added detail on the different events of the feature (e.g. the flow of events for when a patient is deceased). Lastly, each use case contains an alternative flow that describes the behavior of the feature outside of typical functionality (e.g. when the user enters wrong data). The requirements document also contains a reference from each sub-flow to the web page implementing that functionality. For an example of a use case, see the "Traceability in iTrust" section.

After the use cases, the rest of the document comprises of non-functional requirements and constraints. The non-functional requirements describe limitations that all features must adhere to. For example, all features must adhere to HIPAA standards. The constraints section covers the development process, such as the programming language and coding standards. iTrust was written in Java 1.5, and was designed to work with Tomcat v5.5.27 and MySQL 5.0.

The data field formats section covers all of the inputs to the iTrust system and how the field can be validated. For example, the data fields section defines which characters are allowed in a patient's name. Many data fields are defined according to common health care standards. iTrust uses the following standard medical codes:

- ICD9CM for diagnoses
- CPT for procedures
- NDC for drug prescriptions

The iTrust requirements document is stored in a wiki format online. Storing the document in a wiki allows the requirements to be edited in a central location by authorized project maintainers. Each revision of the requirements document is retained so that the entire history of the document is preserved. Using the "diff" feature of the wiki also provides students with the ability to view what has recently changed in the requirements document without having to find changes manually.

4 iTrust Architecture

The iTrust source code is designed around the Model-View-Controller design pattern (Gamma et al., 1994). The goal of this organization is to separate the logic associated with the user interface (i.e. the "view") from the logic of the persistent

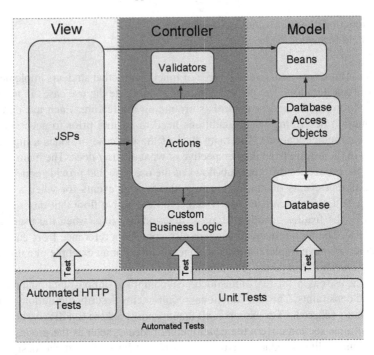

Fig. 2 Overview of the iTrust architecture

storage (i.e. the "model"), while organizing most of the complex business logic in one place (i.e. the "controller"). In iTrust, the view is implemented in JavaServer Pages (JSPs), the controller is implemented in Java, and the model is implemented in SQL and Java. An overview of the iTrust architecture can be found in Fig. 2.

4.1 Source Code Organization

View/JSPs. The primary purpose of the JSPs is to provide a web-based user interface. Each JSP contains Java code, HTML, and potentially some Javascript. Each JSP has a one-to-one mapping to an action class. The JSP instantiates the Action class.

   Controller. The overall purpose of the controller in iTrust is to provide a bridge between the user experience and the persistent storage of the database. Most of the complex logic behind validating data, and processing database query results are implemented in the controller.

   The primary classes in the controller are *action classes.* Representing specific functionality in iTrust, the purpose of an action class is to delegate responsibility to the appropriate classes. Action classes serve as thin mediators between the user interface and the database and business logic. The responsibilities of action classes include:

- Delegating any input validation to a Validator.
- Logging transactions for auditability
- Delegating any custom business logic, such as risk factor calculations
- Delegating database interaction
- Handling exceptions in a secure manner

In addition to action classes, the controller contains *validators*. The sole purpose of validators is to validate any input brought into the system. Since security is a high priority in iTrust, the validators operate on using both whitelist and blacklist techniques for checking input. Additionally, the validators are designed to aggregate all errors in input so that the user is given a full report of all the problems with the input.

Lastly, the controller contains several classes with *custom business logic*. The custom business logic classes are a set miscellaneous Java classes designed for specific use cases. For example, Use Case 14 (UC14) is a feature for determining if a patient is at risk for several risk factors. Many of the queries involved in UC14 are specific to certain risk factors (e.g. having a viral infections during childhood), so the UC14 requires its own business logic.

Model. The model involves the all of the logic related to persistent storage in iTrust. *Beans* are placeholders for data related to an iTrust entity (e.g. Patient). Beans have minimal functionality other than storing data. Other supporting classes load beans from database result sets, validate beans based on input, or any other custom logic needed.

The *relational database* is the sole storage mechanism for iTrust. The database stores all persistent information, including patient records, immunizations, office visits, and transaction logs. The database schema is defined by a set of custom scripts found in the source code tree. The database for iTrust does not contain any foreign keys, as the students who use iTrust do not usually have a background in relational databases and would not be able to debug foreign key constraint violations.

To interact with the database, iTrust employs *database access objects* (DAOs). DAOs are Java objects that interact with the iTrust relational database. Action classes will typically use DAOs to store and query the database. DAOs provide a set of common queries required by the action classes so that database query logic is contained to the DAO layer. Every DAO assumes that the incoming data is valid and any exception is handled by the Action classes. Connections to the DAOs are handled by the DAOFactory, which is a singleton class that utilizes a database connection pool for better performance and reliability. By convention, each database entity maps to a single Database Access Object and a single Bean.

4.2 Testing Artifacts

iTrust contains both automated and manual testing artifacts. All testing artifacts are constantly maintained throughout the development process.

Black Box Test Plan. As a part of their assignments in the graduate and undergraduate software engineering courses, students are required to maintain and develop manual, black box test cases for the functionality of iTrust. The black box test plan is intended to be executed by a software tester using a web browser with no background in the project or how it can be used. The black box test plan is intended to cover each use case and sub-flow, including the exceptional or alternative flow cases.

A subset of the black box test plan is the acceptance test plan. The acceptance test plan is a set of black box, manual test cases that can be executed with passing results by the iTrust customer. When a new use case is developed for a course assignment, the instructors of the software engineering course develop an acceptance test case that corresponds to the use case. The acceptance test plan acts as a tool for grading how well students performed the assignment as well as providing a clarification of certain details of the specification that may be lacking from the requirements specification. Students are then responsible for adding additional black box tests for each use case flow.

Automated Unit Tests. The goal of the unit tests is to test individual iTrust functionality at the Java class level. Students are expected to test both regular functionality and boundary cases for virtually every unit in the iTrust system. When students are assigned faults to fix, they are required to write an automated unit test to ensure that the fault remains fixed. As the iTrust code is being developed, students are required to maintain 80% line coverage of all Java classes. Between semesters, the automated unit test plan is improved and maintained such that 80% coverage is maintained on all relevant classes if the students had not done so. Students are encouraged, but not required to use a test-driven approach to writing unit tests. iTrust uses JUnit for our automated unit tests, and EclEmma for code coverage in an Eclipse environment.

iTrust also contains a number of supporting classes to aid the automated testing process. A test database is set up clean before each unit test on database functionality (i.e. DAO classes), and the test data is a standard data set across all student projects.

There are some packages and classes of the iTrust Java classes for which unit testing does not make sense or is not applicable. The following types of classes are excluded from the 80% coverage requirement:

- *The Server Package*, which contains Java classes that interface with the Apache Tomcat API to provide session time out functionality and other web-server specific features.
- *Test Utilities*, which provide developer-friendly methods for inserting the correct test data into the database.
- *Tag Classes*, which provide custom JSP tags for data fields such as the US state the patient lives in.

Automated HTTP Tests. The automated HTTP tests simulate a user using iTrust in an web browser. Using HTTPUnit,[3] the automated HTTP tests execute on a fully-deployed iTrust system by crafting HTTP requests and checking the responses.

---

[3] http://httpunit.sourceforge.net/

As opposed to the automated unit tests, the automated HTTP tests are intended for regression testing. Students are required to implement HTTP tests based on the acceptance test plan. Thus, each acceptance test case is represented by at least one HTTP test. Students also automate security penetration testing using HTTP tests.

5 Traceability in iTrust

The iTrust project administrators maintain multiple traceability matrices amongst the artifacts. The main three artifacts that are involved in tracing are:

- Black box test plan
- Requirements document
- System archetypes (e.g. JSPs, Actions, Validators, DAOs)

Figure 3 shows an overview of how the test plan, requirements, and system archetypes are traced to each other. The requirements document contains subsections for each use case that trace to the implementing JSP. Students can use this traceability analysis to find the place in the code that implements a given requirement for comprehending the code as well as improved testing. Additionally, the whole traceability matrix is available for students on the wiki for posterity.

To construct the tracing, a software engineering graduate student conducted a manual traceability analysis on iTrust. The procedure was as follows:

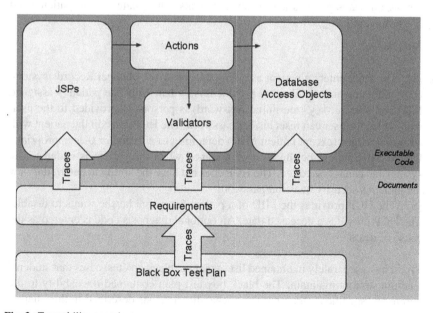

Fig. 3 Traceability overview

1. Examine the first (or next) use case sub-flow in the iTrust requirements document. Record the unique identifier of the use case. For example, UC1S3.
2. Manually perform the action described in the use case. Record the relative URL in the browser window along with the use case and sub-flow. For example /hcp-uap/addPatient.jsp. The observed URLs correspond to JSP files (e.g. addPatient.jsp) contained within the iTrust code base.
3. If the use case cannot be performed, or does not involve any JSPs, enter "No links" for the use case and sub-flow.
4. Inspect the JSP code for the recorded URL. If more than one JSP is involved in executing the described action, for instance when more than one URL is observed in the browser window while executing the action, record each JSP separately on its own line with a trace to the use case and sub-flow in question.
5. Record DAOs, Action classes and Validators separately with their own trace to the sub-flow and use case in question.
6. Return to Step 1.

For an extended example of this traceability analysis, consider iTrust Use Case 1 sub-flow 1, whose traceability results are presented in Table 2.

UC1. Create and disable patients use case

Preconditions:
The iTrust HCP has authenticated himself or herself in the iTrust Medical Records system.

Main Flow:
An HCP creates patients and disables patients. The create/disable patients and HCP transaction is logged.

Sub-flows:

- [S1] The HCP enters a patient as a new user of iTrust Medical Records system. Only the name and email are is provided. An email with The patient's assigned MID and a secret key (the initial password) is personally provided to the user, with which the user can reset his/her password. The HCP can edit the patient with all initial values (except patient MID) defaulting to null and/or 0 as appropriate. Patient MID should be the number assigned when the patient is added to the system and cannot be edited. The HCP does not have the ability to enter/edit/view the patient's security question/password.
- [S2] The HCP provides the MID of a patient for whom he/she wants to disable. The HCP provides a deceased date. An optional diagnosis code is entered as the cause of death.

iTrust has a separately maintained list of manual black box test cases that students and administrators maintain. The black box test plan contained traceability to the requirements specification before the traceability analysis described in this chapter was complete. Students created and developed black box tests for the project as a

Table 2 Traceability results
for Use Case 1 Sub-flow 1

Use Case Subflow	Source Code
UC1S1	/auth/hcp-uap/addPatient.jsp
UC1S1	AddPatientAction().addPatient()
UC1S1	PatientDAO.addEmptyPatient()
UC1S1	AuthDAO.addUser()
UC1S1	PatientDAO.editPatient()
UC1S1	TransactionDAO.logTransaction()
UC1S2	No link

part of their course requirements and included the use case and sub-flow their test case was based upon when creating the test.

This traceability analysis procedure was scoped for the purposes of this case study, and is limited in the following ways:

1. The traceability was conducted manually. We did not look at possible automated approaches since we conducted the analysis exclusively for this case study.
2. The matrix was not checked and confirmed by any other students. Another researcher or developer performing the analysis may arrive at different results.

From the 40 functional requirements in the iTrust requirements specification v18, we elicited 199 use case sub flows that could potentially trace to portions of the code. These 199 sub flows contained 609 separate links to 310 Java methods or JSP files. Of the 199 use case sub flows, 38 did not trace to any code within the iTrust project.

Although we traced the full list of 40 functional requirements, we excluded the set of six non-functional requirements in v18 of the iTrust requirements specification. The functional requirements typically traced to one or two components of each layer of the iTrust architecture. The traceability of the non-functional requirements in iTrust was less straightforward, however. Some of the non-functional requirements trace to every member of certain archetypes in iTrust (e.g. form validation), and others have no direct target (e.g. enabling multiple simultaneous users to be logged in).

6 Summary

iTrust is a patient-centered electronic health record web application used as an educational project in graduate and undergraduate software engineering courses at North Carolina State University. The software development project contains a use case-based requirements document, a black box test plan, automated tests, and source code. The project administrators maintain a manual traceability matrix from the black box test plan to the requirements document, and from the requirements document to the source code. iTrust is an open source software project, and all of its artifacts are publicly-available online.

References

American Recovery and Reinvestment Act of 2009, U.S.C. 111-5 (2009).

Gamma, E., Helm, R., Johnson, R., Vlissides, J.M.: Design Patterns: Elements of Reusable Object-Oriented Software, 1st ed. Reading, MA: Addison-Wesley Professional (1994).

Health Insurance Portability and Accountability Act Privacy Rule. http://www.hhs.gov/ocr/privacy/hipaa/administrative/privacyrule/index.html. Last accessed 4 December 2011 (2002, August)

US Department of Health and Human Services ER Use Case. http://www.hhs.gov/healthit/usecases/. Last accessed 4 December 2011 (2006–2009)

Appendix C: Mobile Phone Product Line Software System Case Study

Waraporn Jirapanthong and Andrea Zisman

1 Introduction

We present in the following a case study for a line of software systems with different mobile phones. The mobile phone product line case study has been developed based on study, analysis, and discussions of mobile phone domains and ideas in http://www.forum.nokia.com/main.html; www.omg.org/technology/documents/formal/xmi.htm. This case study has also been used to evaluate the work in Jirapanthong and Zisman (2009). The various types of documents composing the case study are presented in details in this Appendix. It is worth noting that, when necessary, other documents were created by authors of the chapters in the book, based on the described functionalities of the mobile phone product line case study, to extend the case study and accommodate the need to illustrate or evaluate the works described in those chapters.

The mobile phone product line case study was developed using a feature-based object-oriented methodology. More specifically, we have used an extension of the FORM (Kang et al., 1998) methodology to develop the mobile phone system. A feature-based approach supports domain analysis and design, while an object-oriented approach assists with the development of various product members. The documents in the case study include *feature, subsystem, process,* and *module models* representing product line information; and *use cases, class,* and *sequence diagrams* representing information about product members. Table 1 presents a summary of the documents used in the case study. As shown in the table, these documents represent information in different phases of product line engineering namely *domain*

Table 1 Summary of documents used in the case study

	Domain analysis	Domain design
Product line level	Feature model	Subsystem model
		Process model
		Module model
Product member level	Use cases	Class diagram
		Sequence diagram

analysis and *domain design*, and different levels of specialisations in product line engineering namely *product line* and *product member* levels.

The line of systems in the case study contains three product members (mobile phones), namely PM_1, PM_2, and PM_3, with common and variable characteristics. Product member PM_1 is supposed to be a trendy device and is targeted at young people; product member PM_2 is intended to offer an elegant design and is targeted at business people; while product member PM_3 is targeted at users who enjoy media applications including games and music. Table 2 presents a summary of the various functionalities of these three product members.

Table 2 List of functionalities of the product members

Functionality	PM_1	PM_2	PM_3
F1: Make and receive calls using GSM 900	X	X	X
F2: Make and receive calls using GSM 1800	X	X	X
F3: Make and receive calls using GSM 1900		X	X
F4: Hold and swap a call	X	X	X
F5: Receive and update voice mail	X	X	X
F6: Display and update time and date	X	X	X
F7: Set alarm and time	X	X	X
F8: Record, display, and manipulate call logs	X	X	X
F9: Play games	X	X	X
F10: Update calendar	X	X	X
F11: Add, delete, and update preferences	X	X	X
F12: Add, delete, and update contacts	X	X	X
F13: Include calculator	X	X	X
F14: Take photos using VGA camera	X		
F15: Take photos using VGA camera with 2x digital zoom		X	
F16: FM radio			X
F17: Email system using SMTP, POP3, or IMPA4	X	X	X
F18: Hand-free speaker	X		X
F19: Send and receive text messages	X	X	X
F20: Send and receive multimedia message	X	X	X
F21: Play Real One format tunes and video		X	
F22: Play and record MP3 format tunes			X
F23: Record and update video (clips)		X	
F24: Play 3GPP video format		X	X
F25: Play Real Video format		X	
F26: Access Internet using WAP 1.2.1	X		X
F27: Access Internet using WAP 2.0		X	
F28: Access Internet using WAP XHTML		X	X
F29: Connect via Bluetooth transfer data	X	X	X
F30: Connect via Infrared transfer data	X	X	
F31: Connect via USB			X
F32: Play MIDI formatted tunes	X	X	X
F33: Play AMR formatted tunes	X		X
F34: Play AAC formatted tunes			X
F35: Play MP3 formatted tunes			X
F36: Play WAV formatted tunes			X

Table 2 (continued)

Functionality	PM_1	PM_2	PM_3
F37: Play True Tones formatted tunes		X	
F38: Compose and play MIDI formatted ring tones		X	X
F39: Record and update voice messages	X	X	X
F40: Transfer data via SyncML	X		X
F41: Transfer data via SyncML and TCP/IP		X	
F42: Support CLDC Java technology	X	X	X
F43: Support MIPD Java technology	X	X	X
F44: Support wireless messaging API Java technology		X	X
F45: Support mobile media API Java technology		X	X

We assume that for each line of software system being developed, there is a single instance of feature and subsystem models, but there may have various instances of process and module models and various instances of documents in the product member level (i.e., use cases, class, and sequence diagrams). This assumption is not unrealistic since the product line level represents general characteristics of a group of product members being developed, while the product member level is concerned with the various products in the group. Moreover, for a certain product line,

Table 3 Number of document types and their main elements

Document type	Number of document types	Element type	Number of element types
Feature	1	Features	130
Subsystem model	1	Subsystems	5
Process models	6	Processes	48 (for all 6 process models)
Module models	2	Modules	40 (for all 2 module models)
Use cases	PM_1 = 4	Events	PM_1 = 36 (for all 4 use cases)
	PM_2 = 4		PM_2 = 36 (for all 4 use cases)
	PM_3 = 3		PM_3 = 28 (for all 3 use cases)
Class diagrams	PM_1 = 1	Classes	PM_1 = 23
	PM_2 = 1		PM_2 = 25
	PM_3 = 1		PM_3 = 27
		Attributes	PM_1 = 26
			PM_2 = 26
			PM_3 = 33
		Methods	PM_1 = 78
			PM_2 = 82
			PM_3 = 87
Sequence diagrams	PM_1 = 4	Messages	PM_1 = 114 (in total for all 4 seq. diagrams)
	PM_2 = 4		PM_2 = 128 (in total for all 4 seq. diagrams)
	PM_3 = 3		PM_3 = 95 (in total for all 3 seq. diagrams)

it is possible to have different behaviour for the subsystems represented by different process and module models, and for a certain product member, it is possible to have various ways of using and interacting with the product represented by different use cases, and sequence diagrams.

Table 3 shows a summary of the types and number of documents provided in the case study, and the size of the various documents with respect to the number of their main elements. For the documents representing information of product members (use cases, class, and sequence diagrams), we present the number of these documents and the number of the main elements in these documents for each product member in the case study.

In the following, we give a description of the various types of documents in the case study. The rest of the appendix is structured as follows. In Section 2 we present the product line level documents. In Section 3 we present the product member level documents. In Section 4 we show the feature model in XML format.

2 Product Line Level Documents

2.1 Feature Model

A feature model describes common and variable aspects (features) of a line of applications in a domain. In the FORM methodology (Kang et al., 1998), a feature model is composed of two parts: (a) a graphical hierarchy of features, and (b) a textual specification. Figure 1 presents the graphical representation of the feature model for the mobile phone case study. An example of the textual specification template proposed by the FORM methodology for *Text Messages* is presented in Fig. 2 . The other textual descriptions are shown in XML format in Section 3.

As shown in Fig. 1, a feature is represented by a name and can be (i) *mandatory*, when it must exist in the applications in the domain; (ii) *optional*, when it is not necessary to be present in the applications in the domain; or (iii) *alternative*, when it can be selected for an application from a set of features that are related to the same parent feature in the hierarchy. The features can be classified into four groups, namely: (a) *application capabilities*, signifying features that represent functional aspects of the applications (e.g. calling, connectivity, personal preference, and tool features); (b) *operating environments*, signifying features that represent attributes of the environment in which product members are used and operated (e.g. network, input and output methods, and operating system features); (c) *domain technologies*, signifying features that represent specific implementation and technological aspects of the applications in the domain (e.g. WAP and XHTML2 browser types; specific Java application support like mobile media and wireless messaging application programming interface; SMTP, POP3, and IMAP43 network protocol features); and (iv) *implementation techniques*, signifying features that represent more general implementation and technological aspects of the applications, but not specific for the domain (e.g. PGP and DES encryption methods; AMR, MIDI, and MP3 sound formats; and 3GPP and MPEG4 video format features).

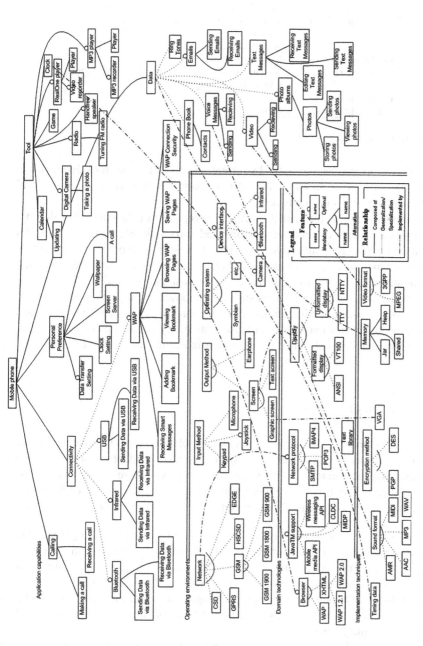

Fig. 1 Mobile phone case study feature model

Feature-name:	Text Messages
Description:	The phone can edit, send, and receive a short text message
Issues and decision:	Text message over mobile phone is a way of communication
Type:	Application capability
Commonality:	Mandatory
Composed-of:	Sending Text Messages, Receiving Text Messages, Editing Text Messages
Composition-rule:	-
Allocated-to-subs:	Messaging

Fig. 2 Textual template for feature model

Features can also be associated by different types of relationships. Examples of these relationships are (i) *composed_of*, (ii) *generalisation/specialization*, and (iii) *implemented_by* relationship types.

As shown in Fig. 2, the textual specification represents (i) a name, (ii) a description, (iii) issues and decisions representing trade-offs, rationale, or justifications for including the feature in an application, (iv) a type such as application capabilities, operating environments, domain technologies, and implementation technologies, (v) commonality indicating if a feature is mandatory, optional, and alternative, (vi) relationship with other features such as composed-of, implemented-by, generalisation/specialization, (vii) composition rule representing mutual dependency and mutual exclusion relationships to indicate consistency and completeness of a feature, if any, and (viii) allocated-to-subsystem indicating the name of a subsystem that contains the feature, if any.

2.2 Subsystem Model

A subsystem model is used at the product line level to represent the main functional groups of a system (internal subsystems), subsystems outside the scope of the system (external subsystems), and how the various subsystems relate to each other in terms of data and control flows. Figure 3 presents the subsystem model of the mobile phone case study composed of five subsystems, as described below.

(a) *Operating System*. This subsystem provides facilities for performing basic tasks such as control of the interaction with all devices, software, and data; support of the interaction between internal applications (e.g. games, multimedia, and PC connective), recognition of internal hardware (e.g. screen, keypad, and Bluetooth) and different types of input data (e.g. air signal, keystroke, screen touch, voice); response to different types of output data (e.g. air signal, screen-display, voice).

(b) *Messaging*. This subsystem manages the exchange and manipulation of messages. It supports two services: *short message service* (SMS) for textual messages, and *multimedia message service* (MMS) for multimedia messages.

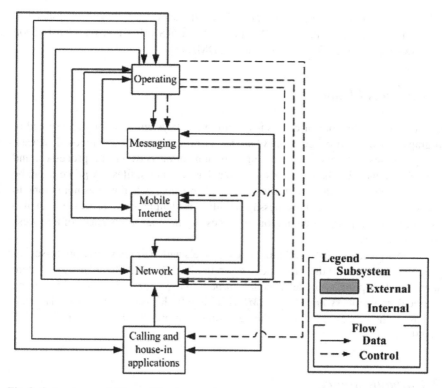

Fig. 3 Subsystem model for mobile phone system

The subsystem interacts with short message service centers (SMSC) or multi-media message service centers (MMSC) to receive and forward messages.

(c) *Mobile Internet.* This subsystem manages the interaction between wireless networks and tools such as plug-in applications (e.g. for online games and for mobile browser) and extra hardware (e.g. mobile game desk and 3G PCMCIA data card) for supporting mobile internet applications. The subsystem supports some special functionalities e.g. editing and browsing mobile web pages by using WML and XHTML techniques. The subsystem is also able to activate 24-hour connectivity and support mobile functions e.g. playing online games, managing personal online data, entertainment, and servicing online banking.

(d) *Network.* This subsystem supports the communication between different network protocols and the maintenance of network coverage for the mobile-phone devices. It manages a network protocol for transferring data over a mobile phone network e.g. GSM, GPRS, HSCSD, CSD and EDGE. It supports different network protocol architectures such as TCP, IPv4, IPv6, MSCHAP v2, IPSec, TCP/IP plug-in framework, WAP stack, and Multiple PDP context.

(e) *Calling and Applications.* This subsystem provides telephony management (e.g. creating and responding to phone calls), supports fundamental functions (e.g. a multimode API), and enables interworking of house-in applications (e.g. electronic games, clock and radio). In particular, the subsystem enables integration

of applications and the creation of advanced data services based on global network standards including GSM (Phase 2), GPRS (r4, Class B), CDMA2000
(1x), EDGE (ECSD, EGPRS), and WCDMA (r4).

2.3 Process Model

The dynamic behaviour of each subsystem in a subsystem model is represented in
a graphical diagram called *process model*. A process model is composed of various processes, messages representing communication between the processes, and
shared data used by the processes (e.g., databases, reports, files). A process can be
resident, when it belongs to the subsystem, or *transient*, when it does not belong to
the subsystem, but exchanges messages with a resident process. Processes can also
be *single* or *multiple*, depending on the necessary number of instances of a process
to perform a task.

Table 4 presents a list of all the process models and their respective processes for
the five subsystems in the case study shown in Fig. 3. For the Messaging Subsystem
there are two process models, namely *process model for SMS* (Short Messaging
Service) and *process model for MMS* (Multimedia Messaging Service). The diagrams of the process models in the case study are presented in Figs. 4, 5, 6, 7, 8
and 9.

2.4 Module Model

Each process in a process model is further refined in a *module model*. A module
model represents a hierarchical structure of the various modules composing a process and their interactions. The modules are classified into four groups related to
the different groups of features, namely: (i) *service modules*, which support the
functionality of the system and correspond to application capability features; (ii)
environment hiding modules, which represent the running environment of the system and correspond to the operating environment features; (iii) *technique hiding
modules*, which represent the technology domain aspects of the system and correspond to the domain technologies features; and (iv) *utility modules*, which represent
general purpose aspects of the system and correspond to implementation techniques
features.

We provide two module models in the case study, namely (a) *module model for
SMS* for process model for SMS (messaging subsystem), and (b) *module model for
mobile internet* for process model for internet subsystem. Figure 10 shows the module model for SMS. Table 5 presents a list of all the modules in this model. The
module model for SMS contains 18 modules which are classified as 3 *service* modules, 1 *environment handling* module, 10 *technique hiding* modules, and 4 *utility*
modules. Figure 11 shows the module model for mobile internet. Table 6 presents
a list of all the modules in this model. The module model for mobile internet contains 22 modules which are classified as 4 *service* modules, 2 *environment handling*
modules, 13 *technique hiding* modules, and 3 *utility* modules.

Table 4 Processes in each process model

Process model	Process name
Process model for operating subsystem	• Recall reception process • Establish the connection process • Control functions process • Display and interact process • Edit information process • Messaging service control process • Making call control process • Maintain logging process • Invoke added-in application process • Detect added-in hardware/software process • IRQ (Interrupt ReQuest) process • IPC (Inter Process Communication) process
Process model for SMS (Messaging subsystem)	• Short messaging control process • Check signal process • Edit process • Short Messaging Service (SMS) control process • Short Messaging Service Center (SMSC) process • Notification process • Update remotely process
Process model for MMS (Messaging subsystem)	• Multimedia messaging control process • Check signal process • Edit process • Multimedia Messaging Service (MMS) control process • Multimedia Messaging Service Center (MMSC) process • Notification process • Update remotely process
Process model for mobile internet subsystem	• Trigger process • Download software process • Launch application process • Restore data process • Maintain reception process
Process model for network subsystem	• Control process • Establish high-range signal process • Check authentication process • Valid equipment process • Find signal process • Forward signals process • Register subscriber process (Roaming) • Handoff process • Establish low-range signal process
Process model for calling subsystem	• Calling control process • Compose a call process • Keep logging process • Check a signal/ reception process • Trigger a receiving call process • Delivery a call process • Forwarding a call to voice mail process • Accepting a call process

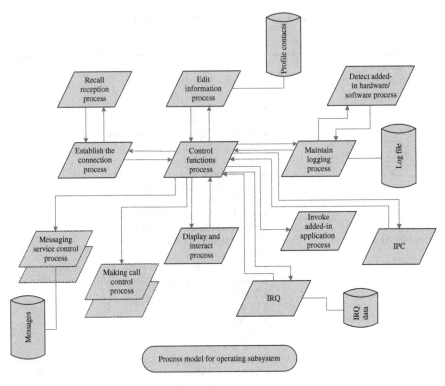

Fig. 4 Process model for operating subsystem

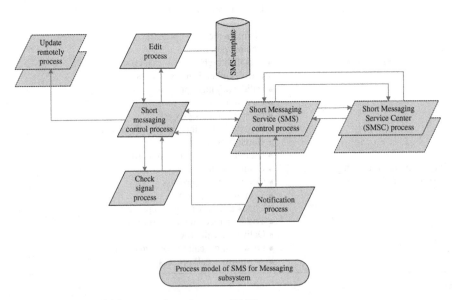

Fig. 5 Process model for messaging subsystem (SMS)

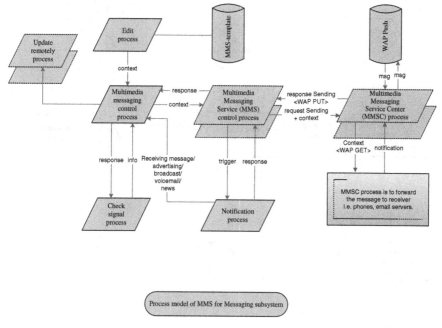

Fig. 6 Process model for messaging subsystem (MMS)

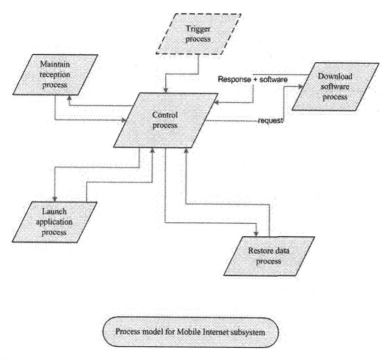

Fig. 7 Process model for mobile internet subsystem

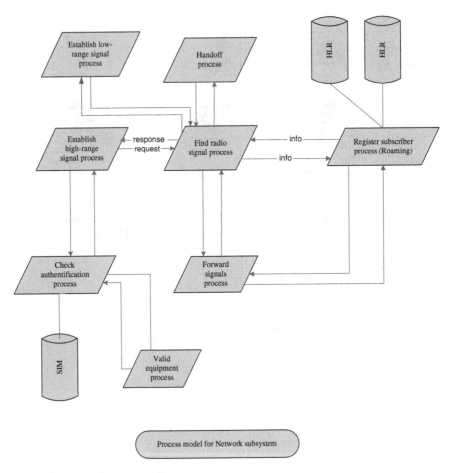

Fig. 8 Process model for network subsystem

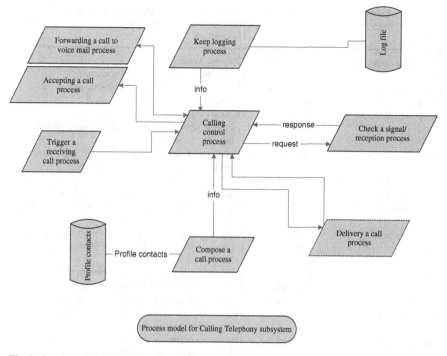

Fig. 9 Process model for calling subsystem

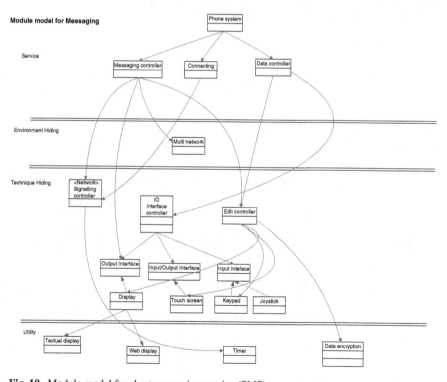

Fig. 10 Module model for short messaging service (SMS)

Table 5 List of modules in short messaging service SMS module model

Module	Type	Description
Messaging controller	Pre-coded	Controls messages
Connecting	Pre-coded	Establishes a network communication
Data controller	Pre-coded	Controls internal data of mobile-phone handset
Multi-network	Pre-coded	Responds to multi-networks
Signaling controller	Template	Provides algorithms for maintaining the mobile-phone reception and supporting different mobile-phone networks
IO Interface controller	Pre-coded	Provides software interfaces for input and output devices of a mobile-phone handset
Edit controller	Pre-coded	Manages editors
Output Interface	Skeleton	Manages output devices of a mobile-phone handset
Input/Output Interface	Skeleton	Manages input and output devices of a mobile-phone handset
Input Interface	Skeleton	Manages input devices of a mobile-phone handset
Display	Pre-coded	Displays data to output devices of a mobile-phone handset
Touch screen	Pre-coded	Manages touch screen of a mobile-phone handset
Keypad	Pre-coded	Manages a keypad of a mobile-phone handset
Joystick	Pre-coded	Manages a joystick of a mobile-phone handset
Textual display	Pre-coded	Manages a textual display of a mobile-phone handset to support displaying text
Web display	Pre-coded	Manages a graphical display of a mobile-phone handset to support displaying web pages
Timer	Pre-coded	Sets and displays the time
Data encryption	Pre-coded	Encrypts and decrypts data

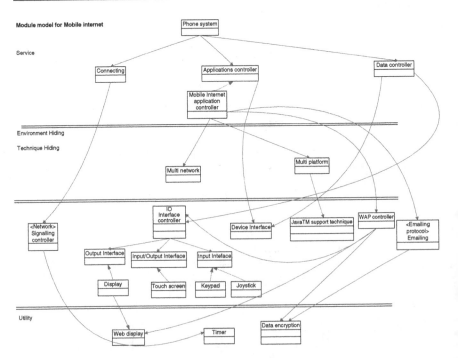

Fig. 11 Module model for mobile internet process model

Table 6   List of modules in mobile internet process model

Module	Type	Description
Application controller	Pre-coded	Controls a running (local) application
Connecting	Pre-coded	Establishes a network communication
Data controller	Pre-coded	Controls internal data of mobile-phone handset
Mobile-phone Internet application controller	Pre-coded	Controls a running Internet application
Multi-network	Pre-coded	Responds to multi-networks
Multi-platform	Pre-coded	Responds to multi-platform applications
Signaling controller	Template	Provides algorithms for maintaining the mobile-phone reception and supporting different mobile-phone networks
IO Interface controller	Pre-coded	Provides software interfaces for input and output devices of a mobile-phone handset
WAP controller	Pre-coded	Controls WAP browsing
Emailing	Template	Provides algorithms for composing emails and supporting different emailing protocols
JavaTM support technique	Template	Manages Java-based plug-ins
Device Interface	Skeleton	Manages interfaces for different devices of mobile-phone handsets e.g. game desk, PDA, computers
Output Interface	Skeleton	Manages output devices of a mobile-phone handset
Input/Output Interface	Skeleton	Manages input and output devices of a mobile-phone handset
Input Interface	Skeleton	Manages input devices of a mobile-phone handset
Display	Pre-coded	Displays data to output devices of a mobile-phone handset
Touch screen	Pre-coded	Manages a touch screen of a mobile-phone handset
Keypad	Pre-coded	Manages a keypad of a mobile-phone handset
Joystick	Pre-coded	Manages a joystick of a mobile-phone handset
Web display	Pre-coded	Manages a graphical display of a mobile-phone handset to support displaying web pages
Timer	Pre-coded	Sets and displays the time
Data encryption	Pre-coded	Encrypts and decrypts data

3 Product Member Level Documents

The three product members in the case study (PM_1, PM_2, and PM_3) are designed and documented in terms of use cases and UML class and sequence diagrams. Use cases are used to represent the functional requirements of the products. One product member can have several use cases. The use cases are specified in natural language following a template that is a variant of the one proposed in Cockburn (1997). The design aspects of the product members are represented as class and sequence diagrams. Each product member has one class diagram, but can have several sequence diagrams. We present below the documents for this case study.

3.1 Product Member PM_1

Use Cases: The four use cases for product member PM_1 are: UC1: Making a call, UC2: Taking a photo, UC3: Sending emails, and UC4: Transferring data. These use cases are described below.

Use Case UC1: Making a call

Status: Common
Region: EU, Africa, Asia Pacific

CHARACTERISTIC INFORMATION
Description: The phone is able to make a call. The user can select a calling phone number from a list of phone numbers, which are restored in the data collection, or enter the number via the keypad. After the user confirms the call, the phone establishes the line connection to create the call. If properly done, the phone dials for a response from the receiver. Otherwise, the phone informs the user of a problem on the connection. In the case that the destination number is engaged, or it is not able to establish a signal, the phone responds with a voice message.
Level: Primary task
Preconditions: The user has selected the function for making a call from the main menu.
Postconditions: The user has finished a call. The phone is ready for next actions.
Primary Actor: The user
Secondary Actors: -

FLOW OF EVENTS
Trigger:

1. The system is ready to make a call.
2. The user selects a phone number from the list of contacts or enters a phone number via keypad.
3. The user confirms making a call.
4. The system establishes the line connection.
5. If the connection is properly set, the phone dials the number to the destination. Otherwise, the phone informs the user about existing problems.
6. If the destination number is engaged or not able to be reached, the phone informs the user.
7. The user confirms by hanging up the call.
8. The phone disconnects.
9. The phone shows the attempt to make a call to the user.
10. The phone keeps a log file of calls made in the data storage.

EXCEPTIONAL EVENTS
None identified at present.

RELATED INFORMATION
Superordinate Use Case: None
Subordinate Use Cases: None

Use Case UC2: Taking a photo

Status: Common
Region: EU, Africa, Asia Pacific

CHARACTERISTIC INFORMATION
Description: The phone is integrated with a digital camera. It enables a user to take and restore pictures from the phone. The photo file is in JPG format. The photo can be taken as one of three optional types: general, night, and portrait. Each of these types are of different size. The pictures stored in the phone can be viewed and deleted afterwards.
Level: Primary task
Preconditions: The user has selected a function for taking a photo from the main menu.
Postconditions: The phone has taken a photo and kept it as a JPG-formatted file in its temporary memory storage in order to be restored in the data collection later on. The phone is ready for capturing future shots.
Primary Actor: The user
Secondary Actors: -

FLOW OF EVENTS
Trigger:

1. The system shows a list of photo types, i.e. general, night, and portrait.
2. The user selects one of the photo types.
3. The system shows the scenario on the screen.
4. The user clicks the button on the phone to capture a snapshot.
5. The system displays the shot that has just been taken.
6. The system pops up a request for restoring the snapshot as a photo in the phone.
7. If the user wants to keep the snapshot, the system restores the photo as a JPG file in the data collection.
8. The system shows the scenario on the screen for other snapshots.

EXCEPTIONAL EVENTS
None identified at present.

RELATED INFORMATION
Superordinate Use Case: None
Subordinate Use Cases: None

Use Case UC3: Sending emails

Status: Common
Region: EU, Africa, Asia Pacific

CHARACTERISTIC INFORMATION
Description: The phone is able to send emails with attachment using different network protocols such as SMTP, POP3, IMAP4. The user can specify the receiver's email addresses by selecting them from a contact list, which are stored in the data collection of the phone, or entered via keypad. The phone can send emails to multiple receivers. The user can attach different file types to the emails including images and photos. The phone keeps a log file of emails sent in the data storage. The user can view and delete the log file later on.
Level: Primary task
Preconditions: The user has selected a function fore sending emails from the main menu.
Postconditions: The phone sends the email to specified receivers and shows a confirmation to the user.
Primary Actor: The user   Secondary Actors: -

FLOW OF EVENTS
Trigger:

1. The system shows an editor composed of a text box for specifying the email addresses of the receivers and a blank note for writing a message.
2. The user inserts a receiver's email address by selecting it from a contact list stored in the data collection of the phone, or entering it via keypad. Note that the user can send the email to multiple receivers by separating the email addresses with ';'.
3. The user can type the message.
4. The user may attach files or notes (.txt), photos (.jpg), and images (.jpg) to the email that are available in the phone. (Note that the event of 2, 3, and 4 are not sequential processes.)
5. The user confirms by sending the email.
6. The phone establishes the connection for sending emails.

7. If the connection is properly set, the phone sends the email via network protocols. Otherwise, the phone informs the user about any problems.
8. After the email is sent, the phone disconnects.
9. The phone shows that an email has been sent and keeps this information in a log file of the phone.

EXCEPTIONAL EVENTS
None identified at present.

RELATED INFORMATION
Superordinate Use Case: None   Subordinate Use Case: None.

Use Case UC4: Transferring data

Status: Common
Region: EU, Africa, Asia Pacific

CHARACTERISTIC INFORMATION
Description: The phone is able to transfer data that are stored in the data collection of the phone via communication ports such as Bluetooth and infrared to another device attached with the same communication port. For example, the user can transfer photos taken by an integrated camera to a computer being attached with a Bluetooth device. Data can be any sort of files or notes (.txt), photos (.jpg), and images (.jpg). The phone can transfer one data item at a time.
Level: Primary task
Preconditions: The user has already selected a function for transferring data.
Postconditions: The system displays the status of data transferred.
Primary Actor: The user
Secondary Actors: -

FLOW OF EVENTS
Trigger:

1. The user selects a data item to be transferred from the data collection.
2. The system shows a list of communication ports for transferring the data item. For PM_1, there are two ports Bluetooth and infrared.
3. The user selects a communication port.
4. The system searches a destination port from a device that is closest to the phone for transferring the data item.

5. If the destination port is found, the system establishes the communication channel between the phone and the device via the communication port. Otherwise, the phone notifies the user about the problem.
6. The system transfers the data item.
7. While transferring, the phone displays the status of transferring the data item on the screen.
8. After completed, the phone disconnects.
9. The phone shows the status of data item transferred.

EXCEPTIONAL EVENTS
None identified at present.

RELATED INFORMATION
Superordinate Use Case: None
Subordinate Use Cases: None

Class Diagram

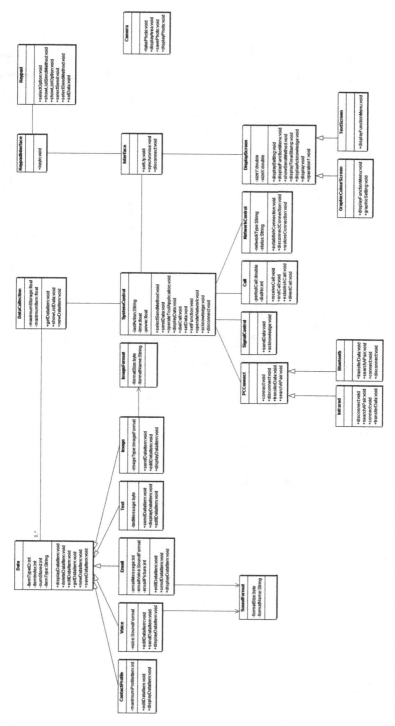

Fig. 12 Class diagram for product member PM_1

Sequence Diagrams

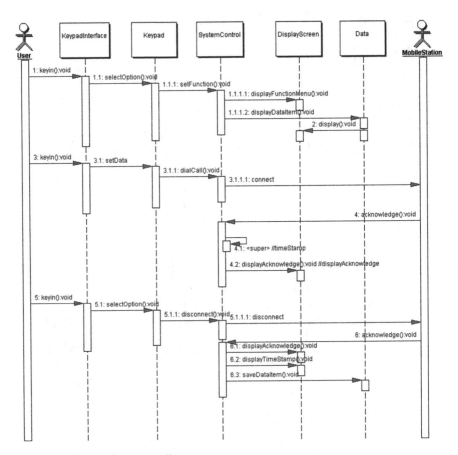

Fig. 13 Making a call sequence diagram

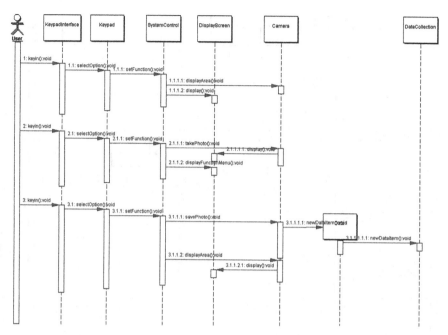

Fig. 14 Taking a photo sequence diagram

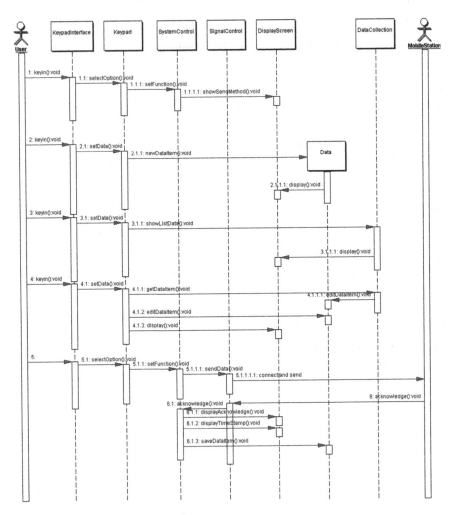

Fig. 15 Sending message sequence diagram

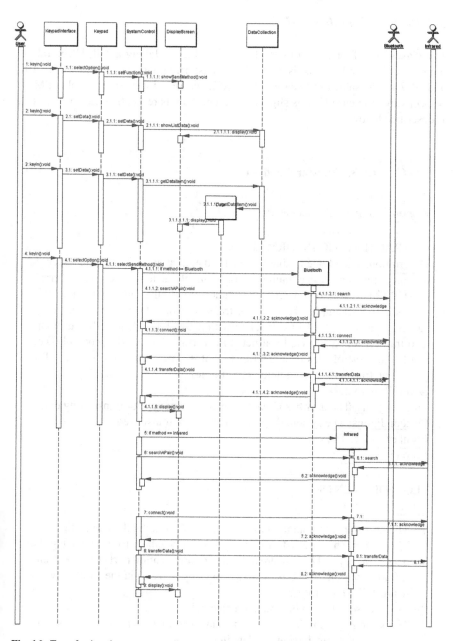

Fig. 16 Transferring data sequence diagram

3.2 Product Member PM_2

Use Cases: The four use cases for PM_2 are: UC5: Making a call, UC6: Taking a photo, UC7: Sending emails, and UC8: Transferring data. Use cases UC5, UC6, and UC7 are the same as use cases UC1, UC2, and UC3 for product member PM_1, respectively. Use case UC8 is slightly different than its respective use case UC4. It is described below.

Use Case UC8: Transferring data

Status: Common
Region: EU, Africa, Asia Pacific

CHARACTERISTIC INFORMATION
Description: The phone is able to transfer data that are stored in the data collection of the phone via communication channels such as Bluetooth, infrared, or TCP/IP network to another device attached with the same communication channels. For example, the user can transfer photos taken by an integrated camera to a computer being attached with a Bluetooth device. The user can also transfer a text file via local network working on TCP/IP protocol. Data can be any sort of files or notes (.txt), photos (.jpg), and images (.jpg). The phone can transfer one data item at each time.
Level: Primary task
Preconditions: The user has already selected a function for transferring data.
Postconditions: The system displays the status of transferred.
Primary Actor: The user
Secondary Actors: -

FLOW OF EVENTS
Trigger:

1. The user selects a data item to be transferred from the data collection.
2. The system shows a list of communication channels for transferring the data item. For PM2, there are not only communication ports Bluetooth and infrared, but the phone is also able to transfer data via the local network using TCP/IP protocol.
3. The user selects a communication channel.
4. The system searches a destination channel from a device that is closest to the phone for transferring the data item.
5. If the channel is found, the system establishes the communication channel between the phone and the device via the communication port. Otherwise, the phone notifies the user about the problem.
6. The system transfers the data item.

7. While transferring, the phone displays the status of transferring the data item on the screen.
8. After completed, the phone disconnects.
9. The phone shows the status of data item transferred.

EXCEPTIONAL EVENTS
None identified at present.

RELATED INFORMATION
Superordinate Use Case: None
Subordinate Use Cases: None

Class Diagram

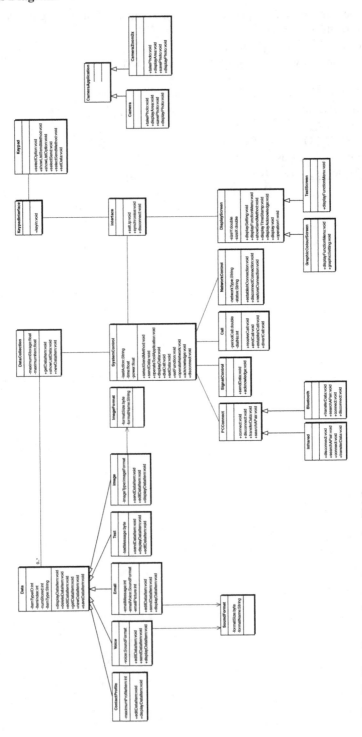

Fig. 17 Class diagram for product member PM_2

Sequence Diagram: The sequence diagrams for product member PM_2 are the same as the sequence diagrams for product member PM_1. An exception is found in the transferring data sequence diagram, which is extended to support data to be transferred using TCP/IP protocol.

3.3 Product Member PM_3

Use Cases: The three use cases for product member PM_3 are: UC9: Making a call, UC10: Sending emails, and UC11: Transferring data. Use cases UC9, UC10, and UC11 are the same as use cases UC1, UC3, and UC4, respectively for product member PM_1.

Sequence Diagram: The sequence diagrams for product member PM_3 are the same as the sequence diagrams for PM_1, for making a call, sending emails, and transferring data.

Class Diagram

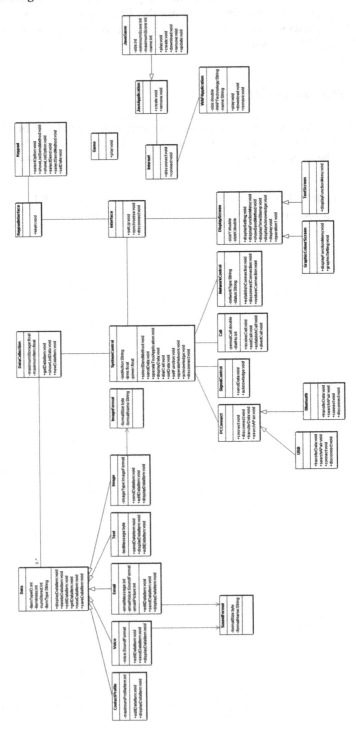

Fig. 18 Class diagram for product member PM_3

4 Feature Model in XML Format

```
<Feature_Model
    xmlns:xsi="http://www.w3.org/2001/XMLSchema-instance">
-<Feature>
  <Feature_name>Bluetooth</Feature_name>
  <Description>Bluetooth enables cost-free wireless connections between elec-
tronic devices within various maximum ranges according to the models of phones.
A Bluetooth connection can be used to send images texts business cards calendar
notes or to connect wirelessly to Bluetooth enabled devices such as computers.
Since Bluetooth devices communicate using radio waves the phone and the other
Bluetooth device do not need to be in direct line-of-sight. The two devices only need
to be within various maximum of distance depending to the models of the phones.
The connection can be subject to interference from obstructions such as walls or
from other electronic devices. Moreover using Bluetooth consumes the battery and
the phone's operating time will be reduced.</Description>
  <Issue_and_decision />
  <Type />
  <Existential>Optional</Existential>
  <Relationship />
  </Feature>
- <Feature>
  <Feature_name>Digital Camera</Feature_name>
  <Description>With the camera customers can take photo or events while on the
move. The photos are automatically saved in the Images application where the cus-
tomers can rename them and organise them in folders. The customers can also send
data to people in a multimedia message as an e-mail attachment or via a Bluetooth
or infrared connection. The camera produces JPEG photos.</Description>
  <Issue_and_decision />
  <Type />
  <Existential>Optional</Existential>
- <Relationship type="Composed-Of">
  <Rel_feature>Taking Photos</Rel_feature>
  </Relationship>
  </Feature>
- <Feature>
  <Feature_name>Edit Text Message</Feature_name>
  <Description>Customers can compose and send the message through net-
work.</Description>
  <Issue_and_decision />
  <Type />
  <Existential>Mandatory</Existential>
  <Relationship />
  <Allocated_to_Subsystem>Messaging</Allocated_to_Subsystem>
  </Feature>
```

- <Feature>
  <Feature_name>Taking Photos</Feature_name>
  <Description>With an integrated digital camera the phone can take photos. The Camera application is opened and customers can see the view to be captured. The screen shows the viewfinder and the cropping lines which shows the photo area to be captured. The customers can also see the image counter which shows how many images depending on the selected image quality fit in the memory of the phone. The lens range is various according to the models of phones. If the distance to the subject of taking a photo is closer than the minimum distance of the lens range it may affect the sharpness of images. The photos are saved automatically in the Images application.</Description>
  <Issue_and_decision />
  <Type>Capability</Type>
  <Existential>Mandatory</Existential>
  <Relationship />
  </Feature>
- <Feature>
  <Feature_name>Connectivity</Feature_name>
  <Description>The phone must be switched on to use the functions in the Connectivity folder. Do not switch the phone on when wireless phone use is prohibited or when it may cause interference or danger.</Description>
  <Issue_and_decision />
  <Type>Capability</Type>
  <Existential>Mandatory</Existential>
- <Relationship type="Composed-Of">
  <Rel_feature>Infrared</Rel_feature>
  <Rel_feature>Bluetooth</Rel_feature>
  <Rel_feature>WAP</Rel_feature>
  </Relationship>
  </Feature>
- <Feature>
  <Feature_name>Infrared</Feature_name>
  <Description>Via infrared customers can send or receive data such as business cards and calendar notes to and from a compatible phone or data device. Do not point IR infrared beam at anyone's eye or allow it to interfere with other IR devices. The infrared ports of the sending and the receiving devices are pointing at the sending device and there are no obstructions between the devices. The preferable distance between two devices is one metre at most.</Description>
  <Issue_and_decision />
  <Type>Capability</Type>
  <Existential>Optional</Existential>
- <Relationship type="Composed-Of">
  <Rel_feature>Sending Data Via Infrared</Rel_feature>
  <Rel_feature>Receiving Data Via Infrared</Rel_feature>
  </Relationship>
  </Feature>

- <Feature>
  <Feature_name>WAP</Feature_name>
  <Description>The phones must be switched on to use this function. Do not switch the phone on when wireless phone use is prohibited or when it may cause interference or danger. Various WAP Wireless Application Protocol service providers on the Internet maintain pages specially designed for mobile phones offering services such as news weather reports banking travel information entertainment and games. These pages use the Wireless Markup Language WML Web pages using the Hypertext Markup Language HTML can not be viewed on the phones. Once the customers have stored all the required connection setting they can access WAP pages. There are three different ways to access WAP pages the homepage of customers' service provider the bookmark from the Bookmarks view and the address of a WAP service.</Description>
  <Issue_and_decision />
  <Type>Capability</Type>
  <Existential>Optional</Existential>
- <Relationship type="Composed-Of">
  <Rel_feature>Receiving Smart Messages</Rel_feature>
  <Rel_feature>Adding Bookmark</Rel_feature>
  <Rel_feature>Viewing Bookmark</Rel_feature>
  <Rel_feature>Sending Bookmark</Rel_feature>
  <Rel_feature>Browsing WAP Pages</Rel_feature>
  <Rel_feature>Saving WAP Pages</Rel_feature>
  <Rel_feature>WAP Connection Security</Rel_feature>
  </Relationship>
  </Feature>
- <Feature>
  <Feature_name>Sending Data Via Bluetooth</Feature_name>
  <Description>There can be only one active Bluetooth connection at a time. Data can be various depending on an application where the item the customers wish to send is stored. For example to send a photo to another device open the Images application. After opening the application the customers can select options of sending data via Bluetooth. The phone starts to search for devices within range Bluetooth enables devices that are within range start to appear on the display one by one. In the case that the customers have searched for Bluetooth devices earlier a list of the devices that were found previously is shown first. The phone is able to start and stop searching of Bluetooth devices before sending data. When the connection has been successfully established the phone is ready to send data If sending fails the message or data will be deleted.</Description>
  <Issue_and_decision />
  <Type>Capability</Type>
  <Existential>Mandatory</Existential>
  <Relationship />
  </Feature>
- <Feature>

<Feature_name>Receiving Data Via Bluetooth</Feature_name>
<Description>When the phone has received data via Bluetooth there will be a tone sound and a pop-up to ask if the customer want to accept the Bluetooth message. If accept the item will be placed in the Inbox folder in Messaging.</Description>
<Issue_and_decision />
<Type>Capability</Type>
<Existential>Mandatory</Existential>
</Feature>
- <Feature>
<Feature_name>Sending Data Via Infrared</Feature_name>
<Description>The sending device has to select the desired infrared function to start data transfer. If data transfer is not started within one minute after the activation of the infrared port the connection is cancelled and must be restarted again.</Description>
<Issue_and_decision />
<Type>Capability</Type>
<Existential>Mandatory</Existential>
</Feature>
- <Feature>
<Feature_name>Receiving data Via Infrared</Feature_name>
<Description>All items which are received via infrared are placed in the Inbox folder in Messaging. The receiving device must activate the infrared port.</Description>
<Issue_and_decision />
<Type>Capability</Type>
<Existential>Mandatory</Existential>
</Feature>
- <Feature>
<Feature_name>Receiving Smart Messages</Feature_name>
<Description>The short message a so-called smart message can be received from the network operator or service provider that offers the WAP service. The message can contain both WAP access point settings and bookmarks such that the customers can view the bookmark and access point information separately.</Description>
<Issue_and_decision />
<Type>Capability</Type>
<Existential>Mandatory</Existential>
</Feature>
- <Feature>
<Feature_name>Receiving Smart Messages</Feature_name>
<Description>The short message a so-called smart message can be received from the network operator or service provider that offers the WAP service. The message can contain both WAP access point settings and bookmarks such that the customers can view the bookmark and access point information separately.</Description>

```
<Issue_and_decision />
<Type>Capability</Type>
<Existential>Mandatory</Existential>
</Feature>
```
- `<Feature>`
```
<Feature_name>Adding Bookmark</Feature_name>
<Description>
```
The customer can add a bookmark in the Bookmark view by only defining the address.`</Description>`
```
<Issue_and_decision />
<Type>Capability</Type>
<Existential>Mandatory</Existential>
</Feature>
```
- `<Feature>`
```
<Feature_name>Viewing Bookmark</Feature_name>
<Description>
```
Viewing Bookmark A bookmark consists of an Internet address mandatory bookmark title WAP access point and if the service requires a user name and password. The phone may have some pre-installed bookmarks for sites not affiliated with the phone company. The company does not warrant or endorse these sites. If the customer choose to access them the customer should take the same precautions for security or content as would with any site. In the Bookmarks view the customer can see bookmarks pointing to different kinds of WAP pages Bookmarks are indicated by the following icons.`</Description>`
```
<Issue_and_decision />
<Type>Capability</Type>
<Existential>Mandatory</Existential>
</Feature>
```
- `<Feature>`
```
<Feature_name>Browsing WAP Pages</Feature_name>
<Description>
```
The phone can show which WAP pages are previously visited. The customers can open a link with various input methods e.g. pressing the joystick entering addresses of WAP pages etc. then they can read and view WAP service messages while browsing.`</Description>`
```
<Issue_and_decision />
<Type>Capability</Type>
<Existential>Mandatory</Existential>
</Feature>
```
- `<Feature>`
```
<Feature_name>Saving WAP Pages</Feature_name>
<Description>
```
A WAP page can be saved to the phone memory and be viewed it offline. The customers can open the Saved pages view from the phone memory. Moreover the customer can start a connection to the WAP service and to retrieve the page again.`</Description>`
```
<Issue_and_decision />
<Type>Capability</Type>
<Existential>Mandatory</Existential>
</Feature>
```

- <Feature>
  <Feature_name>WAP Connection Security</Feature_name>
  <Description>The phone can pop-up an indicator during a WAP connection when the data transmission between the phone and the WAP gateway or WAP service is encrypted and secure. It is up to the service provider to secure data transmission between the gateway and the content server. It is possible that the customer is trying to access or have accessed confidential information requiring passwords for example the customer's bank account. The phone can empty the cache after each use.</Description>
  <Issue_and_decision />
  <Type>Capability</Type>
  <Existential>Mandatory</Existential>
  </Feature>
- <Feature>
  <Feature_name>Tools</Feature_name>
  <Description>Tools</Description>
  <Issue_and_decision />
  <Type>Capability</Type>
  <Existential>Mandatory</Existential>
- <Relationship type="Composed-Of">
  <Rel_feature>Calendar</Rel_feature>
  <Rel_feature>Games</Rel_feature>
  <Rel_feature>Clock</Rel_feature>
  <Rel_feature>Digital Camera</Rel_feature>
  </Relationship>
  </Feature>
- <Feature>
  <Feature_name>Clock</Feature_name>
  <Description>The phone can set and show the time and date. The clock can be Analogue or Digital according to the models of phones.</Description>
  <Issue_and_decision />
  <Type>Capability</Type>
  <Existential>Mandatory</Existential>
  </Feature>
- <Feature>
  <Feature_name>Personal Preference</Feature_name>
  <Description>Personal_Preference</Description>
  <Issue_and_decision />
  <Type>Capability</Type>
  <Existential>Mandatory</Existential>
- <Relationship type="Composed-Of">
  <Rel_feature>A Call</Rel_feature>
  <Rel_feature>Wallpaper</Rel_feature>
- <Rel_feature> Data Transfer Setting </Rel_feature>
  <Rel_feature>Clock Setting</Rel_feature>

```
<Rel_feature>Screen saver</Rel_feature>
</Relationship>
</Feature>
- <Feature>
<Feature_name>Wallpaper</Feature_name>
<Description>The phone can set what is shown on the wallpaper.</Description>
<Issue_and_decision />
<Type>Capability</Type>
<Existential>Optional</Existential>
</Feature>
- <Feature>
<Feature_name>Screen saver</Feature_name>
<Description>The phone can set what is shown on the screen saver bar time and
date or text.</Description>
<Issue_and_decision />
<Type>Capability</Type>
<Existential>Optional</Existential>
</Feature>
- <Feature>
<Feature_name>Calling</Feature_name>
<Description>The phone can connect to landline and mobile phones. During a call
the customer can mute unmute end active call end all calls hold/unhold make a new
call. Moreover if the phone is activated the Call waiting service the network will
notify a new incoming call while the customer has a call in progress.</Description>
<Issue_and_decision />
<Type>Capability</Type>
<Existential>Mandatory</Existential>
- <Relationship type="Composed-Of">
<Rel_feature>Making Call</Rel_feature>
<Rel_feature>Receiving A Call</Rel_feature>
</Relationship>
</Feature>
- <Feature>
<Feature_name>Making Call</Feature_name>
<Description>The phone can make a call by entering the phone number via keypad
or selecting a contact from the Contacts directory.</Description>
<Issue_and_decision />
<Type>Capability</Type>
<Existential>Mandatory</Existential>
</Feature>
- <Feature>
<Feature_name>Receiving A Call</Feature_name>
<Description>The phone can answer an incoming call by any input methods. The
customers can ignore to answer a call by activating as a line busy. The customers
can quickly mute the ringing tone for a coming call. Moreover the customer can
```

direct incoming calls to another phone number. This depends on the network service activated.</Description>
  <Issue_and_decision />
  <Type>Capability</Type>
  <Existential>Mandatory</Existential>
  </Feature>
- <Feature>
  <Feature_name>Input Method</Feature_name>
  <Description>The phone has different ways for entering commands.
</Description>
  <Issue_and_decision />
  <Type>Capability</Type>
  <Existential>Mandatory</Existential>
- <Relationship type="Composed-Of">
  <Rel_feature>Keypad</Rel_feature>
  <Rel_feature>Joy Stick</Rel_feature>
  </Relationship>
  </Feature>
- <Feature>
  <Feature_name>Keypad</Feature_name>
- <Description>A customer can enter data and activate with responses via keypad of the phone.</Description>
  <Issue_and_decision />
  <Type>Capability</Type>
  <Existential>Mandatory</Existential>
  </Feature>
- <Feature>
  <Feature_name>Joy Stick</Feature_name>
  <Description>A customer can browse and select items with a joy stick which can move four directions left right down and up.</Description>
  <Issue_and_decision />
  <Type>Capability</Type>
  <Existential>Optional</Existential>
  </Feature>
- <Feature>
  <Feature_name>Output Method</Feature_name>
  <Description>The phone has a screen as an output showing activating responses to a customer.</Description>
  <Issue_and_decision />
  <Type>Capability</Type>
  <Existential>Mandatory</Existential>
- <Relationship type="Composed-Of">
  <Rel_feature>Graphic display</Rel_feature>
  <Rel_feature>Text display</Rel_feature>

```
</Relationship>
</Feature>
- <Feature>
<Feature_name>Graphic display</Feature_name>
<Description>The screen can display graphic mode including textual contents.
```

The customer can change the contrast of the display to lighter or darker and the colour palette used on the display. The phone has the light sensor to measure the surrounding light. When the light sensor is active and it is bright enough the phone display and keypad lights are automatically shut down. The phone can control the setting of Minimum and Maximum of the sensitivity of the light sensor. Also the function can be set off if the customer does not want to use the light sensor. Moreover the display and keypad lights will shut down if there have been not key presses within a range of time depending on the models of the phones.</Description>

```
<Issue_and_decision />
<Type>Capability</Type>
<Existential>Alternative</Existential>
- <Relationship type="Composed-Of">
<Rel_feature>VGA</Rel_feature>
<Rel_feature>"G"</Rel_feature>
</Relationship>
</Feature>
- <Feature>
<Feature_name>Text display</Feature_name>
<Description>The screen can display responses in textual. The phone has the
```

light sensor to measure the surrounding light. When the light sensor is active and it is bright enough the phone display and keypad lights are automatically shut down. The function can be set off if the customer does not want to use the light sensor. Moreover the display and keypad lights will shut down if there have been not key presses within a range of time depending on the models of the phones.</Description>

```
<Issue_and_decision />
<Type>Capability</Type>
<Existential>Alternative</Existential>
</Feature>
- <Feature>
<Feature_name>Data</Feature_name>
<Description>Data</Description>
<Issue_and_decision />
<Type>Capability</Type>
<Existential>Mandatory</Existential>
- <Relationship type="Composed-Of">
<Rel_feature>Ring Tones</Rel_feature>
<Rel_feature>Photo albums</Rel_feature>
<Rel_feature>Phone Book</Rel_feature>
```

```
<Rel_feature>Text Messages</Rel_feature>
<Rel_feature>Emails</Rel_feature>
<Rel_feature>Voice</Rel_feature>
</Relationship>
</Feature>
- <Feature>
<Feature_name>Photo albums</Feature_name>
<Description>Photo albums</Description>
<Issue_and_decision />
<Type>Capability</Type>
<Existential>Optional</Existential>
- <Relationship type="Composed-Of">
<Rel_feature>photos</Rel_feature>
</Relationship>
</Feature>
- <Feature>
<Feature_name>photos</Feature_name>
<Description>The phone must be switched on to use this function. The phone
can view photos organise delete and send photos and pictures stored. There are
different types of photos Standard or Night or Portrait modes. Photos in Standard
or Night mode are saved in 640×480 pixel VGA format photos. In Portrait mode
are saved in 80×96 pixel format. The phone can store view organise delete and
send photos and pictures stored in your phone. The possible formats of photos in
the phone can be JPEG GIF TIFF MBM BMP WBMP OTA WMP Unsupported or
Unknown.</Description>
<Issue_and_decision />
<Type>Capability</Type>
<Existential>Mandatory</Existential>
- <Relationship type="Composed-Of">
<Rel_feature>Storing Photos</Rel_feature>
<Rel_feature>Viewing Photos</Rel_feature>
<Rel_feature>Sending Photos</Rel_feature>
</Relationship>
</Feature>
- <Feature>
<Feature_name>Storing Photos</Feature_name>
<Description>The phone can store photos including ones taken with the inte-
grated digital camera in the phone itself or ones sent into inbox in a multimedia
or a photo messaging as an e-mail attachment via an infrared or Bluetooth
connection.</Description>
<Issue_and_decision />
<Type>Capability</Type>
<Existential>Mandatory</Existential>
</Feature>
```

- <Feature>
  <Feature_name>Viewing photos</Feature_name>
  <Description>The phone can view an photo with functions e.g. zooming full screen moving the focus rotating.</Description>
  <Issue_and_decision />
  <Type>Capability</Type>
  <Existential>Mandatory</Existential>
  </Feature>
- <Feature>
  <Feature_name>Sending photos</Feature_name>
  <Description>The phone can send photos in a multimedia or e-mail message as an attachment or communication ports like infrared Bluetooth.</Description>
  <Issue_and_decision />
  <Type>Capability</Type>
  <Existential>Mandatory</Existential>
  </Feature>
- <Feature>
  <Feature_name>Text Messages</Feature_name>
  <Description>The phone can edit send and receive a short message photos in a multimedia or e-mail message as an attachment or communication ports like infrared Bluetooth.</Description>
  <Issue_and_decision />
  <Type>Capability</Type>
  <Existential>Mandatory</Existential>
- <Relationship type="Composed-Of">
  <Rel_feature>Sending Text Message</Rel_feature>
  <Rel_feature>Receiving Text Message</Rel_feature>
  <Rel_feature>Edit Text Message</Rel_feature>
  </Relationship>
  </Feature>
- <Feature>
  <Feature_name>Sending Text Message</Feature_name>
  <Description>The phone can send a short message to another phone by pressing a contact via keypad or entering from a list of contacts. The maximum amount of sending short messages and the maximum amount of characters in one short message depend on the models of the phone. The phone can store messages sent previously in the outbox.</Description>
  <Issue_and_decision />
  <Type>Capability</Type>
  <Existential>Mandatory</Existential>
  </Feature>
- <Feature>
  <Feature_name>Receiving Text Message</Feature_name>
  <Description>The phone can receive a short message and store it in the phone memory. The maximum amount of receiving short messages and the maximum

amount of characters in one short message depend on the models of the phone. The phone can store messages received previously in the inbox.</Description>
    <Issue_and_decision />
    <Type>Capability</Type>
    <Existential>Mandatory</Existential>
    </Feature>
- <Feature>
    <Feature_name>Phone Book</Feature_name>
    <Description>PhoneBook</Description>
    <Issue_and_decision />
    <Type>Capability</Type>
    <Existential>Mandatory</Existential>
- <Relationship type="Composed-Of">
    <Rel_feature>Contacts</Rel_feature>
    </Relationship>
    </Feature>
- <Feature>
    <Feature_name>Contacts</Feature_name>
    <Description />
    <Issue_and_decision />
    <Type>Capability</Type>
    <Existential>Mandatory</Existential>
    </Feature>
- <Feature>
    <Feature_name>Emails</Feature_name>
    <Description>The phone can send receive retrieve reply to and forward email. To do so the customer must configure an Internet Access Point IAP correctly and define the email settings correctly. Emails can be attached with photos.</Description>
    <Issue_and_decision />
    <Type>Capability</Type>
    <Existential>Optional</Existential>
- <Relationship type="Composed-Of">
    <Rel_feature>Sending Emails</Rel_feature>
    <Rel_feature>Receiving Emails</Rel_feature>
    </Relationship>
    </Feature>
- <Feature>
    <Feature_name>Sending Emails</Feature_name>
    <Description>The customers can select the recipient(s) from a list of contacts in the phone or write the email address of the recipient. It can send emails to multiple recipients. Moreover the customer can add an attachment to an e-mail. The attachment includes photos sound clip note etc. This function includes replying and forwarding emails.</Description>
    <Issue_and_decision />
    <Type>Capability</Type>

<Existential>Mandatory</Existential>
</Feature>
- <Feature>
<Feature_name>Retrieving Emails</Feature_name>
<Description>The customers can receive emails and store them in the inbox emails. Afterwards the phone can retrieve and delete those emails.</Description>
<Issue_and_decision />
<Type>Capability</Type>
<Existential>Mandatory</Existential>
</Feature> </Feature_Model>

References

Cockburn, A.: Structuring use-cases with goals. Journal of Object-Oriented Programming (JOOP Magazine), Sep–Oct and Nov–Dec (1997).

Jirapanthong, W., Zisman, A.: XTraQue: Traceability for product line systems. Softw. Syst. Modeling J. **8**(1), 1619–1366 (2009).

Kang, K., Kim, S., et al.: FORM: A feature-oriented reuse method with domain-specific architectures. Ann. Softw. Eng. **5**(1), 143–168 (1998).

Nokia: http://www.forum.nokia.com/main.html.

OMA: www.omg.org/technology/documents/formal/xmi.htm.

Appendix D: The Center of Excellence for Software Traceability

The International Center of Excellence for Software Traceability (CoEST) was established in 2005 with the charge to "bring together traceability researchers and experts in the field, encourage research collaborations, assemble a body of knowledge for traceability, and develop new technology to meet tracing needs."

CoEST membership currently includes academic, government, and industrial researchers from across the U.S. and Europe.

Since its inception, the CoEST has engaged in two primary projects, the Grand Challenges of Traceability (GCT) and the Tracy project. The grand challenges, which were presented in chapter "The Grand Challenge of Traceability (v1.0)" of this book, provide a detailed road map of critical research and practice goals. The Tracy project is driven by the grand challenges, and as depicted in Fig. 1, focuses on

equipping the traceability research community through building research infrastructure, collecting and organising datasets, establishing benchmarks, and developing a tool named TraceLab, which will provide support for designing and executing a broad range of traceability experiments.

For further information, or to become a CoEST member, please visit http://www.coest.org.

Appendix E: TraceLab – A Tool for Supporting Traceability Research

TraceLab is a visual experimental workbench for designing and executing traceability experiments.

TraceLab's primary features include:

- A visual environment for designing and executing experiments.
- A component library which facilitates sharing a wide variety of importers, pre-processors, algorithms, analysers, etc. across the traceability community.
- Ability to write components in a wide variety of languages including, C++, C#, and Java, and combined into a single experimental workflow.
- Integration with standard benchmarks for comparatively evaluating new techniques against previous results. Benchmarks utilise community datasets, standardised metrics, and previously published traceability tasks.
- A scalable environment that supports experiments involving extremely large sized industrial datasets.
- Portability across multiple operating systems including Windows, Linux, and Mac OS.

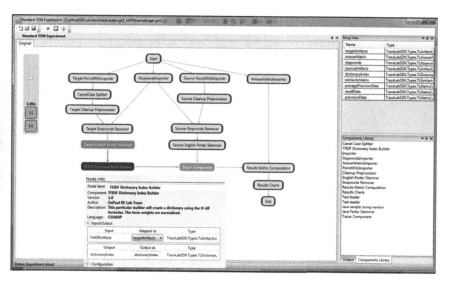

- A simple installation process which allows new users to quickly download and install TraceLab.
- An intuitive user interface which enables new users to execute basic experiments without any formal training.

The TraceLab project is funded under National Science Foundation's Major Research Instrumentation Grant # 0959924. Further information is available at http://www.coest.org.

Index